Twentieth-Century World
Fifth Edition

Carter Vaughn Findley
The Ohio State University

John Alexander Murray Rothney
The Ohio State University

HOUGHTON MIFFLIN COMPANY   Boston   New York

Sponsoring Editor: Nancy Blaine
Associate Editor: Julie Dunn
Associate Project Editor: Martha Rogers
Associate Production/Design Coordinator: Christine Gervais
Manufacturing Manager: Florence Cadran
Senior Marketing Manager: Sandra McGuire

Cover: © Duomo/CORBIS

Printed in the U.S.A.

Library of Congress Control Number:
20001131493

ISBN: 0-618-11532-3

1 2 3 4 5 6 7 8 9-DOC-05 04 03 02 01

Topographical and Political Maps of the World, 2001

ARCTIC OCEAN

ALASKA RANGE

ROCKY MOUNTAINS

CANADIAN SHIELD

NORTH
AMERICA

APPALACHIAN MT.

Mississippi

Rio Grande

NORTH PACIFIC OCEAN

NORTH
ATLANTIC
OCEAN

Tropic of Cancer

Equator

Amazon

ANDES MOUNTAIN

SOUTH
AMERICA

SOU
ATLA
OCE

Tropic of Capricorn

SOUTH PACIFIC OCEAN

Cape Horn

Antarctic Circle

	Sea Ice
	Ice Cap
	Tundra
	Forest
	Grassland
	Desert
	Mountains

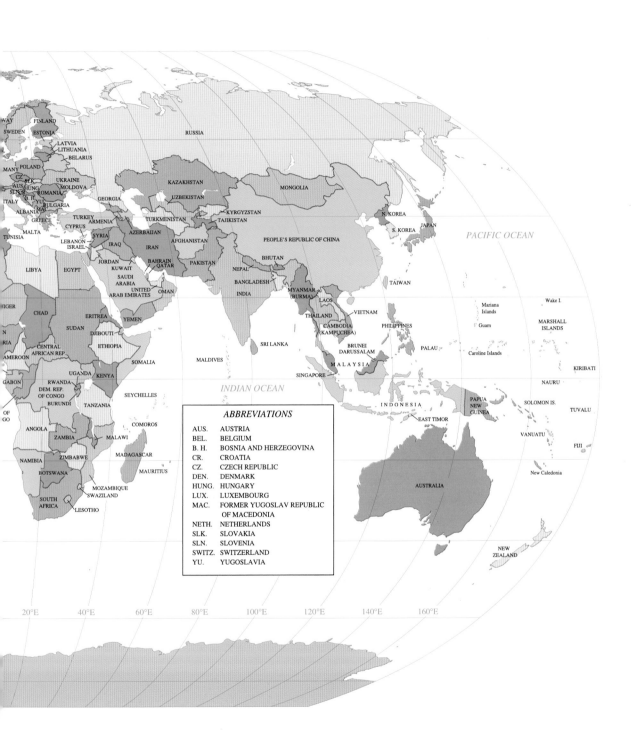

NAY
SWEDEN FINLAND
ESTONIA
LATVIA
LITHUANIA
BELARUS
MANY POLAND
CZ.
AUS HUNG. UKRAINE
SLK ROMANIA
SLN.R.H.
ITALY YU. BULGARIA
ALBANIA MAC.
GREECE
MALTA CYPRUS
TUNISIA
LEBANON
ISRAEL
LIBYA EGYPT
JORDAN KUWAIT
SAUDI
ARABIA
UNITED
ARAB EMIRATES OMAN

NIGER
CHAD ERITREA YEMEN
SUDAN DJIBOUTI
RIA
CENTRAL ETHIOPIA
AMEROON AFRICAN REP.
UGANDA KENYA
GABON RWANDA
DEM. REP.
OF CONGO BURUNDI TANZANIA SEYCHELLES
OF
GO
ANGOLA COMOROS
ZAMBIA MALAWI
NAMIBIA ZIMBABWE MADAGASCAR
BOTSWANA MAURITIUS
MOZAMBIQUE
SOUTH SWAZILAND
AFRICA LESOTHO

RUSSIA

KAZAKHSTAN
MONGOLIA
UZBEKISTAN
KYRGYZSTAN
GEORGIA TAJIKISTAN
TURKEY ARMENIA TURKMENISTAN N. KOREA
AZERBAIJAN AFGHANISTAN S. KOREA JAPAN
SYRIA PEOPLE'S REPUBLIC OF CHINA
IRAQ
IRAN
BAHRAIN PAKISTAN
QATAR BHUTAN
NEPAL TAIWAN
BANGLADESH
MYANMAR
INDIA (BURMA) LAOS
THAILAND VIETNAM
CAMBODIA PHILIPPINES
SRI LANKA (KAMPUCHEA)
BRUNEI
MALDIVES DARUSSALAM PALAU
MALAYSIA
SINGAPORE

PACIFIC OCEAN

Mariana
Islands
Wake I.

Guam MARSHALL
ISLANDS

Caroline Islands

KIRIBATI

NAURU

INDIAN OCEAN
INDONESIA SOLOMON IS. TUVALU
EAST TIMOR PAPUA
NEW
GUINEA VANUATU
FIJI
New Caledonia

AUSTRALIA

NEW
ZEALAND

ABBREVIATIONS

AUS.	AUSTRIA
BEL.	BELGIUM
B. H.	BOSNIA AND HERZEGOVINA
CR.	CROATIA
CZ.	CZECH REPUBLIC
DEN.	DENMARK
HUNG.	HUNGARY
LUX.	LUXEMBOURG
MAC.	FORMER YUGOSLAV REPUBLIC
	OF MACEDONIA
NETH.	NETHERLANDS
SLK.	SLOVAKIA
SLN.	SLOVENIA
SWITZ.	SWITZERLAND
YU.	YUGOSLAVIA

20°E   40°E   60°E   80°E   100°E   120°E   140°E   160°E

Thirty Most Populous Countries

Country	Population (millions)
China	1265
India	1002
USA	276
Indonesia	212
Brazil	170
Pakistan	151
Russia	145
Japan	127
Bangladesh	128
Nigeria	123
Mexico	100
Germany	82
Philippines	80
Vietnam	79
Egypt	68
Iran	67
Turkey	65
Thailand	64
United Kingdom	62
France	60
Italy	59
Ethiopia	58
Democratic Republic of Congo (Zaire)	52
Ukraine	50
Myanmar (Burma)	49
Korea, South	47
South Africa	43
Colombia	40
Spain	40
Poland	39

Source: Data from the World Population Reference Bureau, 2000 World Population data sheet.

Contents

Chapter 4

Restructuring the Social and Political Order: The Bolshevik Revolution in World Perspective 81

Chapter 5

Global Economic Crisis and the Restructuring of the Social and Political Order 102

Chapter 6

Restructuring the Social and Political Order: Fascism 121

Chapter 12

Toward Postindustrial Society: The United States and Western Europe in the Postwar Decades 275

Chapter 13

The Soviet Union, Eastern Europe, and the Collapse of Communism 320

Preface to the Fifth Edition

As "globalization" emerged as a commonplace of political rhetoric around the world in the 1990s, scholars in many fields strove to understand the revolutionary implications of this complex process. Their efforts have produced important results and will continue to do so. However, readers of earlier editions will recognize globalization as only a new form of what *Twentieth-Century World* has taken as its foremost theme ever since its first edition: *global interrelatedness.* This fact epitomizes the importance of both continuity and change in the preparation of this edition. For the benefit of new readers, it may be useful to highlight the basic principles and the new features of the Fifth Edition.

Basic Principles of *Twentieth-Century World*

Global Interrelatedness

Taking the world as its unit of analysis, *Twentieth-Century World* seeks to help students understand how global interrelatedness has evolved, primarily since World War I, but also over the long sweep of world history. No subject of such scale can be intelligible unless organized according to clear principles. Our foremost principle is that the world is a tightly interconnected whole. Today, responsible citizenship requires understanding global interrelationships. To explain these interrelationships, *Twentieth-Century World* emphasizes global patterns of integration and examines issues and events, not as unique occurrences, but in terms of their global linkages. For example, Chapter 4 examines the Bolshevik Revolution not just as a turning point in Russian history but

also as this century's most influential revolutionary experience.

Balanced and Selective Coverage

The authors reject an approach based on Europe or the United States. Instead, this book seeks to balance coverage of both developed and developing societies. In keeping with their emphasis on global integration, the authors also reject the incremental method, which assumes that adding together national histories produces world history. Instead, this book takes a selective and thematic, not an encyclopedic, approach. The goal is to enable students to identify major themes, see them illustrated in selected cases, and thus perceive world history as more than a jumble of details. Selectivity permits meaningful discussion of examples taken up in the book and leaves instructors free to develop alternative examples in class.

A Multifaceted Conception of History

Twentieth-Century World discusses a broad range of subjects—economic, social, political, artistic, scientific, and military—to convey a fully rounded understanding of the contemporary world. Every chapter considers several of these subjects. Certain chapters perform special functions, however. Chapter 1 explains the book's themes. The narrative chapters, beginning with Chapter 2, emphasize political, economic, and social developments. Analyzing such vital future-oriented issues as population, environment, resources, and arms control, Chapter 18 takes a forward look, organized around the book's four themes, at what the world promises to be like as the new millennium opens.

Clearly Stated Themes

The authors have organized this book around four major themes defined in Chapter 1.

1. *Global interrelatedness* and its shifting patterns, from early forms of regional and global integration, to the 1914 world of great powers and colonies, the "three worlds" of the Cold War years, and today's complexly networked and interdependent "global disorder."

2. *Identity and difference,* the struggles of individuals, groups, and societies to assert their identities, a struggle occurring throughout history, but now magnified into multiple layers of contentious identity politics based on nationalism, religion, race, ethnicity, gender, class, and personal preference or disadvantage.

3. *The rise of the mass society,* both in the numerical sense of unprecedented population growth, and in the sense of new, more intense forms of social interaction: mass politics, mass warfare, mass communications, mass consumerism, mass culture.

4. *Technology versus nature,* the ambiguous triumph that has empowered humankind to destroy the earth or to make life on earth unsustainable.

These four themes raise a final question, which is basic to all of world history but especially to today's globalization: How can human beings live together and provide equitably for their needs, without either making unsustainable demands on the environment or conflicting unmanageably with one another?

In addition to the clearly stated themes, other aids to understanding include division of the text into parts, chapters, sections, and subsections, as well as italicization of key terms. An illustrative vignette at the start of each chapter introduces its subject in microcosm and connects that subject to the themes of the book. Maps, illustrations, and a timeline enhance the text, as do suggestions for further reading at the end of each chapter. These aids have been thoroughly revised for the Fifth Edition.

Accompanying the Fifth Edition is a revised Instructor's Resource Manual. In addition to chapter-by-chapter guides to the thematic elements contained in *Twentieth- Century World,* this useful manual also includes, for each chapter, a summary, possible lecture topics, suggested class activities, a list of teaching materials (including audio-visual aids), and approximately thirty multiple choice and five essay questions.

Finally, a new website has been created to accompany the Fifth Edition. This site features resources related to twentieth-century history and is organized around the book's four themes.

New Features of the Fifth Edition

The most momentous changes of the post-1945 era have occurred since the first three editions of this book were published. Communism and the Soviet Union have collapsed, and the Cold War has ended. In addition, apartheid collapsed and the Cold War has ended. In its wake, old conflicts have abated and some new ones have emerged, as Yugoslavia collapsed, majority role came to South Africa, and alignments shifted in the Middle East, where the Arab-Israeli conflict remains the world's most intractable conflict of identity politics. Likewise in science and technology, both the sequencing of the human genome and the leap from isolated computers—each storing and processing its own data—to the global electronic networking of the Internet amounted to revolutionary innovations. Rapid change will surely continue, as economic balances shift, demand for democratization and development increases, and the revolutionary potentials of globalization come into clearer focus. Much of the Fifth Edition has consequently been rewritten to give a full account of these dramatic developments.

Illustrative vignettes introduce each chapter of the Fifth Edition. Their goal is to bring the global down to earth, give added insight into how individuals participate in and help to shape world history, and connect the themes of the book and the subject of each chapter to an episode of human interest.

Part One, fundamentally transformed in the Fourth Edition, has been revised anew for the Fifth Edition. Opening with an updated depiction of the Olympics as a model of globalization, Chapter One condenses narrative coverage of subject matter taken up in the new Chapter Two, sharpens the definition of the four themes, and incorporates recent findings in the study of anticolonial nationalism and in global economic and environmental history. Particular goals of revision have been to bring the discussion of globalization up to date with current understandings of a process whose nature is still controversial and imperfectly understood and to emphasize the concept of a mutually reinforcing relationship between globalization and identity politics.

In Part Two, a new Chapter 2 focuses on the scramble for empire and the other key political, economic, and social themes of late nineteenth and early twentieth century history. This chapter has been introduced to provide students with a more comprehensive background to the post-1914 narrative. Many longtime users of this book will be pleased to find restored in this chapter much of the material comparing imperial Berlin with the Egyptian village of Dinshawai that appeared in the second chapter of the first three editions. To make room for this new coverage, the chapter variously numbered Chapter 6 or 7 on "Western Intellectual and Artistic Life" has been reduced and its material absorbed into Chapter 2.

Chapter Four could not be revised without finding a new answer to an old question

that events of the 1990s had made harder to answer. While the need for an account of the Bolshevik revolution in a history of Russia or modern Europe would pass without question, world historians face a need to explain why they emphasize that revolution and what makes it more widely influential than other revolutions of the twentieth century. All editions of *Twentieth-Century World* have combined an account of the Bolshevik Revolution with a comparative discussion designed to answer that question. Since 1991, however, one also has to ask why, if the Bolshevik Revolution was so important, did the Soviet Union collapse? What bearing does the Soviet collapse have on our old question about the significance of the Bolshevik Revolution? In the Fifth Edition, the comparative discussion of revolutions has been extensively revised to answer this question.

In Part Three, revisions in all chapters have incorporated recent developments in scholarship, particularly on Brazil, Mexico, and China in the 1930s. The vignettes for these chapters take as their subjects three especially dramatic episodes: four Brazilian fishermen's daring voyage by raft to Rio de Janeiro to present their grievances to President Getúlio Vargas, the Aba Women's War in Nigeria, and the crossing of the chain bridge at Luding during the Long March in China.

Parts Four through Six discuss the world from World War II through the year 2000.

In Part Four, Chapter 11, which describes the course of international relations since 1945, and Chapter 12, which describes the domestic history of the United States and western Europe, have been carried forward to the end of the century. The history of the Cold War and the essential political and social developments in the major western nations since the Second World War have been discussed in the context of the two major global economic periods of the postwar era: the three decades of rapid growth after 1945, and the two decades of much slower growth, verging sometimes upon crisis, since the 1970s. With Soviet-American conflict no longer the dominant theme of international rivalry, Chapter 11 turns in its concluding pages to a comparison of today's major contestants for global economic power. This account considers recent Japanese economic difficulties, the dimming prospects for European unity since the Maastricht treaty, and the advantages and limitations of U.S. economic power. Chapter 12 focuses on the challenges posed to western welfare states by economic change since the 1970s. Also in Part Four, Chapter 13 provides treatment of the period of post-Communist or neo-Communist rule in Russia and in three of its former eastern European satellites to the end of the century.

In Part Five, the statistical data used to illustrate demographic, social, and economic issues has been updated throughout. The *Human Development Index* (HDI), a statistic presented in the United Nations Development Program's *Human Development Report* again provides the best comparative measure for assessing development in terms that go beyond the narrowly economic. Beginning with a vignette about a young Afro-Brazilian imprisoned in São Paulo, Chapter 14 incorporates a revised discussion of the tapering off of the Third World population surge of the mid-twentieth century and the high population growth rates that will linger into the next generation. Incorporating advances from recent scholarship, Chapter 14 updates the account of each country discussed, including the election of Vicente Fox as president of Mexico. Starting with a vignette about the connection between the global diamond trade and armed violence in Africa, additions to Chapter 15 pay particular attention to the AIDS epidemic, the transition from the Mandela to the Mbeki presidencies in South Africa, and Nigeria's recent history, for which the latest scholarship offers material for a much-improved account. Chapter 16 combines extensive updating on the latest developments in each of the Middle Eastern countries

discussed, together with a vignette drawn from Turkey's devastating 1999 earthquake and its implications at the personal, national, regional, and global levels. Chapter 17, beginning with a discussion of the Falun Dafa movement and the Chinese government's repression of it, incorporates important revisions on the eclipse of the Congress Party in India, the growing challenge of regional and caste-based parties to India's high-caste politicians, shifting forms of developmental inequality in both India and China, Japan's lingering socioeconomic crisis, the wider Asian economic crisis of 1997, and the implications of recent developments for questions of regional and global hegemony.

In Part Six, Chapter 18 opens with a vignette about the varied celebrations and expectations associated with the start of the year 2000 and then looks ahead to the new century, discussing major problems and prospects in terms of the four themes of the book. Major foci of revision include sharpening the discussion of globalization and updating the analysis of such related topics as human rights, environmental and resource issues, human-induced climate change, and arms control. Much as the beginning of Chapter One invoked the theme of the Olympics, the conclusion of Chapter 18 metaphorically visualizes a "globalization website" as a model for understanding the relationship between the empirical data of contemporary world history and our four themes: globalization, identity and difference, the mass society, and technology versus nature.

Authorship and Acknowledgments

Carter Findley wrote Chapter 1, the comparative material in Chapter 4, Chapters 7 to 9 and 14 to 18. John Rothney wrote Chapters 2 to 6 (with contributions from Carter Findley in Chapter 4), and Chapters 10 to 13. The authors are indebted to the following scholars for valuable comments:

Shannon L. Baker, *SUNY-Cortland*

Terry Crowley, *University of Guelph*

Tom Ewing, *Virginia Tech*

Howard B. Fedrick, *King's College*

Bruce F. Griffith, *Catawba College*

Thomas L. Pearcy, *Slippery Rock University*

Max Riedlsperger, *California Polytechnic State University*

Ralph Violette, *Indiana University-Purdue University Fort Wayne*

James Weland, *Bentley College*

In addition to those named in earlier editions, the authors would like to acknowledge the assistance of the following colleagues: Kenneth Andrien, James Bartholomew, Jerry Bentley, Alan Beyerchen, Ralph Croizier, Jane Hathaway, David Hoffman, R. William Liddle, Patrick Manning, Mark Robbins, Carole Rogel, Leila Rupp, Charles D. Smith, Gaddis Smith, Vladimir Steffel, and Robin Winks. The authors are greatly indebted to the Houghton Mifflin editorial staff. By what they understood, what they showed was not understandable, and what they contributed of their own, thousands of Ohio State students have contributed to the making of this book.

Carter Findley gratefully acknowledges the encouragement of four generations of family members: Inez Vaughn Oliver; Elizabeth and John Findley; Lucia Findley, Clay and Vicki Findley; and Madeleine and Benjamin Findley. John Rothney is grateful for the enduring friendship of Malcolm and Dolores Baroway, Ronald E. Coons, Edward P. Hart, and Richard E. Rogers.

C.V.F.

J.A.M.R.

List of Maps

The Twentieth Century: A Time Chart

	Events and Issues of Global Significance	Scientific-Technical-Intellectual	North America
Pre-1900	Heyday of European world dominance	19th-century materialism, rationalism, and political liberalism increasingly challenged in the 1890s	Spanish-American War (1989) is first assertion of U.S. world power
1900		Freud's *On the Interpretation of Dreams,* 1900 Wright brothers make first powered aircraft flight, 1903 Einstein's "On the Electrodynamics of Moving Bodies," 1905 Picasso's *Demoiselles d'Avignon,* 1907	Presidency of Theodore Roosevelt, 1901–1909 Presidency of William Howard Taft, 1909–1913
1910	World War I, 1914–1918 Paris Peace Conference, 1919		Presidency of Woodrow Wilson, 1913–1921 U.S. declares war on Germany, 1917
1920	League of Nations founded, 1920 First Fascists in power with Mussolini's March on Rome, 1922 Great Depression, 1929	Franz Kafka's *The Trial,* 1924 First nonstop trans-Atlantic solo flight, 1925	Constitutional amendment gives women the vote, 1920 Presidency of Warren G. Harding, 1921–1923 Presidency of Calvin Coolidge, 1923–1929 Presidency of Herbert Hoover, 1929–1933 Wall Street crash, 1929
1930	Global population explosion since 1930 World War II, 1939–1945	Ortega y Gasset's *The Revolt of the Masses,* 1930	Smoot-Hawley Tariff, 1930 Presidency of Franklin D. Roosevelt, 1933–1945 Social Security Act, 1935

Europe	Latin America	Africa	Asia
Franco-Russian alliance, 1894, first step in forming a rival bloc to the Triple Alliance of Germany, Austro-Hungary, and Italy (1879)	Brazil's "Old Republic," 1889-1930	"Scramble" for Africa begins, 1880s Gandhi in South Africa, 1893-1914 Anglo-Boer War, 1899-1902	Meiji Restoration, Japan, 1868 British occupation of Egypt, 1882 Boxer Uprising, China, 1899-1901
Beginning of Anglo- German naval race, 1900 Anglo-French Entente, 1904 First Moroccan Crisis, 1905 Anglo-Russian Entente, 1907 Bosnian Crisis, 1908			Japanese-British alliance, 1902 Russo-Japanese War, 1904-1905
Second Moroccan Crisis, 1911 Italy enters World War I, 1915 Abdication of the Tsar and establishment of the Provisional Government in Russia, March 1917 Bolshevik Revolution, November 1917 Treaty of Brest-Litovsk, 1918 Establishment of the Weimar Republic in Germany, 1919	Mexico's "Great Rebellion," 1910-1920 Radical period in Argentina, 1916-1930	Creation of Union of South Africa, 1910 Unification of Nigeria under British Rule, 1914 French and British seize German colonies, 1914-1915; East Africa campaign, through 1918 France recruits African troops for Western Front	Revolution of 1911, China Gandhi returns to India, 1915 Japan participates in World War I and Paris Peace Conference, 1914-1919 Egyptian "revolution" of 1919 Amritsar Massacre, India, 1919 May Fourth Movement, China, 1919
Russian New Economic Policy, 1921 French occupation of the Ruhr, 1923 Runaway German inflation, 1923 First Labour Government in Britain, 1924 First Soviet Five-Year Plan, 1928 Second British Labour Government, 1929-1931	Growth of artistic interest in developing distinctly national culture in Brazil and Mexico	African National Congress founded, South Africa, 1923	Founding of Chinese Communist Party, 1921 Government of India Acts, 1921, 1935 Mandate system in Syria, Iraq, Palestine, 1922-1923 Turkish Republic founded, 1923 GMD gains control of all China, 1928
"National" government in Britain, 1931-1935 Adolf Hitler named German chancellor, 1933 Popular Front in France, 1936-1937 Munich Agreement, 1938	Getúlio Vargas in power, Brazil, 1930-1945 Presidency of Lázaro Cárdenas, Mexico, 1934-1940	Boom in South Africa, 1933-late 1970s Italy conquers Ethiopia, 1935-1936	Japanese aggression against China, 1931– Japan and China at war, 1937-1940s

(Continued on next page)

The Twentieth Century: A Time Chart (continued)

	Events and Issues of Global Significance	Scientific-Technical-Intellectual	North America
1940	United Nations founded, 1945 Nuclear era begins with bombing of Hiroshima and Nagasaki, 1945 Era of rapid global economic growth, petroleum based, 1945–1973	Germans launch first guided missile, the V-2, 1942	Presidency of Harry S Truman, 1945–1953 Truman Doctrine, 1947 Taft-Hartley Act, 1947
1950	Bandung Conference of Asian-African Nations, stimulates growth of nonaligned movement, 1955 The Antarctic Treaty signed by the U.S., the Soviet Union, and ten other nations, marked an important event in international cooperation, 1959	Explosion of first U.S. hydrogen bomb, 1952 Explosion of first Soviet hydrogen bomb, 1953 Watson and Crick describe the double-helix structure of DNA, 1953 Soviets launch first orbiting satellite, Sputnik, 1957	Korean War, 1950–1953 Presidency of Dwight D. Eisenhower, 1953–1961 U.S. Supreme Court strikes down racial segregation in schools, 1953
1960	Population growth and superurbanization become major Third World issues. Cuban Missile Crisis, 1962 Global wave of protest by the young and disadvantaged, mid-1960s–early 1970s	United States lands first astronauts on the moon, 1969 Computerization becomes widespread in highly developed countries, based on large mainframe computers	Presidency of John F. Kennedy, 1961–1963 Presidency of Lyndon B. Johnson, 1963–1969 Tonkin Gulf Resolution, 1964 Assassination of Martin Luther King, Jr., 1968 Presidency of Richard M. Nixon, 1969–1974
1970	Global population growth peaks near 2 percent, 1970 OPEC oil price increases (1973, 1979) symbolize opening of era of interdependence amid scarcity; slower economic growth with recurrent recessions, 1973–present	SALT I Treaty, 1972 SALT II Treaty, 1979 (not ratified by U.S. Senate)	Watergate scandal, 1972–1974 U.S. Supreme Court strikes down anti-abortion laws, 1973 Presidency of Gerald R. Ford, 1974–1977 Presidency of Jimmy Carter, 1977–1981

Europe	Latin America	Africa	Asia
Winston Churchill, British prime minister, 1940–1945 Labour Government in Britain, 1945–1950 Fourth French Republic, 1946–1958 Marshall Plan, 1947 Berlin crisis, 1948 Foundation of German Federal Republic (West) and German Democratic Republic (East), 1949 NATO founded, 1949	Presidency of Juan Perón, Argentina, 1946–1955 Second Republic in Brazil, 1946–1964	North African Campaigns, 1941–1943 National Council of Nigeria and Cameroons, 1944 Apartheid becomes policy in South Africa, 1948	Japanese alliance with Germany and Italy, 1940 Japanese bomb Pearl Harbor, 1941 Muhammad Reza Shah, Iran, 1941–1979 U.S. occupation of Japan, 1945–1952 China's civil war, 1946–1949 India's independence, 1947; Jawaharlal Nehru, premier, 1947–1964 Israel's statehood, 1948
Hungarian Revolt, 1956 Khrushchev in sole leadership of the USSR, 1957–1964 Foundation of the European Common Market, 1958 Establishment of the Fifth French Republic, 1958	Fidel Castro's regime in Cuba, 1959–	Freedom Charter, South Africa, 1955	Iran's oil nationalization crisis, 1951–1954 Abdel Nasser's regime in Egypt, 1952–1970 Collectivization in China, 1955 Japan's GNP regains prewar levels, 1955 Suez Campaign, 1956 China's Great Leap Forward, 1958–1962 Multiparty democracy in Turkey; Democrat Party in power, 1950–1960 Overthrow of Iraqi Monarchy, 1958
Soviets crush Czech revolt, 1968 "Days of May" in France, 1968	Period of military authoritarianism and economic neocolonialism, mid-1960s–1980s Military rule in Brazil, 1964–1985 Military dominance of Argentine politics, 1966–1983	Decolonization, 1960s South Africa declared a republic, 1960 Sharpeville massacre, 1960 First Nigerian republic falls to military, 1966 Biafran civil war, 1967–1970	China acquires nuclear weapons, 1964 China's Cultural Revolution begins, 1965 Indira Gandhi, premier of India, 1966–1977, 1980–1984 Six-Day War, 1967 (third Arab-Israeli war) Turkey's Second Republic, 1961–1980 Ba'th Party takes power in Iraq, 1968
Nixon visits USSR, 1972 Helsinki Agreements, 1975, climax "Era of Detente"	Presidency of Salvador Allende, Chile, 1973 Presidency of Juan Perón, Argentina, 1973–1974 Major oil discoveries, Mexico, 1974 End of Brazil's economic "miracle," late 1970s Sandinista government in Nicaragua, 1979–1990	Nigeria becomes large oil exporter, 1970s Widespread drought and famine, early 1970s Ethiopian revolution, 1974 South Africa begins giving "independence" to homelands; Soweto incident, 1976 Nigeria returns to civilian government, 1979	Japanese-U.S. trade tensions, 1971–1980s October War, 1973 (fourth Arab-Israeli war) Indian nuclear explosion, 1974; self-sufficiency in grain, 1978 Death of Mao Zedong, 1976 Menachem Begin government in Israel, 1977–1983 Iranian revolution, 1979 Saddam Husayn in power in Iraq, 1979–

(Continued on next page)

The Twentieth Century: A Time Chart (continued)

	Events and Issues of Global Significance	Scientific-Technical-Intellectual	North America
1980	World population reaches 5 billion, 1986 Intermediate Nuclear Forces Treaty (INF), 1987 Montreal Protocol on Substances That Deplete the Ozone Layer, 1987	President Reagan calls for U.S. Strategic Defense Initiative ("Star Wars"), 1983 Desktop personal computer use becomes widespread, mid-1980s Chernobyl nuclear catastrophe, USSR, 1986 First patent of a genetically engineered animal, 1988 Stratospheric ozone depletion found to be global, 1988	Presidency of Ronald Reagan, 1981–1989 U.S. foreign debt becomes world's largest "Black Monday," stock market crash, 1987 Presidency of George Bush, 1989–1993
1990	Conventional Forces in Europe treaty (CFE), 1990 Soviet Union collapses, 1992 Strategic Arms Reduction treaties (START I and II), 1991, 1993 UN Conference on Environment and Development (Rio de Janeiro), 1992 Chemical Weapons Convention (CWC), 1993 Nuclear Nonproliferation Treaty (1968), renewed 1995 Comprehensive Nuclear Test Ban Treaty, 1996 Kyoto summit on global warming, 1997 Protests in Seattle against the World Trade Organization and "globalization," 1999 World population 6.1 billion, 2000	Revolution in global electronic communications technologies, early 1990s Rapid advances in techniques of cloning promise to transform agriculture and animal husbandry, 1996 From its space orbit, Hubble telescope revolutionizes astronomical knowledge U.S. unmanned space mission lands on Mars, 1997 Internet and hand-held devices begin to eclipse the personal computer, late 1990s Human genome sequenced, 2000	Presidency of Bill Clinton, 1993– North American Free Trade Agreement signed, 1993 Bombing of federal government headquarters in Oklahoma City, 1995 U.S. commits troops to peace-keeping mission in Bosnia, 1996

Europe	Latin America	Africa	Asia
Solidarity, independent Polish trade union movement, founded, 1980; forms government, 1989 Gorbachev becomes Soviet leader, 1985 East European countries end Communist dominance of governments, 1989	Argentina restores civilian rule, 1983 Brazil returns to civilian presidency, 1985 Mexican election, 1988, shows erosion of one-party system Chile elects civilian president, 1989	Widespread drought, famine, environmental degradation, c. 1982– Military coups, Nigeria, 1983, 1985 South African Constitution, 1984; township insurrections, 1984–1987	Deng Xiaoping in power in China, 1980–1997 Israel invades Lebanon, 1982 (fifth Arab-Israeli war) Palestinian uprising in occupied territories, 1987–1993 Chinese democracy movement, Tienanmen massacre, 1989 Death of Khomeini, 1989 Turkey's Third Republic, 1983– High-growth Asian economies achieve rapid growth with egalitarian income distributions
Maastricht Treaty to complete West European unity, 1991 Boris Yeltsin, first popularly elected Russian president, 1991, reelected 1996 Return of former Communists to power in Poland, 1993, and Hungary, 1994 Parliamentary election victories of French Socialists and British Labour Party challenge conservative dominance in Western Europe, 1997 Yeltsin resigns as Russian president, replaced by Vladimir Putin, 2000	Argentine economic growth resumes under civilian government, 1991–1992 Scandal topples President Collor, Brazil, 1992 North American Free Trade Agreement, 1993, and other economic integration plans Loss of Soviet subsidies provokes drastic economic decline in Cuba Seven decades of Institutional Revolutionary Party (PRI) rule ended, Mexican election of 1997	Civil war and famine in Somalia; U.S. and UN intervention, 1992 Whites vote to end minority rule in South Africa, 1992 Nigeria's military government ignores results of election supposed to restore civilian rule, 1993 Majority rule in South Africa, 1994; Nelson Mandela elected president Zaire's President Mobutu falls from power, 1997 Election of President Olusegan Obsanjo returns Nigeria to civilian rule, 1999 Thabo Mbeki, elected president of South Africa, 1999	Iraq's annexation of Kuwait, 1990; Gulf War and Iraq's defeat, 1991 Assassination of Rajiv Gandhi, 1991 Israel's 1992 election returns Labor Party to power China's rapid economic growth resumes under "market socialism" Hindu nationalists provoke crisis by destroying Ayodhya mosque (1992) Kobe earthquake, Japan, 1995 Tansu Çiller, prime minister of Turkey, 1993–1996, first woman to head government of an Islamic Middle Eastern country Israel-PLO Peace Accords (1993, 1995) Israeli Prime Minister Yitzhak Rabin assassinated, 1995 India's first lower-caste prime minister, H. D. Deve Gowda, elected 1996 China's Deng Xiaoping dies, 1997 Muhammad Khatami elected president of Iran, 1997 Hong Kong reverts to Chinese sovereignty, 1997 Asian economic crisis, 1997, starting in Thailand New intifada, Palestine, Nov. 2000 Falun Dafa protests and crackdowns, China, 1999– South Korean President Kim Dae Jung's visit to North Korea indicative of growing prospects for reunification, 2000

Twentieth-Century World

PART ONE

Introduction

CHAPTER 1

The Twentieth-Century in World History

EVERY FOUR YEARS, THE OLYMPIC GAMES OFFER THE SPECTACLE OF GLOBAL community organized as a series of sporting competitions. Outstanding athletes win medals and may become celebrities. The many medals won by some countries seem predictable because those countries are populous and powerful. Other countries, sometimes small and poor, make a strong showing in sports for which they have made a great commitment. Television coverage, reaching two-thirds of the world's people in 2000, enables viewers momentarily to share the thrill of victory, a thrill often heightened by moving stories of hardships overcome to win.

Comparisons with previous Olympiads always spring to mind. The percentage of women athletes has doubled since 1980, reaching 42 percent in 2000. The roster of competing countries has grown to 199. Some countries that used to compete no longer exist. Conversely, North and South Korean athletes marched together in the opening ceremonies at Sydney in 2000, symbolizing hopes for reunification. The athletes' racial and ethnic diversity, too, reflects a world of mobility and of identities demanding recognition. In 2000, many Cuban and U.S. athletes were descendants of African slaves, a Ukrainian-born swimmer won gold for the United States in the backstroke, athletes of North African origin competed for France, and sprinter Cathy Freeman, an Aborigine who later won gold in the women's four hundred meter, lit the torch at the opening ceremony, personifying hope for reconciliation between Australians of European and indigenous origin.

The sports are not all we notice. Corruption in the International Olympic Commission might have destroyed the games without diplomatic intervention in the 1990s. Questions about performance-enhancing drugs arise about athletes of all nations, and the variety of drugs is such that there are no tests to detect some of them. The growing size of the games—195,000 people from athletes to volunteers received Olympic credentials in Sydney—threatens their future viability and limits the numbers of cities that can host them. No city can do so without costly public works; Sydney added to this a demand for "green games" with benign ecological impact. The costs of the games places a premium on sponsorships, which threaten to make the games as much a competition among corporations as among athletes. The media's showcasing of U.S. athletes invites questions about how the games look in other countries' broadcasts. New time-keeping technologies alone make it possible to identify the winners in the many events. Ever since Palestinian radicals killed Israelis at Munich in 1972, security worries have haunted the Olympics; fortunately, the Sydney games came off without incident. Politics enters the picture most fascinatingly in the way the medal statistics compare to other rankings among nations. In 2000, the United States won more medals (97) than Russia (88) or China (59), but the twelve former Soviet countries won an astonishing total of 163 medals. Australia (58) won more medals than Germany (57).

Four Themes

As a picture of global interrelatedness, the Olympics provide a good opening point for a discussion of world history. This may not be the picture with the most serious or lasting consequences. Yet through a rapid-fire series of competitions whose winners are proclaimed immediately all over the world, the Olympics illustrate essential features of what we now call "globalization." Once the Olympics fade from television screens, other images—armed conflicts, economic crises, natural disasters—present globalization to us in other, usually less pleasant models. Unmistakably, each of us, wherever on the globe we stand, needs a way to understand these images that succeed each other so rapidly. Is there, then, a way to bring fleeting, fragmentary views of globalization into focus in a view that we can use as a map to help us understand the world around us?

This book aims to fill this need through a study of twentieth-century world history. We organize our study in terms of four themes that are illustrated in the Olympics—and in many other examples. Keeping these four themes in mind will help us understand the twentieth century systematically and selectively, seeing the forest and not only the trees:

1. *Global Interrelatedness.* Especially in a time of globalization, world history is not just the sum of the histories of the world's parts. There is, instead, a pattern of global interconnectedness, which has grown and tightened over time at an accelerating pace. Understanding world history first of all requires analyzing this pattern and how it has changed.

2. *Identity and Difference.* Global integration has increasingly challenged the autonomy

of individual communities. Global interrelatedness, however, has not produced sameness. Peoples all over the world vie to assert their distinct identities, using the very processes and media of globalization for this purpose. Conflict ensues over many issues, including race, ethnicity, religion, class, and gender.

3. *Rise of the Mass Society.* Because the twentieth century has witnessed a population explosion unprecedented in history, all questions about populations and their movements now converge in this question. The growth in human numbers has magnified the impact of political, economic, and technological change to make the twentieth century the age of the masses in everything from politics and war to popular culture.

4. *Technology Versus Nature.* Despite the technological breakthroughs that marked successive thresholds in human history, humanity had little protection from the forces of nature for most of its history. In the twentieth century, accelerating change in science and technology reversed this vulnerability in many respects. This change raises unprecedented questions, however, about whether humankind's seeming triumph over nature has put people at risk of irreparably degrading or even destroying their own habitat.

Key issues of twentieth-century history, these four themes converge on a question that has run throughout human history but seems especially acute today: Can the world's peoples live together and provide with some degree of equity for their members' needs, without either making unsustainable demands on the environment or conflicting unmanageably with one another?

Interrelatedness, identity and difference, the mass society, and technology—the Olympics bring together these themes in a festive picture. Through the selective discussion of spe-cific examples, the rest of this book examines how the themes have interacted, under less than ideal circumstances, to shape the history of the twentieth century. To set the stage for this discussion, the rest of this chapter defines the four themes more fully.

Global Interrelatedness

Large-scale patterns of interrelatedness emerged slowly and for a long time could be only regional or hemispheric in scope. The first global system took shape slowly between 1500 and the 1800s, and the twentieth century has been defined by a protracted crisis that destroyed it. With the destruction of that system, the forces that have shrunk differences of time and distance to produce the emergent system of globalization intensified.

The earliest interregional linkages were necessarily far sketchier than later ones. Two thousand years ago, however, the Central Asian silk route already linked China to the Roman Empire. They had no direct knowledge of each other, yet the Romans already worried about the eastward drain of precious metals to pay for silk. Through the fifteenth century, the silk route was probably the most important route in the world. It helped to spread not only goods but also religions—Hinduism, Buddhism, Christianity, and Islam. It also served as a route for the spread of disease, carrying plagues that reduced populations in China and the Mediterranean region by perhaps a quarter in the second and third centuries C.E., weakening the classical empires.*

---

*Dates in the current international calendar are identified as "C.E.," which stands for "common era." Dates that go back before the current international calendar are identified as "B.C.E.," meaning "before the common era." These designations correspond to "A.D." and "B.C." but are value-neutral in not assuming the Christian outlook implied by "A.D." (*anno domini,* "in the year of the Lord") or by "B.C." ("before Christ").

Kathy Freeman, Sydney, 2000. *She lit the Olympic torch and won gold in the women's 400 meter, symbolizing reconciliation among European and Aboriginal Australians. Thomas Kienzle/©AP-Wide World Photos*

Sea links also developed between the Red Sea and China. Among the goods traded in this network by the fifth century were spices, Indian cottons, sugar (which Indians first learned how to crystallize), the fast-growing rice that stimulated the development of south China, and Chinese products such as silk, porcelain, and the compass, which the Arabs may have been the first to use in seafaring. Indian mathematical advances—notably the concept of zero and the numerals that Euro-Americans call "Arabic" because they got them from the Arabs, who got them from the Indians—spread both east and west. Many crops also spread by this route. Examples include sugar cane; fruits such as oranges, lemons, limes, bananas, and melons; cotton and the indigo to dye it blue.

A much more extensive system of hemispheric integration arose following the Mongol conquests. Based in Central Asia, Chinggis Khan (r. 1206–1227) and his successors created an empire that spread for a time from eastern Europe to China. Catastrophic as Mongol conquest was for those who resisted, survivors found themselves inside an empire where it was possible to transport goods and ideas from China to Hungary safely. Even the Mongol Empire, however, was only one in a set of trading zones that existed between roughly 1250 and 1350, each overlapping one or more of the others. The entire network of exchange covered every place from West Africa and France to China, from south India to Central Asia. By this period, those at far ends of the network knew about one another. However, integration had not yet reached the level where any one power could dominate the whole system. The Mongols controlled the largest trading zone, the Central Asian one. China, then also Mongol ruled, anchored the most productive and advanced zone. The collapse of this hemispheric system followed the transmission through it, from east to west, of the bubonic plague, a catastrophe ironically made possible by the trans-Eurasian links that the Mongols had expanded and consolidated.

Euro-American writers conventionally open the age of global, as opposed to merely regional or hemispheric, interrelatedness with the European voyages of exploration that occurred shortly before the year 1500. It is very important to understand, however, that global integration took centuries and that the major European powers did not achieve global dominance until after 1800.

Between 1500 and 1800, the evolving pattern of global interrelatedness actually included a number of different regional systems that competed and interacted. Centered at Istanbul, for example, the Ottoman Empire (1300–1922) extended its control over the Balkans and Hungary, all of the Middle East except Iran and the lower Arabian peninsula, and most of the North African coast except for Morocco. Under the Safavid dynasty (1501–1722), Iran reached one of its historic high points. India experienced one of its major periods of imperial integration under the Mughal dynasty (1526–1858). China flourished under two of its greatest dynasties during this period: the Ming (1368–1644) and Qing (Ch'ing, 1644–1912). In Japan, this was the period of the Tokugawa shogunate (1603–1868).

The Ottoman Empire, Mughal India, and China were not just states. They also were economic systems that occupied huge spaces unified by the economic and cultural linkages they set up, producing most of their own needs but also engaging in exchanges with other economic systems farther afield. For example, enriched by its conquests and particularly by control of the Nile valley, the Ottoman Empire enclosed huge markets and was traversed by trade routes extending far into the Mediterranean, eastern and northern Europe, the Black Sea region, the Red Sea and Arabo-Persian Gulf, and east as far as India and what is now Indonesia. In the case of Mughal India, to cite but one notable indicator, Indian cotton textiles dominated world markets throughout this period. The greatest economic power of the period was surely China, with its vast exports of tea, silk, and porcelain—superior to other ceramics in durability as well as looks, and still called "china" in English because Europeans did not know how to produce it before the eighteenth century. The economic productivity of China and India was multiplied by the fact that their populations were already exceptionally large. China's rose from around 100 million in 1650 to 410 or 415 million two centuries later. During that period, China accounted for something like 40 percent of the world economy. China's post-1400 shift to a silver-based monetary system pushed the price of silver higher in China than anywhere else in the world. Much of this silver came across the Pacific from Mexico and Peru. In return, China's tea, silk, and porcelain flowed out to ports around the world.

Compared to the great Islamic empires, India, or China, the Europe of 1500 was small, divided, and backward. Even the exceptional transoceanic expansion on which it then embarked was possible only because of technological advances borrowed from other civilizations, especially China, and unforeseeable consequences that followed when Europeans first arrived in the Americas. The key early steps on the long European route to global power were the establishment of a new, world-circling network of sea routes and the early European success in the Americas. Not until the nineteenth century, after the Industrial Revolution, did Europeans establish dominance over Asia and Africa. When they did, they provoked resistance that would destroy European dominance in the twentieth century.

Unlike the huge empires that Islamic or Chinese dynasties—or for that matter the Russian Empire—put together by expanding across land into adjoining territories, the outstanding feature of the European *world system* that now began to take shape was that it was put together through expansion by sea and combined scattered territories in highly unequal relationships. Leading European states formed the *core* of the system. Outside Europe, parts of the world that had been incorporated into this system formed its *periphery.* An essential feature of the system was the *unequal exchanges* among zones of different types. The core powers monopolized the highest-value, highest-skill functions. For the periphery, incorporation meant subordination to one or another of the core powers and forced economic specialization in production of agricultural or mineral raw materials, usually by coerced labor. Ongoing competition among the core powers, both to dominate within the core and to create the largest possible colonial empires in the peripheral zones, gave the system a powerful drive to expand. The resources acquired from their colonies also made the system into a powerful engine to enrich the core powers. Prior to 1800, however, the overseas expansion of this European-centered system mostly occurred in the "new worlds" of the Americas and Australasia, not in Africa or Asia.

The prime factor in limiting European expansion to the "new worlds" can be described in terms of *ecological imperialism.* Europeans did not launch out into the world merely as human beings. They carried with them their culture and technology. They also transported a complex of living organisms, including animals, plants, and disease-causing pathogens. Because Europeans were among many Afro-Eurasian populations that had exchanged technologies, crops, animals, and diseases for millennia, this biological complex was not European but Afro-Eurasian in origin. The various elements of the complex had been brought together by long-term processes of competition and selection in the world's largest zone of interaction, the Afro-Eurasian landmass. If Chinese or Indians had reached the Americas first, they would have produced much the impact that the Europeans did.

When Europeans arrived in parts of the world whose peoples had been out of contact with Afro-Eurasia for tens of thousands of years, it was not just the Europeans, their ships, and firearms, but rather this entire Afro-Eurasian complex, that prevailed. Most lethal were the European-borne micro-organisms that spread smallpox, measles, diphtheria, chickenpox, bubonic plague, and influenza among populations that had never experienced them. The abrupt Spanish conquests of the greatest native American civilizations, those of the Aztecs (1521) and the Incas (1533), were more epidemiological than military disasters. Central Mexico's native American population fell from perhaps 25 million to 3 million in twenty-five years. Similar die-offs followed the establishment of European contact with "insular" populations, as long as there were any left. In Latin America, the conquerors' determination to exploit the survivors as coerced labor caused further mortality, creating the "necessity" to import African slaves. Of all transoceanic migrants in the world system, African slaves outnumbered Europeans until after 1800.

Ecological imperialism was not only a matter of disease. Europeans also introduced plants and animals that they had brought with them, sometimes unintentionally. In suitably temperate climates, these took over, pushing back or sometimes eliminating indigenous species. Europeans brought horses, cattle, pigs, goats, sheep, donkeys, black and brown rats, rabbits, and honeybees to the Americas. They brought wheat, rye, oats, barley, olives, many fruits, and weeds like dandelions and clover. Many of these species had a similar impact in places like Australia. "Neo-Europes" thus came into existence in different parts of the world and became attractive places for European settlement.

One of the most noteworthy features of the European-transported biological complex was that elements from the Americas and Africa were added to it as it spread. Plants that Europeans acquired from native Americans and then spread around the world include maize, squash, beans, potatoes, sweet potatoes, tomatoes, pumpkins, peanuts, cacao, manioc (cassava), tobacco, and various plants used to make dyes or medicines. Likewise, African slaves who were transported to the Americas became involuntary participants in the Europeans' global expansion. By making possible large increases in food production in certain environments, native American crops supported large population increases in places as far apart as Ireland or central Europe (the potato) and parts of China (the sweet potato).

The impact of ecological imperialism in the Americas and Australasia facilitated the establishment of European economic and political domination in those regions. The impact of disease-induced mortality on local cultures assured the dominance of European ideas and beliefs as well, influenced in time, to be sure, by native American and African cultures.

The factors that led to rapid European expansion in the Americas did not work in Africa and Asia, however. A major obstacle in tropical Africa was that Europeans faced a disease environment there that even they could not withstand prior to nineteenth-century medical advances, starting with the use of quinine against malaria. Because Africa is where humans first lived, the symbiosis between humans and their micro-parasites had longest to evolve there. Indigenous populations had developed some natural protections, like the sickle-cell trait against malaria, which Europeans lacked. The African slave trade, which had transported some 12 million Africans across the Atlantic by 1850,* thus depended on contacts at points along the coast between European and African slave traders.

Most of Asia also remained beyond European reach through 1800, not only because of long experience of the technological and biological complex that propelled European advance in the Americas, but also through the major surge of empire building and economic development discussed above. Under these circumstances, major states of the region clearly retained the initiative in organizing their relations with outsiders. The largest Islamic state, the Ottoman Empire, though losing ground militarily by the eighteenth century, dealt with European nations by granting them "privileges" that stated the terms on which they might trade inside the empire. After initial experiences with merchants and Catholic missionaries, China and Japan eventually suppressed Christianity and limited contact with Europeans to a few ports in China's case, to only one in Japan's. Effective responses to pre-1800 conditions, all of these policies proved unwise in the nineteenth century. The Asian environments where Europeans made greatest inroads were ones, like India and island Southeast Asia, where political authority was divided, so that Europeans could not only trade but also work their way into local power struggles, as the British did in India or the Dutch did in what is now Indonesia.

The global triumph of the European system resulted from a dual revolution that occurred in Europe at the end of the eighteenth century as a consequence of the final, British-French struggle for dominance among the core powers. Britain won for various reasons, including its lead in naval power and its greater access to colonial resources. An added factor was that because Britain had already gone through political revolution a century earlier, its parliamentary government already served the interests of the economically dynamic sectors of the population better than did France's absolute monarchy. Even the American Revolution did not slow Britain's ascent, partly because France further weakened itself financially to aid the Americans.

---

*In the same period, the Islamic slave trade transported another 5 million Africans toward North Africa and the Middle East.

Instead the British-French gap widened, as industrial revolution took off in Britain, while political revolution broke out in France.

While Chapter 2 discusses nineteenth-century developments more fully, it is important here to note major implications for global interrelatedness. The greatest technological advance since the invention of agriculture, the *Industrial Revolution* unfolded with late-eighteenth-century breakthroughs that mechanized cotton textile production, made the steam engine a reliable power source, and found in coal a plentiful, low-cost industrial fuel. These innovations made possible the creation of factories, where raw materials, labor, coal, and steam engines were brought together at the command of capital to produce with high efficiency. With this, the core powers began to move beyond *merchant capitalism,* in which businessmen trade in goods whose production they often cannot control, into the far more productive *industrial capitalism,* in which industrialists replace merchants as the key figures. This change hardly benefited everyone, even in Europe. Especially under the brutal conditions of the early factories, industrial workers amounted to "wage slaves," almost as wretched as those on colonial plantations.

What set the Industrial Revolution off from earlier breakthroughs was the mutual reinforcement among its major innovations, especially coal and steam. The development of coal as an industrial fuel opened the age of fossil fuels and greatly increased the amount of energy available for production and transport. The steam engine dramatically increased the demand for iron and steel and for advances in precision engineering, so fostering the rise of heavy industry. Moreover, the steam engine could propel itself as the engine of a railroad train or a steamship. Railways on land soon connected with steamer lines at the ports, creating a global transport network to bring raw materials to steam-powered factories and to distribute goods produced in them. Further improvements in transport and communication, like the telegraph (around 1840), shrank time and distance still more.

The spread of industrialization, from Great Britain to continental Europe, transformed the core powers and the world system. With time, the rise of new sectors like chemicals and steel transformed industry itself. By 1914, to be a great power meant to be one of the handful of European nations that competed with each other in industry and overseas expansion. Outside Europe, several "neo-Europes," including Canada and Australia, had also begun to industrialize. The United States had become the major new contender for great power status. No other country but Japan could make that claim. Industry remained a virtual monopoly of the core countries and some of their overseas extensions. The rise of the modern armaments industry, moreover, industrialized not only production but also destruction, so opening a disastrously wide gap between countries that did and did not have access to advanced military technology. At that, Europe's global dominance reached its zenith.

Meanwhile, following the American experience of 1776, *political revolution* came to Europe in 1789, when the French monarchy collapsed in violent social revolution. By 1793, the French had killed their king, declared a republic based on *popular sovereignty* (that power belongs to the people), and been attacked in retaliation by practically all the rest of Europe. The French response was to create a mass citizen army: the sovereign people mobilized to defend their republic. More highly motivated than the armies they faced, the French not only defended themselves but exported their revolutionary ideas, which eventually spread around the world. Among these ideas, two had especially major consequences for world history.

Nationalism gave emotional fire to the idea that the nation belonged to the people, who therefore should be ready to rise to defend the nation as the French had done. With the overthrow of a monarch claiming to rule by divine right—an idea that goes back to the dawn of civilization—and the substitution of the idea of popular sovereignty, the age of mass politics began. Not only should the people rule, but governments and peoples should speak the same language; the map should be redrawn into nation-states: "Germany for the Germans," and "Poland for the Poles!" In fostering patriotism and citizen participation, nationalism could help to foster democratic politics. However, it also led in many places to bloody conflicts as the number of nation-states rose to the 199 that partcipated in the 2000 Sydney Olympics.

Liberalism, in its "classic" nineteenth-century form, was the most progressive set of ideas current in revolutionary Europe about how a nation should be governed. Classical liberalism aimed to free the individual intellectually through freedom of thought and expression, politically through constitutional government with guaranteed individual rights, and economically through unregulated free enterprise and free trade. By the late nineteenth century, however, industrial labor relations and international competition had begun to create doubts about liberal economics. Shifting emphasis from the rights that preoccupied affluent liberals to the economic relations that made them rich, Karl Marx (1818–1883) predicted the revolutionary overthrow of liberal capitalism when the oppressed "workers of the world" would rise up and throw off their chains. Others less radical sought to protect the disadvantaged by reformist means of the sort that redefined liberalism for Americans of the 1930s or shaped Europe's post-1945 welfare states. Later chapters will discuss these developments.

The effects of the dual revolution on the world outside Europe were not only profound but also ambivalent, because scarcely anyone yet understood that ideas like free trade and nationalism would produce different consequences in colonial environments. The spread of the political revolution to Latin America, for example, made almost the entire region independent—politically but not economically. In-

deed, Latin America remained internally as well as externally colonial: the exploitative racial and class relations of colonial society coexisted with ongoing economic dependency (see Chapter 7).

In sub-Saharan Africa, the slave trade was abolished, but practically the whole continent was colonized. This sudden incorporation into the European system resulted from midcentury medical breakthroughs that enabled Europeans to survive in the interior and from the military technology gap, coupled with agreement by treaty in Europe not to sell guns in Africa. Competition became so keen that the European powers met in congress in Berlin (1884–1885) to define a way to divide the spoils without conflict among themselves. European powers had only to "notify and occupy": announce their claims to one another, then stake them. By 1914 only Liberia and Ethiopia remained independent.

In the Middle East, the Ottoman Empire and Iran remained politically independent but were reduced economically to semicolonial status; the Ottoman Empire also lost many of its provinces—to nationalist movements in southeastern Europe, to colonization in Southwest Asia and North Africa. Further East, despite the Great Mutiny of 1857 and hundreds of smaller episodes of resistance, India had been taken almost entirely under British rule by 1858. China was reduced to semicolonial status after the First Opium War (1839-1842). Japan was forced to open to foreign trade in 1853–1854. In both China and Japan, the forced opening touched off major crises, destabilizing China and provoking the revolutionary crisis that broke out in 1911. In Japan, revolutionary crisis came much sooner (1868) and produced the much faster recovery that enabled Japan to begin to command recognition as a power in its own right by about 1900.

Today some historians speak of a "long twentieth century," beginning in the mid-1800s with crises around the world, such as India's Great Mutiny of 1857 or Japan's crisis of 1868, which signal an increase in reactions against tightening European domination. Other historians, including the authors of this book prefer a "short twentieth century," 1914-1991. Historians of both types see the socialist collapse of 1989-1991 as the end point. The period 1914-1991 was filled with the multiphased terminal crisis of this European-dominated system and with signs of what may be a new system emerging. In the narrowest sense, the crisis that destroyed the old system occurred in three parts, each of which led to the next: World War I (1914-1918), the Depression (1929), and World War II (1939-1945 in Europe but with earlier starts in Africa and East Asia). These crises (discussed in Chapters 3, 5, and 10) produced not only global consequences at the time but also sequels that did not work themselves out until much later. For example, the compound crisis of 1914 to 1945 so weakened the European nations that they had to relinquish control over their overseas colonies, in which independence movements had grown up to press this demand. *Decolonization* continued from 1947 until the 1960s in Asia; in Africa it began in the late 1950s and was mostly over by the mid-1970s. The process turned many former colonies into formally independent nations, which then had to confront the realities of their inability to hold their own in the world economy (see Chapters 14-17), a problem that Latin American states had faced much earlier.

In the meantime, the crisis of 1914 to 1945 had also brought forth new powers and new programs for national and international development. The most important sequel to the passing of European dominance was the emergence of two new powers of much larger scale: the United States and the Soviet Union, which emerged out of the Bolshevik Revolution (1917). The Soviet blend of Marxist internationalism and repression managed, among other things, to hold together this huge, multiethnic state for seventy years past the breakup of Europe's other multinational empires at the end of World War I.

For four decades after 1945 many analysts thought the rivalry between the two nuclear superpowers in itself defined the pattern of global interrelatedness. In particular, as each superpower sought to win allies, it appeared for a time as if a new system of three "worlds" might emerge: the United States and its democratic, capitalist allies made up the "free world"; the Soviet Union and other socialist states formed the "socialist bloc"; and the rest of the world—postcolonial but underdeveloped—constituted the "third world." The supposed system of three worlds collapsed even faster than the Soviet Union, however. By the 1960s, it was clear that neither the "free world" nor the "socialist bloc" was a real unit. In both, the "allies" or "satellites" began to rival their respective superpowers in economic performance, partly because they did not spend as large a part of their resources on military and strategic priorities as did the superpowers (see Chapter 11). This suggested that the real competition was still *geoeconomic* rather than *geostrategic,* that world power was more dependent on economic productivity than military might. By the 1980s, the coherence of the "third world" also began to disappear, as several countries in Southeast and East Asia began to achieve rapid economic growth, while others, mostly in Africa and South Asia, declined economically.

In terms of the economic issues that have shaped earlier world systems, today it seems clear that the world system of the future will have multiple economic "cores." One of them will be centered in North America. One of them will be centered in Western Europe, probably with additions from the former socialist countries; the extent to which the European Union will take precedence over individual nations remains to be determined. East Asia is likely to anchor another regional center. Recent history suggests Japan should lead this region; a longer historical perspective says that China must play this role, although this will require resolving the contradiction between China's still communist political structure and its increasingly market-oriented economy. Whether Russia and the other Soviet successor states can re-emerge as another regional center remains uncertain.

In the sense of having multiple zones, each with its regional center, but with no one zone dominant over all the others, this new world system will resemble pre-1800 global configurations more than it resembles the more recent European-dominated system with its single core region. However there are great differences from both. The greatest difference is that global interrelatedness, after tightening for centuries, has evolved into the new form called *globalization.*

Globalization is the revolution of our times. It continues and intensifies old trends but also transforms them into a new reality. It promises to shape the twenty-first century even more than the Bolshevik revolution shaped the twentieth. Propelled especially by advances in transportation and communications that have radically accelerated change and practically obliterated differences in space and time, globalization affects all phases of life—economics, politics, and culture. Attempts to understand it are also revolutionizing social thought precisely because pre-existing ideas and theories do not suffice to explain it. Instead of older, relatively clear-cut global patterns made up politically of nations and empires, economically of markets and corporations, and culturally of linguistic cultures or systems of beliefs and values, globalization creates a global disorder. The entities that seemed to structure the world before—nation-states and international organizations, business firms, political ideologies, and religious faiths—reappear as if suspended in this global flux. In order to understand globalization, the challenge is not so much to recognize those entities as to analyze this flux and the currents within it.

There are many such currents. There are patterns of migration and ethnic dispersion that have created miniatures of many of the world's nations in the immigrant neighborhoods of the largest cities. There are transfers of technology

that have ended the old monopolization of industry by the most highly developed countries. Global financial flows now reportedly move $1.5 trillion around the world each day—real dollars, virtual dollars? Transmission by satellite creates global flows of electronic media, making images from far parts of the world instantly available everywhere. With electronic mail and the Worldwide Web, instantaneous global communications and library-fulls of information become readily accessible, at least for those equipped with the required technologies. Such enlarged possibilities for the movement of people and ideas make all belief systems—all religions, for example—now truly global, as Californians and New Yorkers join Islamic mystical orders, or as an aged, world-traveling pope blesses the people in scores of places and languages.

Many of the consequences of globalization are benign. Its noblest consequence is to transform "humanity" from an ideal in the minds of sages into something that can be experienced in everyday life. Likewise encouraging, while many of the global patternings of the past were dominated by states and empires, many of the currents associated with globalization are much more voluntaristic and decentralized, as in the case of the global environmental movement or of the Internet, a network of electronic information exchange, operating according to shared conventions, supported at many points around the world, but with almost no center of control.

However, the currents flowing in the global disorder also produce many forms of tension and crisis. The migrants whose far-flung diasporas have begun to deterritorialize national identity are often refugees fleeing from poverty, oppression, or war in their home countries. Stimulated by accelerated developments in the sciences, the technological flows that have brought some form of industrialization to most of the world's countries have also created ever-renewed differentials and inequalities in access to the most advanced technologies. Global fi-

Globalism and religious activism. *A cell phone enables Nachman Biton and a relative in France to pray together at the Wailing Wall in Old Jerusalem.* Nati Harnik/© AP-Wide World Photos

nancial flows have integrated the world's markets more tightly, but not without enlarging gaps between dynamic centers and languishing peripheries. The globalization of the media, while vastly increasing the circulation of information and the possibilities for diversion, has also raised troubling questions about what interests control the media and with what intentions and consequences. Communities of believers, experiencing more complex interactions with those who do not share their commitments, have not always reacted peaceably.

In sum, it is as if the forces of tightening global interconnectedness, intensifying for centuries, have somehow acquired critical mass in the contemporary revolution of globalization. This is the first and foremost fact to notice as the twenty-first century begins. However, it is not the only one. The remaining three themes of this book will raise important questions about

culture, society, and technology. Critical issues in their own right, those three themes gain new dimensions as they become caught up in globalization.

Identity and Difference

Long before the beginnings of recorded history, human beings not only appeared on Earth and began to spread out from their earliest known habitats in East Africa. They also began to form societies and to create artifacts and ideas that they used to structure their ways of life. With time and geographical dispersion, these societies became quite diverse, with differences in tools, languages, beliefs, even physical characteristics. Archeological remains, like the houses built of mammoth bones in the Ukraine 26,000 years ago, or cave paintings as much as 32,000 years old in France, preserve tantalizing evidence of ways of life that vanished long before recorded history began. The difficulty of knowing today exactly what these artifacts meant to their creators suggests, however, that the *cultures* that human communities produce—the combinations of objects and ideas that they create or adopt to structure their way of life— have less consistency of meaning or durability than many of their members may assume. Then as now, cultures are better understood as systems of symbols and meanings that even their creators contest, that lack fixed boundaries, that are constantly in flux, and that interact and compete with one another.

Sometimes, cultural patterns that developed in prehistoric times spread across large regions. Sometimes, too, similar patterns may have been invented independently in more than one region with similar conditions. Agriculture, for example, seems to have developed and spread by both diffusion and independent invention. Wheat-based agriculture was invented in Palestine, Syria, and eastern Turkey and seems to have spread from there. Other types of agriculture, based on other crops that have to be cultivated in other ways, were invented in other places. The fact that some of these systems appeared in places that were not in direct contact suggests independent invention.

Sometimes the spread of particular practices seems to have been associated with specific linguistic groups. The rise of horseback riding and the invention of the wheel and later of the chariot all appear to have occurred between 4000 and 2000 B.C.E. in the steppes (grasslands) near the present border of Russia and Kazakstan, spreading outward from there with the Indo-Europeans. Languages derived from theirs spread all over Europe (English being one) and in Iran and India; but the Central Asian steppe zone was later taken over by speakers of other languages, primarily Turkic, who thus divided the Indo-European zone in two. In Africa, the spread of ironmaking and agriculture was associated with a great migra-

tion of peoples, whose language was the parent of the many Bantu languages still widespread south of the Sahara. The wide spread of languages whose speakers possessed technologies that others lacked suggests that cultural difference could easily give rise to competition and conflict, and that ethnic and linguistic identities, which many of us imagine to be permanent, actually appear and disappear.

History begins with the invention of writing. So say historians, whose primary source for learning about the past is the written records that earlier societies created. The advent of writing followed on the rise of cities and civilizations, momentous developments in the history of human creativity.

The earliest cities grew up in Asia, about 3500 B.C.E. on the Tigris and Euphrates rivers in today's Iraq. The next urban centers emerged about 3000 B.C.E. in Africa, in Egypt's Nile valley. Cities appeared in India about 2500 B.C.E., in China about 1500 B.C.E., and in Central America by 1000 B.C.E. *City* and *civilization* are related concepts: the word *civilization* derives from the Latin *civis* (citizen of a city). The rise of cities became possible once ancient societies had domesticated plants and animals and farmers had begun to settle in permanent villages. Some villages produced enough food to support craftworkers or religious leaders. Specialization of roles and production processes continued; some settlements kept growing in size and complexity, and gradually cities and civilizations emerged. As such growth occurred, craftworkers' need for raw materials and markets gave rise to trade and efforts to expand the city's zone of control. Village shrines grew into temples staffed by religious functionaries wielding wide influence. Organized governmental institutions emerged, with their military forces, tax collectors, and rulers, who reinforced their power by claiming divine sanction for it, if not divinity for themselves. Merchants, priests, and rulers needed ways to keep track of information. The answer was writing, which gradually began to be used also for less practical purposes, such as philosophy and literature. The cities generated most of the ferment that creates great civilizations, but their development required the extension of control over a wider area—not just a city but a kingdom or empire.

Not all civilizations had all these traits. For example, Andean civilizations lacked writing. Specific cases varied, but the traits described above generally appeared as civilizations emerged.

Against the backdrop of ongoing, worldwide cultural creativity and differentiation, the rise of civilization added new complexities. The earliest civilizations were localized in river valleys. Beyond them lived peoples whom the "civilized" saw as "barbarians." With time, the pattern of civilizations isolated like islands in a sea of "barbarism" began to change. As that happened, interactions between centers of civilization and peoples living outside them changed in complex ways.

World historians used to concentrate on the comparative study of civilizations, and some retained the vocabulary of "civilization" and "barbarism." There were many problems about such thinking. The "barbarians" were not always disadvantaged in competing with the "civilized." Nor did everyone who lived in a great center of civilization share fully in it. Privileged elites, almost entirely male, chiefly produced, maintained, and profited from civilization. Most other categories of people who lived within the zone of a given civilization—in proportion as they differed from the privileged elites in race, ethnicity, religion, gender, and social class—had less access to whatever made that civilization memorable. While their influence may have spread across a larger space at a given time, the continuity, too, of large civilizations was not always surer than that of the cultures of smaller, weaker peoples.

With time, the scale of civilizations did increase. Between about 1000 B.C.E. and 500 C.E.,

civilizations arose that projected their influence farther outward and gradually came into contact with one another, as we have seen in the case of Chinese silk exports to Rome. The civilizations of this period also proved *classic* in the sense that they set philosophical or religious standards that endure even still. In this period emerged Greek philosophy, Christianity, Hinduism, Buddhism, and Confucianism. Several belief systems extended their influence beyond their regions of origin. Ancient Greek culture radiated as far as Spain and India. By the end of this period, Christianity had begun to spread from the Middle East to Europe, Africa, and Central Asia; and Buddhism was spreading from India through South and East Asia.

Between 500 and 1500, not only did Eurasia become more tightly interlinked, as noted in the previous section, but new and larger empires emerged. Such was the Islamic empire, which stretched, by the eighth century, from Spain to the borders of China. Spreading into sub-Saharan Africa, Islam, in addition to traditional African religion and Christianity, completed what has been called Africa's "triple heritage" in religion.[1] The largest state of this period was the Mongol Empire. Emerging at a time when weakness and disunity in the major centers of civilization created exceptional opportunities for Central Asia's Turkic and Mongol horsemen to expand by deploying their fearsome military skills, the Mongol Empire became the only premodern empire to rule across Eurasia, from the Baltic Sea to the Pacific. In the thirteenth century, as noted, it became the central zone in a hemispheric system of interlinkage that included much of Afro-Eurasia.

Between 500 and 1500, the civilizations that emerged in the preceding period survived or were transformed to varying degrees, despite invasions by such "barbarian" outsiders as the Germans in northern Europe or the Mongols farther east. While absorbing extensive Buddhist influence in this period, China became the outstanding example of continuity. No other civilization has retained such consistency across such vast stretches of space and time. From the sixth century, too, dates the massive transmission of Chinese cultural influence to Japan, Korea, and Vietnam. In India, cultural continuity was less strong but still significant. Buddhism went into decline from the sixth century on in India, and Hinduism rebounded, partly by absorbing Buddhist ideas. Conquerors from the Middle East introduced Islam into India, as well. In the Middle East, the rise of Islam in the seventh century caused sharper discontinuity than in either China or India. Islam forms a single monotheistic tradition with Judaism and Christianity, and Islamic civilization also absorbed many elements from earlier Middle Eastern and Greek cultures. Yet the rise of Islam marked a break: it abruptly changed the religious map of the Middle East and far beyond, and it established Arabic as the classic language of a major new civilization, in place of older languages of the region. The greatest discontinuities occurred, however, in Europe. There the Roman Empire's collapse cleared the ground for a substantially different civilization, Christian in religion, centered to the north and west of the Roman world, and unable to recover the political unity of the Roman period.

In 1500, if there had been observers equally well informed about all parts of the world, probably only the most perceptive could have seen in Europe's internal disunity the potential to rise to global dominance. China would have impressed all observers by its size, productivity, and brilliance. Islamic civilization would have impressed them as not just brilliant but also the world's most widespread, from West Africa to western China and, in a different line of advance to what we now call the Philippines. Moreover, a series of great regional Islamic empires was developing, centered in the Middle East and India. Even the early European voyages of exploration would not have impressed our imaginary observers. In contrast to the three tiny ships

with which Columbus reached the Americas in 1492, China's Ming dynasty between 1405 and 1423 had launched seven voyages that reached as far as East Africa. The first of these voyages had transported twenty-eight thousand people in sixty-two huge vessels. China's later abandonment of these missions was a rational decision for an empire so productive that it had little to gain from foreign trade, an empire whose Ming rulers had expelled the Mongols but still had to face them across their northern border. As we have seen, China remained preeminent in the world economy through the eighteenth century.

Between the rise of civilization and about 1500, all the processes that shape identity and difference had operated within the zones of individual civilizations or in spaces that separated them (zones of "barbarism," as they were called in ancient times). As the scale of civilizations grew in the way discussed above, those spaces had diminished and increasingly been traversed by patterns of interaction among civilizations—long-distance trade and migration routes, in particular. After 1500, this situation began to change in the fundamental sense that a global network was being put together. This process took several centuries to complete. After 1800, Europe's dual revolution—political and industrial—brought the emerging system to its high point. From then on, all major issues of identity and difference—race, ethnicity, religion, gender, class, and so on—would react not just to local forces but also to the tightening of global integration. Given the structural inequalities of the European-dominated system, the consequences for world history differed in core and periphery but were profoundly significant for both.

Among the privileged power centers of the global system, for example, the centuries-old drive to reorganize political life along the lines of the nation-state climaxed in a wave of unifications and consolidations. Given the fact that practically no European government actually

Latino students in San Francisco protest voter approval of Proposition
187. *California voters deny immigrants access to most state public services,*
1994. © *Bettmann/CORBIS*

had the homogeneous population that the myth of the nation-state idealized, this was no small project. In earlier centuries, many European rulers had used violence to promote religious homogeneity. By 1800, the emphasis for most had shifted to linguistic and cultural homogeneity. War could play a part in promoting this, certainly for disunited nationalities like the Germans and Italians; but so could the use of state power for social engineering through mass education, compulsory military service, and nationalistic indoctrination. Even within the prosperous core nations, however, these changes did not occur without creating new levels of politics defined in terms of identity and difference. Particularist resistances to na-

tional assimilation might be submerged, but few of them—Basques in Spain and France; Welsh, Scots, and Irish in the British isles—truly disappeared. Industrialization created the class politics of owners versus workers, with Marx as the workers' global-minded prophet. Open contradictions in the liberal discourse of the "rights of man" provoked opposition movements like abolitionism and feminism. Even in the core powers of the Eurocentric system, then, issues of identity and difference proliferated.

Societies that passed under European control, directly or indirectly, faced a more complicated situation. Endowed with their own cultures and world-views, they confronted alien

powers whose impact on them was very different from the self-image that those powers promoted to their own people in Europe. Colonial
resistances varied across a vast spectrum, from
evasiveness to violent rebellion, as the global
struggle against subordination opened. Gradually, out of the contradictions between the discourse of liberal nationalism and the practice of
colonial rule, colonial nationalisms began to
emerge. The struggle against colonialism demanded that all these issues be processed into
the form of the mass-mobilizing nationalism
that would eventually seem to triumph with
post-1945 decolonization. All the differences
within the colonial society had to be smoothed
over for that to happen, however. A generation
after decolonization, those differences would
all start to resurface.

With the collapse of the European-centered system in the protracted twentieth-century crises discussed in the previous section
and the transition to the newer pattern of globalization that is now emerging, the global and
the local began to rearticulate in the complex
ways that characterize life today. Today, globalization, in all its growing complexity, comes
down to earth everywhere, grinding against all
the forces of identity politics and provoking
reactions from them. Movements articulated in
terms of nationalism or religion attract most
attention in this connection. Examples include
the self-styled militia movements in the United
States, white supremacists who sometimes also
believe that the nation is being taken over by
"world government," or alternatively the resurgent nationalisms, long surpressed under communism, that have spilled much blood in Bosnia,
Kosovo, and Chechnya. Movements reasserting
religious identities in the face of change are, if
anything, more numerous, ranging from the U.S.
Christian Right to the many Islamic revivalist
movements or India's Hindu nationalism. Religion and nationalism, however, are not the only
issues that shape identity politics. Crosscutting
them are the myriad issues of race, ethnicity,

class, and gender that now intersect hotly in
places like California or south Florida, or that
came into view in South Africa's recent transition to majority rule.

Several decades ago, many observers believed that so many homogenizing forces had
been unleashed through the mass media and
the spread of mass consumerism that the
world would become a "global village." Today it
is clear that globalization produces, not sameness, but newer, stronger assertions of identity
and difference.

Rise of the Mass Society

Twentieth-century population growth has
made the rise of the mass society first of all a
story of numerical increase. Yet the story of
populations is also about their movements and
interactions. It thus includes all the changes that
grew out of Europe's dual revolution and the
global struggle against imperialism. These have
transformed the way people live, creating a
world of mass politics, mass communications,
mass consumerism, and, in time of war, mass
military mobilization. When we speak of the rise
of the mass society, all these meanings are
closely interrelated.

Demographic Transitions

Demography (the study of human populations)
cannot yield exact results for periods before the
advent of modern statistics. Yet demographers
believe that population grew very slowly until
about 1750 and then entered a period of rapid
growth that still continues, although the main
centers of growth, initially in Europe, have
shifted in this century to the developing countries.

Population history includes two, perhaps
three, major transitions. Prior to the invention
of agriculture from 7,000 to 9,000 years ago,
global population probably did not exceed 5 or
10 million. Agriculture increased food supplies

and stimulated population growth, creating the first transition. Still, growth remained slow, and world population had risen to only 500 million by 1750. Birth rates and death rates normally hovered in rough equilibrium at high levels, the chief gaps taking the form of "dismal peaks," when war, famine, or plague caused a spike in the death rate.

Starting around 1750 and continuing in the nineteenth century, the second transition occurred in the European core countries. Initially improvements in food supplies, and later productivity gains from industrialization, supported this transition. The *demographic transition* took the form of a drop, first in death rates, later in birth rates. The transition ended when both rates regained equilibrium at new, lower levels. In between, while the gap between the two rates remained wide, with many more births than deaths each year, a burst of population growth occurred. World population grew from about 1 billion in 1800 to 1.7 billion in 1900. Centered in Europe, this growth was associated with rising living standards made possible by the Industrial Revolution and the increasing integration of the world economy. Europe's population growth also helped bring forth many familiar political and cultural traits of the mass society, to be noted below.

The third transition, so far incomplete, features faster growth in different places. World population soared from 1.7 billion in 1900 to 6.1 billion in 2000. Growth in developed countries fell to replacement levels or less, especially in formerly socialist countries with troubled economies. However, growth took off outside Europe and North America. By the 1980s, 90 percent of each year's growth occurred in developing countries, a change largely caused by modern improvements in public health. After 1970, birth and death rates for the developing countries began to fall; yet the gap between the two rates was nowhere near closing, and both remained at far higher levels than in the developed countries. As a result, the poorer countries'

population explosion would continue for a long time to come. Once again, profound changes followed from this incomplete transition, but they were quite different from those, associated with rising living standards, that had accompanied the second demographic transition a century earlier.

The more than tripling of world population since 1900 has radically altered and intensified human interactions of every kind. Ultimately, some of the biggest issues that this raises cluster around the stresses that such a population explosion places on natural resources. These environmental and resource issues occupy us increasingly in later chapters of this book, starting from the point when the OPEC oil crisis of 1973 ended a quarter-century of exceptional growth in the world economy (see Chapter 16).

Globalization of the Mass Society

Long before its impact on environmental and resource issues reached the acute stage, population growth interacted with other forces to turn the twentieth century, the world over, into the age of the mass society. In Europe, the dual revolution stimulated not only the population growth of the second demographic transition but also modern processes of mass mobilization. The Industrial Revolution, for example, gave rise to the modern industrial working class and stimulated migration from the countryside to industrial towns and cities. By increasing the supply of goods, industrialization helped to launch mass consumerism and new forms of popular culture, while innovations in transportation and communication set people in motion as never before. The political revolution meanwhile transformed people from passive *subjects* of kings into *citizens* with political rights and duties to the nation. Compulsory national education systems, increased literacy, and the rise of modern print media all helped to mold and motivate citizens. With time, mass mobilization sped up in pace and became global in scope. The interlinkages of the European-dominated system launched this process by calling forth colonial nationalisms. Their leaders' task was to convince their followers to reimagine themselves as nations and strive together for independence.

As the twentieth century progressed, innovations that had contributed to mass mobilization in the nineteenth century spread across the world, and new ones—such as the rise of the electronic media and information technologies, or the proliferation of industries catering to mass consumption in clothing, fast food, or commercialized leisure—acquired global scope. In the process, however, an important differentiation in patterns of political mobilization, which had begun to appear in the nineteenth century, also spread.

Liberalism and nationalism, the two great themes of the political revolution, flourished together in only a few countries, producing the kind of democratic mass mobilization that came out of the French Revolution. In Germany and in southern and eastern Europe, from Spain to Russia, the difficulties of achieving unification or overcoming underdevelopment broke these two themes apart. When it came, mass mobilization assumed authoritarian forms, eventually giving rise, under fascism and communism, to some of the most repressive twentieth-century states, which recognized in their people few rights but many duties (see Chapters 4 and 6). The peoples of colonial or semicolonial lands felt the effects of European liberalism economically but not politically. Local elite leaders, realizing the potential of political liberalism and nationalism as counterarguments against imperialism, had to struggle to mobilize their masses in an independence struggle for which the latter were mostly not ready. The normal result was a colonial form of authoritarian mobilization. Few postcolonial governments had the institutional resources to match Nazi or Soviet repression. Yet, with a few notable exceptions,

authoritarian mass mobilization became the norm in the developing world. Achieving greater democratization remained as the critical issue for the post–Cold War era (see Chapters 14–17).

If the rise of the mass society had economic as well as political dimensions in the Europe of the second demographic transition, the same is more true for the developing world of the third. Not only has the twentieth-century population explosion been concentrated in the developing countries, but those countries' rates of demographic and economic growth have diverged, with the highest birth rates persisting in the countries that have fared the worst economically. Among other consequences, this situation has set up flows of migration far larger than, and quite different from, those of the previous century. Much of the migration occurs within or among poor countries. However, much of it also takes the form of movement to the rich countries. They have tried increasingly to protect themselves with restrictive immigration policies (see Chapter 18). Yet the human pressures are ones that latter-day Chinese walls cannot contain.

The result has been to create a world where, for growing numbers of people, it is normal to be stateless or displaced, a migrant or refugee, where diaspora communities—Turks in Berlin, Iranians in Los Angeles—have become as typical as nineteenth-century nationalists imagined cohesive nationalities and cultures should be. Not only have the masses been multiplied and mobilized; in today's contentiously interconnected world they also have been intermingled as never before.

Technology Versus Nature

Across history, changes in the techniques that people use to produce what they need have marked many of the most important developmental milestones. With changes in these techniques have come major shifts, both in the

The world's largest democracy goes to the polls, 1996. *Unusual among developing countries, India continues electoral politics with high voter turnout. Acute social inequality also persists.* © *AP/Wide World Photos*

balance among societies, and in societies' relationship to their natural habitat. Only in the twentieth century, however, did scientific and technological change reach the point where it could not only set up the flows of people, money, and ideas that shape today's tightly networked world, but also fundamentally alter the balance between human societies and their natural environment.

When we think about science and technology, we need to think about "survival technologies," particularly for food production, as well as about more learned pursuits. Throughout prehistory and for much of history, survival technologies, mostly devised by anonymous men and women, were the all-important ones. Humans lived very close to nature, had little control over it, took little from it in the way of nonrenewable resources, and were painfully vulnerable to its forces. Over time, people caused environmental damage through deforestation or overexploitation, probably without realizing what they were doing. For example, the same parts of the Middle East where wheat-based agriculture was invented are today largely bare of trees, partly because of overgrazing, particularly by goats, who eat the bark off young trees and kill them. In general, however, human dependence on the natural world was deeply imprinted on people's thinking.

Not only were many inventions in the realm of survival technology—the different forms of agriculture, for example—among the most important of all time, but some of them are still "state of the art." For example, in postcolonial Africa, well-meant efforts to promote Euro-American-style agro-technology, with large, tractor-tilled fields planted in single crops, succeeded less well than the conventional wisdom of African farmers, often women, who mixed complementary crops in the same field or used "multistory" farming, a technique independently invented in various tropical regions, in which fruit trees of several heights, above-ground crops like corn, beans, and melons, and root crops like yams are grown together. For the world overall, applied science has revolutionized agriculture, yet local knowledge hard won by experience still has its role in maintaining productivity.

For most of history, the development of science and technology was as slow as that of the survival technologies. It was unevenly paced in different parts of the world and little able to change human vulnerability to nature's whims. Despite its technological lead in the nineteenth century, Europe, as we have seen, was not the most highly developed of the world's civilizations in earlier periods. Eleventh-century China achieved technological advances so significant that scholars ask why it did not experience the breakthrough into ongoing, self-compounding innovation that Britain later did. Among China's innovations in that period were the first use of coal as a fuel, advances in iron production, movable type, explosive powder, and the compass. India's shipbuilding was still advanced enough that the British navy ordered ships in India during the Napoleonic Wars, and China still led the world in silk and porcelain in 1800. Another East Asian advantage was that the early creation of a "printed-book culture," coupled with Confucian emphasis on learning, gave China and Japan probably the highest literacy rates in the world, into the nineteenth century. Even so, average life expectancy in the world's most flourishing societies would not have been much over thirty-five in 1800; it was not much

over forty-five in Europe and North America in 1900.

Europe's Industrial Revolution began the shift of equilibrium between humankind and nature that has since continued. The vast growth in the supply of manufactured goods, the increased energy consumption made possible by fossil fuels (first coal, then oil), the creation of a global transport and communication network efficient enough to transport goods over vast distances at low cost, the "opening" of new continents, the expansion of agriculture, improvements in sanitation and public health, and the second demographic transition are parts of this shift. As World War I made clear, however, industrial production techniques could also produce death on unprecedented scale.

The fact that World War I began a period of crisis that led to the advent of the nuclear age shows how radically the balance between humankind and nature has since shifted. On the positive side, continued developments in science and technology have vastly increased food supplies, created whole new categories of goods and services, improved the quality and duration of life in most societies, transformed the media of global networking from the possibilities of iron and steam to those of instant electronic communication, given human beings unprecedented mobility, and supported—just barely—the third demographic transition. With repeated advances in medicine, the world escaped—from the Spanish influenza of 1918 to the onset of the AIDS epidemic in the 1980s— the kind of mass killer disease that plagued earlier ages. On the negative side, however, the ongoing development of science and technology has brought the dangers of the nuclear age, symbolized as much by the risks of Japan's continuing commitment to nuclear-power production or the disaster at the Soviet nuclear plant at Chernobyl (Ukraine, 1986) as by the nuclear bombing of Hiroshima and Nagasaki (1945), the four decades of superpower nuclear

Multistory cropping: Bananas and beans grow together in Rwanda.
Even so, Rwanda and Burundi have become Africa's most crowded nations,
and genocidal conflict between Hutus and Tutsis has resulted.
© *Paul Harrison/Still Pictures*

competition, or the arms proliferation that still continues. Together with the tripling of human numbers, modern technology has raised concerns, scarcely imaginable before 1900, about ecological issues, from the degradation of over-exploited farmland to human-induced climate change. Seen in this perspective, the world of interrelatedness amid difference is also a world of interdependence amid scarcity. Instead of being helpless before the forces of nature, human beings now have the ability to destroy nature and themselves with it.

If the balance between humankind and nature has shifted for the world as a whole, global inequalities in access to science and technology have created added issues for contestation. As we have seen, perhaps the key trait of the Euro-pean-dominated world of the nineteenth century was that industrial production and advanced technology were monopolized, with limited exceptions (like the United States and Japan), by a few European countries. In the twentieth century, this monopoly has eroded, with technologies of destruction spreading more rapidly than those of production. The fact remains that by the time the technologically most advanced countries had begun to make strides in energy conservation and pollution control (about the 1980s), runaway population growth had begun to multiply the impact of both natural resource depletion and reliance on technologies that were often less energy-efficient and more polluting in the poorer countries. Multinational corporations contributed to

Forests destroyed by acid rain in the Czech Republic. *Such sights help explain Europe's "green" politics. Lesser degrees of forest damage are visible elsewhere, including North America.* © *Mark Edwards/Still Pictures*

this condition both by exploiting the poorer countries' depressed wage rates and less strict environmental standards and by exporting labor-intensive operations and often obsolete technologies to them.

Many poor countries had by then begun to develop their own highly trained technical elites to assist in their development efforts, although much of this effort went into weapons programs to enhance state power rather than production to meet human needs. The collapse of the communist regimes revealed, however, that the most degraded environments were in Eastern Europe—grim legacies of the socialist command economies' decades of struggle to overtake the capitalist world in heavy industry and armaments. The human impact of this legacy helps explain why environmentalist "green"

movements emerged all over Eastern Europe by the 1980s, networking with others elsewhere to become another global political linkage.

Its impact magnified by explosive growth in population, scientific and technological change thus entered a new age in the twentieth century. Technology has served as the primary agent in tightening global interconnectedness, accelerating change and interaction through new communications technologies, and giving humankind the ambiguous power both to escape much of its old vulnerability to nature's forces and to degrade or even destroy its natural habitat. The way in which issues of technological change have become integrated into the global landscape of interrelatedness amid difference indicates yet again the conflict potential of the coming world of globalization.

Conclusion: Values for Survival

To the extent that we can contemplate them unmarred by terrorism or commercialism, moments like the Olympics offer uplifting visions of a human community in which competition remains within bounds. Such visions make the world a better place. Yet clearly the world of "globalization" will not be a global Olympic village of harmonious "multiculturalism." Instead, it will be a crowded world of intensified interactions, where groups and individuals vie to assert their different identities, an intensively networked, electronically intercommunicating, but also highly armed, contentious, and ecologically threatened world.

In the midst of all this change, however, some old truths will endure, which humankind will be better able to perceive if they do not lose sight of the inspiring vision of human community. Still as in earliest times, the welfare of human societies will depend on their ability to live together and provide for their members' needs, without either making unsustainable demands on their environment or conflicting unmanageably with one another. Whether or not humankind can meet this need, about which we say more at the end of the book, will be perhaps the key question in the era of globalization.

Note

1. Ali Mazrui, *The Africans: A Triple Heritage* (Boston: Little, Brown, 1986), pp. 44, 81.

Suggestions for Further Reading

Abu-Lughod, Janet L. *Before European Hegemony: The World System, A.D. 1250–1350* (1989).

Barraclough, Geoffrey. *The Times Concise Atlas of World History.* 4th ed. (1992).

Bentley, Jerry H. "Cross-Cultural Interaction and Periodization in World History." *American Historical Review,* 101(3) (1996), pp. 749–770.

Best, Steven, and Douglas Kellner. *Postmodern Theory: Critical Interrogations* (1991).

Chatterjee, Partha. *The Nation and Its Fragments: Colonial and Postcolonial Histories* (1993).

Crosby, Alfred W. *Ecological Imperialism: The Biological Expansion of Europe, 900–1900* (1986).

Eaton, Richard M. "Islamic History as Global History." In *Essays on Global and Comparative History,* edited by Michael Adas (1990).

Geyer, Michael, and Charles Bright. "World History in a Global Age." *American Historical Review,* 100(4) (1995), pp. 1034–1060.

Gunder Frank, André, and Barry K. Gills, eds. *The World System: Five Hundred Years or Five Thousand* (1993).

McClellan, James E., III, and Harold Dorn. *Science and Technology in World History: An Introduction* (1999).

McNeill, John R. *Something New Under the Sun: An Environmental History of the Twentieth-Century World* (2000).

McNeill, William H. *Plagues and Peoples* (1976).

Pacey, Arnold. *Technology in World Civilization: A Thousand-Year History* (1990).

Pomeranz, Kenneth. *The Great Divergence: China, Europe, and the Making of the Modern World World Economy* (2000).

Said, Edward. *Culture and Imperialism* (1993).

Wallerstein, Immanuel. *The Modern World System.* 3 vols. to date (1974–1989).

Wolf, Eric R. *Europe and the People Without History* (1982).

Wolfe, Patrick. "History and Imperialism: A Century of Theory, from Marx to Postcolonialism." *American Historical Review,* 102(2) (1997), pp. 338–420.

CHAPTER 2

Origins of the New Century

AT 11:40 P.M. ON APRIL 14, 1912, THE NEW WHITE STAR LINER TITANIC, *ON HER* maiden voyage from England to New York, collided with a North Atlantic iceberg. When she sank less than three hours later, 1,500 of the 2,200 people aboard perished—with one exception, still the highest death toll in history in a peacetime ocean disaster. Nearly a century later, the *Titanic* continues to haunt us, and not just because of its grim fate. For the ship's story actually symbolizes our central themes of twentieth-century world history. The confident expectations with which she set sail were characteristic of the first years of the new century, but her fate was a warning of how the century would reveal so many of those expectations to be illusory.

The British White Star Line was actually controlled by a huge American trust, assembled to monopolize trans-Atlantic passenger traffic. This was a lucrative objective at a time when a million European immigrants a year were coming to the New World. The *Titanic* was one of three sister ships, half-again larger than any built before, designed to establish a weekly six-day trans-Atlantic crossing.

The interior of the *Titanic* replicated the profound stratification of social groups in the Western world. Two-thirds of its upper deck space was reserved for first class. Its best cabins included two so-called "millionaire's suites," which cost $4,350 apiece. Far below where first-class passengers strolled the deck were the cramped third-class quarters of the immigrants.

The ship was equipped with every mechanical innovation that the late nineteenth century had invented. Almost three football fields long, her hull was divided into sixteen watertight compartments. One shipbuilding journal described her as "practically unsinkable," a clear expression of the early twentieth-century conviction that the *triumph of technology over nature* had been achieved.

On the night of April 14, the *Titanic*'s radio operator was so busy sending and receiving the greetings of the first class passengers that not all of the urgent warnings about ice, radioed by ships ahead, reached the bridge. The captain was asleep while the great ship plunged ahead into the region of ice at the highest speed she had yet registered. Human vigilance backed by the latest technology, it was believed, justified such a challenge to nature's risks.

The end of the story is already familiar to many readers. The collision with the iceberg flooded the hull in a way that the watertight compartments could not contain. The ship would sink. As the danger became more obvious, women and children were loaded into the lifeboats, though in the confusion some boats were left only partly filled, sometimes by men. The lifeboats' total capacity was 1,178 people, 200 more than the outmoded regulations required, but only enough for half of the people on board. And so when the *Titanic* finally sank, the 700-odd survivors in the boats heard an unforgettable chorus of screams from the 1,500 still onboard.

The statistics of those saved and lost reveal much about the stratified society of the early twentieth century. Only 4 of 143 first-class women were lost, compared to almost one-third of third-class women. All but one of first- and second-class children were saved, but two-thirds of third-class children died—a higher proportion than of first-class men. Trapped below, often by locked gates, much of the immigrant third class reached the deck only after the last lifeboat had cast off.

Significantly, although the catastrophe created a sensation around the world, neither press nor public shed many tears over the fate of the third-class passengers. But many commentators recognized how seriously the disaster challenged all the confident assumptions of the time. Recklessly navigated, the *Titanic* had sacrificed safety to a demand for speed and luxury. But nature's iceberg had proved more than a match for all human-kind's technology.

Indeed, the *Titanic* can still be seen as an apt metaphor for the *European-dominated world system* as it entered the twentieth century. That system too steamed confidently ahead, assuming that the century of peace and progress behind it would continue forever, regardless of warnings that terrifying dangers lay ahead. But after April 14, 1912, confidence could never be quite so full. That date marks the turning point from an age of certainty to the twentieth-century's age of doubt.

A "Short" Twentieth Century?

When did the twentieth century begin? The answer seems obvious: it began in 1900 (and ended in 1999 or 2000). But in reality the crucial turning points of history do not coincide so conveniently with the calendar. Looking back over it, some historians have suggested that we should really talk about a "short" twentieth century, beginning in 1914 and ending in 1991. They argue that World War I so drastically altered the world that the twentieth century really began when that war began, just as the collapse of the Soviet Union marked so great a change in history's direction that we can justifiably date the beginning of the twenty-first century from the year of that dramatic downfall.

There is much to be said for the idea of a "short" twentieth century. Yet we really cannot understand the outbreak of world war in 1914 without understanding the diplomatic, political, social, economic, and cultural factors that led up to it. To understand these requires us to go back not just to 1900 but a whole generation before to the nineteenth century. Thus, in this chapter we shall begin our story of the twentieth century as long ago as 1871.

Progress and Optimism, 1871–1914

The year 1871 was memorable in the history of international relations for a dramatic change in the balance among the great powers that controlled the European-dominated world system. Prussia, the most powerful of the forty-odd independent states that until then had made up Germany, defeated France in the Franco-Prussian War and proceeded to create a single German nation for the first time in history. The Prussian unification of Germany thus added a potentially immensely strong great power to share in global dominance with Britain, France, Russia, and the Austro-Hungarian Empire. It also shattered the balance of power that had prevailed among the other four and presaged a

conflict for dominance within Europe (and by extension, in a European-dominated world, for mastery of the whole world) that would eventually lead to war in 1914. (The unification of Italy in the same year was less significant, for even a united Italy had far less potential strength: it was a "sixth great power by courtesy.")

For some historians, 1871 also began what they called a "generation of materialism," because in that year Charles Darwin published his book *The Descent of Man,* the sequel to his 1859 intellectual bombshell, *The Origin of Species.* Like Isaac Newton, the English naturalist was one of those rare figures in intellectual history whose basic idea—the idea of *evolution*—to explain the workings of the natural world not only shook his own specialty—biology—to its foundations but was applied by others to every realm of human thought. According to Darwin, the infinite variety of species living on Earth, including humankind itself, had evolved from one another through adaptations over millions of years. Species were not, as many religions and especially Christianity taught, the individual handiwork of a divine Creator. Life on Earth had a purely material, mechanical foundation, and realism—another idea of which the late nineteenth century was fond—insisted that it be explained in purely scientific terms.

Such an assertion, trumpeted by others more insistent than Darwin himself, provoked enormous controversy in the late nineteenth century, as in some places it still does today, for it implicitly denies any more spiritually inspired vision of the world. But there were many reasons, in addition to inspiration borrowed from Darwin's theory, why the years after 1870 became a "generation of materialism" during which God and organized religion were driven onto the defensive in the Western world.

These years were "materialistic" in the philosophical sense of that term: the world was simply, as one German physicist put it, "matter in motion." But we use this word more generally, to refer to a culture preoccupied with things. In the Western world, material progress was advancing standards of living at an unprecedented pace, as a result of humankind's rapidly improving understanding and mastery of the things in its material environment. It was during these years, for example, that scientists like Louis Pasteur first demonstrated that microorganisms caused infectious diseases, radically altering life expectancy. And such advances were not limited to the realm of medicine. Indeed, there were probably more basic scientific breakthroughs of all sorts in the last generation of the nineteenth century and the first decades of the twentieth than in any similar period in history. Compared with the almost daily revelation of new truths about things, the beliefs of earlier ages seemed increasingly outmoded and irrelevant.

Albert Einstein's equations, for example, published in three groundbreaking papers in 1905, demolished the predictable laws of the "majestic clockwork" model of the universe in which most people had believed since Newton described them in the seventeenth century. Einstein's vision depicted instead a universe of unknowable size whose operations did not fit conventional notions of cause and effect. Later astronomers and physicists whose instruments allowed them to peer further into space and within the atom experimentally confirmed Einstein's theories. That confirmation launched a process of discovery that would ultimately make the twentieth century the age of nuclear energy and space exploration.

At almost the same time, the ideas of the psychologist Sigmund Freud undermined the long-held notion that human beings were rational creatures, asserting that much of our behavior springs from feelings and instincts of which we remain unconscious. As his ideas, today much contested, spread throughout the world after World War I, they destroyed nineteenth-century certainties as completely as Einstein's did. They showed, for example, that the behaviors of the supposedly superior "rational"

people of the Western world often sprang from the same impulses as those of the so-called "primitive" peoples of the non-Western world.

Yet, the Western world's very success at rationally explaining things could be seen as a confirmation of Darwin's theory, which held that species that successfully adapted to environmental challenges survived while those that failed to adapt to change perished. In this light (in a sense Darwin himself would never have endorsed), the whole long history of the rise of the European-dominated world system to mastery over the rest of the world could be interpreted as a triumph of evolutionary progress, which presumably could go on forever, or at least as long as Europeans retained their genius for adaptation. Such a belief explains the climate of unbounded optimism about the human future that dominated both Europe and the United States at the turn of the century.

Social Darwinism and Racist Nationalism

Unfortunately for such an optimistic prospect, Western public opinion by 1900 had become imbued with another key Darwinian hypothesis, often summarized as "the survival of the fittest." In Darwin's vision this catch phrase meant simply that the most successfully adaptive species became the strongest, and therefore survived. Other thinkers, however, rushed to extend the implications of this idea to the relations among human beings within a society, and even between human societies, creating a school of thought that can still be found in political discussion today, although only its critics are likely still to call it "social Darwinism."

The domestic implications of "social Darwinism" are easily drawn. Human progress depends on the triumph of the strong over the weak in the competition for survival. Consequently, any intervention to mitigate this often cruel but natural and essential competition is an unnatural threat to humanity's general progress.

Assertions of this kind were increasingly raised by social Darwinists to challenge the notion put forth during this period that governments should do something to help the weakest in society, the poor, a notion already embodied in legislation by the late 1870s in newly unified Germany.

Even more dangerously, the slogan of "survival of the fittest" was increasingly invoked to justify not merely the European-dominated global system as a whole, but even a drive for supremacy *within* that system. In social Darwinist terms, European mastery of the world seemed easily explicable: the white race had won because it was intrinsically superior to the brown, yellow, red, and black races it so easily overwhelmed in the generations before 1914. But social Darwinists were not content with the concept of a single white "race." Instead, they found among whites a whole assortment of races: the Slavic race, the Teutonic race, the Aryan race, even the "Anglo-Saxon" race, all, naturally, engaged in a competition for survival. Such a contest, ultimately, could only be decided by war. War, therefore, was something not to be feared but to be welcomed. "By war alone," American President Theodore Roosevelt declared, "can we attain the virile qualities." He was echoed by General von Moltke, head of the imperial German general staff, who remarked "Perpetual peace is a dream, and not a pretty dream."

The "Second Industrial Revolution" and the Rise of the Mass Society

When he spoke of "war," Teddy Roosevelt had in mind the kind of war he himself had experienced in Cuba during the Spanish-American War of 1898, when he had galloped up San Juan Hill at the head of his Rough Riders. He did not foresee that, during the period between 1871 and 1914, the growth of technology was mak-ing possible the development of weapons that would make romantic cavalry charges, and indeed cavalry itself, utterly out of date.

An Era of Unprecedented Innovation

Between 1871 and 1914, the techniques and machines developed during the first Industrial Revolution, which began in England in the late eighteenth century and spread through Europe and North America during the nineteenth century, continued to expand across the globe. By now, the coal-fired steam boiler was to be found everywhere in its manifold applications. These years saw the heyday of the steam locomotive, for which track continued to be laid, not only in countries like Russia where development was just beginning but even in countries like England and the United States where extensive railway networks already existed. To fuel the locomotives, the ever-growing fleet of steamships that sustained the European-dominated world system, and the boilers of new industries like steel-making, world coal production grew fivefold in the four decades before 1900.

Historians also recognize a "second Industrial Revolution," beginning around 1890, that employed new sources of energy to build and fuel new sorts of machines. The second revolution used electricity and petroleum to transform machines that had a few years before been the hobbies of eccentric inventors into everyday objects of widespread use. The electric streetcar, for example, transformed time and distance as radically in European and American cities as the railway had transformed them in the countryside. But by 1914 the streetcar's future nemesis could already be seen in the automobiles that wealthier Europeans and Americans were beginning to drive.

The absolute dependence of the later twentieth century upon the internal combustion engine was heralded by the foundation of manufacturing firms still famous today, like Mer-

Assembling Model T Automobiles at the Ford Plant. *This kind of assembly line, along which each worker was responsible only for a single operation, transformed industrial production from skilled craftsmanship into a repetitive, but far more productive, routine.* © Bettmann/CORBIS

cedes (1906) and Ford (1903). In fact, by 1914 Henry Ford had already reduced the hours needed to construct a car from twelve to one and one-half by a new method of production— the assembly line, along which the vehicle moved and took form as each worker performed only one operation on each car as it went by. By this means, Ford's factory could produce a thousand cars, once virtually handmade luxury items, in a day: mass production for the emerging mass society.

In many cases the second Industrial Revolution represented a far more rapid technological exploitation of new discoveries of basic science than earlier ages had ever known. The tremendous growth of industrial chemical production, for example, reflected applications of scientific investigations conducted in rapidly

expanding research institutes, notably in Germany. Similar breakthroughs in medical research pointed the way to large-scale programs of preventive medicine managed by new institutions created to foster public health. Indeed, what is particularly striking about the period is the speed with which new discoveries of all sorts found practical application—for war-making as well as for peaceful purposes. The internal combustion engine, for example, was quickly mobilized, once war came, to power armored vehicles. The most striking symbol of the triumph of technology over nature was the airplane. Man's eternal dream of flight was first realized when the Wright brothers soared over a short stretch of North Carolina beach in 1903. By 1908, the airplane was already in use as a weapon for aerial bombardment as the Italians sought to wrest an African empire from the Turks.

Yet in 1914 only a few thoughtful people recognized the ominous implications of such rapid warlike applications of technological innovation. People felt rather that they were living in a time of wonders. The young English philosopher Bertrand Russell, not yet thirty in 1900, recalled "We all felt convinced that nineteenth century progress would continue, and that we ourselves would be able to contribute something of value." The onrush of change was an inspiration, not a warning.

Industrialization and Urbanization

The second Industrial Revolution drastically altered the shape and size of the cities of Europe and North America, where it was concentrated. In 1900, four-fifths of the world's industrial output came, in very different proportions, from the six European great powers and from the United States. The United States alone turned out a quarter of the world's industrial goods, followed by Britain (18 percent) and Germany (13 percent). Russia, only just entering the industrial race, produced only 9 percent, while the shares of France (7 percent), Austria-Hungary (7 percent), and Italy (2 percent) were relatively insignificant. The remaining one-fifth of world industrial output came not only from some smaller European countries like Belgium but also from a few non-Western states. The most notable was Japan, whose overnight transformation during this period from a feudal to an industrial society will be described in Chapter 9. By 1902, when Britain abandoned its former foreign policy of "splendid isolation" to form an alliance with the Japanese, a quarter of Japanese income already came from manufacturing.

Japanese industrial dynamism, so astonishing to Westerners accustomed to regarding non-whites as racially incapable of such achievements, reminds us that not all of the world's industrial economies were growing at the same pace at the turn of the twentieth century. The American economy was growing the fastest, with an annual growth rate of per capita gross national product of over 2 percent. The Japanese and German economies were also growing rapidly, but not quite so fast (1.5 percent). Britain's growth rate lagged behind all three (only 1 percent) reflecting, many historians believe, a British failure to reinvest sufficiently in industrial plants.

We should not imagine that people anywhere in 1900 were aware of these statistics, many of which have been calculated after the fact by historians. Yet people were aware in an imprecise way of shifts in relative economic strength and were drawing conclusions from those shifts that help to explain why the battle lines of 1914 were drawn as they were. Britain, for example, in 1800 had been virtually the only industrial power, the "workshop of the world." But in 1900 Germany was gaining fast on Britain, while the United States actually produced a larger share of the world's industrial output.

Wherever industry grew rapidly, cities, where most of the factories were concentrated, grew in proportion. The world was still far, in 1900, from the dominance of urban over rural populations that seems natural in the Western world today and is becoming increasingly the norm even in the non-Western world. But in 1914 more than one-third of the British population lived in cities, and in the United States and Germany the urban population ranged over 20 percent. In that year there were over eighty cities in the world with populations greater than a quarter million people, fifteen of them in Britain and twenty in the United States, where almost one-quarter of the people were crowded into cities of at least that size. (Most of the world's other cities over a quarter million were in continental Europe.) As more and more people migrated from the countryside to swell these urban populations, observers began to wonder what impact the completely different environment more and more people were coming to live in might have on the course of politics. As more and more countries granted them the vote, how would these tight-packed new urban masses cast their ballots? How would a city like Chicago, for example, integrate the inrush of immigrants from poverty-stricken and oppressed Poland, which had made Chicago on the eve of World War I the third-largest Polish city in the world?

The Challenge of Democracy

In 1871, democracy—meaning the equal right of every individual regardless of race, wealth, or social status to cast a vote in the choice of those who governed—was limited in Europe to Switzerland, and even there women had no vote. The French revolution of 1848 had supposedly given every Frenchman the vote, but various restrictions, for example on the right to a secret ballot, had considerably limited it in practice. Observers were quick to note that the constitution of newly united Germany, though ostensibly also granting adult males the vote, was rigged in such a fashion that the body thus elected, the *Reichstag,* did not effectively control the government. By 1870 in the United States, most white males had long had a right to vote, although post-Civil War southern legislation quickly ended the short-lived participation of ex-slaves in the political process; in 1914, few southern African Americans would have dared claim such a right.

Between 1870 and 1914, however, the franchise—the right to vote—was gradually extended to wider and wider categories of the male European populations, until at the beginning of World War I universal manhood suffrage had become a reality in most countries. The various restrictions based upon occupations, wealth, or residence that had once riddled the franchise with exceptions had been removed. Only one absolute barrier to voting remained: that of gender. In 1914, true universal suffrage,

including votes for women, was found only in partial forms in a few countries far off the beaten path, like Norway and Australia. Only in 1907 was the first woman member of parliament anywhere elected, again in a country remote from the centers of European power, Finland. The exclusion of women from participation in politics persisted despite the efforts of women's rights groups, some increasingly vocal and militant, to compel a change. In England, in 1903, the House of Commons had laughed down a bill giving the vote to women without even debating it. Mrs. Emmeline Pankhurst's Women's Social and Political Union mounted a campaign of mass civil disobedience and sporadic vandalism that had still failed, by 1914, to persuade the British government to yield, despite its annoyance at the mass arrests of these "suffragettes," its frustration at their hunger strikes in prison, and its acute embarrassment at the public outrage provoked by its attempts to force-feed the strikers. Only after World War I would the franchise be extended to women in most countries, and in France not until 1945.

It is not hard to understand why many societies have denied certain categories of people—or even a whole gender—the vote: they have feared that an enlarged electorate would change the outcome of elections and thus completely alter the political game. In the mid-nineteenth century, though most European countries had been governed by parliamentary majorities, the right to choose these had been carefully restricted by law to voters wealthy and well educated enough to have what was called a "stake in society." Presumably such voters were unlikely to endanger society by electing people who might pass bad legislation.

After 1870, however, industrialization and urbanization continued apace, the incomes even of the lower classes rose, and country after country introduced compulsory elementary school education (as Britain and France did in the 1880s). It became harder to deny the vote to a mass society none of whose members, whatever their wealth, was any longer completely lacking in education.

Perhaps the most dramatic demonstration of the new politics came in Britain in 1909. The House of Lords, the upper parliamentary house composed entirely of peers holding their seats by hereditary right, refused to pass the "People's Budget," intended by the Liberal government to impose much heavier taxes on hereditary landed wealth. Two years of tense constitutional confrontation ended only in 1911 with the passage of a Parliament Bill that ended forever the effective role of hereditary privilege in government in Britain, although the House of Lords, now emptied of most of its hereditary members, survives to this day as a historical curiosity. But with the re-election of the Liberal majority that forced through the Parliament Bill in 1911 after the House of Lords had twice rejected it, the progressive enlargement of the British electorate to include the lower middle class and much of the working class during the past half-century at last bore fruit. The democracy of the mass society prevailed over the age-old idea that the choice of government belonged to an aristocracy of heredity or money.

Yet not all thoughtful observers were confident that the long-hoped-for triumph of democratic politics, at least among men, had created an effective means for solving all the troubling problems emerging with the rapid change of the new century. In the multiethnic Austro-Hungarian Empire, for example, the advent of universal manhood suffrage in 1907 promptly led to parliamentary deadlock as each ethnic group elected representatives of a party speaking its own language and refusing to cooperate with the others. Democracy only magnified nationalistic rivalries. What might its effect be in the industrializing societies of Europe, where economic power had been gathered into fewer and fewer hands, as joint-stock corporations everywhere replaced paternalistic family businesses and the corporations themselves were com-

bined into industry-controlling trusts or cartels? It was calculated that by 1914 three hundred wealthy individuals together controlled most of the German economy. A vote for everyone could hardly fail to bring a challenge by the majority to such a narrow ruling group, and if a democratic challenge failed, might not the mass society turn from democracy to revolutionary violence?

For most of history, the urban working classes had constituted only tiny minorities of national populations. In the few capitals, like Paris, where there had been significant concentrations of them, they had indeed launched terrifying social revolutions. The most recent was the Paris Commune of 1871, an orgy of savagery and destructiveness the memory of which still haunted European minds. Now, however, industrialization and urbanization were bringing these classes closer to the majority in more and more places. Already they were casting their newfound votes for the candidates of socialist parties whose programs directly challenged the capitalistic system on which industrialization had been based. Could these socialistic impulses of an emerging majority be controlled? Some speculated that the only antidote in a mass society to the internationalist socialism of Marxism, which urged workers everywhere to unite against their capitalist masters, would be to educate the masses in social Darwinist nationalism: teaching ordinary Europeans that they could be empowered only by their nation's power, as symbolized by the number of people of other races around the world their nation had subjugated.

The Outburst of Imperialism

So far, this chapter on the world of 1871–1914 has discussed Europeans, and "emigrant Europeans" like Americans, almost exclusively, saying nothing of the peoples of Asia, Africa, and Latin America. The reason for this is not that these peoples were not important. The reason is that the generation between 1880 and 1914 witnessed an unprecedented outburst of European empire building, in which the United States too took its share. At the end of this period of competitive colonization, four-fifths of Earth's surface had passed under European or American control. There were a few scattered cases of successful resistance to this wave of European subjugation of the globe, but not many. In 1914, the imperial dominion of the white race over the world was so extensive that it seemed to most Europeans and Americans, even though it was so comparatively new, as natural a phenomenon as Earth's revolution around the sun.

Empires, of course, were nothing new in history and, as we saw in Chapter 1, had not always been centered in Europe. In 1900, the fading Ottoman and Chinese empires were vestigial reminders of ages in which some nonwhite peoples had dominated vast swathes of the globe. For that matter, from the sixteenth through the eighteenth century Britain, France, and Spain had built and then lost vast empires in the Americas. But never before had European control been extended so far so fast as during the generation between the French seizure of Tunisia in North Africa in 1881 and their establishment of a protectorate over Morocco in 1912.

Scramble for Africa and Penetration of Asia, 1881–1912

Intense enthusiasm for overseas empires had not been a constant of European thought. Indeed, at the end of the Franco-Prussian war the French offered victorious Germany all of France's overseas possessions if they could be allowed to retain the two French European provinces, Alsace and Lorraine, that Germany planned to annex. The German government declined, seeing an assortment of mainly African territories as being of no use to Germany. By 1914, in contrast, disputes over who could claim what colony, as a result of the intense colonialist enthusiasm that blazed up after 1870, had several times brought the rival European powers to the brink of war. In 1870, only one-tenth of the vast African continent was in European hands; by 1914 all *but* one-tenth of Africa had been partitioned among the European powers, including Germany, which by then bitterly resented the fact that the German "place in the sun" was so comparatively small. Africa was not the only colonized place at the beginning of World War I. Russia and Britain divided Persia (the future Iran) between themselves. Britain, France, Germany, Russia, and Japan ruled sizable parts of China in all but name and talked of simply carving up the Chinese Empire among themselves. France completed its annexation of the former Chinese territories that are today included in Vietnam. The march of European empire continued irresistibly. By 1914, the British Empire contained ten black or brown subjects for every Englishman. For every Belgian there were eighty Africans in the Belgian Empire, centered in the Congo (today's Zaire).

Interpretations of the New Imperialism

What explains this sudden outburst of imperialism? Clearly, powerful lobbies worked to influence public opinion with apparently persuasive arguments that acquiring colonies was good policy. However, the growth of popular colonialism in the mass society may owe more to unthinking enthusiasm than to reasonable argument.

The arguments advanced to win support for colonial expansion were of three kinds: economic, moral, and patriotic. According to the economic argument, colonies would provide a safe place for investment and a reliable source of essential raw materials, as well as a protected market, for the nation's industrial sector. Colonies might also provide a new home and labor market for the nation's emigrants, whose talents

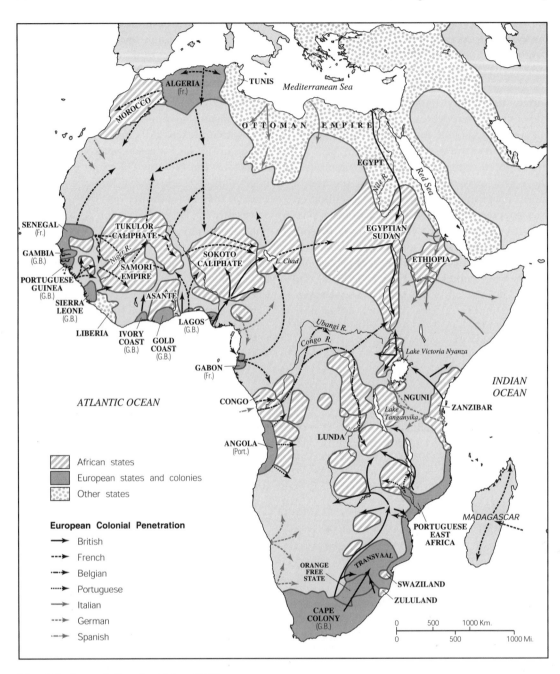

Map 2.1 *Imperialism in Africa, 1914*

and loyalties were lost to their home country when they abandoned it for places like the United States, as they were doing in the millions in the decade before 1914.

Marxists analyzing the outburst of imperialism insisted that the economic argument revealed the real explanation for it. To Lenin, the future leader of the Russian Revolution, empire-building was the final stage of capitalism, a desperate last bid by the world's monopolists to escape the contradictions they had themselves built into their economic system by competitive overproduction and a stubborn refusal to allow workers a sufficient wage to afford the products they made. Colonies, according to this Marxist interpretation, provided investment outlets for the funds capitalists denied to their workers and sales outlets for the products that could no longer be sold in saturated domestic markets.

Certainly if there was ever a time when an economic European-dominated world system prevailed, it was during this era of frantic colonial expansion of 1880–1914, when the European "core" nations (as described in Chapter 1) were hoisting their flags in the remotest regions of the global "periphery" (and the United States was developing a similar economic relationship to Latin America without formally annexing the Latin American states). Yet some historians point out that the impulses behind the drive for colonies were not exclusively economic. They note, for example, that the leadership of the pro-colonialist lobbies did not come originally or exclusively from businessmen, but from intellectuals, and especially academics. Moreover, such lobbies appeared even in countries like Russia and Italy where industrial development was only beginning and there was no shortage of demand for domestic investment and for the new products of industry. These considerations suggest that, powerful as economic arguments for colonialism may have been, they do not entirely explain it. Other motives, reflected in other kinds of argument, also helped attract Europeans and Americans onto the road to colonialism.

Hard as it is for later, more cynical generations to believe, some Europeans and Americans were attracted to imperialism by genuine altruistic feelings: Europeans and Americans had a "civilizing mission" (as the French called it) to teach the backward peoples of the globe the white man's uplifting and improving ways. This mission was most vividly described by the British poet Rudyard Kipling, in famous verses he wrote to urge Americans to colonize and improve the Philippine Islands they had seized from Spain in 1898:

Take up the White Man's Burden—
Send forth the best ye breed—
Go bind your sons to exile
To serve your captives' need:
To wait in heavy harness
On fluttered folk and wild—
Your new-caught, sullen peoples,
Half-devil and half child

Social Darwinism, although Kipling thought it should be mitigated for the "new-caught" peoples of the colonies, echoes through these verses, suggesting a third motive for the outburst of imperialism: sheer patriotic enthusiasm. Simply put, if international relations was a contest for survival, great power status in the contest depended largely on the size of one's empire. Coloring the map of the world red or green or blue proved the power of one's nation, and this was a motive that probably inspired colonialism as much as economic greed and more than missionary altruism. It explains why colonial rivalry continued despite growing revelations that, at least for latecomers to the race like Germany and Italy, most of the alleged advantages of empire were entirely illusory. Although India was indeed the "jewel in the crown" of the British Empire, the German and Italian empires in Africa actually ran at a loss. More Germans emigrated to the United States in one year than ever lived in the German overseas empire. More Italian emigrants lived in New York City than in the whole Italian empire. By 1914 even France, with the world's second largest empire, shipped only 13 percent of its manufactured goods to French colonies and imported only 10 percent of its raw materials from them.

That not all colonies fulfilled the economic expectations held out for them does not mean that stupendous fortunes could not be made from some of them during this zenith of the European-dominated world system. A notorious case that shocked even many Europeans of the time was the private empire created by King Leopold II of Belgium in the Congo in central Africa. At the time, whoever could show he controlled a territory could claim it. In 1885, the great powers entrusted the Congo, known to be rich in rubber and ivory, to a private joint-stock enterprise consisting of King Leopold and other shareholders, originally called the International Association for the Exploration and Civilization of Central Africa. Investors made a killing: shares in the company bought in the 1880s sold by 1914 for sixty-four times their original price. But the Congo was also a story of killing in the most literal sense. Profitability for the shareholders was assured by assigning fixed quotas of rubber to be gathered by the forced labor of the Congolese. Those that failed to meet the quota were savagely punished by systematic mutilations or massacres. Under this system, the Congolese population fell by over a half in a quarter-century. Finally the situation provoked such a scandal that in 1908 the great powers removed the Congo from King Leopold's management and handed it over to the Belgian government. This reversal, however, resulted from the outcry of European public opinion rather than from anything the Congolese could do in their own defense. African or Asian opposition to imperialism hardly counted before 1914.

Rebellion did break out in China, where by 1900 European warships controlled the Chinese rivers, European premises were not under

King Leopold's Congo. *The hands of the youth on the left were destroyed by gangrene after being tied too tightly by soldiers enforcing rubber production quotas. Soldiers cut off the hand of the youth on the right to be able to claim him as one of their quota of "natives" killed. Anti-Slavery International*

Chinese control, and Europeans collected the tariffs and remitted them abroad to pay off Chinese debts. With the covert backing of the dowager empress, a secret society called the Order of Literary Patriotic Harmonious Fists (jokingly dubbed "Boxers" by Europeans) arose to tear up European-built railways, massacre Chinese Christians (and some three hundred Europeans) and lay siege to the privileged quarter in the capital, Beijing, where European diplomatic missions were housed. Within fifty days, however, the siege was broken by a multinational expeditionary force that included contingents from all the European great powers,

Japan, and the United States. The only consequence for China of this lonely example of determined resistance to colonialism, the "Boxer Rebellion," was even deeper humiliation, with even greater financial exactions to be paid to the triumphant Europeans.

The horrors of the colonization of the Congo and the humiliation of the Boxer Rebellion were only two examples of the impact of the European-dominated world system on non-Europeans. Whatever altruistic aspirations may have guided some colonizers, the harsh realities of colonialism were very different. India, for example, was still 93 percent illiterate in 1914, and many of its millions lived on the edge of starvation. In British East Africa (today's Kenya), the good farming land belonged to white settlers. Two thousand of them owned 10,000 square miles, while only half as much was left to the two million African "natives." In such places, as in the Congo and in the European-dominated world system at large, the "white man's burden" was set squarely on the shoulders of the black man (and black woman).

The End of the Spanish Empire and the "American Peril"

Ironically, the only European defeat besides Russia's during this period came with the American victory in the Spanish-American War. By 1880, the United States was more populous than any of the great powers except Russia. By the 1890s, it led the world in the production of coal, iron, and steel. But though the Americans had conquered a continent by vanquishing the Mexicans and uprooting the native Americans they called "Indians," their role during the nineteenth century in the rest of the world had been virtually nil.

The explosion, probably from accidental causes, of the battleship USS *Maine* in Havana harbor in 1898, gave those who favored American intervention in the Cuban revolution against their Spanish colonial masters the excuse for which they had been hoping. In the

"splendid little war" (as the American secretary of state called it) that followed, the Americans easily bested the decrepit Spanish forces, annihilated the Spanish fleet in Manila Bay, and seized the pathetic relics of the once-great Spanish empire, Cuba and the Philippines. (Although the war had ostensibly been fought to free these territories from colonialism, it soon became clear that Cubans and Filipinos had simply exchanged one set of masters for another. The Philippines did not escape American tutelage until 1946; Fidel Castro would argue that Cuba did not escape until his revolution of 1959.)

The same arguments were advanced in the United States for keeping Cuba and the Philippines under American control as Europeans used to justify imperialism. The Philippines, for example, would constitute valuable markets for American products, the Filipinos were Americans' "little brown brothers" to be civilized, and American possession of these overseas territories would call the world's attention forcibly to the growth of American power on a global scale. The days of the nineteenth-century inward-looking America were over. President Roosevelt would soon send a fleet of American battleships around the world to prove it.

Yet Europeans did not recognize the implicit challenge of the Spanish-American War to their global system. When the war broke out, the desperate Spanish appealed for help against the United States to all of the European great powers, but in vain. Only the Kaiser (the German emperor), not a man otherwise known for his political insight, recognized the emerging "American peril" and called for Europe to unite to oppose it. But he found no support for such a strategy even within his own government. Even if the Spanish-American War announced the advent of a huge, seventh, *non-European* great power on the world stage, none of the others was eager to add the United States to its list of potential enemies. It can be argued that the downfall of the European-dominated world system that reached its zenith in 1914 was already heralded by what happened in 1898. But it is not surprising that most Europeans did not recognize this, for as they contemplated, as we shall do in the following section, the differences between their way of life and the life of those around the world whom they had conquered, it must have seemed impossible that European global dominance could ever be shaken.

Two Poles of Experience in the European-Dominated World System

The world of 1914 was an integrated whole dominated by the rapidly changing societies of Europe and North America. Many members of dominant societies saw this global pattern in terms of sharp opposites: superior and inferior. Yet, however different they were in power or rates of change, the societies of the world were connected to one another like points along a spectrum. In 1914, most of humanity found itself at the wrong end of the power spectrum. But even "white men" (and women) were "natives" somewhere. Nothing assured them everlasting dominance.

In many respects, then, differences among societies in 1914 were matters of rates of change. Compared to Europe, many non-European societies were slow to change—and were probably content to be so. Usually, too, the development that they might have generated on their own was thwarted by the European impact, which made itself felt even in remote villages. However, the Europeans' image of their homelands as great powers misled them if it caused them to see such peoples as different in kind or inferior.

To illustrate the nature of the 1914 world and the range of possible contrasts between dominant and dependent societies, it helps to look at representative environments of both types: a European capital and a colonial village.

Imperial Berlin: European Metropolis and Crucible of Change

To understand Europe's world dominance in 1914, we must visit one of its great metropolises, for the economic and intellectual creativity of its urban population was what made European dominance possible. Berlin may seem an obvious choice, because it was the capital of the newest and most powerful of the continental great powers, the German Empire. But a more important reason for choosing Berlin over London, Paris, or Vienna is that it had only recently achieved worldwide prominence. Until the unification of Germany in 1871, Berlin was merely the capital of Prussia, the largest of the German states. Berlin's rapid growth in size and influence came in the half-century before 1914, coinciding with the consolidation of European world dominance. Thus the characteristics of the new century can be seen particularly clearly in Berlin.

Capital of the Germany Nation

An American visitor of 1914 might have felt more at home in Berlin than in the older European capitals. Europeans were invariably struck by Berlin's stark newness. To meet the demand for housing, the city was expanding into the open countryside; streets and apartment buildings were being constructed practically overnight. "You would think yourself in America at the moment a new city was being founded," wrote one astonished French visitor. "In twenty years Berlin will have four million inhabitants and it will be Chicago."

Both Berlin and Chicago had grown to giant size at unprecedented speed. Chicago had doubled its population within fifteen years and by 1914 was the world's fourth-largest city. In 1914, however, the United States was only beginning to assert a worldwide influence corresponding to its economic power. Otherwise we might have chosen Chicago as our representative Western urban environment.

Berlin's growth reflected the consolidation of a national state through war. Many of its monuments commemorated the battles of the Franco-Prussian War of 1870. Glittering cavalry and goose-stepping infantry were on parade everywhere. Berlin's monuments were intended not only to impress the foreign visitor but also to enhance the German people's own identification with their nation. Half a century after German unification, many non-Prussian Germans still identified with their local state or city. But as accelerating economic and social change uprooted more and more people from local backgrounds, Germans, like other Europeans, inevitably came to think of themselves as belonging above all to a national state, whatever their social background.

The City as Crucible of Change

Its role in preparing for war sustained the prestige of the Prussian aristocracy, the top 1 percent of Berlin's society. Titled landowners continued to dominate the army officer corps, in prestige if not in numbers. Observing their arrogant demeanor on the sidewalks of Berlin, foreigners might have wondered why these relics of Prussia's past remained influential in a giant modern city. In culturally conservative societies, the caste of warriors has often been pre-eminent. But Berlin by 1914 was far more than the garrison city for the Prussian Guards. It had become a laboratory and workplace for an innovative society, like the other great cities of Europe and North America. Titled officers might still elbow civilians aside, but it was bankers, chemists, and lathe operators, not generals and colonels, that had made Berlin a world city.

The transformation had taken only two generations. Germany had not joined the world's headlong rush to urbanization and industrialization until after the unification of 1871. As late as 1870, almost half of Germany's

people were still employed, as most human beings have been throughout history, in farming. By the early 1900s, that proportion had dropped to one-third. During roughly the same period, the number of German cities with a population over 100,000 rose from eight to forty-eight. Berlin's population doubled.

Today we take for granted the near-miracles of technology and hygiene that enabled people to find a better life in the city. In the late twentieth century we expect pure drinking water, adequate sanitation and fire protection, safe and dependable transportation systems. In 1914, however, these triumphs of human organization were so new that they seemed remarkable.

Perhaps half of 1914's Berliners had come from the very different environment of villages and farms. Urban life offered in one day a greater variety of new experiences than their former homes could provide in a lifetime. Even a poor Berliner could see the world's great art in a museum, borrow a book on any subject from a library, and marvel at the world's most exotic animals collected in the zoo.

In many ways, Berliners' lives were far freer than those of their rural ancestors. But paradoxically, the complexity of urban life also required the authorities to maintain more control over the individual. The law compelled every child in Berlin to attend school, for example, and hygiene demanded an annual physical examination for each schoolchild. By 1914, such measures had largely eliminated the danger of epidemics in the closely packed population. Detailed records were kept for every child—and for the investigations of meat inspectors, factory inspectors, and building inspectors. More and more government officials were employed in maintaining these records. Watching them at work, a visitor might have admired their efficiency but worried about the potential for bureaucratic interference in individual lives.

The space and time of Berlin were quite unlike those of the village and the farm.

Four levels of traffic in Berlin.   *The different economic activities of a modern metropolis required varied transport: the canal with barges and boats; the street traffic; the freight railway above these; and the electric passenger train taking the fastest route, through a building.*   Album von Berlin *(Berlin, Parnassus, c. 1900)*

Berliners might commute twenty miles to work. To catch their trains, they had to know the time exactly, and so they carried watches. As they rode, most commuters glanced through one of Berlin's cheap newspapers, whose numbers had grown even faster than the city's population.

The large metropolitan newspaper was the first of the twentieth-century mass media. Telegraph and radio enabled it to involve its readers in events on the other side of the world and encouraged them to hold opinions, informed or not, about distant happenings. Not that Berlin-

ers lingered long over their newspapers. Like Americans, they were usually in a hurry, often munching a quick lunch standing up at one of a chain of identical restaurants. Berliners' rapid-fire slang, in which words were often abbreviated to initials, was regarded as very "American" by other Germans.

Like Chicagoans, Berliners in 1914 lived in a highly organized, fast-moving world of strangers. Their horizons extended around the world. Their entirely man-made environment—an "ocean of buildings"—could hardly have been more different from the environment of village and farm, where people still walked most places, recognized most of the people they saw, and told time by watching the sun move across the sky.

Its pace made Berlin exciting. The city welcomed four times as many tourists in 1914 as it had two generations earlier. Some thoughtful people, however, were worried by the growth of the giant twentieth-century metropolis. The German philosopher Oswald Spengler, for example, lamented that urban populations would soon outnumber rural people bound to traditions—"live people born of and grown in the soil." To Spengler, "the parasitical city dweller" was "traditionless, utterly matter of fact, religionless, clever, unfruitful, deeply contemptuous of rural people."

Conservatives in Germany and elsewhere have continued to criticize the great metropolis, the most visible symbol of twentieth-century change. But the very qualities of the metropolis that Spengler disliked—the impersonal crowding together of millions, each person responsible for the speedy performance of a specialized job—made possible rapid development and with it European global dominance.

A city such as Berlin or Chicago was a great human beehive. What might seem a confused swarm of people was actually the intricate interaction of millions of individuals. Together, their efforts yielded the city's products. Berlin was a world leader in such modern industries as electrical equipment, chemicals, and machine tools. Their profits helped supply capital to the city's big banks, which invested around the world from Turkey to Argentina to China.

Berliners' collective efforts also created innovation: an intangible product just as real as machinery and capital. Many of Berlin's huge factories had begun as small workshops where entrepreneurs perfected their discovery of an industrial process such as the making of a synthetic dyestuff. More recently the Kaiser had supported creation of research institutes, backed by both industry and government, to institutionalize the business of discovery. Scientists working in Berlin laboratories had discovered both the bacillus that causes tuberculosis and the x-ray that could detect the deadly disease. A government-sponsored researcher won a Nobel Prize for discovering a cure for syphilis. Such discoveries had made Germany the world leader in science and medicine. Emerging U.S. research universities were designed to follow German models.

Berlin provided the human critical mass for an explosion of creativity felt around the world. The contribution of its millions of workers was as essential as that of industrialists and scientists.

The Social Classes

Not every contribution received equal reward. Berlin in 1914 was a society of layers. Each social class differed sharply from those above and below it in income, lifestyle, and even appearance.

Far outnumbering the aristocrats, who represented the top 1 percent of this social pyramid, the middle classes may have represented almost 40 percent of the population. Wealth varied widely within this group. The richest members of the middle class included many of the three hundred or so powerful company directors who controlled most of German industry. Such men would have been among the few Berliners who could afford a Mercedes or another early automobile. They lived in mansions rivaling those of the imperial family.

Hardly less comfortable were the homes of doctors, senior civil servants, and university professors: ten- or twelve-room apartments overlooking fashionable streets and squares. Guests could confirm their invitation by telephone, ride up in an elevator, announce themselves to a uniformed maid, and await their hosts in a room lit by electricity and warmed by central heating. The lower middle class did not enjoy all these comforts, but even a young

Moving day. *Even in the prosperous metropolis of Berlin, a majority of working-class people like these had few possessions. Still their standard of living was much higher than that of most people in the non-Western world.* Heinrich Zille/Schirmer Verlag, Munich

journalist could find a comfortable apartment by following the building boom out into the suburbs.

At the base of Berlin's social pyramid were the working classes, about 60 percent of the population. They lived much as American workers did. Although Berlin was too new to have extensive slums, the typical working-class couple inhabited a one- or two-room walkup apartment in a cheaply constructed tenement. Often the family took in a lodger, who would occupy a bed in one corner of the kitchen. Landlords were harsh, and evictions were frequent. Moving was relatively easy, for most of a couple's possessions could be loaded onto a small cart.

Most workers spent long hours on the job six days a week. Significantly, workingmen's cut-rate streetcar tickets were good only before 7 A.M. and after 5 P.M.

The life of a Berlin worker was far from desperate, however. Most ate meat—only recently a rare luxury—once a day, with perhaps even a roast goose on Sunday. The family might spend Sunday at the shore of some suburban lake or working in their garden. To attract workers away from the bars, the city rented them suburban garden plots.

German and American workingmen in 1914 differed in two important respects. Berlin's workers were protected by the world's first comprehensive welfare state, and they were virtually all committed socialists. Beginning in the 1880s, the German government had insured workingmen against risks of sickness, accident, and disability. Government benefits also provided "social security" in old age. These benefit plans, which required contributions from both employer and employee, violated the basic principles of nineteenth-century liberal economics, which held that the government should not tamper with the operation of a free-market economy by interfering with employment conditions. Germany's welfare state had actually been constructed in defiance of these liberal ideas by conservative politicians, who hoped to wean Germany's workers from Marxism.

Germany in the Age of Mass Politics

By 1914 this conservative hope appeared to have been disappointed. Five of "Red Berlin's" six representatives to the German parliament, or *Reichstag,* were members of the Socialist party, the nation's largest. In the 1912 elections, a third of the electorate had voted for this party, which still officially followed Marx in advocating revolution to overthrow the middle class, give power to the workers, and abolish private property. The rise of the mass society thus seemed to threaten social revolution.

The typical Berlin Socialist voter, however, was probably not wholly committed to his party's official program. Workingmen wanted to eliminate some relics of Prussia's oppressive past, such as systematic brutalizing of army recruits, and sought such economic benefits as the eight-hour day. They were not so sure that abolishing private property was a good idea or that Marx's idea of class warfare still made sense in a modern society where trade unions were becoming stronger and workingmen had the right to vote.

Yet, despite universal manhood suffrage, Germany was not a real democracy in 1914. The Reichstag had little power. Because its proceedings were not decisive, it was dominated by the petty quarrels and cynical deals of special-interest parties and well-organized lobbies. Germany's first experience with the rise of the mass society was one of corruption and frustration, rather than a lesson in self-government.

Berlin and the Coming Century

Even in a European society accustomed to welcoming change as progress, tradition died hard. In Germany, the global power of a modern urban and industrial economy was entrusted to a backward political system that left power in the hands of one man, the Kaiser, who was known to be unstable. Most Berliners, however, were optimistic about their city's future. Berlin spent a quarter of its budget to provide an elementary education for every child. Like most other Europeans and North Americans, Berliners believed that common schooling would break down whatever cultural differences lingered among the young and would inspire continuing innovation to improve the quality of life.

A newspaper poll showed that the two historical figures Berliners most admired early in the twentieth century were Joseph Lister, discoverer of antiseptics, and James Watt, inventor of the steam engine (both Englishmen). The control of disease had raised German life expectancy from thirty-five to forty-seven years within a few decades, and the new source of energy had revolutionized the German economy. It seemed likely that the talent and energy of Berliners would produce equally miraculous triumphs of technology in the next half-century. In such an era of change, how long could traditional ideas and practices survive? Already the practice of religion was dwindling, so that only a quarter of the babies born in Berlin in 1914 were baptized. Now that science was unraveling the secrets of the universe, many Berliners thought, the values of the superstitious past could be discarded.

A mere thirty years later, devastated by the bombing of World War II, Berlin would lie in ruins. But in 1914 only the most pessimistic of people recognized the dangers that lurked in the very characteristics that had enabled European civilization to conquer the world. The rivalries of national pride would prove disastrous when Europeans in two world wars turned on one another the ferocity they had already shown against Africans and Asians. The advances of science, reinforced by the methods of administrative control that had made Berlin so efficient, would make those wars far more deadly. War's unequal stress on social classes would bring revolution in 1918. The domination of the masses in politics would help give power to leaders such as Adolf Hitler with ideas far more dangerous than the Kaiser's vague dream of extending German influence everywhere.

In twenty years, these developments would fatally undermine the global pattern of European domination. In 1914, however, it still stood triumphant. To see that system from the perspective of non-Europeans is our next task.

Dinshawai, Egyptian Village: Rustic Routine and the Challenge of Colonialism

The characteristic setting for life in the colonial world in 1914 was the village. No single village can typify the colonial countries as well as Berlin did the Western powers. But Dinshawai, in Egypt, illustrates not only how villagers lived but also how European power made itself felt in far parts of the world. An ugly incident that occurred in Dinshawai in 1906 provides a good starting point for a discussion of village life in the Nile Delta at the beginning of the twentieth century. Many features of the village's physical

appearance, its social composition, and its political, economic, and spiritual life are specific to the Nile Delta. But in important respects Dinshawai resembled villages all over the colonial world of the early twentieth century.

The Dinshawai Incident of 1906

Egypt had come under European domination in an unusual way. Politically, Egypt was still a province of the Ottoman Empire. Yet Egypt was no ordinary province. Members of the same family had governed it since 1805, as they would until 1952, and they had acquired powers that made them little less than independent. When the British occupied Egypt in 1882, they did not bother to remove the family of hereditary governors, then known as *khedives,* or to deny—until World War I—the sovereignty of the Ottoman sultan. The British left outward forms unchanged, but they took charge.

What happened at Dinshawai in 1906 has never been entirely clear. People of different cultures perceived the incident differently. It began when British officers, on march through Minufiyyah Province, northwest of Cairo, went pigeon shooting. Western accounts of the incident usually fail to mention that pigeons in Egypt are not wild birds. The peasants raise them for food and build towerlike houses, atop their own houses, for pigeons to rest in. At Dinshawai, a British shot apparently started a fire in some grain on the threshing grounds at the edge of the village. Another shot hit a woman. The villagers sought vengeance, as their code demanded. In the ensuing fracas, several officers and villagers died, and more troops were called in.

The annals of imperialism include many similar episodes. In a sense, they were part of the costs of the game, and it was not always possible for the dominant power to avoid losing. But this time, Lord Cromer, the highest British official in Egypt from 1883 to 1907, decided to exact punishment. He had fifty-two

Pigeon tower, said to be atop the house of Zahran, one of the heroes of Dinshawai, Minufiyyah Province, 1983. *C. V. Findley*

villagers arrested and tried under a regulation against attacks on British army personnel. In keeping with the pretense that the khedive ruled Egypt, prominent officials from Cairo were sent out to serve as judge and lawyers. Thus Egyptians prosecuted Egyptians for attacking foreigners who had inflicted the first injury. Four men were sentenced to death, others to hard labor, and still others to public flogging. The hangings and floggings were carried out on the threshing grounds at the village edge, while the victims' families looked on helplessly.

Egyptians have never forgotten these events. Village bards immortalized them in folk ballads. As a boy, Anwar al-Sadat, president of Egypt from 1970 to 1981, heard his grandmother sing about Zharan, the villagers' hero and one of those hanged. Sadat and others grew up wanting to overthrow those responsible for what had happened—a dream that the 1952 revolution fulfilled. In the Cairo of 1906, intellectuals poured forth their outrage in verse and newspaper articles. As an example of political mobilization, this was a great moment: the first time educated Egyptians supported peasant violence. Critics of British policy as far away as France and England wrote about the incident. Cromer had to retire a year later, and his successor arranged for the pardon and release of the villagers still in prison.

The Village as Rustic Setting

Passing by a village in the Nile Delta in 1906, one ordinarily saw little sign of events as dramatic as those that led to the trials. From afar, the village looked like an indistinct mass of low houses, with a few trees, surrounded by fields. In the Middle East and in most other parts of the world, those who tilled the soil lived together in a village and went out each day to their fields. Very likely, the only structure in the village that differed noticeably from others was the domed and painted shrine of the local saint. The village might have a small mosque or simply an open space at the edge of the fields to use for prayers. The village displayed few signs of occupational specialization. There might be one or two religious functionaries; a barber who also served the villagers' medical needs; and a grocer selling sugar, tea, soap, oil, kerosene, tobacco, and matches. To find other shops or to market their own surplus produce, villagers went to a larger market town down the road.

Many villages lacked streets. Often, there were only one or two lanes, muddy and littered with wastes, because Egyptian villagers had none of the amenities that enabled Berliners to live at close quarters in cleanliness and comfort. Often, the lanes penetrated only part way through the mass of buildings, far enough to give access to the various quarters, where the households of each kinship group were clustered together.

Within the village, the crowded, flat-roofed houses were much like those of ancient times. The villagers still built with the same kind of unbaked mud-and-straw bricks mentioned in the Bible. They still lit their houses with Roman-

style oil lamps and heated them with braziers. Yet a visitor from Berlin or Chicago would have been wrong to think the villagers primitive. Mud bricks are not only low in cost and free to those who make their own but also durable in a hot, dry climate and more efficient insulators than many modern materials. Villagers might have little access to modern technologies, but their traditional ones were sophisticated adaptations to their environment and resources.

Inside the houses, one might find chickens or cows, as well as people. On the rooftop, one might see a pigeon tower, drying crops, or dung cakes for use as fuel. The human and natural worlds were intimately associated.

Village Society

The greatest difference between social life in the village and in the United States or Europe lay in the role of the individual. In the village, the extended kin group was all-important; the individual counted for much less. Death claimed more than a quarter of all infants within their first year, and, partly for that reason, average life expectancy for the entire population barely exceeded twenty years. Most people had little time to make a mark of their own. While life lasted, its quality was not good. Tuberculosis and hereditary syphilis were endemic, as were such parasitic diseases as bilharziasis, hookworm, and malaria. Almost all men of the village contracted parasitic diseases from long work in water and mud.

Social roles also limited the individual. They were highly standardized and little differentiated except in terms of sex and age. The normal routine for the men was fieldwork, including irrigation. Women were in charge of housework, child care, and the milking and feeding of livestock. They also helped in the fields and took produce to sell in the market town. Men had a very limited range of occupational choices. After their years at the village Qur'an school, a few bright boys would go elsewhere for advanced study and become religious scholars. Some would take up barbering, building, or singing in addition to their fieldwork. Choice was almost nonexistent for the women. Uncontrolled fertility dominated their lives. Their standard dress, the long black *gallabiyah* (the same term used for the nightshirtlike outfit of the men) was always full enough to accommodate pregnancy and had two slits at the side of either breast for nursing.

Villagers often married during their teens. A young couple normally remained in the groom's father's household and shared in work. Even after they had children, the young couple acquired little autonomy as long as the older generation lived. The closest thing to independence came with age, when males became heads of extended-family households and their wives thus acquired charge of their daughters-in-law and grandchildren.

To the extent that the short average life expectancy allowed the pattern to be maintained, a villager lived much of his or her life in an extended household that included not only parents and children but also grandparents, uncles, aunts, and cousins. This three-generation household was the meaningful social unit for some purposes, such as farming its own land. But in many respects, even more extended kin groups were the fundamental social units. A village like Dinshawai might have only five or six such kin groups, but each kin group might have had one or two thousand members at the start of this century and today would have several times that many.

The feelings of solidarity associated with common descent were the strongest loyalties that village society knew. Often the founder of the kin group was regarded as a saint. Nothing, except the claim to descent from the Prophet Muhammad, could enhance family prestige more than for one of the domed shrines that dominated the village skyline to be the tomb of the family founder. The kin group preserved its

integrity by arranging marriages, usually within its own circle. The group had a male head, whose functions included dispensing hospitality, solving disputes within the group, and handling relations with the outside world, especially the government. The elders who traditionally ran the village were kin-group heads. When the government created the office of village headman it was usually filled by the leading kin-group head, with the others grouped around him as elders. The unofficial institutions of kin-group leadership thus became the first link in an official chain that extended to Cairo and on to London.

The kin group expressed its solidarity through several physical institutions. The most important was the "big house," which served as headquarters for the kin-group head, guesthouse, meeting place for the leading members of the kin group, and scene for the celebration of marriages, circumcisions, healings, or returns from journeys, especially the pilgrimage to Mecca.

The legendary image of Middle Eastern hospitality was formed in settings like the big house. A visitor with an introduction to a village kin group could rely on this hospitality for accommodation. As the village elders' meeting place, the big house also had an official function. In the Dinshawai trials of 1906, a big house served as courthouse. It still stands today, with an empty weapons rack in a corner to symbolize the importance of defense among the common concerns of the kinsmen who used to meet there.

Other physical expressions of kin-group solidarity included the family tombs, which were vaults built, maintained, and used by the group. Grain for all its members was ground in a cooperative mill. Collectively maintained waterwheels required the group to make joint decisions on their repair and use.

Common activities also reaffirmed kin-group solidarity. The men met to decide issues, such as the sharing of irrigation water. The kin group gathered at the big house for family occasions.

Normally only a few constables, under the control of the village headman, represented the forces of law and order in the village. Disputes over irrigation water, or over injuries to the persons or to the honor of kinspeople, could give rise to feuds that went on for generations, marked by destruction of crops and other acts of violence, including murder. Every kin group included some men ready to sleep in the fields to protect the crops or ready to defend the family against agents of the government. Some of these valiants became village heroes, like Zahran.

The Kinship Society and the World Outside

Because the kin group meant so much, village society de-emphasized not only the individual but also larger social groupings. The sole exception was the common religious bond among all Muslims.

Apart from economic links, the village was relatively isolated from the outside world. Some of the boys went to study at the higher religious schools of the major towns or at the Al-Azhar Mosque University in Cairo; many such scholars never returned. Pious villagers of sufficient means would make the Islamic pilgrimage to Mecca. Their social system was so self-contained, however, that villagers still had little sense of political integration into any entity larger than the kin group. The "politics" that meant most to them concerned matters such as marriage and irrigation or feuds among kin groups.

Villagers knew about the khedive in Cairo and the sultan in Istanbul, and they had some notion of the British. But they also had the apathy of people whose opinion was never asked. Agents of the central government usually came to the village to collect taxes, conscript soldiers, or exact forced labor. In their dealings with officials, villagers tended to be submissive but evasive. The officials generally responded by treating the peasants like brutes.

Economic Life of the Village

In the economic life of the village, agriculture reigned supreme. Tilling one's own land was virtually the only occupation that had prestige among villagers, who were aptly known as *fellahin* ("cultivators"). Many things about Egyptian agriculture seemed timeless, yet European interference had fundamentally changed it during the nineteenth century.

If the villagers had been left to themselves, their economic life in 1906 would have resembled that of many other non-European societies. Villagers would have spent their time cultivating and irrigating their fields, divided into many small plots by the provisions of Islamic inheritance law. Villagers would have consumed some of their produce, used some for hospitality, bartered some, sold some, and yielded up a good part for rents or taxes. They would have given little thought to saving or investment, except to buy more land. Wealth, in their view, would have consisted in having many kinsmen—and land to support them. The delta villager's economic world would have been radically different from the European capitalist's. Instead of profit and growth for the individual, the village would have emphasized the kin group's common interests and the equitable distribution of resources within it.

But delta villagers had not been left to themselves. A new economic order had come into existence, one closer to European capitalist norms than to kin-group communalism. Until the rapid population growth of this century, Egypt produced agricultural surpluses. Since the early nineteenth century, the family that governed Egypt had sought to take advantage of this productivity. The rulers introduced changes in land tenure that led to the formation of huge estates owned by individuals associated with

Villagers tilling the soil with a wooden plow, al-Agami Village, Sharqiyyah Province, 1983. *C. V. Findley*

the government; they undertook large-scale public works to extend irrigation, with permanent irrigation in the delta. Thus, delta agriculture no longer depended on the annual Nile flood, and cultivators could work year-round, producing several crops.

Together with other factors, expensive public works led to tax increases that strained the resources of peasant families. Aiming to maximize agricultural exports, the government introduced new crops—especially long-staple cotton. But cotton cultivation required more investment than did cultivation of other crops,

further straining villagers' resources. And increased emphasis on production for export compounded a problem common to all colonial economies: vulnerability to unforeseen price shifts in world commodity markets. During the U.S. Civil War, for example, when the South could not export its cotton, the price of Egyptian cotton more than tripled. But between 1865 and 1866, when U.S. cotton reappeared on the world market, cotton prices fell by more than half. The collapse of cotton brought ruin to Egyptians and helped push the khedive's government toward bankruptcy, preparing the way for the British occupation in 1882.

More and more village families sank into debt as their taxes and operating costs grew; finally they lost their lands. By 1906, less than a quarter of the rural work force consisted of landowners cultivating their own land. The rest were sharecroppers, tenants, or wage laborers, many of whom had formerly owned land. Some villages now consisted entirely of landless fella-hin, often working for absentee landlords. Peasants who had once cultivated their own fields of wheat, vegetables, and clover spent most of their time growing cotton for the landowners. In the remaining hours, they worked small plots to produce the crops, especially beans and onions, that formed their meager diet.

Agricultural Egypt was being integrated into the world economy under conditions of colonial subordination. Egypt was also becoming a market for goods that its colonial masters had to sell, although villagers were too poor to buy much. Shifting tastes in beverages illustrate this point. Historically, the villagers preferred coffee, consumed in the Middle East long before it became known in Europe. But in 1906 a visitor would probably have been offered tea, for Egypt was then ruled by the British, who dominated the world's tea trade. Today, a visitor is just as likely to be offered a soft drink, such as Coca-Cola.

In the swiftly changing Berlin of 1914, we saw religion's role in people's lives dwindling. In Dinshawai, by contrast, the villagers' lives were imbued with a rich mixture of religious elements, ranging from formal Islam through a variety of customary religious practices—some of which antedated Islam—to a belief in the magical properties of nature that many Westerners would have scorned as "superstitious." Islamic law not only stipulated such observances for Muslims as the five daily prayers and fasting during the month of Ramadan but also regulated many features of daily life, from ideas of cleanliness to rules of inheritance. But the popular practice of Islam included some events that derived from long-held purely local custom: for example, the celebration of local saints' nativity festivals, rites that were at the same time popular fairs, communal celebrations, and religious observances.

Beyond the spiritual teachings of Islam, villagers were drawn closer to their natural world by their belief that it was inhabited by spirits both good and evil. Their belief that nature itself was in some ways holy underlaid many of their attitudes and practices. They loved their land, the foundation of their existence, and found goodness in whatever enriched it and the crops and livestock essential to their survival that it supported. Thus, for example, the muddy canal water that irrigated and fertilized the fields was better to drink than clear water. Such an idea would have horrified the Berliners of the age of Lister. But the villagers of Dinshawai, like peasants around the globe, took for granted that the human and natural aspects of their lives were at one with their spiritual lives, a conviction that inspired every act in the familiar cycle of their generations.

Conclusion: Berlin and Dinshawai

Berlin, with its explosion of creativity, and Dinshawai, with its rustic routine, give an idea of the range of variation between the great powers and the colonial world as of 1914. Berlin flourished as the capital of one great power; Dinshawai suffered as the victim of another. Berlin was a crucible of change; Dinshawai was a living example of slow change. In the Berlin of 1914, the age of national integration and mass politics had begun, despite such anachronisms as the Kaiser and aristocracy. In Dinshawai, the incident of 1906 marked a first step in the villagers' political mobilization. Berlin led in developing modern technology; Dinshawai relied on time-tested technologies adapted to its environment. Berlin represented many of the values that would shape the twentieth century; Dinshawai embodied those that had molded human experience through the ages.

In 1914, the world's Berlins and Dinshawais looked radically different. Yet the global economic relationships that had brought cotton cultivation to the Nile Delta linked them. So did the political domination that brought death to Dinshawai in 1906. Most Europeans and Americans of 1914 would have thought the comparison between Berlin and Dinshawai was all to Berlin's favor. The crises that destroyed the European-dominated global pattern of great powers and colonies left Berlin ruined and divided in 1945; however, the mud-brick houses of Dinshawai still stand intact. Today, in a world where European dominance is a memory and global interdependence increasingly a reality, the values that made places like Dinshawai work command our interest in a way that bids us recognize the shared humanity of men and women everywhere.

Suggestions for Further Reading

Betts, Raymond F. *The False Dawn: European Imperialism in the Nineteenth Century* (1975).

Hale, Oron J. *The Great Illusion, 1900–1914* (1971).

Harriss, John, et. al. *The New Century: A Changing World* (1993).

Hayes, Carlton J. H., *A Generation of Materialism* (1963).

Headrick, Daniel R. *The Tools of Empire: Technology and European Imperialism in the Nineteenth Century* (1981).

Hochschild, Adam. *King Leopold's Ghost: A Story of Greed, Terror and Heroism in Colonial Africa* (1998).

Hoisington, William A. *Lyautey and the French Conquest of Morocco* (1995).

Marcus, Geoffrey. *The Maiden Voyage* (1974).

May, Ernest R. *Imperial Democracy: The Emergence of America as a Great Power* (1961).

On Berlin

Kollmann, Wolfgang. "The Process of Urbanization in Germany at the Height of the Industrialization Period." In *The Urbanization of European Society in the Nineteenth Century,* edited by Andrew Lees and Lynn Lees (1976).

Liang, His-Huey. "Lower Class Immigrants in Wilhelmine Berlin." In *The Urbanization of European Society in the Nineteenth Century,* edited by Andrew Lees and Lynn Lees (1976).

Masur, Gerhard. *Imperial Berlin* (1970).

On Dinshawai

Ayrout, Henry Habib. *The Egyptian Peasant.* Translated by John Alden Williams (1963).

Berque, Jacques. *Histoire sociale d'un village égyptien au Xxe siècle* (1957).

Fakhouri, Hani. *Kafr el-Elow: An Egyptian Village in Transition* (1972).

Goldschmidt, Arthur. *Modern Egypt: The Formation of a Nation-State* (1988).

Richards, Alan. *Egypt's Agricultural Development, 1800–1980: Technical and Social Change* (1982).

PART TWO

Crisis in the European-Dominated World Order

CHAPTER 3

World War I: The Turning Point of European Ascendancy

THE YEARS AFTER WORLD WAR I PRODUCED MANY NOVELS IN ALL LANGUAGES revealing the peculiar horror of soldiers' lives in the front-line trenches. The most famous of these is certainly Erich Maria Remarque's *All Quiet on the Western Front* (1928). The story focuses on a group of German schoolboys from their enlistment in the army under the urgings of their patriotic high school teacher until the very last of them has been killed in France on a day when the official report is that the Western Front has been "quiet."

Like most soldiers, these boys-turned-men talk mainly in matter-of-fact terms about their daily experiences. But on one occasion Remarque, a front-line veteran himself, depicts them in a rare discussion of why the war that is killing them had happened. Wars happen, says one, "mostly by one country badly offending another." A comrade objects: "A country, I don't follow. A mountain in Germany cannot offend a mountain in France. Or a river, or a wood, or a field of wheat." "Don't be stupid," retorts the first. "I don't mean that at all. One people offends the other—." But the second interrupts "Then I haven't any business here at all. I don't feel myself offended . . . ," adding ironically "I can be going home right away."

The old soldier who now leads them suggests, "Just you consider, almost all of us are simple folk. And in France, too, the majority of men are laborers, workmen, or poor clerks. Now just why would a French blacksmith or a French shoemaker want to attack us? No, it is merely the rulers. I had never seen a Frenchman before I came here and it will be just the same with the majority of Frenchmen as regards us. They weren't asked about it any more than we were."

"Then what exactly is the war for?" asks a younger soldier. But though the discussion continues for awhile, his question is never really answered. Finally, one growls, "The best thing is not to talk about the rotten business," and the old soldier agrees, "It won't make any difference, that's sure."[1]

Thus these young men, confronted daily with death, can find no answer to the question why. But the question is still a good one to keep in mind while reading the following chapter. Why, exactly, do wars happen? Why did this one happen?

Causes of World War I

The collapse of Europe's world dominance began with an assassination. It took place on June 28, 1914, in Sarajevo, the capital of Bosnia, then under Austro-Hungarian rule but in the 1990s the scene of savage ethnic strife after the disintegration of Yugoslavia. A nineteen-year-old terrorist, Gavrilo Princip, stepped up to the car in which Archduke Franz Ferdinand, heir to the Austrian throne, was making an official visit to the city. With a shaking hand he pumped bullets into the archduke and his wife, fatally wounding them both.

Because the Austrian government correctly suspected that Princip's terrorist organization, the Black Hand, had the covert backing of the head of intelligence of the neighboring kingdom of Serbia, Austria-Hungary retaliated by threatening and then declaring war on Serbia. The hostilities soon expanded. One after another, honoring commitments made in treaties with their allies, the major powers of Europe entered the most costly war the world had yet witnessed.

In the end, some 10 million young men were killed and another 20 million crippled. In France, more than 1.3 million died, a quarter of all the men of draft age (between twenty and thirty-eight) in 1914; in addition, half the draft-age population had been wounded by 1918.

Death reaped a rich harvest among civilians as well. Millions died from malnutrition in Germany, as the British blockade cut off food supplies, and in Russia, where the still-developing economy could not cope with both total war and normal requirements.

Other consequences of World War I had even longer-lasting significance. To mobilize manpower and materiel, governments extended their control over the lives of citizens, creating a precedent for later government management of society to meet crises. To meet the gigantic costs of World War I, governments resorted to methods of financing that continued to strain the world's economy for generations. The stresses of the war gave communism its first opportunity when V. I. Lenin and the Bolsheviks seized control of the 1917 revolution that had toppled Russia's tsarist government. Thus began the formation of the hostile blocs that divided the world for most of the century, until communism finally collapsed. Above all, the impact of the war and its aftermath helped Adolf Hitler take power in Germany in 1933. The rise of a man dedicated to reversing the outcome of World War I by force probably made a second world war inevitable. From that conflict, Europe would emerge in ruins in 1945, too feeble ever to re-establish control over the rest of the world.

The shots fired by Princip at Sarajevo in 1914 killed not only the heir to the Hapsburg throne but eventually the European-dominated world system. They marked one of the great turning points of history. When the slaughter stopped in 1918, people groped for an explanation of its origins. How could a political assassination, in a town unknown to most Europeans of 1914, have led to such a disaster?

Aggression or Accident?

In the peace treaty they wrote at Versailles, the "winners" of World War I (France, Britain, and the United States) naturally held the "losers," especially Germany, responsible—though it makes little sense to speak of winners and losers after a conflict that mortally weakened every country involved, except the United States. Article 231 of the Versailles treaty placed the blame on decisions made by German leaders between the shooting of the archduke on June 28 and the outbreak of general war in early August.

If we could believe, as the victors claimed at Versailles, that World War I was caused by the deliberate aggression of evil leaders, we would have the key to preventing future wars. Peace could be maintained by preventing people with such intentions from obtaining power, or by constantly resisting them if they already held power. In fact, however, most historians believe that well-meaning, unimaginative leaders in every capital stumbled into World War I. By doing what most people believed was normal for defense, they produced a result none had ever intended.

Ideas cause wars: ideas of how the world is divided and how to resolve conflicts within it. Ideas of nationalism and of alliances underlay World War I. The idea of South Slav nationalism inspired Princip to fire his fatal shot. The local conflict between South Slav nationalism, represented by Serbia, and the Austro-Hungarian Empire escalated into a world war because of European leaders' notion that their nations' safety depended on maintaining credible alliances. These two ideas were reflections of some more basic characteristics of the European-dominated world of 1914. We cannot explain why South Slav nationalists like Princip wanted to destroy the Austro-Hungarian Empire, and why Europe was tangled into alliances that pulled everyone into the conflict, without understanding the nature of international relations in 1914, the assumptions that Europeans made about their obligations to their national communities, and even the general mood. A full appreciation of these factors makes it much easier to understand the link between the shots at Sarajevo and a war of 30 million casualties. If that assassination had not triggered a world war, some similar event elsewhere might have done so.

The Multinational Empire

The shots at Sarajevo might never have been fired had multinational Austria-Hungary not survived into the twentieth century. A state that included people of a dozen ethnic groups seemed out of date to a nationalistic age that believed every ethnic group should have a nation of its own. Austria-Hungary was a mosaic of ethnically diverse provinces collected over a thousand years of wars and dynastic marriages (Map 3.1). Some of these ethnic groups felt they were unfairly treated by the dominant Austrians and Hungarians, and by the twentieth century their rebelliousness had been encouraged by developments on the empire's borders. Nations such as Italy had emerged as independent homelands for some of the ethnic groups that felt oppressed under Hapsburg rule.

In the capital, Vienna, it was feared that a rebellion by another ethnic minority would mean the end of the empire. The nightmare was that the independent kingdom of Serbia would do for the empire's South Slavs what Italy had

The capture of the assassin of Archduke Franz Ferdinand and his wife in Sarajevo, June 28, 1914. *The Granger Collection*

done for its Italians. Since a palace revolt in Serbia had replaced rulers sympathetic to Austria-Hungary with fanatical nationalists, discontented South Slavs within the empire could look across the border for arms and encouragement. Through the assassination of the archduke, Princip and his fellow terrorists, Austrian subjects who sought a nation of their own, aimed to provoke a war that would destroy the Austro-Hungarian Empire.

They succeeded. In Vienna, the Austro-Hungarian government took the assassination as a historic opportunity to eliminate the Serbian menace. On July 23, Austria-Hungary dispatched to the Serbs an insulting set of demands that no independent nation could have been expected to accept.

Alliances and Mobilization

The ultimatum to the Serbs set off a chain reaction that within ten days involved almost all the major powers in war. Government leaders believed that in a showdown the loser would be the first country that did not stand with its allies. A power that proved a weak or disloyal ally would soon have no allies left.

In 1914 Europe was divided into two combinations of great powers: the Triple Alliance of

Map 3.1 Ethnic Groups in Germany, the Austro-Hungarian Empire, and the Balkans Before World War I

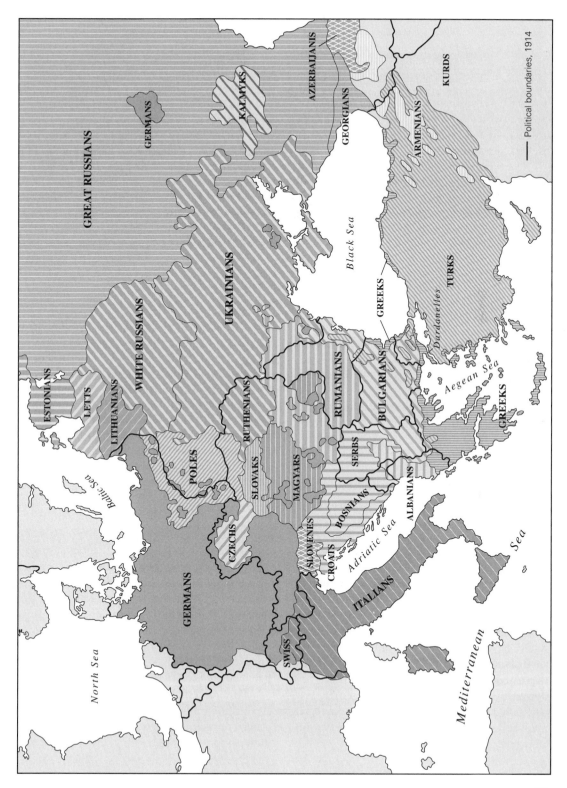

GREAT RUSSIANS

GERMANS

KALMYKS

AZERBAIJANIS

GEORGIANS

ARMENIANS

KURDS

TURKS

Black Sea

GREEKS

Dardanelles

Aegean Sea

GREEKS

BULGARIANS

RUMANIANS

UKRAINIANS

WHITE RUSSIANS

ESTONIANS

LETTS

LITHUANIANS

POLES

RUTHENIANS

SLOVAKS

MAGYARS

SERBS

SLOVENES

CROATS

BOSNIANS

ALBANIANS

CZECHS

GERMANS

SWISS

ITALIANS

North Sea

Baltic Sea

Adriatic Sea

Mediterranean

Sea

—— Political boundaries, 1914

59

Germany, Austria, and Italy and the Triple Entente of France, Russia, and Britain. Ironically, these alliances had originally been formed for defensive purposes. In a clash over European or colonial issues, diplomats had felt their countries would face less risk of attack or defeat if backed by a strong ally.

The events that led to the outbreak of World War I suggest that the leaders had miscalculated. Alliances made it easier, not more difficult, to go to war. The more aggressive partners tended to recklessness because they were counting on allied help. The less aggressive partners were afraid to restrain their ally, lest they appear unreliable and thus find themselves alone in the next crisis. Had the rulers of Austria-Hungary not been sure of German support, they might not have risked war with the greatest Slavic nation, Russia, by attacking Serbia. But the German government essentially gave the Austro-Hungarian government a "blank check" to solve the Serbian problem as it chose. Because of their own blundering foreign policy of the past quarter-century, the Germans felt encircled by unfriendly nations. Ringed by France, Britain, and Russia, the Germans felt they could not let down their one reliable ally.

In the Bosnian crisis of 1908–1909, Russia had challenged Austria-Hungary's annexation of Bosnia but eventually had backed down. In 1914, however, the Russians were determined to stand by their South Slavic kinfolk. When Austria-Hungary declared war on Serbia on July 28 (despite Serbian acceptance of all but one of the demands), the Russians began mobilization. Tsar Nicholas II, who had recently sponsored two international disarmament conferences, would have preferred war against Austria-Hungary alone. Russian military experts, however, explained that their mobilization plan did not permit that kind of flexible response. The tsar had only two choices, they said. He could remain at peace, or he could launch total war on all fronts.

When the tsar chose the latter course on July 30, the events that followed were almost automatic. Though some German leaders began to think of drawing back, it was too late. With the Russian army mobilizing on their borders, they felt forced to launch full-scale war. Germany expected to fight both France and Russia; its only hope of success would be to finish off France quickly before the slow-moving Russians posed too great a threat. Thus German mobilization meant a direct threat to France. The French, outnumbered almost two to one by Germany, believed that their national survival depended on the Russian alliance. Having done little to restrain Russian belligerence, the French responded to the German threat by mobilizing.

Although Britain and France had long been enemies, British rivalry with Germany had recently drawn Britain into a loose alliance, involving some joint military planning, with France. Thus British leaders felt a commitment to help the French. The new friendship of Britain and France, and the cooling of once-friendly British-German relations, resulted above all from the German decision at the turn of the century to build a high-seas fleet. The ensuing arms race convinced the British that the new German battleships were a direct threat to the Royal Navy. Even so, the British public probably accepted the need for war in 1914 only when the Germans invaded neutral Belgium. German military planners, guided by strategic rather than diplomatic priorities, thought the quickest way to defeat France was to attack through Belgium. The British government could now lead its people to war for the moral cause of defending a violated neutral country. Thus, by August 4, all the major European powers but Italy had toppled over the brink into war.

The immediate blame for this catastrophe falls on the monarchs and ministers who made crucial decisions with the aim of either bluffing their opponents into backing down or entering a war with maximum allied help. All considered the preservation of their national interests more important than the vaguer general European interest in maintaining peace. The vital interests of Serbs, Austrians, and Russians justified waging a local war even if it might spread. The Germans and French believed they served their own interests by backing even aggressive allies, because the loss of an ally seemed more dangerous than the risk of war.

In one sense, then, World War I was the result of a series of apparently reasonable calculations, as national leaders decided that each new step toward war was preferable to a backward step that implied national humiliation or isolation. Thus the confrontation was played out to the point of collision.

Nationalism and Interdependence

To avoid the trap into which they fell, Europe's leaders would have had to go against people's perceptions of the nature of the world and against values derived from those perceptions. In a general sense, World War I was caused by the fact that people were nationalists, feeling themselves to be not Europeans but Frenchmen, Germans, Russians, or South Slavs. Although growing global interdependence was making this vision of an ethnically divided continent obsolete, most Europeans knew no higher goal than national self-preservation.

The decade before the war had seen a few steps toward internationalism. An International Office of Public Health and a World Missionary Congress had been created; these institutions recognized that neither disease nor the word of God was restrained by borders. Over half of Europe's trade union members belonged to internationally affiliated unions, united by the idea that workers of all countries had more in common with each other than with their employers. A growing peace movement placed its hopes in the permanent International Court of Arbitration recently established in The Hague. But such expressions of internationalism counted for little against the prevailing nationalism, which exalted individual countries. Many people interpreted international politics the way Charles Darwin had interpreted the world of nature: in the struggle for survival, the weak perished and the strong dominated.

To many people the major European powers seemed already locked in economic struggle for raw materials and markets. Germans resented the fact that their belated achievement of national unity had denied them a colonial "place in the sun" like the empires of Britain and France. By creating a navy to assert its aspirations to world power, Germany came into confrontation with Britain, even though each country was the other's best export customer. Substantial sectors of both economies would have collapsed without the markets provided by the "enemy."

The perception of the world as an arena of conflict rather than interdependence weighed heavily on the calculations of statesmen in 1914. Most people everywhere had learned in school to accept this view. Even Russia was fumbling toward making elementary education compulsory by the time of the war. In parts of Germany all young children had been educated since the early nineteenth century. Britain and France had made their educational systems universal in the 1880s. After school came military service. All the major powers except Britain had universal conscription—the draft.

The patriotism young men learned from their schoolmaster and the drill sergeant was reinforced by what they read in the newspapers. Now that most of the population could read and write, mass journalism entered its golden age. The number of European newspapers doubled in twenty years. And patriotism sold papers. The international conference held at Algeciras in 1906 to deal with a colonial confrontation between Germany and France was the first to be covered by a pack of reporters. Although nations continued to keep their treaties secret, diplomats would henceforth have to negotiate their way out of international showdowns with patriotic public opinion looking over their shoulders.

An Age of Militarism

Hemmed in by public opinion, statesmen struggling to resolve international issues also had to reckon with increasing military influence on decision making. Europe in 1914 was in the grip of *militarism,* the dominance of a military outlook and of the men who embodied it. Of the major heads of state, only the president of the French Republic never appeared in uniform. The German Kaiser, the Austrian emperor, and the Russian tsar always wore uniforms. This custom suggests the supreme prestige of soldiers, especially the generals who commanded the vast armies the draft made possible.

Europe's generals and their allies in industry, finance, and journalism formed a kind of military-industrial complex. The creation of the German fleet, for example, was facilitated by a publicity campaign financed and managed by admirals and shipbuilders. Lucrative contracts were their reward. Such military spending did not mean that a country's leaders were planning aggression. Armaments were amassed in the name of defense, to provide a "deterrent" against attack. These buildups did not prevent war in 1914, however. Indeed they had the opposite effect. Measuring their armaments against those of a potential enemy, some commanders became convinced that they had the upper hand and could risk war. Others feared that they were about to lose their advantage and argued that if a war was to be fought, it should be fought soon. Estimations of this kind were particularly dangerous because military men were specialists trained to think almost entirely in military terms. Such were the advisers who persuaded Nicholas II that partial mobilization

was impractical in 1914. And General Alfred von Schlieffen's strategic masterstroke of launching the German attack on France through Belgium brought Great Britain into the war, thus leading to the German defeat.

Against this background of intense national rivalry and expanding militarism, the decisions statesmen made in 1914 are understandable. None of them had any idea of how long and devastating a war between countries armed with twentieth-century technology would be. Neither did the public. Cheering crowds filled the streets of every European capital in the summer of 1914, greeting declarations of war with delirious enthusiasm.

Europeans had been taught that war was the real test of a nation's toughness. Only those past middle age could remember a war between major powers in Europe. For the young, war meant a short-lived colonial contest that occurred far away, involving someone else, and brought profit and prestige to the victor. For the last ten years, tension had been mounting domestically and internationally. Within each of the major powers, social conflicts had produced strikes and violence. Europe had gone from one diplomatic crisis to another, all ended unheroically through negotiation. Now a crisis had come along that diplomats could not solve, and many people felt relief. The whole society could unite against a common enemy.

As they rushed off to fight that enemy, the soldiers of 1914 could not know that they were embarking on the first of two European civil wars that would end Europe's domination of the world.

Battlefronts, 1914–1918

The war that began in 1914 led to fighting in almost every part of the globe. In Africa south of the Sahara, invasions from British and French colonies quickly captured most of Germany's holdings, though in East Africa a German force continued the battle against a British Indian army until 1918. In the South Pacific, British imperial troops from Australia and New Zealand seized German outposts. Britain's ally Japan snapped up other German possessions and appropriated the German slice of China.

Closer to Europe, the long-decaying Ottoman Empire entered the conflict on the side of the Central Powers (Germany and Austria-Hungary). This move threatened not only Russia's southern flank but also Britain's link to India through the Suez Canal. The British not only fought the Ottomans but also encouraged revolt among the Ottomans' Arab vassals, while making a conflicting promise—the Balfour Declaration—that Ottoman Palestine would become a national homeland for Jews. As a result, the war provoked by the frustrated aspirations of the Serbs, once Ottoman subjects, helped unleash the turmoil of conflicting national aspirations that still torments the Middle East in the twenty-first century.

All these conflicts were extensions of the European battle lines. Only in 1917 did the war become a world war in the sense that whole continents were pitted against one another. Then the weight of the United States, dominant in North and South America, had to be thrown into the scales to match a Germany that had overrun much of continental Europe, penetrated deeply into Russia, and fought Britain and France and their worldwide empires to a standstill.

The Entente Versus the Central Powers

Though hardly anyone in 1914 foresaw the bloody stalemate of the European war, calculation might have predicted such an outcome. The Central Powers and the Entente Powers were rather an even match. Britain's naval might gave the Entente the advantage on the seas. Though the construction of the German fleet had made Britain an enemy, the two nations had only one significant naval encounter,

at Jutland in 1916. There the Germans sank more British ships than they lost but did not risk a second confrontation. Too precious a weapon to be hazarded, the German battleships rusted in port while the British blockade cut Germany off from the overseas world. Against blockade, Germany could muster only its submarines, the weapon that would eventually make the United States another German enemy.

On land the two alliances were more equally matched, despite the Entente Powers' two-to-one advantage in population. Russia's millions of peasants in uniform were so inadequately equipped that some were sent into battle unarmed and expected to find the weapons of dead or wounded comrades. France and Britain could do little to help, for their prewar lines of communication to Russia were blocked by the Central Powers and their Turkish ally. Indeed, Germany's enemies never successfully coordinated their strategies. The war effort of the Central Powers, by contrast, was effectively directed from Berlin.

Since the citizens of each nation were convinced that they were defending their homeland against unprovoked attack, neither alliance had an edge in morale. Both were sufficiently determined to fight the land war to a draw. Thus victory could be achieved only by mobilizing overseas manpower and materiel, either by squeezing resources from the colonial empires or by drawing the world's most powerful neutral nation, the United States, into the conflict. Since British control of the sea lanes gave the Entente Powers better prospects of developing these advantages in a long war, the Germans felt they had to score a quick victory.

Stalemate in the West

The campaign of 1914 failed to produce the hoped-for victory. Germany's initial rush through Belgium carried its advance guard up to the Marne River, scarcely twenty miles from Paris (Map 3.2). The French victory on the

Marne was a very close brush with destruction, but it was a victory.

The Battle of the Marne may have decided the war. By Christmas 1914 the armies' rapid advances and retreats had given way to stationary front lines. Both sides dug into the soil of a corner of Belgium and northeastern France. The French drive against Germany failed, and the Germans reversed the Russian advance on their eastern border. But these successes could not compensate for the loss of German momentum in the west. Germany found itself in the very situation its prewar strategy had tried to avoid: a protracted war on two fronts. Though few sensed it at the time, Germany had perhaps already lost the war. Many million lives were to be sacrificed, however, before that loss was driven home.

During 1915 and 1916 the war was dominated by the futile efforts of both sides to punch a hole in the enemy front. Launched against elaborately fortified lines of trenches, these offensives became massacres. The German attack on the French fortress at Verdun in 1916 cost each side a third of a million men. In the same year the British attack on the Somme River won a few square miles of shell-torn ground at the cost of over a half-million lives. The defending Germans lost nearly as many.

Numbers like these do not convey what life in the trenches was like. Probably no earlier war, and perhaps no later one, imposed such strains on fighting men. Soldiers spent months in a filthy hole in the ground, their boredom interrupted only by the occasional crack of a sniper's rifle or a dogfight between airplanes. (Both sides had quickly learned to put this new technology to military use.) Sometimes the clang of the gas alarm warned the men to put on their masks as a poisonous cloud drifted toward them. When the rumble of artillery fire in the background had risen for a few days or weeks to a roar, they knew they would soon have to go "over the top," out of their trenches and across no man's land toward the enemy's

barbed wire, under a hail of machine gun and heavy weapons fire. The result of these offensives was always the same—failure to break through.

Both sides tried but failed to break through on other fronts. The Entente Powers attracted neutral Italy into the war by promising it a share of the spoils. The Italian challenge to the Austrians soon bogged down, however, giving the Entente's leaders another stalemated front to worry about. They also tried, half-heartedly, to establish a closer link with the Russians by sending an expedition to seize the Ottoman-controlled straits that connect the Mediterranean to Russia's Black Sea ports. Ottoman forces, led by the future creator of modern Turkey, Mustafa Kemal, offered effective resistance. The expedition to Gallipoli proved another fiasco.

The Central Powers also tried to break the deadlock by expanding the conflict. Bulgaria was encouraged to join the German side and successfully invaded Serbia. By 1917 Germany and its satellites controlled most of southeastern Europe, but this success was no more decisive than the continuing German victories against the Russians.

The German submarine effort to cut Britain's ocean lifelines had to be suspended after a U-boat torpedoed the British liner *Lusitania* off the Irish coast in May 1915. Though it was rightly suspected that the ship carried a secret cargo of munitions, most Americans did not believe that excused the drowning of more than twelve hundred people, among them over one hundred Americans. American outrage compelled the Germans to abandon the practice of torpedoing without warning.

Map 3.2 World War I in Europe, ◆
1914–1918

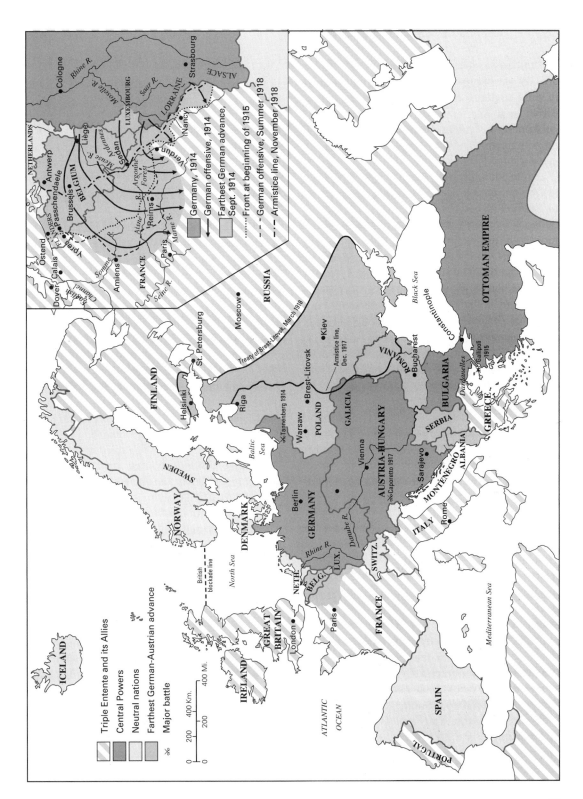

Triple Entente and its Allies

Central Powers

Neutral nations

Farthest German-Austrian advance

⚔ Major battle

0   200   400 Km.
0   200   400 Mi.

ICELAND

IRELAND

GREAT BRITAIN
London •

NETH.
BELG.
LUX.

FRANCE
Paris •

SPAIN

PORTUGAL

NORWAY

SWEDEN

DENMARK

FINLAND
Helsinki •

St. Petersburg •

Moscow •

RUSSIA

Treaty of Brest-Litovsk March 1918

Riga •

⚔ Tannenberg 1914

Warsaw •
POLAND
Brest-Litovsk •

Kiev •
Armistice line,
Dec. 1917

GALICIA

Vienna •

AUSTRIA-HUNGARY

Berlin •

GERMANY

Rhine R.

Danube R.

SWITZ.

ITALY
Rome •

⚔ Caporetto 1917

Sarajevo •

MONTENEGRO
ALBANIA

SERBIA

BULGARIA

ROMANIA
Bucharest •

Black Sea

Constantinople

Dardanelles
⚔ Gallipoli
1915

GREECE

OTTOMAN EMPIRE

British
blockade line

North Sea

Baltic Sea

ATLANTIC
OCEAN

Mediterranean Sea

Germany, 1914

German offensive, 1914

**Farthest German advance,
Sept. 1914**

Front at beginning of 1915

German offensive, Summer 1918

Armistice line, November 1918

NETHERLANDS

Cologne •

Rhine R.

Moselle R.

Saar R.

LUXEMBOURG

LORRAINE

Strasbourg •
ALSACE

Nancy •

Verdun •

Argonne
Forest

Meuse R.

Sedan •

Liège •

BELGIUM

Antwerp •

Brussels •

FLANDERS

Passchendaele

Ypres •

Ostend •

Dover • Calais •

British
Channel

Reims •

Aisne R.

Marne R.

Paris •

Seine R.

Amiens •

Somme R.

FRANCE

The two sides staggered into 1917 with no hope of victory in sight. By now the enthusiasm of 1914 had evaporated, and the mood everywhere was one, at best, of determination to survive. Some people, particularly socialists, urged that the war be stopped by declaring it a draw. But leaders everywhere shrank from such a solution. Without a victory, the previous butchery would seem pointless. And there would be rich prizes for winning.

German industrialists and military men expected to annex Belgium and parts of northeastern France, as well as a hugh swath of Russia. For France, defeat of the Central Powers would mean recovery of the northeastern provinces of Alsace and Lorraine. Victory would enable Italy to incorporate within its borders the remaining Italian-speaking regions of Austria. For Britain it would mean ending the German challenge to its commercial and naval pre-eminence. Hard-liners were now in control in almost every capital, and they used their wartime powers of censorship and arrest to silence doubters. Because technology seemed to have made defensive positions impregnable and offensives unbearable, the weary armies of Europe faced the prospect of apparently endless struggle.

1917: The Turning Point

Two events made 1917 the decisive year of the war. Russia withdrew from the conflict, and the United States declared war against the Central Powers. The net result was an advantage to the Entente side.

Why did the United States enter the war? Idealists point to a U.S. feeling of kinship with the Western democracies. Cynics note that an Entente defeat would have cost the U.S. industrial and financial communities a great deal in contracts and loans. In any case, U.S. entry probably became inevitable when the Germans decided, in January 1917, to resume unrestricted submarine warfare. This was a calculated risk.

The German high command expected that renewed Atlantic sinkings would bring the United States into the war but hoped to starve Britain into submission before American intervention could become decisive. The Germans also tried to incite Mexico to reclaim vast territories lost to the United States in the nineteenth century. The disclosure of this plan by British intelligence showed Americans just how far the Germans were prepared to go.

The entry of the United States marked the turning point of World War I. But it took time for the Entente's new advantages in manpower and materiel to become apparent. Meanwhile, the emergence in Russia of a revolutionary government determined to make peace at any price seemed a devastating blow to Entente hopes. The Bolsheviks believed the war had given them a historic opportunity to make a revolution by fulfilling the yearning of the Russian masses for peace. Even so, they hesitated for a time to pay the price the Germans demanded. The Treaty of Brest-Litovsk (March 1918) required them to hand over a quarter of Russia's prewar European territory, a third of its population, and half of its industrial plant. When Lenin signed, he ratified a decision many Russian peasant soldiers had already made by starting home from the battlefield.

The final phase of the war, from the spring to the autumn of 1918, amounted to a race between trains carrying German troops west to France from the Russian front and ships transporting U.S. soldiers eastward to France. Reinforced from the east, the German spring offensive did break through. Once again the Germans were at the gates of Paris. This second Battle of the Marne, however, was Germany's last gasp. In August the German army's chief strategist, General Erich Ludendorff, admitted to the Kaiser that he had no hope of victory. Germany's enemies were counterattacking its collapsing allies. As the Austro-Hungarian Empire disintegrated, its subject peoples declared their independence.

Inspection of Gurkha Troops by British Officers Before Being Dispatched to the Western Front. *The Gurkhas, recruited from the small Himalayan kingdom of Nepal, have formed part of the British army since the early 1800s. Copyright © The Gurkha Museum, Winchester*

The Hapsburg crown was the oldest but not the greatest to fall in 1918. In Germany, sailors mutinied rather than sail on a final suicide mission. This spark of rebellion set the whole country alight. Deserted even by the generals who had once been his staunchest supporters, the Kaiser fled. Democratic and socialist politicians proclaimed Germany a republic.

It was their representatives who met the supreme commander of the Entente and American armies, French general Ferdinand Foch, aboard his command train. The terms he demanded were stiff. Germany must withdraw its armies, which were still fighting deep in their enemies' territory, behind the Rhine River. Germany must renounce the Treaty of Brest-Litovsk

and hand over much of its railway rolling stock and shipping to the victors. With the British blockade threatening their country with starvation, Germany's representatives had no real choice. Protesting bitterly, they signed an armistice. Thus at 11 A.M. on November 11, 1918, the guns at last fell silent in ruined northeastern France.

Since 1918, there have been other wars, and Americans now celebrate Veterans Day in November, not Armistice Day. We do not always recall that the occasion commemorates men who died fighting what they believed was a war to end war. The generation that first observed November 11, however, was vividly aware that it had survived an experience unparalleled in history, not only for the men in the trenches but even for those who remained at home.

Home Fronts, 1914–1918

World War I was fought on the "home front" as well as on the battlefield. Everyone in each country, not just the men in uniform, was in the battle and had to make his or her contribution to the national effort.

Though the air blitz and guided missile attacks of World War II were foreshadowed thirty years earlier by German bombing raids on London, the technology of 1914-1918 was inadequate to make every citizen a target of enemy attack. In a sense, however, Europe's shops, factories, and farms became another fighting front. As it became clear that neither side was going to win a quick victory, leaders realized that it was essential to harness the efforts of every individual. Unprecedented coordination and coercion would be required. No aspect of people's lives could be left unmanaged.

In this way, World War I had a revolutionary impact on the societies of all the major powers. The new controls imposed on citizens were justified as wartime expedients, and many were relaxed when the war was over. Even so, they established precedents that made the postwar world a very different place. Many of the basic trends in twentieth-century government, politics, economics, and thought can be traced back to the experience of total war in 1914-1918.

War and Government

The war gave a new dimension to the role of government. Before 1914, Western governments had gradually made themselves more and more responsible for the welfare of their citizens, insuring them against old age or disability, limiting their hours of work, forbidding unhealthy workplaces. Germany was the most protective; France and the United States were the least. Every new measure met vigorous op-

position, however, for political thought was still dominated by the basic nineteenth-century liberal conviction that the best government is the one that governs least. Government today is the largest and most powerful organization in society. But in most major European nations in 1914 the "government" was a committee of legislators who exercised limited functions as long as they enjoyed the confidence of a parliamentary majority (or, in Germany and Russia, the confidence of the monarch).

A committee, or cabinet, of ministers oversaw bureaucracies whose numbers and powers varied from one nation to another. Nowhere, however, were bureaucrats very numerous, nor did their responsibilities extend much beyond providing the basic services for which governments had long been responsible. They maintained law and order and raised the modest taxes needed to balance the budget every year, while providing defense and the few other essentials not left to private initiative.

All this changed radically after 1914. Prolonged war demanded a more effective mechanism for planning and decision making than could be provided by the prewar parliamentary system, in which government was essentially a debating tournament. Even in countries with long-established parliamentary traditions, prime ministers emerged who personally exercised wide emergency executive power, tolerating little parliamentary interference: David Lloyd George in Britain and Georges Clemenceau in France. World War I pushed aside even venerable traditions "for the duration." The British Defense of the Realm Act, for example, allowed the government to censor or even silence newspapers, violating one of the most cherished British freedoms.

The number of government employees increased enormously. Twenty clerks had handled the purchase of munitions for the prewar British army. But by 1918, when the draft had put 3 million in uniform, the procurement of arms was the work of a Ministry of Munitions employing sixty-five thousand civil servants. The wartime concentration of power into a few hands and the extension of that power into every sphere of life were most marked in Germany, where the tradition of parliamentary government was weaker and political tradition had long subordinated the citizen to the state.

In Germany, as in the rest of the modern Western world, private economic power had become concentrated in trusts and *cartels** before 1914. Nevertheless, the belief remained strong that the best economy was one of free competition, with a minimum of government interference. Now, cut off by the British blockade from many essential supplies, the German government began to make all the economic decisions. Scarce commodities were rationed, and skilled workers were directed by government order to the jobs where they were needed. The government mobilized the scientific community in fields such as industrial chemistry to develop synthetic substitutes for unavailable imports such as rubber. A government bureaucracy headed by Walter Rathenau, the prewar head of the giant German General Electric Company, oversaw the distribution of available raw materials to the most efficient producers, usually the largest. In the process the prewar economy was altered beyond any hope of restoration.

By the war's end, the German government managed so much of the economy that the system was described as "war socialism." It was operated, ironically, by the conservative military men and industrialists who had been most hostile to socialism before the war. Individual Germans had become cogs in the military machine: every man between the ages of seventeen and sixty was mobilized under military discipline. And the German case is only the most extreme example. In each of the countries involved in the war, government authority was concentrated and expanded.

War, Economics, and Society

In addition to changing ideas about the proper functions of government, the war altered conventional notions of how governments should get and spend money. Traditional methods could not produce the vast sums needed. The British and French governments liquidated between a quarter and a third of their citizens' foreign investments to pay for essential goods purchased overseas, but they still emerged from the war owing enormous debts. In every belligerent country, new taxes were introduced and old ones raised. Nowhere was the resulting income more than a fraction of what governments were spending. They made up the difference by borrowing from their citizens, harnessing the new art of advertising to exhort savers to invest in the war effort. The supply of money was further enlarged by the easiest and most dangerous means of all: printing more of it.

The result was staggering inflation, though its full impact was not felt until after wartime price and wage controls were abolished. Only then did people realize what a new and terrifying financial world they lived in. The budget of the French government, for example, was forty times larger in 1918 than at the beginning of the war. The sum the French treasury had to pay out in interest alone was more than its entire annual budget before the war. The financial legacy of the war made the years 1918–1939 a period of almost constant economic strain.

Such economic changes inevitably produced profound social changes. For some social groups the war meant new opportunities. For example, as U.S. factories tooled up to produce the munitions the Entente demanded, industrialists took labor wherever they could find it. Thus began the migration of blacks from the rural South to the industrial North, a trend that

---

*Cartels are associations of private producers who agree to share markets and fix prices, thus limiting competition.

continued into the post–World War II years, profoundly transforming American life. In the increasingly interconnected world of the twentieth century, sharecroppers from Georgia found jobs in steel mills in Pittsburgh because farm boys from Bavaria were finding death in northeastern France.

European societies that had drafted a large proportion of their male populations, exempting only workers with critical skills, also recruited a "reserve army" of labor by hiring women for jobs monopolized before the war by men. Thereafter it was more difficult to argue that women's place was in the home. In fact, wartime necessity may have done as much as prewar agitation to break down the distinctions between the roles of men and women.

World War I created new opportunities for some groups but ruined others. Governments obsessed with maintaining production proved readier than prewar private employers to engage in collective bargaining. Trade unions thus won greater recognition. But workers felt they had not received just compensation for their contribution to the war effort, and a wave of strikes swept around the world with the coming of peace. In fact, workers' gains were vastly exceeded by the fortunes of profiteers who borrowed to build armaments factories, then paid their debts in a currency depreciated by inflation. Those hit hardest by the war, however, were the people who had lived comfortably before 1914 on a fixed income provided by a pension or on the interest from government bonds. In 1919 an income in British pounds (not by any means the most inflated currency) bought only a third of what it could purchase in 1914.

These economic distortions deepened prewar social divisions. When people had to accept a decline in their standard of living because of inflation, they naturally assumed that others must have gained at their expense. Wartime social upheaval laid the groundwork for the success of postwar political movements based,

like those founded by Mussolini and Hitler, on hatred and an appeal to vengeance.

War's Psychological Impact

The postwar years were marked by a mood of cynicism and disillusionment, an inevitable reaction against the war enthusiasm every government had tried to drum into the heads of its citizens. World War I prompted the first systematic efforts by governments to manage information and manipulate mass emotions. Such efforts were inevitable in twentieth-century society. All the major powers except Russia were approaching universal literacy and universal male suffrage by 1914. People who could read and felt they had a right to vote could not be commanded to blind obedience; they would have to be shown reasons for making the sacrifices the national cause demanded.

Thus each government in World War I mounted a vast propaganda campaign to persuade its public, and potential allies, of the justice of its motives and the wickedness of the enemy. British propagandists convinced a generation that Germany had ordered its soldiers to chop off the hands of Belgian children. But even more damage was done by the *positive* slogans of the propagandists: that soldiers were fighting for the defense of civilization against barbarism, or for democracy against militarism, or for the abolition of war.

The postwar world quickly revealed that these slogans had been hollow half-truths. Postwar cynicism was a direct reaction to wartime campaigns that had played on pride, shame, and fear to mobilize opinion. When the Bolsheviks published the secret Entente treaties, showing that neither side's motives had been pure, when none of the lofty goals for which the war had supposedly been fought materialized even for the "winners," public opinion turned on the leaders whose official news turned out to be lies. The very values that had supposedly motivated the war were discredited. Wartime ideal-

Women riveters in a Puget Sound shipyard. *Wartime labor shortages gave new opportunities to women in many countries, including, in the United States, some women of color.* National Archives

ism, deliberately overheated, turned sour in the postwar world.

The postwar mood also reflected a more basic change in the human outlook. No generation since 1914–1918 has ever matched the nineteenth century's confidence in progress. The world had gone through an orgy of destructiveness that seemed to prove false everything the prewar world had believed in. In the words of a soldier in Remarque's classic novel *All Quiet on the Western Front,* "It must be all lies and of no account when the culture of a thousand years could not prevent this stream of blood being poured out." No wonder the postwar Dadaist movement of artistic rebels mocked the pretensions of the past by exhibiting a copy of the *Mona Lisa* wearing a mous-

tache or suggesting that poetry should henceforth be written by cutting a newspaper into scraps and shaking them at random out of a bag. Such painting and poems might make no sense, but, as the war had just proved, neither did anything else. This was a dangerous discovery, for, as the great Russian novelist Feodor Dostoevski had warned, "If nothing is true, then everything is permitted." Today, when human beings permit themselves cruelties on a scale that earlier ages could not have imagined, we know what he meant.

In every sphere of modern life World War I accelerated trends already visible before 1914 and still powerful today. Politically it stimulated the growth of executive authority and government power. Economically it spurred the concentration of economic power in large corporations increasingly interlocked with government, while destroying forever the comforting idea that money retains a constant value. The war leveled social distinctions between groups and destroyed some groups altogether. In every country, for example, the sons of Europe's landed aristocracies became the second lieutenants of elite regiments and were killed out of all proportion to their numbers. At the same time the war gave greater status to working men and women. By lessening the distances between social classes, however, the war may have heightened tensions, for now hostile classes were in closer contact.

Spiritually, too, World War I marked a turning point. Before 1914, only a minority doubted the nineteenth century's faith in the future. The skeptical mood became general after 1919, as the world began to guess how unsatisfactory a peace had been made.

Peacemaking, 1919 and After

No international meeting ever aroused such anticipation as the conference that convened in Paris in January 1919 to write the peace treaties. Surely, people thought, so great a war would result in an equally great peace.

The Wilsonian Agenda

Many hopes focused on U.S. President Woodrow Wilson. He arrived in Europe to a welcome greater than any other American leader has ever received. Wilson seemed to embody a new kind of international politics based on moral principles, rather than on selfish interests.

Early in 1918, Wilson had outlined American objectives in the war. Some of his Fourteen Points simply called for a return to prewar conditions. Germany must evacuate Belgium and restore its freedom, for example. But other points seemed to promise change in the whole international order. Wilson called for an end to

the alliances that had dragged all the major powers into World War I. He advocated the removal of tariff barriers between nations and a general reduction of armaments. In settling the European powers' disputes over colonies, he declared, the interest of the colonized must be taken into account. The implication was that all peoples had an eventual right to choose their own government. This indeed was what Wilson promised to the subject peoples of the Austro-Hungarian and Ottoman empires. To the Poles, too, Wilson promised a restoration of the country they had lost when Austria, Russia, and Prussia had carved up Poland during the eighteenth century.

For many critics of prewar power politics, the most hopeful of Wilson's Fourteen Points was the last, which proposed to reconstruct the framework of international relations. The countries of the world should form an association—a League of Nations—whose members would pledge to preserve one another's independence and territorial integrity. In this way, the system that keeps the peace in a smaller human community—willingness to obey the law and condemnation of those who defy it—would replace the international anarchy that had brought disaster in 1914.

Wilson had not consulted his allies about any of his proposals. The United States entered the war in 1917 with no obligation, Americans believed, to support the objectives of earlier entrants. The Fourteen Points seemed to promise Europe a just peace and to recognize the national aspirations of colonial peoples. Unfortunately the Paris Peace Conference produced no such results. To the rights of the non-Western peoples it gave little more than lip service. To Europeans it gave a postwar settlement—the Treaty of Versailles—so riddled with injustices that it soon had few defenders.

Colonial Issues in 1919

Four years of world war had undermined European rule over non-Western peoples. In their frantic search for essential war materials, European powers increasingly treated their colonies as extensions of their home fronts. The non-Western peoples were thus subjected to many of the same strains that eventually broke the morale of European populations. In fact, European governments used much greater coercion on their non-Western subjects than they dared try at home. The British, for example, used methods of drafting labor and requisitioning materials that would have been enough in themselves to explain the postwar explosion of Egyptian nationalism. Colonies were also a reservoir of manpower. Almost 1.5 million Indians, for example, fought for Britain, and 62,000 of them were killed in the Middle East, Africa, and the trenches of France. The French recruited in their colonies in sub-Saharan Africa, as well as among the Arab population of Algeria.

To dress a man in your own country's uniform is implicitly to admit that he is not your inferior. The French recognized this by opening French citizenship to Algerians who had fought under the French flag. But many Algerians had greater ambitions than becoming honorary Europeans. Their pride demanded an Algerian nation of their own. The image of European superiority had been drastically undercut by World War I. Hearing the propaganda that Europeans published against each other, non-Western people could conclude that the real savages were their colonial masters. As fighting spread around the world, some non-Western peoples actually saw their European conquerors beaten and driven out. A successful defense often depended on the help of the non-Western population. These developments—economic, military, and psychological—undermined the prewar colonial order and launched a wave of postwar restiveness from Africa to China.

Trusting Wilson's rhetoric of self-determination, some non-Western nationalists journeyed to Paris in 1919 to argue their case. But the peacemakers hardly acknowledged them. They handed over to Britain and France the territories in Africa and the Middle East that had belonged to Germany or to the Ottoman Empire. The only concession to Wilsonian rhetoric was that these territories became "mandates" rather than colonies. This new term implied that Britain and France did not own these lands but held them in trust for the League of Nations. The European country was responsible for preparing the territory for eventual self-rule. In practice, however, there might be little difference from prewar colonial rule. The French, for example, responded to Syrian complaints with tanks and bombers.

Ultimately, the statesmen in Paris not only refused to redefine the power relationship between the world's whites and nonwhites but rejected the principle of racial equality proposed by Japan, the nonwhite great power that could claim a place among the victors. The Latin Americans, the Italians, and the French supported the Japanese. The British, speaking for Australia—a thinly settled white outpost that greatly feared its neighbors on the Asian mainland—opposed the proposal. Without U.S. support, the Japanese initiative came to nothing. It was clear that the peacemakers intended, despite all the noble rhetoric, to re-create the European-dominated world of 1914.

This outcome had a tremendous impact on a whole generation of ambitious young Africans and Asians. Western ideas of democracy were shown to be reserved for Europeans. As the Wilsonian promise faded, some future Asian and African leaders turned instead to the country the Paris peacemakers had outlawed from the international community: revolutionary Russia. Only Lenin and his regime seemed inclined to offer sympathy and support to the wave of protest that swept the colonial world after World War I.

Whatever the intent of the Paris peacemakers, European colonial rule could never again be as secure as it had been in 1914. In Egypt, something close to full-scale revolution broke out against the British. In India, a local British commander in the Punjab demonstrated the firmness of British authority by ordering his soldiers to fire on an unarmed crowd. Brigadier Reginald Dyer's troops killed nearly four hundred people and wounded more than a thousand. A century earlier, this massacre at Amritsar would hardly have been news. In 1919, however, the world reacted with horror. General Dyer was reprimanded by his military superiors and censured by the House of Commons.

Times had changed. Colonialism had acquired a bad conscience, perhaps in part because of all the wartime talk about democracy. By the early 1920s, Britain had launched both Egypt and India on the road to self-government. Indeed the colonial powers had little choice. Bled by four years of war, no European country could devote the same level of resources to colonial pacification as it had spent before 1914. But it took many years and another world war to persuade the British, and even longer to persuade the French, that their empires were too costly to maintain.

The Peace Treaties

The fate of the colonial peoples was a side issue for the peacemakers of Paris, whose real task was to draft the treaties ending the war with the Central Powers and their allies. They produced five such treaties. The Treaty of Sèvres imposed on the Ottoman Empire is discussed in Chapter 9. The three treaties that dealt with southeastern Europe essentially ratified what had happened in 1918. Out of the wreckage of the Austro-Hungarian Empire new nations emerged: Czechoslovakia for Czechs and Slovaks, Yugoslavia for the South Slavic peoples. Balkan nationalists like Gavrilo Princip got what they wanted. Whether their desires were wise remains a question. Most of these new countries remained economically little developed. Their ethnic animosities made cooperation among them unlikely. Miniature versions of the Hapsburg empire they had replaced, most of them contained dissatisfied ethnic minorities within their borders. Even so, most of these

countries felt they had been cheated of the borders they deserved.

These new states were destined for a dismal fate. They were dominated after Hitler's rise by Germany and after his fall by the Soviet Union almost until its collapse. As separate victims of Hitler and Stalin, these countries suffered much more than when they had all belonged to the Hapsburg emperor. But there was no hope of resurrecting his regime in 1919, even if the peacemakers had wanted to. Even today, almost every ethnic group insists on having its own nation: in the 1990s, both Czechoslovakia and Yugoslavia, multinational creations of 1919, disintegrated.

The hardest task in Paris was to decide what to do about Germany. To justify the loss of millions of lives, the statesmen had to ensure that future generations would not have to fight another German war. One approach that appealed to much of European public opinion and to military minds, notably in France, was to destroy Germany's military capability and economic strength. Now that Germany had surrendered, it should be broken up, so that there would be several weak Germanies, as there had been through most of European history.

The emotions that prompted demands for such a drastic solution are easy to understand. Would it have worked? After Russia's collapse, the Entente Powers had not been able to defeat Germany without the help of the United States. Was it likely that this wartime alliance could be maintained indefinitely in the postwar period to hold down an embittered German population? Moreover, in a world of economic interdependence, a country's former enemies are its future trading partners. A bankrupt and broken Germany might drag the whole world's economy down.

Considering such dangers, some concluded that a harsh peace was not the answer. The Kaiser and his regime, who bore responsibility for the war, had been driven from power. Germany was now in the hands of democratic leaders. Why not let it return on relatively moderate terms to membership in a world community ruled by law?

Not surprisingly, this point of view was far more widely held in Britain and the United States than in France, on whose soil the war had been fought and whose richest farming and industrial regions the Germans had devastated. It would be difficult to convince the French to give up their guns. In 1919 the prevention of aggression by the League of Nations was only the dream of idealists.

The peacemakers of Paris failed because of this conflict of views between the wartime allies. It is just possible that World War II might have been avoided if one of these approaches to the German problem had been fully applied. The Treaty of Versailles, however, was a compromise that combined the disadvantages of both approaches. Despite some Wilsonian language, it imposed on Germany a peace no patriotic German could accept. But it did not cripple Germany enough to prevent it from eventually challenging the verdict of 1919 by force.

This outcome may have been inevitable. Wartime alliances usually come apart as soon as the common objective has been attained. Though all twenty-seven countries that had declared war on the Central Powers sent delegations to Paris, most of them, notably the Latin Americans, had made insignificant contributions to the war. The major powers shunted them into the background. Though Italy was considered a major power, it fared little better. Believing that their country had been denied its fair share in the spoils of victory, the Italian delegates left the conference for a time. Neither their departure nor their return could win them a larger share of the remains of the Austro-Hungarian Empire or any of Germany's former colonies.

The important decisions of the Paris Peace Conference were the work of the Big Three: President Wilson, French Prime Minister Clemenceau, and British Prime Minister Lloyd George. Lloyd George was caught in the middle. He could foresee the dangers of a harsh peace,

but he represented an exhausted, bankrupt country, some of whose newspapers had mounted a campaign to "hang the Kaiser." The worst clashes were between Wilson and Clemenceau, who were temperamentally far apart.

Clemenceau Versus Wilson

Clemenceau's determination had made an unmeasurable but real contribution to France's victory. Cynical and sarcastic, the French prime minister cared for nothing but his martyred country. France had suffered, he believed, as a result of incurable German aggressiveness; in time the Germans could be expected to attack again, and only force would stop them. All the talk about new principles in international affairs left him cold. "Fourteen Points!" he snorted. "Even the Good Lord only had ten points." Yet Clemenceau knew that France's safety depended on British and American support, especially since Russia had disappeared into a dark cloud of communist revolution.

Wilson, the sublimely self-confident former professor, believed that his country had no selfish motives—a position easier to maintain in relation to the United States' role in Europe than to its role in Latin America. He thus spoke from a position of moral superiority that Clemenceau, and others who did not believe that morality ruled international affairs, found hard to endure. Wilson spoke with the zeal of a missionary from the idealistic New World to the corrupt Old World. But he may not have spoken for U.S. public opinion. The congressional elections of 1918 had gone against his party, and a reversal of wartime enthusiasm would soon lead the United States back to its traditional isolation from European affairs.

Only the necessity of producing some conclusion enabled two such different men to hammer out a treaty both could sign. When its terms were published, both were bitterly attacked by their countrymen. French hard-liners condemned Clemenceau for not insisting on the territorial demands they thought essential to

Paul Nash, **The Menin Road *(1918).*** *The painting reveals the English artist's horror at the landscape of modern war: trees stripped bare by gunfire, earth cratered by shells, soldiers dwarfed by destruction. Imperial War Museum, London*

French security. Many of Wilson's advisers thought he had too often given in to European-style power politics, sacrificing the principle of a people's right to choose its own government.

Wilson's supreme goal was the creation of the new international organization, the League of Nations. Clemenceau could hardly take the idea seriously, for Wilson could not promise that membership would require any nation, least of all the United States, to help a future victim of aggression. The same difficulty arose when the United Nations was created in 1945. Sovereign nations proved unwilling to subject their freedom of action to international authority.

In return for French agreement to the establishment of the League, Wilson allowed Clemenceau to impose severe penalties on Germany. The German army was to be limited to a hundred thousand men. Germany could have neither submarines nor an air force. Characteristic of the compromise nature of the treaty, this virtual disarmament of Germany was described as the first step toward the general disarmament called for in the Fourteen Points. The Treaty of Versailles was full of provisions intended by Clemenceau to weaken Germany. The new Republic of Austria, the German-speaking remnant of the former Hapsburg state, was forbidden to merge with Germany, though a national vote made it clear this was the solution preferred by most Austrians.

With the Russian alliance gone, Clemenceau intended to surround Germany with strong French allies to the east. The new state of Czechoslovakia was given a defensible mountainous border that put millions of Germans under Czech rule. The Poland the Paris peacemakers resurrected included a "Polish corridor" cutting through German territory to the Baltic Sea. Such terms made sense if the aim was to cripple Germany. But they flouted Wilsonian principles, and the Germans complained that the principle of self-determination had been honored only when it worked against them.

The Paris peacemakers also demanded that Germany should pay reparations. The word implies that Germany was to repair the damage its war had caused—not an unreasonable demand. But the bill drawn up by the victors was so astronomical—132 billion gold marks—that the Germans would still be making huge payments today if anybody were still trying to collect them.

The old idea of collecting large sums from a defeated enemy may have been outdated in the twentieth century, when national economies were so interdependent. If the Germans had to turn over everything they earned, they would be unable to buy the goods the victorious nations wanted to export. The economists who raised such questions were drowned out by the insistence that "the Germans will pay." Indeed when the Germans did not pay enough, soon enough, French and Belgian armies reoccupied German territory to collect what was due. Germans then concluded that reparations were not a bill for damages but an excuse for Germany's enslavement.

To prevent another German invasion like those of 1870 and 1914, many Frenchmen felt German territory should be amputated in the west as well as in the east. In particular, they wanted to detach the Rhineland—the region between the French-German border and the Rhine—and place it under reliable French control. (Map 3.3 makes clear why the French would have liked to control this territory.) Even as the conference was meeting in Paris, renegade Germans working for the French tried to establish a separate Rhineland Republic, though the effort soon collapsed. The Rhineland issue provoked the bitterest of the many quarrels of the Paris conference. Wilson, backed by Lloyd

George, warned that taking the Rhineland from Germany would create a permanent German grievance, comparable to Germany's taking of Alsace-Lorraine from France in 1871. Speaking for a country that had suffered casualties at thirty-six times the American rate, Clemenceau insisted that French control of the Rhineland was essential for French security. But he finally agreed to a compromise. The Treaty of Versailles stipulated only that the Rhineland be demilitarized. The Germans would keep it but could not fortify it or station troops there. In return for this concession, Wilson and Lloyd George signed a separate treaty committing their countries to help France if it was again attacked by Germany.

After months of argument, the Treaty of Versailles was complete. The victors handed it to the Germans to sign—or else. Germany's representatives were horrified. Their contacts with Wilson before the armistice had led them to expect a compromise peace. Now they were told to confess that Germany alone had caused the war, as Article 231 of the treaty proclaimed, and to pay a criminal's penalty.

By accepting the Treaty of Versailles, Germany's new postwar democracy, the Weimar Republic, probably signed its own death warrant. But its critics, like Adolf Hitler, never explained how the republic's representatives could have avoided the "dictated peace" of Versailles. Germany had lost the war. Because the fighting ended before Germany had been invaded, many Germans did not recognize this harsh reality. They saw the Treaty of Versailles as a humiliation to be repudiated as soon as possible. The treaty's reputation among the victors was hardly better. French hard-liners charged that Clemenceau had conceded too much and thrown France's victory away. "This is not a peace," said Marshal Foch, "but an armistice for twenty years."

The pessimism of these critics was confirmed within six months as the United States repudiated the agreements its president had negotiated. In November 1919 the Senate

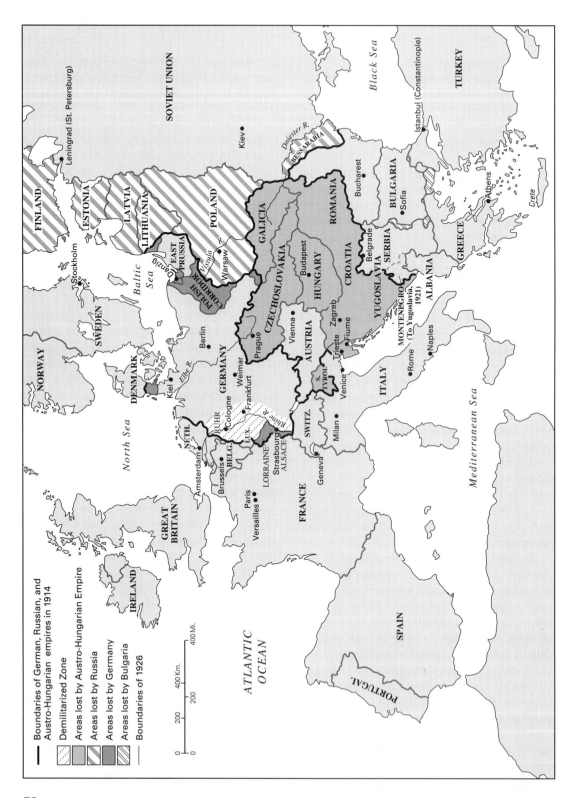

Boundaries of German, Russian, and
Austro-Hungarian empires in 1914
Demilitarized Zone
Areas lost by Austro-Hungarian Empire
Areas lost by Russia
Areas lost by Germany
Areas lost by Bulgaria
Boundaries of 1926

SOVIET UNION

FINLAND

Leningrad (St. Petersburg)

Black Sea

TURKEY

Istanbul (Constantinople)

Kiev

Dniester R.

BESSARABIA

ESTONIA

LATVIA

LITHUANIA

POLAND

GALICIA

ROMANIA

Bucharest

BULGARIA

Sofia

Stockholm

EAST
PRUSSIA

Danzig

POLISH
CORRIDOR

Vistula R.

Warsaw

Brzura

CZECHOSLOVAKIA

Budapest

HUNGARY

CROATIA

Belgrade

SERBIA

YUGOSLAVIA

ALBANIA

GREECE

Athens

Crete

SWEDEN

Baltic Sea

Berlin

GERMANY

Weimar

Prague

Vienna

AUSTRIA

Zagreb

Fiume

Trieste

MONTENEGRO
(To Yugoslavia,
1921)

Rome

Naples

NORWAY

DENMARK

Kiel

Elbe R.

Frankfurt

S.
TYROL

Venice

ITALY

Mediterranean Sea

North Sea

NETH.

Amsterdam

BELG.

Brussels

LUX.

RUHR

Cologne

Rhine R.

Strasbourg

ALSACE

LORRAINE

SWITZ.

Geneva

Milan

Paris

Versailles

FRANCE

GREAT
BRITAIN

IRELAND

ATLANTIC
OCEAN

SPAIN

PORTUGAL

400 Mi.

400 Km.

200

200

0

0

78

refused to ratify the Treaty of Versailles or the treaty promising American help to France. Americans were increasingly impatient with Europe's messy, faraway problems. The Old World, which had seemed so close in 1917–1918, again became remote: another world, a week away by the fastest ship. The 1920 presidential election was won by a likable, small-town newspaper publisher from the Midwest, Warren G. Harding. The choice reflected Americans' longing for a return to what Harding called "normalcy"—the way things had been before the United States became involved in a European war.

This American return to isolationism suggests the fatal weakness in Wilson's vision of a new world order. As an international organization, the League of Nations could keep the peace only if its members committed themselves to use force against any country determined to be an aggressor. Yet Wilson himself could offer no such commitment on behalf of the United States. The Senate's rejection of the Treaty of Versailles showed that Americans, like other people, still insisted on judging international conflicts in terms of their national interests. With no power of its own, the League of Nations proved pathetically inadequate to the task of keeping the peace when international tensions mounted again in the 1930s.

The limitations of the League were particularly serious because the balance of power in Europe had been destroyed. The collapse of Austria-Hungary had left a vacuum of power in Central and southeastern Europe. Russia was in the hands of revolutionaries who encouraged the overthrow of all other governments; no one could form an alliance with such an outlaw regime. Indeed the new states the peacemakers had created in Eastern Europe were intended to

contain not only Germany but the Russian communist threat. Britain, like the United States, now decided that the costs of getting involved in Europe outweighed the likely benefits. Using as their excuse the American failure to honor Wilson's commitment, the British also repudiated their pledge to defend France. This left an exhausted France alone (except for resentful Italy) on the continent with Germany. And Germany, though disarmed and diminished, was still the same nation that had held off the British Empire and two other major powers for most of the war. Its fundamental strengths—its numbers and its highly developed economy—could be mobilized by some future regime less willing than the Weimar Republic to accept the Versailles verdict.

World War I did not end until U.S. troops became combatants, along with many from the British overseas empire. If peace were to be maintained by some renewed balance of power, that balance had to be global. But many people in all countries were unable to draw this conclusion. Americans tended to see their intervention in international politics as a choice rather than as a necessity of the twentieth-century world. Over the next decades, they continued to come and go as they pleased on the world stage. Similarly, the British Empire soon became the British "Commonwealth of Nations," whose members did not automatically follow where Britain led. It would take a second world war to persuade all these peoples that they had a permanent stake in the global contest for power.

Conclusion

Although it is sometimes said that wars do not settle anything, World War I resolved several prewar questions, though hardly ever in the way the people who started the war had hoped. It settled the fate of the ramshackle Austro-Hungarian, Russian, and Ottoman empires. It showed that Europe, the smallest though the most developed of the continents, could not indefinitely dominate the globe. The war also

◀ **Map 3.3 Post–World War I Boundary Changes**

settled prewar uncertainties about the possible limits of government power over individuals. The disciplined fashion in which millions had marched to their deaths showed that power was virtually unbounded. At the same time, the war settled some questions about inequalities of civil rights based on birth or sex. Distinctions among citizens had given way to the demands of total mobilization (though discrimination had certainly not disappeared in 1918). And certainly the war gave a shocking answer to the prewar question of whether progress was inevitable. The art of surgery, for example, had advanced significantly during the war—prompted by improvements in the design of high explosives to blow people to pieces. It was hard to see this as "progress."

World War I also created a whole new set of postwar questions. If the fall of the Austro-Hungarian Empire proved that multinational states could not survive and that each people must have its own country, how could nations be established for all the hundreds of peoples around the world? And what would happen in places such as Ireland, Palestine, and South Africa, where more than one people claimed the same territory as their home? What would happen if government expansion continued? If the mobilization effort had created a greater social equality, would that eventually mean equal rights for everyone or an equal loss of freedoms? Would the mechanization of human life, so dramatically accelerated by the war, result in greater comforts or greater dangers?

By the mid-1920s some optimists thought they could see hopeful answers to all these questions. They found them in a country that was seeking to replace the European-dominated world system with a new system based on worldwide revolution. There, in Russia, an experiment in unlimited government power was taking shape. The country's goal was said to be the creation of a society based on literal equality. Its officially anointed heroes were its steelworkers and tractor drivers, whose machines would modernize a peasant land and make it the model for the twentieth century. Like those optimists of the 1920s from the West, but with a more analytical eye, we shall next look at the Union of Soviet Socialist Republics (USSR)—the country that emerged, after the Bolshevik Revolution of 1917, under Lenin and Stalin.

Note

1. Quotations from Erich Maria Remarque, *All Quiet on the Western Front* (1928), Fawcett Crest edition, pp. 203–207.

Suggestions for Further Reading

Eksteins, Modris. *Rites of Spring: The Great War and the Birth of the Modern Age* (1990).

Falls, Cyril. *The Great War* (1959).

Feldman, Gerald D. *Arms, Industry, and Labor in Germany* (1966).

Fussell, Paul. *The Great War and Modern Memory* (1975).

Horne, Alistair. *The Price of Glory* (1979).

Joll, James. *The Origins of the First World War* (1984).

Kaiser, David. "Germany and the Origins of World War I." *Journal of Modern History,* 55 (September 1983).

Lafore, Laurence. *The Long Fuse* (1965).

Mayer, Arno J. *The Politics and Diplomacy of Peacemaking* (1968).

Mee, Charles. *The End of Order: Versailles 1919* (1980).

Nicolson, Harold. *Peacemaking, 1919* (1984).

Remarque, Erich Maria. *All Quiet on the Western Front* (1929).

Tuchman, Barbara. *The Guns of August* (1988).

Williamson, Samuel R., Jr. *The Origins of a Tragedy, July 1914* (1981).

CHAPTER 4

Restructuring the Social and Political Order: The Bolshevik Revolution in World Perspective

THROUGHOUT HISTORY, GREAT REVOLUTIONS BEGUN BY PEOPLE WHO BELIEVED they were forever changing the world for the better have often ended in systematic massacre and crushing dictatorship. Noting this pattern, many historians have concluded that revolutionary attempts to change the direction of history are always inherently evil, or at least tragically misguided.

But historians always know how the story ended; vision in hindsight is always perfect. To understand an event like the Russian Revolution, we need to know how it appeared to the people actually living through it. For this purpose, no source offers more insight than the novel *Darkness at Noon,* written by Arthur Koestler, a former Communist who left the party in the late 1930s.

The central figure of Koestler's novel is N. S. Rubashov, a figure closely modeled on a real old Bolshevik, one of those middle-class Russian intellectuals who had lived in exile in Western Europe. After World War I gave the Bolsheviks the opportunity to return to Russia and seize power, Rubashov had been a high official of Lenin's regime. But *Darkness at Noon* finds him in the late 1930s in one of Stalin's prisons, awaiting the fate of an enemy of the revolution—execution, after a public confession of antirevolutionary crimes he had not committed. In anguish, Rubashov wonders why the bright noonday of successful revolution of 1917 has become the terrifying darkness of twenty years later. How had a movement launched in hopes of ending the cruelties of human life become itself so cruel?

An answer is given him by one of the secret policemen charged with his interrogation: Gletkin, a much younger man of peasant background who has known only the Stalinist phase of the revolution. He asks Rubashov if he had had a watch as a boy, and when Rubashov replies that of course he had, Gletkin continues:

> *I . . . was sixteen years old when I learnt that the hour was divided into minutes. In my village, when the peasants had to travel to town, they would go to the railway station at sunrise and lie down to sleep in the waiting room until the train came, which was usually at about midday; sometimes it only came in the evening or next morning. These are the peasants who now work in our factories. For example, in my village is now the biggest steel-rail factory in the world. In the first year, the foremen would lie down to sleep between two emptyings of the blast-furnace, until they were shot. In all other countries, the peasants had one or two hundred years to develop the habit of industrial precision and of the handling of machines. Here they only had ten years. If we didn't sack them and shoot them for every trifle, the whole country would come to a standstill, and the peasants would lie down to sleep in the factory yards until grass grew out of the chimneys and everything became as it was before.*[1]

The achievement of the ends Rubashov had dreamed of, Gletkin is saying, justify the cruelest of means to attain them, for if the Russian revolutionary experiment fails, humanity will be left with no hope of a better future. Whatever threatens the success of the revolution, be it peasant backwardness or the humanitarian reservations of intellectuals like Rubashov, must be ruthlessly destroyed.

In the chapter that follows, it is suggested that among the revolutions compared, it was the ones inspired by this kind of ruthless commitment, the Russian and the Maoist Chinese, that were most successful in transforming the societies. Is the lesson of history then that it is the most merciless revolution that really changes things?

The End of Tsarist Russia

World War I not only began the decline of European world dominance. This "European civil war" also opened the way for the triumph of a revolutionary movement in Russia: Bolshevism, committed in principle to destroying the social and economic bases of the European-dominated system worldwide. The Bolshevik Revolution of 1917 therefore influenced world history, as well as Russian history. This chapter explains why Russia's prewar tsarist regime was vulnerable to revolution, how Lenin and the Bolsheviks seized power, and how Stalin in the 1930s began to transform the Soviet Union into an industrial superpower.

This chapter also has a comparative goal. Russia's revolution was the early twentieth century's most important revolution but not its only one. By 1917, revolutions had also occurred in Iran (1905), the Ottoman Empire (1908), Mexico (1910), and China (1911), challenging the dominance of Europe's great powers or (in Mexico) of the United States. The question that arises is, Why did Russia's revolution prove the most influential?

We shall argue that the Bolsheviks defeated internal and external enemies and established their independence, while none of the earlier revolutions proved as decisive either in winning independence from great-power dominance or in restructuring society. The earlier revolutions fell short partly because they lacked leadership or organization comparable to Lenin's and, more important, because they had essentially nationalist goals. Aiming to free one country, they offered no model for transforming the world. Mexico's revolution illustrates this problem (see also Chapter 7).

The Bolshevik Revolution, by contrast, claimed to liberate Russians by implementing a set of relatively simple ideas about history and politics—Marxism-Leninism—that were equally applicable everywhere. Economic forces determined the course of history, in Marx's view. Capitalist industrial societies emerged when middle-class interests overthrew feudal societies dominated by monarchs and aristocrats. The middle-class capitalists then created the means of their own eventual destruction by exploiting industrial workers (the proletariat). Eventually, Marx said, workers would rebel and overthrow capitalism in a revolution inaugurating the communist dictatorship of the proletariat. As imperialistic capitalism spread its control over the world, the revolutionary potential would become an international, ultimately a global, one.

Lenin modified Marxism for a country where industrial workers made up only about 1 percent of the population. His innovation was to insist that the proletariat be guided in establishing its dictatorship by a tightly organized and disciplined party in which power flowed from the top down, a system he called "democratic centralism."

After 1917, people in colonial or semicolonial countries inevitably asked themselves whether Marxism-Leninism was an effective way to shake off European domination. Although the situation of colonial peoples differed fundamentally from that of workers in industrial societies, the global dominance of capitalist societies had created a powerful connection between the two groups. In Russia, Marxism-Leninism had provided a way to topple despotism in one of its European homelands. Could it do as much in colonial lands? Could other ideas produce such results?

Non-Western leaders' answers to these questions varied widely. At one extreme, in India Mohandas Gandhi produced an ideology of mass mobilization that rejected both colonialism and violent revolution. His career illustrates what could be accomplished through a reformist, not a revolutionary, approach to national independence and regeneration. His ideas could be borrowed and used successfully in

Harnessed women dragging barges on the Volga River. *In a Tsarist Russia already rapidly industrializing, human beings were still being used as beasts of burden.* David King Collection, London

other countries. Could his movement have succeeded, however, if European dominance had not been weakened by the shocks of world war and depression?

At the other end of the spectrum from Gandhi, Mao Zedong (Mao Tse-tung) was perhaps the most important non-Western political leader of the twentieth century (see Chapter 9). His early career shows how much Marxism-Leninism could do, compared with the less radical ideology of Sun Yat-sen and the Chinese Nationalists, to revive the world's most populous nation. But first Mao had to adapt Marxism-Leninism to the Chinese setting by formulating the ideas that later became known as Mao Zedong thought. Mao's ideas provide the best example of the influence of the Bolshevik Revo-

lution on the wider world, and of the limits and ambiguities of that influence.

Russia has always loomed menacingly over Central and Western Europe. In the nineteenth century, however, Russia was dreaded by Europeans not as the homeland of revolution but as the crusher of revolutions. Russian troops repeatedly snuffed out the Poles' hopes for independence. Russia's tsar saw himself as Europe's policeman and played an equally autocratic role at home. Even as it had expanded five thousand miles across a continent, subjecting a hundred nationalities to its rule, the Russian Empire never departed from its inherited political system. Its law was the will of the tsar, whose secret police still curbed freedoms taken for granted in Western Europe or North

America—freedom of speech, press, association, and self-expression.

Society and Politics

At the beginning of the twentieth century, Russia was still socially and economically backward. Nine out of ten Russians were still peasants. Until 1861 their grandparents had been serfs, literally the property of the aristocrat or the state whose land they worked. Even now the peasants were Russia's "dark people," largely illiterate, often lacking sufficient land to feed themselves. Their tradition was one of endurance, interrupted periodically by violence, as in the six hundred separate serf rebellions of the first half of the nineteenth century. Between the peasants at the bottom of Russian society and the wealthy, untaxed aristocracy at the top was a small middle class. The economic functions of a middle class—commerce and industry—had developed slowly in nineteenth-century Russia. Until 1830 there had not even been a paved road connecting Moscow and St. Petersburg, the empire's two principal cities.

In the early twentieth century, middle-class political liberals hoped to convert the tsarist autocracy into a Western-style constitutional monarchy. But by 1900, many intellectuals had despaired of any peaceful evolution of Russia's government. So grim was the tsarist record of repression and resistance to change that Social Democrats believed Marxist revolution offered the only hope. Other revolutionaries favored the distinctively Russian politics of assassination that had killed one tsar and dozens of high officials since the mid-nineteenth century. Many revolutionaries paid for their political beliefs with their lives or with long terms in Siberian prisons. Others fled Russia to await the coming of revolution. The tsarist regime was happy to see them go. There was no room for people influenced by Western notions of freedom and tolerance in a society that used the state-domi-

nated Orthodox church to control popular opinion, that imposed rule by Russians on the many ethnic minorities, and that repeatedly persecuted Jews. To official Russia, Western ideas were alien and dangerous.

The Western Challenge

Russia, however, could not do without Western ideas. If it was to remain a great power as its rivals modernized, Russia had to modernize too. This lesson had been painfully driven home in the mid-nineteenth century when Britain and France defeated Russia in the Crimean War. One of the war's consequences was the tsar's decision to emancipate the serfs in 1861—a decision inspired less by humanitarian concern than by economic calculation. A modernized agricultural system no longer based on serfdom might produce more grain for export, and grain was what Russia had to exchange for the products of Western ingenuity. By the turn of the century, Russia had become a large exporter of grain, even in years, such as 1891–1892, when famine killed millions of peasants.

Apart from the large loans it received from Western Europe and particularly from France, Russia could finance its industrialization only by exporting food even while its own people went hungry. Although it claimed to be a great power, preindustrial Russia stood in almost the same colonial economic relationship to Western and Central Europe as the dependent peoples of Africa and Asia. By the 1890s progressve ministers had persuaded the tsar that Russia must undertake a crash program of industrialization.

The program produced impressive economic results. Russian industry doubled its output from 1900 to 1913, raising the nation from near insignificance among industrial powers to fifth rank. Russia still had a long way to go, however. Its per capita income was one-sixth that of the United States, one-third that of Germany.

The social consequences of rapid industrialization were explosive. The capital needed for development was literally wrung out of the peasantry, already burdened by the debt they owed their former masters for emancipation. Their taxes increased 50 percent in a decade. A more immediate danger to the government was the condition of Russia's rapidly growing cities. As in almost every other country, the first phase of industrialization was a grim era for workers. The Russian factory worker often returned home after an eleven-and-a-half-hour day under relentless supervision to a hovel he shared with ten other people. He could not protest such conditions to anyone, for strikes, like unions, were illegal. Many Russian factories were huge places where the worker had no human contact with his employer, only with his fellow employees. In such settings, though propaganda could circulate only secretly, the Marxism of the Social Democratic party gained ground among the urban working class.

The massacre of hundreds of working people on Bloody Sunday (January 22) triggered the Revolution of 1905. Their peaceful attempt to petition the tsar—the "Little Father," Nicholas II (r. 1894–1917)—by gathering outside his palace in St. Petersburg ended in a hail of bullets. The uprising that followed was inconclusive, a dress rehearsal for the Revolution of 1917. Nevertheless, it revealed the deep disaffection of almost all of Russian society.

Military defeat had already exposed the regime's weaknesses. The tsar's advisers had led him confidently to war with Japan in 1904, expecting to defeat the "little monkeys" easily and end their interference with Russian expansion in East Asia. The Russo-Japanese War turned out instead to be the first major defeat of a European great power by a non-Western people. Admiral Heihachiro Togo's battleships sank much of the Russian fleet in a single battle. It was just one in a seemingly endless series of revelations of the tsarist government's incompetence. By the time Russia sued for peace, the government had been wholly discredited.

After Bloody Sunday, Russia's cities became the scene of continuous strikes and demonstrations until the army could be moved back from the front to restore order. Reinforced by violence in the countryside, this wave of revolt compelled the tsar to yield concessions, including a constitution. He even promised that the new parliament, or Duma, would have real power. But the tsar's heart was never in such promises; he had come to the throne denouncing petitions for reform as "senseless dreams." He intended to rule Russia exactly as his forefathers had ruled. As his government gradually regained control of cities and countryside, he took back most of the concessions he had made.

Thus Russia was still an autocracy as it entered World War I. The electoral system had been rigged to give the Duma, which was virtually powerless, a conservative majority. The parliament consequently provided no real outlet for the grievances of the middle class, workers, or peasants. Despite the failure of the 1905 revolution, the tsarist system seemed doomed to fall before long.

Lenin's Russia, 1917–1924

Revolutions seldom begin among people who have no hope. Like many others, the one that occurred in 1905 was a "revolution of rising expectations." Rapid modernization had showed Russians the possibility of change. It also increased their frustration with a government that seemed both incompetent and oppressive. People seem able to endure a harsh, efficient government or an inept government that is not harsh. But they will rebel against a government that combines harshness and ineptitude if its defenders lose confidence. That is what happened to the tsarist government in March 1917.

World War I proved disastrous for Russia. As German armies drove deep into Russian territory, the government showed itself incapable of mobilizing society for total war. It was so frightened of losing control that it prohibited the patriotic efforts of citizens to organize to help the war effort. In 1915 the tsar took personal command of his armies, asserting his autocratic responsibility. But his bureaucracy could not organize Russia's industrial and transport systems to supply those armies. The home front was no better managed. Shortages of food and fuel led to ceaseless protests. The prestige of the imperial family vanished as it became known that a sinister monk, Grigori Rasputin, had acquired such a psychological hold on the tsar and his wife that he virtually dominated the government.

By the spring of 1917 the only support remaining to the autocracy was its forces of law and order, and they were wavering. When the troops disobeyed orders to fire on food rioters in Petrograd (formerly St. Petersburg), joining the rioters instead, Nicholas II could do nothing but give up his throne. Four years would elapse before it became clear to whom power had passed.

The Provisional Government

As often happens in revolutions, the people who first came into power could not hold on to it. The Provisional Government of Duma liberals that proclaimed itself the tsar's successor immediately enacted reforms. It prepared to convene a democratically chosen Constituent Assembly to give Russia a real constitution. Nevertheless, the government quickly became almost as unpopular with the masses as the tsar had been. It could not bring order out of the chaos into which Russia had fallen. Its leaders insisted on continuing the war to fulfill the commitments the tsar's government had made to Russia's allies, even as millions of peasant soldiers declared *their* war over by simply starting to walk

home from the front. Moreover, an explosion of grassroots democracy challenged the Provisional Government. Workers and soldiers everywhere elected *soviets* (councils) to govern each factory and regiment. These soviets in turn elected a hierarchy of Councils of Workers' and Soldiers' Deputies that amounted to a rival governmental authority.

In this confused situation one of the most formidable figures of modern times saw his opportunity to change the course of history. Vladimir Ilyich Ulyanov, better known by his revolutionary name Lenin, was forty-seven in 1917. Child of a middle-class family, he had been a revolutionary at seventeen, when his older brother was hanged for conspiring to assassinate the tsar. In exile since 1900, he had taken a leading role among Russian Social Democrats abroad.

Lenin combined tactical brilliance and ruthlessness. He was certain that he knew how to make a revolution that would change the world, and he was prepared to use any means and to destroy any opposition. Thus in April 1917 he accepted the offer of the Kaiser's generals to send him from Switzerland through the German battle lines into Russia. Their intent was that Lenin should undermine the Provisional Government's continuation of the war, and he did not disappoint them. As soon as he arrived in Russia, he announced that the revolution should provide "peace, land, and bread." The Provisional Government, having failed to produce these, should be overthrown and replaced by giving "All power to the soviets."

Lenin believed that his faction of the Social Democratic party, the Bolsheviks, with its base in the soviets, could now seize power and make Russia's revolution real. The rival Menshevik faction believed that Russia must industrialize further before it could have the proletarian revolution Marx envisioned. But Lenin saw the possibility of capturing power *now* by giving Russia's masses what they demanded: End the war, even by accepting defeat. Give the peasants

Lenin addresses Red Army troops in Moscow, 1920. *The uniformed officer to the right of the rostrum is Trotsky. After Trotsky became an "unperson" under Stalin's dictatorship, Soviet propagandists painted him out of this famous picture. Keystone Collection/Archive Photos*

the land many were already beginning to seize. Feed the starving cities, imposing whatever controls were necessary.

Second Revolution, 1917

So exactly did Lenin's program correspond to the aspirations of war-weary Russians that Bolshevik representation in the soviets continued to climb through 1917. In vain the Provisional Government tried to fight back. Ineffective, torn by dissension, threatened both by tsarist generals and by Bolsheviks, it could not endure. Hardly a shot was fired in its defense during the

second (November) revolution of 1917. When Bolshevik soldiers occupied government headquarters, it was all over. Lenin had been right, and everyone else wrong. The Bolsheviks, a tiny minority of Russian society, could capture the power the tsar had let fall.

As often happens in revolutions, power had passed from the moderates to a small band of dedicated extremists with a vision of an entirely changed society. Only after four more years of civil war, however, did the Communist party (as the Bolsheviks renamed themselves early in 1918) secure its victory. Lenin swiftly implemented changes that inevitably turned much of his country and the world against him. He made peace on Germany's terms in the Treaty of Brest-Litovsk in March 1918, surrendering Russia's most fertile and industrialized regions and a third of its population. He abolished private ownership of land.

It was more difficult to meet the goal of providing bread from Russia's war-ravaged economy, though he sent the army to seize food from recalcitrant peasants. But Lenin did not hesitate to decree complete economic reorganization. In the name of "War Communism," he nationalized Russia's banks. He confiscated industries and merged them into giant government-controlled trusts. He repudiated Russia's foreign debts. Private property was not the Communists' only target, however. They attacked the patriarchal family by establishing legal equality of women with men, easing conditions for divorce and abortion, and providing for universal compulsory education.

Lenin did not seek popular consent to these changes. He knew that many of them would not have commanded majority support. Indeed, the Bolsheviks won only about 25 percent of the votes cast for the Constituent Assembly, which the Provisional Government had ordained. Lenin's solution to this problem was simply to dissolve the Assembly on the first day it met. So vanished the only democratic parliament Russia had ever known, unmourned by most Russians.

Parliamentary democracy was not part of the Russian tradition. Since the 1905 revolution, soviets *had* been part of the Russian tradition, and in theory the Council of People's Commissars, dominated by Lenin, now governed as the delegates of the All-Russian Congress of Soviets. In reality, the soviets had served their purpose, and Lenin had no intention of letting them continue their disorderly experiments in direct democracy. He quickly brought them under control of the Communist party.

Invasion, Civil War, and New Economic Policy

In concentrating power in the hands of a few, Lenin was following his deepest instincts. He had always believed that a revolution was made by a small elite—a party "like a clenched fist"—that directed the masses. In 1918 to 1921, moreover, his regime was fighting for its life against enemies within and without. Russia's former allies sent in 100,000 troops (British, French, Japanese, and 7,000 Americans) to occupy strategic points in Russian territory. The goal was first to bring Russia back into the war and later, as Winston Churchill put it, "to strangle Bolshevism in its cradle." Most of the troops were withdrawn by 1919, but their presence symbolized the world's refusal to recognize the Communists as Russia's masters. This refusal encouraged some non-Russian nationalities within the former tsarist empire to rebel, and raised the hopes of several high-ranking tsarist officers, who mobilized "White" armies to march against the new "Red" regime. Against these multiple enemies the Red Army, led by the brilliant Leon Trotsky as commissar for war, fought at one time on two dozen fronts.

The White counterrevolution failed. The mutual suspicions of the White leaders made cooperation impossible. Moreover, fighting to restore the old tsarist order, they could not win the support of the majority of Russians. However disillusioned they might become with Communist rule, the people had gained from the revolution.

There was soon much reason for disillusionment. In his fight for survival Lenin had not hesitated at any step. He re-established the secret police, for example, and demanded the shooting of hostages. He ordered the murder of the captive tsar and his family. In protest against the iron rule of his party dictatorship the sailors at the Kronstadt naval base rebelled in March 1921. Though they had once been ardent

Bolsheviks, Lenin crushed their uprising without mercy. Within four years, "heroes" of the revolution had become "traitors."

Many of the world's revolutions have followed a similar path from enthusiasm to disillusionment. In the resulting atmosphere of cynicism, the extremist leadership has often been overthrown by leaders less bent on total change. Lenin's pragmatism told him that he must temporarily slow the pace of revolution to consolidate Communist rule. The revolution's enemies had been beaten, but the economy was a shambles. Thus in 1921 his New Economic Policy (NEP) ended War Communism by re-establishing the free-enterprise system in agriculture and retail trade, though not in heavy industry.

There was no corresponding relaxation of political control from the top, however. In 1922, the Communist state became, ostensibly, a federal state, the Union of Soviet Socialist Republics, a concession to the nationalist demands of the former tsarist empire's many non-Russian minorities. In fact, however, Moscow ruled everywhere through the All-Union Communist party. After 1921, disagreement with the party line meant expulsion from the party. To the distress of some old Bolsheviks, by the time Lenin died in 1924 the party was becoming the privileged, conformist bureaucratic machine that governed the Soviet Union until the 1990s.

At the end of his life Lenin seemed clearly to regret that he had created a party dictatorship rather than a truly egalitarian society. For this reason, his defenders try to dissociate him from the later totalitarian regime of Joseph Stalin. It was Lenin, though, who laid the foundations for the one-party police state that Stalin built. Lenin could hardly have done otherwise. His genius had been to see how his party could capitalize on war-weariness, land hunger, and economic chaos to take power. But only for that brief interlude did the Bolshevik vision of the future coincide with the ideas of most Russians. Once in power, the Bolsheviks had to use force to turn their vision into reality. To do that required re-creating the kind of authoritarian rule the revolution had just overthrown. The only means to the Communist end were means that mocked that end—a paradox that partly explains why communism eventually failed.

Stalin's Soviet Union, 1924–1939

The realities of the Soviet Union (USSR) were never anticipated by Marxist theory. Communism had won its first great victory not by a worldwide workers' revolution but by imposing a party dictatorship on a largely peasant country. There was no clear Marxist prescription for what to do next. After Lenin died, leaving no clear successor, the question of the USSR's future direction divided the Communist party leadership.

In this debate, which became a power struggle, the advantage lay with the man who dominated the bureaucratic machine. This was General Secretary of the Communist party Joseph Stalin (1879–1953). Though a Bolshevik since his youth, Stalin came from a background very different from that of most of the men who surrounded Lenin. Son of a cobbler and grandson of serfs, Stalin had emerged from among the "dark people." Like them, he had little to say. When he did speak, it was often in the peasant's earthy proverbial language. He had never lived in the West and had none of the old Bolsheviks' fluency in Marxist theory. By 1927, however, Stalin's ruthless ambition allowed him to gain control of the Communist party and Soviet state. The party congress of that year forbade any deviation from the party line as Stalin defined it. This final blow to party discussion drove many idealistic old Bolsheviks into retirement or exile. Some of them concluded that the Russian Revolution, like earlier revolutions, had convulsed an entire society only to end up in the dictatorship of a tyrant.

Soviet "crash industrialization." *Under the gaze of a giant portrait of Stalin, the Molotov plant in Gorky turned out two hundred cars daily in the 1930s.* Sovfoto/Eastfoto

Socialism in One Country

Because the world had not yet followed Russia into revolution, Stalin was convinced, the task of Marxists was to strengthen "socialism in one country." This could be done only by making the Soviet Union a mighty industrial power. As he declared in 1931, "We are fifty or one hundred years behind the advanced countries. We must make good this lag in ten years. Either we will accomplish this or we will be crushed."[2]

The USSR's first Five-Year Plan, launched in 1928, made it clear that Stalin intended to squeeze capital for industrialization out of agriculture, just as the last tsars had done. To make agriculture more productive, Stalin believed, required smashing the rural society that had developed under the NEP. Wealthy peasants (*kulaks*) were to be "liquidated" and the millions of family farms abolished. Surviving rural Russians were to be massed on collective farms a thousand times bigger than the typical peasant holding, better suited for efficient mechanized agriculture. The immediate results of this agricultural revolution were catastrophic. Peasant resistance to collectivization reduced agricultural productivity to nothing, and Russia endured mass starvation during 1931-1933, only the first of the Stalinist horrors of the 1930s.

Meanwhile the industrial sector grew enormously—by a factor of three during the 1930s, according to one evaluation. Production rose at an annual rate of 14 percent. The Soviet Union rose from fifteenth to third rank worldwide in production of electricity, fulfilling Lenin's definition of communism as "socialism plus electricity."

The contrast between this frenzied Soviet development and the stagnation of the Western economies during the Depression was striking. Soviet propaganda attributed the nation's accomplishments not only to Stalin's genius but to the heroism of Soviet workers like the miner Stakhanov, who supposedly exceeded his production quota by 1,400 percent in 1935. Some Western visitors came away marveling at such achievements. But shrewder observers could guess at some of the human costs.

Soviet workers, who had no right to strike, were not spurred to produce by any hope that their low earnings would purchase consumer goods. Hardly any were available. Soviet workers were goaded to productivity by all the managerial tricks of early industrial capitalism, including piecework rather than hourly pay. They could not change jobs. Any protest meant arrest and deportation to one of the large projects being built with slave labor. Under Stalin, some 12 million Russians were prisoners on such sites, or in Siberian camps—*gulags*—or in jails—far more than the tsars had ever incarcerated.

Assessing the Soviet Experience Under Lenin and Stalin

On the eve of World War II, the Soviet Union projected two sharply contrasting images to the world. The image of progress emphasized the great dams, factories, even whole new industrial cities sprouting across the land. But there was also the image of terror, particularly during the great purge of 1936–1938, when Stalin got rid of most of the surviving old Bolsheviks. Courtroom cameras filmed them cringingly confessing to improbable crimes against the state before disappearing forever.

Defenders of Stalin's historic role explain that these contrasting images are inseparable. The factories, they maintain, could not have been created so quickly without the threat of the prison camps. By forcing the discipline of modernity on Russian society, Stalin transformed a largely peasant nation into an industrial superpower in just two decades. Because we cannot rerun history to see the results of alternative approaches, we cannot know whether the Soviet Union could have industrialized quickly without Stalin's inhumanity.

For world history, the important consideration is the import of what Lenin and Stalin did. They showed that it was possible to break away from the European-dominated world system. The Soviets did so both politically, by rejecting Western liberal democracy, and economically, by undertaking their own industrial development. Western capitalist societies had industrialized over several generations, as their citizens slowly adjusted their lives to the rhythms of the machine age. The Soviet Union seemed to provide a model for accelerating this process and overcoming economic dependency rapidly. In the Bolshevik model, modernization was imposed from above by force. But for the vast majority of the world's people, who had never known Western-style liberal democracy, authoritarian modernization was not necessarily unattractive. Comparing the results of the Russian Revolution with those of less radical revolutions and independence movements elsewhere, the aspiring revolutionary might well find the Bolshevik model more attractive.

Contrasts in Revolution and Mass Mobilization

The Bolshevik Revolution of 1917 helped open the twentieth century and became that century's most influential revolution. Seventy-odd years later, the failure of Soviet Communism helped close that century in 1989–1991. This sounds paradoxical; yet it is not hard to explain.

As noted in the introduction to this chapter, the Bolshevik Revolution combined a globalist ideology with an effective model of organization, leadership, and mass mobilization—a combination that was bound to inspire imitation elsewhere. Yet the Soviet example would have had to be followed much more widely than it was to escape eventual failure. Some of the reasons for this are internal to the Soviet system; others take the form of major forces at work in world history: nationalism, capitalism, and imperialism. Most countries that did not follow the Soviet example—and some that did—were chiefly motivated by nationalism. Nationalisms all share resemblances; yet, each asserts the uniqueness of a particular people. Nationalisms assert identity and difference, in contrast to Marx's globalism. In colonial or semicolonial countries, moreover, the struggle against imperialism increased the need to mobilize all the people, irrespective of class origin, against the foreign threat. The Bolshevik Revolution of 1917, like the French Revolution of 1789, created sharp breaks in history by not only toppling an old regime but also liquidating the social class that had supported it: as the French say, to make an omelette you have to break eggs. In contrast, colonial and semicolonial societies, while seldom able to escape violence among their own people entirely, saw a greater need to mobilize all their national forces in a united front against the foreigner in what was often a national liberation struggle more than a revolution. Nationalist appeals served quite well to hold together such a common front, while Marxist-style class conflict could only divide it. In countries like China and Vietnam, where anti-colonial nationalisms did assume Communist forms, they had a nationalistic coloration that Marx would not have liked. Elsewhere, the "social-isms" of the developing world—Arab socialism, Afro-socialism—tended to be ideologies for national development that incorporated only some Marxist themes, especially the critique of capitalism and imperialism. The prevalence of Euro-American imperialism as an issue in the world's revolutions and liberation struggles points finally to the fact that it was capitalism, not communism, that did most to shape the world system of the twentieth century. Even the twentieth century's most dramatic revolution and the Soviet state that emerged from it never came close to changing that fact (see Chapter 11).

In sum, the Bolshevik Revolution provided the twentieth century's most influential model of revolution but did not dominate the century's history overall. The remainder of this chapter will amplify these points by comparing two countries that did not borrow from Soviet example, Mexico and India, with one that did, China.

The Mexican Revolution

The Mexican revolutionaries of 1910 faced a daunting task. Like Latin America in general, Mexico after a century of independence was still an agrarian country with a poorly integrated society. Different regions and social classes had conflicting interests. Three-fourths of Mexicans tilled the land, but only 2 percent of them owned the land they tilled, and the proportion of owners was declining. Most rural Mexicans were illiterate; perhaps a third of them were native Americans who spoke no Spanish. Landlessness, mining, and early industrialization had created a working class, small but badly exploited and open to radical ideas. Middling landowners (*rancheros*), business and professional interests in the towns, and intellectuals provided elements of a middle class. Though disunited, they played key roles in running the economy, articulating ideas, and providing revolutionary leadership. At the top stood the wealthy few, often owners of plantations (*haciendas*), with vested interests in export-oriented agriculture and mining.

In 1910, Mexico had been ruled for three decades by Porfirio Díaz (1830–1915) and his wealthy clique. Starting out as one local boss among many, Díaz had risen with backing from U.S. interests. Mexico developed spectacularly under him in some ways. Railroad mileage increased more than fortyfold, and national income doubled in the decade before the international financial crisis of 1907.

Díaz, however, became the kind of conservative ruler who undermines himself by encouraging change without distributing its benefits equitably. As he and his cronies aged in office, young Mexicans saw their ambitions frustrated. As export-oriented estate agriculture spread, some native American communities lost all their land except what was under their houses. Mexico's ability to feed itself declined, while enterprises set up to export raw materials did not provide enough jobs to employ the landless. Most hated was the regime's subservience to U.S. interests. By 1900, half of all U.S. foreign investment was in Mexico. Its railroads had been laid out to move goods to the ports or to the U.S. border, not to bring Mexicans closer together. By 1910, 130 of Mexico's 170 largest enterprises were foreign controlled. U.S. investors had bought over 100 million acres, and

Pancho Villa's army attacks. *Denounced by Americans as a "bandit," Villa was seen by many Mexicans as a revolutionary leader challenging American power in northern Mexico.* © Bettmann/CORBIS

fifteen thousand American settlers had begun expelling Mexicans found living on "their" land. Díaz once sighed, "Poor Mexico! So far from God, so near the United States!" Other Mexicans responded more militantly: "Mexico for the Mexicans!"

Clear-cut nationalist grievances eventually united the Mexicans against Díaz and unleashed a decade of violence that no leader or movement controlled. Before the storm ended, Mexico experienced mass mobilization against Díaz, class conflict among the revolutionary forces, and U.S. intervention. Leading the charge against Díaz in 1910 were wealthy landowners whose interests had been hurt by his policies. Moderate constitutionalists, they soon found

themselves surrounded by forces of other kinds. Central authority broke down; regional and class interests came to the fore; and Mexico lapsed into violence and anarchy, as leaders from different regions mobilized to seize the capital and the presidency.

The contrasts among its revolutionary leaders and movements show how far Mexico was from having any leader of Lenin's stature or any organized revolutionary movement. Francisco Madero, who raised the call to arms against Díaz, was a wealthy northerner, a nineteenth-century liberal who saw the cure to Mexico's ills in political democracy. Becoming president in 1911, he was soon murdered (1913). Popular imagination was more gripped by leaders like

Francisco "Pancho" Villa from the northern state of Chihuahua, a leader of peasants and workers from a region of landlessness and foreign-owned export businesses. Emiliano Zapata came from Morelos, just south of Mexico City, where the spread of export-oriented estate agriculture had destroyed the native American communities within living memory. (Zapata spoke the native American language Nahuatl as well as Spanish.) His peasant movement aimed to restore a balance by giving a third of the haciendas to the landless peasants, with compensation to the owners. This was scarcely a radical demand, compared to the Bolsheviks' abolition of private property, although it did reflect native American demands for community and access to the land. Still, Zapata frightened the constitutionalists, who had him killed in 1919. The man whose presidency (1920–1924) opened the postrevolutionary period, Álvaro Obregón, was different. He ran on a platform mentioning both agrarian reform and security for foreign investment. From the northwest, he had kept ties to U.S. interests during the revolution, and they saw his election as the signal to accept the new Mexico.

With such diverse goals and leaders, what did the revolution accomplish for Mexico? There were winners and losers, and Mexico did change appreciably. Peasants and industrial workers lost, but so did big landowners and capitalists. Forced to choose between radicals and moderates, foreign interests also made concessions. The middle class won from the revolution a government open to their interests and ambitions. The 1917 constitution reflected their liberal, nationalist, inclusive outlook. It also gave the defeated some recognition. It granted workers the eight-hour work day, overtime pay, and restrictions on child labor. It promised rural Mexicans agrarian reform and the breakup of large estates. Perhaps most important of all, Article 27 of the constitution provided that the soil and subsoil rights belonged to the nation, as did the right to define property rights. Foreign

interests had to accept this, although Obregón later exempted mines and oil wells owned by foreigners before 1917 from nationalization. With a tradition of rebellion unparalleled in Latin America, Mexico's peasants and native American communities could see in Article 27 a recognition of their historic struggles for land. Some of them, consequently, have never used the term *revolution* for the events of 1910–1920 but have saved that name for the land redistributions that did not occur on significant scale until 1936 (see Chapter 7). Such were the bases of the postrevolutionary political order that survived in Mexico for the rest of the twentieth century.

Mexico's was the first Third-World uprising against U.S. interference. It improved Mexican social conditions without totally restructuring them. It renegotiated Mexico's dependence on the United States without severing it. Unlike the Bolsheviks, the Mexicans did not offer the world a model to follow. In their own ways, however, many other developing countries lived through analogous national struggles against imperialism. Had China's national struggle been won by the Nationalists (see below) rather than the Communists, the outcome would have resembled the Mexican experience more closely than the Bolshevik model.

An Indian Alternative

Indians had challenged British rule from its inception in many ways, including violent rebellions great and small. A national political organization, the Indian National Congress, had formed in 1885 as a confederation of local or regional political figures. Against this background, Mohandas K. Gandhi (1869–1948) emerged to play a critical—though never uncontested—role in achieving Indian independence. Although nonrevolutionary, his ideas and methods offered a significant alternative model for national mobilization against imperialism.

Gandhi was the son of an official who worked for the Hindu ruler of one of the "native states" that the British allowed to survive under their rule. Earlier the family had been grocers. The name Gandhi was the term for the subcaste of grocers in the larger Banya subcaste of shopkeepers, which belonged in turn to the Vaisya caste of traders and farmers. This was one of the four original castes, with many later subcastes, into which tradition divided all Hindus, except the casteless Untouchables, at birth. Gandhi's early life reflected the force of tradition in these and other details, including the extended family household into which he was born and his marriage, arranged by his parents when he was about twelve.

To assure his future, however, Gandhi's family decided he must complete his education in England, leaving his wife and newborn son behind. His mother, a strict vegetarian Hindu, made him vow not to touch wine, women, or meat while away. Because he had crossed the "black waters," the elders of his subcaste pronounced him an outcaste.

Gandhi arrived in England in 1888, aged nineteen. Over the next three years, he completed legal studies and qualified as a barrister (lawyer); he also discovered a world of new ideas. At first, he tried to blend in, paying much attention to dress and taking dancing lessons. Then, realizing that he could never become English, he sought out people with whom he had something in common: vegetarians and enthusiasts of different religions. He read widely in religious texts, ranging from Christ's Sermon on the Mount to the great Hindu scripture the Bhagavad Gita or "Celestial Song," which he read first in English. In both, albeit in different terms, God summons human beings to a life of selfless dedication to others. This, not law, became Gandhi's lasting lesson.

Returning to India at twenty-one, Gandhi had trouble readjusting to his uneducated wife, Kasturbai, and lacked the self-confidence to suc-

ceed in legal practice. Soon frustrated, he leapt at a chance to go to South Africa to represent an Indian merchant in a case there. He had gone through religious rites to be received back into his caste, but now he set out across the "black waters" again. Spending most of the time from 1893 to 1914 in South Africa, he developed the methods that he later applied in India.

One of his first experiences in South Africa was to be thrown off a train, even though he had the proper ticket, because a European objected to his presence in a first-class compartment. Having thus discovered the discrimination to which all non-Europeans were subject, he began to mobilize the Indian community against the discriminatory laws. Having planned to stay only a year, he remained in South Africa to continue this work.

Over the next twenty years, he worked out a distinctive way of life and political action. He read widely, studying the scriptures of Hinduism and Islam, India's two most widespread religions; the works of Henry David Thoreau, the U.S. apostle of civil disobedience; and the later writings of the Russian novelist and pacifist Leo Tolstoy. Gandhi made his personal life increasingly ascetic. He formulated his principles as *brahmacharya*, self-restraint (including chastity within marriage); *satyagraha*, truth-force, a concept he developed to refer to the moral force of passive resistance; and *swaraj*, self-rule. To Gandhi, that meant not just political independence but a moral regeneration that would unite Indians of all religions and castes and lead to economic self-sufficiency. His ability to express partly new concepts in Hindu categories enhanced Gandhi's appeal, as did his selfless way of life. A man who cleaned latrines as a spiritual discipline and led ambulance units in hazardous service during the Boer War, Gandhi could convince people that his motives were unselfish.

No solitary ascetic, he organized communal settlements that became models for the *ashrams* (religious retreats) he later created in India. Promoting a life of egalitarian self-reliance, he became a mass mobilizer, championing women's and Untouchables' interests. Self-reliance and latrine cleaning were part of his attempts to get Indians to forget differences of religion and caste, which condemned Untouchables to do jobs that Hindus classed as unclean. Gandhi also became a political leader and mobilizer. Staging his first great passive-resistance campaigns in South Africa against laws that required Asians to carry special registration certificates and that made only Christian marriages valid, he won some concessions from the government.

Returning to India in 1915, Gandhi soon took up the cause of Indian independence, discussed more fully in Chapter 9. In India, Gandhi elaborated his idea of self-reliance into a Constructive Program. It sought to revitalize village India by getting villagers to breed cattle, improve hygiene, take up useful crafts such as beekeeping or pottery, spin and weave their own cloth, form cooperatives and village assemblies, overturn hereditary obstacles to learning, learn Hindi so that India could have one national language, and eliminate discrimination against Untouchables, whom Gandhi called *harijans* or children of God. He also advocated women's equality, prompting the Indian National Congress party to adopt a bill of rights (1931) calling for equality without regard to religion, caste, or sex. Politically, he worked through the Congress Party to organize passive-resistance campaigns. Identifying with the poor by traveling among them and living the life of a Hindu holy man, he gained such authority that he could command the attention of a crowd with a gesture or halt intercommunal violence by fasting. His followers hailed him as a *mahatma* ("great soul"), even as a manifestation of divinity.

Neither a revolutionary nor a politician himself, compared to those who are he shows an unusual combination of strengths and weaknesses. He and his followers used nonviolence as a powerful instrument for change. They were effective organizers, drawing on familiar forms of activism at both elite and mass levels to create an unprecedented India-wide movement. Yet his goals for social and political change were limited. For Hindu society, they did not go beyond ending discrimination against Untouchables and women. Such appeals to reason could not prevail against caste, which is sanctioned in Hindu sacred texts. Although he sought unity among members of India's religions, he never seemed to see how his overtly Hindu ideas and style irritated some non-Hindus. His Constructive Program anticipated later rural development concepts, and he correctly saw that industrial labor was dehumanizing. However, his idea of escaping economic dependence on Britain by reviving hand spinning and weaving was backward looking.

Gandhi's strength lay in bridging the gap between Indian and foreign ideas, which he expressed through symbols familiar to the masses, and in organization. Many younger nationalists, including Jawaharlal Nehru, who became independent India's first prime minister, found Gandhi mystifying. They valued Gandhi for his ability to mobilize the masses, who could not yet understand the elites' more "advanced" reformist-socialist ideas, which would have to prevail after independence if India was to develop. Gandhi was sincerely committed to the people; many elite nationalists were authoritarian mobilizers. For them, Gandhi was only an instrument.

Fifty years after his death, his few remaining disciples thought India's rulers had more in common with the British than with Gandhi. Yet his ideas, far from forgotten, influenced people all over the world. The fact that India still functioned as the world's largest democracy, with honest and efficiently run elections and high

Mao Tse-tung and his wife in 1936. *The first Chairman of the Chinese Communist Party married a movie actor from Shanghai, Lin Ping. Fox Photo Collection/Archive Photos*

the form known as Marxism-Leninism-Mao Zedong thought.

After Lenin, the next person to have as profound an impact as a Communist revolutionary was Mao Zedong (Mao Tse-tung, 1893–1976).* For much of Mao's life, however, this importance was far from obvious. In 1911, a revolution toppled the entire combination of imperial institutions and Confucian ideology that had dominated China for two millennia. The causes of this revolution were European imperialism, which had undermined China's imperial government without establishing direct foreign rule (except in some enclaves), and the nationalism that developed among Chinese in reaction. The crisis that ensued was so vast and profound that not one, but two movements were launched to create a new order in China. Not before 1949 did it become clear whether the winner would be the moderate, inclusive mobilization of the Nationalists under Chiang Kai-shek or the radical, peasant-based movement of the Communists under Mao. The essential challenge facing China's leaders was to restore order and unity, reassert China's independence, and meet the challenges of mass politics and economic development in a fast-changing world.

Unlike many Chinese leaders, even Communists, Mao came from a peasant family. His authoritarian father, with whom he often clashed, was a "rich" peasant, owning about three acres, producing five or six tons of rice a year, and trading in grain. This relative affluence

voter turnout, suggested that Gandhian mobilization had a profound impact and that India's elite intellectuals, lacking Gandhi's populism, may have judged the political potential of poor Indians too negatively.

China

In adapting Marxism to colonial or semicolonial societies, China played the most important role. China under Mao showed that communism could succeed in a country even less industrialized than Russia had been. This success required rivaling the Bolsheviks in organization and mobilization while changing their ideology into

*Following current usage, we use the Pinyin, rather than the Wade-Giles, system for the rendering of Chinese names and terms. At the first appearance of each name or term, however, the Wade-Giles version is shown in parentheses following the Pinyin. The only exceptions are cases where the two forms are identical or cases in which the identity of individuals who are well known by the Wade-Giles spelling would be obscured by the Pinyin form. Two such individuals mentioned in this book are Sun Yat-sen and Chiang Kai-shek; the Pinyin forms of their names are Sun Yixuan and Jiang Jieshi.

enabled Mao to go to school, where he began by memorizing Confucian classics. But education was changing in China, along with everything else. By his mid-twenties, Mao had moved in and out of various schools and studied for a time on his own. He gained exposure to both traditional Confucian learning and popular literature, from some of whose Robin Hood-like heroes he learned military strategies that he later used. He read Western literature in translation and wrote for newspapers. Many Chinese were taking a new interest in the army as a way to combat imperialism, and Mao too was briefly a soldier.

When other future Communist leaders, like Zhou Enlai (Chou Enlai, 1898–1976, later premier of the People's Republic), went to France to study during World War I, Mao stayed behind, perhaps because he was not good at languages. Mao remained close to China's common people and dealt with foreign ideas only in Chinese. These factors may explain why it was he who naturalized Marxism into the Chinese setting.

Ultimately, Marxism was the intellectual influence that affected Mao most. In 1918, when the Bolshevik Revolution had attracted attention in China, Mao joined a Marxist study group at Beijing (Peking) University. Its members did not understand Marxist theory and had not yet committed themselves to it. Following the war of 1914–1918 among the imperialist powers, however, they sensed that the Bolshevik model offered a way to reorganize China and improve its place in the world.

On May 4, 1919, a massive student demonstration broke out in Beijing to protest Japanese encroachment on China and the decision of the Paris Peace Conference to support Japan's claims. The demonstration gave rise to an ongoing May Fourth Movement, which promoted new ideas. In his native Hunan province, Mao took an active role and helped organize the Chinese Communist Party (CCP) in 1921.

Mao and his colleagues were still unsure how to launch revolution in China. It hardly had the urban working class that Marx assumed. Mao's work in the countryside convinced him of the peasants' revolutionary potential. But party leaders of the 1920s thought peasants only wanted land and would drop out of the revolution once they got it.

The CCP sought help from the Soviet Union through the Communist International or Comintern, founded in 1919 as a "general headquarters" for world revolution. Unfortunately, the Soviets did not understand China. Comintern advice varied from bad to disastrous, especially after Stalin shifted priorities to "socialism in one country." Because Marx had held that the overthrow of feudalism (in China, the imperial system) should lead to a period of bourgeois capitalism before the proletarian revolution, the Soviets called on the CCP to ally with the larger Nationalist party, the Guomindang (GMD, Kuomintang), which despite its attempts to include everyone was mainly supported by middle class and landlord interests.

GMD leader Sun Yat-sen (1866–1925) agreed that Communists could join the GMD and work within it as individuals, and Mao and other Communists did join. GMD-CCP collaboration continued until Sun's successor, Chiang Kai-shek, turned violently against the CCP in 1927, killing thousands. Still, Stalin continued for months to advocate GMD-CCP cooperation. The influence of Moscow-trained leaders in the CCP remained a problem into the early 1930s.

Surviving the GMD terror, Mao again went south. He joined other Communists to form the Jiangxi (Kiangsi) soviet, of which he became chairman, in the mountains on the border between Jiangxi and Hunan provinces. Isolation from the CCP Central Committee and Comintern representatives in Shanghai helped Mao develop his own ideas of organization and tactics, emphasizing rural base areas, agrarian revolution, and development of the Red Army.

In 1930, Chiang Kai-shek launched campaigns against the Jiangxi soviet, eventually forcing the Communists to strike out on the

Long March (see Map 9.3). During this six-thousand-mile trek from Jiangxi to a new base in the northwest, Mao emerged as the CCP leader. Only a fraction of the hundred thousand people who set out on the Long March survived. At Yan'an (Yenan), their base from 1935 to 1947, Mao finally came to grips with Marxist theory, evaluating it in terms of Chinese experience.

So began the modification of Marxism-Leninism that later became known as Mao Zedong thought, the main themes of which underscore its potential for conflict with Soviet ideology. One theme was Mao's emphasis on will. Mao had become a Marxist out of excitement over the 1917 revolution, without knowing Marx's ideas about the stages of history. For Mao, revolution emerged from will and activism, not from predetermined levels of economic development. From this idea followed his belief in thought reform as a way to bring people into conformity with the party line. This implied an idea of class struggle that made class more a matter of how one thought than of how one earned a living. If Mao's ideas made a muddle of Marx's stages of revolution, so be it: China would have permanent revolution.

A second Maoist theme was nationalism—anathema to Marx but essential in Chinese thinking. Mao's nationalism showed in his closeness to China's traditional culture and his hostility to the Comintern and Soviet Union—early reasons for the Sino-Soviet split of the late 1950s. Mao saw the real enemy of the revolution as imperialism, identified class struggle with national struggle, and would allow willing Chinese of any class origin to join the revolution.

Perhaps the most important Maoist theme reflected his origins: *populism,* or championship of the common people. Mao's radicalism showed most clearly in his romantic faith in the peasants' revolutionary potential. Since this belief conflicted with Marxist theory, Mao became distrustful of theorists and experts in general. Differing also from Lenin's idea that the vanguard party could impose revolutionary consciousness on the workers, Mao came to believe in a "mass line," a revolutionary consciousness among the peasant masses, which the party must understand before it could guide them. This idea shaped a commitment to mass mobilization that enabled the CCP, unlike the GMD, to succeed among the peasants, who might not have responded to communism otherwise.

Like most Chinese of the time, Mao also saw that overcoming imperialism required an effective military. Such a force must be able to survive among the people, as it had during the Long March, without alienating them. That meant treating peasants like human beings, paying for supplies, and a host of other things not done in the past.

Mao's ideas enabled the CCP to survive through World War II, during which it again cooperated with the GMD against the Japanese. His ideas enabled the CCP to win support while the GMD crumbled, setting the stage for the civil war (1946–1949) that gave the Communists control of the country. Chapter 17 shows how Mao's thought left its mark on the People's Republic of China. After 1991, China remained with Vietnam, North Korea, and Cuba as the last officially Communist states. During the preceding four decades, however, elements of communist or at least socialist thought had been adopted throughout much of the developing world because of their value, which Chinese like Mao had sensed as far back as 1918, in challenging Western imperialism.

Conclusion: Revolutions Compared

Revolutions vary widely in scope. Some affect only domestic politics. Some also restructure society and economy. Others transform culture as well. Internationally, revolutions may or may not transform a society's place in the global configuration.

The examples in this chapter suggest that for a country with a domestic history of exploitative social and economic relationships, the only real revolution is a social one that not only changes politics but also "cracks eggs" (or heads) by redistributing wealth and power. The Bolsheviks did this in Russia; so did the Maoists in China. In colonial or semicolonial countries, common-front nationalist movements like Mexico's elite revolutionaries, China's Nationalists, or India's Congress Party, could not afford anything so radical. To succeed, any far-reaching revolution also needs a coherent ideology—a program for action such as Marxism-Leninism gave Russia, or Mao's adaptation of it gave China. The comparisons discussed above also show that Lenin was right about the importance of effective leadership and a well-organized movement or party.

For a country in a subordinate position in the global pattern of power relationships, moreover, a revolution does not triumph until it transforms those external relationships. Mexico made limited gains in this respect. The Bolsheviks succeeded by breaking links of debt and investment that had made the tsarist regime, though supposedly a great power, dependent on Western Europe. Both the GMD and the CCP advanced China's struggle against imperialism.

The Soviet experience with revolution was so influential in the twentieth century that it was difficult to discuss the requirements of successful revolution without referring to it. Gandhi's significance lies in showing another way. Although his movement did not produce revolution, it included the aspiration to socioeconomic and cultural change, the ideology to chart a course for change, the charismatic leader, strong organization, mass mobilization, and the intent to transform India's place in global power relationships. The main limiting factors were that he sought to reform Indian society but could not eliminate the inequality of the caste system and that his method perhaps also assumed a certain type of adversary, accessible to moral arguments. The method worked against the British and in some other settings, like the U.S. civil rights movement. Could it have worked against someone like Hitler or Stalin?

Notes

1. Quotations from Arthur Koestler, *Darkness at Noon,* Bantam Books edition, pp. 182-183.
2. Quoted in Theodore H. Von Laue, *Why Lenin? Why Stalin? A Reappraisal of the Russian Revolution, 1900-1930* (Philadelphia: Lippincott, 1964), p. 212.

Suggestions for Further Reading

Carr, E. H. *The Meaning of the Russian Revolution* (1979).

Chatterjee, Partha. *Nationalist Thought in the Colonial World: A Derivative Discourse* (1986).

Crowley, James B., ed. *Modern East Asia: Essays in Interpretation* (1970).

Green, Martin. *The Origins of Nonviolence: Tolstoy and Gandhi in Their Historical Settings* (1986).

Guha, Ranajit. *Elementary Aspects of Peasant Insurgency in Colonial India* (1983).

Hart, John Mason. *Revolutionary Mexico: The Coming and Process of the Mexican Revolution* (1987).

Knight, Alan. *The Mexican Revolution.* 2 vols. (1986).

Malia, Martin E. *The Soviet Tragedy: A History of Socialism in Russia, 1917-1991* (1994).

Mehta, Ved. *Mahatma Gandhi and His Apostles* (1976).

Schram, Stuart. *Mao Tse-Tung* (1966).

——. *The Thought of Mao Tse-Tung* (1989).

Snow, Edgar. *Red Star over China.* Rev. ed. (1968).

Von Laue, Theodore H. *Why Gorbachev? The Rise and Fall of the Soviet System* (1993).

CHAPTER 5

Global Economic Crisis and the Restructuring of the Social and Political Order

TO POOR FARMERS AROUND THE WORLD, THE GREAT DEPRESSION OF THE 1930S, the subject of this chapter, seemed as inexplicable as the natural disasters like drought that periodically impoverished them. Why should a price collapse in distant Wall Street force down prices until the farmers went broke? The fate of farmers in the part of the southwestern United States that came in these years to be called the Dust Bowl was even worse, for their economic disaster was compounded by a real natural disaster: dust storms. From 1934 to 1940, such storms darkened the American skies from the Rockies to the East Coast and made life in places like the Oklahoma Panhandle literally unsustainable.

Ironically, these storms could be described as nature's vengeance for human imprudence in plowing the grazing lands of the Great Plains, uprooting the prairie grasses that had held the soil in place. The storms completed the ruin of the region's small farmers, already devastated by the Depression's falling prices. As farmers lost crop after crop to the dusty winds and could no longer pay off their loans, the banks foreclosed their mortgages, leaving the farmers no choice but to uproot themselves and flee with their few remaining possessions in search of a better life, perhaps in California.

The sufferings of these "Okie" fugitives from the Depression Dust Bowl are unforgettably described in John Steinbeck's great novel *The Grapes of*

Wrath (1939). Its very first pages give a quiet description of what a day in the Dust Bowl could be like:

> The air and the sky darkened and through them the sun shone redly, and there was a raw sting in the air. During a night the wind raced faster over the land, dug cunningly among the rootlets of the corn, and the corn fought the wind with its weakened leaves until the roots were freed by the prying wind and then each stalk settled wearily sideways toward the earth and pointed the direction of the wind.
>
> The dawn came, but no day. In the gray sky a red sun appeared, a dim red circle that gave a little light, like dusk; and as that day advanced, the dusk slipped back toward darkness, and the wind cried and whimpered over the fallen corn.
>
> Men and women huddled in their houses, and they tied handkerchiefs over their noses when they went out, and wore goggles to protect their eyes.
>
> When the night came again it was black night, for the stars could not pierce the dust to get down. . . . In the morning the dust hung like fog, and the sun was as red as ripe new blood. All day the dust sifted down from the sky, and the next day it sifted down. An even blanket covered the earth. It settled on the corn, piled up on the tops of the fence posts, piled up on the wires; it settled on roofs, blanketed the weeds and trees. . . . Men stood by their fences and looked at the ruined corn, drying fast now, only a little green showing through the film of dust. The men were silent and they did not move often. And the women came out of their houses to stand beside their men—to feel whether this time the men would break. . . .[1]

The Deceptive "Normalcy" of the 1920s

The triumph of communism in Russia challenged the European-dominated global pattern of 1914 in three ways. It offered an alternative to the liberal capitalist model for the organization of an economy, society, and government. It severed the links that had subordinated Russia economically to Western Europe. It encouraged revolutionaries everywhere who dreamed of restructuring their own societies and freeing them from foreign domination.

This challenge to the pre-1914 order produced panic that the communist "disease" might spread. Politicians blamed communists for the 1919 wave of strikes in which workers protested their loss of purchasing power under wartime wage controls. In the United States, the postwar "Red Scare" led to the so-called Palmer raids, in which Wilson's attorney general rounded up and deported foreigners without regard to their rights. In France, the right-wing parties won a landslide victory in the elections of 1919 partly by playing on voters' fear of "the man with a knife between his teeth"—a hairy and terrifying Communist depicted on conservative election posters.

By the mid-1920s, however, it seemed clear that the Russian Revolution was not going to spread. Conservative forces overturned the communist regime established in Hungary after the Hapsburg collapse. The new German republic crushed communist attempts to seize power in 1919 and 1923. Arguing that communist subversion was still a threat probably helped British Conservatives defeat the first Labour cabinet in 1924. But by then Europeans and Americans were beginning to see communism as a Russian abnormality.

People could more easily believe that the Russian Revolution had not changed the course of world history because some semblance of prewar politics and economies seemed re-established by the late 1920s. In the great democracies, politicians whose very ordinariness reassured people that nothing had changed replaced dynamic wartime leaders like Wilson and Clemenceau. Humorist Will Rogers said of Calvin Coolidge, who became the U.S. president after Harding's death in 1923, that "Silent Cal" did exactly what Americans wanted: nothing. His administration was reminiscent of the nineteenth century, when U.S. presidents had been relatively inconspicuous. In Britain and France, too, conservative prime ministers—Stanley Baldwin and Raymond Poincaré—held power for much of the 1920s. They also were committed to the pre-1914 view that the government's role in a free society should be minimal.

After the mid-1920s, some nations' economies seemed to have regained or exceeded

their prewar levels. By 1929, for example, U.S. industrial production was 75 percent greater than in 1913. British factories in 1929, however, were producing only 10 percent more than they had before the war. The war had seriously weakened the British economy, around which the world economy had pivoted throughout the nineteenth century. Nevertheless, Britain took the controversial step of returning to the gold standard in 1925—that is, the British government again offered to sell gold for an established price in pounds. As a result, the pound became overvalued, making British exports too expensive for many countries to buy. But deeply felt psychological need, rather than economic calculation, motivated the return to the gold standard. By the mid-1920s, people wanted to see World War I as a short and accidental interruption of "normalcy"—President Harding's word—rather than as the beginning of a grim new era of change. So Britain declared that the pound would once again be "as good as gold."

Because people wanted so much to believe that World War I had not fundamentally changed the world, they ignored the ominous structural faults that were the war's legacy to the global economy. Wartime demand had everywhere expanded both agricultural and industrial capacity beyond peacetime needs. By the late 1920s prices were beginning to fall and unsold goods and crops to pile up. The prewar pattern of international finance was replaced by an absurd system of overextended international credits that reflected political pressures rather than economic good sense. For example, in order to pay their huge war debts to the United States, Germany's other former enemies insisted that the Germans pay them reparations. When the Germans insisted they could not afford to pay, American bankers lent them the money, as they also lent other Europeans money to pay their debts. This was all very well as long as the lenders felt sure they would get their money back, but it would prove calamitous when that confidence was lost, dragging the whole developed world into economic ruin.

Thus the prosperity of the late 1920s rested on fragile foundations. Because the economies of the developed world were so interdependent, a catastrophe in any one of them would quickly spread to the rest. When prices on the New York Stock Exchange collapsed in October 1929—the biggest loss stocks have ever experienced—the eventual result was a worldwide Great Depression far worse than any earlier downturn.

In economic terms, a *depression* is a time when curves on all the graphs—prices, wages, employment, investment, international trade—head persistently downward. After 1929 all these variables dropped to, and stayed at, unprecedentedly low levels.

The Great Depression wrecked more than the global economy. By 1932, with one American in four and two Germans in five unable to find jobs, much of the world was living in psychological depression. Economists, business leaders, and politicians admitted they could not find a cure. No experience from the pre-1914 world was relevant to an economic disaster so big and long lasting.

Gravely eroded by World War I, the foundations of the European-dominated global pattern were further undermined by the Depression. The dependent peoples of the world had already seen their European masters locked in a death struggle that left none unscathed. After 1929, Asians, Africans, and Latin Americans saw that the technological dynamism of Western civilization had not averted an economic calamity that engulfed them too. The Depression of the 1930s cruelly drove home to the dependent peoples the extent of their economic subordination and further discredited the Western claim to rule the globe by right of cultural superiority. Though most colonial peoples would win political independence only after the second "European civil war" (World War II), 1929 like 1914 was a fateful date on the way to the post-1945 "end of empire."

In the developed Western nations, despair and rage led people to reject many of the economic and political ideas taken for granted until the crash, and stimulated frantic demands for new ideas that could put people to work again. Now interest in the communist alternative truly began to develop. When European and American coal mines were closed for lack of sales while unemployed people froze to death for lack of coal, the Soviet idea of a government-planned and -managed economy suddenly seemed to make more sense.

In Western Europe, political parties had emerged since 1917 that accepted the need for socialism but argued that it was not necessary to destroy parliamentary democracy in order to institute government ownership and management of the economy. In Britain and France, the Great Depression would provide a first test of this idea of achieving socialism through democracy.

Still found today in Europe and much of the rest of the world, democratic socialism was never a strong movement in the United States. Its most successful presidential candidate, Eugene Debs, won no more than 6 percent of the vote in 1912. Yet many critics of President Franklin D. Roosevelt, elected in 1932, attacked his New Deal programs as "socialistic." Though incorrect, the label reflected the deep controversy the New Deal provoked among Americans. All agreed that it profoundly changed the bases of American life—but was it for better or for worse?

What role the federal government should play in controlling the U.S. economy is still a matter of hot controversy. Americans tend to debate that issue without placing it in historical context or drawing comparisons with the experiences of other nations. But, as we shall see, in the light of world history the New Deal is best understood as the U.S. answer to a worldwide problem revealed after the Wall Street crash.

From Wall Street Crash to World Depression

In the summer of 1929, American ingenuity seemed to have produced an economy invulnerable to the ups and downs of economic history. The new president, Herbert Hoover, an engineer and self-made millionaire, proclaimed, "We in America today are nearer to the final triumph over poverty than ever before in the history of any land . . . we shall soon with the help of God be in sight of the day when poverty will be banished from this nation."[2] Such confidence seemed justified when all but 3 percent of the work force had jobs and manufacturing output had risen by 50 percent in a decade.

At the New York Stock Exchange on Wall Street, the mood was euphoric—and why not? Stock prices were climbing with unprecedented speed, as much in June and July alone as in all of 1928. After Labor Day the rise slowed, but few of the million or so Americans speculating in stocks were disturbed. They trusted authorities like the president of the National City Bank, who declared, "Nothing can arrest the upward movement of the United States."

In October, however, the bottom fell out. October 29 was the worst day in the history of the exchange. As panic-stricken investors tried to sell, an unheard-of 16.5 million shares were dumped. Some found no buyer at any price. Within two months American stocks lost half their value. Paper millionaires in August were bankrupt by Christmas.

The impact of this disaster was not limited to investors or even to Americans. As business leaders' confidence sagged, they reduced production, throwing employees out of work. As the unemployed stopped buying anything but necessities, reduced demand put more people out of work. As the unemployed failed to pay what they owed to banks, the bankers called in the loans they could collect. Because U.S. banks had made huge loans to Europe, panic spread there. After one of Vienna's leading banks, the Credit-Anstalt, failed in the spring of 1931, the cycle of fear and economic paralysis spread quickly into neighboring Germany and from there to the rest of the continent.

By 1932 the Depression was everywhere. In the United States its symptoms were padlocked factories, vacant stores, deserted transportation terminals, and empty freight yards. City streets were relatively empty, for many people now had no place to go. On the sidewalks were unemployed people attempting to sell apples for a nickel or simply seeking a handout. The fortunate were those who were still working, though at reduced wages, and those who still had their homes, though they might have lost their savings. Others, homeless, huddled in improvised shantytowns bitterly called Hoovervilles or rode the rails in empty freight cars, crisscrossing the country in a hopeless search for work.

Such were the human realities behind the grim statistics. In the United States, gross national product had fallen by nearly a half, and the number of suicides had increased by a third. Things were as bad in Düsseldorf as in Detroit. Worldwide industrial production in 1932 stood at only two-thirds of its 1929 level. World trade had fallen by more than half.

Nothing better illustrated the twentieth-century global pattern than the Depression's impact on parts of the world whose peoples knew nothing of stock markets and little of industrial development. Because natural rubber prices fell 75 percent from 1929 to 1932, for example, fewer jobs were available on the rubber plantations of Ceylon (now Sri Lanka). Because Western manufacturers were ordering less rubber for automobiles and appliances, half the Indian laborers who had worked on the Ceylonese rubber plantations had to return jobless to their homeland.

*A **Depression-era "Hooverville."*** *Even once solidly middle-class people lost their homes—note the properly attired man reading a magazine.* Museum of the City of New York

The Depression stretched to the ends of the earth. What was worse, it seemed to go on forever. The world's earlier economic crises had often been short and sharp, followed quickly by recovery. But despite politicians' assurances that prosperity was "just around the corner," the current economic decline seemed beyond remedy. How had this disaster of unprecedented size and duration occurred?

Origins of the Crisis

Economics is not an exact science. Moreover, the history of an economic crisis cannot be discussed without evaluating opposing economic policies. For these reasons, explanation of the Depression is controversial. Although historians generally agree on why the stock market crashed, they differ as to what the crash implies about the structure of the U.S. economy. Still more controversy surrounds the relation of the crash to the worldwide slump. In attempting to explain the crisis, we shall move from the surest ground to the most contested: from Wall Street to the U.S. economy and finally to the world scene.

Stock Market Collapse

The Wall Street crash that triggered the Depression was the collapse of a house of cards. It ended a decade of speculation that involved dangerous though hidden risks for the speculators, the bankers who lent them money, and the brokers who sold them shares. During the 1920s all three groups began to assume that financial paper like shares of stock had a value of its own that could only increase. Buyers bought stock "on margin," paying only 10 percent of the price and borrowing the rest from the broker; they expected the stock's value to increase fast enough to allow them to pay off the loan. Often the initial 10 percent was lent by bankers who accepted the stock itself as collateral while investing their depositors' money in similar shares. Shady financiers created glittering opportunities for these eager investors by launching holding companies whose only assets were paper ones: shares of other companies. They also bribed financial advisers and newspaper columnists to circulate tips that would stimulate a rush to buy shares in these paper creations.

The stock market's climb owed as much to psychology as to economics. For example, people borrowed money at high rates of interest to purchase the stock of Radio Corporation of America (RCA), not because they expected to collect dividends—RCA had never paid any—but because they were sure its price would continue to soar. And while the optimism lasted, its price quintupled in a single year.

Once the mood changed, and people became convinced that the market could only go down rather than up, the plunge was as steep as the climb had been. As prices fell, brokers demanded a larger margin. When speculators could not pay, their shares were dumped onto the market, further depressing prices. Meanwhile the holding companies melted away as their paper assets became worthless.

In one sense, the 1929 crash was the inevitable end of a financial boom generated within the small world of Wall Street. But it had a devastating impact on the entire U.S. economy. It wiped out much investment capital and made investors cautious about risking what they still had. The resulting damage to individual purchasing power, to international lending, and

to trade would not be repaired in the next ten years.

Mass Production and Underconsumption: Basic U.S. Economic Flaws

Many economic historians believe the Wall Street crash was only a symptom of basic flaws in the U.S. economy that inevitably would have produced a depression at some point. These flaws were not apparent at the time. Throughout the 1920s, U.S. industry continued the rapid growth stimulated by the war. By 1929 there were 26.5 million automobiles on American roads, compared to 1.3 million in 1914. Once a curiosity, radio became an industry of mass entertainment. Americans in the Far West and the Deep South listened to identical network programs. In 1929, expenditures on radios were forty times the level of 1920, when they were first mass-produced. The apparent affluence represented by American ownership of automobiles, radios, and other gadgets did not surprise visiting Europeans. They knew that World War I had transformed the United States from a debtor nation to the principal creditor of the rest of the world. With industry booming and the rest of the world owing them money, Americans thought nothing could be wrong with their economy.

But the distribution of wealth in U.S. society may have been too unequal in the 1920s to create demand for all the goods that industry was pouring forth. Some domestic markets were becoming glutted with unsold goods as early as 1926. The productivity of American factory workers rose by almost 50 percent in the 1920s, as mergers created firms large enough to afford more efficient machinery. But firms' cost savings were channeled primarily into corporate profits, which tripled during the decade. Prices were not substantially reduced, and even in unionized plants, wages rose less than profits.

Thus the purchasing power of the U.S. labor force was not greatly increased. Nor was the boom creating jobs. The number of Americans employed remained fairly constant through the 1920s. In some industries mechanization actually reduced the number of jobs steeply while increasing output. The problem of *technological unemployment*—of human workers displaced by machines—dates back to the beginning of mass production.

In human terms, these trends meant that the average American might be able to maintain a car in the 1920s but not to trade it in for a new one. Industrial expansion proceeded on the assumption that consumers could afford to keep buying indefinitely, though the 20 percent of Americans who worked in agriculture did not realize even the modest gains of industrial workers.

World War I had been a bonanza for American farmers, who vastly expanded their acreage to provide the food once grown on European battlefields. When European production revived after the war, the world's markets were soon glutted with agricultural produce. Long before the Wall Street crash, world farm prices had collapsed to about half their level of 1919. When the Depression began, the wages of American farm and factory workers were farther apart than they had been in 1910.

While some of the poor were getting poorer, the rich were getting richer. The proportion of total U.S. income earned by the wealthiest 5 percent of the population had grown since 1910 from a fourth to a third. In 1929, almost a fifth of American income was collected by the top 1 percent. Wealthy people's purchases of yachts and jewelry could not sustain a boom.

The United States had developed an economy of mass production without a corresponding society of mass consumption. The concentration of wealth had been less important during the nineteenth century, when Americans had been building and equipping a nation of continental dimensions. Now, however, the railroads the tycoons had built were all finished. Stringent postwar laws restricted immigration, which had increased the American population by as much as a million people a year before World War I. With nation building complete and population growth greatly reduced, the possibilities for constructive investment were less obvious. There was no guarantee that the wealth increasingly concentrated in fewer hands would be invested in ways that benefited the economy as a whole. The stock market boom, like an earlier craze for buying Florida land, showed that too much money was at the discretion of people who could afford to spend it foolishly. The purchasing power of most consumers was far more limited. The shrewdest investors recognized these warning signs. In 1928, when they noticed that company profits were not increasing nearly as rapidly as stock prices, they began the trickle of selling that became an avalanche in October 1929.

Maldistribution of income also helps explain why the Depression persisted so long. Although the economy would remain stagnant without investment, the wealthy few who could afford to invest were afraid to do so. The vast majority of Americans confined their expenses to necessities. Thus a vicious circle developed. With no hope of sales, there was no inclination to invest. With no investment, there were no jobs, no income, and consequently no sales.

The Spread of the Depression

If the Depression resulted from weaknesses in the U.S. economy and society, how did it spread to the rest of the world? Historians disagree on this question. But it is clear that the U.S. crash and U.S. government policies in reaction to it were the final blows to a world economic order already mortally weakened by World War I.

The European-dominated global pattern of 1914 was centered on Great Britain. Because the British were committed to free trade, many goods could enter their country tariff-free, even when British industry and agriculture were suffering from an economic downturn. British wealth had been so great that the bankers of the City of London continued to make long-term loans to the rest of the world regardless of the fluctuations of the British economy. When investment opportunities at home were limited by an industrial slump, British investment abroad actually increased. Whenever a banking crisis threatened anywhere in the world, bankers turned to the London banks for prompt help. After the Wall Street crash, however, it became clear that Britain could no longer play the central role in the global pattern and that the United States, Britain's logical successor, would not do so.

Britain had been the first nation to industrialize. In 1914 its industrial plant was already outmoded in comparison with those of its later-starting competitors. During World War I, Britain sold many of its overseas assets to buy arms but nevertheless amassed huge debts to the United States. The war enabled nations like Japan to invade British markets. Whereas over three-fifths of India's imports in 1914 came from Britain, by 1929 fewer than half did.

Britain's weakness became obvious when the Depression struck. After nearly a century of free trade, it adopted protective tariffs in 1932. A year earlier, the drain on British gold reserves had forced Britain to stop paying gold for pounds. Once again off the gold standard, and with a depreciating currency, Britain itself was in too much trouble to help reinflate the world economy with new investment. A large British loan might have saved Vienna's Credit-Anstalt after the recall of American loans and might have forestalled the economic collapse of Central Europe. But the Bank of England would offer only a comparatively small loan, to be repaid in weekly installments: hardly the terms of a long-term offer of salvation.

Britain could no longer be the world's financier, and the United States declined to take on any such responsibility. Throughout the 1920s the U.S. government rejected European arguments that war debts and reparations destabilized international payment balances and should be canceled. Not until 1932 were these economic reminders of wartime hatreds abandoned. The German economy increasingly relied on short-term American loans to make its reparations payments—which in turn were needed by Britain and France to pay their American debts. Germany was already in trouble before October 1929, as U.S. bankers reclaimed their money to invest it on Wall Street. After the crash, demands for immediate repayment completed the damage.

In 1930, Congress passed the Hawley-Smoot Tariff Act, imposing the highest import duties in history. Ignoring protests from thirty countries, President Hoover signed it into law. Now foreign countries could no longer sell their goods in the American marketplace to earn dollars to buy American products. Nor could they borrow dollars, for after the crash American banks became much more cautious lenders. Meanwhile, U.S. producers found they sold less abroad, for many countries retaliated by shutting their doors to U.S. products.

Because the United States produced nearly half the world's goods, it was the obvious candidate to assume Britain's former role of financial leadership. But instead of providing a market and loans in a crisis, the U.S. government signaled that in a world depression, it was every nation for itself. In such an atmosphere, what were the weak to do?

The Depression in the Developing World

The peoples of the developing world, whether living in colonies or in technically independent countries such as those of Latin America, were even less able to combat the Depression than were Europeans and North Americans. The more a developing country's economy had been integrated into the European-dominated global pattern, the more it suffered after 1929.

Those who fared best were the new nations whose principal economic activity was still subsistence agriculture—growing food to feed themselves. By 1929, however, many countries of Latin America, Africa, and Asia were economically dependent on their sales of agricultural or mineral products to Europeans or Americans. In many cases a single crop or mineral constituted most of a country or colony's exports.

The world agricultural glut had cut into export earnings well before 1929. To many crop-exporting countries the Depression was the final blow. The price of rice, the principal export of Siam (today Thailand), fell by half within a year. As the factories of Europe and the United States shut down, the bottom fell out of the market for industrial raw materials like copper and tin. The value of Chile's exports fell by 80 percent, and that of other Latin American exports by at least half. Despite international efforts to restore prices by agreeing to limit production, the countries that had earned their living by selling such goods as tea, rubber, and copper remained in deep trouble throughout the 1930s. Unable to sell, they could not buy what their trading partners might offer, nor were they credible risks for loans. Their wealth of natural resources was now worthless. In two years, for example, Brazil burned or shoveled into the ocean enough coffee to fill the cups of the whole world for a year. Although Brazil had been ostensibly independent since the 1820s, the Depression showed that its economic well-being was at the mercy of prices set in markets it did not control.

The experience of India, still a British colony, suggests that colonies beginning to develop economies less dependent on a few commodities might actually benefit from the Depression's impact on their masters. After World War I, British industry never regained its prewar dominance of Indian markets. When Britain in response to postwar unrest granted its colony power to manage its own economic affairs, India promptly erected tariff barriers to protect its infant industry from foreign competition. In the twenty-five years after India opened its first large steel mill in 1913, Indian steel production grew more than eightfold. Though raw cotton remained India's principal export, its own cotton-spinning industry grew rapidly, encouraged both by protective tariffs and, after 1930, by Gandhi's campaign to boycott British goods. In 1939 modern textile mills—largely owned by Indians, not Englishmen—produced almost three times as much cotton cloth as the primitive hand looms Gandhi's campaign had encouraged.

India did not escape the Depression entirely. In 1939, total steel consumption, including imports, was still less than in 1929. Agricultural exports fell, partly because of a 15 percent growth in population in the 1930s. (The population explosion began in much of Asia during this period, as these countries' rates of population growth overtook those of Europe and North America.) The need to feed many more people encouraged the overcultivation and exhaustion of Indian soil. Already one could foresee the question that became critical for India during the 1980s: Could industrialization raise the standard of living among so many hungry mouths? Even so, India came through the Depression far more easily than countries wholly dependent on raw-material exports.

Britain, France, and the Dilemma of Democratic Socialism

An astute observer in the 1930s might have realized that if the rest of the dependent world followed the Indian example and made its own cloth and steel, the global pattern of European and North American dominance would eventually collapse. Today, in fact, the American steel

Indian boycott of British products, 1931. *Preparing to burn an effigy of the British cotton cloth industry, these followers of Gandhi were protesting colonial dependency.* Popperfoto/Archive Photos

industry has shrunk as steel imports have increased—some from countries like Brazil and India. Few foresaw this development in the 1930s, however. Europe and North America still made the economic decisions. If a remedy for the Depression was to be found, it was up to them to find it.

The Failure of Economic Liberalism

As the Depression deepened, it became clear that the old remedies were not working. According to the liberal school that dominated economic thinking throughout the nineteenth century, governments could do little about a depression. They could no more legislate their way out of a depression, President Hoover declared, than they could "exorcise a Caribbean hurricane." What governments could do was *deflate*. If people were not buying, the remedy was to push prices down to a level low enough to stimulate demand. This also meant driving down the price of labor: wages. If people lacked confidence in the future of their money, the way to restore it was to balance the government's budget. Since a depressed economy produced fewer tax receipts, government would have to reduce its expenditures and raise taxes.

Most economic historians agree that these measures actually made the Depression worse. Higher taxes further reduced the public's purchasing power. With government spending also limited, there was no stimulus to boost confidence and revive the economy.

As the 1930s dragged on, the failure of traditional politics and economics drove more and more Europeans into a search for alternatives. The longest-established alternative was Marxism, which had always warned that capitalism was ultimately doomed by its failure to pay workers enough to buy the things they made. Now that the warning seemed to have come true, the Marxist alternative had much appeal. In a society where income was evenly distributed and the government planned and controlled production, Marxists argued, a disaster like the Depression could not have happened. Nor would government be indifferent to the sufferings of the jobless. But although many Europeans were attracted to a vision of a fairer social system, they shrank from the Soviet model of violent revolution and totalitarian government, preferring instead the nonrevolutionary socialist path.

The Socialist Alternative

To combine a socialist economy with political democracy was the central hope of the Social Democrats, or Socialists. In the 1930s, as today, they constituted the principal opposition to conservative or liberal parties in many countries with a democratic political tradition.

The Bolshevik Revolution had caused a split in all pre–World War I Marxist movements. To be allowed to affiliate with the Comintern, non-Russian Socialist parties had to accept the Soviet model of change. Many Socialists, however, were already sick of Bolshevik methods. At the 1920 annual convention of the French Socialist party, for example, a minority led by Léon Blum, a future prime minister, walked out rather than accept Moscow's control. The majority accepted Moscow's terms and became the French Communist party. Blum and his followers refounded the Socialist party. Germany's Social Democratic party broke apart during the war, and in the chaotic first years of the postwar republic, the German Socialist party (SPD) and the German Communist party (KPD) fought each other in the streets.

Deep differences of principle divided socialists and communists. To communists, it was a dangerous illusion to believe that it would be possible to create a socialistic society by winning an election. Why, communists asked, would capitalism yield to anything but force? Socialists, in contrast, believed that Lenin had made an unacceptable sacrifice of political freedom to achieve the socialist goal of a society based on economic equality.

Who was right? The Depression provided several tests of the idea that a socialistic society could be created through democratic politics. In Scandinavia the formula proved partially successful. After socialist electoral victories, Denmark, Norway, and Sweden developed a kind of "mixed" economy. Although most businesses were still privately owned, the mixed economy made government responsible for protecting all citizens' welfare "from the cradle to the grave." The high taxes needed to sustain the welfare state have recently prompted protests. Nevertheless, Scandinavian Socialists and their political opponents have seemed until recently to agree on the necessity for this "middle way" between capitalism and socialism.

The record of democratic socialism during the Depression was much more disappointing in larger countries such as Britain and France. The failures of the British Labour party and the French Popular Front were not entirely their own fault. But their experience shows some of the obstacles to establishing socialism within a democratic system.

Britain

When leaders of the British Labour party formed the first "socialist" cabinet in European history in 1924, middle- and upper-class Englishmen were filled with anxiety. Supported chiefly by working-class voters organized by Britain's increasingly powerful trade union movement, Labour had made an official commitment to socialism in 1918. The party's prime minister, Ramsay MacDonald, was the illegitimate son of a Scottish tenant farmer—a very different kind of person from the aristocrats and conservative businessmen who had previously occupied his office. But the fears of the well-to-do were soon allayed, as they saw that Labour was not going to make many changes. MacDonald's government, which lasted less than a year, made no attempt to convert Britain to a socialistic economy. Its most radical measure was to construct public housing with controlled rents, a measure continued by the Conservative government that replaced it.

To the second Labour government, formed after elections in 1929, fell the task of finding a remedy for the Depression. By 1931, one Englishman in four was unemployed. Unemployment benefits—"the dole"—were meager. Nevertheless, conventional economic wisdom demanded that this burden on the budget be reduced. A majority of the Labour cabinet resigned in 1931 rather than accept such a cut, which they saw as a betrayal of Labour's responsibility to the poor. MacDonald formed a new cabinet, composed largely of Conservatives but called a "National" government because all parties were represented in it. The Labour party expelled MacDonald as a traitor but remained crippled by its internal divisions. Labour did not get another chance to govern until after World War II. Meanwhile, under the governments of MacDonald and his Conservative successor Stanley Baldwin, the country muddled through the Depression without imagination. There would be no experiment in democratic socialism until after 1945.

In 1929 as in 1924, most Labourites wanted to preserve the political consensus that had enabled English men and women of all classes to live together in democracy. Their party was

an uneasy alliance of trade unionists (the majority) and middle-class intellectuals. However much they hated Britain's class society, the trade unionists were not sure it could be replaced by a socialist alternative within the existing democratic framework of Crown and Parliament, which most of them cherished. MacDonald's cautious policies corresponded to their views, not those of Marxist intellectuals. Even the Labour ministers who broke with MacDonald when he agreed to inflict deflation on the unemployed in 1931 did not urge the socialist alternative. If the British Labour party was an example of a democratic socialist movement, it clearly reflected the basic dilemma of democratic socialism: If a majority of society, or even of a social democratic party, is mistrustful of the profound change associated with socialism, then how can the goal of a socialist society be attained under a system respectful of majority rule?

France

In France the question of creating socialism within democracy presented itself somewhat differently. Here the ideas of Karl Marx had more influence than in Britain. While bitterly opposing each other until the mid-1930s, both French Socialists and French Communists proclaimed their allegiance to his ideas. Dividing the votes of France's Left,* they allowed the conservative Right repeated victories. Those French who wanted a different society, particularly members of the urban working class, became deeply frustrated.

---

*The use of the terms *Right* and *Left* to designate opposing political beliefs dates back to the parliament of the French Revolution of 1789. Supporters of the king and of the existing society happened to sit on the right side of the hall, supporters of the revolution and of change on the left. Ever since, opponents of change—conservatives— have been described as the Right, and proponents of change—from progressives to radicals—have been the Left.

In 1935, however, faced with the threat posed to the USSR by Germany after the arch anti-communist Adolf Hitler became German dictator, Stalin imposed a complete reversal of policy upon the Comintern and the Communist parties of Europe. Instead of reviling Socialists, Communists henceforth were to ally with them and other democratic parties in a Popular Front against the fascist threat. In France, after the formation of the Popular Front, Communists and Socialists united with the middle-of-the-road, nonsocialist Radical party to back a single candidate in each electoral district in the general election of 1936.

The victory of the Popular Front aroused tremendous hope in the French working class. At last, it seemed, a reunited Left could impose a socialist alternative to the capitalistic economy that had collapsed. But the Socialist party leader, Léon Blum, faced the same dilemma as British Labour when he became France's prime minister. Some of those who had voted for the Popular Front wanted it to make France a socialist country. But the majority, including supporters of the Radicals, did not want a socialist France. If Blum did not implement a socialist program, he would be undercut by his Communist allies. But if he did, he would lose the support of Radicals, whose votes he also needed to maintain a majority coalition in parliament. Both groups would turn on him unless he found a way to relieve the Depression.

Blum hoped to escape from this dilemma by improving the conditions of the French working class enough so that its rising productivity and purchasing power would stimulate recovery. Thus, when a wave of strikes followed the victory of the Popular Front, he pressured French employers into making such concessions as the forty-hour workweek, annual paid vacations, and workers' rights to bargain collectively. Although he encouraged working-class demands, Blum moved very slowly toward actual socialism. He took over from private ownership only the railways, munitions factories, and the Bank of France.

Blum's efforts to conciliate all groups in French society ended by satisfying none. Productivity fell with the establishment of a shorter workweek. Meanwhile, fearing a socialist tax collector, the wealthy sent their money abroad for safekeeping. Reluctant to aggravate their fears, Blum did not impose strict controls to keep money from crossing the border. Many poor voters concluded he was not really committed to socialism.

With productivity declining and investors frightened, France remained mired in depression while Blum's coalition of Communists, Socialists, and Radicals quarreled over the direction he should take. One year after coming to power, Blum, no longer able to muster a parliamentary majority, resigned.

France's experiment with democratic socialism ended on an ambiguous note. Some Popular Front legislation had a lasting effect on French society. Annual paid vacations brought the first working-class families to France's beaches, for example, shocking the middle-class people who had always had these resorts to themselves. Yet Blum's inability, after winning a majority in democratic elections, even to begin to create a socialistic society, raises questions about the possibility of democratic socialism. It may seem that his failure resulted from the particular French circumstances of 1936, notably the need to satisfy a coalition of groups with very different aspirations. Yet this was a problem likely to confront all democratic socialists in power. To give a genuinely socialistic direction to the French economy, Blum would have had to defy the rules of the democratic game, which require a parliamentary majority. Using undemocratic means, however, would have violated his convictions. Moreover, it would have confirmed the communist view that social change can be imposed only by revolution.

Conventional economic thinking had proved to be of little use in countering the

A sitdown strike at General Motors, 1937. *In the United States, as in Europe, workers simply moved into factories and refused to leave until their demands were satisfied.* © *Bettmann/CORBIS*

Depression. But Europe had not found an effective democratic alternative. How much more successful was the United States?

The New Deal in Global Perspective

President Franklin D. Roosevelt promised Americans a New Deal after his election in 1932. Despite the charges of Roosevelt's critics, the New Deal was not socialistic in any sense that European socialists would have understood. Nevertheless, the measures Roosevelt adopted to combat the Depression fundamentally altered the role of government in American life, setting a pattern that persisted without real challenge until the inauguration of President Ronald Reagan in 1981. Today most Americans

seem to resent and distrust the role of the federal government in their lives. Relatively few recall how that federal role developed in response to the worst economic collapse the country had known. Americans turned in desperation to government in 1933 because all other sources of leadership were helpless.

Roosevelt was inaugurated in March 1933, almost four years after the Wall Street crash. A quarter of the work force was unemployed. Farmers were threatening to hang bankers who tried to repossess their farms. Bankers had just closed the doors of all U.S. banks after a wave of failures created panic among depositors. Public opinion, the business community, and even Congress were ready to follow wherever Roosevelt led. He had already made it clear that he would seek "broad executive power to wage a war against the emergency, as great as the power that would be given to me if we were in fact invaded by a foreign foe."

During the first "Hundred Days" of the New Deal, Congress passed whatever legislation the administration proposed. The banks were reopened, with depositors' savings guaranteed by a Federal Deposit Insurance Corporation (FDIC). A Federal Emergency Relief Act replenished the funds used by states and cities to relieve the distress of one out of seven Americans.

The "Roosevelt Revolution"

Beyond such rescue measures, Roosevelt tried to attack the basic problems of the American economy. The descendant of generations of aristocratic Hudson river valley landowners, he was not committed to any particular doctrine. He was as skeptical of the theories of economics professors as of the platitudes of businessmen. Launched helter-skelter, the New Deal's programs were usually vote-catching, often ineffective, and sometimes inconsistent. Nevertheless, the whirlwind of activity rekindled hope. Skillfully projecting his cheerful optimism in radio "fireside chats," FDR became a hero to a majority of Americans.

The New Deal's congressional supporters attacked the farm problem by legislating limits on production. The Agricultural Adjustment Act (AAA) paid farmers not to contribute to the glut. Thus began the federal administration of farm markets that continues today.

To combat mass unemployment, the federal government became an employer of last resort. The Civilian Conservation Corps (CCC), for example, hired idle young men and set them to work on improving the American environment.

To promote industrial recovery, the New Deal allowed business to escape some of the stress of free-market competition. In 1931 the president of General Electric had called for the establishment of government-enforced cartels

to fix prices and regulate competition in every industry. The National Recovery Administration (NRA) met this demand by establishing "codes of fair competition" in some eight hundred industries. These rules were designed to limit competition so that all businesses might survive. When the Supreme Court struck the NRA down as unconstitutional, the New Dealers retorted by creating a series of "little NRAs" in separate industries.

Such legislation, and loans from the Reconstruction Finance Corporation (RFC), helped to keep many businesses afloat. Nevertheless, most business leaders came to hate Roosevelt and the New Deal, perhaps because the Roosevelt administration also supported labor, especially in the so-called second New Deal after 1935. The Wagner Act endorsed trade unions and collective bargaining, prohibited employers from opposing unionization, and set up a National Labor Relations Board (NLRB). The Fair Labor Standards Act of 1938 established a forty-hour week and a 40-cent minimum hourly wage.

Even this summary list of New Deal legislation suggests how much the role of the federal government, and its impact on the individual, had grown. A host of new agencies was created—like the SEC (Securities and Exchange Commission), intended to prevent the kind of Wall Street malpractices that had led to the crash. How effective were these laws and agencies?

Evaluating the New Deal

The New Deal did not end the Depression. Unemployment still stood at 17 percent in 1939. Only the need to make weapons for a new world war provided jobs for virtually every American man who wanted one, and for some women too.

Today, as in the 1930s, the New Deal remains controversial. Conservatives think its basic mistake was to attempt, vainly, to alter the normal operations of a free-market economy.

Spending more money than the government had collected, Roosevelt began the system of federal budget deficits that became so enormous toward the end of the century. Deficit-financed government investment to restart the economy had been recommended as a depression remedy by the most innovative economist of the day, the Englishman John Maynard Keynes. But conservatives argued that deficit spending was a double mistake. It proved ineffective, and it taught Americans to rely on an overgrown federal government rather than on their own efforts.

Such criticism is rejected by liberals, the New Deal's most ardent supporters. Their support has given a special American twist to the word *liberalism*. Unlike their nineteenth-century European predecessors, New Deal liberals favored an active role for government in social and economic life. Liberals see in the New Deal a sensible progressive adjustment of American institutions to the new reality of a world depression. In this view, by humanizing and democratizing the economy, and above all by restoring people's hope, the New Deal became one more chapter in the continuous success story of American history.

This interpretation was challenged, especially in the 1960s, by the historians of the New Left. Looking back from the decade of the Vietnam War and ghetto riots, they wondered whether American history really was a success story. In their view, far from undermining American capitalism, as conservatives charged, the New Deal had given it a new lease on life by alleviating its worst abuses. Liberals were equally mistaken, according to the New Left, when they applauded the New Deal for its concern for the common people. Ordinary people actually benefited little. It was the big farmers, the future founders of agribusiness, who were helped by government management of the marketplace.

Organized labor tripled its membership between 1933 and 1941, unionizing one of four American workers, but organized labor was al-

most entirely white and male. Unorganized labor—like blacks and women—did not fare so well. Moreover, the New Deal did not eliminate "unjust concentrations of wealth and economic power," the professed goal of one piece of legislation. In 1941 the poorest 20 percent of American families collected 4.1 percent of American personal income, compared with 3.5 percent in 1929. The richest 20 percent were still collecting 49 percent of national income in 1941, a small decline from the 54 percent they earned in 1929 and a very long way from the equal shares prescribed by socialism.

There is some truth in each of these conflicting assessments of the New Deal. The federal government did grow: it had 50 percent more employees in 1937 than in 1933. Federal spending rose from 3 percent of the gross national product in 1929 to 14 percent a decade later. The deficits required to pay these employees and fund this spending were unprecedented—though minuscule compared with the deficits of the 1980s. The rich did pay more taxes: the rate in the highest income bracket went up from 20 to 79 percent. Nevertheless, the New Deal was far from a social revolution. At the end of the 1930s, Roosevelt admitted, one-third of Americans remained "ill housed, ill fed, ill clad."

Those same words can be cited as evidence that the New Deal had created a norm of government responsibility for the economic well-being of its citizens. Though he was probably more hated than any other twentieth-century American president, Franklin Roosevelt was also more loved. He was re-elected to an unprecedented four terms. Above all, his popularity was inspired by his willingness to mobilize the forces of government against economic disaster (though the New Left historians are correct in asserting that New Deal benefits were unequally distributed).

After the New Deal, the federal government became a "guarantor state."[3] Before 1933 the American government had guaranteed its citizens practically nothing. Thereafter, at least until the 1970s, the federal government sought to guarantee more and more to all citizens: an education for the young; a safe and adequately paid job for adults, with compensation if the job was lost; an adequate standard of living; and medical care for the elderly.

Such guarantees of the quality of life were evidence of the new social role the New Deal assigned to the federal government. It also set a precedent for an enhanced governmental economic role. Government was henceforth held responsible for guaranteeing that there was sufficient demand for the economy's products to avert a return to Depression conditions, even if this meant spending more than its income in tax revenues. So widely accepted did this Keynesian idea of the creative possibilities of government deficit financing become that by the 1970s even the conservative Republican president Richard Nixon could declare, "We are all Keynesians now."

Moreover, government henceforth was expected, by taxing some and spending on others, to effect a degree of redistribution of the wealth of society, guaranteeing that the rich did not become too rich or the poor too poor. Some observers believe that only these enlargements of the role of government as social and economic guarantor—enlargements sooner or later matched everywhere in the developed world—rescued Western capitalism from the doubt and discredit into which it fell during the harsh years of the Depression.

Conclusion: The Global Trend Toward the Guarantor State

The New Deal was the American example of a worldwide trend toward enlarging governments' responsibility for their people. Perhaps the emergence of the guarantor state was inevitable in democratic societies, once World War I had shown that a government could coordinate an entire society and the Depression had reduced whole peoples to despair. Though democratic socialism failed in Britain and France during the 1930s, both countries eventually established welfare states more elaborate than the one the New Deal created. So did other developed industrial nations and even some Third World countries.

Despite the current disenchantment with big government, the guarantor state may have become indispensable in the complex, mobile, urban societies of the late twentieth century. Who else today will take care of young and old as the extended family did before 1914 in villages of the non-Western world?

The growth of government power can pose grave risks, however. Democratic socialism and New Deal democracy were not the only possible answers to the Depression. President Roosevelt once declared: "My desire is to obviate revolution. . . . I work in a contrary sense to Rome and Moscow." If he could not make the New Deal work, in other words, the American people might turn from democracy to another model of government and society. We already know the Moscow model. We must now examine the model that began in Mussolini's Rome: fascism, which seemed on its way to conquering the world in the 1930s.

Notes

1. Quoted from John Steinbeck, *The Grapes of Wrath,* Penguin edition, pp. 5–6.
2. Quoted in Robert L. Heilbroner, *The Making of Economic Society,* 6th ed. (Englewood Cliffs, N.J.: Prentice-Hall, 1980), p. 140.
3. The term *guarantor state* is taken from Carl N. Degler's essay "The Establishment of the Guarator State," in Richard S. Kirkendall, ed., *The New Deal: The Historical Debate* (New York: Wiley, 1973).

Suggestions for Further Reading

Childs, Marquis. *Sweden: The Middle Way* (1936).

———. *Sweden: The Middle Way on Trial* (1984).

Colton, Joel. *Léon Blum: Humanist in Politics* (1987).

Galbraith, John Kenneth. *The Great Crash* (1988).

Heilbroner, Robert L. *The Making of Economic Society*. 7th ed. (1985).

Johnson, Paul. *Modern Times: The World from the Twenties to the Eighties* (1983).

Kent, Bruce. *The Spoils of War: The Politics, Economics, and Diplomacy of Reparations, 1918-1932* (1990).

Kindleberger, Charles P. *The World in Depression, 1929-1939*. 2d ed. (1986).

Kirkendall, Richard S., ed. *The New Deal: The Historical Debate* (1973).

Latham, A. J. H. *The Depression and the Developing World, 1914-1939* (1981).

Orwell, George. *The Road to Wigan Pier* (1937).

Taylor, A. J. P. *English History, 1914-1945* (1985).

CHAPTER 6

Restructuring the Social and Political Order: Fascism

FOR PEOPLE WHO COULD READ ENGLISH BUT NOT GERMAN, IT TOOK A LONG TIME for Hitler's own written statement of his ideas to become accessible. Written in prison after his unsuccessful bid for power in 1923, his book *Mein Kampf* ("My Struggle") appeared in Germany in 1925–1927. An abridged English edition, containing less than half of the text, did not come out until 1933, when German conservatives, as we shall see in this chapter, made the Fascist revolutionary chancellor of Germany. And it was only in 1939, when Hitler was about to precipitate a second world war, that a full English translation was published. The ten noted American historians and journalists who sponsored its publication announced in their introduction "Here . . . for the American people to read and judge for themselves, is the work which has sold in Germany by the millions, and which is probably the best written evidence of the character, the mind, and the spirit of Adolf Hitler and his government." By then, however, it was perhaps too late. As you read the story of Hitler's rise in the following pages, it is worth speculating whether the course of history would have been different if more people outside Germany had had access to *Mein Kampf*. After all, in a Europe where many ethnic Germans lived under the rule of other "races," the implications of such a statement as the following, from Chapter II of Volume II, were not that hard to draw:

> *The German Reich, as a State, should include all Germans, not only with the task of collecting from the people the most valuable stocks of racially primal elements and preserving them, but also to lead them, gradually and safely, to a dominating position.*[1]

The Varieties of Authoritarianism After 1918

The word *fascism* derives from the Italian *fascio (di combattimento)* and originally referred to the street-fighting combat groups of an Italian political movement. But in the 1920s and 1930s the fascist label was applied indiscriminately to virtually every government in the world that was clearly neither democratic nor socialist. As a term of abuse, the word *fascist* is still carelessly used to refer to almost anybody politically to the right of center. To deal precisely with such an ambiguous concept, this chapter begins by defining fascism. It then discusses the two most important fascist regimes, those of Mussolini in Italy and Hitler in Germany, and shows how Hitler's rise prepared the way for World War II. Like other models of social and political organization that developed in Europe, fascism influenced political movements in other parts of the world. As strictly defined, fascism may seem to have perished in World War II. But the stresses that produced European fascism can lead to a similar phenomenon anywhere.

The years between the world wars were not healthy ones for democratic government. Initially the new states of eastern and southeastern Europe created from the ruins of the German, Austrian, and Russian empires all had democratic constitutions. Within a few years, however, most of those governments were forcibly replaced by some form of authoritarian or dictatorial rule. Poland became a dictatorship in 1926. After years of chronic political chaos, the kings of Yugoslavia and Rumania abrogated their countries' constitutions and became dictators in 1929 and 1938, respectively. In the other least-developed corner of Europe, a 1926 military coup in Portugal paved the way for the dictatorship of Dr. Oliveira Salazar, an austere economics professor. His regime lasted from 1930 to 1968—long enough to become an accredited part of the "free world" through its membership in the North Atlantic Treaty Organization. In Spain, General Francisco Franco led the army in rebellion against the Popular Front government of the Spanish Republic in 1936. After a three-year civil war, Franco established a dictatorship that endured almost as long as Salazar's, until Franco's death in 1975.

All these governments were sometimes called fascist. But their appearances were deceiving. Though most borrowed language from fascism and occasionally mimicked fascist rituals, fundamentally these regimes were simply dictatorships by conservatives. Challenged by real or imagined threats of democracy or socialism, the long-established elites of these little-developed countries—landowners, the church hierarchy, the army officer corps—abolished politics and began to govern by force. Their goal was to restore or perpetuate their own rule by forestalling all change. Once they had consolidated their power, they usually domesticated and sometimes annihilated the fascist movements whose slogans and cooperation they had borrowed.

Borrowings from Left and Right

The old elites feared fascism's revolutionary potential. Authentic fascism—the fascism preached by Mussolini and Hitler and their imitators around the world—did not fit into the usual political categories of Left and Right. It borrowed some of the ideas of both. Like the right-wing regimes established in places like Portugal, fascism was ferociously hostile to liberal democracy and Marxist socialism. Like most conservatives, fascists were intransigent nationalists. Moreover, fascists proclaimed their determination to restore law and order in society, using whatever force was needed—another favorite conservative theme.

Yet much about fascism should have alarmed a genuine conservative. Like movements of the Left, fascism was avowedly revolutionary. Fascists said they intended to smash the existing order of things, including much that conservatives held dear. Fascists often declared that their mission was to replace capitalism with a "national" socialism, although this bore little resemblance to the Marxist variety, which stressed international worker solidarity.

Fascism's leaders were young men, drawn not from the old elites but from the middle and lower strata of society. They sought power by mobilizing mass movements whose disciplined readiness for violence was symbolized by their uniforms. Italian Fascist Black Shirts and German Nazi Brown Shirts had counterparts around the world, from the tan shirts of the Lebanese Phalange to the green shirts of the Brazilian Integralistas.

Once in power, many fascists aspired to a new kind of unified society, ruled by an all-powerful state that would mold every individual's life. None of these themes is conservative, and some were clearly borrowed from the Left, indeed from the far Left.

Faced with this basic ambiguity in fascism's nature, historians and political scientists have long argued about how to interpret it. Most would probably agree, however, that fascism is a revolutionary movement whose mass appeal is achieved by invoking largely conservative values. Fascism triumphant was a revolution from the Right.

Economic and Social Change and the Growth of Fascism

Why did people on the Right, who usually oppose change, flock to join fascist movements that promised to change everything? Some powerful trends that underlay fascism's success were already apparent in European society and culture before World War I. The war, its aftermath, and the Great Depression accentuated these trends, bringing Mussolini to power in 1922 and Hitler in 1933.

One such prewar trend was the impact of social and economic change on the groups in every society least able to defend themselves. These groups included small businessmen, small farmers, and self-employed craftsmen. Before 1914 they saw themselves as being crushed between big business and big labor. Chain stores belonging to anonymous corporations reduced the sales of the corner shopkeeper. The exchanges of a worldwide economy meant that the small dairy farmer in northwest Germany had to compete with New Zealand butter brought halfway around the world in refrigerated ships. Ingenious machines designed for high-speed mass production threatened the livelihood and status of handworkers everywhere.

Parliamentary politics, which often seemed a mysterious and corrupt game benefiting only the politicians, offered no protection against these looming dangers. Nor could these people turn to Marxist socialism, for they were proudly respectable citizens who looked down on proletarian factory workers, who voted Marxist. These middle-class groups and low-level office workers—the fastest-growing component of society in much of Europe in 1914—derived their sense of security from identification with such apparently solid institutions as the German monarchy. When World War I swept these institutions away and the following decade of uncertainty led into the Depression, these groups stampeded into fascist movements that promised to restore order and security.

Paradoxically, however, fascism also drew support from groups that had found the complacency of pre-1914 European society unbearably confining. In 1914, Europe had not had a major war for fifty years. The younger generation found itself in a world without prospect of the glorious conflict that patriotism taught it to value. Moreover, for the first time in history, medicine was beginning to cure as many patients as it killed. As the older generation lived longer and longer, young people's wait for opportunity was indefinitely prolonged. Fascist ideas reflected the impatience and quest for adventure of this prewar younger generation.

This generation was inspired by an intellectual revolt against many of the dominant ideas of the nineteenth century, such as scientific materialism and parliamentary democracy. The prophets of this revolt saw in the civilization of the world's great cities a symbol of decay rather than progress. The routine of technological society had produced, they complained, a contemptible kind of human being: selfish, complacent, weak, irreligious. Parliamentary democracy had given political authority to the clever people who knew how to manipulate these gullible masses. They had tamed even the threat of revolutionary socialism. The time was coming to sweep all this away, to replace what one fascist derided as "the politics of ink, saliva, and ideology" with a real politics of "soil, flesh, and blood."

This contrast between the artificial and the real sums up fascism's revolt against modernity. While capitalists and socialists argued about what should become of "economic man," fascists held up the ideal of "heroic man," strong and cruel, joyful believer in the destiny of his nation or race. Fascists, Mussolini declared, were "against the easy life," because only a life of continuous hardship and struggle, like that of peasants of earlier centuries, could retrieve modern human beings from the decay of a world grown too comfortable. Only a movement dedicated to such a life of primitive virtues could reunite nations divided by the strife between social classes of the twentieth century.

Without World War I, such ideas might have remained confined to the fringe of European society. It was the war and its aftermath that made them meaningful to millions and decisively encouraged the growth of fascism. Their experiences in the trenches of World War I deeply affected the first fascists, those who joined up in the hard days before their movement won power. The more thoughtful of them found in the war's horrors a reason to condemn the whole prewar way of life. At the same time, the anguish of life on the front line produced a camaraderie among young men who in peacetime Europe would have been kept apart by sharp class distinctions. As veterans, many of these men tried to prolong this wartime sense of classless camaraderie by joining paramilitary street-fighting movements dedicated to smashing the prewar social order that had condemned them to the battlefronts. In its place they wanted to install the kind of government World War I had brought to the home front of every belligerent: one that would use centralized authority to impose a united society and a controlled economy.

Such movements emerged in all the countries that fought in World War I. Only in Italy and Germany, however, did they win control of the government. Why did those two societies prove especially vulnerable to the fascist temptation?

Both Italy and Germany were new nations, united only in the second half of the nineteenth century. Defeat—or, for Italy, a victory that seemed like defeat—in World War I revealed their internal fragility and external helplessness. Both Italy and Germany were rocked by near civil war at the very moment they were humiliated by the Versailles settlement. Frustrated nationalism and widespread fear of a Bolshevik-style social revolution thus reinforced the appeal of fascism.

Neither Italy nor Germany had the kind of long-established liberal or democratic institutions that gave some confidence to the English and the French. Faced with social chaos or economic disaster, the Italian and German middle classes preferred to abandon their feeble newborn democracies for the strong government the fascists promised. They acquiesced in a revolution that they hoped would end the disturbing changes brought by the war—a revolution from the Right.

We now turn to an examination of the fascist experience in particular cases, first Italy, then Germany. Six years after Adolf Hitler came to power, his National Socialist regime had drawn the nations into a new world war. By then, as we shall see, fascism's apparent success had spawned a host of imitations throughout Europe and beyond.

The Original Fascism: The Italian Model

Italy gained little from its alliance with the winners of World War I. This disappointment was the last in a series of frustrations since the unification of the nation in 1870. Italy's status as the sixth great power was a fiction. The country remained desperately poor. The Italian south was notorious for the backwardness of its huge landed estates. Recent industrialization in the north had added urban social tensions to the age-old clash between peasants and landowners.

Nor could Italians take much pride in their constitutional monarchy. The nation's parliamentary system, long based on corrupt bargains and rigged elections, faced paralysis after every Italian male became eligible to vote in 1912. This mass electorate did not provide support to the traditional liberals and conservatives; it divided its support between two mass parties, Socialists and Catholics. Each was strong enough to prevent the other (or anyone else) from governing, but they were separated by differences too deep for compromise.

The Versailles settlement gave Italy far less of the disputed territories on its borders than Italians felt their country deserved. Only nine thousand square miles compensated for the loss of 600,000 young men. Moreover, this "mutilated" victory brought Italy the same economic dislocations and social unrest that other nations faced. Cabinets based on parliamentary coalitions that typically collapsed after a few months did little to combat the fourfold increase in the postwar cost of living, the sevenfold increase in the public debt, and the

rising rate of unemployment. When discontented workers seized control of factories in the fall of 1920, the contagion of revolution seemed to have spread from Russia to northern Italy.

Benito Mussolini (1883–1945) skillfully mobilized his compatriots' anxiety and disgust. Since his adolescence he had been a rebel against Italian society, though originally, like almost all rebels, on the Left. At the outbreak of World War I, he was a leading Socialist journalist. But he disagreed with the Socialist party's position that Italy should stay out of the war, and broke with the Left permanently over that issue. For Mussolini the violence of war was a promise of revolution. In war, a proletarian nation like Italy might throw off its dependence on the more developed industrial nations. When Italy entered the war on the Anglo-French side in 1915, partly as a result of Mussolini's agitation, he promptly joined the army.

The war won as little for him as for his country. As a demobilized veteran, Mussolini became a spokesman for his comrades' rage for something better. On March 23, 1919, with about 145 friends, including former *arditi* (shock troops) whose black uniform he adopted, Mussolini founded the first Fascio di Combattimento.

The Rise of Fascism

During its first year, Mussolini's Fascism, championing such radical causes as votes for women and the eight-hour workday, attracted little attention. Its real growth began when frightened conservatives recognized its potential to suppress social disorder. Industrialists, landowners, and the army rushed to bankroll the movement, whose brutal *squadristi* beat up strikers and other troublemakers, often forcing them to drink nearly fatal doses of castor oil. By late 1922, growing as fast as the unemployment lines, Fascism had a membership of over 300,000. Its leaders loudly demanded at least a

Mussolini harangues the crowd. *In a characteristic pose on a visit to a provincial city in 1930, the Duce promises Italians a return to the greatness of ancient Rome. The photographer captured the essence of authoritarian mass mobilization.* *UPI/Bettmann—CORBIS*

share in the government. With Fascist thugs controlling the streets of many major Italian cities, their threat of a march on Rome, the capital, seemed plausible.

Yet Mussolini did not take power by violence. Power was handed to him. Rather than challenge so formidable an enemy of their own enemies—Socialists and Communists—the king and his conservative advisers decided to name Mussolini prime minister. In October 1922, Mussolini "marched" comfortably on Rome in a railroad sleeping car, with a royal invitation to head a fourteen-member cabinet including only three Fascists.

For a time he appeared content with this role, although many of his followers called for a "second wave" of revolution to transform Italy's society and political system. Behind his bluster, Mussolini was a hesitant adventurer—a "roaring rabbit," as he was once called. It took a major threat to his new position to force him into the final steps to dictatorship. Fascists close to Mussolini kidnapped and murdered a Socialist member of parliament, Giacomo Matteotti, who had exposed Fascist misdeeds. In reaction to this scandal, Catholic and some liberal politicians began to boycott parliament, hoping to force Mussolini to resign. Instead, this show of opposition apparently pushed him, after months of wavering, to establish a dictatorship.

By 1926, after dissolving opposition parties and independent unions, establishing strict press censorship, and reducing parliament to subjection, Mussolini appeared to be Italy's only master. Whenever he appeared on the balcony of his Roman palace, frenzied crowds saluted him as leader with cries of *"Duce! Duce!"* A similar, if more restrained, enthusiasm was expressed by many foreign visitors. Fascism, it appeared, had taught the formerly "undisciplined" Italians to "make their trains run on time." Mussolini's propaganda machine proclaimed that his genius had created a successful alternative to both capitalist democracy and Soviet communism. A closer examination of the regime's record and its relationships with various groups in Italian society, however, suggests that this was a gross exaggeration.

Fascist Myth Versus Fascist Reality

Fascism's remedy for social conflict was the corporatist society. This concept derived from Catholic social thought, which had always been troubled by the ruthless individualism of the free-enterprise system and took models for social organization from the precapitalist past, notably from the guilds of the Middle Ages. Fascist *corporatism* sought to unite members of the same economic calling, both employers and employees, by abolishing political parties and geographical election districts. In place of these divisive institutions, "corporations" were to be established for each sector of the economy. In these institutions representatives of bosses and workers could resolve their differences in an atmosphere of mutual understanding.

Mussolini eventually created twenty-two such corporate bodies and in 1938 replaced his rubber-stamp parliament with a Chamber of Fasces and Corporations. Far from fulfilling Catholic hopes of social reconciliation, the system was a façade disguising the repression of

Italian labor. The leaders of big business effectively controlled the corporate bodies. Italian workers, forbidden to strike, had little voice in them. By 1939, workers' real wages—the purchasing power of what they had earned—had fallen below the level of 1922.

Workers, who tended to be Socialists, had never been Fascism's best supporters. Small businessmen were generally much more enthusiastic, but even they got little help from the Mussolini regime when the Depression struck. Government planning consistently favored big businesses. Small ones were allowed to fail while their larger competitors got loans from the Agency for Industrial Reconstruction. The effort to build an efficient industry took precedence over Fascist rhetoric about preserving the little man. Perhaps the best rewarded of Fascism's early supporters were the students and white-collar workers who found jobs in the expanding party and government bureaucracies.

Fascist propaganda declared that these bureaucracies gave new unity and direction to Italian life. In reality Mussolini's movement never began to achieve his totalitarian dream of integrating every individual into society. Long accustomed to political cynicism, many Italians simply went through the Fascist motions. In Sicily, for example, members of the Mafia put on black shirts and continued business as usual.

Nor was the Mafia the only group beyond Mussolini's control. In 1929 he tried to placate the Catholic church by signing a treaty that ended the long quarrel over Italy's seizure of Rome, the pope's city, as the national capital. But the church objected to Mussolini's efforts to enroll children and young people in Fascist youth movements that rivaled the Catholic ones. Though much overshadowed, king and court also remained a potential rival power center. And despite all the talk about a new social order, the leaders of industry continued to direct the economy much as before, in cozy consultation with the higher bureaucracy. The

Duce had not fully realized his boastful slogan: "Everything for the state, nothing against the state, no one outside the state."

The original Fascist regime in Italy bore some striking resemblances to systems like Franco's and Salazar's because such conservative groups as the church, the court, and big business remained influential. By the mid-1930s, Fascism appeared to be a gigantic bluff even to some of its original supporters. It did not save Italy from the Depression. After 1929 Italians who had emigrated to the United States sent less money home—a heavy blow to the Italian budget. Despite Mussolini's emphasis on public works projects, all his construction sites could not provide jobs for the many who fled the poverty-stricken countryside for the cities.

Mussolini's policies were crippled by contradictions. It made little sense, for example, to try to keep people on the overpopulated farms while encouraging Italians to have more children. But Fascist ideology insisted on both agricultural self-sufficiency and an ever-growing population to make Italy strong. Similarly, the goal of an "autarkic" economy, independent of foreign suppliers, had patriotic appeal. But in practice the Fascist regime restricted the purchasing power of the working-class majority without planning systematically for investment—hardly a recipe for economic growth.

Mussolini raged as he became entangled in the contradictions between Fascist myths and hard reality. In 1935 he turned again to violence, launching an invasion of Ethiopia to avenge Italy's humiliating defeat there in 1896 (Map 6.1), a rare victory of Africans over Europeans. Instead of establishing an Italian empire, however, this adventure began the undoing of Fascism. For a country as underindustrialized and poor in raw materials as Italy, war would eventually mean dependence on a more powerful ally. Hating (and spurned by) the domineering democracies, Britain and France, Mussolini eventually turned to his fascist neighbor, Nazi Germany. Its leader had come to power much

as Mussolini had. But Hitler had created a far more terrifying regime. In the end, he would drag Mussolini with him to destruction.

From Weimar Republic to Third Reich

In Germany as in Italy, fascism owed its success to a masterful demagogue who mobilized popular anger against a feeble democracy during a period of upheaval. In Germany too, the conservative establishment handed the fascist leader supreme power in the expectation of exploiting his movement. Hitler had a far greater impact on world history than did Mussolini, however. From the moment a leader determined to reverse the humiliation of Versailles took power in Germany, another European "civil" war became likely. That conflict brought the final collapse of European domination of the world.

Weakness of the Weimar Republic

Like Fascism's, the story of Nazism's triumph begins with the end of World War I. The conditions imposed on Germany by the Versailles settlement were an enormous liability for the new Weimar Republic. Right-wing propaganda implanted in the minds of many the lie that the war would not have been lost if the German army had not been "stabbed in the back" by Republican "November criminals," who had allegedly preferred revolution to victory. The Weimar Republic's first five years were a constant struggle for survival against attacks from both Left and Right. In 1919 the Socialist-dominated government mastered Communist uprisings only by using both the old imperial army and

Map 6.1 German and Italian Expansion, 1935–1939   ♦

ICELAND

Germany and Italy
Italian possessions in Africa before 1935
German aggressions, 1935–1939
Italian aggressions, 1935–1939

0   200   400 Km.
0   200   400 Mi.

NORWAY

SWEDEN

FINLAND

North
Sea

DENMARK

ESTONIA

LATVIA

Baltic Sea

Memel
LITHUANIA

Moscow

IRELAND

GREAT
BRITAIN

London

ATLANTIC
OCEAN

NETHERLANDS

Danzig

EAST
PRUSSIA

SOVIET UNION

Berlin

POLISH
CORRIDOR

Warsaw

Brussels

GERMANY

BELGIUM

SUDENTENLAND
1938

RHINELAND
1936

Paris

Weimar

POLAND

LUXEMBOURG

Nuremberg

Prague

Munich

CZECHOSLOVAKIA
1939

FRANCE

SWITZERLAND

Vienna

AUSTRIA
1938

HUNGARY

ROMANIA

PORTUGAL

SPAIN
(Civil War, 1936–1939)

Madrid

Barcelona

ITALY

YUGOSLAVIA

Black
Sea

BULGARIA

Rome

ALBANIA
1939

GREECE

TURKEY

Mediterranean Sea

LIBYA

ERITREA

AFRICA

ETHIOPIA
1935–1936

IT. SOMALILAND

A F R I C A

private armies of right-wing veterans (Freikorps). The old army remained unsympathetic to the republic, however. When several of the Freikorps backed the attempt of a right-wing bureaucrat, Wolfgang Kapp, to overthrow the government in 1920, the army refused to move against them. The republic defeated Kapp only by calling out its worker supporters in a general strike.

This sequence of events already revealed the Weimar Republic's fatal weakness. On paper it was a model of democracy. Its bill of rights guaranteed freedoms never before recognized in Germany, including the vote for women. But in reality the republic was aptly described as a "candle burning at both ends." It faced a continuous Communist threat on its Left and also had to contend with a hostile Right that included many of its own officials, as the Kapp putsch proved. In truth the German revolution of 1918 had hardly been a revolution at all. Far from stabbing the army in the back, the Republicans had merely occupied the political vacuum temporarily created by its collapse. They did not shatter the old power structure, for they needed the empire's bureaucrats and officers. Many of these, though ostensibly serving the new government, remained as contemptuous of democracy as they had been before 1914.

The republic might have endured if it had won the support of the German middle classes. But this group lost its savings when a terrifying wave of hyperinflation—the worst ever recorded anywhere—destroyed the value of the German currency overnight in 1923. Soon 1 billion marks was worth only about 25 cents, and many people blamed the republic. Few recalled that the imperial government had begun the inflation by printing floods of money to fight the war. Meanwhile, to force the payment of reparations, France occupied the Ruhr, Germany's industrial heartland, thus compounding the financial crisis.

To many, the Weimar Republic appeared to be on the point of collapse in 1923. Commu-

nists threatened a rising in Saxony. In Bavaria, Adolf Hitler led his Nazi storm troopers from a Munich beer hall in an attempt to overthrow the Bavarian state as a prelude to destroying the central government. The Beer Hall putsch was a fiasco. The police fired on the advancing Nazis, killing several, and arrested Hitler, who was sentenced to a five-year prison term. This apparent failure marked a turning point in the career of one of the most sinister figures of modern history.

Born in Austria, the son of a minor customs official, Hitler (1889–1945) left his provincial birthplace for Vienna at the age of eighteen. Failing to get into art school, he drifted, like many unsuccessful migrants to the great metropolis, into a lonely and marginal life. From his observations of Viennese society and politics, he developed two basic beliefs. The German nationalists there, who despised the multiethnic Hapsburg monarchy, taught him the necessity of uniting the Germans of Europe into one nation. Viennese anti-Semitism persuaded him that Jews were Germans' worst enemies in the worldwide struggle for survival. Though Hitler exploited these themes to move the masses, these were also his deeply held beliefs. World war and genocide would later prove how sincerely he meant them.

When World War I broke out, Hitler chose to fight not for the Hapsburgs but for Germany. Though he did not advance beyond the rank of corporal, he thrived in the army as he never had done in civilian life, winning decorations and commendations. The worst day in his life was the one in November 1918 when, lying wounded in a hospital, he heard the news of Germany's defeat. Later, drifting in bewilderment like so many demobilized veterans, he came to Munich, where army intelligence hired him as a political agent. His job was to infiltrate an obscure group called the National Socialist German Workers party—Nazi for short. Hitler soon took it over from its founder, a locksmith whose aim was to combine German nationalism with a socialism dedicated not to Marx's proletarian revolution but to the protection of respectable little men in the middle—like locksmiths.

German society included millions of people to whom such a mixture would appeal. Hitler had exceptional gifts for reaching such an audience. Films of his speeches show that he had an uncanny ability to rouse crowds to frenzy by expressing their rage and frustration. He articulated the grievances of the many Germans who believed their nation was destined by racial superiority to rule Europe but was now disarmed and held captive by a conspiracy of alien forces: Jews above all but also Communists, Socialists, Catholics, and democratic politicians. It was wholly irrational to attribute Germany's misfortunes to the cooperation of such ill-assorted groups or even to any one of them alone. But Hitler knew that emotion, not reason, wins political commitment.

For a time Hitler's message of hate went unheeded as a renewed currency and a reviving economy gave the Weimar Republic a respite after 1924. Hitler served only eight months of his prison sentence, an indication of the Weimar judges' leniency toward right-wing revolutionaries. He emerged from prison to find Nazism largely forgotten. In the 1928 elections, his party won only twelve seats in the Reichstag, with only 3 percent of the popular vote. It remained largely a refuge for a hard core of veterans unable to readjust to civilian life. They reveled in the brown-shirted uniforms of the Nazi storm trooper brigade, or SA (for *Sturm-Abteilung*).

From Hindenburg to Hitler

It was the Depression that finally doomed the Weimar Republic and gave German fascism its opportunity. As in Britain, parliamentary factions became deadlocked over the issue of reducing government spending by cutting unemployment benefits. A government based on a Reichstag majority became impossible.

After 1930 the president of the republic, the aged Field Marshal Paul von Hindenburg, governed with the emergency powers given him by Article 48 of the constitution. Thereafter the political battle was fought in two places: between the SA and the uniformed brawlers of the other parties in the streets, and among rival factions in the circle of conservative intriguers who surrounded Hindenburg.

Desperate economic circumstances intensified political violence in the streets. By 1932, two of five trade union members were unemployed, and another was working short hours. Meanwhile, trying to break the political deadlock, the government held one election after another. In this atmosphere of economic despair and political frenzy, the extremes gained at the expense of the middle-of-the-road parties. The Communist vote rose dramatically but not nearly as fast as the Nazi totals. The Nazis had 12 seats in the 550-member Reichstag in 1929, 107 in 1930, and 230 in the summer of 1932.

Sensing that momentum was with them, some Nazis urged Hitler to overthrow the republic. But he had learned from Mussolini's experience and his own failure in 1923. As leader of the largest party, he could simply wait for the conservatives around Hindenburg to offer him a deal that would enable them to end emergency government under Article 48. On January 30, 1933, an agreement was reached: Adolf Hitler became chancellor of Germany as head of a coalition government whose eleven members included only three Nazis.

Many groups share the blame for this development. Conservative German politicians sneered at Hitler's "gutter" following but still tried to use his mass movement for their own purposes. Convinced that the Socialists were their real enemies, the Communists joined the Nazis in attacking the republic. Yet it should not be forgotten that Hitler could claim power because so many Germans backed him. Careful comparison of election results shows that the Nazis had relatively little success among working-class Socialist voters or the Catholic voters of the Center party. Many Nazi votes came at the expense of the conservative middle-class parties, which were virtually wiped out. Others were cast by new voters, especially the young. A third of the Nazi party's membership was made up of young people between eighteen and thirty.

Disgusted with the floundering of the Weimar government, which could not restore sanity to an economy gone crazy for the second time in ten years, these voters saw a striking contrast in Nazi dynamism. They also expected Nazi force to restore law and order to a turbulent political scene. Eighty-two people had been killed and hundreds wounded in six weeks of street fighting in one German state alone. If the price of an end to chaos was the establishment of a dictatorship, many were prepared to pay it—indeed looked forward to it.

The Nazi State

Dictatorship was not slow in coming. When a fire devastated the Reichstag building less than a month after Hitler's inauguration, the Nazis proclaimed that Germany was faced with a Communist plot. As a "defensive measure against Communist acts of violence," they "suspended" constitutional guarantees of personal freedom—never to be restored. As the first concentration camps opened to hold Communists and other Nazi enemies, the Reichstag convened to consider an Enabling Act that empowered Hitler to make laws, even unconstitutional ones, on his own authority for the next four years. With Communist members of parliament under arrest, only the Socialists were there to vote against the proposal. Combining his Nazis' votes with those of the Catholic Center party and what remained of the other parties of the Right, Hitler won an easy victory.

Now invested with unlimited authority, Hitler swiftly destroyed most of the institutions of a free society. He outlawed rival political

parties or prodded them to dissolve themselves. He abolished the federal system, making Germany a country with an all-powerful central government for the first time in its history. When Hindenburg died early in 1934, Hitler simply absorbed the president's office into his own. Never was the Weimar constitution modified. The "constitution" of the new Third Reich was simply whatever the Nazi *Führer* (Leader) commanded.

He gave a fearful demonstration of the extent of his power in the summer of 1934. By then, many Nazis, especially in the SA, were complaining that the political revolution had not gone far enough. Taking the socialism of National Socialism seriously, they were impatient to see Germany's old elites displaced. The SA's leaders dreamed of replacing the old officer corps, dominated by aristocrats, with their own street brawlers. Their demands forced Hitler to choose between some of his earliest supporters and the conservative and army leaders who had just given him power. He favored his most recent benefactors, ordering his black-uniformed SS bodyguards to massacre his most troublesome SA followers. When this "Night of the Long Knives" (June 30, 1934) was over, Hitler bluntly warned the Reischstag that if anyone "raises his hand to strike the State, then certain death is his lot."

Nazi Society and Economy

The Nazis overhauled German life and institutions through a process of "coordination" (*Gleichschaltung*) designed to compel obedience by peer pressure. To prevent individuals from combining to oppose the regime, Hitler ordered the Nazification of every organized activity in Germany, right down to clubs of stamp collectors and beekeepers. He dissolved the labor unions and made every German worker a member of the Nazi Labor Front—without, of course, any right to strike. He ordered the consolidation of the Protestant denominations into a single church under Nazi domination. In addition to bringing these older institutions under control, the Nazis also created new ones, such as the Hitler Youth, to enroll whole categories of the population.

All these groups were organized according to the *Führerprinzip*, the idea that authority comes from the top down and must be obeyed without question. Nazi society thus became an example of mass mobilization carried to its most extreme and authoritarian form. Until 1938 the army high command seemed exempt from "coordination." But in that year Hitler took advantage of trumped-up scandals involving the most senior officers to retire them and take the supreme command into his own hands. Unlike Mussolini's Italy, Nazi Germany seemed to have fulfilled the fascist revolution; the prefascist power structure was forced into obedience.

Joseph Goebbels, Hitler's propaganda minister, described the Third Reich as "one great movement of obeying, belonging, and believing." Historians have shown that this image was only partially accurate. Behind the façade of totalitarian efficiency was a bureaucratic nightmare of confusion and rivalry. Hitler was bored by the routine of government and ignored it, while deliberately encouraging organizational enmities that only he could resolve. Nevertheless, the accomplishments of his regime, particularly its economic achievements, were enough to make it genuinely popular with a majority, at least until war came in 1939.

Six million Germans were out of work in 1932. By 1938, the figure had dropped to 164,000 and was still declining. Three factors contributed to this success. First, the Nazis—unwitting Keynesians—used government spending, even at a deficit, to restart the economy. These appropriations went originally for public works—the Nazis built the world's first network of superhighways—and later almost exclusively for rearmament. By 1938 the Nazis were committing at least half the budget—far more than any other country—to an arms

buildup. Second, they brought the economy under tight government control. The government fixed prices, established production quotas, and allocated raw materials according to a Four-Year Plan, practically abolishing the forces of the marketplace. The third anti-Depression tactic was an effort—called for by the Plan—to make Germany's economy self-sufficient. The chemical industry, for example, was stimulated to develop synthetic substitutes to replace imported oil and rubber.

Together these policies produced a full-employment economy that contrasted sharply with the stagnation of the democracies. Not that all Germans fared equally well. Industrial workers, who had never been enthusiastic Nazis, were the least rewarded. The fate of farmers and small businessmen was only marginally better, though they had provided much of Nazism's voting strength. Their earnings increased faster than those of factory workers but not nearly as fast as industrial corporate profits, which grew fourfold in the 1930s. Nazi promises to safeguard the little man proved hollow. The flight from the farm continued, and the number of small businesses actually declined faster than in the 1920s.

Like Fascism, Nazism proved a disappointment to those who had supported it as a conservative revolution against change. In practice, Nazism proved to be a means of forcing rapid modernization by mobilizing the German masses under totalitarian control. Under the Third Reich, change actually accelerated, further eroding German small-town and rural society. The reason is quite simple. Hitler's goal was a powerful Germany. That meant a Germany equipped for war by the latest technology, which only large corporations could supply. The little people who had flocked to Hitler in fear of change could contribute little to that goal. He sacrificed them ruthlessly to the needs of war.

Despite these disappointments, when Hitler's war came in 1939 and left Germany in ruins by 1945, the victors who occupied it at

Hitler Youth Drummers and Trumpeters Salute the Fuhrer. *The
designers of Nazi propaganda strengthened young people's feeling of belonging
by engaging them often in grandiose occasions of public pageantry.*   © *AP-Wide
World Photos*

war's end were astonished to discover how
uncritical many ordinary Germans still were of
the Nazi leader. How, the victors wondered,
could Germans still uphold the virtues of Hitler
after the disaster he had brought them?

Perhaps the simplest answer is that most
people hate to admit they have been wrong. But
the victors also forgot that they had heard most
about Nazism from its victims and opponents,
many of whom had fled. For most Germans,
however, the Nazi period, particularly compared to the Weimar Republic, had been a positive experience, at least until Germany began to
lose the war, which they were told had been
launched by their enemies. Hitler had promised
to restore law and order and end unemployment, and he had done so. Under him, many
Germans lived better lives, in material terms,

than they had ever known. Nazism gave many a
sense of inclusion in the national community:
the Hitler Youth provided summer camps for
children of all classes and kept them out of
trouble.

True, Nazism had ended the democratic
freedoms of assembly and of the press, but not
many ordinary Germans insisted upon attending opposition rallies or reading opposition
newspapers. The regime abandoned programs,
like euthanasia or sterilization of mental patients, that aroused what little protest was to be
heard. True, persecution was meted out to unpopular minorities like Jews, but the ordinary
German had no contact with those officials
who were responsible, such as the secret police.
Indeed, postwar Germans who knew something of the American experience during the

war enjoyed pointing out that few Americans had protested when 112,000 Japanese Americans were suddenly deported en masse to unknown destinations after Japan attacked Pearl Harbor. Indeed, why should they protest? The maltreatment of ethnic minorities was simply a matter of "politics," and politics was something a wise person with real troubles of his or her own should stay away from.

Such was the reasoning about Hitler that foreign investigators frequently encountered among the unrepentant majority of postwar Germans. These attitudes, it must be emphasized, do nothing to *excuse* those Germans who joined the Nazi party as a career move or the far larger number who just went along because everyone else was. But such attitudes do much to *explain* why Hitler found so much support in the German mass society.

The Road to War

Compared to the causes of World War I, the causes of the European part of World War II have provoked little debate. The story of European international relations between 1933 and 1939 is the story of how Hitler dismantled the Versailles treaty piece by piece, unresisted by the democracies, until they finally went reluctantly to war in defense of Poland. Although one might conclude that Hitler was the cause of World War II, the leaders of the democracies are often also blamed for giving in to him. Even today, this interpretation remains an important historical model in the minds of foreign policy planners. The lesson American leaders felt they had learned from the sorry outcome of the 1930s was surely one reason for the prolonged U.S. involvement in Southeast Asia in the 1960s and 1970s. The lesson appeared to be that any failure to resist an aggressor nation, even in the remotest and most unimportant-seeming place, simply emboldens it to further aggression. More recently, too, the world situation has been ana-lyzed by analogy to the 1930s, for example, in justifying U.S. intervention in the Persian Gulf war in 1991. We need to know precisely what happened in the 1930s if we are to judge the aptness of these analogies.

Design for Aggression

Sometimes the suggestion is made that the democracies' failure to resist Hitler in the 1930s was the more inexcusable because his book, *Mein Kampf,* made no secret of his objectives. This rambling, unreadable work, written during his short stay in prison, clearly revealed his basic beliefs. Hitler was a "social Darwinist," who applied to human life the evolutionary vision of nature as a struggle among species for the survival of the fittest. For Hitler, history was a struggle for survival among biologically distinct races. The German race would not be able to compete effectively unless all Germans were brought within one country—a program that implied the destruction of independent Austria, Czechoslovakia, and Poland, where many "racial Germans" lived. Because France had consistently blocked German unity, another French war was probably essential. Yet Hitler's ambitions for the Germans did not stop with their unification, for he believed that all the lands they inhabited were overcrowded. They must conquer additional *Lebensraum*—living space—in the east, taking land from the racially inferior Slavs, particularly of the Soviet Union.

Mein Kampf thus does contain a kind of "design for aggression." Moreover, we know that Hitler vaguely contemplated still further struggles—ultimately, perhaps, a war with the United States for mastery of the world. Yet we cannot really blame democratic statesmen for not taking the message of the book seriously. Many politicians out of power have made promises that they later failed to keep. *Mein Kampf* was dismissed as this kind of propaganda.

Hitler's Destruction of the Versailles System

As chancellor, Hitler at first proceeded very cautiously in foreign policy. He had no predetermined timetable for destroying the Europe of the Versailles treaty, though this remained his goal. Instead he took advantage of opportunities as they arose, avoiding risks and accepting whatever successes circumstances gave him. His speeches stressed his own experiences of the horrors of war and his determination to prevent a new one. He was always careful to stress that the changes Germany sought in the Versailles settlement were only what was "fair." Hitler's rhetoric appealed to the guilty consciences of many people in the democracies. They had forgotten that the Versailles treaty had been intended not to be fair but to weaken and control Germany.

Arguing that the Versailles treaty had called for all countries to disarm but only Germany had been forced to do so, Hitler withdrew Germany from international disarmament talks and the League of Nations in the fall of 1933. He used a similar justification in 1935 when he announced the creation of a German air force, or Luftwaffe, forbidden by the Versailles treaty, and the expansion of the German army to five times its permitted size.

Perhaps encouraged by the failure of Britain and France to counter these challenges, Hitler began moving troops in the spring of 1936. In violation of the Versailles treaty and later agreements, he "remilitarized" the German Rhineland. This strengthening of Germany's western defenses would make it much harder for the French to move into Germany—the only action they could take to help Germany's eastern neighbors if Hitler threatened them. But the French confined themselves to an ineffectual protest. On the eve of their Popular Front experiment, they were divided domestically and dreaded a new war after the fearful toll the last one had taken of their youth. They surrendered European leadership to Britain. The British could see nothing wrong with Hitler moving German troops into German territory. So Hitler got away with it.

It is sometimes suggested that the Rhineland crisis of 1936 was the one time when Hitler could have been stopped without much bloodshed. Armed resistance to remilitarization might have forced him to retreat, destroyed his prestige, and perhaps prompted the German generals to overthrow him. But it is not clear that the German generals would have had the courage to mount a coup. Moreover, Hitler's ambitions were not his alone. Most Germans wanted to reverse the Versailles treaty. Their country had territorial ambitions long before Hitler came to power, as illustrated by the peace Germany imposed on the Russians in 1917. A rebuff in the Rhineland might not have toppled Hitler. Even if it had, he might have been followed by a German government no more peacefully inclined.

In 1937, Hitler directed his generals to be ready for war in connection with his next move. This precaution proved unnecessary, for the democracies did not oppose his annexation (*Anschluss*) of Austria in the spring of 1938. After he marched in, Hitler arranged a plebiscite in which a majority of Austrians approved the annexation. This result eased the consciences of people in the democracies, who thought in terms of national self-determination rather than strategic realities.

The annexation of Austria left Czechoslovakia in the position of a man with his head in the lion's mouth. By September 1938, Hitler was preparing to devour the Czechs. The complaints of the more than 3 million Sudeten Germans whom the Versailles settlement had placed under Czech rule served as his justification this time.

The Czech situation brought the most severe of the prewar crises, for France and the Soviet Union were committed by treaty to protect the Czechs. At every Czech concession

Hitler tours the Sudetenland after the Munich pact removed it from Czech rule. *If there were Sudeten Germans who did not welcome going "home to the Reich," they are not in this photograph.* *Keystone Collection, London—New York*

Hitler escalated his demands and threatened a solution by force. He was not bluffing. In May he had issued secret orders stating his "unalterable intention to smash Czechoslovakia by military action in the near future."[2] But he was also willing, grudgingly, to let the democracies deliver Czechoslovakia to him without war.

The British prime minister, Neville Chamberlain, obliged him. Chamberlain made three frantic trips to Germany to negotiate a settlement. In Munich, with Mussolini's encouragement and France's acquiescence, Chamberlain and Hitler made terms. The Czechs, who were not represented, lost their defensible mountain frontier regions, where the Sudeten Germans (and nearly a million Czechs) lived.

The Munich agreement made *appeasement* a dirty word and Chamberlain's umbrella a symbol of surrender. But in 1938, most Europeans were relieved by this settlement. They were not eager to go to war again. It is in hindsight that Chamberlain's sacrifice of the only remaining democracy in Eastern Europe has been condemned.

Often such condemnation has been made without any understanding of Chamberlain's position. He was no admirer of Hitler, whom he regarded as half-crazed. Nor was he simply yielding to threats. He was pursuing a deliberate policy of peacefully eliminating sources of conflict. He foresaw correctly that another bloodbath like World War I would mean the end of the European-dominated world order. He had little faith in help from the Soviet Union, whose communism seemed to conservatives a greater menace than Germany's anti-communist Nazism, or from the United States, whose citizens clearly wanted to avoid further involvement in Europe. In this perspective, the sacrifice of a small remote country seemed a lesser evil than a new war.

Chamberlain's error was to believe that Hitler, like most people, would prefer peace to war, especially if his grievances were satisfied. In fact, Hitler was glad to get what he demanded without war. But if Chamberlain had not appeased him, the war that began in September 1939 would probably have begun in September 1938, and the British would have been even less well prepared than they were a year later.

When Chamberlain returned to Britain, he announced that the Munich agreement heralded "peace in our time." But in the spring of 1939, Hitler seized what was left of Czechoslovakia. In retaliation, the British government promised support to Poland, clearly destined to be his next victim. Even so, Hitler probably did not expect his invasion of Poland to produce full-scale war, which German planning anticipated would come only in 1943 or 1945.

In August 1939, preparing to attack Poland, Hitler cynically signed an agreement with the Soviet Union that ensured Germany would not have to fight on two fronts. In return, this Nazi-Soviet pact guaranteed Stalin a share of the Polish spoils and at least temporary immunity from German attack. Hitler probably calculated that such odds would prove daunting to Britain and France, and indeed those countries hesitated to respond for almost two days after German troops crossed the Polish border on September 1. But the Poles refused to have a surrender negotiated over their heads, as had happened to the Czechs. And so, with the British and French declarations of war on September 3, Europe's second world war began.

The Record of the 1930s and the Lessons of History

What "lessons of history" are to be learned from the story of the 1930s? Winston Churchill, soon to become Britain's prime minister, had systematically condemned each successive failure to curb Hitler. The prestige of his wartime leadership has lent much weight to the lesson he preached: the need for timely resistance to dictators. Yet it cannot be proved that following Churchill's policy would have allowed Europe to avoid war or even to fight on terms more advantageous to the democracies. We cannot know what would have happened if Hitler had been forced to back down in 1936. And by 1938 he was eager to fight. In historical perspective, Churchill's lessons no longer seem so certain.

Ironically, Neville Chamberlain in 1938 was convinced that *he* had learned the lessons of history. How incredible it was, he said during the Munich crisis, that the British government should be issuing gas masks to its civilians and digging trenches in London "because of a quarrel in a faraway country between people of whom we know nothing." Clearly he was remembering the origins of World War I. The lesson Chamberlain had learned from 1914 was that great wars began when great powers were dragged into them by alliances with quarrelsome small powers like Serbia—hence his determination to defuse a similar crisis, as he saw it, by opening a dialogue.

Perhaps there was no way to stop German expansion except by war. Hitler was in a hurry, believing that destiny called him to realize Germany's ambitions and that his own days were numbered. It may be that the fascist revitalization of Germany, always potentially the strongest power on the European continent, forced the democracies to choose between war and submission. As we shall see, Germany's power was finally destroyed only when the country was invaded and dismembered, as French hardliners had wanted to do in 1919. Chamberlain at Munich may have been wrong to believe that negotiation allowed the democracies to avoid both war and surrender. But no one can be certain that earlier resistance to Hitler would have offered a way out of the dilemma.

War or submission? Our views of what should have been done to stop Hitler in the 1930s are influenced by hindsight—by knowledge of World War II and the ghastly sufferings the Nazis inflicted. We find it difficult to imagine how Chamberlain could have believed it wise to accommodate Germany in hope of avoiding a conflict that seemed to him the greater evil. Perhaps the greatest wisdom is to realize that the lessons of history do not repeat themselves exactly. Chamberlain correctly recognized that World War I resulted from the great powers' failure to manage a peripheral crisis effectively. The origins of World War II, however, lay rather in the limitless ambitions of a revived Germany. Before applying the lessons of history to the present and future, we need to examine carefully the validity of the analogy linking our own situation with the past.

Despite the rapidity of twentieth-century change, 1914, 1939, and our own times do have one thing in common. Now as then the world is divided among sovereign nations that acknowledge no law except that of self-preservation, by force if necessary. In such a world, fascism, with its glorification of patriotism and violence, found imitators almost everywhere.

Fascism Around the World

As Hitler systematically overturned the obstacles to German power set up by the Versailles system, the momentum of fascism seemed irresistible. In imitation of this success, fascist or fascist-inspired movements appeared all over the world—testimony to the power of the European-dominated global configuration in shaping the ideologies of other countries as well as their economies.

Other European Fascist Movements

Few of these fascist movements succeeded in capturing power, and some did not even command much attention. In developed northwestern Europe, British, Dutch, and Scandinavian fascists were insignificant political forces. In linguistically divided Belgium, ethnic tension produced two fascisms, one speaking Flemish and the other French, that together captured 20 percent of the vote in 1936. Militant right-wing leagues rioted in Paris in 1934, arousing fears of a fascist coup in France. But they were conservative rather than revolutionary, tamely submitting to dissolution by Léon Blum's government.

In southeastern Europe, by contrast, substantial fascist movements included the Hungarian Arrow Cross and the Romanian Iron Guard. In both Hungary and Romania, however, the conservative dictatorships were at least as ruthless as the fascists. Corneliu Codreanu, leader of the Iron Guard, was "shot while attempting to escape" after King Carol II suspended the Romanian constitution and threw him into jail. When

Capture of Defenders of the Spanish Republic.   *Hands in the air, they are led away by Nationalist army troops loyal to General Franco.*   © *Hulton-Deutsch Collection/CORBIS*

the Iron Guard attempted to regain control, the army crushed it.

In Spain, the fascist Falange was not nearly so powerful a force as the Iron Guard was in Romania. It failed to win a single parliamentary seat in the fateful election of 1936 won by the leftist coalition, the Popular Front. Among the groups who backed General Franco's Nationalist revolt against the Popular Front government of the Spanish Republic, the Falange was far less numerous than traditional conservatives: monarchists and Catholics. For many people, it was the intervention of Mussolini and Hitler on the Nationalist side in the ensuing savage three-year Spanish Civil War (1936–1939) that turned resistance to Franco into a crusade against the international march of fascism. As the fascist dictators poured in arms and reinforcements for Franco, idealistic volunteers from many countries formed "international brigades"—among them the American Abraham Lincoln Brigade—to defend the Spanish Republic. Many

became disillusioned as the republic, abandoned by the governments of the democracies, became more and more reliant on Soviet aid and thus fell increasingly under Communist control. When Stalin left the republic to its fate and Franco won the civil war, he soon made it clear, now that he no longer needed Italian or German aid, that he was no more inclined to a revolution from the Right than to one from the Left. Though his regime had adopted some of the slogans and trappings of fascism, Franco relegated the Falange to political insignificance. His ultimate legacy to Spain was not fascism but, oddly in the 1970s, the restoration of the monarchy.

The Brazilian Integralistas

An even harsher fate than the Falange's befell the most interesting of the Latin American fascist movements, the Brazilian Integralistas. After borrowing many of their slogans, dictator

Getúlio Vargas prudently outlawed his fascist allies.

The Depression caused a collapse of Brazilian coffee prices. The resulting crisis dealt the final blow to Brazil's republican government, which had been run by a tiny minority of the wealthy. In 1930 it was overthrown by Vargas, an ambitious provincial governor. This coup marked the beginning, not the end, of political uncertainty. The new constitution of 1934 extended the right to vote, launching Brazil on the perilous new course of democratic politics in a time of growing social unrest. An abortive Communist coup in 1935 expressed the discontent of urban and rural workers.

Amid similar anxieties, the middle classes of Italy and Germany had turned to fascism. In Brazil the urban lower middle class and small landowners made up three-quarters of the Integralista movement founded by Plinio Salgado in 1932. The movement copied many aspects of European fascism, from its emphasis on centralized and authoritarian government and a corporatist economy to the stiff-armed salutes exchanged by its green-shirted militia. But it also reflected Brazil's particular circumstances. In this fervently Catholic country, the fascist motto was "God, Country, and Family." Moreover, Salgado explicitly condemned the racism of some European fascisms as inappropriate for a country with Brazil's mixed racial heritage.

As Brazil's first truly national political party, the Integralistas initially expected to take power by legal means, the only ones Salgado admitted. They were also encouraged by the tacit support they received from President Vargas, whose speeches stressed themes similar to theirs. But Vargas refused Salgado's offer of Green Shirt help against the Communists. He would tolerate no armed power to rival his own. The Integralistas would not, he explained, "Hindenburg" him. In 1937 he carried out a new coup d'état and established a more authoritarian political system, the Estado Novo (New State). To their horror, the Integralistas discovered that the new system's press censorship

and prohibition of political parties applied to them, too. When some of them attempted a coup against Vargas in 1938, the ensuing shootout marked the end of the movement.

The Integralistas failed partly because of their own political naiveté. Trusting in Vargas and nonviolence, Salgado had none of Hitler's cunning. But the parallel failures of fascist movements in Mexico and Chile suggest that Latin American societies still lacked some of the essential ingredients for successful fascism. None of these countries had experienced the mass mobilization and disruptive horror of World War I. Indeed, Latin American armies rarely fought wars. They devoted their time to politics instead, providing their own brand of authoritarian rule. Moreover, despite some industrialization, most of Latin America in the 1930s had not yet developed mass movements of the proletarian Left, such as those that had made fascism attractive to the European middle classes. For all these reasons, fascism failed in Latin America in the 1930s.

The Lebanese Phalange

The 1930s produced short-lived proto-fascist movements in the Middle East: Blue Shirts and Green Shirts in Egypt, Gray Shirts and White Shirts in Syria, Khaki Shirts in Iraq. Arabs under British and French rule had reason to copy the political style of Germany and Italy, the enemies of their enemies. But in the Middle East, the social groups that constituted the core of European fascism were too small or too strictly controlled to permit Arab fascism to develop fully. Nonetheless, at least one such movement founded in the 1930s survives today, a reminder of the permanent temptation of fascism for people who feel that history has wronged or is threatening them.

Five young Western-educated Christian Arabs founded Al Kata'ib, otherwise known as the Lebanese Phalange, on November 21, 1936. Their leader was pharmacist Pierre Gemayel, captain of the Lebanese soccer team at the 1936

Berlin Olympic Games. Gemayel had been struck by German discipline, which contrasted sharply with the bitter division of his homeland.

Historically, the name *Lebanon* referred not to a state but to a region within Syria. Mountainous Lebanon had long been a refuge for religious minorities. When the League of Nations gave France control of the region after World War I, France created the Republic of Lebanon, which contained some seventeen religious sects. Maronite Christians, like Gemayel, who had important historic links to the Papacy and France, were the largest sect, though they represented less than a third of the population. Most of the rest were Muslims. Most Muslims resented Maronite dominance, which they believed rested on foreign support. Then and now, many Muslims even resented the French-imposed idea that Lebanon should be a country separate from Syria and the rest of the Arab world.

In such a situation, the task of Gemayel's Phalange was obvious. It recruited Maronite students, apprentices, shopkeepers, and minor bureaucrats into a militia that could defend their community and the Maronite-dominated Lebanese order. Their slogan was "God, Country, and Family"—the same as that of the Brazilian Integralistas. Members between the ages of eighteen and thirty-five were organized into 600-man "phalanxes," which carried out military drills in their tan shirts. The motto, the military trappings, and the early insistence of the Phalangists that they were not a political party, all link this movement with fascistic movements elsewhere. After Lebanon became independent from France in 1943, the Phalange gradually evolved into a political party. Yet it never lost its military dimension and still had seventy thousand men under arms a generation after Pierre Gemayel's visit to Berlin. In the Lebanese civil war that began in 1975, the Phalange played a leading role in defending the Maronite position.

Conclusion: The Permanent Temptation of Fascism

To what extent has fascism survived into our own time? For decades after World War II, it appeared that fascism had arisen in response to a specific set of conditions in the aftermath of World War I and had ended with the destruction of the regimes of Hitler and Mussolini in 1945. Their defeat, it was supposed, had discredited most of the ideals and symbols associated with them. Thus the survival into our own time of the Lebanese Phalange, which may never have fully met our definition of fascism, could seem to be merely a historical curiosity.

Yet postwar appearances have proved deceiving, for fascism is really best understood as a response to the central themes of the twentieth century defined in this book. Fascism's nationalism appeals to the resentment of peoples who feel oppressed or cheated by history. Its revolutionary conservatism is a violent protest against the erosion of culturally conservative societies by the acceleration of change. Fascists boast that they can succeed where democracy always fails, in combining the politics of a mass society with effective government. Ideologically, fascism curiously mingles the twentieth century's mania for futuristic technology with its uneasy suspicion that human beings are losing touch with their natural environment. Above all, fascism offers its adherents a set of values—belief in the nation and the leader—that can prove comforting in an age when, as we saw in Chapter 2, most values have come into question.

Since fascism claims to have answers to central problems of modern life, we should not be surprised that movements resembling interwar fascism continue to appear. The most pessimistic observers of the Soviet Union's collapse fear that the eventual successor of communism will be not today's fragile democracy but various blends of nationalism and fascism. Most disturbing, the 1990s saw a resurgent neo-Nazism in newly reunified Germany. The mobs of young Germans who brandish swastika-like symbols and persecute ethnic minorities were born long after Hitler's death. But like his followers in the 1930s, they are driven by economic despair and frustration with ineffectual government. Their numbers remind us that in times of trouble, fascism remains for many a tempting alternative to democracy.

Notes

1. Adolf Hitler, *Mein Kampf* (New York, 1941), pp. vii, 601.
2. Quoted in Alan Bullock, *Hitler: A Study in Tyranny,* rev. ed. (New York: Harper & Row, 1964), p. 408.

Suggestions for Further Reading

Adamthwaite, Anthony. *The Making of the Second World War* (1979).

Bullock, Alan. *Hitler: A Study in Tyranny.* Rev. ed. (1971).

Cassells, Alan. *Fascism* (1975).

De Grazia, Victoria. *How Fascism Ruled Women: Italy, 1922-1945* (1992).

Hiden, John, and John Farquharson. *Explaining Hitler's Germany: Historians and the Third Reich.* 2d ed. (1989).

Hilton, S. *"Ação Integralista Brasileira:* Fascism in Brazil, 1932-1938," *Luso-Brazilian Review,* 9 (December 1972).

Kershaw, Ian. *The Nazi Dictatorship: Problems and Perspectives of Interpretation.* 3d ed. (1993).

——. *Hitler, 1889-1936: Hubris* (1999).

Laqueur, Walter, ed. *Fascism: A Reader's Guide* (1976).

Mayer, Milton S. *They Thought They Were Free: The Germans, 1933-1945* (1955).

Payne, Stanley G. *A History of Fascism 1914-1945* (1995).

Smith, Denis Mack. *Mussolini: A Biography* (1982).

Taylor, Alan. *The Origins of the Second World War* (1983).

Weber, Eugen. *Varieties of Fascism* (1982).

PART THREE

Latin America, Africa, and Asia: The Struggle Against Colonialism

CHAPTER 7

Latin America's Struggle for Development

IN 1941, FOUR POOR FISHERMEN—KNOWN AS TATA, JERÔNIMO, MANUEL PRETO, and Jacaré—boarded a raft at Fortaleza in the coastal state of Ceará in northeastern Brazil. Made of a half-dozen balsa wood logs with a rudder and a triangular sail, the raft (*jangada*) was what local fishermen used. As they headed out from shore, the four *jangadeiros* looked more like ragged, weather-beaten wind surfers than like mariners starting a long sea odyssey. Yet that is what they intended. Their minds were on Brazil's president, Getúlio Vargas, the "father of the poor," whose appeals to the "workers of Brazil" had given his countrymen a new sense of citizenship. Tata, Jerônimo, Manuel Preto, and Jacaré planned to sail 1,600 miles southward around Brazil's eastern bulge to Rio de Janeiro to ask Vargas to help people like them. They had a lot to tell. Just south of the equator, Brazil's northeast is an arid, impoverished place, so poorly connected to Rio that it was still hard to go there except by sea. Fishermen of Ceará usually did not even own their rafts and had to divide each day's meager catch into two piles, one for them and one for the raft's owner.

Sharing tasks at sea and stopping along the coast for supplies, the four reached Rio after sixty-one days. Fashionable sunbathers waved surprisedly, boats came out to meet them, a small plane carrying a radio announcer flew overhead, and newsreel cameras whirred as a crane lifted them—raft and all—out of the water. Still dripping, the four were taken to Vargas, who embraced them and promised the benefits they sought. National heroes and international celebrities after a trip that "thrilled all of Brazil" as Brazilian journalist Edmar Morel later recalled, the four stayed in Rio several months. *Time* magazine hailed their voyage as a heroic one that "wrought a political miracle." Orson Welles, age twenty-five but already a famous film maker, arrived in Brazil a few months later on a U.S. government-

145

sponsored, wartime mission to strengthen "hemispheric solidarity"; Washington was worried that Vargas had Nazi sympathizers in his government. Fascinated by the four *jangadeiros'* exploits, Welles decided to film a re-enactment, using all local people as the actors. However, Jacaré, whose political activism in Rio had begun to alarm the Vargas government, was suddenly killed when a large wave overwhelmed the raft in Rio harbor. Welles's focus on Brazil's poor, not only the fisherfolk of Ceará but also the samba musicians and dancers who streamed out of the *favelas* (shanty towns) around Rio at Carnival, further worried the Vargas government, concerned about Brazil's image abroad. Welles lost the financial support of his Hollywood studio and never finished his film; the footage was only rediscovered decades later. As for the "political miracle" that *Time* magazine had proclaimed, Gegê—another nickname for Vargas—did take an unprecedented interest in the needs of the Northeast, although his programs produced more patronage for people who worked in them than improvements for outlying parts of this huge, poorly integrated country.

Decades later, friends and relatives recalled the "great peaceful voyage." It had not wrought a miracle. Yet, like many other episodes in Latin American history of the period, it vividly illustrates how even the faraway and forgotten were becoming caught up in the quickening rhythms of national and global interconnectedness, political mass mobilization, and global communications.[1]

Continental Overview: The Illusion of Independence

In the colonial era, Brazil was integrated into the European-dominated world system as a Portuguese colony; almost all the rest of Latin America became Spanish colonies. Most of Latin America won political independence in the early nineteenth century. Economic dependence has proven harder to shake off. Latin American countries differ markedly; yet in this and other respects, they also share important traits, both internally and externally. This chapter begins with an overview of society, economy, and politics in Latin America. In external

politics, the dominant outside power is the United States, rather than the European countries. Following the continental overview, we shall take up the themes it develops by looking more closely at three of the most important Latin American countries—Argentina, Brazil, and Mexico—through 1945.

Latin American Societies

To a large extent, the Latin American nations' similarities and problems stem from the way their populations developed. The proportion of people of native American and African, as opposed to European, origin was much higher in Latin America than in English-speaking North America. When the Spanish reached the mainland following Columbus's voyages of 1492–1504, perhaps 60 million native Americans inhabited the region, mostly in present-day Mexico, Guatemala, and Peru. By 1850, probably over 9 million Africans had been imported as slaves to Latin America and the Caribbean islands. In contrast, fewer than 1 million Europeans immigrated to Latin America in the colonial era.

The epidemiological aspect of ecological imperialism made disease a major factor in shaping Latin America's population, causing die-offs of 90 percent or more among some native American peoples in the sixteenth century. Malaria and yellow fever afflicted non-natives, too. By 1800, South America's population may have fallen as low as 20 million. In the long run, differences in mortality rates made the impact of European migrants on the region's population mix greater than their initial numbers implied.

Another factor shaping Latin American identities was the mixing of peoples and cultures. In some countries, most people—in Brazil virtually all—are of mixed ancestry. The human blend varied across time and space. The importation of Africans ended with slavery. European immigration increased thereafter, confirming Argentina's comparatively European aspect, in particular. Still, the mix of colonial times prevailed, in varying proportions, over most of the continent.

Latin American societies did not become integrated, however. Spanish and Portuguese settlers had a capitalist outlook, but one wedded to ideas of class and privilege developed in Europe in earlier centuries. In the colonial period, the superiority that Iberians born in Europe felt over people of Iberian stock born in the Americas added complexity to this picture. Europeans of either type had not come to work the land with their hands. They came as con-

querors who would exploit the resources of the New World by commanding the labor of others. Instead of pushing aside native Americans, as North American settlers did, Spaniards and Portuguese settled where they could exploit indigenous people in greatest numbers; or they brought in African slaves. The Spanish and Portuguese crowns supported settlers' aspirations by issuing large land grants, thereby laying the foundation for the huge estates that continue to exist. The melding of peoples began with sexual exploitation of the conquered.

Meanwhile, the conquerors elaborated their ideas about social relations into a virtual caste system. At the top stood European-born Iberians, followed by colonial-born Iberians, then mixed-bloods of all types. Last came black slaves and native Americans. At independence, Latin American countries proclaimed legal equality, and a few nonwhites rose into the elites. But discrimination persisted, and those who were, or could pass for, white still dominated the rest.

Latin American Economies

Because Latin American economies remained primarily agricultural, the most important expression of white dominance lay in the great estates known as *fazendas* in Brazil, *estancias* in Argentina, and *haciendas* in other Spanish-speaking countries. Some estates were unimaginably vast. The Díaz d'Avila fazenda in colonial Brazil was bigger than some European kingdoms. Around 1900, the Terrazas-Creel clan of the state of Chihuahua, Mexico, owned 7 million acres. By 1914, urban middle and working classes were forming and assuming important roles. But Latin American society still consisted mostly of small landowning elites and huge peasant masses.

The gulf between elite and mass was wide in every respect. Members of the elite were well dressed, well fed, relatively well educated, European in culture as well as origin, and keen to

Slaves raking coffee beans, Brazil, 1880. *Brazil was the last country in the Western Hemisphere to abolish slavery (1888).* *From H. L. Hoffenberg,* Nineteenth-Century South America in Photographs. *Reproduced by permission*

preserve a way of life that assured them power, wealth, and leisure. The poor were ill fed, ill clad, largely illiterate, and attuned to folk cultures in which native American and African elements and older communal ways played a major role. Among elite and mass alike, women were repressed by factors ranging from the elites' refined etiquette to the crude cult of male dominance (*machismo*) in all classes.

The rural population was generally poor and subordinated to the owners of the great estates. Most rural folk were either small subsistence farmers or free peasants who lived in independent villages but worked part-time for hacienda owners to make ends meet. In Brazil and Cuba, many of the rural poor were slaves until slavery was abolished in the late 1800s. In the highlands of Spanish America, many people were debt peons working full-time on the haciendas. The difference between slave and peon was often slight, thanks to the debt servitude promoted through the hacienda store. Many hacienda owners paid their peons with scrip or tokens usable only at the store, which charged inflated prices to force the peasants into permanent indebtedness. By law, peasants could not leave the hacienda as long as they owed money. They responded sometimes passively, sometimes rebelliously, a combination to which the elites reacted with a mixture of paternalism and fear. No wonder hacienda agriculture was inefficient. Critics have labeled the hacienda world one of "internal colonization."

In Latin America's economic history internal colonization went with external dependency. Europeans first came to South and Central America seeking new routes to Asia. They stayed to exploit the mineral, agricultural, and human resources of the New World "Indies." Following the then-widespread economic philosophy of *mercantilism,* Spain and Portugal each set out to monopolize its colonial trade so as to assure the mother country a positive trade balance. The trade restrictions never fully succeeded, but they implanted on Latin American economies a pattern they have never completely shaken off: supplying raw materials to more powerful economies abroad and importing finished goods.

Latin American elites profited from this arrangement and have done much to perpetuate it. One legacy of economic colonialism was that imitation of highly developed economies occurred more in consumption than in production. Consuming European products was easier than mastering advanced production techniques. Such behavior increased demand for imports and deepened dependency but did not jeopardize the elites' positions as middlemen.

In the long run, Spain and Portugal were too weak to remain the dominant outside powers in the region. When Latin American countries won independence in the early nineteenth century, they opened their ports to world trade—that is, to British industrial goods. As the greatest maritime power and the only industrial

power of the day, Great Britain had aided Latin American independence movements with this end in view.

Free trade set in motion a sequence of events that became familiar around the colonial world: the ruin of local merchants and manufacturers, accumulation of foreign debt by local governments, and eventual bankruptcy or near-bankruptcy, with the risk of intervention by foreign governments to protect their citizens' investments. Such events did not fail to provoke conflict over economic policy, but supporters of free trade won in the long run. Major steps toward industrialization occurred in Latin America in the late nineteenth century, but they were often the work of foreign capital and tied the local economies more tightly into the global economy. The railroad networks, for example, developed in typical colonial style. They were designed to drain products of the interior toward the ports, rather than to link regions and countries to serve Latin American needs.

Over time, Latin America's focus of dependency shifted toward the United States. In 1823, President James Monroe announced the policy that became famous as the Monroe Doctrine: the United States would regard any European attempt at colonization of the independent Americas as a threat to its own peace and safety. At that time, the United States lacked the strength or the interest to protect Latin America. The dominant outside influence remained that of Great Britain, which sought economic dominance rather than political control. In the early twentieth century, however, U.S. interest and investment began to outstrip the British, especially in the Caribbean. The Panama Canal (completed in 1914) symbolizes this growth. The United States was prepared to use military force to protect such investments, as it did in Cuba during the Spanish-American War (1898).

By 1914 it was clear that the Latin American states' independence was limited, whether politically or economically. The powerful industrial nations had indeed established colonial economic relations the world over. The fact that a country could achieve political independence but remain economically dependent was simply a variation, often called *neocolonialism,* on the theme.

Economic dependency has many disadvantages for countries that suffer from it. In Brazil, for example, a long series of export products— dyewood, sugar, gold, diamonds, tobacco, cotton, cacao, coffee, rubber—succeeded one another as the major determinants of prosperity. There were several reasons for these changes. Mineral resources do not last forever, nor does demand for a given country's production of a crop. Cheaper sources may be found elsewhere. New processes or products, such as synthetics, may wipe out demand entirely. Even when such changes do not occur, the colonial economy remains at risk because it has little or no influence over the price of its exports, which is determined far away in international trade centers. During the Great Depression, for example, the value of Latin American exports fell about two-thirds between 1929 and 1932.

Because Latin America's ties to the outside world were economic more than political, the 1929 Depression marked a clearer turning point in the region's history than either world war. Industrialization efforts had begun earlier and been stimulated by import shortages during World War I. After 1929, however, the virtual stoppage of international trade created an opening for a major push to escape economic colonialism. The larger Latin American countries intensified their efforts to industrialize, first through *import substitution* (local production of previously imported goods), then through development of *heavy industry.* High tariffs and other measures were used to protect the budding industries from competition. These policies produced unexpected consequences, and the relation between agricultural and industrial development was not well thought out. But

a new era in Latin America's economic history had begun.

Politics and International Relations

Nineteenth-century revolutions freed most of Latin America from European rule, but the new states did not fit local reality. By 1914 the independent Latin American countries were officially all republics (Map 7.1). But political reality was determined not so much by fashionable ideas like republicanism and liberalism as by Iberian traditions of absolutism and Catholicism and by local conditions. The absolutist heritage made it seem natural for presidents to dominate the legislative and judicial branches and interfere in local government in ways unheard of in the United States. Catholic social thought supported executive dominance in the sense of favoring strong government as a means to assert moral values and harmonize social relations.

Translated into Latin America's poorly integrated societies, the result of these ideas fell short of the ideal. Power generally belonged to elite factions and military strongmen (*caudillos*), usually representing regional more than national interests. The caudillos rigged elections. They told legislators what laws to pass and judges what decisions to render. They kept administration inefficient and corrupt. Their military forces did little but interfere in politics. To preserve the elites' wealth, the caudillos kept direct taxes very low. Well into the twentieth century, import and export duties provided half of the revenues of many governments. With such narrow resource bases, governments could not have done much for the masses, even had they wished to.

Map 7.1 Latin America, 1910 ◗

UNITED STATES

ATLANTIC
OCEAN

MEXICO
Mexico City • • Veracruz
Havana
CUBA
BR. HONDURAS
Guatemala JAMAICA HAITI
GUATEMALA
HONDURAS
NICARAGUA
COSTA RICA
PANAMA
DOMINICAN REP
PUERTO RICO
CARIBBEAN SEA

Caracas
VENEZUELA
BR. GUIANA
DUTCH GUIANA
FR. GUIANA

• Bogota
COLOMBIA

Quito •
ECUADOR

Amazon

PERU
Lima •

BRAZIL

• Bahia

PACIFIC
OCEAN

La Paz •
BOLIVIA

MINAS GERAIS

PARAGUAY

SÃO PAULO
São Paulo •
RIO DE JANEIRO
Rio de Janeiro •

Paraná

RIO GRANDE
DO SUL

Valpariso •
• Santiago
CHILE
Buenos Aires •
ARGENTINA
URUGUAY
Montevideo •

Bahia Blanca •

PATAGONIA

Independent nations

0   1000 Km.

0   1000 Mi.

FALKLAND/MALVINAS ISLANDS

In time, new leaders won power by attempting broader political mobilization. The decades preceding the Depression of 1929 produced a wave of nineteenth-century-style liberal leaders such as revolutionary Mexico's elite politicians (see Chapter 4), who demanded political rights and freer elections but not fundamental social change. In Latin America as elsewhere, the Depression exposed these liberals' incapacity to cope with economic crisis. In 1930–1931, twelve Latin American countries underwent changes of government, mostly by military intervention. Power was passing to a new type of authoritarian mass mobilizer, such as Lázaro Cárdenas in Mexico, Getúlio Vargas in Brazil, and Juan Perón in Argentina, all of whom applied corporatist policies.

Under *corporatism* (as noted in Chapter 6), the state organizes or "incorporates" interest groups defined by occupation—combining owners and workers without regard to class differences—and bases representation on these occupational groups, rather than on constituencies defined by geography or population. While sometimes confused with fascism, corporatism lacks the militarism, ideological elaboration, or totalitarian goals of fascism. Corporatism allows occupational groups and traditional interests like the Church their own spheres of operation. Rooted in precapitalist social structure and Catholic social thought, corporatism aims to use the state to protect individuals from excessive competition and to harmonize, not deny, different class interests. Corporatism thus contrasts with liberal individualism, Marxist classism, and fascist totalitarianism. Fascism perverted the benevolent intentions of corporatism—not that Latin American corporatists always did better. Yet through World War II, corporatism provided a way to mobilize, from the top, workers and peasants who had previously had little political voice. By combining corporatism and populism (commitment to the common people),

Cárdenas, Vargas, and Perón became their respective countries' most popular leaders and still remain so.

These developments strengthened the Latin American states' power domestically, but international politics still reflected their historical dependency. Their most important economic relations were always with countries outside the region. Partly to compensate for their poorly developed relations with one another, Latin American states joined in international agreements and organizations, such as the Pan American Union (1889)—although U.S. sponsorship made it an object of suspicion—and later the League of Nations.

Latin America's biggest international problem was U.S. aggressiveness. Size and distance helped protect countries like Argentina and Brazil, but Caribbean countries, especially the smallest, lay fully exposed to this danger. For example, while Woodrow Wilson argued for national self-determination at the Paris Peace Conference, five Caribbean nations—Cuba, the Dominican Republic, Haiti, Nicaragua, and Panama—were under U.S. rule, a policy that Washington deemed vital to protect U.S. interests. Later, under the Good Neighbor Policy (1933), the United States backed away from interventionism. But the corollary of this policy was reliance on pro-U.S. regimes, often brutal dictatorships such as Nicaragua's Somoza regime (1936–1979).

The Latin American states eventually entered World War II on the U.S. side. Mostly, they provided bases, supplies, or intelligence, although Brazilian troops did fight in Italy. The war illustrated that U.S. interests were global in scope, rather than hemispheric like those of most Latin American states. Tensions continued to arise from this disparity, as well as from further U.S. interventions, especially in Caribbean countries such as the Dominican Republic, Guatemala, Nicaragua, and El Salvador.

Context of the Struggle for Independence and Development

Lack of social integration, agrarian inequity, caudillo politics, corporatist-populist mass mobilization, external economic dependency—these common traits provide the background against which Latin American states evolved in the interwar years. As we look more closely at Argentina, Brazil, and Mexico, we shall see that they shared not only these traits but also developmental patterns reflecting the major themes of twentieth-century world history. All three nations experienced both major growth in demand for political participation and widespread mobilization from the village world into national life. Eventually, each country produced a charismatic leader responsive to these changes. The main economic theme, especially after 1929, was the attempt to break out of dependency through a technology-based strategy of industrialization aimed at import substitution followed by development of heavy industry. This development strategy proved as problematic as authoritarian political mobilization. Still, the progress made and the limits encountered, both political and economic, essentially defined the basis for Latin American development in the post–World War II era.

The Amazing Argentine

Argentina's economy and political system developed in parallel stages. In the colonial period, economic interest centered on the Andean region, which supplied agricultural and manufactured products to the nearby silver-mining centers of what is now Bolivia. By the late eighteenth century, with the decline of the silver mines, the economic center began to shift to the pampas, grassy plains near the coast, lying inland and southward from Buenos Aires and containing some of the world's richest soil. The agricultural system that developed on the pampas spread to the windy plateaus of Patagonia in the south and to the northern lowlands, tying the country into a unit dominated by the port-capital, Buenos Aires.

The foundations for agricultural prosperity were created by accident in the sixteenth century, when Europeans introduced horses and cattle to the New World. Some animals escaped and flourished on the pampas. By the eighteenth century, horsemen known as *gauchos* had begun hunting these animals for their hides. The elites began to form herds and stake claims to vast, inefficiently managed landholdings. Gradually, people learned to exploit Argentina's natural resources more intensively, always with political results. In the 1780s the introduction of meat-salting plants made it possible to export meat, as well as hides. This development increased the commerce of Buenos Aires, heightened resentment of Spanish commercial restrictions, and led to the proclamation of independence at Buenos Aires in 1810, in the interior in 1816. Politically, independence brought regionalism and caudillo politics.

In the mid-nineteenth century, the rise of sheep raising and wool exports opened a new chapter. Since a given amount of grazing land could support four or five times as many sheep as cattle, sheep raising led to more intensive use of established grazing lands near Buenos Aires, and cattle raising shifted to new lands to the south and west. The growth of the sheep economy attracted European immigrants, and the extension of the frontier climaxed with a military campaign against the Araucanian people of Patagonia in 1879–1880.

This campaign, which added 100 million acres of new grazing land, coincided with the development of techniques for transoceanic shipment of chilled meat. These two events touched off a major boom in the 1880s. Over the next fifty years, "the amazing Argentine" became a leading export economy. But the exports were mostly agricultural, the trade was

Gauchos branding cattle on the Argentine pampas, 1880. *These cowboys'*
costumes and customs helped give Argentine culture a distinctive stamp. From
H. L. Hoffenberg, Nineteenth-Century South America in Photographs. *Reproduced with*
permission

largely foreign controlled, and Argentina's profits were poorly distributed among the populace. Argentina experienced growth but not
balanced development.

The boom of the 1880s made Buenos Aires
one of the first New World supermetropolises.
Henceforth the city dominated the nation politically and economically. By 1914, Buenos Aires
had a population of 1 million, and the province
of Buenos Aires contained 46 percent of Argentina's population. The rail network converged
on the city, which was by far the most important port.

Radiating out from Buenos Aires, land-use
patterns assumed a distinctive form. This emphasized livestock and grain production on

huge estates with small numbers of laborers,
often immigrants who lacked the rights of
citizens. This pattern of development distinguished Argentina from other Latin American
countries in an important way: Argentina never
acquired a large peasant class, and land reform
never became a key issue, as it often did elsewhere.

Politically, the period after 1880 was one of
oligarchical domination by the National Autono-
mist party (later known as the Conservatives),
whose corrupt politicians ruled in the interest
of large landowners and foreign capitalists. In
1889–1890 as the boom collapsed, a protest
movement emerged from the growing middle
class, itself a byproduct of urbanization. With

this movement, Argentina's twentieth-century political history began.

The Radical Period

By 1892, the protest movement had taken form as the Radical Civic Union with Hipólito Yrigoyen as its charismatic leader. Not really radical, the party did not attack economic inequity. Yrigoyen and other Radicals were middle-class reformers with economic interests in the export sector. Both self-interest and nineteenth-century liberal ideas limited their grasp of socioeconomic issues. Yet their demands for honest elections and broader power sharing amounted to calls for further political mobilization. In 1912, seeing that genuinely leftist forces were forming, the Conservatives tried to steal the Radicals' thunder by granting their demands—votes for all adult males and the secret ballot.

The Radicals profited from these reforms by winning the election of 1916. Yrigoyen assumed the presidency, and the Radicals remained in power until 1930. Under the gaze of political opponents of the Right and Left, foreigners with economic interests in the country, and their own middle-class supporters, who were eager for power and patronage, the Radical leaders proved unprepared to solve the social and economic problems that emerged, especially in times of crisis, from the inequities of Argentina's export economy. For example, when the economic pressures of World War I led to strikes, Yrigoyen first supported the strikers but then yielded to Conservative and British pressure and used force against them. In 1930, the Great Depression again spotlighted the Radicals' inability to cope with economic crisis, and a military coup toppled them. The Radicals had tried to broaden political life. But their vision was not yet broad enough to meet the needs of most Argentines in times of hardship.

The Depression and the Infamous Decade

Just as economic change had correlated closely with earlier political milestones in Argentina, the same occurred again in the 1930s. Until the Depression, its agriculture-based export economy had made "the amazing Argentine" Latin America's most dynamic economy. Thereafter, the emphasis was increasingly on industrialization. World War I had stimulated industry by creating needs for import substitution and even opportunities to supply the Allies' wartime needs. The Depression made expanding domestic production still more important because the price of Argentina's exports fell faster than the prices of the goods it had been importing. The Conservative politicians who succeeded the Radicals in 1930 restricted imports to protect Argentine industry and fought to defend their share of the British market for agricultural goods. One development with future implications was that U.S. manufacturers reacted to discriminatory import restrictions by establishing plants in Argentina.

Such changes essentially ended the Depression for Argentina by 1936. World War II provided another economic stimulus. An inflationary export boom ensued, and the war left Argentina with $1.7 billion in foreign exchange reserves. Argentina was now an industrial as well as an agricultural country. Because industry was concentrated around Buenos Aires, industrialization further heightened the dominance of the country's one great city.

The period known as the "Infamous Decade" (1930–1943) marked a move away from democracy but ended with a further step toward authoritarian mass mobilization. The Depression ended the agrarian elite's control of government, fragmented the upper class politically, and allowed the state to assume greater autonomy and dominance over society. Politically, the period featured a Radical-Conservative coalition, with the military in the background. In a 1943 coup, however, generals took over the government, thus completing the trend toward a dominant state uncontrolled by any broad sector of society.

The officers behind the 1943 coup were ultraconservative nationalists, strongly influenced by recent events in Europe, especially Spain and Italy. They were eager for industrialization but fearful of radicalism among Argentina's workers and immigrants, of whom the latter made up a larger percentage of the population than in the United States. A few days after the coup, the Department of Labor was turned over to Colonel Juan Perón (1895–1974), a respected officer who had long argued for military-led industrialization. Ultimately, to the displeasure of many Argentine conservatives, Perón turned out to be one of the most effective political mobilizers in Latin American history.

The Rise of Perón

Urgrading his department of Ministry of Labor and Welfare, and taking a corporatist-populist approach to preventing the working-class revolution that many officers groundlessly feared, Perón encouraged workers to organize under state control and supported them in negotiations. Wages increased, expanding demand for goods and stimulating industrialization. Perón also created a system of pensions and health benefits. In return for these gains, the unions became part of a corporatist apparatus that Perón controlled. All the while, his power (and conservative resentment of it) grew.

Perón was an impressive figure, and his readiness during speeches to pull off the jacket that Argentine politicians had always worn and identify with the shirtless workers (*descamisados*) won him acclaim as "Argentina's Number One Worker." His opponents overthrew and jailed him in 1945 but, bewildered by the demonstrations that followed, released him. He then retired from his government and military posts,

organized his followers as the Labor party, and campaigned for the presidency in 1946. In one of Argentina's most honest elections, Perón won with 56 percent of the popular vote.

The story of what followed belongs to the postwar era (see Chapter 14). Yet Perón's rise to power, his charisma, and that of his politically active wife, Eva Duarte Perón, decisively advanced the trend, observable ever since the Radicals' heyday, toward broadened political participation. Events would show that this was still mass politics in the authoritarian mode.

Brazil from Empire to New State

Brazil has such great natural promise that it has been known for centuries as the "land of the future." Unfortunately, the struggle to fulfill this promise has encountered most of the difficulties found elsewhere in South America, together with some distinctive problems.

Colonial Brazil presented the spectacle of a huge colony—now the world's fifth-largest nation in population—dependent on a tiny mother country, Portugal, which itself slipped into dependency on the most powerful economy of the day, Britain. During the Napoleonic Wars, which shaped the European background for Latin American independence, the Portuguese government responded to its danger in a unique way: fleeing to its most important colony. Rio de Janeiro became the imperial capital from 1807 to 1821. This episode led to a political consolidation that enabled Brazil to weather the transition to independence, and later crises, without loss of unity or much political violence. Another consequence was that the Portuguese court, which fled to Brazil in British ships, opened Brazil to free trade and British economic domination.

When the king returned to Portugal in 1821, he left his son, Pedro, as regent in Brazil. Frictions soon developed between colony and mother country, and Pedro declared independence in 1822. In what amounted to a bloodless coup, he assumed the title emperor of Brazil.

For decades, he and his son, Emperor Pedro II, ruled in alliance with slave-owning coffee planters concentrated in three adjoining states: Rio de Janeiro, Minas Gerais, and São Paulo. The alliance was so close that when Brazil abolished slavery in 1888 (the latest emancipation date in the Western Hemisphere), Pedro II fell in a bloodless coup a year later. Emancipation alienated slave owners, who got no compensation for losing their "property." The regime of crown and coffee had already alienated other groups, including military officers and especially the urban populace, from which a commercial-professional middle class and an industrial proletariat would soon emerge.

The Old Republic

The period from 1889 to 1930 is known as the "Old Republic." At first it resembled Argentina's Radical period, in that the urban elites replaced the coffee interests as the politically dominant group. By 1893, however, the new government's clumsy efforts to stimulate the economy and promote industrialization, coupled with shifts in coffee prices, had produced economic crisis and revolts. The government could cope with these only by striking a deal with the coffee planters of São Paulo, who controlled a well-trained militia: support against the rebels in return for the presidency at the next election. Thus in 1894 the political emergence of the urban middle class, which came only later in other Latin American countries, ended for the time being, and the coffee interests regained the ascendancy.

After 1894 the Old Republic turned regressive. With no political parties in existence, the two richest coffee states, São Paulo and Minas Gerais, made a deal to monopolize the presidency. The small size and geographical concen-

tration of the electorate helped make this deal possible. Illiterates could not vote, so the electorate never exceeded 5 percent of the adult population before World War I. Since education and wealth went together, over half of the electorate lived in just four of twenty states: São Paulo, Minas Gerais, Rio de Janeiro, and Rio Grande do Sul.

Securely in power, the coffee interests abandoned the industrialization efforts of 1889–1894. Economic policy concentrated on the agrarian interests of the leading export-producing states. A major government concern was coping with the oversupply that resulted from the spread of coffee production. In 1906 the government set up a system of valorization: large government coffee purchases to drive prices up. This helped Brazil's growers, although no measure taken by a single producing country could overcome the uncertainties of the global commodities markets. Another problem was lack of diversification in agricultural exports. Brazil's second most important export of this period—rubber, which rose from 10 percent of exports in 1890 to 39 percent in 1910—was not cultivated but collected from trees growing wild in Amazonian jungles. When the British began to cultivate rubber in Asia, they destroyed Brazil's position in the world market in a few years.

Between 1910 and 1930, the Old Republic's dominant political alignment fell apart. When the president unexpectedly died in office in 1909, Brazil's first hotly contested presidential race developed. Neither candidate was from one of the big states, and new demands for democratization were heard. After the election, the country faced revolts fed by resentment of oligarchical rule. World War I relieved tension by touching off an agricultural export boom and boosting industrial production. But the boom collapsed soon after the war.

Politicians from São Paulo and Minas Gerais continued to occupy the presidency by turns, but scattered events in the 1920s showed that discontent was spreading. In February 1922 a Modern Art Week was organized in São Paulo to celebrate the centennial of independence. Young artists used the occasion to express rebellion against European forms and determination to develop a Brazilian culture. Here, as later in Mexico, cultural nationalism had political significance, for it meant a growth of interest in the common people. The year 1922 also saw the formation of the Brazilian Communist party. Perhaps more important, army officers began to join the opposition. A handful of junior officers revolted at a fort on Copacabana Beach at Rio de Janeiro and fought to the death for their ill-defined cause. Their seemingly foolish heroics started a series of revolts that lasted until 1930, culminating in the overthrow of the regime. The ideas of the "lieutenants' movement" gradually became widely held demands for revolution, modernization, national integration, and expanded political participation. Soon even the Catholic church was taking an active concern in the plight of workers.

The Depression Destroys the Old Republic

When coffee prices were high, the government could contain such pressures, but a drop in prices threatened the status quo. When the Depression drove coffee from 22.5 cents a pound in 1929 to 8 cents in 1931, making valorization unworkable, things fell apart. The 1930 presidential election destroyed the Old Republic.

The trouble began when the outgoing president selected another man from his state, São Paulo, to run instead of allowing Minas Gerais its turn at the presidency. The Minas Gerais politicians then joined opposition groups all over the country in a Liberal Alliance, which selected Getúlio Vargas, from the southernmost state of Rio Grande do Sul, as its presidential candidate. As always, the incumbent president's candidate won. But when the congress refused to seat some Liberal Alliance overthrew the government. Coming to power

with military backing, Vargas dominated Brazil from 1930 to 1945 and again from 1951 to 1954.

Vargas and the New State

Until 1945, Vargas ruled first as head of the provisional government (1930–1934), then as elected president under the 1934 constitution, and after his 1937 coup as dictatorial head of the "New State" (*Estado Novo*). At first he ruled "provisionally" in the sense that the new constitution was still under preparation. Even so, he established absolute power, cracked down on Right and Left extremists, began to assert the power of the central government over the states in new ways, and cultivated political support among industrial and white-collar workers. He created new ministries for health and education and for labor, industry, and commerce. He paid unprecedented attention to the problems of the Northeast. The elites' confidence that he was theirs freed him to concentrate on corporatist mobilization of the masses.

In 1934, the Constituent Assembly completed the constitution, approved it, and elected Vargas president. The people did not get to vote on either the constitution or Vargas, who thus, said his opponents, became Brazil's "Third Emperor." Political violence from Right and Left and barracks revolts provided him the pretext to reorganize the military and assert federal control over the state militias, furthering his consolidation of central government power. His 1935 National Security Law created a police state. Civil liberties were diminished, and little was done to improve housing or public health. Yet political rhetoric carefully tuned to the masses, astute use of emerging media (radio and newsreels), and official sponsorship of both soccer (*futebol,* previously an elite sport) and samba as symbolic ways to participate in national life won many Brazilian hearts.

Otherwise unable to keep power beyond the end of his constitutional four-year term, Vargas staged a coup against his own government in 1937 and introduced his New State. By now, Vargas believed that only he could achieve national integration. Lowering state flags and raising the national flag, Vargas ended the autonomy of the states. He suppressed independent labor unions and outlawed strikes. Spokesmen for the regime called for "docile submission" to state authority. Now, even members of the government had their phones tapped and their mail opened. In a country with no history of political parties, Vargas did not create one. Politics still meant administration, for which Vargas created a new, federal superagency, the Administrative Department for Public Service (DASP in Portuguese). Politics also meant patronage, which is why the four fishermen from Ceará sailed all the way to Rio to appeal to Gegê, the "father of the poor." Vargas lacked the intent or the means to achieve totalitarian control over such a huge country. Authoritarian but no fascist, he took advantage of a coup attempt by Brazil's real fascists, the Integralistas (see Chapter 6), to eliminate the opposition throughout the country.

For Vargas, nationalism meant not only asserting central power over the states but also development and economic independence. Brazil's first head of state to visit far parts of the country, he called for a "March to the West" to colonize the interior. He founded regional institutes to foster production and sale of agricultural commodities and a social security system as good as any in Latin America, though far from universal in coverage. Using Brazil's neutrality to elicit U.S. aid during World War II, he built Brazil's first steel mill at Volta Redonda, a planned industrial city that symbolized economic independence. Eventually entering the war in 1942 on the Allied side, Brazil became the only Latin American country to send troops to fight.

The end for the Estado Novo came when fighting fascism abroad raised demands for democratization at home, forcing Vargas to call elections for 1945. Vargas's new turn toward democracy alienated the military, and they de-

posed him after fifteen years of support. One of the generals who had led the coup emerged as president, and a new constitution was drawn up. Vargas was elected senator from two states and congressman from a half-dozen others. There would be more to hear from him politically. But the part of his career most significant for Brazil's political and economic development was over.

Mexico and Its Revolutionary Legacy

The revolution of 1910 overshadowed Mexican history throughout the first half of the twentieth century. Chapter 4 has already raised the question of how the Mexican Revolution compares with other revolutions. We must reconsider some aspects of the crisis to understand its significance for Mexico through World War II.

Mexico's Revolutionary Experience

The main problem about Mexico's revolution was that it expressed in politics the Latin American societies' lack of integration. Like the Berkeley-educated Francisco Madero, who called for the republic to "rise in arms" in 1910, many revolutionary leaders came from the elite class. Their ideas, like those of the Argentine Radicals, seldom went beyond political liberalism. Any thought of social and economic change that would upset their interests, which were largely tied to the export sector, was enough to turn most of them into defenders of law and order. Leaders from other classes did identify with the masses, and their appeals roused passions that could not be ignored. Yet the only prominent leader with a consistent social program was the southern caudillo Emiliano Zapata. His slogan of "Reform, Liberty, Justice, and Law" would not have sounded radical to the Bolsheviks, but it did express native Americans' vital interest in seeing their rights to land and to the maintenance of their communal way of life recognized in post-revolutionary Mexico.

Although many hopes were doomed to disappointment, the rising against the regime of Porfirio Díaz plunged Mexico into a decade of brutal violence. More than anything else, it is this impact on the populace, and the vast military and political mobilization that accompanied it, that justified Mexicans in remembering what they went through as an epic struggle. Within a few years, the army numbered a quarter-million, twelve times its size at the fall of Díaz. Vast forces also mobilized in different regions to fight against government troops. Those drawn into the struggle found their lives transformed—and not necessarily for the worse. Hacienda peons and mineworkers escaped into a life of adventure as revolutionary soldiers or, in the case of women, as camp-following *soldaderas,* many of whom also fought. By their testimony, these men and women found these experiences far preferable to their former lives. This does not mean, however, that the revolution they served, served their interests very closely.

At the top, the rebellion pursued a zigzag course under different presidents. First came Madero, elected in 1911. He showed his faith in political democracy but never developed a program for social or economic reform; he also appointed many conservative relatives to high office. Madero was murdered in 1913 by one of his generals, Victoriano Huerta. Assuming the presidency himself, Huerta faced revolts by all the regional leaders. U.S. president Woodrow Wilson was determined to undermine him. In 1914, the U.S. Marines occupied Veracruz. Huerta saw that he could not regain control and resigned. A chaotic period followed, from which Venustiano Carranza emerged as president, partly because Woodrow Wilson gave U.S. recognition to him as the most conservative contender. Angry that he was not the one recognized, Pancho Villa raided Columbus, New Mexico, provoking the punitive expedition that

General John Pershing led into Mexico in 1916–1917.

As these events unfolded, the revolution progressed through three phases. The initial mass mobilization to overthrow Díaz (1910–1914) extended into widespread conflict among revolutionary forces and the destruction of U.S. interests. The second phase (1914–1916)—that of class conflict, U.S. intervention, and worker defeat—included the U.S. occupation of Veracruz in 1914, which set up a vast flow of weapons to the Constitutionalist forces led by Carranza and ended with the urban workers' defeat by middle-class interests. The final phase of synthesis and reorganization included the adoption of the 1917 constitution, pacification of most of the countryside, and the coup that brought Álvaro Obregón to the presidency in 1920. With its concessions to workers and peasants in matters such as land reform and labor relations, the 1917 constitution provided a charter for reconstruction—at least on paper.

Reconstruction and Depression

Two presidents, Álvaro Obregón and Plutarco Calles, dominated the reconstruction period, which lasted until 1934. Taking only limited steps toward fulfilling the constitution, they distributed some 11 million acres of land in the 1920s, mostly as communal lands (*ejidos*) for native American villages. That sufficed to worry hacienda owners but not to satisfy the land-hungry. In education, there were significant efforts to develop rural primary schools to teach native Americans Spanish and draw them into national life. The new interest in rural Mexico also had a profound effect on the arts. Artists such as Diego Rivera (1886–1957) and David Alfaro Siqueiros (1896–1974) were commissioned to paint murals in public buildings. Inspired by indigenous cultures and meant for the people, their works stimulated nationalist feeling and won international acclaim.

Calles in particular enacted important measures for business and industry. Road building, electrification, and the founding of the Bank of Mexico all assisted economic development. Government subsidies and high tariffs on imports also stimulated the growth of consumer-goods industries. But U.S. interests still found ways to flourish inside Mexico's tariff walls, as in 1925 when Ford opened an automobile assembly plant organized on terms highly favorable to the parent company. And frictions continued with U.S. oil companies, which feared that the constitutional restrictions on foreign control of natural resources might yet be applied to them.

In the later 1920s, just as Argentine Radicals and Brazilian coffee oligarchs seemed to run out of ideas, Mexico's reconstruction lost momentum. Aggravated during the revolution, church-state conflict gave rise to a unique church "strike"—no religious services for three years—and a guerrilla war between government forces and Catholic Cristeros. Many Mexican peasants refused to lay down their arms as long as the revolution's promises of land remained unfulfilled. In 1928, even the presidential election degenerated into violence. Two candidates were executed for starting rebellions before the election, and the winner, Obregón, was assassinated by a Cristero before taking office.

Only Calles had enough influence to run the government, but a constitutional amendment prevented any president from succeeding himself. He arranged for puppets to serve Obregón's term while he pulled the strings. Calles also organized the National Revolutionary party (PNR in Spanish, 1929), which, with changes of name, dominated Mexican politics until 1997. The creation from the top of a single mass party in support of the regime suggests the influence of corporatism, if not also European fascism. The virtual suspension of land reform and other social programs in the later Calles years also indicates a shift to the right, which the Depression confirmed. Fortunately for those who still believed in the revolution, a progressive wing was forming in the PNR.

Cárdenas and the "Revolution of the Indians"

The PNR nominated Lázaro Cárdenas, former party chairman and progressive leader, for the presidency in 1934, and he was duly elected. Calles proved unable to control the new president. Democratic in style, Cárdenas made himself accessible to peasants and workers. When Calles made threats, Cárdenas deported him.

Cárdenas brought the revolution to Mexico's native Americans, albeit at a price. Now, even people in the far southern state of Chiapas experienced partial agrarian reform, unions, and abolition of debt peonage. Cárdenas distributed 49 million acres of land, roughly twice as much as all his predecessors, most of it as communal ejidos. The government also provided other facilities—roads, credit, electrification, medical care. The historical patterns of the hacienda system and peasant servitude had been broken. The price was that Mexico's corporatist state had now incorporated societies that had their own forms of communal organization, which now underwent change and deformation. Communal leaders became the first links in the chain or authority that led to the state and federal capitals; instead of landlords, the peasants now faced the government. Still, the land distribution under Cárdenas was the "revolution of the Indians," some of whom laid down their weapons only when they got their land deeds.

Considering how Article 27 of the 1917 constitution had linked the issues of rights to the land and control of the mineral rights coveted by foreigners, Cárdenas's concession of land to the Indian communities led logically to a new assertion of economic independence in 1938. When controversy with U.S. oil companies flared after a strike by Mexican workers, Cárdenas went on the air to announce nationalization of the companies' holdings. The assertion of economic independence created a sensation all over Latin America. The oil companies were outraged; but because the administra-

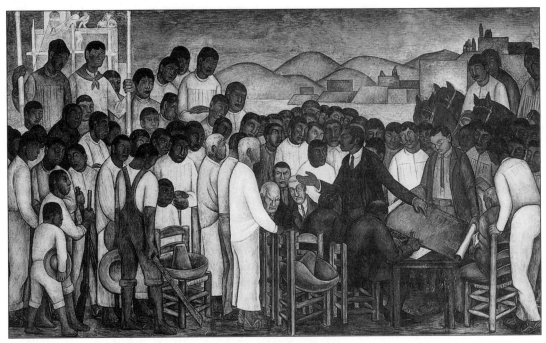

***Diego Rivera,* Distribution of the Land to the Peasants.** *This*
Indian-inspired work illustrates one of the most important issues raised by
Mexico's revolution. Instituto Nacional de Bellas Artes de Mexico/Art Resource, NY

tion of Franklin D. Roosevelt had decided on a policy of nonintervention in Latin America, they had to settle for monetary compensation.

A few days after the oil nationalization, Cárdenas moved to consolidate his domestic support by reorganizing the official party, with agrarian, labor, military, and "popular" (essentially middle-class) sectors. One reason for the long-term dominance of Mexico's single party, known since 1945 as the Institutional Revolutionary party (PRI in Spanish), may be that Cárdenas's corporatist-populist approach to mass mobilization kept workers and peasants separate, in competing sectors.

The events of 1938 marked a high point for Cárdenas. Conservative fears over his policies prompted a flight of Mexican capital abroad and a scaling back of reform during his last two years in office. World War II opened a long period of rapid economic growth but con-

firmed the rightward political shift. After Cárdenas, the revolution, supposedly institutionalized in the PRI, became increasingly a conservative force.

Conclusion: Charismatic Leaders and Their Policies Compared

By World War II, three of Latin America's most important countries had produced memorable charismatic leaders: Perón, Vargas, and Cárdenas. We can sum up the significance of the first half of this century for their countries by comparing these men and their policies.

Each came to power only after demands for mass political participation had already produced changes in his country. The Argentine Radicals' electoral victory in 1910, the urban elites' brief ascendancy in the early years (1889–1894) of Brazil's Old Republic, and Mexico's revolution of 1910 all signified such a broadening. Yet then and later, most politicians had but limited concern for the common people. Neither Madero in Mexico nor Yrigoyen in Argentina had clear policies for attacking socioeconomic, rather than political, problems. Even Zapata made only limited demands.

More than anything else, the Depression exposed such leaders' inadequacies and called forth a new approach. The collapse of the markets for Latin American exports toppled both the Argentine Radicals and the coffee oligarchs of Brazil's Old Republic. Coming after the church-state crisis of the 1920s and the 1928 election violence, the Depression also heightened the confusion of the later Calles years in Mexico.

Out of this disruption, Perón, Vargas, and Cárdenas emerged to carry political mobilization into a new phase. In doing so, they displayed important common characteristics and policies. They all took an authoritarian, corporatist-populist approach to mass mobilization. In Argentina, Perón's followers, drawn largely from the state-controlled labor movement, became the largest party, though not the only one. Vargas's New State monopolized political life, allowing no parties. Cárdenas contributed to the development of Mexico's corporatist single party.

Pursuing nationalist developmental goals, Perón, Cárdenas, and Vargas expanded the state's economic role and pushed for industrialization to overcome the effects of the Depression and economic dependency. Assuming power with Argentina's drive for industrialization already well launched, Perón championed the working class, thus creating for himself a wider base of support than earlier politicians had enjoyed. Vargas ended the coffee interests' political dominance, carried Brazil into the age of heavy industry, and shifted power to the cities, where both the middle class and workers benefited from his authoritarian

paternalism. In Mexico, which also undertook centralized economic planning, Cárdenas transformed land tenure, promoted significant industrialization, and nationalized petroleum.

To break out of economic dependency, Latin American leaders of the Perón-Vargas-Cárdenas era pursued a state-led industrialization strategy aimed first at import substitution behind high tariff barriers and then at heavy industry, without necessarily reforming the agricultural sector. How sound was this strategy?

Adopted when high tariffs prevailed globally, the protectionist import-substitution strategy produced some positive results. Yet neglect of the agricultural sector was unwise. An agricultural policy aimed at reducing inequality in the countryside would have enlarged the market for industrial products by increasing the majority's income. A development policy that increased the efficiency of agriculture could also have helped to provide both capital for industrial investment and food for a population who increasingly worked in factories rather than fields. Finally, rural mass education would have produced a more skilled and productive labor force.

A sound approach to industrialization would have required starting with agriculture and fundamentally changing Latin America's historical pattern of internal colonization. Argentina was a partial exception because it lacked the large peasant class found in other Latin American nations. Mexico was also exceptional because its reforms, especially under Cárdenas, met some of this approach's requirements. But Argentina and Mexico were only local variations in an agrarian problem of continental scope, still unsolved today.

The high import duties typical of the Depression posed another danger to the import-substitution strategy: the protected industries might not develop the ability to compete in international markets. Until domestic need for basic consumer goods had been met, only Mexicans, or Brazilians, or Argentines had to put up with the inferior goods. But a time would come—in the 1960s for these countries—when domestic demand for light industrial goods had been met and industrialization could proceed only by mastering more advanced technologies or facing the competition of world markets. By then, too, U.S. manufacturers' response to the creation of protective barriers (setting up subsidiary firms in Latin America) would show that protectionism offered no sure way to overcome economic dependency.

In time, the state's expanded role in the economy also produced troubling consequences. During the Depression, state initiative may have looked like the only way to advance Latin America's struggle against economic dependency. Then many countries made comparable choices. By 1970, however, the state sectors had grown so much that they accounted for 30 percent or more of all goods and services produced in some Latin American countries, compared to 2 percent in Japan or 4 percent in the United States. This growth vastly expanded government payrolls, injected bureaucratic inefficiencies into the economy, and raised the stakes and bitterness of political struggle. Like the consequences of authoritarian mass mobilization, those of state-led industrialization remained key issues after World War II.

Because most Latin American nations enjoyed political, if not economic, independence when most of Africa and Asia was still struggling against European rule, the problem of choosing effective economic development strategies arose earlier for Latin America than for most other parts of the colonial world. The Depression similarly highlighted questions of economic strategy for the powerful nations of Europe and North America, as noted in Chapter 5. With the collapse of European colonialism after 1945, an increasingly populous and interdependent world would find its attention fixed more and more on problems of resources and productivity such as those discussed here. Many developing nations would repeat Latin America's economic mistakes. Few would do better.

Note

1. "It's All True," based on an unfinished film by Orson Welles, Paramount Pictures; Robert M. Levine, *Father of the Poor? Vargas and His Era*, Cambridge, 1998, 108, 186.

Suggestions for Further Reading

Burns, E. Bradford. *A History of Brazil.* 3d ed. (1993).

Hart, John Mason. *Revolutionary Mexico: The Coming and Process of the Mexican Revolution* (1987).

Keen, Benjamin, and Keith Hayes. *A History of Latin America.* 6th ed. (2000).

Knight, Alan. *The Mexican Revolution.* 2 vols. (1986).

Levine, Robert M. *Father of the Poor? Vargas and His Era* (1998).

Loveman, Brian. *Chile: The Legacy of Hispanic Capitalism.* 2d ed. (1988).

Mallon, Florencia E. *Peasant and Nation: The Making of a Postcolonial Mexico and Peru* (1995).

Meyer, Michael C., William L. Sherman, and Susan M. Deeds. *The Course of Mexican History.* 6th ed. (1999).

Nugent, Daniel, ed. *Rural Revolt in Mexico: U.S. Intervention and the Domain of Subaltern Politics* (1998).

Rock, David. *Authoritarian Argentina: The Nationalist Movement, Its History, and Its Impact* (1993).

Skidmore, Thomas E., and Peter H. Smith. *Modern Latin America.* 4th ed. (1997).

CHAPTER 8

Sub-Saharan Africa Under European Sway

IN NOVEMBER 1929, AT OLOKO IN SOUTHEASTERN NIGERIA, MESSENGER MARK Emeruwa approached a poor woman, Nwanyeruwa, and asked if she had been counted. "Has your mother been counted?" she retorted. They scuffled, and she ran to tell the village women's association, who sent out palm fronds to call a protest meeting. So began the Women's War that lasted into December, spread over two provinces, and left scores of Nigerians dead, all but one of them female. This is often called the "Aba Women's War." The largest actions occurred there, but not the first or the bloodiest. Nigeria's British rulers called this not a war but "riots," depreciating the resistance. In addition, there was a Riot Act, and, once a riot proclamation had been read, troops could fire. They did. The women fired on did not oppose British rule, not yet. They did oppose its local henchmen.

The British could not understand the Women's War. They had perfected their "indirect" method of rule in northern Nigeria, then imposed it on the South. Finding no chiefs there through whom to rule indirectly, they did not ask how local peoples managed their affairs. Instead they named "warrant chiefs," giving them warrants of appointment. These chiefs headed "native courts" with messengers like Mark. The chiefs also had administrative tasks such as census-taking and taxation. Past taxation had taken indirect forms, such as customs duties or compulsory labor. The men might have to carry the goods or even the persons—in litters on poles—of the British. Some warrant chiefs also liked to be carried. Direct taxation of men had started in 1927. The rate was low, but the people were poor. The prices of palm products, their exports, were falling, while increased duties raised import prices. Direct taxation, however, required an accurate headcount. That is what the messenger who accosted the poor woman was working on. There was no plan to tax women, yet that rumor had spread. Although the British were oblivious to it, counting people violated local religious scruples, and taxing women was an explosive idea. The women had cause to resent chiefs and messengers who aided the endeavor.

What was a "Women's War"? The Ibo and Ibibio peoples historically managed their affairs in decentralized ways, without forming states. If gender roles were highly differentiated and men dominated in some ways, women had major entitlements. Economically, they produced specific "women's crops," owned all domestic animals, engaged independently in trade, and controlled their own property. Socially, they had densely networked associations. Marrying outside their native village but retaining ties to their kin, women were in the best position to coordinate action among villages. The women's associations had recognized means of protest, symbolically marked in ways that commanded respect—from all who knew the symbols.

If their rights were violated, the women would "sit on" or "make war" against the offender. A throng of women, clad in a short loincloth draped with ferns and palm fronds, their bodies smeared with pigments, large pestles in their hands, inspired dread as they marched to demand redress. Ferns symbolized protection from evil spirits; palm leaves, invincibility; young palm leaves, peace; and the pestles, the power of the female ancestors. The women would dance and mock their adversary in song. They might also pull his house down. The men stood back: to interfere was sacrilege. Oloko's women "sat on" their warrant chief and toppled him.

In mid-December, after having wrecked the native court, the women of Opobo faced their district officer, ironically named Whiteman. He was backed by reinforcements, including a machine gun. The women demanded his signed agreement to their demands, including no taxation of women, in six typed copies, one for each of their towns. During the typing, more women arrived, new demands were voiced, and some women broke a fence. Whiteman nodded to the soldiers. They fired two volleys, leaving thirty-two dead and more wounded. Stampeded by the firing, other women drowned in the river.

Although it was soon quelled, the Women's War made a difference. British reports compared it to women suffragists' lawbreaking in England and found it "without precedent . . . in the history of the British Empire." In time, the warrant chiefs were replaced by better local administration. Anthropologists were sent to study the region's peoples. The goal was to control them better; the result was to start writing their histories. Mass movements by Nigeria's women continued, proving that indigenous peoples cannot just be colonized: they have their own interests and their own ways to assert them.[1]

Continental Overview: African Diversity, European Domination

Over three times the size of the United States, Africa includes the sites in Kenya where the oldest human fossil remains have been found, as well as the monumental remains in the Nile valley of one of the first great civilizations. Ancient African cultures left behind a rich "triple heritage,"[2] combining indigenous, Semitic, and Greco-Roman elements. Religiously, this heritage expresses itself in Africa's traditional, Islamic, and Christian faiths. In modern times, the triple heritage appears, too, in the interplay of indigenous, Islamic, and Western influences. Africa's past includes much to glorify. Sub-Saharan examples of monumental scale include the remains of Great Zimbabwe and the empires of Ghana and Mali; all three names have been reused to designate modern republics. Subtler expressions of African creativity range from masterpieces in sculpture to widely influential musical styles, the consensual democracy of village Africa, and some African peoples' success at living together without creating states.

African societies have also historically had strong ties to the outside—to the Mediterranean, to the Islamic lands to the east, and to the Americas. Yet understanding the last five hundred years of Africa's history requires recognizing not only its vastness and creativity but also the painful fact that its integration into the modern world has occurred, unfortunately for its peoples, at the price of drastic exploitation and dependency—keynotes of the modern Western part of Africa's triple heritage.

This history of exploitation contains a major paradox, for compared to the Americas and parts of Asia, most of Africa was late in becoming integrated into the European-dominated global pattern. The European voyages of exploration began decades before Columbus, as Portuguese navigators inched their way down Africa's coast. Asia was the principal source of the silks and spices the explorers sought, but Africa also produced precious goods such as gold and ivory. How could Africa remain long outside the sphere of European control?

Disease and topography hindered Europeans in Africa, as did the presence of strong African kingdoms controlling trade to the interior. In the Americas, as noted in Chapter 1, diseases introduced by Europeans helped to ensure European triumph over local populations lacking immunity. Until the advent of modern tropical medicine, however, Europeans could not resist the diseases endemic to Africa. Yellow fever and malaria caused high death rates among newly arrived Europeans. Diseases spread by the tsetse fly made animal transport impracticable in many places. Topography, too, slowed European penetration of the continent; the rivers mostly had high cataracts near the coast, and existing paths were not suitable for wheeled vehicles. Much of European trade with Africa had to connect near the coasts with commercial and political systems controlled by Africans or, in East Africa, by Arabs.

Firearms spread into Africa *from both Europe and the Ottoman Empire.*
The Benin bronze (left) shows the firearm in Portuguese hands. The wooden
sculpture (right) shows the firearm in African hands. Left: Werner Forman
Archive/Art Resource, NY Right: Collection Wereldmuseum Rotterdam, The Netherlands

In the late nineteenth century, however, advances in tropical medicine and military technology made possible an unstoppable European advance into the African interior. To study what followed, this chapter presents an overview of Africa and its history through 1945, followed by closer looks at two of the larger colonies—Nigeria and South Africa. The remainder of this overview examines Africa in terms of key dimensions of its diversity—topography, modes of environmental adaptation, language, social organization, state formation—and some common traits, before examining Europe's impacts and African responses. The more detailed discussions of Nigeria and South Africa then consider how the major themes of twentieth-century history have been illustrated, both in a *peasant colony* like Nigeria, where Africans did not have to contend with large numbers of Europeans, and in a *settler colony,* like South Africa, where they did.

African Diversity

Among many indicators of African diversity, the most basic are ecological differences that divide the continent into zones running across it roughly east and west. Northernmost, Algeria and Morocco have a small coastal zone with a Mediterranean climate like Spain's or Italy's. Below this zone, the Sahara extends from the Atlantic Ocean to the Red Sea; this desert is only the African part of a dry zone that continues across Asia to China. Below the Sahara, desert grades into savanna (a zone of grassland and scattered trees), running from Senegal in the west to the southern Sudan, from which the same environment also extends to the southeast. Next comes the tropical forest, found in a coastal strip running from Senegal through Nigeria, then widening to the east and south to cover the Congo (Zaire) river valley. Pockets of rain forest recur farther south and east. South of the Congo river valley, much the same zones as in the north appear in reverse order: a zone of woodland and shrub; a savanna zone; an arid zone including the Kalahari Desert to the west and grassy steppes in eastern South Africa; finally, a small zone of Mediterranean climate at the Cape of Good Hope. These regions produce many valuable products: rubber, cacao, palm oil, ivory, gold, and diamonds.

One way to classify African peoples is according to how they adapt to their environments, how they survive and obtain food. We can distinguish four adaptations, all of which also exist in other parts of the world. The two more common are agriculture and pastoralism; the two less common are fishing, and hunting and gathering. Most societies have combined various of these activities and have also traded.

In the most ancient way of life, hunting and gathering, people subsist on wild plants and animals, without either agriculture or animal husbandry. This way of life survives for a few Africans like the San of South Africa's open grassland. Hunting-and-gathering communities must remain small and migratory in order to find subsistence year-round. In such communities, which never exceed a few hundred members, the need for chiefship has never been felt. Decision making and control of conflict are communal tasks. Communal egalitarianism and highly developed skills for taking advantage of difficult landscapes are notable features of this way of life.

The first communities to settle permanently in one place were probably fisherfolk, located along rivers, lakes, or the ocean, which provided an adequate food supply year-round. A permanent food supply permitted the formation of larger communities, specialization of roles, and the emergence of chiefs. Few fisher communities survive, but they probably provided the setting for the development of a sedentary (as opposed to migratory) lifestyle, such as later became known in agricultural communities.

Agriculture has long been the most widespread of the environmental adaptations. Cultivating plants and domesticating animals enabled farmers to use the environment more intensively than hunter-gatherers and to spread over more of the landscape than fisherfolk. Agricultural productivity permitted formation of larger societies in which people's roles and statuses became more differentiated, trade began, and the chiefship evolved into kingship. As noted in Chapter 1, this is the process out of which civilizations emerged.

Where conditions were, or became, too dry for agriculture, as in the Sahara, pastoralism appeared. This way of life depends on herding livestock, such as sheep or camels, in zones too arid to support year-round grazing. Pastoralism is a migratory or nomadic way of life, requiring intimate knowledge of the environment because the community's survival depends on knowing how to find grass and water year-round. Chiefship is sometimes an important institution in the pastoralist community, which is normally an extended kin group. But some pastoralist groups have stateless societies in which elders keep order with no formal government. In Africa as in other parts of the world, pastoralists and agriculturalists sometimes clashed over use of the same environments and resources, but they also complemented each other, exchanging agricultural for animal products, for example.

However African societies adapt to the environment, language also differentiates them. Africa has over eight hundred languages and many more dialects. Virtually all of them belong to five language families with common structural traits that indicate a common origin. The Afro-Asiatic family includes the Arabic and Berber languages of North Africa, various languages of Somalia and Ethiopia, and Hausa, widely spoken in West Africa. In western South Africa and adjacent territories are the speakers of the Khoisan languages. The Nilo-Saharan family is found in a zone running from Chad, through the southern Sudan, to the eastern side of Lake Victoria. The fourth language family, Austronesian, is of Southeast Asian origin. This family is found on the island of Madagascar, whose people migrated from Indonesia long ago, bringing a language closely related to Malayo-Polynesian. Africa's most widely dispersed language family is Congo-Kordofanian. Languages of this family, including over four hundred Bantu languages, are spoken across much of the savanna belt of West Africa, the forest zone, and most of the southern part of the continent. Widely spoken in East Africa, Swahili has a Bantu structure but contains many borrowings from Arabic. Finally, several European languages—English, French, Portuguese, Dutch-derived Afrikaans—remain in use. European languages provide common media of communication in regions that might otherwise lack one. But these languages also served as European tools for dividing and ruling Africa.

Variations in concepts of kinship provide yet another way to classify African societies. Historically, some societies were patrilineal, organizing themselves in terms of descent relationships among males; some were matrilineal; and some recognized bilateral kinship. Some societies preferred marriage among kin (endogamy); some preferred marriage among nonkin (exogamy). African societies differed vastly in scale, from bands of a few hunter-gatherers to huge kingdoms ruling many kin groups. Some societies developed complex variations on the kinship theme. For example, the Lunda people of Central Africa practiced perpetual succession (each successor to an office took the name, as well as the title, of the original incumbent) and positional kinship (later occupants of the offices assumed the same kin relationships to one another as the original incumbents had had). If originally several chiefs were brothers, generations later the chiefs bore the same names and were still considered brothers. For many societies, in Africa as elsewhere, nonkin relationships could serve to extend the range of kinship ties. For example, while some African societies may have used slaves for little but their labor, others used them to expand the master's household. The contrast with the plantation slavery of the Americas could be radical. The Ijaw people of the Niger Delta, for example, developed an organizational form known as the canoe house, which began as an extended family plus the family head's slaves. The slaves were treated as members of the household and might succeed to its headship.

Kinship and its extensions, such as slavery or blood brotherhood, were certainly not the only meaningful social relationships. Religious bonds were also extremely important. The Sokoto caliphate of northern Nigeria was one of many African states to grow out of an Islamic reform movement. Groups defined in terms of age and sex were also important. Southeastern Nigerian women used such associations to launch their war in 1929. The Zulu regiments of nineteenth-century South Africa consisted of contemporaries who went through initiation rites together as youths. A Zulu ruler bent on military expansion could use these age-grade societies to separate young fighters from their kin and form them into units dependent on himself alone.

While some African societies succeeded in living stateless, the Zulu example points to the importance of state-formation—another major dimension of African diversity. For example, Ethiopia, the ancient Christian empire, was re-unified between 1855 and 1889. It was the easternmost of a line of states that extended, as of 1800, just south of the Sahara, all the way to the Atlantic coast. Many of these were Muslim, and some—like the Sokoto caliphate in northern Nigeria—had emerged from Islamic revivalist holy war (*jihad*) movements. South of the equator, the large Kongo kingdom that flourished in the sixteenth century had disintegrated, but several other states had emerged. Further east, six states, including Buganda, Rwanda, and Burundi, flourished around 1800 in or near what later became known as Lake Victoria. Large centralized states also existed in what are now Zimbabwe and southern Mozambique. In South Africa, the Zulu and other nations emerged in the early nineteenth century, expanding and clashing with consequences felt two thousand miles to the north.

Christian Ethiopia, Islamic states in the west and east, states following traditional religions in the forest regions and south—Africa's triple religious heritage played a critical role in state-formation. So did economics, as states rose and fell in response to shifting opportunities to trade either commodities like ivory and gold, or slaves. From the sixteenth century on, the spread into Africa of firearms also contributed decisively to state-formation and to the ability of some peoples to enslave others.

One approach to the study of Africa is, then, to classify its societies along dimensions like those mentioned above—the different environments, environmental adaptations, languages, kinship structures, political systems, or religions. However, it is also important to consider shared traits in African history.

Common Traits

Among African societies' common traits, two had especially important implications for the twentieth century: the effects of ethnic and kinship divisions on efforts at large-scale political integration, and the problems created by Africa's relative insulation from the impact of European expansionism until the late nineteenth century.

Especially because they often coincided with linguistic, cultural, and political differences, rivalries among kinship and ethnic groups and among the states of the precolonial period made it easier for Europeans to take power in Africa. As Europeans consolidated their control in the late nineteenth century, most African societies—despite many forms of resistance to be discussed below—proved too underdeveloped technologically to escape subjugation. Africa then had some states that were relatively large and powerful, many microstates of village size, and stateless societies. The larger monarchies were often easiest for Europeans to master, since if they could defeat the ruler, his subjects became theirs. As Nigeria's Women's War implies, stateless societies were hardest to subdue, because practically the only way to gain control was to make each member of the society submit.

As Europeans established control, they consolidated African societies into larger entities, destroying or subordinating pre-existing states in the process. The arbitrary boundaries imperialists drew mostly still survive as those of Africa's independent nations (Map 8.1). Because these boundaries reflected European interests, ignoring and cutting across those of Africans, the European-defined colonies and the states that emerged out of them after independence had an artificial quality in African eyes. In any given colony, Africans of different ethnic backgrounds would unite to oppose European rule, but most Africans had difficulty shifting their primary loyalty from kin and ethnic group to the larger colony and later nation. The western education of the African elites who imported and propagated nationalism opened another gap. In political consciousness, as well as in language and ethnicity, colonial nationalists might differ from the masses they sought to

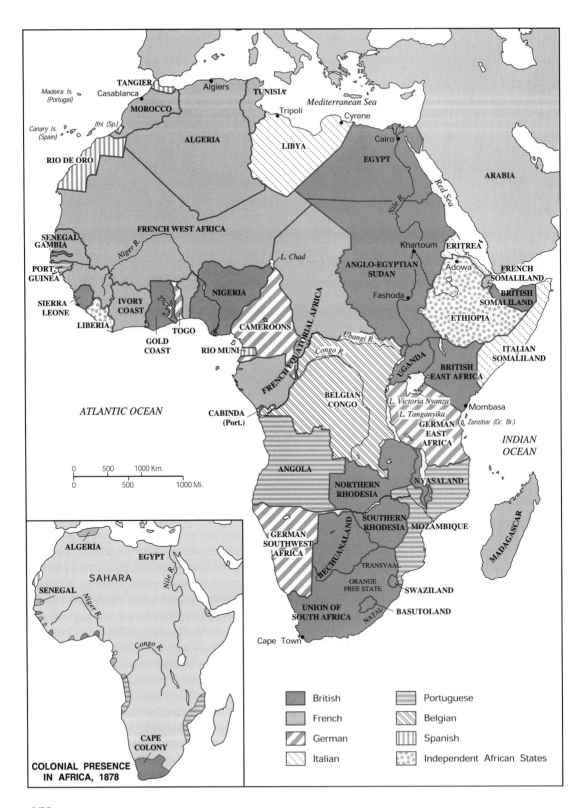

Madeira Is.
(Portugal)

TANGIER
Casablanca

Ifni (Sp.)

Canary Is.
(Spain)

RIO DE ORO

MOROCCO

ALGIERS

TUNISIA

Mediterranean Sea

Tripoli

Cyrene

ALGERIA

LIBYA

EGYPT

Cairo

Nile R.

Red Sea

ARABIA

FRENCH WEST AFRICA

SENEGAL
GAMBIA

Niger R.

PORT.
GUINEA

L. Chad

Khartoum

ERITREA

ANGLO-EGYPTIAN
SUDAN

Adowa

FRENCH
SOMALILAND

BRITISH
SOMALILAND

SIERRA
LEONE

IVORY
COAST

NIGERIA

Fashoda

ETHIOPIA

LIBERIA

GOLD
COAST

TOGO

CAMEROONS

RIO MUNI

FRENCH EQUATORIAL AFRICA

Ubangi R.

Congo R.

UGANDA

BRITISH
EAST
AFRICA

ITALIAN
SOMALILAND

ATLANTIC OCEAN

CABINDA
(Port.)

BELGIAN
CONGO

L. Victoria Nyanza

L. Tanganyika

Mombasa

Zanzibar (Gr. Br.)

GERMAN
EAST
AFRICA

INDIAN
OCEAN

0   500   1000 Km.
0   500   1000 Mi.

ANGOLA

NORTHERN
RHODESIA

NYASALAND

MADAGASCAR

GERMAN
SOUTHWEST
AFRICA

BECHUANALAND

SOUTHERN
RHODESIA

MOZAMBIQUE

TRANSVAAL

ORANGE
FREE STATE

SWAZILAND

NATAL

BASUTOLAND

UNION OF
SOUTH AFRICA

Cape Town

ALGERIA

EGYPT

SAHARA

SENEGAL

Niger R.

Nile R.

Congo R.

CAPE
COLONY

COLONIAL PRESENCE
IN AFRICA, 1878

British

French

German

Italian

Portuguese

Belgian

Spanish

Independent African States

172

mobilize. Splits in independence movements resulted from such gaps, as could the subordination of postindependence national politics to ethnic and regional interests. These are generic problems of colonial nationalism and state building. No European state fully lived up to the nation-state ideal; the nations that colonialism created did so far less.

African societies also suffered from the lateness and abruptness with which the European impact hit much of the continent. It may seem strange to argue that Africa suffered by being insulated from the full impact of imperialism until the late nineteenth century. Yet Europe had begun to develop so rapidly, in its technologies of production and destruction, that insulation from European expansionism tended to make its impact more destructive when it could no longer be averted.

Integration into the Europe-centered Global Pattern

Africa's integration into the European-dominated world progressed in several stages. The transatlantic slave trade dominated the first. Africans were already trading in slaves when the Europeans appeared off their coasts. The European export of African slaves quickly began and grew as Europeans spread the plantation system of agriculture in the Americas. In the end, perhaps 12 million slaves were exported to the Americas, mostly from West and Central Africa. Many died. An older, Islamic slave trade across the Sahara and the Red Sea also continued, accounting for perhaps 5 million people during the period of the transatlantic trade. Africans thus became widely dispersed in the world, a fact with major consequences for today's identity politics.

◀ *Map 8.1 Africa, 1914*

Though Europeans were long unable to enter Africa's interior, the slave trade produced profound changes there too. Slave trading played an important part in the economies of various African states; West African examples include Asante, which also exported gold and ivory, and Dahomey. In West Central Africa, the Imbangala people specialized in the slave trade for over two centuries. Accustomed to trading in prisoners of war and criminals and knowing little of the nature of slavery across the Atlantic, many Africans were little more shocked by the trade than were Europeans.

In the nineteenth century, "legitimate" trade in industrial, agricultural, and mineral products replaced slaving as Africa's main tie to the world economy. The change owed more to economics than to abolitionism. Britain's abolition of the slave trade (1807) coincided not only with growing interest in human rights but also with the Industrial Revolution. British ships had new products to take to Africa, and British demand for raw materials began to exert a stronger pull on African exports than did American demand for slaves.

African societies had to reorient themselves as trade shifted in character and grew in volume. In the Niger Delta, which had been the most prolific source of slaves for export, the volume of legitimate trade increased 87 percent between 1830 and 1850. At the same time, Europeans began to extend the influence of their coastal representatives: consuls, explorers, missionaries, and merchants. There were also efforts to resettle freed blacks in Africa—the British settlement at Sierra Leone (1787) and the U.S. settlement in Liberia (1822). The pace of European involvement was quickening.

The 1880s marked the critical phase in consolidation of European control. Several factors combined to start what Europeans called the "scramble for Africa," as noted in Chapter 2. By 1914, only Liberia and Ethiopia remained independent. In a continent where precise linear boundaries were scarcely heard of, Europe-

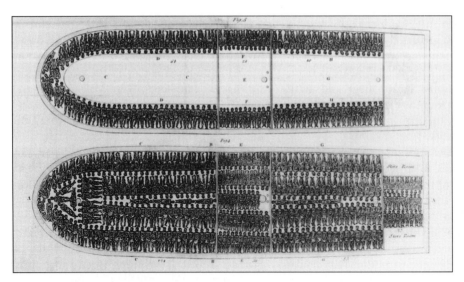

Inhuman conditions in the Trans-Atlantic slave trade. *An abolitionist visual aid, this diagram shows how slaves were packed on shipboard for the rough crossing. Many died. Still the traders made large profits on the survivors.* Fotomas Index

ans carved out colonies as they pleased. The resulting territorial divisions reflected the perspective of someone entering from the coast. Togo was just a thin strip running in from the sea. The Belgian Congo, in contrast, was a vast interior expanse, but it too had an outlet to the sea. Capital cities grew up on the coast as beachheads of imperialism. Everywhere, boundaries cut across patterns of settlement and economic life that mattered to Africans. European imperialists did not care. Their aim was to plant the flag and claim their "place in the sun." Virtually all of Africa was thus divided into dependencies of seven European states (see Map 8.1).

Although World War I weakened European power, and Woodrow Wilson's principle of self-determination attracted attention around the world, European dominance of Africa appeared to become even stronger during the interwar years. Defeated Germany lost its colonies, but they were entrusted to Belgium, France, South Africa, and Britain under mandates from the League of Nations. Mandates theoretically differed from colonies, for the powers that held

the mandates were accountable to the League of Nations. Because the League was not a strong organization, not all mandatory powers lived up to their obligations. Not until 1990 did South Africa give up control of Namibia (the former German colony of South-West Africa), which it had continued to administer despite United Nations resolutions revoking its mandate (see Chapter 15). European empire building in Africa did not stop, even with the mandates. In 1935, Mussolini's Italy invaded Ethiopia—the last campaign in the conquest of Africa and the first for Africa in World War II. Italy held Ethiopia only until 1941. During those few years, Liberia was the only independent African nation, and it was a virtual colony of the Firestone Rubber Company, which owned millions of acres of plantations.

The Impact of Colonial Rule

Inside the colonies and mandates, political and economic conditions varied. The biggest difference was that of settler colonies and peasant colonies. Settler colonies developed regimes that allowed political participation to whites but few rights to Africans. In peasant colonies, Europeans, few in number, viewed government as a matter of administration, not politics, and scarcely allowed questions of political participation to come up. There were also differences of national style in colonial administration. As compared to the British, French administration was more centralized, allowing local chiefs no real power and their people no political rights. Yet conditions everywhere were enough alike to permit generalizations.

In an era when many Europeans thought their racial superiority to other peoples was a matter of scientific fact, the foremost trait of colonialism was racism and lack of understanding of Africans. Europeans were likely to dismiss Africans who acquired a Western-style education as "trousered natives" and all others as "savages." Educated Africans did risk becoming alienated from their own peoples. The French and Portuguese encouraged just that by offering full citizenship rights to individuals who met certain cultural standards. The Portuguese called such people *assimilados* (assimilated). The French used the patronizing term *évolués* (ones who have "evolved").

All forms of colonial rule were disruptive. Where white settlers were not present to contend for power, the organization of colonial rule ranged from military despotism to the British ideal of "indirect" rule—a policy choice recommended by the limited investment that Europeans were willing to make in colonial administration. The impact of indirect rule varied greatly, depending on whether or not there were local rulers who could be taken under "protectorate" and tied into a colonial hierarchy with only a few Europeans at the top. Nigeria's Women's War illustrates how poorly "indirect rule" worked in historically stateless African societies. There, troubles with "warrant chiefs" and court clerks showed how the European impact extended below the local rulers to the grassroots level. The fact that Europeans usually lacked the concern or language skills to control the chiefs and their agents enabled them to become corrupt petty tyrants. Anthropology, now an established scholarly discipline, was then only emerging, all too often as an applied science frankly in service to colonialism.

Colonial administrators cared little for political development or social needs. The administrators at first relied on missionaries to meet such needs as education or public health and only slowly broadened the range of government functions. Some imperialists acknowledged a responsibility to prepare the people of their colonies for self-government in the remote future, but they felt no responsibility to develop the colonies' resources for the benefit of the populace. They exploited those resources for the world market.

In Africa the colonial economic pattern assumed even starker contours than in Latin America, and no country except South Africa came close to moving beyond economic dependency. African prosperity, too, rested on single-crop agriculture or exports of raw materials produced by mining. Working conditions were scandalous and highly unequal for Africans and whites. In 1939, black South Africans in mining or industry received one-eighth the wages of whites in the same jobs. Export agriculture centered on such crops as palm kernels and palm oil, peanuts, cotton, rubber, and cacao. Plantations did not totally dominate agriculture, especially in West Africa. Yet even independent African producers suffered indirect exploitation by the varied interests—trading companies, local middlemen, banks, shippers, insurance companies—that stood between them and the faraway markets for colonial goods. The governments had intimate links to these interests and aided them by such means as requiring forced labor or imposing taxes that could be paid only in money, thus forcing Africans to produce new crops for export or to hire out as wage laborers.

One principle of colonial administration was that each colony should be financially self-sufficient. In the Belgian Congo, this policy degenerated into an "economy of pillage." Everywhere, colonial economies were at the mercy of fluctuating commodity prices. The Depression of 1929 underscored this fact so strongly that Britain and France began to consider economic diversification and improvements in public welfare for their colonies. But few practical improvements emerged before World War II. Economically, far from preparing Africa for independence, colonial rule led to what radical critics call "the development of underdevelopment."

African Responses to Imperialism

African responses to Europeans have a long history. Even before the late nineteenth century, many African economic systems and states had developed as responses to European-created changes. Some religious movements, too, expressed African reactions against Europeans. Whereas many Africans adopted Christianity in European forms, others joined anti-European movements that grew out of African traditional religion, Islam, or Christianity itself. One such movement began when Nongqause, a Xhosa girl in South Africa, saw in a vision in 1856 that, if her people would destroy their cattle, their ancient heroes would be reborn and the Europeans would be driven into the sea (starvation resulted instead). Opposition to Europeans also took the form of Islamic *jihad* movements— such as that of Muhammad Ahmad, who claimed to be the Mahdi (the leader who would restore justice to Muslims at the end of time) and who successfully fought off the British in the Sudan of the 1880s—and Africanized churches like the one founded in the Belgian Congo by Simon Kimbangu (d. 1951), a black prophet for a black people. One hallmark of the movements based on Christianity or African religions was the prominent role women took as leaders, even founders—such as Kimbangu's

precursor in Africanizing Christianity in the Congo, Donna Beatrice (martyred 1706).

To respond to European inroads, African rulers had a range of choices, from armed resistance to accommodation. By defeating the Italians in 1896, Ethiopia became the only African country to defend itself successfully against imperialism, until it fell to Mussolini in 1935. But other nineteenth-century kingdoms, such as the Zulu of southern Africa and the Asante of what is now Ghana, managed to resist colonial occupation for decades. Some ethnic groups—the Maures of Mauritania and the Nuer of the Sudan, for example—managed to resist the Europeans until the 1930s. Faced with European encroachment, African men and women responded with an outburst of creativity and leadership, organizing resistance movements based on ideas and symbols drawn from indigenous belief systems, Islam, or even European ideologies.

Even where armed resistance was not totally successful, it was seldom entirely futile, for it forced thinly staffed European administrations to see that their power was limited and partly dependent on indigenous military and police forces. Not only resistance but accommodation, too, might have advantages for Africans, by enabling them to influence the terms of colonial rule.

After colonization, Africans created new institutions to pursue their interests. In Senegal, public letter writers helped develop a communications network linking the French-educated urban leaders to the rural populace. In South Africa, efforts to form broadly based African political organizations began during the 1880s.

World War I also affected Africa in important ways. Thousands of Africans from the French colonies served on the western front, as noted in Chapter 3. Because African territories under German and Allied control shared borders, there was some fighting in Africa. The Allied seizure of Togo, Cameroon, and South-West Africa presented little difficulty, but the campaign for German East Africa lasted for most of the war and involved many African troops. For Africans as for other colonial peoples, the spectacle of a brutal war among their colonial masters shattered the myth of European supremacy.

Consequently, Africans grew more assertive after World War I. In West Africa, wartime pressures provoked widespread rioting in Sierra Leone, and a political association, the National Congress of British West Africa, was formed in 1920. In the towns, recent migrants from the countryside began to form voluntary associations, alumni groups, dance societies, sports clubs, and religious or ethnic associations. Such groups provided needed support for people who were not yet at home in town. The societies served, too, as communication channels between town and hinterland. In time, the societies became channels for political mobilization, as political organizations grew out of them. In the sense that the educated elites who led the nationalist movements had acquired political ideas different from those of most of their compatriots, political mobilization in Africa displayed elite-mass gaps like those seen in the authoritarian mobilizations of India or Latin America (see Chapters 4 and 7). One sign of Africans' limited adjustment to the new colonial boundaries was that nationalism also focused at first on larger entities: unity for English- or French-speaking West Africa, or unity for all Africa (Pan-Africanism), which appealed to Africans as a response to colonial racism.

World War II precipitated the end of colonial rule. In 1935 Italy's attack on Ethiopia—the ancient Christian kingdom whose culture and independence symbolized for blacks everywhere all that colonialism denied them—started a trend of radicalization. From 1941 to 1943, North Africa provided the stage for major campaigns. All Africans suffered from wartime shortages and restrictions. Far more than in World War I, Africans were drawn into forces fighting around the world. They saw that Europeans were not all governors and generals:

many were peasants and privates who bled and died as they did. Broadened awareness and increased confidence reinforced existing pressures for political mobilization. For nonsettler colonies such as Nigeria, the age of independence was coming, although it did not open for most until the 1960s. For settler colonies such as South Africa, the struggle would be longer and harder.

Nigeria Under the British

Nigeria today is Africa's most populous state and one of its most important. Like most African nations, it is a colonial creation and shares the diversity of the continent as a whole. Nigeria's peoples speak several hundred languages or dialects from various language families. Four peoples have been especially prominent in Nigeria's modern history, however. The Hausa and Fulani live in the semiarid northern savanna, where Muslims form a majority. In the forest near the coast, where traditional religions historically prevailed, are the Yoruba in the west and the Ibo in the east.

Unification Under British Rule

Nigerian history had unifying factors even before Europeans arrived. Yet their coming reoriented the economy toward the sea, rather than toward the old trans-Saharan trade routes, and tied Nigeria's regions together. Through the early nineteenth century, the main theme in the reorientation was the slave trade, which drew many of its victims from the Ibo lands of the southeast and the Yoruba lands of the southwest.

For a long time, Europeans had little effect on northern Nigeria, which still responded more to stimuli coming from other Islamic lands across the Sahara. The most important event of the century preceding British rule was one of the Islamic revival movements then sweeping the Islamic world. The movement began among Fulani townspeople, turning them against the Hausa rulers under whom they lived. Led by the religious activist Usman dan Fodio, the movement erupted in 1804, toppled the Hausa kings, and established a caliphate—the term implies a state organized strictly according to early Islamic practice—centered at Sokoto. When the British eventually took control in northern Nigeria, they did so by defeating the Sokoto caliphate.

First, the British had to take the coastal zone. This occurred as slaving gave way to legitimate trade. Not all of Africa had commodities, other than slaves, that Europeans valued. But the Niger Delta had several. The most important was palm oil, used for soapmaking (hence the name "Palmolive") and as a lubricant. By mid-century, British naval and consular personnel had become assertive in regulating trade. In 1861, the British annexed Lagos on the western coast and soon after appointed a governor. Lagos later became the capital of all Nigeria, a fact that gave the Yoruba people of the vicinity exceptional prominence in Nigerian politics.

European interest also extended into the interior. In 1854 an exploration mission, using quinine against malaria, penetrated nine hundred miles inland without the fearful loss of life seen in earlier attempts. Missionaries and merchants then enlarged their efforts. The original missionaries in southwestern Nigeria were "recaptives," people recaptured from slavery, like Bishop Samuel Ajayi Crowther, who had been educated in Sierra Leone and had returned to work among his Yoruba people. Nonetheless, the confrontation of cultures by 1900 had assumed the conflict-ridden form depicted in Chinua Achebe's aptly named novel about what happened when the first whites arrived in an Ibo village: *Things Fall Apart* (1959).

It was traders who put Nigeria together economically and politically. In the 1870s the companies trading on the Niger River combined into the United African Company. The British government gave it the right to make treaties with local chiefs. After the Berlin African Congress of 1884–1885, the British claimed the territory around the Niger. By 1900 they had established several protectorates in what is now Nigeria and created a military force, the West African Frontier Force, to operate in the interior under command of Frederick Lugard. He more than anyone consolidated British rule in Nigeria.

In 1900, rivalry with the French to the west and desire for greater coordination inside Nigeria led the British government to take over the functions of the trading company, then known as the Royal Niger Company. The country was reorganized into the Lagos Colony and separate Northern and Southern Protectorates, with Lugard as governor in the north. In the south, British control was a reality. In the north, Lugard's mission was to make it so.

Lugard had only a small force with which to conquer the Sokoto caliphate, which, though in decline, presented a huge target. This situation suggested to Lugard the policy of *indirect rule,* which he is often credited with creating, though the British had long used it in India. The strategy was to defeat the rulers of the caliphate, then take over their government apparatus and dominate their former subjects through it. Superior technology enabled Lugard to achieve military success by 1903 and then consolidate indirect rule in the north. In 1912 he was appointed governor-general with the task of "amalgamating" Nigeria under a single administration, a task formally completed on January 1, 1914.

Development Under the British

Between 1900 and 1914 the consolidation of British rule quickly broke down accustomed ways of life. Economic development was extensive, although starting from income levels so low that the results were impressive only on a colonial scale. Political amalgamation created a huge free-trade area. Local rulers were deprived of trade tolls they had collected; but trade grew, and the distribution of wealth and power shifted. A major integrating factor was the railway. When it reached Kano, a key city of the Sokoto caliphate, in 1911, peanut shipments from that town rose to 19,288 tons, up from 1,179 tons the year before. Amalgamation also gave Nigeria its first uniform monetary system.

Cultural and administrative change accompanied economic development. Missionaries challenged traditional beliefs but offered the country its first common system of literacy. Initial suspicion of missionary education waned as people saw that it offered opportunities in economic life and in the administration. Western-educated Nigerian men who moved into low-level central administrative jobs became the first Africans oriented to thinking of Nigeria as a whole. In the north, where the Sokoto caliphate survived under British protection, indirect rule made government less flexible and more autocratic. More serious consequences followed when Lugard's attempt to introduce his pet policy to the south led to the appointment of warrant chiefs among the stateless peoples there.

Change slowed between the world wars. The administrative system, introduced abruptly on the eve of World War I, evolved only gradually after 1918. Economic change slowed as well, especially after 1929. Nigeria still had only 1,903 miles of railroad track in 1945. Foreign trade grew in value from 0.2 British pounds for each Nigerian in 1900 to 1.3 pounds in 1945—a substantial rate of increase yet at low levels that indicate minimal purchasing power. By World War II, industrialization had barely begun outside of mining. Low per capita incomes limited the internal market for industrial products and made it difficult for the governor to raise revenue to support development projects. As in all colonial economies, severe fluctuations in export prices hindered development, a point illustrated by the link between the Depression and Nigeria's Women's War of 1929.

The Rise of Nigerian Nationalism

Nigerian political activism emerged as a demand for participation, not independence. The National Congress of British West Africa, a political association founded in 1920, included representatives of four British colonies: Gambia, Sierra Leone, Gold Coast (now Ghana), and Nigeria. Its demands included an end to racial discrimination in civil service appointments, control of specific administrative functions, and the opening of a university in West Africa.

In 1920, Europeans still felt they could reject such demands outright. Yet small concessions occurred. The Lagos town council became elective in 1920. More important, under the constitution of 1922, elected African representatives joined the colony's legislative council, though they were outnumbered there by the governor and his staff. Comparable provisions appeared in the constitutions of Sierra Leone (1924) and the Gold Coast (1927). Political parties quickly formed at Lagos to contest the seats, and newspapers sprang up to support the parties.

At first this political activity remained largely localized at Lagos, among the Yoruba people. In other regions nationalist politics emerged only later, or in different forms. In the north, as in the princely states of India, indirect rule fossilized the political forms of a bygone era. In the southeast the main problem was resentment of warrant chiefs, which boiled over in the 1929 Women's War.

In the 1930s the Depression, the growing integration of the country, and modest gains in education stimulated the emergence of new political movements. One of the first, the West African Students' Union formed in London, greatly influenced later nationalist leaders. The Nigerian Youth Movement, in turn, formed at Lagos in 1936. It became an organization of national importance under leadership of Dr. Nnamdi ("Zik") Azikiwe, a U.S.-educated Ibo, the first prominent non-Yoruba politician. The

Nigerian Youth Movement suffered because of quarrels among its leaders, and the fact that different leaders came from different peoples injected ethnic rivalries into the national movement.

As the 1930s wore on, Nigerian nationalists pressed for economic and social, as well as political, concessions. World War II, which stimulated growth in the economy and the labor movement, heightened these demands. In 1944, after virtual disintegration of the Nigerian Youth Movement, Azikiwe founded the National Council of Nigeria and the Cameroons (NCNC), a confederation of trade unions, small parties, ethnic associations, and other groups, to pursue these goals. When the British introduced a new constitution in 1947 without consulting Nigerians on its terms, virtually all the nationalists attacked it. With colonial-style political mobilization well advanced, Nigeria began to move, not toward participation but toward independence.

As concerned British-Nigerian relations, the transition to independence would prove relatively easy. To close the elite-mass gap in education and political awareness, or to divide power among Nigeria's peoples and regions so as to ensure peace and unity, would prove greater challenges.

South Africa: A History of Two Struggles

Two struggles shaped today's South Africa. One was between two white communities—the British and the Afrikaners, who are largely of Dutch origin—for political control. The other was between Europeans, of either community, and Africans. While Africans strove to remain autonomous as peasants or wage laborers, European farmers wanted to exploit African families as farm workers, and white mine owners wanted cheap male labor for the mines.

White settlement in South Africa began almost accidentally when the Dutch East India Company set up a station at the Cape of Good Hope on the way to its possessions in what is now Indonesia. In 1657 the company allowed colonization of the countryside. Gradually, a Dutch-speaking, slave-owning agricultural community developed, favored by the moderate climate near the Cape. Over generations, the Boers (Dutch for "peasant" or "farmer") spread out, coming into conflict with African peoples. As Europeans expanded from the sparsely settled territories in the west into the more thickly settled territories of the Bantu-speakers in the east, these conflicts became serious. Adapting their Calvinist faith to justify their intentions, the Dutch identified white dominance with the will of God. Enough racial mixing occurred to form a "colored" population—the South African term for people of mixed ancestry—but racial mixing remained less extensive than in Latin America.

Dutch expansion to the east worsened existing competition for land among the Bantu-speaking chiefdoms there. By the early nineteenth century, a people that needed more land for its cattle could expand only at the expense of its neighbors. One people, the Zulus, did this with dramatic results, referred to in Zulu as the *mfecane* (crushing) of the peoples.

The Zulus' rise to military power was the work of Shaka (1787-1828). Becoming chief in 1816, he reformed an existing system of military organization based on age-regiments. He tightened discipline over his regiments and improved their tactics and weapons. In addition, he expanded the powers of Zulu kingship and enlarged the scope of war into a total effort to wipe out his enemies' resistance and incorporate the survivors into his own kingdom. In 1818, Shaka embarked on a career of conquest. The effects were felt far and wide. Some peoples fled his forces, clashing with one another. Some fled toward Cape Colony, worsening conflict with the Dutch. Some started their own campaigns of conquest, extending as far as Lake Victoria. The mfecane became one of the most widely felt upheavals of nineteenth-century Africa. The Zulus remained an independent nation on the Indian Ocean coast of Natal into the late 1870s, and a Zulu rising occurred as late as 1906. At least two other states emerging from the mfecane—the Swazi kingdom and Lesotho—proved strong enough to resist both Zulus and Europeans.

Meanwhile, conflict had developed within South Africa's white population. The democratic ideas that swept Europe and the Americas in the late eighteenth century also influenced the Dutch at the Cape of Good Hope, awakening a concern for individual rights (their own, at least) and republicanism. Then, as a consequence of the Napoleonic Wars in Europe, Cape Colony came under British control, permanently so in 1806. The ideas of Dutch rights and republicanism became ways to express anti-British feeling.

British settlers started arriving in 1820 and disapproved of much the Dutch said and did. British missionaries were shocked at the way the Dutch treated Africans. The British soon abolished slavery and enacted other reforms. In 1853 they granted the Cape Colony a constitution that allowed for parliamentary government and a nonracial franchise for males, although a property qualification limited black registration. Ultimately, British-Dutch differences gave rise to Afrikaner nationalism and spurred the development of Afrikaans, derived from Dutch, into a language in its own right.

Many Dutch had had too much of British policy long before 1853. By the 1830s, some had decided on migration (*trek* in Dutch) beyond the frontiers of Cape Colony. They would create a republic, their ideal political form, where they could assure "proper relations" between blacks and whites. Their frustrations and the mfecane interacted, for the Dutch learned that lands to the east of Cape Colony had been depopulated and turned into grazing land by the Zulus. By

1839, Dutch migrants had defeated the Zulus and set up a republic in Natal. Unwilling to accept this arrangement, the British annexed Natal in 1845. But the Dutch migrated again and created the republics of the Transvaal and the Orange Free State to the north. The British recognized these states in 1852 and 1854. At that point, the area now covered by South Africa consisted of two British colonies (Cape Colony and Natal), the two Dutch republics, and numerous African chiefdoms and kingdoms.

In the late nineteenth century, both the black-white struggle over land and labor and the Afrikaner-British struggle for political dominance intensified. The land struggle proved tragically unequal, as it did in many other cases where capitalistic and communalistic economic outlooks confronted each other in the age of European expansion. Whites took much land by conquest and much by other means. They entered the struggle for land armed with tools and ideas unfamiliar to Africans: surveying instruments, title deeds, and the very ideas of individual ownership and a market for land sales. Conquest empowered the whites to create a legal environment that enforced their ideas. In some cases, unwary Africans traded land rights for guns or liquor or, where formerly communal lands had been divided into individual holdings, lost their land through inability to adjust their way of life quickly to the new conditions. For those who lost their land, exploitation as farm workers or miners was hard to avoid. In a few cases, African rulers avoided annexation by getting their kingdoms made protectorates of the British crown. By this means, Swaziland, Bechuanaland (now Botswana), and Basutoland (Lesotho) remained separate as High Commission Territories when the Union of South Africa was formed in 1910. They acquired formal independence in the 1960s.

Competition for the land and its resources was also a major factor in the Afrikaner-British struggle. In 1867, diamonds were discovered near the junction of the Orange and Vaal rivers, just outside the western edge of the Orange Free State. That discovery began a race between the British—who won—and the Orange Free State to annex the diamond territory. Then, in 1886, gold was found in the Transvaal at Witwatersrand, near Johannesburg. An influx of gold-hungry outlanders (*uitlanders*) ensued, and the building of railway lines toward the mining centers accelerated. South Africa had four thousand miles of track by 1899. Afrikaners felt threatened, for most of the great entrepreneurs were British. The outstanding example was Cecil Rhodes (1853–1902), who acquired vast wealth from gold and diamonds, served as prime minister of Cape Colony in the early 1890s, and directed British expansion into the regions that became Northern and Southern Rhodesia (now Zambia and Zimbabwe), thus blocking Afrikaner dreams of expansion to the north.

In the 1890s, Anglo-Afrikaner tensions reached a climax. Rhodes tried to destabilize the Transvaal government by inciting the outlander gold seekers to revolt. In 1895 a raid led by a Rhodes agent, Leander Starr Jameson, tried to raise a revolt but failed. Reactions to this episode finished Rhodes's political career. But because major nations' monetary systems were based on gold, the British government took over the struggle to control South Africa and provoked a showdown. War broke out in 1899 and lasted until 1902.

Compared to other colonial wars, the Boer War proved trying indeed. Afrikaner commandos used guerrilla tactics deep in British territory. Not prepared for that kind of war, the British responded brutally, burning farms and moving civilians into concentration camps, where over twenty-five thousand died of disease. The war turned into one of attrition, which the Afrikaners could not win. The British got peace on their terms in 1902, after a bitter foretaste of twentieth-century conflicts.

The Union of South Africa: Politics and Economy

The Boer War set the stage for South Africa's unification. Having bullied the Afrikaners, the British now yielded to many of their demands. The Afrikaners found, too, that they could get more through conciliation—for example, by soft-pedaling their wish for a republic. In 1910, after long negotiation between the two white communities but no consultation of nonwhites, the four colonies became the Union of South Africa under a constitution that recognized the union as a dominion (a term used for former colonies that won autonomy within the British Empire). A governor-general, representing the British monarch, headed the government, which had a two-chamber parliament. Dutch and English were both official languages. Because the British feared that extending the colorblind franchise of the Cape Colony to the entire country would wreck the union, voting rights were left as they had been in each of the colonies before union. As a result, nonwhites remained permanently disenfranchised in Transvaal and the Orange Free State. Peace with fellow whites mattered more to the British than votes for Africans, whose cheap labor mattered most of all.

So began the Union of South Africa, as the country was known until it became a republic and broke with the British Commonwealth in 1961. Three trends dominated the country's development through 1945. The Afrikaners, the majority among whites (about 60 percent in the 1970s), gained political control. The rights of nonwhites—the real majority—were steadily reduced. Finally, thanks to mineral wealth and exploited black labor, the country grew from an economy based on mining to one combining mineral exports with industrial self-sufficiency. South Africa's industrialization was a rare achievement in the colonial world, but one with grim social and political costs.

The Union's political life began auspiciously. The first two prime ministers, Louis Botha (1910–1919) and Jan Smuts (1919–1924), belonged to the South African party. Boer generals who had fought the British, they now tried to unite the white communities. They also participated in the Paris Peace Conference and influenced the emerging concept of the British Commonwealth. Smuts suggested the mandate concept that the League of Nations adopted, and South Africa acquired South-West Africa (Namibia) as a mandate. Smuts gained renown as a world-class statesman.

The untroubled mood of 1910 did not last long. Facing an economy dominated by English-speakers, Afrikaners struggled to win political predominance and then reshape South Africa to suit them. Founding the National party in 1913, J. B. M. Hertzog symbolizes the first phase of this push. His movement opposed South Africa's participation in World War I and later other ties to Great Britain. It steadily hardened on racial issues. When mine owners tried to cut costs by admitting blacks to jobs previously held by whites, the white workers rebelled in the Rand Rebellion of 1922 under the paradoxical slogan "Workers of the World, Unite for a White South Africa." The political consequences of the Rand Rebellion helped Hertzog achieve power in 1924. The policies of his government (1924–1933) were those of Afrikaner nationalists opposed to both British and blacks. He expanded the Afrikaner role in government, which had previously been dominated by English-speakers. He recruited Afrikaners into government service, made Afrikaans (as well as Dutch) an official language, and required it to be taught in school. Taking advantage of the British Statute of Westminster (1931), which turned the empire into a Commonwealth and gave the dominions complete independence to make laws and conduct foreign relations, he moved toward greater independence from Britain. Given English-speakers' control of the private sector, he used state intervention to expand Afrikaner roles in economic development. For example, the South African Iron and Steel Corporation, a government firm set up in 1927, both created jobs for Afrikaners and used the country's abundant coal and iron ore to gain economic independence.

While South Africa's gold exports made the impact of the Depression relatively slight and brief, Hertzog was only able to remain in power after that (1933–1939) by forming a coalition with Jan Smuts's South Africa party. Hertzog's alliance with moderates infuriated hard-line Africaners, who found new leadership in Daniel Malan and his Purified Nationalist party. The example of European fascism compounded South African racism, and extremist organizations proliferated in this period.

Several milestones measure changes in racial policy. The Native Land Act of 1913 confined African landownership to native reserves, which were based on former chiefdoms and contained only 7 percent of the land for 78 percent of the population. A system of passes controlled Africans' movements elsewhere in the country, and the Native Urban Areas Act of 1923 imposed residential segregation. The Native Representation Act of 1936 effectively removed Africans in the Cape Province from the common voter rolls. Thereafter, Africans in each province voted separately to select whites to represent them in parliament. Another law of 1936 enlarged the native reserves, but only to 13 percent of the country's land surface, while extending segregation elsewhere. To reduce white unemployment, special laws barred non-whites from better jobs (the "color bar"). The doctrine of apartheid ("apart-ness") had not yet been proclaimed as such; but its bases were in place.

In September 1939, the Smuts-Hertzog government split over the question of war with Germany. The British governor-general asked Smuts to form a new government. This brought a relative moderate to power one last time. Committing itself to the war, the Smuts government (1939–1948) moderated some of Hertzog's racial policies, for labor needs could only be met by hiring blacks without regard to the color bar (though still at lower wages). Smuts also created a "Native Laws" Commission, whose 1948 report urged concessions. Since blacks were already incorporated in the economy, the report urged their inclusion in the country's political life, too. Alan Paton's impassioned novel, *Cry the Beloved Country,* also from 1948, dramatizes the same issues and needs.

Most whites, however, saw the 1948 report as a bombshell. Hertzog's Nationalists and Malan's Purified Nationalists had by then reunited. The more extreme Malan had captured party leadership, and his Nationalists won the 1948 election. The Nationalists then unveiled their doctrine of apartheid, which elaborated Hertzog's policies into a program of strict racial separation.

Nonwhite Responses to the Consolidation of White Supremacy

For nonwhites, political developments between 1910 and 1948 meant steady erosion of rights, against which protest proved less and less effective. Part of the problem was disunity, for the nonwhite category included three types of people, all referred to in South Africa as "black." These three types are racially mixed coloreds, Asians (mostly Indians, who originally came to South Africa as migrant workers), and Africans, who belong to numerous ethnic groups. White governments reinforced this fragmentation by legally defining the status of different groups in different ways and by setting up separate "native reserves" for specific African ethnic groups. In the preunion period, nonwhites' rights had also differed from one colony to another.

Nonwhites' political activity developed first in the relative freedom of Cape Colony. There, in 1884, John Jabavu founded the first African political newspaper. An Aborigines Association was founded in 1882 to encourage cooperation among religious denominations, an effort partly motivated by the proliferation of separatist churches. In 1902 the colored population of the Cape established the African Political Organization, which formed branches outside Cape Colony, becoming the first political organization for nonwhites from all South Africa.

Natal was the original center for the Indian population, and laws discriminating against them were passed there in the 1890s. Chapter 4 noted the importance of Gandhi's South African years (1893–1914) for his development and his contributions to the South African Indian community. Gandhi formed the Natal Indian Congress in 1894, patterned after the Indian nationalist movement. His passive-resistance campaigns also won concessions from the Union government in the Indian Relief Bill of 1914.

The fact that the Union of South Africa was created without consulting nonwhites gave new impetus to political mobilization and cooperation among nonwhite communities. In 1909 a South African Native Convention met to protest the terms of union. In 1912 the South African Native National Congress was formed. Its name was shortened in 1923 to African National Congress (ANC), and it is still the most influential political organization among South African blacks. Influenced by Gandhi, the ANC long remained a small organization dominated by moderates. Its goal was not revolution but political participation and equal rights. It remained committed to nonviolence for almost half a century. Gradually, however, the worsening political situation led to radicalization and broader efforts at political mobilization. The Native Representation Act of 1936 was a special shock that helped to bring forth new leadership. Alfred

How whites wanted to see Africans in South Africa. *This man obligingly shows the pass that was supposed to regulate his movements outside the native reserves.* Juda Ngwenya/Reuters—Archive Photos

Xuma, a U.S.-educated physician, became president of the ANC in 1940 and broadened it into a mass movement of national scope. During World War II, a still more radical generation formed the Congress Youth League and toppled Xuma from ANC leadership in 1949.

The ANC and the many other political organizations that emerged during the interwar years all faced common problems. One was agreeing on how to respond to government policy changes. Even a measure as drastic as the Native Representation Act of 1936 divided nonwhites. Some thought it was to their interest to cooperate in the procedures of indirect representation provided by the law. Others opposed cooperation. The question of political

methods was also difficult. Some have asserted that Gandhi's nonviolence and passive resistance are ideal methods for a people confronting oppressors who use superior force to impose morally indefensible policies. Yet when South African blacks tried the same methods, whites responded with violence, not concessions. Smuts, the scholar-statesman, was personally impressed by Gandhi. Hertzog candidly admitted that whites' fears of being deluged by the African majority lay behind his segregationist policies. One of the greatest dangers to nonwhite unity lay in exclusive African nationalism, opposed to other nonwhites as well as to whites. In fact, a movement of this type, the Pan-Africanist Congress, eventually broke off from the ANC.

As the end of World War II opened a new global era, South Africa's racial gulf was widening. It was also beginning to attract criticism abroad. A sign of the change was the leadership of newly independent India (1947) in attacking South African racism at the United Nations.

By then the Afrikaners had won political control from the British, and the whites together had wrested control of the land from the Africans. South Africa had diversified economically and embarked on a sustained period of economic growth. But these accomplishments rested on a radical denial of majority rights, an injustice that had begun to isolate South Africa in world opinion.

Conclusion: Africa and Imperialism

While the dominant trend of modern African history through 1945 was integration into the European-dominated global system, even in the heyday of imperialism, internal as well as external forces shaped African history. The ongoing dynamism of Africa's "triple heritage" expressed the diversity of African identities, assuming either indigenous African manifestations, as in the rise of the Zulus; or Islamic forms, as in jihad movements like the Sokoto caliphate; or Christian forms, as in Ethiopia's long history or in the proliferation of Africanized churches. Nigeria's Women's War symbolizes women's centrality to the continent-wide assertion of African identities and interests against alien rule. In time, new forms of political mobilization, like the Nigerian Youth Movement, the National Council of Nigeria and the Cameroons, or South Africa's ANC emerged alongside traditional ones. As European powers reshaped Africa political geography, and as the mounting impact of the three great global crises of the 1914–1945 period provoked suffering and gave Africans a new awareness of the wider world, elements of the new Africa that would emerge after decolonization began to take shape.

In the early twentieth century, apologists for imperialism justified it as preparation for independence. Applied to Belgian or Portuguese colonies, that idea was a mockery. French colonies were better run but also denied their African subjects basic rights. The British probably came closest to the ideal, but the Nigerian and South African cases show this was not very close.

In Nigeria, unification produced a burst of development just before World War I, but gradually the pace slowed, especially during the Depression. British attempts to extend indirect rule by appointing warrant chiefs in the south, and the abandonment of this policy after the Women's War, revealed uncertainty over how to prepare Nigeria for self-government. Limited economic development showed that the real goal of colonialism was to exploit the country's economic resources. Under the circumstances, nationalist political mobilization proved surprisingly gradual, largely because of the elite-mass educational gap and the country's ethnic complexity.

South Africa clearly illustrates the differences that large numbers of European settlers could create. In sub-Saharan Africa, this was the country with the largest proportion of European settlers. Competition among the two white communities worsened the situation. English-Afrikaner competition for political control, and European-African competition over land and labor, thus formed the distinctive themes of the country's history. Between the formation of the Union of South Africa in 1910 and the end of World War II, the Afrikaners gained political control, black rights were steadily eroded as the foundations of apartheid were laid, and the economy developed from reliance on mineral exports to reliance on mining plus industry. The nature of white rule makes it even more surprising here than in Nigeria that the nonwhites' political goals remained so moderate. Gandhi's influence, not just on the Asian community but also on the African National Congress, is especially noteworthy.

Perhaps South Africa's most exceptional trait, in comparative world perspective, is its attempted denial of the processes of political mobilization that have made the twentieth century the age of the mass society. Complicated by British-Afrikaner competition, however, the whites' struggle to dispossess and dominate the Africans made it impossible to mobilize the masses, producing polarization instead. The polarization appeared first among whites as they rallied behind steadily more uncompromising leaders. The African majority's radicalization in the opposite sense was only beginning by World War II. The intricacy of South Africa's discriminatory legislation, and the fact that the majority would have to face not a few colonial troops and administrators, as in Nigeria, but rather all the political and military institutions of a sovereign state, would make the inevitable struggle more painful.

Still, all over Africa, resistance to colonialism had never ceased, and national political mobilization was growing in such a way that colonialism and white settler rule would not indefinitely survive the collapse of European global dominance in World War II.

Notes

1. P. Chike Dike, ed., *The Women's Revolt of 1929: Proceedings of a National Symposium to Mark the 60th Anniversary of the Women's Uprising in South-Eastern Nigeria,* (Lagos: Nelag and Co., 1995); Nina E. Mba, "Heroines of the Women's War," in *Nigerian Women in Historical Perspective,* ed. Bolanle Awe (Lagos: Sankore Publishers, 1992), pp. 73–88; Judith Van Allen, "Aba Riots or Igbo Women's War? Ideology, Stratification and the Invisibility of Women," in *Women in Africa,* ed. Nancy I. Hafkin and Edna G. Bay (Stanford: Stanford University Press, 1976), pp. 59–85.

2. Ali Mazrui, *The Africans: A Triple Heritage* (Boston: Little, Brown, 1986), pp. 44, 81.

Suggestions for Further Reading

Achebe, Chinua. *Arrow of God* (1969).

——. *Things Fall Apart* (1959).

Afigbo, A. E., et al. *The Making of Modern Africa.* 2 vols. (1986).

Crowder, Michael. *The Story of Nigeria* (1978).

——, ed. *West African Resistance: The Military Response to Colonial Occupation.* Rev. ed. (1978).

Curtin, Philip, Steven Feierman, Leonard Thompson, and Jan Vansina. *African History* (1978).

Hafkin, Nancy, and Edna Bay, eds. *Women in Africa* (1976).

Mazrui, Ali. *The Africans: A Triple Heritage* (1986).

McCarthy, Stephen, *Africa: The Challenge of Transformation* (1994).

Oliver, Roland, and Anthony Atmore. *Africa Since 1800.* 4th ed. (1994).

Paton, Alan. *Cry, the Beloved Country* (1948).

Rodney, Walter. *How Europe Underdeveloped Africa* (1974).

Taylor, Stephen. *Shaka's Children, A History of the Zulu People* (1994).

Thompson, Leonard. *A History of South Africa.* Rev. ed. (1995).

CHAPTER 9

Asian Struggles for Independence and Development

SO VAST WAS THE CRISIS FOLLOWING THE 1911 COLLAPSE OF THE CHINESE EMPIRE that not one but two attempts at national mass mobilization emerged. They cooperated at times but fought at others, as when Chiang Kai-shek's Nationalists (Guomindang, GMD) forced the Communists (CCP) out of their southern bases. Fighting Chiang's "Whites" all the way, the "Reds" embarked on the Long March (1934–1935) into the interior as far as Tibet, then back to a new northern base at Yan'an. Setting out in defeat with a hundred thousand people, the Reds spent 368 days en route, marched nearly six thousand miles, crossed eighteen mountain ranges and twenty-four rivers, broke through ten provincial warlords' armies, and crossed territories of six indigenous peoples, some of them hostile to all Chinese, Red or White. The march became a huge propaganda tour, during which the Communists "taxed" the rich and roused the poor. All the way, the Nazi-supplied GMD air force followed and attacked. The greatest danger came far in the interior, at a crossing on the Dadu (Tatu) River.

The Reds first approached the Dadu at Anrenchang, managing to ferry nearly a division across. But as rising flood waters slowed the task, the Reds realized that GMD forces would crush them before they could finish it. The Reds had no choice but to march over a hundred miles west and try again at Luding (Luting). Its bridge offered the last crossing east of Tibet. Desperate to get there quickly, the Reds set out on May 23, 1935, at times in sight of the Whites marching on the other side to head them off. One Red commander, Yang Chengwu, recalled that the road "twisted like a sheep's gut," through mountain gorges so steep-sided that "your cap fell off when you tried to look all the way to the top," while the other side of

Traditional chain bridge in southwest China. *During the Long March, Communists crossed a similar bridge under hostile fire from a similar walled town at the far end. Into the Middle Kingdom, photograph by Auguste François. Copyright Réunion des Musées Nationaux/Art Resource, NY*

the trail dropped to the river far below. At times, the road narrowed to a trail, nearly impassable from heavy rains. Political agitators worked steadily to keep the men going. To keep marching at night, like the Whites across the gorge whose torches they could see, the Reds also lit torches. Luckily, they took the precaution of preparing their buglers, if challenged, to answer with the bugle calls of GMD units the Reds had defeated. The Reds reached the western end of the Luding bridge on the morning of May 25.

Across the deep gorge stretched an archaic bridge of over a hundred meters, made entirely of chains, two on each side for rails, and nine for a roadbed. There should have been planks across the nine chains, but the Whites had ripped most of them up and carried them into Luding, a walled town at the far end of the bridge. Machine guns and mortars in Luding were aimed at the bridge. To cross, the Reds formed an assault squad of twenty-two volunteers. With tommy guns on their backs and twelve grenades each on their belts, the volunteers advanced hand over hand along the chains, covered from behind by heavy fire. More troops followed the assault squad, laying planks and advancing at the same time. The Whites on the other side returned fire, and the bodies of men who had been hit plunged into the river. The Whites also set fire to the remaining planking at their end. But some Reds got across and started hurling grenades. After more hours of fighting, the Whites retreated. The Communists had survived the severest trial of the Long March.

"We're bound to win because ours is a people's army," they concluded. Compared to the GMD, it was, and they did. For its survivors, the Long March became the great bonding experience; its veterans provided most of the major leaders of the People's Republic through Deng Xiaopeng (d. 1997). One of the most dramatic episodes in modern Asian history crystallized one of the great twentieth-century themes: the revolutionary power of mass mobilization accompanied by effective organization and motivation.[1]

Asian Centers of Civilization

Defined by geographers as extending from the eastern Mediterranean coast and Russia's Ural Mountains to the Pacific, Asia is not a distinct or coherent unit. It is really part of the larger Afro-Eurasian landmass and can be distinguished by only arbitrarily chosen criteria. Perhaps for this reason, a tendency exists today to use the name "Asia" only for the region from Pakistan to Japan; yet even this smaller "Asia" presents the same problems of arbitrary definition and internal heterogeneity as the larger one. Based on the principle that all human societies are comparable—a precondition for the study of world history—this chapter considers the history of Asia in the larger sense. For the post-1945 period, to avoid having one chapter of excessive length, we shall subdivide Asia into the Middle East (Chapter 16) and South and East Asia (Chapter 17).

This chapter's conclusion will argue that Asian societies' responses to twentieth-century challenges depended on four factors that express the impact on those societies of the four great themes of contemporary world history. First, in the years leading up to 1945, tightening *global interrelatedness* challenged Asian societies to adapt and respond to the European imperialist onslaught. Second, on the level of *identity and culture* the critical need in most countries was to develop or consolidate consensus about national identity; independent countries needed, as well, basic consensus about the organization of their political life. Third, the *rise of the mass society* usually merged in Asia with the effort to mobilize the entire populace for the struggle against imperialism. Fourth, centering on *technology* but extending beyond it, an economic strategy that could overcome the effects of imperialism was required in every country before the victory over imperialism could be consolidated. To illustrate these points, this chapter presents a comparative overview followed by fuller discussion of three major Asian centers of civilization. Chapters 16 and 17 will show that the same factors that proved most critical for the pre-1945 history of these societies remained critical thereafter, while also assuming new dimensions.

Asia contains three of the zones where the world's most influential civilizations have emerged: the Middle East, South Asia, and East Asia. Other parts of Asia have also been important in world history: the Central Asian arid zone through which the silk routes passed, or Southeast Asia, especially its spice-producing islands. Here, we begin by surveying Asia in terms of its diversity, major unifying themes in its history, and the process of its integration into the European-dominated world system in the nineteenth century.

Asian Diversity

Marked ecological differences underlie and have helped to shape the diversity of Asian societies and their histories. Seen from space, the entire Earth's most striking terrain feature is the belt of desert and semidesert (steppe) that extends from Northwest Africa nearly to China's Beijing.[2] A salient feature of this arid belt is that its eastern part, extending from Ukraine to China, lies farther north and is less arid than its western part; the latter extends across North Africa to the Middle East, which forms the central part of the dry belt and connects its eastern and western extensions (see the color topographical map at the front of this book). North of the Asian, eastern part of the arid belt lie forests and ultimately the Siberian tundra. To the south of the Asian part of the dry belt lie the high, cold mountains of Tibet and western China. South and east of the mountains lie better-watered regions, whose climates

range from subtropical to tropical as one moves southward from central China and northern India to the equatorial islands of Southeast Asia.

Cultural criteria distinguish five major zones important in world history: (1) Central Asia consists of the arid belt of steppe and desert through which the silk routes ran, a zone historically important as a medium of communication for those who knew how to traverse it and as the site for the emergence of nomadic empires. (2) Southeast Asia, including both the mainland zone lying east of India and south of China and the islands of the Indonesian and Philippine archipelagos, has historically been subject to influences from the two powerful zones that border it. Important both for its own products, including rice and spices, and for the sea routes that traverse it, Southeast Asia has been hindered from matching the power and influence of India or China by the dispersal of its islands and the division of its mainland regions by mountains. (3) Southwest Asia—which, together with Egypt, is more commonly referred to as the Middle East*—forms the central part of the arid zone. In addition, its river valleys were the sites of the oldest civilizations. In the seventh century, Islam emerged in this region; rapid, far-reaching Islamic conquests unified not just the Middle East but nearly the entire Afro-Eurasian arid belt for the first and only time. (4) South Asia or the Indian subcontinent, historically protected from the north by the Himalayas and from the east by the Burmese

---

*The expression *Middle East* is objectionable because it defines the region from a European viewpoint; the fact that the same region is sometimes called the *Near East* adds to the confusion. Yet we shall use *Middle East* for want of a concise alternative. In terms of today's political geography, the Middle East consists of Turkey, Iran, the Arab lands of Southwest Asia, Israel, and Egypt; some authorities add Sudan and Afghanistan. *Southwest Asia* would be a better name for the region, except that Egypt, one of its most important countries, is in Africa. *North Africa* (Libya, Tunisia, Algeria, Morocco) is an extension of the Middle East, sharing both Islamic faith and Arab culture with Egypt and the Arab countries of Southwest Asia.

jungle, was invaded several times from the northwest. Home to the cults that became known collectively as Hinduism, as well as to Buddhism and a number of other religious movements, South Asia was historically a major center of productivity with important links by sea to both East and West. (5) East Asia, finally, with China as its self-styled "middle kingdom" and Japan as its other most important country, was long the world's most productive region and acquired a significant measure of cultural cohesion through the spread of Confucianism and other cultural traits from China.

The fact that three of these five zones—the Middle East, South Asia, and East Asia—are among those in which the world's most influential civilizations arose, while the other two—Central Asia and Southeast Asia—have played very different but also important roles in world history, indicates something of Asia's complexity. Internally, too, each of these regions displays intricate variegations. As the home of the oldest civilizations, Southwest Asia is a veritable ethnographic museum. Internally, not to speak of the farther reaches of the Islamic world, the region has developed three linguistically differentiated Islamic high cultures, expressed in Arabic, Persian, and Turkish. Dense with religious and ethnic minorities, the region has also seen some of its peoples whose histories extend back to pre-Islamic times re-emerge as claimants to national identity and statehood in modern times; the Zionist movement that led to the creation of the state of Israel offers the most successful example, while the history of the Armenian people offers perhaps the most tragic. In South Asia, while Hinduism and a range of shared historical experiences have created many commonalities, factors of language, ethnicity, religion, and caste have created so many cleavages that the mobilization of a unified nationalist response against imperialism required overcoming exceptional obstacles. In East Asia, finally, while ethnic Chinese make up over 90 percent of China's population, that country has scores of ethnic minorities, mostly in its border regions. The surrounding lands, which China's rulers historically sought to make into tributary satellites, spoke languages unrelated to Chinese in some cases (Mongolian, Manchu, Japanese, Korean) and invariably resisted Chinese pretensions to hegemony.

In terms of the Asian societies' adaptation to the conditions of the modern world, one of the most important expressions of their diversity was that almost none of them—with the chief exception of Japan—fulfilled the ideal of ethnic and cultural homogeneity that supposedly characterizes the modern, Western-derived concept of the nation-state. As in Europe, each country's internal diversity has challenged its nationalist mobilization movements in distinctive ways. The fact that European imperialism had significantly different impacts on various parts of Asia has accentuated this fact.

Common Traits of Asian History

Before considering the impact of imperialism, it will help to point out some major common traits. One of the most salient has been the persistent drive for large-scale integration. Geographical factors hindered this process in Southeast Asia. In Central Asia, aridity and sparseness of settlement permitted political integration only in the form of the generically short-lived nomadic empires of conquest; the thirteenth-century Mongol Empire is the greatest example. In all three of the major Asian centers of civilization, however, the push for large-scale integration was strong and persistent. All three of these regions became centers for the propagation of value systems that exerted great influence as cultural unifiers—the monotheistic religions in the case of the Middle East, Hinduism and Buddhism in the case of India, Confucianism in the case of China. Each of these three regions also showed a recurrent thrust toward large-scale forms of social or political integration.

Experiencing greatest prosperity when strong dynasties maintained peace and unity, the Chinese were the most successful in maintaining political integration. While India had fewer episodes of large-scale imperial unification, the Maurya (322-185 B.C.E.), Gupta (4th century C.E.), and Mughal (1526-1858) dynasties all unified large parts of the subcontinent, as did the British from about 1800 to 1947. In between, Hinduism and the caste system provided cultural and social frameworks that accommodated Indian diversity while also imposing their own distinctive stamps on it. Symbolic of the starkest inequality to outsiders, and often the object of Indians' attempts to renegotiate caste status or rebel against the system by creating alternative cults or religions, the caste system (introduced in Chapter 4) provided a kind of India-wide grid in which Indians of diverse origins could reckon their status in relation to one another. For Muslims, centered in the Middle East but found from West Africa to the Philippines, the drive for unity became an article of faith. The entire Muslim community (*umma*) was supposed to be a religious and political unit. Probably more enduringly than India but less so than China, the central parts of the Islamic world did enjoy large-scale, if not complete, political integration—for example, under the Abbasid caliphate (750-1258) or the Ottoman Empire (1300-1922), at least when those states were at their height. Even when unity was lacking, Islamic religious law, the *sharia,* created an important degree of uniformity in Islamic societies everywhere.

For all three of Asia's major centers of civilization, as noted in Chapter 1, the period 1500-1800 coincided with a major resurgence of empire-building under indigenous dynasties: the Ottomans, ruling most of the Middle East, North Africa, and southeastern Europe; the Safavids of Iran (1500-1736); the Mughals in India; and the Ming (1368-1644) and Qing (1644-1912) dynasties in China.

A consideration of what disunity could mean helps to show why large-scale, and especially political, integration was so important for Asia's great civilizations. In a vast region where so many peoples and cultures interacted and competed, fragmentation meant vulnerability. The loss of effective central control in the Middle East between the ninth and fifteenth centuries, or the anarchy that preceded the rise of China's Ming dynasty in the fourteenth, reinforced the assumption that a large, centralized state was needed to maintain the order required for civilization to flourish. Border defense reinforced the need for concentration of state power; the clearest symbol of this was the Great Wall of China, maintained and guarded by China's rulers to protect their agricultural lands from raids by the nomadic steppe peoples to the north.

Only in exceptional circumstances, it seems, could a society combine security with politcal decentralization. Western Europe, isolated at the far end of Eurasia and too primitive for much of its history to attract covetous eyes, illustrates this point in general terms. Perhaps the best examples, however, are two island nations at the extreme ends of Eurasia: Britain, which idealized political decentralization to a unique degree; and Japan, where reverence for the state was much stronger but where political fragmentation under the Tokugawa shogunate (1600-1867) could easily have opened the way to conquest if it had not been for over a hundred miles of sea separating Japan from the nearest point of mainland Asia (see Map 9.3). If, as many scholars think, the most democratic societies are those in which multiple power centers historically coexisted, then it is not hard to see why Japan eventually became one of Asia's few democracies.

If the will to survive dictated over much of Eurasia that the individual's best interest lay in subjection to a great ruler, at least the Asian civilizations' achievements remained unmatched for most of history. We have noted some of the many innovations that came to Europe from Asia. China, with its vast production of tea, silk, and porcelain, was surely the most productive and creative Asian country of all. Yet most of Asia historically produced goods that Europeans coveted, and the original thrust of Europe's overseas expansion was to gain direct access to and control of these markets.

Integration into the European-dominated World System

The most important fact about this European effort is that it had but limited success before 1800. As noted, Asian empires dominated the scene until then. China, in particular, not only dominated its own regional "world economy," but—with its vast output of products valued around the world and its huge demand for silver—had more impact on the global economy than any other single country.

Both before and after 1800, different parts of Asia experienced the European expansion in different ways, depending on the specific European powers with which they became entangled and on their own characteristics and ability to resist. Central Asia was divided between the Russian and Chinese empires between the sixteenth and nineteenth centuries. Partly because many of the sought-after spices were grown on small islands, island Southeast Asia became an early focus of European expansion, particularly by the Dutch, despite considerable local resistance. In India, Europeans were initially minor players in a political scene where the late Mughal Empire's lack of central control created opportunities to exploit local rivalries. By 1800, the British had bested the French as rival contenders and had begun to put together the power base in the northeast, around Calcutta, from which they gradually extended their control. Further west, the Ottoman Empire began after 1699 to lose outlying European provinces to Austrian or Russian expansion. After 1800, the Ottomans lost others to Balkan nationalism and to European colonialism in North Africa. After 1800, both the Ottoman Empire

and Iran (ruled by the Qajar dynasty, 1796–1925) retained nominal independence but were reduced to semidependency by European interference in their political and, especially, economic affairs. In East Asia, China and Japan had successfully dealt with the Europeans for centuries by excluding them or severely limiting contact. The Industrial Revolution and rapid widening of the technological gap between Asia and Europe turned this policy from a success into a disaster, however. The British reduced China to a semicolony following the First Opium War (1839–1842), and a U.S. mission forced Japan to "open" to the outside world in 1853–1854.

Asian societies of the nineteenth century responded to the multifarious challenges of European imperialism by mobilizing movements of renewal and resistance. Varying among themselves, these movements tended to represent the efforts of cultural elites to motivate and activate populations whose accustomed forms of political awareness and action differed markedly from the elites' own. The common result, as in Latin America and Africa, was authoritarian mobilization, in which the elites strove to maintain national unity, suppressing or re-educating dissident voices in the name of "the people." In Asia as elsewhere, the result of such mobilization was often to postpone demands for fuller democratization until after 1945.

To illustrate these patterns, we shall examine the three major Asian centers of civilization in the order in which they felt the impact of European imperialism: first India, then the Middle East, then China and Japan.

India Under the British

About half the size of the continental United States but far more densely populated, India is a large country. Its population, already 250 million by the 1920s, was second only to China's but much more diverse, speaking hundreds of languages from four different language families;

some fifteen of these languages count as major ones. India is also religiously diverse. Among its half-dozen religions, the Hindus are by far the most numerous, although the Muslims (the largest minority) had long been politically dominant prior to the establishment of British rule. The consolidation of British rule, by 1858, added one more complexity to this landscape.

British Rule in India

Until 1858, India was ruled by the British East India Company, the officially chartered trading company that had monopolized British trade with India. During the early nineteenth century, company rule not only unified India but also introduced many changes. The British abolished *sati,* the ritual suicide of Hindu widows on the cremation pyres of their husbands, and promoted English-style education. They proclaimed the ideas of nineteenth-century liberalism through the Charter Act of 1833. Politically, the act promised equal rights for all Indians, including the right to administrative employment. Economically, the act abolished the company's monopoly over most branches of trade and opened India to unrestricted British immigration and enterprise. The political promises of the act were not fulfilled, but the economic ones were. Free trade had come to India.

Pre-1858 British policy produced mixed results. Intervention in matters of Hindu or Muslim religious belief helped provoke widespread revolt in 1857. This crisis provoked lasting distrust of the "natives," a racist turn in British attitudes, and a decision by the British government to take control away from the East India Company. In the long run, because Britain was the only industrialized state at the time, free trade was more devastating than the revolt. For an unindustrialized country like India, free trade meant the collapse of production by hand, massive unemployment, and economic subordination.

When crown rule replaced company rule in 1858, India assumed the status in the British Empire that it held until independence in 1947. With its huge markets and large production of spices, tea, and other goods, India was the "jewel of empire." Queen Victoria became sovereign over the country, assuming the title "empress of India" in 1877. A viceroy represented her there. In London, where the Colonial Office managed most of Britain's overseas dependencies, another ministry, the India Office, managed India alone. Its head, the secretary of state for India, was a member of the prime minister's cabinet.

In India, crown rule had a conservative impact in some ways. British control over the Indian army tightened. Many local princes were left in place (indirect rule). But technological modernization continued, as steamships, telegraphs, and railroads tied India more tightly into the imperial system. As usual, colonial administration siphoned off much of the country's wealth. By 1892, about a fourth of the Indian government's annual expenditures went for overseas expenses. Indians had little to say about this.

From 1858 to 1947, Indian participation in public affairs expanded but slowly. Indians had become eligible for certain appointments in the civil service in 1854. But until 1921, the examinations required for appointment occurred only in England, not in India. The first steps toward giving Indians some control of local affairs, and representation on the councils of the viceroy and of the governors of Bombay and Madras, also took place during the first half-century of crown rule. But not until 1907 were the first Indian members appointed to the council of the secretary of state for India in London.

Far-reaching change began only after World War I. In 1917, Secretary of State for India Edwin Samuel Montagu promised gradual steps toward "association of Indians in every branch of the administration," "development of self-governing institutions," and "responsible government." Delivery on these promises came with two acts of the British Parliament, the Government of India acts of 1921 and 1935. These acts broadened the franchise and transferred nearly all government responsibilities at the provincial level, as well as some at the central-government level, into Indian hands. In 1935 some 35 million men and women, one-sixth of the adult population, were eligible to vote. Although the 1935 act at first dissatisfied nationalists, large sections of it were included in independent India's constitution of 1950.

Indian Responses to Imperialism

The slow expansion of the Indian role in public affairs would not have occurred without mounting political pressure from Indian society, which was undergoing complex transformations at many levels. A continuing dynamic of peasant political activism produced some hundred insurgencies during the nineteenth century; these expressed opposition to Indian elites as well as to the British. Cultural renaissances began in different languages, in Bengal and other regions, as Indians re-examined their situation in a changing world. Movements of religious revival or reform, and voluntary associations ranging from student clubs to chambers of commerce, formed in towns and cities. In 1885—very early by colonial standards—India acquired a political movement of national scale, the Indian National Congress.

Initially a loose coalition of local interests more than a political party, the Congress party was Hindu dominated from the start, and tensions with Muslims and other communities soon arose. The Hindu majority, however, had certain qualities that enabled it to respond effectively to India's political situation. The Hindus had not been sorry to see the British end the earlier Muslim domination. Hinduism lacked the doctrinal definition or closedness of some other religions, and Hindus could absorb Western ideas into their outlook with less sense

of conflict than could Muslims. Finally, there was charismatic leadership, furnished by Muhammad Ali Jinnah (1876–1949) to the Muslims and, even more, by Mahatma Gandhi (1869–1948) to the Hindus. In the long run, the British had to make concessions. Among the many who contributed to this outcome, Gandhi holds a unique place even though his was never the only voice or message in Indian nationalism.

Gandhi and Nonviolence

Chapter 4 has examined Gandhi's background and ideas. When he returned to India in 1915, he was already known for his work in South Africa and his writings. He soon began applying his nonviolent techniques on behalf of the poor and dispossessed, demonstrating how he differed from the elite, authoritarian mobilizers who dominated many colonial nationalist movements. When the British prolonged the wartime suspension of civil liberties into the postwar years, after having promised reforms that eventually became policy in the Government of India Act of 1921, Gandhi called for a nationwide campaign of civil disobedience. The ensuing tensions climaxed in 1919 at Amritsar, where the British commander, who had forbidden gatherings, led the massacre of a crowd that had peaceably assembled to celebrate a Hindu festival. Outraged, the Congress party then abandoned cooperation with the British and brought Gandhi to leadership of the movement.

In 1920 Gandhi opened a nationwide campaign of noncooperation—refusal to work for the British, pay taxes, use British products, associate with the British at all. He predicted that this strategy would produce self-rule by the end of 1921. When it did not, disillusionment spread, and violence broke out. The British imprisoned Gandhi in 1922. By the time of his release in 1924, enthusiasm for noncooperation had waned, and Hindu-Muslim tensions had

Mahatma Gandhi and his wife, Kasturbai, on their return to India, 1915. Peter Ruhel/Archive Photos

homespun cloth he wore and tried to popularize. With this program went further reformist efforts to improve the lot of women, whom Gandhi regarded as having greater capacity for nonviolence than men, and Untouchables. Meanwhile, India's industrialists—including wealthy Gandhi disciples who bankrolled his experiments in communal poverty—pursued goals of import substitution and heavy industrial development. In a sense, Gandhi and the industrialists pursued the same goal: self-sufficiency. The industrialists took the same developmental path that most developing countries chose, but Gandhi knew better how to capture the people's imagination.

Gandhi was politically astute. By conducting local campaigns in many regions and championing the interests of many groups, he acquired a unique national following. Striving for unity at high levels as well, Gandhi strove to maintain solidarity across religious or ideological lines, as when he worked in 1928 to elect Jawaharlal Nehru as president of the Congress party, even though the younger man's reformist socialism placed him well to Gandhi's left. Later, though Gandhi disliked certain features of the Government of India Act of 1935, he decided that Congress members should participate in elections and take office. Congress leaders had waited so long for power that many misused it. Muslims protested, but they had fared poorly at the polls while the Congress won a smashing victory. Soon Jinnah and many other Muslims shifted to demanding a separate state. Meanwhile, officeholding unquestionably helped prepare the Congress leadership for independence.

With time, especially under the stress of World War II, Gandhi's hold over the masses weakened, but it never vanished. As British rule approached its end and preparations were made to divide the country into separate Hindu and Muslim states, he sought to restrain violence and maintain goodwill among religious communities. He had always opposed the

increased dangerously. Yet, significantly, the non-cooperation campaign had confronted the British with India-wide political hostility as never before.

Later Gandhi mounted two more large civil disobedience campaigns: in 1930–1932 against the British salt monopoly and salt tax (salt was a major dietary requirement for poor workers in this hot country) and in 1940–1942 in protest against the fact that Indians were forced to fight in World War II as British subjects. But during the 1920s and 1930s, he also took a different route, through his Constructive Program, symbolized by his spinning wheel and the

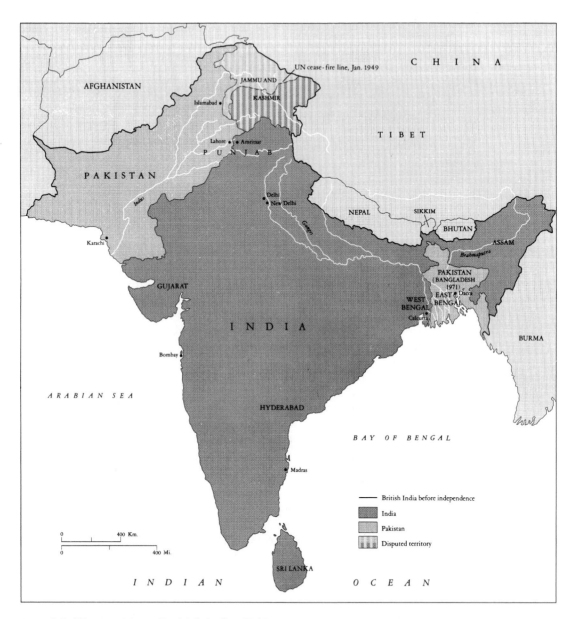

Map 9.1 The Partition of British India, 1947

"vivisection" of India. But on August 15, 1947, India and Pakistan became independent as separate states (see Map 9.1). The Muslim state, Pakistan, combined two widely separated terri-tories under a single national government. The mood of India had shifted away from Gandhi's vision. In January 1948 he was assassinated by a member of a Hindu revivalist movement—a sign of tensions that would resurface in more dramatic form in the 1980s.

Even in his own country, Gandhi's methods have not been the ones most used to solve the political and economic problems of peoples trying to escape from colonialism. Yet his memory lives on. His nonviolent principles have exerted a far-reaching influence, from the African National Congress in South Africa, to Martin Luther King, Jr., and the U.S. civil rights movement, the European anti-nuclear movement of the 1980s, and popular movements working for development in South Asia today.

The Middle East and North Africa in the Era of European Expansionism

Unlike India, most of the Middle East survived to World War I without being brought under direct European rule. But this region had special significance for European colonialism from the beginning. Before 1500, the Europeans' prime source for Asian goods had been the Islamic ports of the eastern Mediterranean. Knowing that many of those goods were produced farther east, Europeans had sought access to their sources, thus opening the age of oceanic exploration that brought Columbus to the Americas and the Portuguese to India.

After 1800, the impact of Europe's dual revolutions, industrial and political (see Chapter 1), provoked not only nationalist revolts in the Ottomans' Balkan provinces, such as Greece and Serbia, but also widespread economic change. In the wake of the Ottoman-British free-trade treaty of 1838, the Ottomans sank into debt, bankruptcy, and foreign financial control (1881). Ottoman producers survived as best they could, adapting and adjusting in sophisticated ways. The Ottoman government also made vigorous efforts at reform, laying the basis for the rise of the Turkish Republic in the 1920s. At times, Europeans recognized Ottoman ef-

forts. During the Crimean War (1854-1856), several European states allied with the Ottomans against Russia, symbolically accepting the Ottoman Empire as an equal in military alliance (1854) and as a member of the European family of nations in the Treaty of Paris (1856). More often, the great powers regarded this partly European empire to the east as the "sick man of Europe." When they wished, they took outlying provinces. France helped itself to Algeria (1830) and Tunisia (1881). Britain took Cyprus (1878) and occupied Egypt (1882). When not grabbing territory, the European powers cooperated to preserve the Ottoman Empire, whose condition so favored their interests. Iran was in sorrier shape, chiefly because the government was weaker even after the revolution of 1905-1911 introduced a supposedly constitutional monarchy. In Iran the dominant outside powers were Russia and Britain. In sum, by 1900, the Ottoman Empire and Iran had no more real independence than the Latin American republics.

Political Fragmentation and the Drive for National Independence

After World War I, European control seemed to grow stronger as Europeans divided the territories of the Ottoman Empire, much as Africa had been divided after 1885, and asserted political dominance over much of the Middle East. This region, which until recently had known only two states of consequence, the Ottoman Empire and Iran, suffered political fragmentation, which maps still reflect (see Map 9.2). Uncomfortable with this innovation, many Middle Easterners have since sought to re-create unities of larger scale, such as historically prevailed in the Middle East and in other great Asian centers of civilization. For the short run, however, a more immediate problem was to recover independence at what appeared on the region's redrawn map as the "national" level. As this struggle began, European control proved less solid in some places than at first appeared. For illustrations, we shall look first at Iran, then at Ottoman successor states.

Iran During World War I, although Iran declared neutrality, it suffered from fighting and foreign occupation. Afterward, while the Bolsheviks took the Soviet Union temporarily out of the imperialist game, the British tried to fill the gap. In 1919, they prepared a treaty that would have made Iran a virtual British protectorate. When Iranian and foreign opposition forced abandonment of this idea, the British withdrew.

Shortly afterward, a military officer, Reza Khan, emerged as shah (r. 1925–1941), founding the Pahlevi dynasty. Iran's first effective modernizing ruler, Reza Shah founded the nation's army, its modern educational system, and its railway network—all long overdue reforms. But he also set the example of despotism and greed that ended in revolution against his son, Muhammad Reza Shah (r. 1941–1979). Reza had to abdicate in 1941, when the British and Soviets occupied Iran—a measure he patriotically opposed—to use it as a conduit for war aid to the Soviet Union. Becoming shah under such circumstances, young Muhammad Reza only slowly regained his father's power (see Chapter 16).

The Succession to the Ottoman Empire

The consequences of World War I were more serious for the Ottoman Empire, which had entered the war on the German side. During the war, Britain and its allies began planning to liquidate the empire. Ultimately, they made too many plans. To start an anti-Ottoman revolt in the Arabian peninsula, the British encouraged Arab aspirations to independence in certain territories. To smooth relations with France, Britain agreed to divide some of those territories into zones that the two powers would control directly or indirectly. Then, in 1917, Britain aligned itself with the Zionist movement by issuing the Balfour Declaration, which declared that Britain favored establishment of a "national home for the Jewish people" in Palestine and would support efforts to realize this goal on certain conditions. Many Zionists, and many of their opponents, interpreted the declaration to mean British support for the creation of a Jewish state or even a British promise of such a state.

At the peace conference, it proved impossible to reconcile all these commitments. British and French interests won out in the Treaty of Sèvres. The Zionists managed to get their goals recognized. The Arabs were not so lucky. Nor were the Turks at first.

The treaty disposed of every part of the former empire. Istanbul and the straits that flowed past it, connecting the Black Sea with the Aegean, were to form an international zone. Other regions on the edges of what is now the Republic of Turkey were to go to various foreign powers or to local non-Turkish peoples (the Kurds and the Armenians). The Turks were to have only what remained. Mandates from the League of Nations assigned Syria, including what is now Lebanon, to France and Iraq to Britain. A special mandate, including many Zionist goals, gave Britain control of the territory that is now Israel and Jordan. Other provisions of the treaty recognized the British position in Egypt and Cyprus.

Thus direct European domination came to parts of the world that had not known it before, and the struggle for political independence became the main theme of the interwar years in the former Ottoman territories. As examples, we shall consider the cases of Egypt, Palestine, and the Turkish Republic.

Egypt In Egypt, a nationalist movement predated the British occupation of 1882. Nationalism re-emerged in anti-British form in the 1890s and erupted in what Egyptians remember as the revolution of 1919. Unable to suppress this uprising, and unwilling to negotiate with the nationalists, the British unilaterally declared the country independent under a constitutional monarchy (1922–1923). But they attached conditions that required negotiations. Not until 1936 could the British and the Egyptian nationalists agree on these conditions. Abolition of foreigners' exemption from Egyptian law (*extraterritoriality*) followed in 1937. Although Egypt was supposedly fully independent after 1936, the British retained a "preferential alliance," giving them special rights in wartime. During World War II they exercised these rights with full force, nullifying Egypt's independence and discrediting the Egyptians who had negotiated the 1936 treaty.

In *Midaq Alley* (1947), Naguib Mahfouz, an Egyptian novelist who has won the Nobel Prize for Literature and been physically attacked by Egypt's Islamic militants, uses the metaphor of prostitution to symbolize the combination of socioeconomic stress and political cynicism into which World War II then plunged the country. Egypt's experience showed just how elusive independence could be for a colonial country. The leader for a new push for independence would emerge in Gamal Abdel Nasser, in 1952 (see Chapter 16).

Palestine How the League of Nations mandates worked out depended on local conditions and the policies of the European power in charge. One familiar theme was that boundaries drawn in some cases by Europeans had little relation to local social and economic realities. The British adhered to the mandate ideal fairly successfully in Iraq. The French did not try to in Syria and Lebanon. In Palestine, the British failed.

The mandate concept required preparation for self-government. But Palestine included two communities with incompatible goals: the Zionists, mostly immigrants from Europe, and the local Arabs. The Arabs' goals were at first less clear-cut: Palestinian nationalism emerged only gradually. But an international Zionist movement had been active even before World War I.

Its goal was to redevelop Palestine as a Jewish homeland with a Jewish culture and all the social and economic institutions needed for self-sufficiency. The idea of a Jewish state had been current in the movement at least since one of its founders, Theodor Herzl, had published a book called *The Jewish State* in 1896. But for a long time, an independent Jewish state seemed a remote goal. Not until May 1942 did the Zionist movement in general formally commit itself to the demand for a sovereign "Jewish commonwealth" after the war.

After World War I, Palestinian Arabs began to realize what extensive Jewish immigration could mean for them. Outbreaks of violence began in 1920 and culminated in the Arab Revolt of 1936–1939. The British struggled to satisfy both sides. The mandate permitted them to specify that the terms of the Balfour Declaration would apply only to part of the mandated territory. In 1922 they exercised this option, setting aside the territory east of the Jordan River to be an Arab state, now known as the kingdom of Jordan. West of the river, British difficulties in bridging the Arab-Zionist gap continued. They grew worse after the rise of Nazism in Europe increased the demand for unlimited Jewish immigration. Ultimately, the British could not devise immigration and land policies that satisfied both Zionists and Palestinian Arabs, who feared that they would become a minority in their homeland.

By the time World War II broke out, the Zionists bitterly resented the British. They hated the Nazis still more, however, and backed Britain in the war. But resentment of British policy played a major role in prompting the Zionist demand of May 1942 for a sovereign state. Later, as the horrors inflicted on European Jewry became known more fully, Zionist feeling grew even stronger. By the time the war ended, the British could no longer manage Palestine. They decided to turn it over to the United Nations as successor to the League of Nations, and withdraw.

In the ensuing melee, Zionist organization and will proved decisive, even after five Arab countries sent in forces to support the Palestinians against the new state of Israel, which declared its independence on May 14, 1948. The story of this remarkable state receives fuller attention in Chapter 16.

Turkey   Among Middle Eastern countries, Turkey came closest to defying the apparent postwar strengthening of European power. Sure that the multinational Ottoman Empire was finished, the Paris peacemakers did their work as if the Turkish people, among whom the empire had arisen, were also finished. Yet a mass-based Turkish nationalist movement, led by a charismatic general named Mustafa Kemal, emerged from the collapse of the empire and took up arms in 1919. Its goal was to create a nation-state and prevent the carving up of what is now Turkish territory.

By 1922 the military effort had succeeded so well that attempts to divide the territory were abandoned. The nationalists then destroyed what was left of the imperial government and declared a republic, with Ankara as capital (see Map 9.2). The Western powers convened a conference to negotiate a new peace, in which they renounced the commercial and legal privileges they had enjoyed under the Ottomans (1923). Through its nationalist revolution, Turkey had become the only defeated power of World War I to force revision of the peace terms.

But the "national struggle" of 1919–1922 was only the beginning of revolutionary change in Turkey. With Mustafa Kemal as president, the republic went on from political to social and cultural changes that were revolutionary in many respects. After a century of agony over the clash of Western and Islamic civilizations, the new state sought to overcome the conflict by turning its back on the heritage of Islamic empire. Instead, while keeping many late Ottoman reforms, it became a pro-Western, secular, nationalist republic.

In the early twentieth century, only one Asian country, Japan, was more successful than Turkey in learning from the West, but no other remade its culture so completely in the process. Geography gave Turkey a unique potential for such reorientation, for it lies immediately next to Europe and part of its territory is in Europe. This potential gave a distinct stamp to the Turkish effort at state formation, the most successful such effort among Muslim societies in the interwar period.

Turkey's Westernizing reforms began in 1924 with abolition of the institutions that had made Islam an official part of the imperial political system. Henceforth, as in the West, religion was to be a matter of private conscience. The old religious bureaucracy, religious courts, and religious schools were abolished or drastically modified. The legal system was almost completely secularized through adoption of Western-style codes.

Social and cultural reforms of other types followed, building on Ottoman movements for sociocultural change, including an active Ottoman women's movement. Western dress was prescribed for men. For women, veiling was not forbidden but discouraged. Polygamy was abolished, and civil marriage became mandatory. Major efforts were made to improve education for women and bring them into professional and public life. As political mobilizer, Mustafa Kemal played an important role in advancing Turkish women, who became eligible to vote in local elections in 1930 and in national ones in 1934—exceptionally early dates by comparative standards. Another important social reform was the adoption of Western-style family names, which became compulsory in 1935. It was then that Mustafa Kemal acquired the surname Atatürk, "father Turk." Among other things, the

Map 9.2 The Middle East,   ▶
1920s–1930s

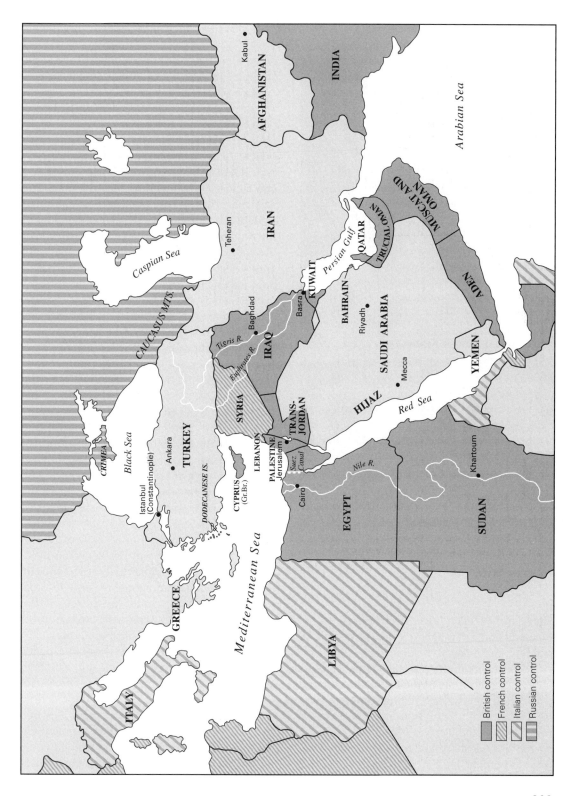

203

Heroes of Turkish Independence, 1922.
*Mustafa Kemal (left), first president of Turkey
(1923–1938), with his deputy Ismet (president,
1938–1950). In 1935, under Turkey's surname
law, they become Mustafa Kemal Atatürk and
Ismet Inönü.   The Mansell Collection/© TIMEPIX, Inc.*

family names aided government efforts to implement modern systems of census registration,
taxation, and military recruitment.

To strengthen the national character of its
culture, Turkey adopted the Latin alphabet and
launched a language revolution to purify Turkish by removing many Ottoman borrowings
from Arabic and Persian. Simultaneously, the
spread of education doubled the literacy rate,
from 11 percent of the population in 1927 to 22

percent in 1940. The cultural inheritance of the
Ottoman Empire became inaccessible to generations schooled only in the new language.

By Atatürk's death (1938), Turkey had experienced a cultural revolution and much social
reform, but no social revolution. Turks had experienced extensive political mobilization, but no
radical redistribution of wealth and power. Several factors contributed to this outcome. One
was that Turkey had extensive uncultivated
lands and distributed these in small holdings to
the rural poor. Through the 1950s, expansion of
the cultivated area was as important a factor in
Turkish economic growth as was industrialization. Except in the southeast, landholding remained much less concentrated than in many
other countries. A substantial minority of rural
households owned no land or had to supplement what they owned by renting or share-
cropping other fields; yet land reform never
became a burning issue in Turkey. Under the
circumstances, sons of the late Ottoman bureaucratic and military elite, like Atatürk, continued to rule Turkey until 1950, and the
"populism" they preached served for authoritarian mobilization of masses who had not yet
found their own voices.

In a different sense, the replacement of the
multinational empire by a Turkish nationalist
state also compensated for the lack of a fundamental restructuring of Turkish society. Yet this
substitution left important problems unsolved.
The collapse of the empire had turned once-in-
ternal nationalist antagonisms into international problems. Despite the peace of the
Atatürk years, lasting tensions between Turks
and Greeks or Armenians illustrated this fact.

While not revolutionary, economic policy
under Atatürk featured a critical innovation. In
1932, Turkey became the first developing state
(Mexico being the second) to adopt central
planning for economic development. Inspired
partly by Soviet practice, Turkey's policy differed in that the state took responsibility only
for key sectors of the economy, leaving others

in private hands. As in Latin America, the industrial drive aimed first at import substitution, then at heavy industry. The first five-year plan accomplished its goals in a number of fields, and the second produced an iron and steel mill, if an inefficient one. In the 1930s, industry's share of gross national product almost doubled, reaching 18 percent. A Turkish managerial class also began to develop; it would play a major economic and political role after 1945.

Not all Turkish reforms were equally successful, but together they created a new concept of a Turkish nation and helped mobilize the populace into citizenship. This intent is clear from the organization of Atatürk's followers into the Republican People's party (1923) and from the nationwide creation of "people's houses" (*halkevi*) and "people's rooms" (*halkodasi*) as political and cultural centers.

Democratic values played a key role in the mobilization process. Like other major Asian cultures, Turkey had no heritage of political pluralism. Under Atatürk it was a one-party state. But he and many others believed Turkey should be democratic. Atatürk encouraged experiments with opposition parties. After 1945, his successor, Ismet Inönü, authorized formation of a second party. When this Democrat party won national elections in 1950, the Republican People's party stepped aside, opening an era of two-party—soon multiparty—politics. Turkey's democratization has since faced many obstacles, but it remains an outstanding chapter in the history of the developing countries.

Comparison with Japan shows a wide developmental gap between the two countries. The causes of this gap must include Turkey's low starting levels in terms of economic and human resources (witness the low literacy levels). Yet Turkish success in creating a new order was impressive. It is little wonder that Atatürk became an inspiration to Middle Eastern leaders of his own and later generations, from Reza Shah in Iran to Nasser and Anwar al-Sadat in Egypt.

China and Japan: Contrasts in Development

Continuing to develop at their own rhythms, the easternmost of the great Asian centers of civilization did not feel any threat from European expansion until much later than either India or the Middle East. Until after 1800, China almost entirely limited its European contacts to trading posts at Guangzhou (Canton); Japan confined its contacts with both Europeans and Chinese to the port of Nagasaki. Both countries suppressed Christianity. The Chinese had traditionally seen their "middle kingdom" as the center of a world economy or world system of its own, with culturally inferior, tributary peoples around their frontiers. More conscious of their debts to other peoples, the Japanese excluded foreigners out of a desire to avoid foreign domination and escape acknowledging Chinese superiority on Chinese terms.

In the mid-nineteenth century, isolation ended as Westerners forcibly "opened" China and then Japan. British merchants first went to China from India. Initially, the trade was profitable to the Chinese. The only way the British could achieve a positive trade balance with China was to import Indian opium, thus fostering drug addiction in China. When the Qing government tried to stop the drug traffic, the British responded with talk of free trade—and with force. The First Opium War (1839–1842) was a sordid affair. Europeans had the means to exert force and goods to sell but no intention of accepting the status of "barbarians" owing tribute to the Chinese emperor.

The British used their victory to create the unequal treaty system, which completely turned the tables on China. This system, which remained in force until 1943, reduced a formally independent country to semicolonial status. The unequal treaties were patterned after the commercial concessions in the Ottoman Empire but eventually went further. By the late nineteenth century, China had made many treaties, and the number of Chinese ports open to foreign trade had grown to about fifty. Extraterritoriality (meaning that foreigners were subject only to the law of their home country) not only covered foreigners wherever they went in China; but in the treaty ports, everyone, including Chinese residents, was subject to the law of the controlling European power. Opium was legalized. Restrictions on missionary activity were eliminated. Tariff rates were set low by treaty, so that the Qing government lost part of its power to raise revenues. As the government slipped into debt to foreign interests, its revenues were placed under foreign control as security for the loans. At the end of the century, as doubts about the Qing dynasty's survival increased, Europeans widened their goals from treaty ports to gaining *spheres of influence*— zones where a given power's interests took precedence.

At midcentury, Japan had seemed headed for a fate no better than China's. The United States took the lead in "opening" Japan. Naval missions commanded by Commodore Matthew Perry visited the country in 1853 and 1854 to press U.S. demands. Over the next few years, the unequal treaty system was established in Japan, too.

The process of "opening" was similar in both countries, but later events differed greatly. China's development remained among the least successful in Asia. Japan's quickly became the most successful.

China's Crisis of Authority

China was slow to respond to outside challenges for many reasons. One was the country's vast size and its population of 300 to 400 million people by the early nineteenth century. Even after many ports had been opened to foreign trade, most Chinese lived in the interior, far from foreigners. Culturally, China was more homogeneous than other large empires. A monolith with great inertia is very hard to move. While the Chinese had learned much from other cultures over the centuries, their rich intellectual tradition and self-centered world-view gave them many ways to explain external challenges. More than other Asian cultural centers, China first reacted to the West with a reinterpretation of its own dominant value tradition, Confucianism. Only at the end of the nineteenth century did China begin significant borrowing from Western cultures.

The Qing Dynasty and the Western Challenge   The decline of the Qing dynasty (1644–1912) complicated China's reaction to the Western challenge. The Qing were not Chinese but Manchu, a tiny minority trying to rule the world's most populous country. Partly in reaction against European pressures, a series of provincial rebellions broke out in the second half of the nineteenth century, complicating the dynasty's problems. The Taiping Rebellion (1850–1864), the most serious, probably caused 20 million deaths, more than World War I. Unable to quell such disturbances with its own forces, the Qing government had to rely on forces led by the local gentry. Thereafter the central government began to lose control of the provinces, and local affairs became militarized. At the turn of the twentieth century, anti-foreign sentiment again boiled over in the Boxer Uprising, a movement that mobilized the young and poor, including women, and had the backing of the powerful empress-mother. When the foreign powers intervened, putting down the Boxers and imposing disastrous terms that inflamed nationalist resentments, the Qing regime lost all credibility.

Under the circumstances, serious reform efforts began slowly. Once underway, they further weakened the regime. In the 1860s, as part of an effort to reassert Confucian ideals of government, the Chinese had made their first experiments in defensive westernization. They tried to obtain modern military technology and organized something like a foreign ministry and a system to train interpreters. Japan's victory in the Sino-Japanese War of 1894 revealed how much more rapidly Japan had changed; this triggered a new seriousness in Chinese reform efforts. A burst of reform ensued in 1898, soon frustrated by the empress-mother's opposition. But the catastrophic end of the Boxer Uprising left her and her supporters no choice but to carry through many of the reforms thwarted only a few years earlier.

The last decade of Qing rule thus brought major change. The examination system that had capped traditional education was replaced by new schools with a mixed Chinese-Western curriculum. Efforts were made to create new military schools and forces. Changes in administration included the creation of ministries and attempts at legal and budgetary reform. Under a plan to create a constitutional system, elective provincial and national assemblies came into being. Meanwhile, widespread demand to nationalize China's developing railways helped politicize the populace.

Revolution was on the way. Sun Yat-sen, China's first professional revolutionary, and others were at work by the 1890s. In 1905 Sun helped found a United League, intended to bring together all opposition elements. When revolution broke out in 1911, however, it was not only the work of this organization. The elective provincial and national assemblies played a critical role, becoming rallying points for opponents of the dynasty. Another essential factor was a government plan for nationalizing the railways on terms favorable to foreigners. When the assemblies' protests against the plan went unheeded, fifteen provinces proclaimed their independence in the fall of 1911. The provincial military forces that had grown up since the mid-nineteenth century then assumed a leading role in overthrowing the Qing regime. Sun returned from abroad to assume the provisional presidency of the Chinese Republic. The three-year-old emperor, bowing to the "mandate of Heaven . . . mani-fested through the wish of the people," abdicated in February 1912.

Nationalists Versus Communists

Recent emperors had been weak, but their office had remained the focus of authority. With the fall of the dynasty, the entire combination of imperial regime and Confucian values came into question. What could hold China together? The revolutionary leadership set out to expand the United League into a National People's party (Guomindang, GMD) and made an attempt at parliamentary government. But the GMD had great difficulty gaining control of the country. Sun relinquished the provisional presidency of the republic to General Yuan Shikai (Yuan Shih-k'ai) after the general forced the emperor to abdicate. But Yuan turned into a dictator and would have made himself emperor if he had not died in 1916. After 1912, real control of much of China passed to local "warlords," military men with their own armies. The GMD did not regain control of China until 1928. Even then, GMD control proved only an episode in China's authority crisis, which continued through the civil war of 1946–1949.

Japanese expansionism worsened China's problems. During World War I, Japan tried to exploit China's weakness by occupying the German positions on the Shandong (Shantung) Peninsula and presenting twenty-one demands, which would have given Japan far-reaching control. China resisted some of the demands but had to accept a treaty recognizing Japan's claims in Shandong, southern Manchuria, and eastern Inner Mongolia. After the war the Paris Peace Conference failed to restore Chinese interests; this failure provoked the May Fourth Movement (1919), a patriotic outburst that marked a new phase in the growth of Chinese nationalism (see Chapter 4).

Students, male and female, were prominent in the movement, for the new schools had done much to promote political mobilization. New political ideas were also spreading, including

Student demonstration, Peking, November 29, 1919. *China's May Fourth Movement opened a new phase in mass politicization. Its memory helped provoke the student-led Tienanmen Square demonstrations of 1989. From the exhibition "China Between Revolutions." Photographs by Sidney D. Gamble, 1917–1927. Copyright 2001, the Sidney D. Gamble Foundation for China Studies*

Marxism. The GMD tried to keep abreast of the changes and absorb the newly politicized elements of the population. Still, in 1921, the Chinese Communist party (CCP) was founded. The GMD and the CCP became leading forces in the struggle to create a new order.

At first, in line with Soviet thinking on Asian national revolutions, the CCP worked with the larger and stronger GMD in hopes of gaining power through it. Sun Yat-sen himself became

interested in the Soviet model, tried to reorganize the GMD along Soviet party lines, and was eager for Comintern aid. Believing he could control the Communists, he accepted them as members of the GMD. One example of this collaboration occurred at the Huangpu (Whampoa) Military Academy. There, Chiang Kai-shek, who later succeeded Sun as head of the GMD, was superintendent, and Zhou Enlai (Chou Enlai), later premier of the People's Republic of

China (1949–1976), had charge of political education.

In the 1920s, during the struggle against the warlords, the GMD-CCP relationship degenerated. A year after Chiang succeeded to GMD leadership in 1925, he launched his Northern Expedition to reunify China. By 1928, this campaign had been so successful that foreign powers recognized the Nationalist regime and began to give up some privileges of the unequal treaties. Meanwhile, GMD-CCP tension worsened to the point of civil war in 1927, and the Communists were defeated for the time being. Many Communists were killed, and many were forced underground or into exile.

For the next several years the Communists struggled to survive. In time they would emerge as China's most effective mass mobilizers. The key to their success was the idea, discussed in Chapter 4, that the revolution could be based on the peasantry, rather than on the proletariat, which scarcely existed in China. Mao Zedong did not invent this idea, but it came to dominate CCP policy as he became leader of the party during the Long March (1934–1935). Mao expressed his understanding of the relationship between mass mobilization and the military struggle in memorable terms: "such a gigantic national revolutionary war as ours cannot succeed without universal . . . mobilization. . . . The popular masses are like water, and the army is like a fish. How . . . can it be said that when there is water, a fish will have difficulty preserving its existence?"[3]

Meanwhile, the GMD faced huge problems in governing China. Chiang spent much of his time manipulating GMD factions. In a country with no tradition of political pluralism, he tried to turn his party into a political machine that would include everyone important. He had only limited control over the GMD military and the countryside. Based on Sun's Three People's Principles—nationalism, democracy, and "people's livelihood" (a classical concept sometimes equated with socialism)—the GMD ideology also lacked the clarity of communist thought. Largely urban oriented, the GMD regime failed to win over the peasantry. The GMD's economic development efforts, too, almost solely benefited the modern sector of the economy, centered in the coastal cities. Agriculture, in which some 80 percent of the populace worked amid widespread landlessness and exploitation, remained nearly untouched except where the Communists gained control.

Japanese Aggression The GMD also faced Japanese aggression in Manchuria, whose population was almost entirely Chinese. However, the Japanese claimed interests there and were the region's leading foreign investors. In warlord days, Japan wielded power in Manchuria behind a front of Chinese rule, but the spread of Chinese nationalism challenged that. In 1931, Japanese officers in Manchuria responded by attacking the Chinese at Mukden. The Japanese then created the puppet state of Manchukuo (see Map 9.3) and extended their control southward into northern China.

As in 1918, Japanese aggression inflamed Chinese nationalism. Chiang knew he was not strong enough to take on Japan, and the Communists posed a more direct threat to his government. But his strategy of military campaigns against the Communists, rather than against the foreign invader, roused Chinese resentment until Chiang had to form a second common front between GMD and CCP in 1937. By then, a full-scale war between China and Japan had begun. For China, it was the beginning of World War II.

War brought with it virtually genocidal Japanese attacks on the Chinese and became, as well, the midwife of Communist revolution. Japanese attacks forced the Nationalists into the interior, cutting them off from their support in the coastal cities. The landlord class, which had supported them in the countryside, either had to flee with them or remain helpless behind. That left the Communists to extend their bases,

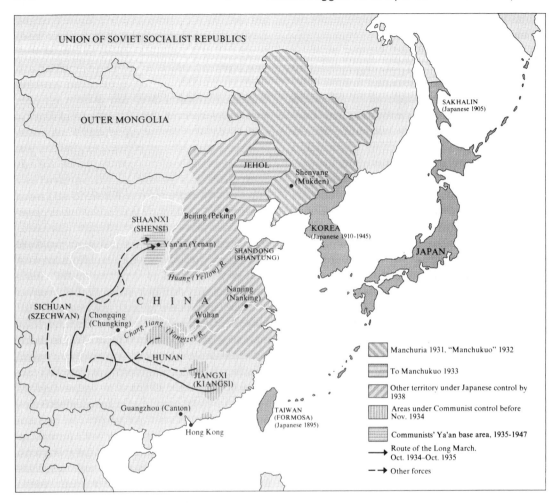

Map 9.3 China and Japan in the 1930s

undermine the landlords' two-thousand-year domination, and apply their skills in guerrilla warfare. With the GMD unable to defend the nation, the Communists began to seem like the real nationalists. The invading Japanese forces, heavily armed but badly provisioned, were completely unprepared to cope with the huge numbers of both GMD soldiers who surrendered and civilians who fell into their hands when they captured Chinese cities. The result was the massacre of hundreds of thousands of Chinese and the rape of many women, not only during the "rape of Nanjing," but in many places. By the time of Japan's defeat, GMD authority had declined to a point that set the stage for Communist triumph in the civil war of 1946–1949.

Japan's First Rise to Great-Power Status

U.S. commodore Matthew Perry's visits to Japan in 1853 and 1854 sparked a crisis that illustrates basic differences between Japan and China.

Shanghai railroad station bombed by the Japanese, 1937. *A bloodied, abandoned infant, wailing amid the wreckage, symbolizes China's plight.*
© *Bettmann/CORBIS*

Those differences explain why Japan's response to the West differed so from China's.

Whereas in China the emperor remained the central political figure despite dynastic decline, real power in Japan had for centuries belonged to a leading member of the warrior class, the *shogun,* though the emperor retained legitimacy and prestige. In China, the leading elite was that of scholar-officials, who served the emperor; in Japan, it was the warrior class of the *samurai.* Although many of them had become civilian bureaucrats in fact, samurai felt superior to commoners and jealously guarded their monopoly of warlike skills and privileges. But they differed vastly in wealth and power. After the shogun, the leading samurai were the lords (*daimyo*) of large and supposedly autonomous domains, numbering 260 in the nineteenth century. Each daimyo had many samurai

retainers. It took a strong shogun to control this system. By the 1850s the shogunate was in decline. The need to respond to U.S. demands provoked its final crisis.

Japan needed consensus about such a controversial question. Most Japanese wanted the foreigners repelled, but the nation lacked the strength to do so. The shogun found himself forced to make treaties with the United States and other powers, granting privileges of the sort that foreigners enjoyed in China. The shogun's inability to apply the policy that most Japanese wanted, and economic disruption following the country's sudden opening, brought the shogunate into question. Samurai discipline began to collapse. The emperor's prestige remained intact, however, and in 1868 a rebellion broke out under the slogan of "restoring" the rule of the emperor. The shogunate fell.

Revolution by Way of Restoration This event is called the Meiji Restoration, after the emperor. The Meiji emperor (1867–1912) did not wield real power, which the men who made the rebellion retained. The changes they introduced mark the beginning of modern Japan and deserve the name "revolution."

Major changes began with the organization of the central government system. In 1868 a Council of State was created, with various ministries under it. The revolutionary leaders soon assumed control of these ministries. In the same year, the imperial capital was moved from Kyoto to Tokyo, which under its old name "Edo" had been the shogun's center. The next priority was to reassert central government authority over the autonomous domains; otherwise, Japan could produce no coordinated response to the Western challenge. The new leaders persuaded the daimyo to return their holdings voluntarily to the emperor. At first the daimyo were allowed to stay on as governors; but soon the domains disappeared entirely as the country was redivided into prefectures, the basis of the centrally controlled system of local government that still exists. The next step was to create a modern army and navy. The leaders of the revolution came from daimyo domains in which experiments in military modernization predated the revolution. The new leaders made such experimentation a national policy. They also undermined the status of the lower samurai by making military service compulsory for all men (1873). Thus the new government eliminated Japan's old social class distinctions almost entirely.

A key problem for the new regime was finance. Existing revenue had been inadequate for the shogun. Because the new regime did not have good enough credit to borrow abroad and did not want to, Japan escaped the slide into bankruptcy and foreign financial control that other Asian countries experienced in this period. The new government limited its borrowing to the internal market and worked to improve its finances by reforming its monetary, banking, and taxation systems. Land tax reform gave landownership in the countryside to the peasants who actually paid the tax. Its effect was to stimulate growth in agricultural output and provide capital for the first phase of Japan's modern economic development.

At first, economic growth was fastest in traditional sectors—agriculture, commerce, and handicrafts. Stimulants to growth included domestic security, expansion of foreign trade, national economic unification, and improvements such as modern shipping, telegraphs, and railways. A distinctive combination of government leadership and private enterprise developed as well. The government led in certain fields of industry, later selling many of the enterprises it founded to private investors. Even in the Meiji period, however, individual initiative probably contributed more to industrialization than did government.

In fact, Japanese readiness to respond to opportunities for economic growth was extraordinary by any standard. Even before the Meiji Restoration, Japan may have had an adult literacy rate of 40 percent, Asia's highest. Because of the country's isolation and ethnic homogeneity, its commerce remained essentially in the hands of Japanese, as opposed to foreigners or unassimilated minorities. Outside the samurai class, the Japanese had a long history as eager businessmen. After 1868, even former samurai assumed important roles in business. In time, Japanese business and industry developed a dual character, with both huge conglomerates (*zaibatsu*, "financial cliques") and small enterprises. By the early twentieth century, Japan's industry was diversified and strong, and the economy had enjoyed a quarter-century of significant growth.

By 1900, then, Japan had responded to the Western challenge more successfully than any other non-Western country, including ones that had faced serious challenge far earlier. The contrast with China reflected major differences between the two. Japan lacked China's size and inertia but was at least as uniform in culture and more so in population. Japan had no vast interior isolated from contact with foreigners, and Japan had more of a history of cultural borrowing. Once Japan was "opened," revolution quickly followed, provoking rapid change in many fields. For example, Japanese writers produced popular books about the West, introduced journalism, and translated Western literary successes. Japanese were popularizing Western ideas on a large scale by the 1860s and 1870s, much before the Chinese and almost as early as the Ottomans, whose contacts with Europe went back centuries earlier. Japan's government fostered cultural development by becoming Asia's first to develop a Western-style, national, secular school system, from compulsory elementary schools through universities. Primary school enrollment grew from 28 percent of school-age children in 1873 to 96 percent in 1905.

Japan as a Great Power Its leaders wanted Japan to gain acceptance from the major powers as an equal. This concern had important implications for internal politics. Japanese leaders, like other non-Western leaders of the time, assumed that representative government had something to do with the success of the great powers. They also had to contend with demands from former samurai for political participation. As a result, the Meiji regime introduced representative bodies at the prefectural level in 1878. Political parties emerged in the 1880s. In 1889 the country received a constitution, drafted along German lines.

The constitution of 1889 vested supreme authority in the emperor, who held vast executive, legislative, and military powers. Ministers were responsible to him, rather than to parliament. As in Germany, the chief of staff remained independent in matters of command from the army minister. Thus the military was not under civilian control. There was a parliament, known in English as the Diet, with two houses. The budget and all permanent laws required approval of both houses, although the govern-

ment could keep operating under the last year's budget if the Diet failed to pass the new one. The constitution gave the people numerous rights, usually with restrictions.

Compared to Japan before 1868, the constitution was a remarkable change. But it contained problems. It did not say who would exercise the many powers formally vested in the emperor. In practice, the top civil and military officials did so. The constitution also did not clearly regulate relations among the various power centers. What if the Diet tried to assert control over the cabinet, as is normal in parliamentary systems? What if military commanders used their independence to launch operations that the cabinet opposed? Both these things eventually happened, and the latter produced tragic results.

Their wish for recognition as a great power also led Japan's leaders to pay great attention to foreign policy. Their method, typical of the time, was imperialist expansion. By 1895, they had seized the Ryukyu Islands and made war against China, winning Taiwan and other concessions. These gains were economically significant, for Japan was losing self-sufficiency in rice. From then on, it could supply its needs with cheap rice from its dependencies.

Japan's diplomatic gains were more important. Impressed by Japan's rise, Western powers began to conclude new pacts surrendering the unequal treaty privileges. In 1902, Britain made an alliance with Japan on a footing of formal equality; this was the first peacetime military alliance between an Asian and a European power. Most astonishing was Japan's victory in the Russo-Japanese War of 1904–1905—the most dramatic pre-1914 defeat of a European state by a non-Western one. Japan then expanded its interests in Manchuria and annexed Korea (1910).

By 1914, Japan had risen from semicolonialism to nominal equality with the great powers and had acquired its own overseas dependencies. Siding with the British in World War I, it did little militarily but used the occasion to pick up German possessions in China and the Pacific. Japan was the only non-Western power to sit with the victors at the peace conference. There the great powers showed that they still did not accept Japan as an equal, for when it tried to get a clause on racial equality inserted into the Versailles peace treaty, U.S. and British opposition thwarted the effort. But the conference did aggravate Chinese nationalist resentment by leaving Japan the territories it had taken in China.

Democratization or Militarism? Between the world wars, Japan's growth into a great power continued. From 1914 until World War II, the economy grew spectacularly. The record was marred by unimpressive performance from 1920 to 1932. But Japan was already recovering from the Depression by 1932, earlier than any other major power. By 1940, less than half of Japanese workers were employed in agriculture, and some zaibatsu firms had grown into the largest financial empires in the world. In the economy, as in other spheres, Japan no longer simply imitated the West. By the 1930s, for example, the Japanese had designed and produced the biggest battleships ever built.

Political parties grew in influence during this period. At first, this development seemed to strengthen the influence of parliament over the cabinet. Although it never became a principle that the majority leader in the Diet would become prime minister, from 1924 to 1932 the prime minister was always the head of one of the two major parties. Suffrage was broadened in 1925 to include all men of twenty-five and older (women did not get the vote until 1947). Through 1937, the popular vote showed public support for democratization.

Yet Japan was not destined to consolidate its democracy during the interwar period. One reason was that the bureaucracy wielded more power than in most democracies. The main reason was lack of civilian control of the military. Various factors—the Depression, conflict with

China over Manchuria, the rise of fascism—led the military to assert its independence in ways that upset the liberal trend.

The Depression contributed by calling down blame for economic distress on the parties and the big firms. Rightists and militarists asked whether Japan could afford to depend on world markets or should expand its empire. By 1931 the army was also concerned that Chinese Nationalist progress threatened its position in Manchuria. Two Japanese colonels organized a plot, not without high-level complicity. A Japanese-staged railway bombing at Mukden became the pretext to attack Chinese troops in Manchuria, and the conflict spread. The Manchurian episode seriously affected the Japanese government's credibility. Repeatedly, the government announced it had limited the scope of conflict, only to have further military initiatives follow. By 1932, Japan had been condemned by the League of Nations, had withdrawn from it, and had moved beyond Manchuria to occupy parts of Inner Mongolia. Inside Japan, extreme rightists went into action, using violence against the Left and the liberals. By 1937, when war with China began, militarists had essentially captured control of the cabinet. Japan's naval commanders, meanwhile, resented treaty limits on Japan's and other states' sea power. By 1937, Japan had withdrawn from the disarmament system and begun a naval buildup.

Japan never acquired the charismatic dictator, mass movement, or clear-cut ideology of a fascist regime. But it moved toward authoritarianism and militarism. Japan's aggression in China and its naval expansion upset relations with the United States and Britain, and many of the Japanese responsible for these developments preferred Fascist Italy and Nazi Germany. In September 1940, impressed by German victories, Japan signed an alliance with Germany and Italy. The alliance bound each country to go to war against any nation attacking any one of them. Japan had committed itself to the Axis, a decision that would bring it to virtual destruction in World War II.

Conclusion: China, India, Turkey, and Japan Compared

With the integration of Asia into the European-dominated world order, no Asian country entirely escaped the effects of European expansion. In reaction, independence movements emerged everywhere. A comparison of Asia's two most populous countries, China and India, and of its two most dynamic independent nations of the interwar period, Turkey and Japan, suggests that the outcome of these struggles depended on several prerequisites. These are adaptability in response to the imperialist challenge, consensus about national identity and the forms of political life, mass mobilization to support the drive for independence, and formulation of a development strategy that could overcome economic colonialism. Comparing the four countries illustrates the significance of these points.

During the interwar period, China probably endured the worst fate of all these countries. It had to survive not only a change of dynasty but also the collapse of its historical synthesis of imperial regime and Confucian value system. The crisis that began with the Qing dynasty collapse in 1911 would not end until 1949. Meanwhile, consensus about national identity was not a major issue for the hundreds of millions who were ethnically and culturally Chinese, despite their differences of dialect. Achieving consensus on how to organize a new political order proved extremely hard, however. The effort produced two rival nationalist movements. Its effects worsened by Japanese aggression, their rivalry led to the civil war of 1946-1949 and to the creation of two regimes—the People's Republic on the mainland and the Republic of China on Taiwan—each professing to be the real China. The prolonged

political struggle showed how hard it was to mobilize China's huge population. In this, the GMD failed, but the CCP under Mao succeeded, ultimately as mass mobilizers authoritarian-style. After 1949, revitalization of the economy remained one of the greatest challenges for the Communists.

India, in contrast, could not forge a broad enough consensus about national identity to prevent partition into separate Hindu and Muslim states in 1947. Yet Indians made important gains in other respects. Gandhi symbolized the Hindus' openness to new ideas. Selflessly committed to the poor, he pioneered, through his Constructive Development program, the kind of rural development that most nationalist leaders of his era neglected. He played the critical role, too, in creating a sense of national unity among a population highly fragmented by language, religion, caste, region, and modes of political awareness. This response to India's diversity helped to forge a constitutional consensus that, if fragile, has made independent India the world's largest democracy. India experienced no revolution in social structure, but some of the pre-1947 social reforms—the mobilization of women and Untouchables, or the extension of the vote to both sexes—were major gains. Clearly not all Indians responded to the same signals. Gandhi's methods remained a moral inspiration to people around the world. Yet much more would be heard in India after independence from the Hindu militants who assassinated him, from business interests who saw India's economic future not in hand spinning but in industrialization, and from elitist nationalists like Nehru who expected to guide the masses mobilized by Gandhi toward a reformist-socialist future of their devising, not his.

In Turkey, despite a century of vigorous reform under the late Ottoman Empire, the resistance of Islamic tradition to alien ideas was such that—as in China—really reorienting the country required the drastic means of cultural revolution. Geography made Turkey unique in its potential for the reorientation toward the West that Atatürk carried out. Because of the Ottoman Empire's collapse and the success of the Turkish independence movement (1919-1922), Atatürk's Turkey came through this readjustment with relatively high levels of consensus about national identity and democratic government. Change stopped short of revolution in Turkey's social structure, however. For most Turks, the shift from polyglot empire to Turkish Republic, the many social and cultural reforms, and the authoritarian mobilization of the Atatürk years probably seemed revolutionary enough. The availability of uncultivated land and its distribution to smallholders also spared Turkey the acute agrarian problems found in India or Latin America. Turkey's policy of state initiative in developing key industries set an example that most other developing countries emulated through the 1960s. Yet in the long run this policy could not match the productivity of Japan's distinctive approach.

Japan performed superlatively along all four dimensions considered here. It was uniquely successful in quickly turning its encounter with imperialism to its own advantage. By the interwar period, Japan's mastery of modern ideas and techniques, as in industrial production, had gone beyond cultural borrowing to a synthesis between Japanese tradition and Western or now international ways. One of the world's few countries historically endowed with the homogeneity of the nation-state ideal, Japan had no need to redefine national identity. A redefinition of constitutional principles did occur with the Meiji Restoration—really a revolutionary change. But the fact that the Japanese could conceptualize the shogunate's elimination as a re-emphasis on another institution of ancient and unimpaired legitimacy, the imperial throne, greatly eased their transition. Socially, Meiji Japan experienced significant structural change with the destruction of the samurai, the elimination of the old class distinctions, and the land tax reform, which gave landownership to

the peasant cultivators. Thereafter, the cultural homogeneity, high literacy, and business spirit of the Japanese contributed to an extraordinary economic transformation. By the 1920s, Japan could supply many agricultural needs from its colonies and had become internationally competitive in industry. A nation-state with a powerful industrial economy and a colonial empire, Japan had become a great power. Some problems remained unresolved, especially the lack of civilian control over the military. These flaws would bring Japan to defeat in World War II—the final crisis of the European great powers it had come to resemble—before its extraordinary rise resumed.

Notes

1. Edgar Snow, *Red Star Over China* (New York: Random House, 1938); *Stories of the Long March* (Beijing: Foreign Languages Press, 1958).

2. Jay Apt, "The Astronauts' View of Home," *National Geographic* (November 1996), p. 14.

3. Quoted in Michael Gasster, *China's Struggle to Modernize,* 2d ed. (New York: Knopf, 1983), p. 78.

Suggestions for Further Reading

India

Brown, Judith M. *Modern India: The Origins of an Asian Democracy.* 2d ed. (1994).

Chatterjee, Partha. *The Nation and Its Fragments: Colonial and Postcolonial Histories* (1993).

Guha, Ranajit. *Elementary Aspects of Peasant Insurgency* (1983).

Lal, Deepak. *The Hindu Equilibrium.* Vol. 1, *Cultural Stability and Economic Stagnation: India, c. 1500 B.C.-A.D. 1980* (1988).

Mehta, Ved. *Mahatma Gandhi and His Apostles* (1983).

Wolpert, Stanley. *A New History of India.* 6th ed. (2000).

The Middle East

Cleveland, William L. *A History of the Modern Middle East* (1994).

Goldschmidt, Arthur, Jr. *A Concise History of the Middle East.* 6th ed. (1999).

Richards, Alan, and John Waterbury. *A Political Economy of the Middle East: State, Class, and Economic Development.* 2d ed. (1996).

Zürcher, Erik J. *Turkey: A Modern History* (1998).

China and Japan

Duara, Prasenjit. *Rescuing History from the Nation: Questioning Narratives of Modern China* (1995).

Fairbank, John K., Edwin O. Reischauer, and Albert M. Craig. *East Asia: Tradition and Transformation* (1978).

Honda, Katsuichi. *The Nanjing Massacre: A Japanese Journalist Confronts Japan's National Shame.* Trans. Karen Sandness (1999).

Reischauer, Edwin O. *Japan: The Story of a Nation.* 4th ed. (1989).

Schram, Stuart. *The Thought of Mao Tse-Tung* (1989).

Spence, Jonathan. *The Search for Modern China.* 2d ed. (1999).

PART FOUR

World War II, Superpower Rivalry, and the Post–Cold War World

CHAPTER | 10

World War II:
The Final Crisis
of European
Global Dominance

THE FIRST YEAR OF WORLD WAR II IN EUROPE, AS WE SHALL SEE IN THIS CHAPTER, could not have gone better for Adolf Hitler. His armies overran most of Europe, leaving only Britain continuing the fight against him. In the summer of 1940, as his *Luftwaffe* (air force) prepared to destroy the Royal Air Force as preclude to an invasion, Hitler declared that he had won the war and was willing to offer Britain peace: "I can see no reason why this war need go on." His public speech was followed by private Nazi peace feelers through neutral channels. The British reply, however, was uncompromising:

> On October 12, 1939, His Majesty's Government defined at length their position toward German peace offers. . . . Since then a number of new hideous crimes have been committed by Nazi Germany against the smaller States upon her borders. Norway has been overrun, and is now occupied by a German invading army. Denmark has been seized and pillaged. Belgium and Holland, after all their efforts to placate Herr Hitler, and in spite of all the assurances given to them by the German Government that their neutrality would be respected, have been conquered and subjugated. In Holland particularly, acts of long-prepared treachery and brutality culminated in the massacre of Rotterdam, where many thousands of Dutchmen were slaughtered, and an important part of the city destroyed.
>
> These horrible events have darkened the pages of European history with an indelible stain. His Majesty's Government see in them not the slightest cause to recede in any way from their principles and resolves

as set forth in October, 1939. On the contrary, their intention to prosecute the war against Germany by any means in their power until Hitlerism is finally broken and the world relieved from the curse which a wicked man has brought upon it has been strengthened to such a point that they would rather all perish in the common ruin than fail or falter in their duty. . . . [I]t will always be possible for Germany to ask for an armistice, as she did in 1918 . . .[1]

Though the reply was issued in the name of all the King's ministers, the language was clearly that of the Prime Minister, Mr. Churchill. But was this the right answer to give Hitler? Some people doubted it then, and recently a few historians who were not even born in 1940 have attracted attention by suggesting that it was not. Do you agree? When you have read the whole chapter, ask yourself what Europe might have been like if the British had not continued to fight Hitler in 1940.

From Phony War to Operation Barbarossa, 1939–1941

The habit of looking at the twentieth-century world from the perspective of European dominance is hard to shake. Even now, a half-century after that dominance collapsed at the end of World War II, Western historians often date the war from Hitler's invasion of Poland in 1939. Americans often date the war from the Japanese attack on the U.S. fleet at Pearl Harbor on December 7, 1941. By then Britain had been fighting Germany for a year alone, while German armies overran most of Europe. Britain found an ally against Hitler only when he invaded the Soviet Union on June 22, 1941, the day the war begins in Russian history books.

For many non-Europeans, however, World War II dates from well before 1939. For the Chinese, it began in 1931 against the Japanese in Manchuria. For the Ethiopians, virtually the only Africans not under European rule, it began with the Italian invasion in 1935.

The significance of these differing dates is that what we call "World War II" was the convergence of originally separate drives for empire into one conflict. One drive began with Hitler's war with Britain and France over Poland, one of the last two surviving creations of the Versailles system. This last of Europe's "civil wars" became a German campaign for "living space," which culminated in a Hitlerian empire stretching across Europe.

Another drive for empire began with Japan's penetration of China in the 1930s. Profiting from Hitler's attack on the European colonial powers, the Japanese extended their control over a large part of the East Asian mainland and the islands of the southwest Pacific, including the Dutch East Indies and the Philippines.

By the end of 1941, the German and Japanese drives for empire had converged to make World War II a conflict of continents. It pitted Europe, under Hitler's rule, against the worldwide British Empire, which also had to face much of Asia, under the dominance of Japan.

Had Germany not attacked the Soviet Union, and had Japan not attacked the United States, those other two continent-size powers might not have been drawn into the struggle. Until Hitler attacked, Stalin had adhered to the Nazi-Soviet Pact of August 1939. A clear majority of U.S. citizens favored neutrality in the war until the Japanese attacked them.

Russian and American participation brought World War II to a turning point by mid-to-late 1942. Until then, the so-called Axis Powers (Germany, Japan, and Italy) had achieved an unbroken series of victories. German armies surged to the northern tip of Norway, to the shores of the Greek peninsula and the Black Sea, and over much of the North African desert. The Japanese swept to the eastern frontiers of India and to the arctic fringes of North America in the Aleutian Islands.

Even in this early period, however, the Axis leaders made fateful mistakes. Hitler failed to defeat Britain. He neither invaded it nor cut its lifelines across the Atlantic and through the Mediterranean. Meanwhile, he repeated Napoleon's fatal blunder of invading Russia while Britain remained unconquered. The Japanese leaders did not join in this attack on their enemy of the war of 1904–1905 but tried to avert U.S. interference with their empire building by destroying the U.S. Pacific fleet. After the attack on Pearl Harbor, it was Hitler who declared war on the United States, not the United States on Hitler.

These uncoordinated Axis attacks forced together what Churchill called the "Grand Alliance" of Britain, the Soviet Union, and the United States. Together, these dissimilar Allies were too strong for the Axis. Consistently victorious through most of 1942, the Axis encountered nothing but defeat thereafter. Germany and subjugated Europe had been a match for Britain, despite the troops sent by British dominions, such as Canada, Australia, and New Zealand. But the Russian war destroyed Hitler's

armies, and the U.S. agreement to give priority to Germany's defeat made it certain. After mid-1942, the Americans, the British, and their allies also steadily pushed the Japanese back. When the Soviet Union, after Hitler's defeat, joined Japan's enemies in 1945, Japanese prospects became hopeless, even without the awful warning of two American nuclear attacks—the first in history and the last, so far.

Throughout the war, the Axis Powers failed to cooperate effectively. They also did not mobilize their home fronts as effectively as the Allies. Despite German rhetoric about uniting the peoples of Europe and Japanese claims to be leading an Asian crusade against imperialism, neither Germany nor Japan was able to mobilize the enthusiasm of a majority in the lands they overran. Instead their treatment of conquered peoples was marked by cruelty and greed, which inspired even civilians to abandon passivity for active resistance.

After World War I, people quickly concluded that most of the slogans for which they had fought were hollow. After World War II, the revelations of Japanese and Nazi brutality kept alive the sense that this second global conflict had been fought for a just cause. But although the war defeated evil regimes, this struggle of continents also destroyed the power of Europe as a whole and the European-dominated global system. Within a generation after 1945, even Britain, bankrupt and exhausted in victory, would grant independence to most of its Asian and African colonies. From this "end of empire" would soon emerge the Third World of countries reluctant to subordinate themselves to either the United States or the Soviet Union, the only great powers left after 1945.

Not only in the already threatening conflict of these two superpowers does the world of 1945 foreshadow most of the rest of the century. Even more intensively than in 1914–1918, the pressures of total war expanded the powers of governments, transformed societies, and revolutionized the economies of the world. Moreover, with official encouragement, scientists produced a weapon so incomparably deadly that thoughtful people wondered whether human beings still had a future. We still live with that unprecedented uncertainty of 1945. In this respect as in most, World War II marks the turning point of the twentieth-century world, though few people foresaw this transformation when Hitler's armies crossed the Polish border on September 1, 1939.

The German attack on Poland underscored the revolutionary impact of the internal combustion engine on warfare. *Blitzkrieg* (lightning war) used fast-moving masses of tanks, closely supported by aircraft, to shatter opposition. The gallant charges of Polish cavalry could not stop them. Within a month Poland ceased to exist. Russian troops moved in to occupy the eastern half of the country, where a majority of the population were not Poles but Ukrainians. The Russians deported over a million Poles eastward, most to their deaths. Stalin now had a common border with his German ally, some two hundred miles west of the former Soviet-Polish frontier. He also regained control of the strategic Baltic seacoast by annexing the three small nations of Latvia, Lithuania, and Estonia, former provinces of the tsarist empire that had declared their independence after the 1917 revolution.

The Phony War and the Fall of France

Meanwhile the British and French did nothing, though they had declared war on Poland's behalf. The French army and a small British contingent moved into defensive positions and bombarded the Germans with propaganda leaflets. For the moment, they were unwilling to attack, and Hitler was unready. The resulting "phony war" profoundly damaged the morale of Germany's enemies, especially the French. Governments that had gone reluctantly to war now debated where to fight it. Defeatists who had argued it was crazy to go to war for Poland now declared it was even crazier to fight after Poland had been destroyed. Communist propaganda explained the war as a conflict between equally greedy imperialist powers. Meanwhile Hitler conquered Norway, whose location was strategically essential in an Anglo-German naval and air struggle (Map 10.1). The Norwegian king and his ministers fled to London, the first of many governments-in-exile to find sanctuary there. Hitler established a puppet government headed by Vidkun Quisling, a Norwegian fascist. His name has become a generic term for traitors who do a conqueror's dirty work.

The lull ended when Hitler launched the blitzkrieg westward on May 10, 1940. Horrified by the destruction of Rotterdam—the first European use of aerial bombardment to terrorize the population of a large city—the Dutch soon surrendered. Belgium held out little longer. No one had expected these small countries to withstand Hitler. The great shock of 1940 was the fall of France.

The country that had held off Germany for almost five years in 1914–1918 now collapsed within six weeks, suffering over a quarter-million casualties. Such losses are proof that despite the prewar quarrels that had continued through the phony war, many of the French still believed in their country's cause. What they lacked was not courage but the weapons and especially the leadership needed for mechanized war. France's elderly generals had ignored the warnings of the soldier-scholar Charles de Gaulle that the machine had revolutionized warfare. Unable to hold a line as they had in 1914–1918, they could only surrender.

Map 10.1 World War II: ◆
The European Theater

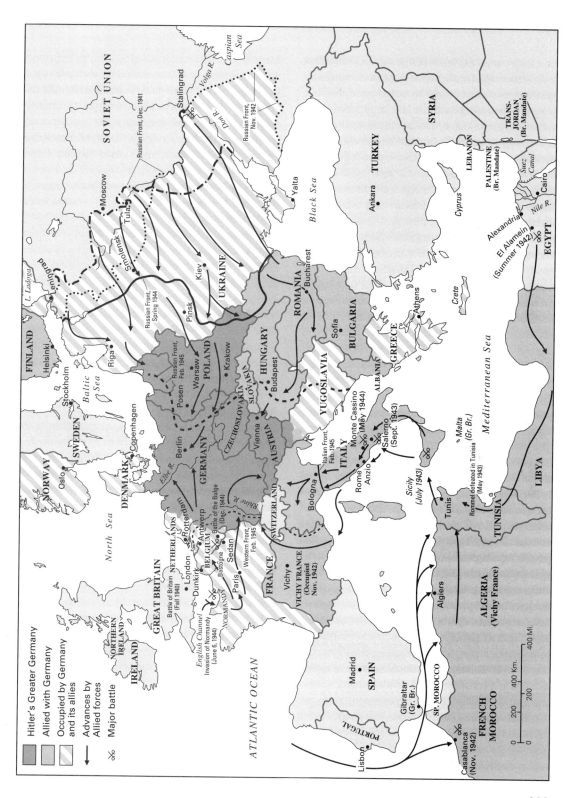

SOVIET UNION

Caspian Sea

Volga R.

Russian Front, Dec. 1941

Stalingrad

Russian Front, Nov. 1942

Don R.

Moscow

Tula

Smolensk

Leningrad

L. Ladoga

FINLAND

Helsinki

NORWAY

Oslo

SWEDEN

Stockholm

Baltic Sea

Copenhagen

DENMARK

North Sea

IRELAND

NORTHERN IRELAND

GREAT BRITAIN

Battle of Britain (Fall 1940)

London

Dunkirk

English Channel

Invasion of Normandy (June 6, 1944)

NORMANDY

Paris

Sedan

Rotterdam

Antwerp

Bastogne

Battle of the Bulge (Dec. 1944)

NETHERLANDS

BELGIUM

Western Front, Feb. 1945

Rhine R.

Elbe R.

Berlin

GERMANY

Posen

Warsaw

POLAND

Krakow

Russian Front, Feb. 1945

Russian Front, Spring 1944

Pinsk

Kiev

UKRAINE

Riga

CZECHOSLOVAKIA

Vienna

AUSTRIA

SWITZERLAND

SLOVAKIA

HUNGARY

Budapest

ROMANIA

Bucharest

Sofia

BULGARIA

YUGOSLAVIA

ALBANIA

GREECE

Athens

Black Sea

Yalta

Crete

TURKEY

Ankara

SYRIA

LEBANON

PALESTINE (Br. Mandate)

TRANS-JORDAN (Br. Mandate)

Cyprus

Suez Canal

Cairo

Nile R.

Alexandria

El Alamein (Summer 1942)

EGYPT

Mediterranean Sea

Malta (Gr. Br.)

Monte Cassino (May 1944)

Salerno (Sept. 1943)

Anzio

Rome

ITALY

Bologna

Italian Front, Feb. 1945

Sicily (July 1943)

Tunis

Rommel defeated in Tunisia (May 1943)

TUNISIA

LIBYA

Algiers

ALGERIA (Vichy France)

FRANCE

VICHY FRANCE (Occupied Nov. 1942)

Vichy

ATLANTIC OCEAN

PORTUGAL

Lisbon

SPAIN

Madrid

Gibraltar (Gr. Br.)

SP. MOROCCO

FRENCH MOROCCO

Casablanca (Nov. 1942)

Hitler's Greater Germany

Allied with Germany

Occupied by Germany and its allies

Advances by Allied forces

Major battle

400 Mi.

400 Km.

200

200

0

0

223

Hitler savored his revenge for the Versailles treaty, forcing the French to capitulate in the very railroad car where Foch had accepted the German surrender in 1918. Hoping to make the French reliable satellites, he allowed them to keep their fleet and colonies. There would still be a French government in the southern two-fifths of the country, where German columns had not penetrated. Thus the little resort of Vichy replaced Paris as the capital, and Marshal Philippe Pétain, a hero of World War I, set up an authoritarian regime to replace the fallen democratic republic. Stunned by defeat, most Frenchmen at first accepted this dictatorship. Few heeded the radio appeal of General de Gaulle, who had fled to London, for Frenchmen to join him in continuing the battle overseas.

"Their Finest Hour"

Within a few weeks of Hitler's attack, the British found themselves all alone against him. Hitler publicly proposed peace. He had never really wanted a war with the British Empire. His onslaught, coming after the British failure to keep the Germans out of Norway, had discredited Neville Chamberlain's government. The new prime minister, Winston Churchill, replied that Britain would make peace if Hitler gave up all his conquests.

Churchill combined apparently contradictory traits into a remarkable personality—the last great figure of the age of European global dominance. Child of an old, aristocratic family, he had been a political maverick throughout his forty years in the House of Commons. As First Lord of the Admiralty at the beginning of both world wars, he had been at the center of the British military establishment, yet he remained a consistent champion of military innovations. Excluded from government through the 1930s because he opposed appeasing Hitler, he became Britain's leader chiefly because the policies he had criticized had failed. But the vision, energy, and determination that had made

him a loner were now the qualities Britain needed.

Steeped in history, Churchill did not always see the future clearly. He had opposed concessions to Gandhi as resolutely as he opposed them to Hitler. Churchill's understanding of the past, however, gifted him with words to unite Britain's class-ridden society in old-fashioned patriotism. The battle of France was over, he declared on June 18:

I expect that the Battle of Britain is about to begin . . . Hitler knows that he will have to break us in this island or lose the war . . . [If] we fail, then the whole world . . . will sink into the abyss of a new Dark Age. . . . Let us therefore brace ourselves to our duties, and so bear ourselves that if the British Empire and its Commonwealth last for a thousand years, men will say "This was their finest hour."[2]

Since Churchill ignored Hitler's prophetic warning that the British Empire would not long survive another world war, the Nazi leader reluctantly ordered his staff to plan an invasion. As his generals and admirals wrangled over how to carry the blitzkrieg across twenty miles of the English Channel, the Luftwaffe offered the alternative of bombing Britain into submission.

Through the summer of 1940 the Battle of Britain raged in the English skies. Just as it was devastating British air bases, the Luftwaffe made the mistake of switching its target to London. Thus Londoners became the first to prove, as the citizens of Tokyo and Berlin later confirmed, that people can continue to live and work under the stresses of nightly air raids. Meanwhile the Royal Air Force, aided by a radar early-warning system in operation only since 1939, shot down two Germans for every plane it lost. Unable to establish air superiority, Hitler "postponed" his invasion of Britain—a delay that proved to be permanent.

The Battle of Britain may have determined the entire future course of the war. Hitler now faced the prospect of a long war, requiring a level of preparedness he had told his planners to expect only in 1944 or 1945. Moreover, though Britain was as incapable of attacking Germany as Germany was of attacking Britain, Britain might find an ally. Striving, while half-prepared, to eliminate such potential allies, Hitler was drawn into an ever-widening, eventually global, war he could not win.

Mediterranean Campaigns

The failures of Mussolini provoked the first dispersions of German strength. Having remained neutral, except for a belated attack on defeated France, the Duce decided that Italy would risk less by joining the general war than it would by failing to profit from Germany's victories. In September 1940, he struck from Libya, Italy's North African colony, at the British in Egypt. A month later, he invaded Greece. Both attacks were fiascos. The British pushed the Italians out of Egypt; the Greeks pushed them out of Greece. Hitler had had little notice of the Italian plans—only one example of the general Axis failure to coordinate strategies. But he had to retrieve Mussolini's failures. If he did not, the British might overrun North Africa and return to the European mainland by way of the Balkans. In the spring of 1941, German troops arrived in North Africa to stiffen the Italians. Hitler thus involved himself in a seesaw desert battle that would end in an Axis defeat two years later. Almost simultaneously, he invaded Greece and Yugoslavia, quickly defeating them.

Neither of these campaigns proved decisive. Hitler never really accepted the idea that the way to defeat Britain was to cut its Mediterranean link to the Empire at both ends—at Gibraltar and at the Suez Canal. Though the Spanish dictator Franco coveted Gibraltar, he was too wily to let Hitler draw him into the war. Hitler never gave the Afrika Korps sufficient means to dislodge the British from Egypt. Most of the Balkan countries had already become economically dependent on Germany before the war began. The campaign to reinforce this dependency militarily delayed for five critical weeks the blow Hitler thought would decide the war: invasion of the Soviet Union.

Operation Barbarossa

In December 1940, Hitler decided to "crush Soviet Russia in a quick campaign even before the end of the war against England."[3] The failure to defeat Britain had reinforced his long-standing purpose of expanding German "living space" at Russian expense. Though Stalin had lived up to the Nazi-Soviet Pact, to "crush" him was the only sure way to prevent him from changing sides.

Because the Soviet Union and the West became antagonists after World War II, few Westerners realize the size of the Russian contribution to the conflict Russians call "the Great Patriotic War." (In fact, until the Anglo-American invasion of occupied France in the summer of 1944, 90 percent of the troops fighting Hitler's armies were Russians. In the course of the war, 80 percent of the German soldiers killed died on the Russian front.)

On June 22, 1941, 4 million German and allied troops began crossing the Soviet frontier in Operation Barbarossa. They constituted the biggest invading army in history. Within three weeks they had advanced two-thirds of the way to Moscow, taking a million prisoners. Surprised by the attack, despite ample warnings, Stalin could only trade space for time, retreating deeper and deeper into the vastness of Russia. Hitler's optimism—he had neglected to equip his armies with warm clothing or antifreeze—seemed justified. But in December 1941, "General Winter" took command, halting the German advance only twenty miles from Moscow. The blitzkrieg had stalled, and Barbarossa proved to be no quick campaign.

Stalin counterattacked, in weather of thirty degrees below zero, with troops transferred from Siberia, where they had been guarding against a Japanese attack. His spies in Tokyo had reassured him that the Japanese would honor their nonaggression pact with the Soviet Union. A coordinated Axis strategy would have forced Stalin to fight on both fronts. But to the extent they listened to Hitler at all, the Japanese agreed with him that their interest lay in attacking the United States.

Meanwhile, on the other side, Churchill, a lifelong anti-communist, pledged all-out British help to the Soviets when they were invaded. "If Hitler invaded Hell," he explained, "I would at least make a favorable reference to the Devil in the House of Commons."[3] He understood that mutual interests dictated Allied cooperation. No such commitment bound the Axis Powers together. The attack on Pearl Harbor on December 7, 1941, surprised Japan's allies as much as its victims.

The Japanese Bid for Empire and the U.S. Reaction, 1941–1942

By the 1930s, as we saw in Chapter 9, Japan had produced the most successful non-Western response to European global dominance. Both the ancient and the modern elements of that response inclined the Japanese toward empire building. Aloof from democratic politics, the Japanese officer corps still lived by the code of *Bushido,* the way of the warrior, whose fate was to die for the emperor. Many leaders of big business saw more practical reasons for war. Japan was an overcrowded set of islands practically devoid of essential raw materials and dependent on exports for survival. The impact of the Great Depression had confirmed these harsh realities.

Economic greed inspired the Japanese thrust into China in 1931. Mere territorial ambition, however, does not explain the bestial cruelty with which the Japanese army treated Chinese noncombatants, especially after it overran the capital Nanjing (Nanking) in 1937. Japa-

nese soldiers competed enthusiastically in the speedy beheading of masses of civilians, who were also used for bayonet practice or doused with gasoline and burned alive. At least a quarter-million Chinese, from infants chopped to pieces to old women raped and slaughtered, perished during these six weeks of methodical atrocities, still remembered as the "Rape of Nanking." Its ruthlessness is only partly explained by Japan's harsh military code, which taught young soldiers to attach no value to their own lives, let alone to the lives of Japan's enemies and inferiors, who peopled the rest of the world.

A similar feeling of rage that Japan was a superior nation humiliated by inferiors had grown among military-industrial circles since the League of Nations had condemned Japanese aggression in invading China. This feeling was heightened by the constant rebukes of the United States, whose traditional insistence on an "open door" for American trade in East Asia clashed directly with Japanese ambitions. In 1940 President Roosevelt reinforced his moral condemnations with an embargo on scrap iron and weapons for Japan. In July 1941, after the Japanese took advantage of the fall of France to seize French Indochina, he extended the ban to include oil and steel. In the ensuing negotiations, the United States made it clear that the U.S. condition for lifting the ban was Japanese withdrawal from China. Thus the Japanese were faced with the choice of giving up the imperial ambitions upon which they had staked their future or overcoming U.S. opposition by diplomacy or force.

Pearl Harbor

As negotiations failed to resolve the embargo issue to Japan's satisfaction, power within the Japanese government shifted to the military-industrial advocates of war against the United States and the European colonial powers. Japan's decision to enter the war was not

The "Rape of Nanking." *Civilian corpses strew the streets of the Chinese city after the Japanese army overran it on December 14, 1937. National Archives*

prompted by any sense of solidarity with the fascist powers. Hitler had not warned the Japanese he would invade Russia, despite the German-Japanese pact signed in 1940, nor did the Japanese consult him before Pearl Harbor. Rather, the war they planned had three objectives: to break the stranglehold of embargo, to end interference with their conquest of China, and to build an overseas empire that would give Japan the supplies and markets it lacked.

Early on Sunday morning, December 7, 1941, Honolulu awoke to the roar of explosions. The surprise Japanese air attack sank or damaged much of the U.S. Pacific fleet at its moorings in Pearl Harbor. Having disabled their most-feared enemy, the Japanese quickly overran Hong Kong, the Dutch East Indies, Burma, and Malaya. The surrender of the great base at Singapore dealt a lasting blow to the prestige of the British Empire in East Asia. By May 1942, American and Filipino resistance in the Philippines had also ended in surrender (Map 10.2).

At the time of Pearl Harbor, U.S. intelligence had cracked the Japanese codes and was expecting an attack someplace. Why then was the Pacific fleet so unprepared? No credible evidence supports the allegation that Roosevelt deliberately allowed the attack so that outraged public opinion would accept war. Several factors contributed to the disaster: the secrecy that shrouded the Japanese strike force, the racist

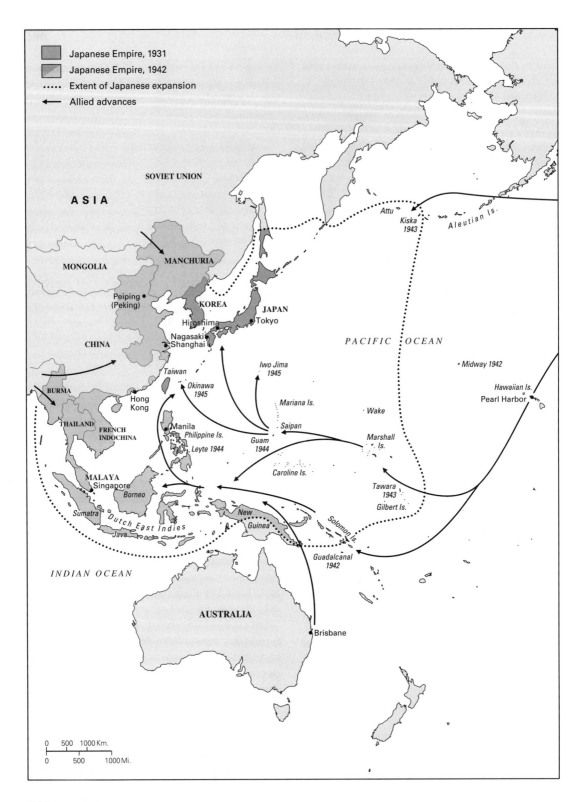

overconfidence of commanders who believed the "little yellow men" would not dare attack Hawaii, and the habits of peacetime routine. The Federal Bureau of Investigation, for example, failed to alert Roosevelt that it had intercepted a German spy whose mission was to assemble detailed information about Pearl Harbor, to be passed on, undoubtedly, to the Japanese.

The End of U.S. Isolation

Pearl Harbor unquestionably simplified Roosevelt's foreign policy problem, which arose from the clash between two enduring characteristics of American thinking about foreign relations. Protected by oceans and bordered by far weaker neighbors, Americans, unlike Europeans, had little experience of adjusting foreign policy to the necessities of the balance of power. The threat to Britain of a Europe dominated by Germany, for example, spurred Churchill's opposition to Hitler far more than his distaste for Nazi politics. Americans, with their strong Puritan heritage, were more likely to judge others in moral terms. This view implied that the United States should help "good" countries and oppose "bad" ones. By the late 1930s most Americans probably judged Nazism and Japanese imperialism to be bad. But an equally powerful American tradition urged against any "entangling alliance" abroad. The widespread feeling that the United States had been led into World War I under false pretenses had reinforced this tradition. To prevent its happening again, Congress had passed a series of neutrality acts aimed at preventing any peripheral involvement in foreign wars that could be used to justify U.S. intervention.

◀ *Map 10.2 World War II:
The Pacific Theater*

In keeping with this isolationist sentiment, Roosevelt had proclaimed U.S. neutrality in 1939. Despite his growing conviction that the United States' vital interests required opposition to both Japan and Germany, he could not do more than public opinion would permit. Thus in the fall of 1940, when Britain desperately needed escort ships for its Atlantic convoys, Roosevelt could only trade Churchill fifty obsolescent U.S. destroyers for ninety-nine-year U.S. leases on six British bases in the Western Hemisphere.

In the spring of 1941, polls showed that no more than one American in five favored entering the war. By then Britain had sold all its dollar holdings at a loss in order to pay for munitions. U.S. legislation stipulated that foreigners could buy arms in the United States only on a "cash-and-carry" basis. Roosevelt now persuaded Congress to pass the Lend-Lease Act, empowering him to lend or lease the British whatever they needed. However, the act stipulated that U.S. ships must not enter combat zones. In August, Roosevelt and Churchill met at sea and promulgated the Atlantic Charter. This document set forth the kind of general principles Americans liked to affirm, including the right of self-determination. Churchill could only accept it, though he tried to insist to Roosevelt that the charter, which implicitly repudiated Britain's right to rule over other peoples, did not apply to the British Empire.

Thus step by step Roosevelt edged Americans toward war. As U.S. warships escorted convoys across the Atlantic, there were clashes, despite Hitler's orders, with German submarines. These encounters enabled Roosevelt to declare that the country was already virtually at war. Even after Pearl Harbor, however, he did not ask Congress to declare war on Germany. Hitler solved Roosevelt's dilemma by aligning himself with the Japanese, against whom Americans had been roused to fury. Vastly ignorant of the United States and contemptuous of its racially mixed society, Hitler saw no reason not to declare formally a war that had already begun in the Atlantic.

The Turning Points, 1942

Churchill immediately recognized the significance of the Pearl Harbor attack. From that moment he knew Britain would not lose the war. With the formation of the Grand Alliance, the tide of war began to turn in mid-to-late 1942. By the spring of 1943, the Axis had lost battles in Pacific jungles and North African deserts, in the snows of Russia and the storms of the North Atlantic.

The momentum of the Japanese seemed irresistible in early 1942. Their planes bombed northern Australia. Their fleet raided Ceylon. But in May 1942, in the Battle of the Coral Sea, the U.S. Navy parried the threat to Australia. A month later, a smaller U.S. force repelled the huge Japanese fleet sent to take Midway Island, only eleven hundred miles from Hawaii. In August, U.S. Marines landed on Guadalcanal in the Solomon Islands, a British possession occupied by the Japanese. Six months of fighting in the steamy, malarial jungle ended in an American victory. It was the first in the long-running battle that would lead from island to island to Japan itself.

In November, at El Alamein, less than one hundred miles from the Suez Canal, the British counterattacked and drove the Germans out of Egypt. Retreating westward, the Germans encountered the British and American troops that had landed in Operation Torch in French North Africa. Caught between these two fires, the Germans surrendered in Tunisia in May 1943. Meanwhile, enraged by the French failure to resist the landings, Hitler ordered the total occupation of France. This invasion shattered the illusion of the Vichy regime's independence. The French began to realize that the only independent French regime was the one de Gaulle soon installed in North Africa.

The war in the Soviet Union also reached a turning point in November 1942 with the sav-

age house-to-house battle of Stalingrad. Hitler refused to allow any retreat. In three months he lost a half-million men. Thereafter the Soviet advance did not halt until it reached Berlin.

Despite these Allied successes, Churchill was still haunted through the spring of 1943 by the one German threat he really feared: the submarine campaign against ocean convoys. In the first years of the war the North Atlantic crossing demanded a quiet heroism of every merchant seaman. For fifteen days they battled through mountainous seas, dreading what they called "the hammer": a torpedo slamming into their ship to send it to the bottom in minutes. In the eighteen months after the fall of France, Britain lost a third of its prewar merchant tonnage. The British convoys dispatched through the Arctic to supply north Russian ports confirmed the Grand Alliance at a terrible cost in ships and lives. By late 1942, however, the Americans were building ships faster than the Germans could sink them. By deploying more escorts and wider-ranging aircraft, and by perfecting submarine detection by underwater radar, the British destroyed an unprecedented forty-one submarines in March 1943. A turning point had been reached on the Atlantic sea lanes, too, allowing the Allies to bring the full weight of their home-front production against the Axis.

The Home Fronts

Even more than in World War I, the home front was a real fighting front in World War II. Not only were civilians much more subject to attack by enemy bombers, but victory or defeat depended largely on the government's success in organizing their productive skills for the war effort. This was a war between economies as well as between armies. Churchill actually created a Ministry of Economic Warfare. Its responsibilities included organizing sabotage of the German-dominated European economies and denying Hitler vital raw materials by offering neutrals a better price for goods they would otherwise have sold to Germany.

Allied Mobilization

Victory in this war of economies was really decided, however, by the relative success of the two sides in mobilizing their home fronts. The Churchill all-party government, depending on a parliamentary majority, felt it could ask at least as much of its citizens as more authoritarian regimes imposed on theirs. The British National Service Act of 1941 put every adult from eighteen to fifty at the government's disposal, to be sent to work wherever he or she was needed. The government controlled prices and rationed such essentials as food and fuel. It paid part of the soaring costs of war by deducting compulsory savings from every paycheck. By 1945 it had allocated one-third of the British work force to war industry.

The Soviet government took equally drastic steps. Though the Five-Year Plans of the 1930s had begun locating industry farther from Russia's European border, German armies had seized one-third of the Soviet industrial plant by late 1941 and threatened another third. Stalin's response was to move some fifteen hundred entire factories eastward and to order the destruction of whatever had to be left behind. In 1942 he mobilized every Soviet citizen between sixteen and fifty-five. With 22 million men in uniform, more than any other combatant, the slogan "Women to the Tractors" came true. At the war's end, three-quarters of the Soviet Union's agricultural workers, and half of those working in war industries, were women. By 1943, despite invasion, these industries were turning out more tanks and planes than German factories were.

Hitler's European Empire

The mobilization of the German home front began late and was less thorough. Although Germany began the war woefully short of such essential weapons as ocean-going submarines, easy victories prompted Hitler actually to cut war production. Only at the end of 1941, when it became clear that Germany was in for a long war, did he order total mobilization. Such were the rivalries of the Nazi hierarchy, however, that production of some nonessential consumer goods continued to increase into 1944. Moreover, Hitler's views precluded drafting women, who were supposed instead to stay home and breed children for Germany. During World War II the German female labor force hardly increased at all (while in the United States the number of working women rose by one-third).

Foreigners from conquered Europe increasingly filled places at the machines that German women might have been assigned. By 1944, more than 7 million foreigners represented a fifth of the German work force. Most of them had been rounded up and brought to Germany virtually as slaves.

The need for labor was not what originally inspired the Nazis to shift huge numbers of people around Europe, however. From the moment of victory in 1940, they began to rearrange the ethnic map of the continent in accordance with their notions of racial hierarchy. The Nazi "New Order" decreed that "racial Germans" living elsewhere should be moved to Germany, where European industry was henceforth to be concentrated. The peoples of the rest of the continent were to be reduced to colonial dependency. The harshness of their fates would depend on how much "Nordic blood" the Nazis thought they had. The fortunate peoples of northern and western Europe, who supposedly had a measure of it, were subjected at first only to puppet governments like Quisling's and to systematic confiscation, through the payment of "occupation costs," of much of what they produced.

In Nazi eyes, non-Nordic peoples like the Poles and Russians were subhuman, fit only for enslavement. After erasing Poland from the map, the Nazis closed Polish schools and massacred the educated elite. They subjected the rest of the Polish population between the ages of eighteen and sixty to forced labor. Forced to wear a purple "P" on their clothing, Poles faced the death penalty for having sex with a German. As for the Soviet Union, Hitler declared his intention to "Germanize the country by the settlement of Germans and treat the natives as redskins," to be killed or herded onto reservations like American Indians.[5] Eighty percent of the Soviet prisoners taken by Germany died of overwork and starvation.

Historically, most empire builders have justified their conquests as the means of spreading some idea of general benefit to humankind. Nazi ideology is remarkably barren in this respect. The Nazi vision of the future depicted a Nazified, static world stretching from the Atlantic far into the Eurasian landmass. Thousand-mile expressways and oversized trains would connect the monumental fortresses from which the German racial masters would rule their enslaved inferiors. By implementing this vision as his armies advanced, Hitler made enemies even of ethnic minorities within the Soviet Union who had initially welcomed the Germans as liberators from Stalin. As the war began to go against the Nazis, Europe eventually became one large prison. Its restive populations made as small a contribution to the Nazi war effort as they dared.

Those carried off to the labor camps established by the SS or German industry could not choose how hard they worked. Nazi-occupied Europe did not only contain camps intended to work people to death, however. The Nazis designed some camps for the immediate extermination of minority groups they deemed unfit to live on any terms. Among these were Gypsies, Jehovah's Witnesses, homosexuals, and especially Europe's Jews.

The Holocaust

Long before the war, the Nazi Nuremberg Laws (1935) had deprived German Jews of their civil rights, and storm troopers had wrecked their businesses and places of worship (1938). But the war provided the opportunity for the "final solution" of what the Nazis called "the Jewish problem." After Poland's defeat, its 3 million Jews were sealed into walled urban ghettos. Special extermination units accompanied the German army into the Soviet Union. But their primitive massacres, in which thousands were shot and hastily buried dead or alive in mass graves, struck Heinrich Himmler, the head of the SS, as unnecessarily harrowing as well as inefficient.

Himmler called on modern technology to equip the extermination camps opened in 1941–1942 with a kind of production line of death, including specially designed gas chambers and crematoria. Into these camps the Nazis slowly emptied the Polish ghettos. They also deported Jews from the rest of Europe "to the east," never to return. So essential did the Nazis consider this task of extermination that they continued it even when Germany was on the brink of defeat. Sometimes they gave trainloads of deportees destined for the death camps the right of way over ammunition trains for their retreating armies.

Six million Jews perished in this Holocaust. The camp at Auschwitz probably established the killing record: a million people, not all Jews, in less than three years, twelve thousand in a single day. The rest of the world did little to hinder the slaughter. Such indifference reinforced the Zionist argument that Jews could be safe only in a country of their own that they could defend themselves.

When the extent of these crimes became known after the war, some explained them as the result of a uniquely German sadism. Unfortunately, however, the underlying causes of these attempts to wipe out whole peoples arose from characteristics of human thinking not at all peculiar to the Germans of the 1940s. Human beings have always been too ready to deny the humanity of other people by stereotyping them, to believe that the problems of their own group could be solved by eliminating such a dehumanized enemy, and to excuse from moral responsibility those who are "just following orders."

To acknowledge that these common human traits helped make the Holocaust possible is not to deny its unique horror but to recognize the kinds of thinking that humanity has to unlearn if it is to escape future holocausts.

The Defeat of the Axis, 1943–1945

Italy was the first of the Axis Powers to fall. British forces had ousted the Italians from Ethiopia in 1941. The alliance with Germany that had sent 200,000 Italians to the Soviet front had never been popular. When British and U.S. forces crossed from North Africa to invade Sicily in July 1943, even many leading Fascists concluded that it was time for Italy to change sides. Within two weeks of the landing, the king ejected Mussolini from office and had him arrested.

When Italy surrendered to the Allies in September, Hitler's armies turned northern Italy into another German front line. German paratroopers rescued Mussolini from imprisonment and made him the head of a puppet state. Stubborn German resistance slowed the Allied advance up the Italian peninsula to a crawl. When the Germans finally surrendered in the spring of 1945, Italian anti-Fascist guerrillas executed Mussolini and hung his bullet-riddled body by the heels in a gas station as an object of public contempt.

Dreading another slaughter of British troops in France like that of World War I, Churchill had imposed his preference for attacking Italy rather than mounting the cross-Channel invasion favored by U.S. military planners. Italy, he said, was the "soft underbelly" of Hitler's Europe. In actuality the Italian campaign proved

far from easy. Yet Stalin did not admit that fighting there amounted to a real "second front" that could reduce German pressure on the Soviet front by dividing German forces. Stalin's complaints help explain the compromises Churchill and Roosevelt made when they met him in Tehran, the Iranian capital, late in 1943. The location was symbolic of the Grand Alliance, for some American lend-lease supplies reached the Soviets through the Persian Gulf and the Trans-Iranian Railway.

At Tehran the "Big Three" recognized their need for each other's help. They therefore tended to put aside any issue that might divide them. Churchill and Roosevelt were keenly aware that Stalin commanded most of the soldiers actually fighting Germans. Having put him off in 1942, and again in 1943, they now gave him a firm date in 1944 for the cross-Channel invasion of France. Roosevelt and Stalin rejected as a dangerous diversion Churchill's suggestion that the United States and Britain also attack another "underbelly" in the Balkans, so as to "join hands with" the Soviets. In return for the second front, Stalin pledged Soviet support for a postwar world organization to replace the League of Nations and a Soviet declaration of war against Japan soon after Hitler was defeated.

Stalin made it clear that he intended to keep the territories annexed by the Soviet Union in 1939. Though the Soviets had severed relations with the Polish government-in-exile in London, Churchill concurred with moving the Polish-Russian border westward and compensating Poland at Germany's expense. Roosevelt, characteristically mindful of the large Polish-American vote in the coming presidential election, preferred to avoid discussing territorial adjustments until the war was won. Like Woodrow Wilson, he envisioned a totally new postwar world order, in which the new United Nations would decide such questions. At Tehran, in fact, the president began to feel he had at least as much rapport with Stalin, who agreed

The liberation of Buchenwald concentration camp, 1945. *From the bare
shelves on which they slept, starving slave laborers stare at the U.S. Army
cameraman, hardly believing that freedom has come before death.*
© *Bettmann/CORBIS*

with him that World War II should end European global dominance, as with Churchill,
champion of the British Empire.

Thus the outlines of the postwar world
remained largely undefined as Hitler found himself between the closing jaws of a gigantic vise
in the summer of 1944. While the Soviets drove
his armies out of their homeland, the Americans,
British, and Canadians hit the beaches of western France on D-day, June 6. Operation Overlord
was a technological and managerial feat as well
as a military one. The Allies towed entire artificial harbors across the English Channel to provide ports for the landing of a million men in a
month. Four pipelines laid on the seabed
pumped fuel for the Allied advance across
northern France.

In August, French and U.S. tanks reached
Paris, where fighting had already begun between the forces of the underground Resistance movement and the retreating German
garrison. General de Gaulle, the lonely exile of
1940, returned to be acclaimed as his country's
liberator.

While Parisians rejoiced, the people of German cities had few illusions about the war's
outcome by late 1944. When the Royal Air Force
discovered early in the war that it could not hit
precise targets such as particular factories, it
adopted a policy of simply loosing its bombs
indiscriminately on the populations below. In
the summer of 1943, a week of incendiary raids
on Hamburg had generated fire storms that
killed fifty thousand and left a million homeless.

Hiroshima, August 6, 1945. *Controversy continues over whether it was necessary to level whole cities with the world's first atomic weapons. Some historians have argued that the American decision to do so reflected a desire to end the war with Japan before the Soviets, entering it only in 1945, could claim a share in the victory.* National Archives

The strategic effectiveness of this "saturation bombing" is doubtful. Postwar studies have shown that air raids did not even begin to slow German war production until the summer of 1944, when American "precision bombing" started. Even then, postwar polling revealed, only a bare majority of Germans would have favored surrender.

The last months of Hitler's Germany provide an eerie demonstration of the capacities of human determination—or madness. Hitler withdrew to an underground bunker in Berlin, from which he issued orders forbidding retreat to units that had already ceased to exist. To the end he hoped that his new secret weapons would save him. In addition to the world's first jet aircraft and robot flying bombs, these weapons included V-2s, missiles carrying one-ton warheads. Five hundred V-2s, crude prototypes of today's weapons, fell on London alone. Too few of them had been produced too late, however, to reverse the outcome of World War II.

Eventually Russian tanks overrode the elderly men and teenage boys Hitler had mobilized as a last line of defense and began shelling the ruins above his bunker. Only then did Hitler admit that the war was lost. On April 30, 1945, after marrying his mistress and writing a will blaming the Jews for his failure, he shot himself. She took poison. SS men burned their bodies in the courtyard above while the Russian shells continued to fall. Only then was the spell of this man, who had risen from obscurity to command the largest European empire ever known, finally broken. A week later, Germany surrendered.

Like Hitler, the Japanese warlords failed to mobilize their home front as effectively as the Allies had done. Just as the Nazis claimed that their conquests were building a united Europe, the Japanese asserted that they were establishing a "Great East Asian Co-Prosperity Sphere" and were reserving Asia for the Asians. These claims were belied by the cruelty of their occupying armies, however. Like the Germans, the Japanese people displayed great tenacity as defeat closed in on them.

In China the Japanese withstood the Nationalist armies of Chiang Kai-shek, despite heroic American efforts to arm him by airlifts over the Himalaya Mountains. But by the time of Germany's surrender, a British army including African and Indian troops was driving the Japanese from the Southeast Asian mainland. The Americans had begun the reconquest of the Philippines, and their bloody island-to-island campaign had won them air bases within easy striking distance of Japan itself. A single air raid by General Curtis Le May's B-29s on March 10, 1945, burned nearly half of Tokyo to the ground, killing or maiming 125,000 people.

Nevertheless the Allies dreaded the invasion of Japan. They expected suicidal resistance of the sort displayed by the kamikaze pilots, who deliberately crashed their planes into American warships. Considering the gloomy estimates of American casualties, Harry S. Truman, who had become president at Roosevelt's death, unhesitatingly ordered the dropping of the first atomic bomb on Hiroshima on August 6, 1945. This single bomb, tiny in comparison with today's nuclear weapons, destroyed at least 100,000 people. The only other atomic bomb then in existence fell on Nagasaki three days later. In the meantime, the Soviets had hastened to declare war and invade Japanese-held Manchuria. On August 15, the Japanese people heard over the radio, for the first time

ever, the voice of the emperor, announcing defeat. World War II was over.

The Revolutionary Impact of World War II

A World Divided into Three

The distribution of global power for most of the rest of the century was already taking shape in 1945. Hitler's defeat left Europe divided down the middle into blocs dominated by his two strongest enemies, the United States and the Soviet Union. In the next decade, Western Europeans would begin to recognize that recovery depended on European economic cooperation and political unity, not on a vain attempt to re-establish global dominance. As former colonies won independence, a host of new nations emerged in Asia and Africa to form a Third World seeking to stay out of the superpower conflict that divided Europe.

The Yalta Conference and the Postwar World

Despite the Nazis' hopes, the Grand Alliance against them held together until they were defeated. Allies usually tend to diverge as soon as their common goal is in sight. Knowing this, and fearing a Soviet advance into the vacuum left by Germany's collapse, Churchill approached Stalin to propose a deal in southeastern Europe. The Soviets would be dominant in Bulgaria and Romania, Nazi allies already invaded by Soviet armies. Britain would dominate in Greece. Each would have a half-interest in Hungary and Yugoslavia. Stalin seems to have been agreeable. He did not object when British troops crushed a communist attempt to seize power in Greece and imposed the monarchist government that had spent the war in London.

But after June 1944, for the first time, there were more American than British soldiers fighting Hitler. Churchill became the junior partner

The Big Three at the Yalta Conference, February 1945. *Winston Churchill (left) and Stalin (right) flank President Franklin D. Roosevelt. Already, Churchill feared that Roosevelt had a "slender contact with life."* National Archives

of the Western Allies. Henceforth it would be the Americans who set the tone in relations with the Soviets, and they contemplated no such deals. American military planners were preoccupied with the military objective of ending the war, not with seeking advantage for some postwar conflict between allies. They rejected as "political" Churchill's feeling that it would be desirable for the Western Allies' armies "to shake hands with the Russians as far east as possible" and even to beat them to Berlin.

The Big Three met for a second time at Yalta in the southern Soviet Union in February 1945. Once again the emerging differences among the Allies were papered over with ambiguous formulas. Roosevelt had reacted to Churchill's

deal with Stalin as Woodrow Wilson had reacted to European power politics a generation earlier. He insisted that the Allies guarantee free postwar elections everywhere in Europe. In Poland, elections were to be held by a new government that would somehow merge the Poles of the London government-in-exile into the pro-Soviet regime the Soviets recognized.

Stalin accepted these proposals but told a confidant, "Any freely elected government in eastern Europe would be anti-Soviet and that we cannot permit." He could not believe the Americans would not understand this, or that they intended the pledge of free elections everywhere as more than propaganda. In fact, U.S. foreign policy is often made by such a statement of principle, and Americans were outraged at Stalin's violations of it. From these differing perspectives eventually arose the East-West confrontation Churchill had tried to avoid.

Critics have sometimes accused the dying Roosevelt, who survived Yalta by only two months, of conceding too much to Stalin. Such criticism forgets the actual situation at the time of the Yalta conference. The war was not over. The Western Allies had yet to cross the Rhine, and the Soviets were already a hundred miles from Berlin. Expecting to need Soviet help in the final campaign against Japan, Roosevelt accepted Stalin's demands for Chinese territory. Expecting to withdraw U.S. troops from Europe as rapidly as they had left after World War I, Roosevelt secured whatever postwar commitments he could. Though he clearly overestimated his personal influence on Stalin, in early 1945 Roosevelt saw no reason to doubt his cooperation. Nor would American public opinion then have favored opposition to Stalin, for since 1941 Americans had been encouraged to see the Soviets as allies fighting the good fight.

In the end, as Churchill had expected, the realities of power, not declarations of principle, determined the division of the postwar world. For Stalin, the war before the German invasion of the Soviet Union had been a contest between equally dangerous capitalist powers. His country had narrowly escaped being defeated by one of them. Afterward, as a victor, he attempted to win control of as much territory as possible between the Soviet Union and the other capitalist powers. He expected the Americans to do the same. As Stalin said, "Everyone imposes his own system as far as his army can reach." And in fact until 1990—except in Germany, where the Americans withdrew westward some one hundred miles to the U.S. occupation zone agreed to at Yalta, and in Austria, from which the Soviets withdrew in 1955—the European frontier between the "free world" and the Soviet bloc ran

where the respective armies stood at Hitler's defeat (Map 10.3).

The End of the European Empires

Even more than Europe's division into two blocs, the rapid dissolution of its colonial empires after 1945 revealed how World War II had ended European global dominance. In 1939, a quarter of the world's people, most of them nonwhite, lived under the British flag. They produced three-quarters of the world's gold; half of its rice, wool, and tin; and a third of its sugar, copper, and coal. France's overseas empire was twenty-six times larger than France itself, with three times the population. The Dutch ruled an empire with a population nine times larger than that of the Netherlands. Few of the colonial peoples enjoyed in 1939 even the limited self-government the British had conceded to India. Almost everywhere, however, a nationalist elite had emerged who had absorbed from their European masters the modern political ideal of a self-governing national state. World War II showed them that the Europeans could be beaten. In Asia especially, the Japanese not only drove the Europeans out but claimed to foster colonial nationalism—though they ultimately ruled these former colonies at least as harshly as the Europeans had. Moreover, the war left Europeans too exhausted for vigorous efforts to restore colonial rule. Wherever they attempted such a restoration, they encountered the opposition of both the Soviet Union and the United States.

Americans took seriously Article 3 of the Atlantic Charter, which proclaimed "the right of every people to choose the form of government under which it desires to live." As promised, they granted independence to their

Map 10.3 USSR Western Border   ▶
Changes, 1914–1945

	Areas lost by Russia after 1917
	German territory to Poland, 1945
	Acquired by Soviet Union, 1939-1945
	Soviet satellites
	Communist, nonsatellite nation
——	"Iron Curtain" after 1950

NORWAY

SWEDEN

FINLAND

Helsinki

G. of Finland

Leningrad

Stockholm

ESTONIA

Moscow

LATVIA

BALTIC SEA

LITHUANIA

SOVIET UNION

DENMARK

Copenhagen

Gdansk (Danzig)

Hamburg

Elbe R.

Berlin

Vistula R.

Warsaw

WHITE RUSSIA

NETHERLANDS

EAST GERMANY

POLAND

Kiev

WEST GERMANY

Prague

UKRAINE

Dnieper R.

Bonn

CZECHOSLOVAKIA

Dniester R.

Rhine R.

Munich

Vienna

BESSARABIA

SWITZERLAND

AUSTRIA

HUNGARY

Budapest

CRIMEA

Po R.

RUMANIA

BLACK SEA

YUGOSLAVIA

Belgrade

Bucharest

Danube R.

ITALY

ADRIATIC SEA

BULGARIA

Sofia

Istanbul

CORSICA

Rome

Tirane

Ankara

ALBANIA

SARDINIA

GREECE

AEGEAN SEA

TURKEY

SICILY

Athens

CYPRUS

MEDITERRANEAN SEA

239

Philippine dependents in 1946, and they expected others to do likewise. Whether this attitude reflected the United States' own history as a colony, as Americans often asserted, or its eagerness to penetrate more non-Western markets, as embittered Europeans complained, the effect was the same. In 1945 and 1946, U.S. agents encouraged Ho Chi Minh and other Indochinese nationalists to resist the reimposition of French rule after the Japanese departure. When the Dutch refused to recognize the independent Republic of Indonesia established in their former East Asian empire as the Japanese left, U.S. pressure through the United Nations forced them to abandon their military intervention. Over three hundred years of Dutch colonialism came to an end in 1949. The United States began to reverse its anti-colonial pressure only in the 1950s, when it began to perceive colonial nationalists as communist agents or dupes.

The Soviet Union also supported the non-Western drive for independence. Under this double pressure, Europeans gave up their empires more or less gracefully. The British habit of indirect rule simplified Britain's surrender of formal power in Burma (1948), Malaya (1957), and much of sub-Saharan Africa (after 1957). The Commonwealth provided a kind of club within which former colonies could preserve a loose affiliation with Britain, though not all chose to join it. Thus the rich and gigantic empire of 1939 dwindled to a few bits and pieces by the 1970s.

After the debacle of 1940, the French found it harder to relinquish the overseas symbols of great-power status. France was almost the last European country to remain involved in colonial warfare. It fought for eight years (1946–1954) to hold Indochina and another eight (1954–1962) to hold Algeria—all in vain.

The War and Postwar Society

In several respects, the end of World War II marked the beginning of the world we know today. Unlike the temporary controls of World War I, lasting changes in the relationship between government and the individual emerged from the experience of wartime government or, in German-occupied Europe, from social conflict between those who collaborated with the Nazis and those who resisted them. The war also did much to stimulate the technologies that now pervade our lives.

In much of Europe, World War II laid the foundations of the postwar welfare state. In Britain the wartime government had made great demands on citizens but had also assumed unprecedented responsibility for them. The population became accustomed to the provision of extensive social services—and to the high taxes needed to pay for them. When the Labour party defeated Churchill's Conservatives in the elections of July 1945, the new government moved rapidly to nationalize much of private industry and to implement such wartime proposals as a compulsory social security program and free secondary education.

On the continent, the ideas of the underground Resistance movements provided much of the impetus for postwar social change. Resistance originated with the lonely decisions of individuals that Nazism was intolerable and that they must oppose it somehow. Gradually they found others who felt the same way and began publishing clandestine newspapers, smuggling downed Allied airmen to safety, or transmitting intelligence to London. As Resistance movements grew with Germany's defeats, they inevitably became politicized. Because the regimes that collaborated with Hitler—like Pétain's Vichy government—were drawn from the prewar Right, the Resistance inclined to the ideas of the Left. This was true even of Catholic Resisters, who later founded Christian Democratic parties committed to programs of social reform.

In France, for example, General de Gaulle, like the leftist thinkers of the Resistance, was convinced that the defeat of 1940 reflected basic weaknesses of France's society and economy. The provisional government he headed until 1946 set out to transform both. It imposed government ownership of the big insurance companies and the coal, steel, and energy industries. It laid the foundations of the system that still sets goals for the French economy today: cooperative development of five-year plans by industry, labor, and government. And it greatly expanded the prewar welfare state. Thus one legacy of World War II was the idea that government has a comprehensive responsibility for the quality of its citizens' lives.

The War and Postwar Technology

The war was even more revolutionary in its acceleration of the pace of technological innovation. The Battle of Britain was an early clash in what Churchill called "the wizard war" (because it seemed magical to laymen): German electronics experts devised a guiding beam for bombers, and British engineers found ways to deflect it. In this war of scientists the most formidable feat was the transformation of what was still, in 1939, only a concept of nuclear physics into the bomb dropped on Hiroshima in 1945. To turn its design into an actual weapon, the Manhattan Project constructed whole new factories employing 120,000 workers, including the first entirely automated plant in history. The total cost came to some $2 billion. Ever since, government-sponsored research has continued to demonstrate the possibilities of invention on demand, at vast cost.

Nuclear weaponry was only the most dramatic example of the technological breakthroughs stimulated by the needs of war. In 1940, the British invented *operations research,* the statistical study of war, a discipline that would profoundly influence postwar ideas of industrial management. In 1943 U.S. factories began to mass-produce the pesticide DDT and the antibiotic penicillin. Before long these two substances had fundamentally altered the conditions of human life. The application of DDT in Ceylon after the war, for example, reduced the death rate by half in one year by wiping out disease-bearing insects. Penicillin and the sulfonamides were the first of the wonder drugs that since 1945 have virtually eliminated infectious diseases in areas where the drugs are available.

Conclusion: The High Point of U.S. Power

Even in the United States, where no battles were fought, World War II had a revolutionary impact. After Pearl Harbor, formerly isolationist Americans threw themselves into the war effort with an enthusiasm that no war since 1945 has generated. U.S. industrial production quadrupled as assembly lines turned out over a quarter-million aircraft and vast quantities of other goods. Such feats demanded substantial relocations of population, as new factories opened in under-industrialized regions like the South and the Pacific Coast. Everywhere new opportunities drew rural people to the cities. The demand for labor led to Roosevelt's creation of the Fair Employment Practices Commission, the first federal agency charged with protecting minorities from discrimination.

By 1945, war-induced patterns of migration and economic growth had produced a society very different from the one Americans had known in 1941. The war effort carried over into peacetime, too, for the development of military technology had acquired a dynamic of its own. In 1945 the U.S. and Soviet military establishments raced to capture Hitler's missile designers. Those efforts marked the beginning of what has been called the "warfare state," dedicated to developing new technologies of destruction. World War II had already hinted what a future war fought by such means might be like. Almost half of its 50 million dead were civilians (compared with only 5 percent during

World War I). Many of these were victims of indiscriminate aerial bombing—a weapon that had seemed so terrible in imagination that many people in the 1930s believed that it never would be used or that it had made war itself unthinkable. World War II proved otherwise, and after 1945 the use of aerial bombing was taken for granted in all nations' defense planning.

The outcome of World War II suggested that future combatants in such a full-scale war would have to be as populous and industrially powerful as the United States, which then had more than 140 million people. Former great powers with populations of 40 to 50 million, like Britain and France, were already dwarfed. On this superpower scale, the only possible rival to the United States was the Soviet Union. A Soviet challenge seemed unlikely, however, for that country was exhausted and devastated. It had lost 20 million people, sixty times more than the United States had lost.

In the face of such Soviet weakness, the United States had probably reached in 1945 the high point of its twentieth-century power. So strong was the U.S. position that Americans redesigned the world's political and economic systems to their own specifications.

The United Nations, the new international organization launched in October 1945 to replace the failed League of Nations and intended to guarantee the postwar peace, perpetuated the name given to the wartime anti-Axis alliance and the principles enunciated in 1941 in the Atlantic Charter by Churchill and Roosevelt. Four of the five permanent members of its executive arm, the Security Council, corresponded to Roosevelt's notion of the "four policemen"—the United States, Britain, the Soviet Union, and China—who together had the strength to enforce law and order upon the world. (General De Gaulle's assertiveness added France to the list.) Significantly, the United Nations established its headquarters not in Europe, where the League had had its seat, but in New York—clear recognition that the inspiration for the organization, as for much of its structure, was American.

Similarly the new International Monetary Fund, designed to balance international payments, and the World Bank, established to make loans to needy nations, conformed to the specifications of the U.S. delegation to the international financial conference held at Bretton Woods, New Hampshire, in 1944. Though ostensibly international, both institutions were actually subject to U.S. influence.

In many ways, then, the destiny of the world after 1945 seemed to be in American hands. World War II marked the climax of an incredibly swift U.S. ascent to world power. Until the 1890s, the United States had been seen as a second-rate power, not even accorded full ambassadorial representation by the great powers. Over the next half-century, it began to play a world political role corresponding to the fantastic growth of its economy. But the U.S. advance to world power had been interrupted by apparent retreats, like the return to isolationism after 1918. Today, when U.S. armed forces are stationed in more than a hundred countries around the world, it is hard to imagine the situation of 1940, when the Pentagon had not been built and the U.S. army was smaller than that of Belgium. It was World War II that marked the turning point to the global involvement Americans have learned to live with. For U.S. power did not long remain unchallenged. Only a few years after the war's end, the United States and the Soviet Union found themselves locked in Cold War confrontation.

Notes

1. Quotations from Winston S. Churchill, *Their Finest Hour* (Boston: Houghton Mifflin Company, 1949), pp. 259, 261–262.

2. Winston S. Churchill, *Their Finest Hour* (Boston: Houghton Mifflin, 1949), pp. 225–226.

3. Alan Bullock, *Hitler: A Study in Tyranny,* rev. ed. (New York: Harper & Row, 1964), p. 574.

4. Winston S. Churchill, *The Grand Alliance* (Boston: Houghton Mifflin, 1950), p. 370.

5. Peter Calvocoressi and Guy Wint, *Total War: Causes and Courses of the Second World War* (New York: Penguin Books, 1972), p. 212.

Suggestions for Further Reading

Bratzel, John F., and Leslie B. Rout, Jr. "Pearl Harbor, Microdots, and J. Edgar Hoover." *American Historical Review* (December 1982), pp. 1342–1351.

Browning, Christopher. *Ordinary Men: Reserve Police Battalion 101 and the Final Solution in Poland* (1991).

Calvocoressi, Peter, Guy Wint, and John Pritchard. *Total War: Causes and Course of the Second World War.* Rev. 2d ed. (1988).

Chang, Iris. *The Rape of Nanking: The Forgotten Holocaust of World War II* (1997).

Churchill, Winston S. *The Second World War.* 6 vols. (1986).

de Gaulle, Charles. *War Memoirs.* 3 vols. (1955).

Feis, Herbert. *Churchill, Roosevelt, Stalin* (1967).

Fourcade, Marie-Madeleine. *Noah's Ark: A Memoir of Struggle and Resistance* (1981).

Hersey, John. *Hiroshima* (1946).

Horne, Alistair. *To Lose a Battle: France 1940* (1979).

Hughes, Terry, and John Costello. *The Battle of the Atlantic* (1977).

Liddell Hart, Basil H. *History of the Second World War* (1980).

Lukcas, John. *Five Days in London, May 1940* (1999).

Millett, Allan R., and Williamson Murray. *A War to Be Won: Fighting the Second World War* (2000).

Prange, Gordon W. *At Dawn We Slept: The Untold Story of Pearl Harbor* (1981).

Rupp, Leila J. *Mobilizing Women for War: German and American Propaganda, 1939–1945* (1978).

Wright, Gordon. *The Ordeal of Total War* (1968).

CHAPTER 11

From the Cold War to the Global Marketplace: International Relations Since 1945

"HISTORY REPEATS ITSELF," PEOPLE OFTEN SAY. BUT FEW PROFESSIONAL HISTORIANS would agree. After all, if later generations regularly found themselves facing exactly the same choices earlier generations had faced, but already knowing what the results of those choices were, life for the decision-makers faced with choices would be much simpler. Professional historians know that history *never* repeats itself exactly. Does this mean, then, that decision-makers can learn nothing from history? The story of the Cuban Missile Crisis, the climactic confrontation of the U.S.-Soviet Cold War described in this chapter, suggests otherwise.

When President John F. Kennedy learned in October 1962 that Soviet leader Nikita Khrushchev, contrary to his own public statements, was secretly installing in Cuba nuclear missiles capable of hitting American cities, the world came as close as it has so far to a nuclear World War III. By coincidence, however, as he faced this supreme crisis Kennedy had just been reading a history book—Barbara Tuchman's *The Guns of August*—a book well worth reading today. In it Tuchman tells the story of the series of miscalculations by the leaders of the great powers that led from the assassination of Archduke Franz Ferdinand of Austria-Hungary in July 1914 to the outbreak of World War I at the end of August. What Kennedy learned from the book was how the leaders of Europe made miscalculations during the crisis that forced their potential enemies into positions from which they could not back down short of war. Kennedy was determined, while holding firm in defense of American safety, not to repeat this mistake by placing the Soviet leader in such a situation. "I am not going to follow a course," he told his brother Robert, "which will allow anyone to write a comparable book about this time, *The Missiles of October* . . . If anybody is around to write after this, they are going to understand that we made every effort to find peace and every effort to give our adversary room to move. I am not going to push the Russians an inch beyond what is necessary."[1]

It can be argued that this historical insight helped guide Kennedy through his own crisis to the peaceful resolution of a confrontation that could have escalated into nuclear war.

History does not "repeat itself." But reading history offers each new generation some parallels to ponder as it faces its own, sometimes anguishing, choices.

Interpreting International Relations, 1945–2000

After the defeat of the Germans and the Japanese, the victors of World War II hoped that they had established peace for good. In one sense they were soon disappointed. Within five years the two superpower winners, the United States and the Soviet Union, were confronting one another in a Cold War that many feared would culminate in actual war. In the 1950s, this bipolar conflict of the two superpowers seemed the dominant theme of international relations, defining every confrontation around the world.

Looking back over the whole period since 1945 from the perspective of the year 2001, however, we can see that the confrontation of the superpowers was not the only factor at work in international relations. While the nuclear stalemate dominated the headlines, the half-century of the Cold War also witnessed a wave of global economic change unparalleled in speed and scope since the Industrial Revolution. Change took two forms: an explosion of new technologies changed *how* things were produced, and the tightening bonds of global economic integration changed *where* things were produced. This tidal wave of change continued unabated, moreover, from the globally prosperous years of the 1950s and 1960s into the more troubled economic period that began in the 1970s. The impact of change dramatically altered the balance of economic advantage in the world from the pattern of 1945.

Only after the collapse of the Soviet Union in 1991, however, did most people begin to assess the balance of world power not in terms of weapons or alliances but rather in terms of economic strength or weaknesses—"geo-economic" power. As we shall see in the last section of this chapter, in the 1990s people began to see international relations as a contest between economies. This contest pitted the United States against a Europe striving for unity and against Japan (and other dynamic nations of East Asia). Some historians indeed argue that this multipolar contest will be seen in retrospect as a more important development of the second half of the twentieth century than the Cold War itself.

The long standoff between the two nuclear superpowers does, however, help to explain why the world managed to live for a half-century after World War II without having to face World War III. Neither superpower dared strike the other because the other's nuclear retaliation would have been so devastating. The cost to the economies and societies of both of sustaining this nuclear stalemate proved so debilitating, however, that by the 1990s the Soviet Union (as we shall see in Chapter 13) collapsed and disintegrated, while the supposed Cold War "victor," the United States, was beset (as Chapter 12 will show) by grave economic anxieties undreamed-of in the heady days of triumph in 1945.

Thus we live today in a multipolar world, much more reminiscent of the pre–World War II world than of that of the Cold War. This was an outcome not foreseen by those who waged the Cold War.

Publicly, the leaders of both superpowers asserted that their confrontation was between political and economic systems. The U.S. government declared, and most Americans believed, that confrontation with the Soviet Union was essential to the defense of political democracy and what is called the free-enterprise system. The Soviet government proclaimed, and most Soviet citizens believed, that confrontation with the United States was essential to the defense of revolutionary socialism.

Clearly the systems of the two superpowers were very different. Despite the differences, however, some aspects of the U.S.-Soviet confrontation suggest that it was not fundamentally driven by ideology. To counter Soviet influence, for example, the United States supported regimes around the world that had little more regard for freedom than a communist regime would have. Nor did the Soviet Union consistently support communist regimes and movements. In the 1960s the two largest communist

powers, the Soviet Union and China, became open enemies. In the same decade, the democracies of Western Europe were becoming increasingly impatient with U.S. direction.

What was really at stake after 1945 was the world distribution of *power.* The conflicting ideologies of the superpowers concealed the real nature of this contest. As the wartime Grand Alliance dissolved in suspicion, American policymakers came to assume that the Soviet Union's aims, like Hitler's, were unlimited: the creation of a universal empire by conquest and communist revolutions. Soviet policymakers expected U.S. capitalism to envelop and try to destroy the homeland of communism.

Each side feared an ideological crusade by the other. But in practice neither superpower was willing to let ideological goals override its interests. The nonaligned nations of the world soon came to see the U.S.-Soviet confrontation as a power struggle, regardless of ideology. In 1955 at a conference in Bandung, Indonesia, many of these nations declared their unwillingness to line up with either superpower.

This perspective of the nonaligned Third World sometimes surprised Americans. Americans were still significantly influenced by the idea that had lain at the heart of their earlier aloofness from international affairs: the sense that the United States was a uniquely superior society that might be defiled by contact with a more sordid world. This notion reinforced a strong impulse to improve the world and make it conform to the U.S. model. If the United States could no longer remain aloof from the world, then the world had to be made a safer place for U.S. ideals. Americans did not understand that other nations perceived these ideals as a smokescreen covering the use of U.S. power to promote U.S. economic interests.

The Soviets approached the postwar world in much the same spirit. They too tried to impose their ideals on their neighbors and on as much of the rest of the world as possible. Because both U.S. and Soviet policies were embodied in alliances, the world for a time came to resemble less the 1930s than the pre-1914 European world of armed alliances, confronting one another in successive crises.

During the period of postwar international relations, from the end of World War II to Stalin's death in 1953 and from 1953 to the Cuban missile crisis of 1962, the dominant theme was the bipolar confrontation of the two giants. This Cold War was an unequal contest, though the Americans, who dominated it, did not always see it that way. It pitted the United States, dominant in Latin America and Western Europe, against the Soviet Union, which controlled (beyond its own vast territories) only the band of adjacent lands overrun in World War II. The crises of the Cold War all occurred along this periphery of Soviet control—in Korea, in southeastern Europe, in Iran, in Berlin. In every case the Soviets' attempt to expand their perimeter was rebuffed, as was their probe of the U.S. perimeter in support of Cuba in 1962. The Soviets' strength was still so inferior that when President Kennedy gave them an ultimatum, they could only retreat. The Cuban missile crisis seemed to confirm American primacy in the world.

The 1960s—a decade that did not truly end until 1973 with the withdrawal of U.S. combat troops from Vietnam—exposed the limits of the two giants' power. The Vietnam debacle shattered American self-confidence, appearing to prove that the United States could not defeat Third World revolutionaries determined to pull their country out of the U.S. orbit. Meanwhile, a prosperous Western Europe, spurred by a France once more led by General de Gaulle, increasingly challenged American economic dominance. Soviet power also seemed to be eroding in the 1960s. It was then that relations between the Soviet Union and China flamed into open hostility.

In the 1970s and the first half of the 1980s, there were several dramatic reversals in the climate of superpower relations. With international politics evolving toward multipolarity as Western Europe and China asserted themselves, the United States and the Soviet Union at first seemed to have achieved *détente*—the word then employed to describe relaxation of tensions. But *détente* proved fragile. Within a few years relations soured again. Through most of President Reagan's first term there seemed little prospect of improvement.

Few people who attended the inauguration in 1981 of so staunch an anti-communist as Ronald Reagan could have imagined that the world's television audiences would see him strolling arm-in-arm through Moscow's Red Square with Soviet leader Mikhail Gorbachev as he neared the end of his second term in 1988. The U.S.-Soviet accommodation symbolized by their Moscow embrace came too late for the purpose for which Gorbachev had attempted it: the economic and political revitalization of the USSR. Rather than reinforcing the USSR, Gorbachev's reforms proved the prelude to the collapse of the Soviet Union and its dissolution on December 25, 1991, into fifteen separate and independent republics.

The administration of U.S. President George H. W. Bush, elected as Reagan's successor in 1988, could thus proclaim that U.S. steadfastness had produced a Cold War victory and opened the way to a "New World Order" under American leadership. The economic realities of the 1990s, however, made it clear that the "victory" was won at great cost to the United States.

The Cold War to 1953

Allies in World War II, the United States and the Soviet Union did not become opponents overnight. The Cold War developed gradually between 1945 and 1950. There has been much controversy over who was to blame. Most historians now agree that the Cold War began as the Soviet Union, seeking to expand in accordance with historic Russian ambitions, aroused American fear that it would contest the emerging U.S.

world dominance created by European and Japanese collapse. Each side reacted to successive challenges by taking new steps that it regarded as defensive but that appeared to the other as new threats. A dynamic of confrontation developed.

There were three stages in this process. During the first stage, which ran from Hitler's defeat to the spring of 1947, cooperation was curiously mixed with growing antagonism. Communists held seats in coalition governments in Western Europe, noncommunists in Eastern Europe. Expecting a permanent peace, the United States reduced the number of Americans in uniform. The Soviets also demobilized. American soldiers handed over Soviet refugees in their jurisdiction to the Soviet authorities. As Truman and Stalin had agreed, the Soviets collected reparations from the other three occupation zones—American, British, and French—into which western Germany had been divided.

In the meantime, however, the Soviets sought to expand into areas that Russia had long coveted. They encouraged separatist movements in northwestern Iran and demanded a revision of the historic agreement by which Turkey controlled the passage to Russia's warm-water ports on the Black Sea. In the past, Britain had often pushed the Russians back. Bankrupt postwar Britain, however, could no longer play this role.

In February 1947, the British indicated they could no longer afford to give aid to Turkey, or to the royalist government Churchill and British troops had installed in Greece, under attack from Communist guerrillas. Unwilling to allow Soviet pressure in southeastern Europe to succeed, American policymakers took a step that marked a second stage in the development of the Cold War. On March 12, 1947, President Truman announced that the United States would aid the Greeks and Turks. It would be American policy, he declared, "to support free peoples who are resisting subjugation by armed minorities or by outside pressures."[2] This Truman Doctrine marked a major turning point in the history of American foreign policy. The U.S. president had offered an open-ended commitment to forestall revolution or aggression anywhere.

Prostrate Western Europe, where cooperation between Communists and the other parties in coalition governments broke down in the spring of 1947, seemed especially vulnerable. In June, Secretary of State George Marshall committed the United States to rebuilding the European economy. His offer of aid was extended to all the war-torn countries, including the Soviet Union. Americans, who saw the Marshall Plan as an act of spontaneous generosity, could not understand why the Soviets walked out of the Paris conference convened to implement it.

In fact, unsurprisingly, the Marshall Plan was designed as much in U.S. economic self-interest as for Europe's benefit. It required its recipients to accept U.S.-made goods, shielding the U.S. economy from a postwar slump. In effect the Marshall Plan tied the European market securely to the U.S. economy. It is not surprising that the Soviets rejected such subordination in a U.S.-dominated world.

Integration into the U.S. economic orbit brought Western Europeans a rapid postwar recovery. By 1952, when Marshall Plan aid ended, European industrial production was a third higher than it had been before World War II.

Two separate European economies began to emerge: one oriented to the Atlantic, the other to the Soviet Union. Now Europe was truly divided by the "Iron Curtain" that Winston Churchill had described in 1946. In February 1948, a coup d'état in Czechoslovakia overthrew the last Eastern European coalition government and imposed a communist dictatorship. President Truman responded by encouraging the formation of the Brussels Pact, including Britain, France, and the "Benelux" countries (Belgium, the Netherlands, and Luxembourg). As the two blocs solidified, a key uncertainty was the fate of divided Germany.

Early in 1947, the Americans and British merged the economies of their two occupation zones. Clearly, it was only a matter of time before a western German state dependent on the United States emerged as a barrier to any further Soviet ambitions in Central Europe.

The growth of a resurgent Germany aligned with a hostile United States was a terrifying prospect for the Soviets. Stalin's countermove, in June 1948, was to cut off access to Berlin, which lay deep within the Soviet occupation zone of Germany. The ruined former capital, itself partitioned into zones, was to be used as a Soviet chip in the international poker game. But Truman raised the ante by airlifting all the needed supplies—including coal—into Berlin. Once again the Soviets backed down, abandoning their Berlin blockade after a year. When the Federal Republic of West Germany was created in May 1949, the Soviets could only counter by establishing a communist-led German Democratic Republic in East Germany.

The U.S. strategy of containing the Soviet Union had not yet led to major American rearmament. The United States remained confident in its monopoly of the ultimate, nuclear weapon. When the Soviets exploded an atomic bomb in July 1949, a major reassessment was required. According to "NSC-68," a secret planning document prepared by the U.S. National Security Council in April 1950, the Soviet Union was a rampant aggressor bent on overrunnng all of Europe and Asia. To counter the threat, "NSC-68" declared, the United States must develop a thermonuclear bomb and European air bases from which the Strategic Air Command could deliver it. In Europe, U.S. troops should reinforce the North Atlantic Treaty Organization (NATO) formed to link the United States, Canada, Denmark, Norway, Iceland, Italy, and Portugal to the countries of the Brussels Pact (Map 11.1). Moreover, it would be necessary to rearm West Germany, despite the reluctance of Europeans whose countries had been ravaged by German armies. The implementation of "NSC-68" marks the third and final stage in the development of the Cold War. For the first time in its history, the United States began massive peacetime preparations for war.

The sudden attack of North Korea on South Korea in June 1950 seemed to confirm the need for such preparations. The defeat of the Japanese in 1945 left Korea divided between Soviet and American occupying armies. Each superpower established a client regime, north and south of the thirty-eighth parallel of latitude. U.S. Secretary of State Dean Acheson, however, had publicly excluded South Korea from the list of countries the United States was prepared to defend.

Thus emboldened, the North Koreans attacked. This seemed to be a clear case of aggression and an opportunity for the United Nations to demonstrate its ability to restore peace. Any one of the five permanent members of the UN Security Council could paralyze action by exercising a veto. At the time of the Korean attack, however, the Soviet representative was boycotting Security Council meetings to protest the UN's refusal to recognize the Chinese Communists in place of Chiang Kai-shek's regime. In the Soviets' absence, the United Nations prescribed collective action against aggression in Korea.

In fact, the so-called UN forces mustered to meet the North Korean attack were 50 percent American (and 40 percent South Korean). They were successful in containing the North Koreans' initial headlong advances. Then the American UN commander, General Douglas MacArthur, became overconfident. He moved his forces close to the Chinese border. Fearing an American attempt to reverse their revolution, the Chinese rushed 200,000 "volunteers" into the Korean War. They soon pushed the UN forces back to the line where the conflict had begun. Forced to choose between this Korean standoff and the unknown risks of full-scale war

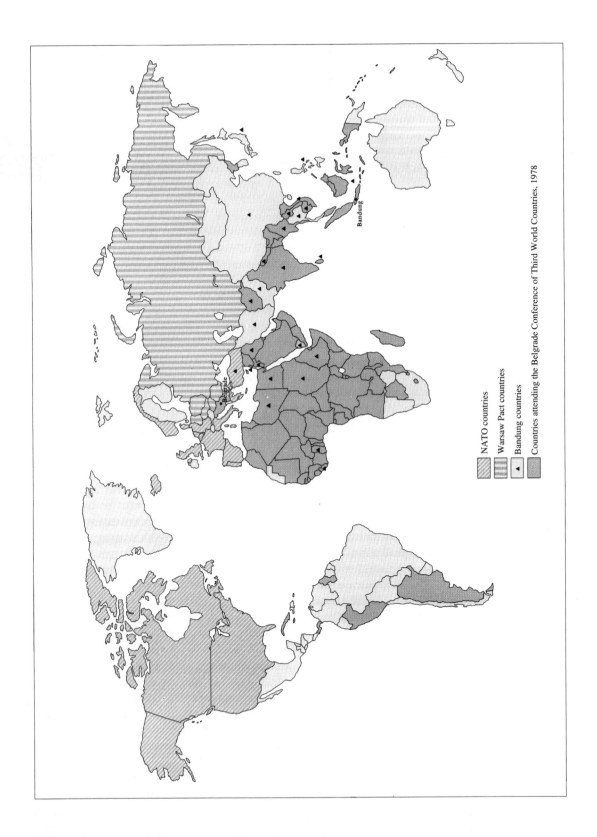

Bandung

Belgrade

NATO countries

Warsaw Pact countries

Bandung countries

Countries attending the Belgrade Conference of Third World Countries, 1978

with China, President Truman agreed in June 1951 to begin negotiations for a cease-fire, finally signed in June 1953.

This outcome of the Korean "police action"—after the loss of fifty-four thousand American lives—illustrated how frustratingly inconclusive peripheral bipolar conflicts could be. But the experience stimulated the American government to extend its guarantees wider still: to the Philippines, Australia, and New Zealand. During the 1950s, it gave a quarter of a billion dollars annually to Chiang Kai-shek's Taiwan, no small factor in that country's "economic miracle." The key to securing the Pacific was Japan, which now, like Germany, changed rapidly from an American enemy into an American friend. In 1951–1952, the United States signed a peace treaty and withdrew its occupation troops. Many American servicemen remained in Japan, however. Japanese bases were a key link in the chain the United States had drawn around the Soviet Union from Norway through Greece and Turkey (added to NATO in 1952) to South Korea and Taiwan. Americans saw this strategy as *containment* or the defense of freedom—though strongman regimes like that of South Korea were hardly free. But to the Soviets it undoubtedly looked like *encirclement.* It would be up to Stalin's successors after his death in 1953 to find ways to break out.

The Containment of Khrushchev, 1953–1962

The Soviet leaders who succeeded Stalin were anxious to reduce international tensions so as to reallocate arms spending for domestic investment. It was not clear, however, how their conciliatory gestures would be received in

♦ *Map 11.1 NATO, the Soviet Bloc, and the Third World*

Washington. President Eisenhower's secretary of state, John Foster Dulles, had come to office in 1953 arguing that mere containment of the Soviets was not enough. Dulles professed to see international relations as a contest between good and evil, in which the Soviet rule over Eastern Europe should not go unchallenged. He did not, however, explain how the United States could drive the Soviets out of that region without going to war. Dulles could back up his aggressive language only by threats of "massive [nuclear] retaliation" for any Soviet transgression. That threat became far less credible, however, when the Soviets exploded their hydrogen bomb in 1953, only nine months after the Americans detonated their first such weapon. For many years the United States retained an advantage in capabilities for delivering the fearsome new weapon. Nevertheless, the Soviet hydrogen bomb, rapidly evening up the arms race, was a vivid reminder that the two superpowers could not wish away each other's power.

The new Soviet leadership had to try to reach accommodation with the United States without alienating factions within the communist bloc that insisted the Americans were not to be trusted (the Chinese, for example). For this reason, Soviet policy alternated between concessions and intransigence through the 1950s. In 1955, for instance, the Soviets countered the entry of West Germany into NATO by forming the Warsaw Pact, an alliance of their Eastern European client states—but they also met with Western leaders in Geneva, in the first "summit conference" since 1945. Proposals at Geneva to de-escalate the nuclear arms race failed to overcome each side's suspicions that the other would cheat in any process of negotiated disarmament. Still, the discussions marked a departure from Cold War unconditional hostility. So did such Soviet concessions as withdrawal from Austria, on condition that it remain nonaligned.

Two simultaneous international crises in 1956 revealed that while the two superpowers

Khrushchev visits an Iowa farm, 1959.   *Recognizing his country's agricultural failures, the Soviet leader (left) hoped improved relations would enable him to borrow the techniques of U.S. agribusiness.   Elliot Erwitt/Magnum Photos*

might warily negotiate with each other, they would tolerate no independent initiatives from their allies or satellites. When Hungary rose in revolt against Soviet domination in October, the Soviets sent in armored columns to crush the uprising. Despite the encouragement the Hungarian rebels had received from CIA-financed radio stations such as Radio Free Europe, the United States could do nothing for them. For all of Dulles's talk of "rolling back" Soviet rule, the United States would not intervene in a region tacitly conceded to lie within the Soviet sphere of influence.

The U.S. government in October 1956 brought pressure not against the Soviets but against its own allies—the British, French, and Israelis—when they provoked the other inter-national crisis of that month by invading Egypt in retaliation for President Nasser's seizure of the Suez Canal. Nikita S. Khrushchev, who had emerged as the Soviet leader, threatened a nuclear war, but Eisenhower's warnings to the U.S. allies were far more effective in ending the invasion. The future of the Arab world lay with Nasser-style Third World nationalism, U.S. policymakers decided, and not with a resurgence of European influence in the region. Thus nations on both side of the world's bipolar divide received sharp reminders in 1956 of their dependency—the Hungarians, of course, far more tragically than the British and French. Meanwhile, Khrushchev alternated blandishments and threats in his efforts to force the United States to recognize Soviet equality.

The Soviet Union and Berlin

A perennial bone of contention was the status of Germany and its capital. By surviving the siege of 1948, Berlin had become a symbol of freedom, a democratic and affluent island in a totalitarian and destitute sea. The official position of the West German government was that Germany should be reunified by free elections, with Berlin again becoming the capital. Official U.S. policy supported this scenario, though privately American policymakers, like those in Western Europe and the Soviet Union, were doubtless content to see Germany remain divided. Fearful of the power that West Germany alone contributed to the U.S.-led NATO alliance, the Soviets repeatedly tried to force the United States to recognize the permanent division of the country, including the Soviet domination of East Germany. Their lever once again was the vulnerability of isolated Berlin. Late in 1958 Khrushchev threatened unilaterally to end Berlin's privileged status as a free city within communist East Germany. Encountering united Western resistance where perhaps he had hoped to expose disunity, he canceled this Berlin ultimatum in March 1959.

Confrontations of this sort alternated with attempts at communication. On a visit to the United States later that year, Khrushchev met with President Eisenhower at Camp David, Maryland. Those talks produced little except agreement for another summit meeting in Paris. The president and the premier made no progress on disarmament, though by now the Soviets had created a strategic bomber force (still far smaller than the U.S. Strategic Air Command) and both nations were hard at work developing ballistic missiles. Khrushchev aborted the Paris summit meeting as soon as it convened, by revealing that the Soviets had shot down an American high-altitude U-2 spy plane over Soviet territory.

In June 1961, this turn toward renewed confrontation was followed by an ultimatum to U.S. president John F. Kennedy. Within a year, Khrushchev declared, he would sign a peace treaty with East Germany and relinquish to the East Germans control over access to Berlin. A few months later he ordered the erection of a wall separating East and West Berlin to end the hemorrhage of Eastern European labor and talent from the Soviet empire. Kennedy's only response was to draft more young Americans and send some of them to West Berlin. Forced to choose between acquiescence and war, the United States preferred to acquiesce.

The Cuban Missile Crisis

Though it solved a Soviet problem, the Berlin Wall was hardly a Soviet success. Presumably challenged by Soviet and Chinese hard-liners to achieve more successes, Khrushchev took a step in 1962 that brought the world as close as it has yet come to nuclear war. He ordered the installation of Soviet missiles in Cuba.

The ultimate cause of the Cuban missile crisis was the Cuban Revolution of January 1959, in which Fidel Castro overthrew the right-wing, U.S.-backed dictatorship of Fulgencio Batista. The United States reacted by virtually excluding sugar, Cuba's principal source of export income, from the American market and by denying Cuba most American goods. Castro retaliated by seizing control of economic assets in Cuba—sugar mills, oil refineries, banks—that were largely American owned. In such a situation, Cuba and the Soviet Union inevitably drew together. Khrushchev saw opportunities to extend Soviet influence by helping developing countries. Castro had no alternative ally. By the end of 1960, the Soviet Union had agreed to buy half of Cuba's sugar crop and to provide Castro with the essentials the U.S. embargo denied him.

Unwilling to tolerate a Soviet client state ninety miles off U.S. shores, the Eisenhower administration ordered the CIA to develop a secret plan for overthrowing it. But the plan, executed in April 1961, proved a deeply humiliating fiasco for President Kennedy. Castro's forces easily killed or rounded up the fifteen hundred Cuban refugees the CIA landed at the Bay of Pigs. Contrary to Washington's expectations, the Cuban population did not rise up to welcome the invaders.

Castro's demands for Soviet protection against a renewed American attack undoubtedly encouraged Khrushchev's decision to send missiles to Cuba. But he had other motives for taking such a tremendous gamble. Soviet missiles in Cuba would put much of the United States at the same nuclear risk the Soviet Union already faced from American missiles in Turkey and Western Europe. They could be used as bargaining chips against a German settlement. Their emplacement would prove to Khrushchev's critics that he could get tough with the Americans.

In October 1962, when U.S. aerial reconnaissance revealed that launching sites were under construction in Cuba, a terrifying thirteen-day crisis began. Few voices in the U.S. administration called for negotiation; most favored some show of force. Rather than attacking the launching sites without warning, as some recommended, Kennedy chose to impose a "quarantine" on Cuba. That term was used because a naval blockade amounted to a declaration of war. In fact, however, the U.S. Navy blockaded Cuba; it was prepared to stop and search approaching Soviet ships that might be carrying the missiles. As television news plotted the course of those ships, the world waited and wondered whether a clash on the high seas might lead to nuclear war. Kennedy himself is reported to have thought that the odds of war were at least one in three, and at worst even. The suspense ended only with the news that the Soviet ships were turning back.

Once again, and this time very publicly, Khrushchev had to back down. He paid for this humiliation in 1964 when his colleagues in the Politburo, the Soviet cabinet, fired him. Whatever credit he might have earned for ending the crisis was negated by the fact that he had provoked it. In exchange for his retreat he had received a tacit U.S. commitment not to invade Cuba and to remove American missiles (already obsolete) poised on the Soviet border in Turkey. But the Soviet Union had visibly failed in an attempt to project its power as close to American borders as U.S. power hemmed in its own frontiers.

Challenges to Bipolarity, 1962–1973

During the Cuban missile crisis, most of the world stood on the sidelines, at risk of destruction if the two superpowers clashed. This episode vividly illustrated the continuing danger for other nations of "annihilation without representation." That danger helps to explain the theme of the next decade of postwar international relations: the beginning of the breakdown of the bipolar world into a multipolar one. An economically resurgent Western Europe increasingly challenged U.S. leadership. At the same time, the U.S. assumption that Moscow orchestrated every move of world communism proved stunningly false as the Soviet Union and the People's Republic of China moved from mistrustful friendship to the verge of war.

First Steps Toward the Integration of Europe

The first steps toward Western European economic resurgence were taken while the continent was still rebuilding after the war. As the Cold War undercut the parties of the Left, power passed to Christian Democratic leaders. Their shared Catholic faith, transcending national loyalties, helped them to see that the European nations had become dwarfed and obsolete in a world of superpowers. Only by merging into a "United States of Europe" could

Europeans regain even part of their former power. The first institutional embodiment of European integration was an economic one: the European Coal and Steel Authority, established in April 1951. It merged the mines and steel mills of France, West Germany, Italy, and the Benelux countries. This proved to be only the first of many such supranational European organizations. In 1957 the same countries signed the Treaties of Rome, establishing the European Economic Community (EEC). Its members committed themselves to creating a "Common Market," designed to combine Europe's many national economies into one big one.

The Gaullist Challenge to U.S. Leadership

Though scornful of the federal model of European integration favored by the founders of the EEC, General de Gaulle, as president of France from 1958 to 1969, tried to make multipolarity a reality by compelling Western Europeans to abandon their dependency on the United States. He aimed to make a revived Europe, led by France, a power to reckon with in the world again.

Western Europe's subordination to an American NATO commander, de Gaulle maintained, was frightening and unconvincing: frightening, because as the Cuban missile crisis showed, in a confrontation with the Soviet Union the United States would not consult its allies before acting; unconvincing, because as the Soviet Union developed its nuclear capability, it was no longer credible that the United States would risk destruction to save Europe from a Soviet attack. Therefore de Gaulle did all he could to foster an independent European defense system. He gave the highest priority to developing delivery systems for France's nuclear weapons, developed over U.S. objections. Meanwhile he refused to allow the installation of NATO nuclear weapons on French soil, withdrew French forces from NATO command, and

Charles de Gaulle in 1965. *The French president votes in his village's town hall beneath his portrait as Free France's leader during World War II.* © *AP-Wide World Photos*

in 1966 ousted NATO from France. Similarly, when the British agreed in 1962 to replace their obsolete nuclear bombers with U.S. missiles, de Gaulle retaliated by vetoing Britain's application for membership in the EEC.

In hopes of restoring European economic independence, de Gaulle attacked the international monetary system created under American auspices at Bretton Woods in 1944. Under this system, the dollar had become the world's principal means of exchange. De Gaulle argued that the dollar's privileged status enabled the

United States to escape the discipline the world economy enforced on other currencies. The United States could ignore growing inflation and an ever-growing imbalance in the payments it exchanged with other countries. Its worldwide role protected the dollar from depreciating even when Americans spent more abroad than they earned. The endless outflow of dollars enabled U.S.-based multinational companies to buy heavily into the economies of other countries. Until the world monetary system could be revised, de Gaulle's remedy for France was to demand payments in gold, largely depleting the U.S. supply.

Many Americans denounced de Gaulle as an enemy. In fact, however, Gaullist foreign policy was only the most outspoken expression of a widespread European aspiration to break free of the post-1945 bipolar system.

Playing the China Card

In January 1964, de Gaulle's France extended diplomatic recognition to the People's Republic of China. To many Americans, this seemed another example of Gaullist unfriendliness. American policy was that "China" meant Chiang Kai-shek's refugee regime on Taiwan. De Gaulle, however, was bent on enlarging the number of players in the global power game, and recognizing China was one step in this process. Only in this way, he believed, could the world escape endless bipolar confrontations or the equally grim prospect of an agreement between the superpowers to rule the world, such as had occurred at Yalta in 1945.

By 1964, communist China was turning out not to be the obedient creature of Moscow once imagined. Mao Zedong was convinced that the Soviet Union was becoming a nonrevolutionary society closer in outlook to the capitalist nations than to China. At the same time, the Soviets, whose economic aid had always been meager, reneged on their promise to equip China with nuclear weapons. In 1960, as Sino-

Soviet relations worsened, Khrushchev withdrew the Soviet technicians sent to facilitate Chinese development. By the mid-1960s, border clashes revealed the depth of hostility between the two communist giants. As de Gaulle saw, the West now had an opportunity to draw closer to a potentially powerful enemy of the Soviet Union, thus complicating Soviet calculations. Unfortunately, it would be nearly a decade before the United States could play this "China card" in the international game. For American leaders had become obsessed with victory on another Asian front—in Vietnam, where they mistakenly believed they were resisting Chinese expansion.

The American Misadventure in Vietnam

The total costs of the Vietnamese conflict, the United States' longest and most expensive war, are not easily reckoned. Over fifty-seven thousand Americans and hundreds of thousands of Vietnamese died. Total American expenses have been calculated at over a trillion dollars. Less tangibly, the lost war dealt a blow to Americans' self-confidence from which they began to rally only in the 1980s. The United States' obsession with Vietnam, and then its apparent renunciation of power when it withdrew, hastened the transformation of international relations to a multipolar system. Thus the Vietnam War must be regarded as a pivotal event. Certainly its impact was far out of proportion to the importance of this Southeast Asian country. The tragedy unfolded in four acts.

The first act, the end of French rule in Vietnam, involved the United States only tangentially. Vietnam had been part of the French empire at the beginning of World War II. The Japanese defeat of the colonial powers created a power vacuum at the war's end when Japan itself was defeated. Vietnamese nationalists seized the moment to reclaim independence. Their leader was Ho Chi Minh, who

The war in Vietnam: A conflict of two ages. *A column of American tanks overtakes a peasant's oxcart. The war frequently juxtaposed the world's most advanced technology with one of its most ancient. Living as they did in different ages of human development, the oxcart driver and the tank commander were ill-equipped to comprehend one another's beliefs and purposes, a failure that foreshadowed the war's tragic outcome.* © *Bettmann/CORBIS*

as a young emigrant to France in 1919 had vainly petitioned the Paris Peace Conference for self-determination for his country. Disappointed by the indifference of Western leaders, he became a founding member of the French Communist party. The French had no intention of surrendering Vietnam to the Vietminh, the name given the movement Ho founded when he returned to his country in 1941. Negotiations between them ended in bloody clashes in 1946, the prelude to eight years of war.

American sympathies in this conflict shifted with events. U.S. undercover agents had cooperated with Ho's resistance to the Japanese. During the Cold War, however, Americans began to perceive Ho as a creature of Moscow, rather than as a nationalist fighting for liberation. The French took advantage of this shift to enlist U.S. aid against Ho. By 1954 the United States was paying three-quarters of France's war costs, and three hundred American advisers were in Vietnam. Though Vietnam's mineral wealth was sometimes cited as the reason for U.S. involvement, the real explanation seems to have been the *domino theory*. In this view the countries of Southeast Asia were like a row of dominoes standing on end: push one over and all the rest would fall to communism.

This theory became critical when the Vietminh defeated the French at the Battle of Dien Bien Phu early in 1954. A new French cabinet indicated its intention to get out of Vietnam as swiftly as possible. An international conference

in Geneva agreed to partition Vietnam temporarily, though it was to be reunited after free
elections within two years.

These Geneva accords mark the beginning
of the second act of the American drama in
Vietnam. Having refused to sign them, Washington felt free to disregard them. The promised elections, which all agree would have
given a majority to the Vietminh, were never
held. Instead, as had happened elsewhere
around the periphery dividing the spheres of
the superpowers, two countries emerged. As it
protected South Korea, the United States took
under its protection the Republic of South Vietnam. Its president was Ngo Dinh Diem, a fervent
anti-communist from the country's Catholic
minority.

Diem's regime was corrupt, and its contempt for the country's Buddhist and peasant
majorities soon provoked revolt. In 1960 a National Liberation Front (FLN in French) began
guerrilla operations in South Vietnam's jungles
and villages. From the start, though the FLN
claimed to be a multiparty, strictly southern
movement, it received supplies and direction
from Ho Chi Minh's North Vietnam.

This situation gave the Kennedy administration an opportunity to test its theory that
guerrillas could be beaten by tactics of counterinsurgency, including programs to "win the
hearts and minds" of a peasant populace by land
reform and social change. By 1963, twelve thousand American advisers were in South Vietnam,
helping Diem's army regroup peasants to prevent the FLN from living among them. However,
the Diem regime's continued repression of Bud-
dhists and other "enemies" made it impossible
to claim that the United States was defending
democracy in South Vietnam. Early in November, with U.S. encouragement, elements of the
South Vietnamese army overthrew Diem.

The third act of the Vietnam tragedy began
a few weeks later when Vice President Lyndon
Johnson succeeded Kennedy. To understand
why Johnson turned American involvement

into a tragedy by vastly increasing the U.S. commitment to Vietnam, it is necessary to examine
the perceptions of the policymakers who advised him.

In the context of twentieth-century history,
Ho Chi Minh is a familiar type. He was only one
of many leaders who mobilized mass movements against the European-dominated world
system. Ho had warned the French that even if
they killed ten of his men for every French
soldier killed by the Vietminh, he still would
win. And he did.

U.S. policymakers, however, looked at the
Vietnamese situation through a veil of American
preconceptions. Americans knew, and cared to
know, practically nothing of Vietnamese history,
culture, or language. They had little understanding of how colonial rule had left societies throughout the developing world—not just
Vietnam's—divided between small European-
ized and wealthy elites, made up of people like
Diem, and an overwhelming majority of impoverished peasants who could be mobilized by
champions of national independence and social
change. Unable to recognize how this colonial
legacy heightened the potential for revolution
in Vietnam, Americans saw in the country a
"cornerstone of the free world," a place to
"stand up to" the Soviet Union and China. Before
it became an American nightmare, Vietnam was
an American fantasy—and the mightiest nation
on earth was prepared to invest powerful energies in making the fantasy a reality. The policymakers who directed those energies wanted to
make sure that events conformed to their preconceptions, because their careers and reputa-
tions were at stake. For such reasons many
young men sometimes die.

Within a year of Johnson's 1964 pre-elec-
tion promise not to expand the U.S. commitment, there were 200,000 American troops in
Vietnam. When North Vietnamese patrol boats
clashed in the Tonkin Gulf with U.S. warships,
Johnson seized the occasion to force a resolution through the Senate giving him virtually

unlimited powers to expand a war against the North Vietnamese without declaring it. Out of 100 senators, only 2 voted against the resolution. While American infantrymen sweated through search-and-destroy missions in the South Vietnamese countryside, the U.S. Air Force dropped on Vietnam, North as well as South, nine times the tonnage of bombs dropped throughout the Pacific during World War II. This was massive support indeed for the dozen-odd mostly military governments that succeeded one another by plot and coup in the South Vietnamese capital, Saigon, between 1963 and 1965.

But it did not work. The North Vietnamese matched the Americans escalation for escalation, infiltrating regular troops into the South to back up the FLN. One of the many ironies of this terrible story is that both sides were obsessed with the "Munich analogy"—belief that surrender to aggression would mean never-ending subjection to it, as in 1938. American failure in Vietnam, Johnson and his advisers deeply believed, would expose the United States to a never-ending series of communist aggressions. The prime minister of North Vietnam, Pham Van Dong, declared in 1966, "Never Munich again, in whatever form." *He* meant that Vietnam had been cheated of total independence twice, in 1946 and 1954, and had no intention of negotiating anything away again.

In this contest of wills, the turning point for Americans came with the FLN offensive during the Vietnamese month of Tet, in January 1968. The Tet offensive ended in military defeat for the FLN, but it was a psychological success. The nightly television news depicted an apparent American debacle. Coordinated FLN operations showed that not even the American Embassy in Saigon was safe from guerrilla attack. After Tet, influential figures in the administration joined campus protesters in doubting that victory could ever be achieved. Faced with these doubts, Lyndon Johnson declared he would not seek re-election.

The election of 1968 opened the final act of the drama: the slow facing up to the reality of defeat. The successful Republican candidate, Richard M. Nixon, knew the war could not be won. His "secret plan" for Vietnam turned out to consist of trying to cut U.S. losses by beginning withdrawal while trying to bomb the North Vietnamese into a settlement that would save American face. For four years negotiations dragged on in Paris. At last the United States agreed to essentially the same terms the North Vietnamese had held out for from the beginning: prompt U.S. withdrawal, with few effective guarantees for South Vietnam.

South Vietnam did not long survive the departure of the U.S. combat troops in 1973. Nixon's plan for "Vietnamization" of the war—preparing the South Vietnamese to defend themselves—proved illusory. In April 1975 the North Vietnamese army entered Saigon. U.S. helicopters lifted the last Americans out of the embassy compound, while U.S. Marines pried loose the clutching hands of desperate South Vietnamese supporters who wanted to fly away too. It was a scene remarkably like that of the French departure from Vietnam twenty years earlier.

In 1975 most Americans probably considered the nation well out of Vietnam, even at such a price. With the passage of time, however, myths have grown up, as often happens when a nation has suffered a defeat. One is almost reminiscent of the "stab-in-the-back" legend of post-1918 Germany in blaming defeat on civilian irresolution. It alleges that the Vietnam War was lost not by the army but by Washington's unwillingness to fight with sufficient determination. In crude terms, this view holds that "Next time, we should go in with everything we've got!"

As we have already seen, however, the lessons of history are not always clear. Certainly, bitterness toward Washington by some Vietnam veterans is understandable. They neither caused the war nor failed in their duty—but after anguishing experiences they returned to an indifferent or hostile home front. Moreover, the extension of North Vietnamese rule to the whole country in 1975 belied the assurances of antiwar protesters that an FLN victory would bring freedom to South Vietnam. The unlucky South Vietnamese exchanged a regime of stark social inequality and fast-changing dictatorship under Diem and his successors for Soviet-style scarcities under the dictatorship of Ho Chi Minh's successors.

Had the United States gone all out for victory, some argue, none of this would have happened. But the implications of such a statement demand careful analysis. In pursuit of victory the United States extended the Vietnam War to the rest of Indochina, devastating once-neutral Laos and Cambodia (Kampuchea). What further steps would have been involved in "going all out"? The United States could have gone to war with China, which was supplying the North Vietnamese (as was the Soviet Union). But none of the presidents who had to face the Vietnamese nightmare was willing to risk the American public's reaction to such steps. Far from favoring war with China, most Americans later welcomed improvement of Chinese-American relations. Meanwhile, once the Americans were gone, relations between Vietnam and China, traditional enemies, deteriorated into actual war in 1979.

If the risks of enlarging the war outweighed the possibilities of thereby winning it, could the United States have made a greater effort in Vietnam itself? This question cannot be answered without doing something American policymakers rarely did: understanding the mentality of their opponents, particularly their different understanding of *time*. To Americans of the television era, a year is a very long time, and three years of inconclusive fighting by large American forces in Vietnam proved insupportable by 1968. To the Vietnamese, nearly a century of French colonialism had been a mere interlude; their history is one of a thousand years of resis-

tance to the Chinese. Even if the American forces had concentrated on defeating the North Vietnamese regular army instead of the FLN guerrillas, the resulting "victory" would probably not have been definitive. Vietnamese resistance would doubtless have continued, requiring an American occupying army. And Americans have shown little enthusiasm for commitments that would keep draftees indefinitely at risk. In the light of these considerations, the idea of victory in a place like Vietnam becomes elusive and problematical. Perhaps the best way of achieving victory would have been to follow the wise counsel of a senator who advised Johnson simply to announce that the United States had won—and then withdraw as quickly as possible.

Multipolar Détente Versus Renewed Confrontation, 1973–1984

After the Vietnam War, international relations were marked by an exploration of the possibilities and limits of diminished tension—détente—in a multipolar world. Through the mid-1970s, détente made it possible to set aside many of the festering issues of the Cold War. From the mid-1970s to the mid-1980s, however, Soviet-American relations took another sharp turn for the worse.

The Making of Détente

American diplomacy during the period of relative détente until 1976 was orchestrated by Secretary of State Henry Kissinger. Now that the revolutionary ardor of the Soviet Union and China had diminished, Kissinger believed, the United States could maneuver between them to secure its own interests and the balance of power. Though he too ritually denounced the Soviet Union on occasion, Kissinger did not see the world's future as the triumph of American right over communist wrong. Rather he envisioned an everlasting process of adjustment of interests among five centers of power: the United States, the Soviet Union, China, Western Europe, and Japan, now emerging as an economic superpower.

The most spectacular result of this idea was the reversal in Chinese-American relations. The process wound its way from secret negotiations to a solemn state visit by President Nixon to China early in 1972. His televised toasts to Chinese leaders marked a dramatic contrast to the decades during which the United States had ignored the existence of the People's Republic. The new friendship of the two countries raised deep concern in the Soviet Union, which by the early 1970s was maintaining up to a quarter of its armed forces in the east against possible Chinese attack.

The United States and the Soviet Union in the World Economy

Partly because of Soviet concern about China, President Nixon was warmly received when he visited Moscow in May 1972, three months after his trip to Beijing. But many motives, both international and domestic, impelled the Soviets toward détente.

On the international plane, the Soviet Union had overcome the inferiority in nuclear weaponry so evident during the Cuban missile crisis. Each superpower now had enough nuclear warheads to destroy the other many times over. When President Nixon admitted there was no possibility that the United States could win a nuclear war, the Soviet Union could feel it had finally been accepted as an equal.

Domestically, however, Soviet society by the 1970s had weaknesses that could be addressed, if at all, only by achieving détente with the United States. The Soviet economy was in increasing trouble (see Chapter 13). The Cold War also imposed severe strains on the U.S. economy. On August 15, 1971, Nixon had reacted dramatically to the decline of the dollar. He ended the dollar's convertibility at fixed rates to gold or foreign currencies. Henceforth, currencies would "float," exchanged at whatever rate the markets thought best. By this unilateral action, the United States destroyed the Bretton Woods system on which it had insisted in 1944. By refusing to pay in gold, the United States was repudiating part of its debts by depreciating the dollar. Its ability to do so without provoking protest was a testimony to continuing American economic power. But its need to do so suggested that American economic power was no longer what it had been in 1944.

Thus, when Nixon met Leonid Brezhnev in Moscow in 1972, both leaders recognized their nations' limitations. Their meeting produced an agreement based on the Strategic Arms Limitation Talks (now known as SALT I) held over the previous three years. Both sides would retain the monstrous stockpiles of nuclear weapons they had already built, but future production of certain kinds of weapons would be limited. Modest though it was, this agreement was a sign of the "spirit of détente," which soon stimulated a large increase in trade between the Western and Soviet blocs.

Détente for Europeans

This increased flow of goods reflected the détente that had developed between the subordinate states in each of the superpowers' spheres of influence. While the United States was preoccupied in Vietnam, Europeans east and west had seized the initiative to begin melting down the Iron Curtain that divided their continent. The credit belongs primarily to West German Chancellor Willy Brandt. Brandt's first step was to calm Soviet fears by signing a nonaggression treaty with the USSR in 1970. He also accepted Poland's western border with

Germany. In 1972 the two Germanies acknowledged each other's legitimacy. Finally, in 1973 West Germany formally renounced the Munich Agreement of 1938 that had dismembered Czechoslovakia. This period of détente climaxed in 1975 at the European Security Conference in Helsinki, Finland, where all the European countries, Eastern and Western, and the United States promised to honor each other's existing borders.

Critics of the Helsinki treaty contended that the East got considerably more out of it than the West. In return for Soviet promises to guarantee basic human rights, which soon proved valueless, the West acknowledged Stalin's expansion of the Soviet perimeter in Eastern Europe.

Yet, as de Gaulle had foreseen, the Soviet Union's rule in Eastern Europe had become so difficult that the USSR found détente essential. Behind a façade of communist solidarity, the Soviets were trying to maintain Eastern Europe in a situation of dependency. Such a situation was wholly incongruous. Still developing economically itself, the USSR could not provide its satellites with capital. Meanwhile, some of the satellite states had reached a higher level of economic development than the Soviet Union but remained politically repressed. Thus, both the poor and the more affluent economies of Eastern Europe had economic reasons to complain of Soviet rule by the 1970s.

To the extent that détente offered an economic alternative to Soviet dependency, it was seized eagerly by the communist leadership of the various Eastern bloc countries. Moscow's tolerance of their growing indebtedness to Western banks suggested it had no better solution. As economic exchanges with the global economy multiplied, the life of Eastern Europe was unavoidably altered. By the 1980s it was clear that its peoples, like those of Western Europe, desperately wanted to perpetuate détente.

The Carter Years: Détente Dissolved

President Jimmy Carter came into office in 1977 anxious to maintain détente. He left office with détente in shambles. Perhaps the rapid chill was inevitable, given the continuing rivalry of the superpowers.

The Carter administration completed negotiations with the Soviets in 1979 for a second Strategic Arms Limitation Treaty (SALT II). Though this treaty was never ratified by Congress, both parties continued to abide by its provisions. Despite these continuing contacts, Carter's foreign policy advisers convinced him that the Soviet Union was taking advantage of détente. They were alarmed by growing Soviet involvement in the rivalries among African independence movements. Except for their sponsorship of Cuba, the Soviets had not previously committed themselves in countries so far from their borders. American policymakers found it unacceptable that the Soviets should feel free to intervene on a global scale.

The Carter administration's greatest indignation, however, was reserved for the Soviet invasion of Afghanistan in December 1979. The situation in this undeveloped mountain nation bore certain ironic resemblances to that of Vietnam, with the very important difference that Afghanistan lay on the Soviet Union's southern border. A series of pro-Soviet governments had displaced the former nonaligned regime. Many Afghans held them in contempt. When fighting broke out, the Soviet puppet government could control the capital, the cities, and the main roads, but it could not control Muslim tribesmen in the hills, who had a proud historic tradition of warfare against all invaders. The Soviets were unable to master their resistance, despite extensive use of the kind of tactics—saturation bombing, helicopter gunships, napalm—employed unavailingly by the United States in Vietnam. There was little the United

States could do for the Afghan rebels except secretly send them arms. But Carter took the initiative in several expressions of outrage, including stopping the sale of grain to the Soviets and boycotting the 1980 Moscow Olympics.

None of these measures had any effect on Soviet policy, but they did contribute to the end of détente and the renewal of bipolar confrontation. At the same time, however, the United States was discovering the power of the previously powerless—small countries rich in raw materials.

The OPEC Challenge and the Iranian Revolution

In 1973, when the Organization of Petroleum Exporting Countries (OPEC) embargoed the sale of oil to the West to protest its support for Israel, stocks on the New York Stock Exchange lost $100 billion in value in just six weeks. Even supposedly reliable U.S. allies among the oil producers, like the shah of Iran, were quite unapologetic about their new attitude. Oil prices quadrupled between 1973 and 1975.

Worse followed in the oil-rich Persian Gulf. The shah's regime was overthrown in 1979 by a massive opposition front whose religious leadership regarded the United States as the "great Satan" of the world. After the shah fled to the United States, Iranian militants seized the American Embassy in Tehran, taking sixty Americans hostage. All of the United States' might could not help the hostages. For many months, television brought before Americans the humiliating spectacle of their fellow countrymen paraded before the cameras by enemies filled with the Third World's rage against superpower dominance. President Carter was quite unfairly blamed for the hideous dilemma of a hostage situation—whether to sacrifice the hostages or give in. He succeeded in negotiating their release only minutes before Ronald Reagan was sworn in as president in January 1981.

Return to Confrontation

Reagan represented the right wing of the Republican party, which had been deeply suspicious of Kissinger's design for détente. During his first term, Soviet-American relations continued the deterioration begun during the Carter administration. Reagan ordered a record military buildup, which included preparation for the militarization of space. And he denounced the Soviet Union in language reminiscent of that of John Foster Dulles.

At the same time, the Reagan administration seemed keenly aware that while Americans liked a president who would "stand up to the Russians," they would be unsympathetic to belligerence that imposed sacrifices—such as the draft. Reagan preferred confrontational rhetoric to actual confrontation. In Latin America, the United States sent aid to the "Contra" rebels seeking to overthrow the revolutionary Sandinista government in Nicaragua, but no American troops.

When Reagan did send troops, it was to a Caribbean island, a place without strategic importance and also without risk. The U.S. invasion of Grenada in October 1983 easily overthrew a new Marxist government that vainly aspired to change Grenada's typical Third World economic dependency on the export of cocoa, nutmeg, and bananas. Grenada provided just one more example of how the tragic and perhaps insoluble problem of Third World poverty could be perceived by U.S. policymakers as a challenge to the capitalist West by the communist East.

Reagan-Gorbachev Summitry

Many Americans, including President Reagan, interpreted the U.S. intervention in Grenada as a successful countermove, after years of failure, against the spread of Soviet influence in the Caribbean. Perhaps it was this "success," combined with the renewed American self-confidence produced by economic recovery and Reagan's military buildup, that prompted the president to announce in a speech on January 16, 1984, a far less confrontational approach to relations with the Soviet Union. Once he had denounced it as the "evil empire." Now he spoke of his hope of reaching an understanding with the Soviets, based on a reduction in nuclear armaments.

Reagan's offer of negotiations was gladly accepted by Mikhail Gorbachev when he became the Soviet leader early in 1985. In 1986, in Reykjavik, Iceland, they came close in their face-to-face conversations to envisioning the scrapping of all nuclear weapons, until the professional caution of their military advisers restrained their enthusiasm. Nonetheless, the first steps were taken toward elaborating a treaty to eliminate ground-based "intermediate nuclear forces" (the INF treaty). Though the treaty mandated the destruction of only a small portion of both sides' vast nuclear arsenals, it included the medium-range missiles the United States had only recently persuaded the often-reluctant Europeans to install on their own territories. The formal signing of this treaty, with its unprecedented provisions for on-site inspections by both sides to verify that the weapons were actually destroyed, was the principal achievement of another Reagan-Gorbachev summit held in Washington late in 1987.

No similar breakthrough on substantive issues marked the Moscow summit of the summer of 1988. Reagan would not sign Gorbachev's proposed joint pledge not to attempt to resolve any future superpower conflict by military means. His advisers felt that such a pledge would inhibit American shipments of arms to the anti-communist forces rebelling against the governments of Angola, Nicaragua, and Afghanistan. (Gorbachev had already begun withdrawing Soviet troops from Afghanistan, boldly cutting the losses of nearly a decade of futile Soviet intervention and leaving the Afghan communist government to fend for itself.) Despite the absence of substantive results, the world drew comfort from the spectacle of this friendly encounter in the Soviet capital.

How are we to explain this apparent thaw in nearly a half-century of Cold War, coming in the second term of the most outspokenly anti-communist U.S. president? Much of the explanation can be found in the respective visions of world realities held by the two men who brought it about. Gorbachev's most innovative pronouncement regarding foreign policy was his frank admission that the advent of nuclear weapons had invalidated all the old Marxist-Leninist ideas about the conflict of nations. In Lenin's time, a major war such as World War I had been a necessary precondition for the social revolution the Bolsheviks had made. Today, though, the prospect of nuclear war "called into question the very survival of the human race." In such a situation, to strive for military superiority was pointless.

Even more essential to explaining Gorbachev's foreign policy is the fact that, as we shall see in Chapter 13, he saw his mission as the revitalization of the Soviet Union by a total renovation of its economy and institutions. Such a goal could be attained only if relaxation of tension with the United States enabled the Soviets to devote most of their resources to investing for domestic development, rather than arming for external confrontation. Gorbachev criticized his predecessor Leonid Brezhnev for failing to recognize that a nation cannot be powerful abroad if it is in economic decline.

Clearly President Reagan did not recognize, in approaching negotiations with the Soviets, any similar American economic weakness—though in light of the largest U.S. government and international trade deficits in history and the Wall Street crash of October 1987, the worst since 1929, many Americans did not agree that their economy was as robust as he believed. Consciousness of a need to reorient U.S. investment priorities does not explain Reagan's acceptance of a Cold War thaw. Perhaps the best explanation is the simplest: Reagan changed his mind. For all his ideological language, he proved, as did Gorbachev, to be basically a pragmatist. Recognizing that the advent of Gorbachev and his plans for reform marked a potentially historic turning point for the Soviet Union, Reagan was prepared to renounce his adamantly anti-Soviet stance and explore what negotiations could achieve.

The End of the Cold War

If Gorbachev hoped that by achieving accommodation with Reagan he could reform the Soviet economy, he was soon disappointed. The astonishingly rapid collapse of the Soviet bloc within six years of his coming to power in 1985 provides one more illustration of the historical generalization that no time is more dangerous for a decrepit authoritarian regime than when it attempts reform. As we shall see in Chapter 13, Gorbachev recognized that he could not achieve economic change without granting a measure of independence to the Soviet satellites and a degree of political participation to Soviet citizens. But in doing so, he unleashed pent-up demands for national freedom and democracy that had been growing for decades and raged far beyond his expectations or his ability to control them.

The year after his triumphant Moscow summit with Reagan, 1989, began the most fundamental changes to the global configuration since 1945. The largest street demonstrations since 1953 in East Germany forced the tottering communist regime there to open the Berlin Wall in November. Once opened, it did not remain standing for long. For better or for worse for the world, Germany was effectively reunited when, in September 1990, representatives of its two former governments signed a treaty by which the Federal Republic in effect absorbed East Germany. Meanwhile,

the other former Soviet satellites proclaimed their independence, so that by June 1991 both the Warsaw Pact and Comecon, the mechanisms for Soviet political and economic control of Eastern Europe, no longer had any function and dissolved themselves.

No more than in Eastern Europe could the genie of nationalism be forced back into the bottle within the Soviet Union itself. The new political institutions provided a forum in which one Soviet ethnic minority after another could express its frustration at continuing economic failure by demanding independence from Moscow. Under their secessionist pressure the Union of Soviet Socialist Republics simply broke apart into its constituent republics, no longer soviet or socialist. Soon no role was left for a central government. At the end of 1991, Gorbachev resigned as president of a Soviet Union that had ceased to exist, leaving behind a loose federation that awkwardly called itself the "Commonwealth of Independent States."

Such a stunning collapse of one of the antagonists naturally brought an end to the bipolar Cold War confrontation that had appeared to dominate international relations since 1945. In September 1991, President George Bush ordered an end to the twenty-four-hour alerts in the underground silos where for a generation Air Force officers had awaited the order to launch nuclear Armageddon by dispatching U.S. missiles against Soviet targets. In February 1992, at yet another summit, Bush met Boris Yeltsin, president of the largest of the Soviet successor states, the Russian Republic. Together they formally proclaimed an end to the Cold War. The unequal terms on which it ended were reflected in the arms treaty the two signed in June. Both sides agreed substantially to reduce their nuclear arsenals; but while the Russians surrendered their land-based multiple-warhead missiles, the key to the former Soviet deterrent, the Americans retained their submarine-based warheads of the same type, the essential element of U.S. defenses. Desperate for American economic aid to prevent his famished country from sinking further into chaos, Yeltsin was in no position to insist on a better deal.

And so, some people claimed, the Cold War had ended with a complete U.S. victory. Or had it?

The Post–Cold War World System: U.S. Hegemony or "Geoeconomic Multipolarity"?

The Panama Invasion and the Persian Gulf War

The collapse of the United States' only military superpower rival naturally tended to embolden American leaders to assert U.S. power. President Bush's first such assertion came in a part of the world where the United States had always insisted on acting regardless of the USSR: Central America. In December 1989 he dispatched U.S. troops to seize the dictator of Panama, General Manuel Noriega, a long-time U.S. ally now accused of complicity in drug traffic. U.S. helicopter gunships flattened Noriega's headquarters in the slums of the Panamanian capital. Between 202—the official U.S. count—and up to 4,000 Panamanian civilians, according to critics, lost their lives. Noriega's eventual sentence by a Miami court seemed to Bush supporters to justify the operation, though within less than a year cocaine traffic through Panama had returned to preinvasion levels. Within a few months of December 1989, Panama vanished as completely from the U.S. front pages and evening news as Grenada had done after Reagan's invasion of 1983. U.S. intervention in Latin America, after all, is an old story.

President Bush's next crusade against a dictator—the Iraqi leader Saddam Hussein—took American troops in far greater numbers much farther from home: to the Persian Gulf War, which resulted from Saddam's occupation of Kuwait in August 1990.

Saddam might be forgiven some surprise at the violent U.S. reaction to his invasion of his neighbor, for the Reagan and Bush administrations had given him substantial help in his long war against Iran. Even after that war ended in 1988, Iraq received some $2 billion in U.S. aid, though some in Washington were aware that Saddam was diverting these funds to his ambitious arms program, which included both poison gas and nuclear weapons.

Even though the American public knew none of these facts, it was not easy for the Bush administration to portray the Iraqi-Kuwaiti conflict in the familiar terms of evil versus good. Saddam's regime was a monstrously cruel dictatorship, but the Emirate of Kuwait was no democracy. Eighteen families, including that of the ruler, the emir, controlled 90 percent of the $100 billion in oil revenues that Kuwait had invested in Western banks.

Nor was Saddam without genuine grievances against Kuwait. The border between it and Iraq had been imprecisely penciled in on a map by the British colonial administrator of the region in the 1920s. Worse, from Saddam's point of view, Kuwait was dumping its oil onto world markets at prices below those stipulated by OPEC to curry favor with Western governments. Since Iraq too depended heavily on oil sales, Saddam calculated that every dollar off the OPEC price cost his country $1 billion. Thus he had no lack of motives for overrunning his little neighbor.

President Bush, however, soon decided that Saddam must be chastised as Noriega had been chastised. For the first time since the beginning of the Korean War, the United States was able to mobilize the UN Security Council against an aggressor. Gorbachev's faltering USSR could only go along as the Council voted to dispatch a vast multinational army, largely composed of young Americans, to the Persian Gulf. Their mission was, ostensibly, to reinforce the economic sanctions voted against Saddam.

The road back from Kuwait. *As the Iraqi army fled homeward on the night of February 25, 1991, American bombers and helicopters poured down a devastating fire on the fugitives. Dawn revealed a roadway lined with an endless caravan of carnage. © Peter Turnley/CORBIS*

Bush argued a number of themes against critics of his policy. Sometimes he spoke of the "lessons" of the 1930s—that aggression must be resisted everywhere. He directly compared Saddam to Hitler, an apt comparison of character but not of power, since Iraq with its population of 18 million was hardly an equivalent of the Third Reich. Administration officials were more candid when they explained that what they were really defending in the Persian Gulf was "the American way of life," or even "jobs," both

synonyms for cheap oil. By 1990 the U.S. economy had become dependent on foreign sources for half its supply. (Unlike Japan, which had responded to the oil price shocks of the 1970s by planned reductions in per capita energy consumption, the United States during the Reagan years virtually abandoned the idea of conservation.)

When Saddam defied the UN deadline to evacuate Kuwait, Bush, arguing that sanctions had failed, promptly ordered a long-planned attack. For six weeks the United States and allied air forces pounded both the Iraqi army in Kuwait and its essential facilities within Iraq. When they finally launched a ground attack on February 24, 1991, the war was over within a hundred hours. Outnumbered, abandoned by Saddam's fugitive commanders, the Iraqi army was simply massacred from the air as it stampeded home from Kuwait, suffering casualties perhaps a thousand times greater than the allies. U.S. combat casualties totaled 146.

After such a lopsided victory, many Americans expected that the allied armies would overthrow Saddam. But Bush decided otherwise. The cease-fire agreement required Iraq to complete its withdrawal from Kuwait and to surrender its chemical and nuclear weapons but not to change its government. In fact, by early 1992 most of the Americans deployed in the Persian Gulf had gone home. Iraq, despite the continuing pressure of embargo, was returning to something like normal life. Saddam seemed as firmly in control as ever. Sober calculation had suggested to the Bush administration that if Saddam were overthrown, Iraq might collapse, altering the delicate Middle Eastern balance of power.

The returning American victors of the Gulf War received heroes' welcomes. President Bush exulted that their success proved that the United States had at last "licked the Vietnam syndrome" of hesitating to commit forces overseas. Some commentators even suggested that victory in the Persian Gulf signaled the beginning of a post–Cold War "New World Order" to be imposed by the United States.

Yet the mood of the American public was far from what might be expected after two victories like the collapse of the Soviet Union and the expulsion of Saddam from Kuwait. Their pessimism reflected Americans' growing recognition that military power exerted against the USSR and Iraq alike had yielded only hollow victories, for, as a widely current bitter joke had it, "The Cold War is over; it was won by the Japanese."

Geopolitical Versus Geoeconomic Power

Indeed, though some American commentators gloated that the collapse of the Soviet Union had left only one superpower standing, there were almost as many to point out that the way the United States paid for the Gulf War revealed the real distribution of economic power in the post–Cold War world. Though the United States supplied the bulk of the troops for Operation Desert Storm against Saddam, it could muster only 10 percent of its $61 billion cost. The rest of the money had literally to be begged from U.S. "allies" like Germany and Japan, who offered no troops though they were far more dependent on Persian Gulf oil than was the United States. Burdened by a debt that had tripled in the 1980s, the United States was also becoming a less effective competitor in the global marketplace. The vast military buildup of the Reagan years may indeed have finally convinced Gorbachev that the Soviet Union could not sustain the military confrontation of the Cold War. But while the United States was deploying the world's most sophisticated weapons, in the 1980s the already small American share of world exports of automobiles fell by 10 percent, of machine tools by 35 percent, and of semiconductors by 39 percent.

Militarily, the United States might be the only remaining superpower, but economically, the standard by which post–Cold War world power is measured, the United States found itself challenged in the new century by two geoeconomic superpowers: united Europe and Japan.

Seeing this contest for power as a rivalry of *national* economies may be a naive oversimplification. Now that five *multinational* corporations today control more than half of the global market in products ranging from automobiles to electronic components, and another five such multinational conglomerates provide over half of the world's supply of oil, personal computers, and multimedia,[3] it might seem pointless to compare the achievements and failures of mere national, or even regional economies. Nevertheless, commentators and editorialists discussing the competition for geoeconomic power continue to scan national statistics to determine whether the United States, the European Union, or Japan is ahead in the race. In these terms of comparison, who then is in the lead? Fully to answer that question will require close study of the impact of post-1945 technological innovation and tightening global integration on the societies and economies of the three contenders: the United States and Western Europe in the next chapter, and Japan and its East Asian counterparts in Chapter 17. Yet it is appropriate to conclude our discussion of the half-century of the Cold War with a brief look at how prepared its vast changes left the three potential geoeconomic superpowers for the challenges of the twenty-first century.

"United" Europe: Geoeconomic Superpower?

Membership in the European Economic Community, renamed the European Union in 1993, has grown substantially since its foundation by France, West Germany, Italy, and the Benelux countries in 1957. Between 1973 and 1986, Britain, Ireland, Denmark, Greece, Spain, and Portugal joined. During 1995, Austria, Finland, and Sweden were added, bringing total membership to fifteen nations. A dozen additional countries, mainly in the former Soviet bloc, are now candidates for membership.

Even with only twelve members at the beginning of the 1990s, united Europe appeared to be a formidable geoeconomic contender. A third of the world's trade circulated within or across its borders. The value of its combined industrial production exceeded that of the United States, Canada, and Mexico together by over 20 percent. On the foundation of economic unity, Europeans seemed to be building political unity. An all-European elected parliament continued to meet regularly in the French

city of Strasbourg, though its powers were still overshadowed by those of the Union's bureaucrats at its headquarters in Brussels. In December 1991, the Union's leaders signed a treaty in the Dutch city of Maastricht that was intended to take Western Europe a momentous step further toward economic unity and power. They committed themselves to creating, before the year 2000, a common European currency, the euro, to replace the pounds, francs, and marks with which Europeans had traded for centuries. Though this commitment fell short of what the most ardent advocates of European integration wanted—more powers for the European parliament and a single European central bank— French president François Mitterrand exulted that at Maastricht "a great power is being born, one at least as strong commercially, industrially and financially as the United States and Japan."

From the perspective of the new century, however, the achievement of this goal of Maastricht seems less certain. In the forty years that have gone by since the European Union began, the clarity of its original objectives has been obscured. The end of the Cold War has undermined the argument that economic unity was the necessary corollary of NATO military unity against the Soviet troops on Western Europe's borders. The shared vision of Europe as a common home that helped inspire the original six members has been diluted as more and more nations, with their disparate societies, economies, and political preferences, have been admitted. As membership has grown, there have been more and more demands for special treatment, for exemptions from the common rule. On January 1, 1998, for example, passport examination at borders within the Union was scheduled to cease, but in fact only seven member nations accepted this symbol of a truly multinational community.

This kind of reluctance to subordinate national preferences to common policies grew as the prosperity of the 1950s and 1960s gave way to the more troubled period of global economic history beginning in the 1970s. The Union had begun as a confederation of nations all committed to the prevailing political model of Europe in the 1950s: the full-employment guarantor state. But as economic times grew harder, consensus on maintaining this political model began to break down. A substantial wing of the British Conservative party—"Euro-sceptics"—never accepted the loss of sovereignty Union membership implied. They bitterly protested the dictates of Brussels bureaucrats, especially their insistence on maintaining the social safeguards of the guarantor state, which British governments in the 1980s were the most eager of all in Europe to attack. Ironically, by the mid-1990s many French and Germans mistrusted the European Union for the opposite reason: it seemed to threaten the very survival of the guarantor state.

The Maastricht treaty stipulates that for a nation to be eligible to adopt the common currency mandated for the new century, it must reduce its government deficit below 3 percent of gross domestic product (GDP). This requirement gave an additional argument to conservative governments, especially in France and Germany, who insisted that successful competition in the global marketplace required cutting the benefits of the guarantor state, which had sustained Western Europe's comfortable postwar way of life, with its high wages, ample pensions, long paid vacations, and restricted working hours. The attempt of the French government to impose such cuts on workers for the government-owned railway system provoked paralyzing strikes late in 1995 that one newspaper correctly described as "the first revolt against globalization"—that is, against the government's assault on laws that protected French pay and working conditions from being pushed down to levels dictated by the global labor market. Similar strikes threatened to disrupt the German economy. In the minds of the protesters the idea of European union, once seen as the means to make Europe economically powerful enough to challenge the United States and Japan, had become merely an excuse to lower European living standards to those of the poorer parts of the world.

Even more distressing to Europeans who had always believed that European union was the only means of restoring the continent's power was the revelation that Union members could not or would not take concerted action to stop the tragedy unfolding in the 1990s on Western Europe's own doorstep, in Bosnia. The ethnic civil war among Serbs, Croats, and Bosnian Muslims into which Yugoslavia disintegrated in 1991 became a conflict of sickening cruelty, marked by genocidal atrocities reminiscent of those of the Nazis, though smaller and less systematic. Yet the members of the Union could not agree on action to stop this European horror unfolding only a few hundred miles from their capital cities. Some members did contribute troops to the pathetically outnumbered peacekeeping force the United Nations sent to Bosnia in 1992. When one of the warring Bosnian factions contemptuously took the peacekeepers hostage, NATO retaliated with ineffective air strikes, mainly by U.S. planes. But that was all Europe did. Europeans watched passively as the Bosnian Serb army overran one of the UN "safe havens"—Srebrenica, left undefended by Dutch peacekeepers—then marched thousands of Muslims who had taken refuge there off to massacre. Only when the United States, which thus far had contributed only aircraft to pacifying Bosnia, brokered a treaty among the Bosnian factions and committed twenty thousand ground troops early in 1996 to enforce it did the killing stop.

Once again, thoughtful Europeans lamented, Europe in the 1990s had been reduced to calling in the Americans to end a European war, as had happened on a far larger scale in 1917–1918 and in 1944–1945. To many, this failure suggested how hollow the idea of European union really was. Perhaps because for forty years bureaucrats and politicians had focused mainly on its economic advantages, they had failed to instill Europeans with a sense of community and shared responsibility for ending the Bosnian tragedy next door. Thus each nation had consulted only its own interests, which were to contribute as few troops and as little aid as possible.

Lacking a sense of shared responsibility, some observers wondered, did the European Union really amount to more than a commercial convenience for a collection of divided and irresolute middle-size nations? If not, then despite its enormous potential, the European Union might in the long run prove an ineffective geoeconomic contender against Japan and the United States.

Japan and the United States as Geoeconomic Competitors

The challenger for geoeconomic supremacy that Americans have been most aware of has been not Europe but Japan. In the 1980s, a nation that Americans had once perceived as a reliable Cold War subordinate came to be seen as posing almost as serious an economic threat to American world dominance as the Soviets had appeared to pose militarily. Shocking surprises like the purchase of New York's Rockefeller Center symbolized how rich the Japanese had become. To explain Japanese success, American critics of their own country's economic policies pointed to many things the Japanese did better. Though numbering fewer than half the American population, they regularly invested more in plants and equipment than Americans did. Their per capita expenditure on research and development, the key to success in an age of headlong technological innovation, ranked first in the world among large industrial countries, while the United States, if military research and development were subtracted from its total, ranked tenth and falling.

Such comparisons, these critics argued, showed that Americans must reorient their national priorities along Japanese lines, develop-

ing geoeconomic, not military power. The key to sustaining American global predominance in the post–Cold War world, they insisted, was to be found not in the high-tech weaponry that had crushed Saddam Hussein's army but in better schools, more sensible investment priorities, less inequality between bosses and workers, less thoughtless consumption of nonrenewable resources—all characteristics of Japanese society that helped explain its success.

By the mid-1990s, however, many American observers, noting growing Japanese setbacks, became much more critical of the Japanese system. Japanese economic growth virtually stopped, and unemployment rose in 1996 to the unheard of rate, for Japan, of 3.8 percent. The stock market virtually collapsed, and some of the giant Japanese banks, undermined by ill-judged loans, had to be bailed out by the government. Symbolically, in late 1995 the Mitsubishi Corporation, after losing $1 billion, abandoned its ownership of Rockefeller Center.

Despite these setbacks, Japan could not yet be counted out as a geoeconomic contender. All the foundations that long supported Japanese economic success were still in place. The Japanese still led the world in manufacturing, notably of automobiles, electronic equipment, ships, and steel. They remained the world's largest spenders for private research and development, and they planned in 1996 to increase public expenditure by 50 percent. Japanese households still saved a percentage of their annual income four times greater than the American rate. By the criterion of per capita Gross National Product (PCGNP), the Japanese in 1998 were still the world's economic champions, with a PCGNP of $32,350, compared to $29,240 in the United States and $26,570 in Germany. (However, all three were outproduced by the five million citizens of Denmark, whose PCGNP was $33,040.)

Such statistics remind us that though there may be "only one remaining superpower" in the post–Cold War world in a *military* sense, such a statement is not accurate in *geoeconomic* terms, though the United States may now hold a lead over Europe and Japan. Certainly American cultural influences are the most widespread in today's world. Ninety percent of the messages on the newest and fastest-growing medium of communication, the Internet, are in English, a language now spoken around the world by more people for whom it is a second language than by native speakers. The American media conglomerate MTV now beams programs like *Beavis and Butthead* to a quarter-billion television sets in seventy countries, though it faces growing competition from local imitators in many of them.

Moreover, in the late 1990s there was evidence that some American industries apparently beaten in global geoeconomic competition were recapturing a share of the market. The American steel industry, for example, once thought doomed by cheaper foreign production, doubled its exports between 1994 and 1996, its best performance since before World War II. Such an accomplishment suggests that the erosion of American geoeconomic power from its predominant position of 1945 might not be destined to continue indefinitely, though that predominance will never be regained.

It is important to note, however, that American steel's recovery has not been painless. The industry has become competitive again because the hours of work needed to produce a ton of American steel have fallen to 4.2 from 12.49 in twenty years, reflecting a downsizing of the industry's labor force that has made the remaining steelworkers far more productive. Spurred by global competition and downsized by labor-saving new technologies—the hallmarks of the economic history of the second half of the twentieth century—American steel can now contribute successfully to the race for geoeconomic power. But the industry can no longer provide the kind of highly paid and secure job for a steelworker's son today that his father took for granted a generation ago. This bleak fact reminds us that beyond the bare

statistics, we need to consider the impact of geoeconomic change, or "globalization," on the lives of societies and individuals around the world.

Conclusion: Globalization—For Whom?

The arms race of the Cold War period inspired such deep concern among the world's peoples, especially its younger generations, that many rallied to movements challenging their government's arms policies even to the point of violent protest. Children of the 1950s, absurdly taught that they could protect themselves by crouching under their school desks at the moment of a nuclear blast, grew up in the 1960s to become supporters of organizations advocating nuclear disarmament—even unilateral nuclear disarmament—by demonstrations that sometimes provoked harsh police repression. The demonstrations prompted no country to disarm itself, but the moral pressure exerted by the younger generation certainly did much, by the 1970s, to delegitimize the 1950s notion that nuclear war was just another potential strategic option.

The youthful protest movement against "the bomb" waned with the emergence of détente as a US-Soviet nuclear confrontation became more improbable. (It should be noted, however, that the collapse of the Soviet Union has not removed its missiles and that nuclear weapons continue to proliferate, raising the possibility that the first actual nuclear war might be between India and Pakistan.)

At the end of the twentieth century, however, there was growing evidence that young people of many countries were beginning to mobilize against a phenomenon of the 1990s that some interpreted as almost as dangerous to Earth's well-being as "the bomb"—the economic threat of "globalization."

We shall reserve a full discussion of this complex phenomenon for the final chapter of

A protest march against the meeting of the World Trade Organization in Seattle, December 1999. *Protest sometimes led to more violent scenes of confrontation between the demonstrators and the Seattle police, armed with batons and tear gas. Antoine Serra/© CORBIS-SYGMA*

this book. To close this chapter on twentieth-century international relations we shall simply note the possible parallel that may now be emerging with the anti-nuclear movements of an earlier generation. Many young people today do not accept the pro-globalization arguments of such champions of the movement as the Clinton administration: that the creation of a single global marketplace encourages international investment and trade, promoting growth, jobs, and competitiveness while lowering consumers' costs. Rather they see globalization as the creation of multinational corporations—aided and abetted by international institutions like the World Bank, the International Monetary Fund, and the World Trade Organization—to manage the global economy in their own inter-

ests, rather than those of Earth's peoples, particularly poor nations and poor people within rich nations. They point out that the rules of the World Trade Organization limit the power of national governments to control economic developments within their own borders that their own people perceive to be harmful.

In November 1999, when the World Trade Organization scheduled one of its periodic international meetings in Seattle, it was greeted by some 50,000 protesters, young people supported by some labor organizations like the Teamsters and the AFL-CIO. They successfully prevented the organization from transacting its business, at the cost of some violence. For those who could remember nuclear disarmament rallies of a generation earlier, the sight of the

Seattle police clubbing and pepper-spraying youthful demonstrators was eerily reminiscent.

Such confrontations are not the only tactic these young protestors envision to bring the process of globalization under democratic control. They plan to make full use of globalization's own technical foundations—such as the Internet—to develop contacts around the world, with the aim of creating international organizations numerous and powerful enough to confront the multinational corporations and their international bureaucratic allies on an equal footing. Such a goal may seem today the visionary quest of a tiny minority, scoring only such slight symbolic victories as persuading their universities not to endorse the products of firms like Nike, whose athletic shoes they charge are produced by Third World workers employed at substandard wages.[4]

If, however, the terms on which globalization becomes a reality become a central issue of the world's political life early in the twenty-first century, the protest of Seattle may come to be seen as merely an historic beginning. For now, the issue remains who will be the winners, and who the losers, in this process of globalization that accelerated so dramatically in the last decade of the twentieth century.

Notes

1. Quoted from Robert F. Kennedy, *Thirteen Days: A Memoir of the Cuban Missile Crisis* (New York: W. W. Norton, 1969), pp. 62, 127.

2. Quoted in William R. Keylor, *The Twentieth-Century World: An International History* (New York: Oxford University Press, 1992).

3. David C. Korten, "The Limits of the Earth," *The Nation*, July 15-22, 1996, based on figures from *The Economist.*

4. For continuing coverage of the ideas and plans of anti-globalization groups, see the website www.alternet.org.

Suggestions for Further Reading

Beschloss, Michael R. *The Crisis Years: Kennedy and Khrushchev, 1960-1963* (1991).

Blight, James G., Bruce J. Allyn, and David A. Welch. *Cuba on the Brink: Castro, the Missile Crisis and the Soviet Collapse* (1993).

Hogan, Michael J., ed. *The End of the Cold War: Its Meaning and Implications* (1992).

Karnow, Stanley. *Vietnam: A History* (1983).

Keylor, William R. *The Twentieth-Century World: An International History.* 3d ed. (1996).

Lafeber, Walter. *America, Russia, and the Cold War, 1945-1990.* 7th ed. (1993).

Leffler, Melvyn P. *A Preponderance of Power: National Security, the Truman Administration and the Cold War* (1992).

——— , and David S. Painter, eds. *Origins of the Cold War: An International History* (1994).

Lewis, Gordon K. *Grenada: The Jewel Despoiled* (1987).

Luttwak, Edward N. *The Endangered American Dream* (1993).

MacDonald, Callum A. *Korea: The War Before Vietnam* (1987).

Maier, Charles S., ed. *The Cold War in Europe* (1996).

Mastny, Vojech. *The Cold War and Soviet Insecurity: The Stalin Years* (1996).

Reynolds, David. *One World Divided: A Global History since 1945* (2000).

Wolff, Michael, Peter Rutten, and Alfred F. Bayas III. *Where We Stand: Can America Make It in the Global Race for Wealth, Health and Happiness?* (1992).

Wrong, Michela. *In the Footsteps of Mr. Kurtz* (2000).

CHAPTER 12

Toward Postindustrial Society: The United States and Western Europe in the Postwar Decades

A GENERATION HAS NOW PASSED SINCE "THE SIXTIES," THE EVENTFUL DECADE whose story forms a central part of this chapter. Though we know it as a time of rebellion, we tend to think such a characterization refers to the growing-up years of the baby-boomers climaxed in the fabled open-air rock concert at Woodstock. We do not always remember that the sixties were also a time of violent, destructive upheaval in America's inner cities. The toll of these disturbances was 189 killed, over 7,000 injured, nearly 60,000 arrested and nearly $160 million in property damage.[1]

The pattern for the riots was set one hot summer night in August 1965 in Watts, the vast African-American ghetto that stretches south from central Los Angeles. The arrest of a black motorist by white police officers led to protests and then a confrontation between the police and an angry crowd that escalated into six days of rioting that was quelled only by sending in 14,000 troops. Thirty-four people were killed, most of them poor and black, a fact that suggests they had not been as well armed as those who shot them. The 1,000 people injured included 136 firemen hurt battling some 600 separate blazes, sometimes under sniper fire, while watching crowds chanted "Burn, baby, burn!" Two hundred buildings worth over $40 million went up in flames.

When the nationwide wave of rioting had subsided, there was a short-lived interlude during which social scientists, at the behest of politicians, searched for answers to why it had happened. They found that despite its landscape of bungalows lining palm-decorated streets, Watts was as segregated a ghetto as that of any northeastern city. Half of its population were jobless and lived on public assistance, and half of its children were being raised by single parents. Though the riot had been sparked by a traffic stop, half of the population of Watts had no cars, though the nearest hospital, and the nearest jobs, were ten miles away.

A presidential commission concluded that the United States was becoming "two nations," one affluent and white, the other poor and black. If the implication of such studies was that social conditions in Watts explained the riot there, events nearly a generation later in virtually the same neighborhood suggested that little had changed. In March 1991, a neighbor videotaped police beating an intoxicated black motorist, Rodney King, landing sixty-one blows in less than a minute and a half. When four of the arresting officers were tried and acquitted by an all-white suburban jury for the beating in April 1992, south-central Los Angeles again erupted. This time 58 people were killed: 27 blacks, 17 Hispanics, and 11 whites. The 2,300 injured included some white motorists who had blundered into the neighborhood and had been dragged from their vehicles and beaten. Some 17,000 had been arrested for looting or arson, and the property loss rose to over $1 billion. In 1992, however, there was little of the outcry and sociological inquiry of 1965. Perhaps this meant that most Americans now took the idea of "two nations" pretty much for granted.

The Stages of Post-1945 Economic Transformation

As we compare in this chapter the internal histories of the United States and of the Western European democracies since the end of World War II, we shall discover that a single fundamental issue has underlain most of the political debate in these countries. That issue is how much power and responsibility should be entrusted to the government of the guarantor state. This kind of government, foreshadowed in the 1930s by Roosevelt's New Deal, became the norm throughout the Western world after 1945 as people became convinced that governments were responsible for managing economies and societies to guarantee a decent standard of living for all citizens.

In Western Europe, as we have seen, this responsibility had long been championed by democratic Socialists. Indeed, the immediate postwar regimes of the Left, such as the Labour party in Britain, brought the guarantor state into being. To such democratic Socialists it seemed only natural, on the grounds that management in the public interest would be more generally beneficial than private management for individual profit, to extend the responsibilities of the state to include ownership of the basic means of industrial production. Thus British Labour "nationalized" Britain's coal mines, steel mills, and railways. Left-dominated governments on the continent took similar steps.

In the United States, no such substantial movement in favor of socialism ever developed. Neither the New Deal nor subsequent governments advocated nationalizations or even the development of government-managed comprehensive health care. Nonetheless, American conservatives continued regularly to denounce the "big government" created by the New Deal. American "liberals," by contrast, insisted that reaching the goal of an equitable and livable society for all citizens required an active role for government.

The vocabulary of U.S. politics today shows us that over sixty years of argument since 1933 have not resolved this debate. People's judgments of the guarantor state, both in the United States and elsewhere, depend very largely on how its costs and benefits impinge on their own personal economic situations. The essence of the guarantor state is *redistribution:* from the taxes it collects it distributes payments of all sorts to support a variety of programs, from road construction to welfare. People tend to see the payment they collect as their just due and the payment that goes to someone else as a handout.

Given this human tendency, it is remarkable that through the 1950s and 1960s a kind of political consensus accepting the necessity of the guarantor state prevailed in the United States and throughout Western Europe. In the United States, only the most extreme conservatives advocated abolishing such essential pillars of the guarantor state as the Social Security

system. Even in the 1960s, a decade of widespread challenge to existing beliefs and institutions, only a few radical students attacked the state as an oppressive institution. Many protesters in the United States—blacks and women, for example—actually sought to enlist the state on their side.

More recently, however, the postwar consensus in favor of the guarantor state has everywhere broken down. In the 1980s in the United States and in Britain, President Ronald Reagan and Prime Minister Margaret Thatcher built political careers by denouncing the guarantor state, though neither succeeded in demolishing it. Their triumphs, like most of the major political developments in the Western world over the past half-century, reflect the dramatic impact of the total transformation of the global economy since 1945.

This global economic transformation unfolded in two stages. The first ran from 1945 to the early 1970s; much of the world is still living in the second. An appropriate date to divide these stages is 1973, when the Organization of Petroleum Exporting Countries (OPEC) drastically increased the price of the world's prime energy source. We shall see that the two stages of economic transformation were differentiated by many factors besides the price of oil. Nevertheless, cheap energy fueled the unprecedented economic boom of the 1950s and 1960s. And the stage since the oil price rises of the 1970s, though not nearly as devastating in much of the world as the Great Depression of the 1930s, has marked the first time since then that in some places, at some times, key economic indicators have dropped to near-Depression levels.

The Thirty Glorious Years

The French remember the first stage of postwar economic transformation as the *trente glorieuses,* the "thirty glorious years" from 1945 to the mid-1970s. These were years of unprecedented economic growth, not just in France but throughout the developed world and in many developing countries. The world's manufacturing output quadrupled, and world trade in manufactured goods expanded tenfold. Meanwhile, unemployment rates rarely exceeded 3 percent of the work force—in Western Europe in the 1960s, they averaged 1.5 percent. So general was economic well-being that by the late 1960s, some critics, complained that this "affluent society" had created mindless conformity.

What factors explain these thirty glorious years? Economists generally recognize that capitalistic economies cycle between boom and slump at reasonably predictable intervals. According to this kind of timetable, by the end of World War II an upturn was due. Yet it cannot be assumed that the postwar boom, whose dimensions were unprecedented, was somehow automatic. Though deliberate postwar policy choices helped global economic recovery, an explosion of technological innovation and of global economic exchanges explains the "thirty glorious years."

The victorious policymakers at the end of World War II were determined not to repeat mistakes they believed had produced economic disaster after World War I. At the Bretton Woods Conference in 1944, they agreed to establish international financial institutions, the International Monetary Fund and the World Bank, that they hoped would help keep the world economy from spiraling downward out of control. Moreover, though the American economy vastly dominated the world in 1945, American leaders soon recognized that restoring the purchasing power of the rest of the world was essential, not only to prevent the spread of communism but also to provide markets that would sustain American prosperity. Thus the Marshall Plan helped to fuel the postwar boom.

Policy changes designed to promote thriving economies were not limited to international programs, however. Everywhere in the developed world—even in the United States— postwar leaders believed that their national economies could not be left to the kind of unpredictable surges that had plunged the world into Depression in the 1930s. They therefore assigned to the guarantor state a new role: to use government surpluses or deficits in the manner prescribed by Keynesian economics to stimulate an economy that balanced the needs of employers, employees, and consumers.

Countless such new products—long-playing records, tape cassettes, and transistorized radios, for example—flooded the world's marketplaces in the 1950s and 1960s, as the wartime technological revolution continued. During the thirty glorious years, the production and consumption of manufactured goods increasingly became global in scale. Throughout the world, the need for farm labor shrank as agriculture mechanized. Millions worldwide flocked from the countryside to industrial cities in search of a higher standard of living, creating vast new markets. This did not yet mean that every industrial or industrializing country became a competitor for the same customers in a global marketplace. The United States, for example, exported no more than 8 percent of its gross domestic product (GDP) during these years. In most countries during the thirty glorious years, the expansion of demand as cities mushroomed and standards of living steadily rose seemed to provide an ever-growing market at home. Indeed, it appeared to some that the world had found the secret of everlasting prosperity. But from the 1970s on it became painfully clear that this was not to be. A second stage of the postwar global economic transformation had begun.

Economic Transformation During and After the 1970s

It can be argued that factors inherent in the fantastic growth of the years from 1945 into the 1970s undermined its foundations. The continuing boom in demand drove prices of everything—not just oil—higher and higher, leading to an unacceptable rate of inflation. Consumer discontent prompted governments to try to retard the rise in prices by raising interest rates, making money harder to borrow, and by limiting their own expenditures, thus slowing growth.

Nearly full employment during the thirty glorious years encouraged workers in every country to demand ever-higher pay. For this problem, the new global scope of industrial activity offered employers an increasingly obvious remedy. If workers in the developed countries demanded unacceptably high wages, their jobs could simply be moved to places in the world where people were willing to work for far lower pay. Already by the mid-1960s, the booming American electronics industry, for example, had begun manufacturing many of its components overseas. Such shifts of employment, along with the recovery of the Western European and Japanese economies, help explain why the American economy no longer loomed like a giant over the rest of the world as it had in 1945. By 1980, the combined European and Japanese economies were 60 percent larger than the American economy—a total reversal of the situation at the end of World War II.

By that date, however, economic analysts were beginning to argue that it was pointless to compare the size of national economies. World manufacturing and trade were now dominated by "multinational" corporations employing workers in dozens of countries. This range of activity made them largely invulnerable to control by any national government. Nor did their executives, whatever their national origins, identify with the interests of any country in particular: their only objective was to maximize corporate profits for their shareholders.

The combined effect of these developments was to destroy the foundations of the boom economy of the 1950s and 1960s. Faced with the power of multinational corporations, national guarantor states increasingly lost control of their economies and could no longer sustain the prosperous balance among employers and investors, workers, and consumers. As economic growth slowed in most of the world in the 1970s and later, the perception grew that the advantages of one of these groups was only obtained at the expense of another. In these harsher times, the generous benefits paid by the guarantor state to the unemployed or the poor, for example, seemed less and less justifiable to the taxpayers.

By the 1990s, indeed, few economists had much good to say about the guarantor state. Their profession was now dominated by an influential school centered at the University of Chicago. They saw the guarantor state not as the outcome of centuries of social progress, as many had regarded it in 1945, but as an unfortunate interlude of misconceived policy, too influenced by socialistic ideas. For these economists, it was not only impossible but undesirable to try to control the natural forces sweeping the globalizing marketplace. It would be economically self-defeating, they argued, for governments to prevent corporations from relocating jobs to low-wage countries, whatever the misery they left behind. For it was only by maximizing their cost-effectiveness by such relocations that multinational corporations could ultimately foster the growth of the global economy. Absolute free trade, said the Chicago economists, was the only cure for the global slowdown since the 1970s. Whatever impedes free trade—inefficient state-owned monopolies, labor unions, protective tariffs, overpopulated payrolls—must be ruthlessly swept out of existence. All of these changes are in fact happening today. State-owned industries everywhere—not just in the former Soviet bloc—are being "privatized." Union membership everywhere, particularly in the private sector, is dwindling to levels not seen since before the Depression. Groups of nations not only in Europe but in North America, Latin America, East Asia, and even Africa are eliminating tariffs and combining in free-trade associations. And managers everywhere are wondering whether they must preserve their competitiveness by ruthlessly "downsizing" their payrolls, following the example set by American management from the late 1980s onward.

Public opinion did not always grasp the impact of this post-1973 stage of postwar economic transformation or realize that the rapid growth of the 1950s and 1960s could not be sustained. In the developed countries the change seemed at first to be no worse than a repetition of the usual capitalistic cycle from recession to recovery and back. In fact, the rapid growth of the postwar years could not be recovered. Since 1973, rates of growth have returned to pre–World War I levels and have been further depressed by serious recessions in the early 1980s and early 1990s. Yet the reappearance on city streets in the 1980s of multitudes of homeless people, a sight uncommon since the Depression, did not at first suggest that the global economy had passed a turning point in the early 1970s. Only when people whose education had always assured them of secure careers began to fear that downsizing threatened their own futures did public opinion take account, in the early 1990s, of how dramatically the world economy had changed.

Two of the trends that had stimulated that first boom stage of the postwar economic transformation continued into the second. Technological innovation and economic globalization continued to hurtle forward. But now people were not so sure that their effects were always beneficial. The average employee began to wonder whether these trends meant losing his or her job to a machine or to a lower-paid worker in some distant land.

The reply of champions of an unfettered capitalistic global economy had always been that workers displaced by technological innovation, like workers displaced by the exporting

of their jobs, would soon find new employment as innovation and globalization created new opportunities. This no longer seemed so certain in the mid-1990s. Some doubters wondered where the jobs to replace those lost to technological change and globalization would be found. In a world in which the bottom line of the corporate balance sheet was the only criterion in economic decision making, some critics argued, the "end of work" was at hand.

In this grim view, the post-1970s stage of the postwar global economic transformation signaled grave new implications of the central themes of the twentieth century and of this book. The principal consequence of the emergence of a new world system based on a truly global economy might be to leave Americans, Europeans, and Japanese competing for jobs in a worldwide labor pool that included the peoples of the still-developing world, who expected a far lower standard of living. Similarly, "humankind's triumph over nature" through the acceleration of technological innovation might lead, ironically, to a new century in which machines would make the labor of much of humankind superfluous—a hollow triumph indeed.

Postindustrial Society and the Guarantor State

Already during the postwar boom of the 1950s and 1960s, technological change had a powerful impact on life in the Western world. Inventions that the New Deal generation only barely anticipated—television and the computer—profoundly reshaped the patterns of people's daily lives. A majority of Americans, Europeans, and Japanese, in fact, today probably feel more at home in the artificial electronic environment these machines have created than in the natural world of farms and fields their ancestors inhabited.

The kind of society created by these new technologies, first in the United States but soon after in Europe and Japan, is one the planners of the guarantor state as recently as 1945 could not have foreseen. It promises to be as different from the period between the mid-nineteenth and mid-twentieth centuries—when vast numbers worked at the machines of heavy industry—as that industrial era was from earlier centuries, when most people were farmers. In this new *postindustrial* society, a majority of people earn their living neither on the farm nor in the factory but in shops and offices, providing "services" that range from flipping fast-food hamburgers to processing the computerized data of large corporations.

Because nothing is more fundamental to society than the ways people earn their living, the advent of a postindustrial society has profoundly affected the patterns of relations between the races, the social classes, the generations, and the sexes. Because such changes are never easily accepted, they carried serious implications for politics. To the extent that the guarantor state both in the United States and in Europe tried to accommodate change by meeting some of the demands of such protesters as the young and women, it became the target of conservative backlash. Resentments grew deeper still with the slowdown of the world economy after 1973. The general postwar assumption had been that by using the taxing and spending mechanisms Keynes had recommended, the guarantor state could fine-tune Western economies. But by the late 1970s it became clear that Keynesian management was not working. Blame for the unpredictable combination of rising inflation and rising unemployment was increasingly cast on governments. The resulting discontent provided a bonanza of votes in the 1970s for the conservative opponents of the guarantor state.

Thus, ironically, at the very moment that Western governments seemed to have become most responsive to democratic control, they were confronted with electorates increasingly mistrustful of government. The years since

World War II have seen the climax of another central theme of the twentieth century: the mobilization of a mass electorate by democratic politics. When France, the last of the major democracies, gave women the vote in 1945, the right to general electoral participation was almost complete. It only remained to extend the vote to eighteen-year-olds, as many countries did in the 1970s in response to youth revolts. With the collapse of the Spanish and Portuguese dictatorships, politics everywhere in the West seemed to have become democratic.

The troubling question that had already emerged in the 1950s and 1960s, however, was the extent to which these expanding political systems offered voters genuine alternatives. The principal differences between the parties that alternated in office seemed limited to details of how the guarantor state should manage the economy, and in whose interest. In no country did any significant party any longer advocate truly revolutionary change. The prevalence of protest—sometimes violent protest—in the 1960s suggested that many Americans, Europeans, and Japanese doubted whether their votes really counted for anything. In the emerging postindustrial global economy, dominated by huge government and multinational corporate bureaucracies, did the individual's choice make any difference?

In the 1970s and 1980s, the most significant development was the emergence of leaders and movements that challenged the postwar consensus by boldly denying the effectiveness of the guarantor state. On the Left in Europe the so-called Green parties warned that technological change was making the global environment uninhabitable. Far more effectively on the Right, leaders such as Reagan and Thatcher argued that rather than being the means of social improvements, governmental bureaucracies were the principal obstacles. This view came to be widely shared in the 1980s. Only the Socialist government of France's François Mitterrand, in 1981 and 1982, tried briefly to reassert the role of the guarantor state, but the pressures of a global system being pushed in the opposite direction by Thatcher and Reagan soon forced him back into line. Thus the bitter argument of the 1930s over the merits of a governmental role in managing the economy and improving the society, muted by the prosperity of the 1950s and 1960s, broke out by the 1990s with renewed vigor.

Political Developments in Postwar Western Europe and the United States

To trace the impact of the two postwar stages of economic transformation on the politics of Western Europe and the United States, and especially on public opinion concerning the guarantor state, it is not necessary to chronicle the history of every country. Rather we shall use examples, comparing Britain, France, and the United States. A period of *conservative political dominance* (from the early 1950s into the early 1960s) followed the short era of social reform immediately after World War II. Behind the appearance of immobility of the 1950s, however, accelerating technological and social change was fundamentally altering U.S. and Western European society.

The stresses of change burst out in protests that made the 1960s, a *decade of upheaval.* Some who protested—such as blacks in the United States—were demanding their share in newly affluent societies; others were challenging the notion that society's only goal should be affluence.

In the early 1970s, these combined revolts produced a period of conservative *backlash against the apparent collapse of authority.* Conservative values, however, could not cope with the economic slump that followed the rise in OPEC oil prices. Europeans and even the Japanese discovered, as Americans already had, that their heavy industries could not compete with products turned out in developing coun-

tries with lower labor costs. As the withering of their traditional industries brought them into the postindustrial age, the peoples of the developed world restlessly voted governments, whether of the Left or the Right, out of power in rapid succession.

With the fundamental disarray of the world's economy masked by a partial recovery that benefited principally the United States, the theme of the 1980s became *revulsion against the guarantor state.* But as even the U.S. economy sank into recession in the early 1990s under Reagan's successor George H. W. Bush, a period of *economic anxiety and the quest for an alternative politics* opened. As even middle-class people everywhere began to face the consequences of global economic transformation, such as massive layoffs, they became increasingly disenchanted with all the familiar parties and leaders, who seemed ill equipped to cope with economic crisis. While some, finding no one to vote for, stopped voting, others voted for political alternatives they once would have ignored. In the United States in 1992, voters drove George Bush from the White House by dividing a majority of votes between his Democratic challenger Bill Clinton and independent Ross Perot. Two years later they repudiated Clinton in his turn, by electing conservative Republican congressional majorities pledged to destroy the guarantor state, only to reject this extreme antidote to economic anxiety by re-electing Clinton president in 1996. In the Western Europe of the 1990s, too, especially in France, Austria, and Italy, substantial numbers voted for leaders or movements who in language sometimes reminiscent of fascism voiced disenchantment with conventional politics as the solution to economic problems.

Thus, as the twentieth century ended, ongoing global economic transformation continued to agitate politics in the Western world, particularly on the central issue of the survival of the guarantor state. While some insisted that the new global order had made it obsolete, others, especially in Europe, saw it as a shelter from the whirlwinds of economic change.

The United States and Western Europe in the Cold War Era

To a considerable extent, bipolar confrontation with the Soviet Union shaped U.S. and Western European politics in the two decades following World War II. The momentum for postwar social reform died as the perceived necessity of resisting communism at home and abroad discredited the Left and brought moderate centrist or even right-wing governments to power by 1949 on the European continent and by 1952 in Britain and the United States. These governments, however, did not reverse the postwar expansion of the guarantor state.

In the United States the principal beneficiaries of this expansion were veterans. The GI Bill of Rights gave them educational grants, loans, and jobs. Although this was in reality a government reapportionment of income in their favor, an entire generation of Americans perceived it as a right.

Generosity to veterans did not mean that conservatives intended to leave the New Deal intact. The Taft-Hartley Law of 1947 prohibited some of unions' most effective tactics. By upholding the anti-union right-to-work laws of the South, the law spurred the flight of industry from the unionized Northeast and Middle West to what would later be called the Sunbelt. Thus, the end of World War II, when a third of nonfarm labor was unionized, marked the high point of the union movement in U.S. history.

This law proved to be as far as U.S. conservatives could go in actively reversing the New Deal. President Harry Truman, re-elected in 1948, called for the establishment of an American national health insurance system comparable to the systems that most other developed countries established after World War II. But a coalition of conservative Republicans and southern Democrats blocked enactment of Truman's proposals. Thus, though established programs of the guarantor state continued, Congress resisted their extension to other groups, such as the ailing poor.

The last years of the Truman administration were overshadowed by a crusade by Republican conservatives, led by Senator Joseph R. McCarthy of Wisconsin, to root communists out of the U.S. government. The climate of fear created by his hounding of persons with leftist associations lingered long after his Senate colleagues repudiated him. Henceforth, while the range of respectable political opinions in Western Europe continued to extend from socialists or even communists on the Left to conservatives on the Right, in the United States the comparable range was from moderate to conservative.

Republican nominee Dwight D. Eisenhower swept to victory in the presidential election of 1952. Under Eisenhower, as under Truman, the U.S. guarantor state grew slightly, rather than shrinking as Republicans hoped. Haunted by fear of runaway inflation, Eisenhower held it to a level of about 1 percent a year maintaining the federal budget largely in balance. In his farewell address he warned, as only a former commander of Allied forces in Europe in World War II could, against the dangerous growth of the "military-industrial complex." The alliance of big business with the Pentagon, he declared, threatened not only war but economic ruin through uncontrollable inflation.

This prophetic warning was uncharacteristic of a president whose bland political style made the 1950s synonymous with political conformity. In Western Europe, similarly reassuring leaders from the past provided a sense of postwar continuity. In Britain the seventy-seven-year-old Churchill led the Conservatives back to power in 1951. They held it under his successors until 1964. The political life of the new

Federal Republic of Germany was dominated until 1963 by "the old man," Chancellor Konrad Adenauer, leader of the centrist Christian Democratic party. In France, no such dominant figure emerged after de Gaulle withdrew in disgust from postwar politics in 1946. The postwar Fourth Republic was governed after 1947 by the kind of unstable and short-lived coalition cabinets of the Center and the Right that had dominated prewar political life. Their inability to deal with rebellion in Algeria brought de Gaulle back to power with a Fifth Republic in 1958.

Like President Eisenhower's administration, these European governments maintained, but did not greatly expand, the activities of the guarantor state. However, behind the appearance of political continuity, technological change in the 1950s was fundamentally altering Western societies.

The Acceleration of Change

The postwar economic boom led to a tremendous expansion throughout the Western world, which increasingly included Japan. The U.S. gross national product (GNP) doubled between the end of the war and the early 1960s. Despite recessions, real wages (taking inflation into account) rose 20 percent during the eight years of Eisenhower's administration alone. Fully a third of American families had been living in poverty (by the official definition) in 1940, and over a quarter of them were still officially poor in 1950. By 1960, however, only about one American family in five was to be found below the poverty line.

Western Europe shared in the 1950s boom. By the end of the decade, the continent produced a quarter of the world's industrial goods, though even West Germany's "economic miracle"—a growth in industrial production of over 100 percent—was outstripped by Japanese expansion. Although their standards of living were still only half of U.S. levels, Europeans'

pay envelopes reflected the boom. Real wages doubled in Europe between 1950 and 1966.

In the midst of growing affluence, the ways in which Americans and Europeans earned their living were changing. In the mid-1950s the number of U.S. nonfarm workers employed in blue-collar jobs dropped below the number of white-collar office workers for the first time. This was a momentous turning point. Once office workers began to outnumber workers in factories, commentators began to talk of the United States as a postindustrial society. U.S. industrial employment was not yet contracting. But jobs in the service sector—government, retailing, finance, insurance, health care—increased by over 200 percent between 1945 and 1970. The number of local government employees tripled.

Western European societies soon followed the United States into the postindustrial age. In the mid-1950s the farming, industrial, and service sectors of the French economy, for example, employed almost equal numbers of workers. By 1970 the postindustrial service sector, expanding much more rapidly than industrial jobs, employed almost half the French population.

Changing technology explains why industrial employment in the Western world peaked by the 1970s. Cheap energy made it advantageous for industry to replace workers with machines.

The Computer Revolution and the Knowledge Explosion

Machines replaced workers in complex tasks as well as in simple ones, reflecting the increasing speed with which new knowledge found practical application.

The computer is probably the most revolutionary of those machines. In 1936, Alan Turing, a British mathematician, first sketched the concept of a machine that could almost instantly solve calculations that would take human beings a lifetime. Electronic technology and wartime need transformed this idea into actuality. During World War II, Turing was one of the British code-breakers who designed machines to uncover by high-speed computation the random settings of German ciphering machines.

The first programmable digital computers ultimately derived from these wartime machines. The invention of the transistor soon made possible the development of ever-greater calculating capacity in ever-smaller machines. By the 1980s, worldwide computer capacity was doubling every two years, with over 5 million machines in use in the United States alone.

People who have grown up with computers may find it difficult to imagine what life was like in the very recent past without them. In one sense the computer is simply one more machine with which human beings have harnessed nature to their purposes. This machine uses electrons moving in billionths of a second to manipulate numerical symbols. It is a kind of assembly line of information, producing conclusions as earlier assembly lines produced automobiles.

In fact, however, the computer is a wholly new kind of machine. It produces not goods or energy but information, the most important commodity in a postindustrial society. By the 1980s, half of the American work force was engaged in processing information of one sort or another.

The computer may have potential for harm as well as for good. Since the 1950s, critics have warned that its capacity to store information about every individual could reinforce bureaucratic control of human life. The ultimate impact of the computer remains to be seen. Some believe the personal computer will restore to the individual some of the creative autonomy of craftsmen. Others feel computers directly threaten jobs. In this gloomier scenario, the service sector of postindustrial society will provide a dwindling number of jobs to low-paid operators performing repetitive tasks before a

video terminal under conditions of discipline reminiscent of the industrial assembly line.

Whatever its ultimate impact, the computer has proved to be an essential tool in the postwar knowledge explosion. By 1960, the U.S. government was spending 10 percent of its budget on research, compared to less than 1 percent before World War II. Such government expenditures powerfully influenced the shape of society. The knowledge explosion helps to explain why so many people by 1960, not only in the United States, were doing different jobs and living in different places.

The Flight to the Suburbs

As more and more of the population moved into service-sector occupations such as computer programming, people moved inexorably from farm and city to the suburbs. Machine technology in agriculture made it possible to produce far greater yields with ever-fewer farmers. As agribusiness produced huge stocks of food, what had remained in 1945 of the distinctive rural life of the small farmer faded away. Only 9 percent of Americans still lived on farms in 1960, compared to 17.5 percent in 1945. By the 1980s, French and West German farmers made up equally small minorities of their populations.

The distribution of population within the metropolitan areas to which these formerly rural people were migrating reflected the dispersion that postindustrial employment made possible. The policies of the U.S. federal government accelerated flight to the suburbs in the 1950s. The Federal Highway Act of 1956 revolutionized transportation. Fueled by an apparently limitless supply of cheap petroleum, automobile ownership tripled in the United States. By the early 1970s, there was almost one car for every two Americans. Unlike public transportation, the automobile conformed to Americans' longing for a private life. Since the suburban house fulfilled a similar aspiration, jobs and stores followed the new freeways to the new suburbs.

The landscape of the suburbia of the 1950s was semistandardized. An architecture of mass production produced neighborhoods that looked the same from one region of the country to another.

This willingness of Americans to conform to a single suburban lifestyle shocked Europeans. They were accustomed to a society where the ways of life of regions and social classes remained distinct. But by the 1960s the institutions of American suburbia were beginning to appear in Europe, too. The spread of fast-food chains and supermarkets provoked patriotic Europeans to decry the "Coca-colonization" of their societies by powerful U.S. corporations. Though U.S. multinationals did market their products aggressively in Europe, it was really the transformation of European societies that made such marketing possible. European firms were producing ten times as many automobiles for newly affluent consumers in the mid-1960s as they did in the late 1940s, for example. The resulting congestion of its ancient cities encouraged Europe's suburban sprawl. By 1980, half of France's nonrural population lived in suburbs developed after World War II. Like suburban Americans, suburban Europeans turned increasingly to the electronic entertainment provided by television.

Television: The Electronic World-View

Television has proved to be as momentous a postwar innovation as the computer. It has basically altered the way viewers form their *cognitive maps,* their way of understanding reality. As the world increasingly becomes a single audience for the same programs, television may prove to have the same impact everywhere.

In 1949 there were still only a million television sets in operation in the United States. By 1960 there were 46 million sets, watched for an average of five hours a day in 90 percent of American homes. As the mass audience grew, so did the U.S. networks' advertising sales—by a phenomenal 50 percent a year in the 1950s. To keep such a lucrative audience in front of their sets, television executives limited most programming to a predictable staple of quiz shows, comedies, and crime thrillers.

Such programming, endless commercials, and perhaps the very nature of the electronic medium itself have unquestionably affected the American consciousness. The average child has spent twice as much time in front of a television set as in the classroom. While growing up, most children watched some thirty thousand repetitive and frequently violent "electronic stories." Television gave a deceptive impression of mirroring reality, allowing people to "see for themselves."

Television broke down the barriers between politics and entertainment. In 1960, people who heard Richard M. Nixon and John F. Kennedy's presidential debate on the radio thought that Nixon had clearly worsted Kennedy on the issues. But the glamorous Kennedy, more skillfully made up, projected a better image to those who watched television, and he won the election.

By the late 1960s, Americans were increasingly taking their political cues from television, rather than from the party leaders and influential opinion makers who had earlier guided them. Molding the politician's image—what he or she *appeared* to be—became crucial. Political and other advertising used the same technique: endless repetition of simple and emotionally appealing themes.

Television has also shaped the political thinking of Americans through its treatment of news. The percentage of prime-time programming devoted to public affairs has fallen by almost one-third since the late 1970s as the U.S. networks have increasingly come under the control of corporate managements more inter-

***Buying the Colonel's Kentucky Fried Chicken
in Tienanmen Square, Beijing.*** *Since many
Chinese, like this soldier of the People's Liberation
Army, still do not have automobiles, this otherwise
familiar facility has a bike-through window.* ©
Dave Bartruff/CORBIS

ested in profits than in loss-making documentaries about contemporary issues. What interpretation of video events television commentators
supply often concentrates on exposing politicians as self-seeking bunglers. Television thus
has confirmed many Americans' view of politics
as a dirty business rather than as the mechanism
for managing a complex society. In this way,
television has contributed to the steady decline
since 1960 in the number of Americans who
vote for president.

It is likely that television will have the same
overwhelming impact on other postindustrial

societies as it has had in the United States. In
1980, there were 63 television sets for every
100 Americans, but only 33 for every 100 West
Germans and 29 for every 100 persons in
France.[2] But television sets are continuing to
proliferate around the world at incredible
speed. Even in China, where in 1985 only 10
percent of the still largely rural Chinese population had a television set, by 1995 80 percent
owned one. In the same decade the proportion
of Chinese city dwellers with *color* televisions
rose from under 20 to 90 percent.

Thus far, the television medium has clearly
not realized the hopes of its early years. Culturally, television faithfully reflected growing
global integration. It shrank the world to the
dimensions of a "global village." But traffic
within the "village" was virtually a one-way
street. Twenty percent of British TV and 50
percent of French TV programming was imported, mainly from the United States. The number of people outside the United States who
watched U.S.-made serials like *Dallas* far exceeded the number of Americans who could
find on their TV screen a window into the lives
of their fellow "global villagers" in Europe and
the Third World. In fact, except in moments of
international crisis, American television largely
ignored other countries. In an interdependent
world where human survival depends on
greater public understanding of complex issues,
television offered instead an escape into a
world of illusory images—network sitcoms or
rock videos.

The 1960s Challenge
to Authority

Though television entertainment reinforced
the escapism of the postindustrial suburban
middle class, television news thrived on the
dramatic images of protest in the 1960s. The
first of the successive revolts that dominated
the news came in the southern United States, as

blacks protested its segregated society. Within a few years, television had shown young people throughout the world how to challenge authority by, for example, occupying a place and refusing to leave—the sit-in.

Protests against the Vietnam War reflected the growing integration of the Western world: a march on the Pentagon in Washington, D.C., in October 1967 occurred simultaneously with demonstrations in Amsterdam, Berlin, Oslo, Paris, Rome, and Tokyo.[3] Some of those who demonstrated were attacking not only the war but the technological, inhuman society that they blamed for the war's continuation. Thus challenged by young Americans and faced with a no-win situation in Vietnam, President Lyndon B. Johnson had to abandon his ambitions to expand the guarantor state and did not run for re-election. In France the student and worker revolt of May 1968 so discredited General de Gaulle's government that he too had to retire within a year.

The Black Rebellion

Television images of policemen assaulting unresisting civil rights demonstrators brought home the conflict between American ideals and the realities of black life. Below the Mason-Dixon Line, the law segregated blacks from whites in their daily activities. Even getting a drink of water was segregated, with separate fountains for "White" and "Colored." Intimidation prevented any challenge to this system through the political process.

Blacks also faced discrimination outside the South. The postwar mechanization of agriculture in the southern states reduced employment there and accelerated northward migration. As whites moved out of the inner cities of the Northeast and the Middle West, blacks moved in.

In the South the black revolt could be dated from December 1, 1955, when Mrs. Rosa Parks refused to give up her seat on a city bus in Montgomery, Alabama. Mrs. Parks was already sitting in the "colored" rear section of the bus. The law required her to yield her seat to any white person who had none.

Martin Luther King, Jr., a Baptist minister, began his rise to leadership of the civil rights movement by organizing a boycott of the bus system to bring economic pressure on segregation. King had been deeply impressed by Gandhi's success in compelling change in India by nonviolent resistance. The Southern Christian Leadership Conference, which King founded in 1958, helped spread this tactic throughout the South. The first southern sit-in occurred in 1960 when blacks refused to be ousted from a segregated lunch counter in Greensboro, North Carolina. Within two months, the movement had spread over nine southern states.

Media attention to these nonviolent demonstrators soon brought the weight of worldwide disapproval against southern segregationists. Federal legislation overruled the state statutes that provided the basis for southern segregation. King then turned his attention to the plight of blacks in the northern urban ghettos. Here it was not enough to reassert political rights; the problem was to provide economic advantages for a minority. But such advantages, many white Americans believed, could come only at their own expense. As a result, King made little progress by 1968, the year he was assassinated.

Some blacks had always doubted that white America would yield to moral persuasion. As King's drive for economic equality stalled, more and more began to see their struggle as part of a worldwide conflict. They identified with the African nationalists then winning their independence from the white dominance of the European world system. In 1966 the Student Nonviolent Coordinating Committee, founded in 1960 by whites and blacks to bring Gandhian pressure on southern segregation, expelled its white members and adopted the slogan "Black Power." Henceforth, "The Movement," as young people of the 1960s sometimes called their revolt, was divided.

The Rebellion of the Young

The principal theaters of the youth revolt were college campuses. At the University of California at Berkeley in the autumn of 1964, students protested the arrest of distributors of political literature. The student organizers of the Free Speech Movement argued that the academic environment could not be insulated from the emotional issues of race and war then dividing the country. For the next eight years, Berkeley students intermittently disrupted the usual academic routines.

This pattern of disruption was matched on many U.S. campuses. It reached a climax of horror in 1970 when nervous National Guardsmen opened fire on students demonstrating at Kent State University in Ohio. Four young people were killed.

Campus unrest and even violence were not limited to the United States. Throughout the world, students copied the methods of their American counterparts to protest what they saw as U.S. racism at home and imperialism in Vietnam. The German movement Students for a Democratic Society (SDS), like the U.S. organization of the same name, insisted that in the age of the mass society, democracy had become a sham. Since no political party anywhere, not even socialists, questioned the quality of life under the capitalist guarantor state, the young could challenge the managerial elite who actually controlled postindustrial society only by demonstrating in the streets.

This revolt among students who did not risk, as American students did, being drafted for an overseas war baffled many observers. Conflict between generations, like conflict between the sexes and between social classes, has been a constant in history. But this young generation lived in the most prosperous societies the world had ever seen. Why should they rebel?

A partial explanation for the rebellion is that the large size of the baby-boom generation of the 1960s and its relative affluence made the usual generational conflict worse worldwide. When student protests began, American, Western European, and Japanese youth—in their late teens and on the verge of adulthood but not yet accepted by their societies as adults—were the most numerous age group in the population. This generation had grown up with higher expectations than its predecessors'. Before World War II, for example, only 15 percent of Americans between the ages of eighteen and twenty-one had gone to college. By 1960 one-third of the same U.S. age group was attending college. Many Western European societies too were approaching this proportion. This extension of adolescence into college years brought young people both benefits and liabilities.

The benefits often included continuing parental support. The price for that support was continued subordination. Yet such dependency seemed unreasonable to young people raised in postindustrial suburban households in which both parents worked. In their absence, young people found role models within their own generation; they developed their own uniform—T-shirt and blue jeans—and their own music. Rock-and-roll began as a celebration of adolescent defiance of adult authority. The grandest rock concert of all brought nearly a half-million to Woodstock, New York, in August 1969. It was the celebration of a generation apart, aptly called "the Woodstock Nation." Many of this generation, reared in affluence and enforced conformity and identifying with each other and with generous ideals, rose in revolt.

Moreover, the Woodstock Nation extended throughout the world, and its members watched one another on television. Attacking a worldwide society they believed to be economically integrated by multinational corporations, some leaders of the youth rebellion

***An American soldier draws a peace symbol on a helicopter landing pad
in Vietnam.*** *By 1972, many soldiers sympathized with the movement at home
to end the war, and some officers feared that discipline in the U.S. Army was
near collapse.* © *David Burnett/Contact Press Images*

hoped to generate a protest movement that was
equally integrated globally.

Television helped to link the protest movements. The original nucleus of protest in France
was provided by students at a suburban branch
campus of the University of Paris who had been
horrified by the daily spectacle of the carnage
in Vietnam. But what fired the revolt of the
French young was the changing nature of
France's university system. The technocrats of
de Gaulle's government decreed a vast expansion of higher education. Like many American
students, however, French students found the
new campuses to be oppressive environments.

Campus activists played on this feeling of pow-
erlessness to provoke confrontations with university authorities.

Student occupation of the main campus of
the University of Paris in May 1968 provoked a
crisis that paralyzed the whole economy. Half of
France's work force went on strike. The Gaullist
government finally resolved the crisis only by
decreeing an inflationary 10 percent wage hike.
Thus pacified, the workers went back to work,
leaving the students alone to face police repression. Nevertheless, the "events of May" had destroyed de Gaulle's credibility as the defender
of law and order.

The French explained the youth revolt of 1968 much as Americans did. Conservatives dismissed it as the misbehavior of a spoiled younger generation. More tolerant commentators blamed the revolt on the stresses of adjusting the university system to a democratic mass society. New Left sympathizers discovered more basic causes. Scornful alike of technocratic capitalism and of communism, these critics saw the French students as a vanguard of revolt against postindustrial society worldwide. The younger generation everywhere, in the New Left view, was refusing to become a new white-collar proletariat.

Understanding the youth revolts of the 1960s requires weighing the merits of all these explanations. The generation coming to adulthood, buoyed by growing affluence and low unemployment, tended to take these blessings for granted. These young people questioned whether a comfortable lifestyle and a dull job were life's only goals. Assuming the economy would continue to prosper, they idealistically sought to assure that everyone would benefit from this growth, and set their expectations higher than any government could meet. Their increasingly shrill protests inevitably produced a backlash, but not before their rebellion forced the political retirement of both Charles de Gaulle and Lyndon Baines Johnson.

The Limits of the Guarantor State: The Great Society

President Johnson aspired to make the United States a Great Society for all of its citizens. To many Americans, such a program seemed long overdue, since the country lagged far behind the guarantor states of Western Europe in providing social services.

Johnson's plans in 1965–1966 involved the federal government in improving the environment. Federal grants would support the cleansing of the nation's water supply, for example, and help rebuild its decaying mass transit systems. Medicare and Medicaid finally realized Truman's aspirations, giving elderly Americans some measure of security against dying untreated and penniless.

Johnson could see that even when guaranteed legal equality, blacks had no hope of becoming equal members of U.S. society so long as most of them were poor. Thus the Great Society launched programs designed to rescue blacks from a "culture of poverty" similar, in the eyes of social planners, to that of the Third World. The Equal Opportunity Act of 1964, for example, fostered such ventures as a Job Corps and community action programs to stimulate economic development in the ghettos.

In today's disillusioned atmosphere, it is fashionable to decry these programs as failures. Certainly they were inadequate to fulfill Johnson's grand goal of eliminating poverty. Critics pointed out that they provided opportunities for corruption and filled ghetto dwellers with unrealistic hopes. Revolutions coincide with rising expectations. The wave of rioting that swept black areas of inner cities in the mid-1960s can partly be explained as the result of the misleading impression given by the Great Society that things were going to change.

By 1968 the ghettos seemed out of control. Johnson declared he would not run for re-election; the young carried their protest against the Vietnam War to the streets outside the Democratic convention in Chicago. The majority of Americans who regarded these protesters as spoiled and unpatriotic had no love for Johnson either. To suburban Americans, he was responsible for handouts to rioting blacks. Richard Nixon's victory in 1968 brought a Republican to the presidency.

Johnson had thought that the U.S. economy was strong enough to support both a huge military commitment abroad and a Great Society at home. Professional economists had assured him that there was no risk in running a budget deficit to reduce unemployment. As Johnson left office, however, it was already clear that this had not been good advice. As inflation increased, so did unemployment. This *stagflation*—rising prices in a stagnant economy—became the central economic problem of all the developed economies in the 1970s as they entered a second stage of the postwar global economic transformation.

The Women's Liberation Movement

The early 1970s saw the climax of yet another revolt: women increasingly demanded that in the postindustrial era they no longer be confined to the stereotyped roles of earlier times.

In the United States the most recent chapter of women's struggle for equality dates from the end of World War II. Veterans were demobilized and sought jobs that women had filled. Women were encouraged to be homemakers.

As so often happened in the 1950s, however, accelerating social change was quietly undermining apparent certainties such as the exclusively domestic role of women. To help support the suburban lifestyle, more and more women returned to work. In 1940, only 15 percent of American married women had been employed outside the home. By 1960, almost a third of them had jobs. As female employment grew, more women sought educational qualifications. The number of U.S. female college graduates doubled in the 1960s. It was largely among such women that the liberation movement found its members.

To liberate women from male domination, women's groups revived the demand for an Equal Rights Amendment (ERA) to the U.S. Constitution. To free women from economic dependency, they called for a national system of day care and the elimination of laws forbidding abortion. To enforce such demands, groups such as the National Organization for Women (NOW) mounted a campaign to raise the consciousness

of women and to turn their gender solidarity into political power.

This political mobilization paid off. Federally imposed quotas required affirmative action by employers to ensure that women were sufficiently represented among their employees.

Under such government pressure, women penetrated in considerably greater numbers into professions once reserved for men. The percentage of U.S. lawyers who were women more than tripled during the 1970s, from 4 percent to 14 percent. The proportion of women doctors doubled, from 9 percent to 20 percent—a far cry from the 1930s, when most U.S. hospitals would not admit a female intern.

Similar pressures produced similar results in Western Europe. In France, for example, the proportion of women among the younger generation of doctors rose even higher, to over a third. This represented a remarkable change in a country where, until the mid-1960s, a woman had to obtain her husband's legal permission to open her own bank account or run her own business. In 1974 the French parliament legalized abortion, one year after a historic U.S. Supreme Court decision upheld this most controversial of women's rights.

As economic opportunities for women grew, their tolerance for a subordinate role in marriage declined. By the 1980s, one French marriage in six ended in divorce. The U.S. divorce rate was far higher: half of all marriages. Fully half of American women were single, compared to only a quarter of them in 1960. The kind of household that Americans had taken for granted only a generation earlier—father, dependent mother, two or more children—by the 1980s represented only 12 percent of U.S. households, and this proportion was still declining.

The acceleration of change in such a fundamental institution as the family naturally produced a backlash. In 1982 the ERA failed to secure ratification. In the 1984 U.S. presidential campaign, the Republican party platform de-

Women demand the right to an abortion, 1977. *Though the leading figure is costumed as an American comic-strip character, this march was in New Zealand.* Westra/Magnum Photos

manded that future federal judges be pledged to oppose abortion. European conservatives similarly attacked women's liberation as destructive of the social order. Faced with such adverse reactions, the women's movement seemed in retreat by the 1980s. A younger generation of women appeared to take the hard-won victories of women's liberation for granted.

Nevertheless, it seems unlikely that women in postindustrial societies will ever return to the domesticity the 1950s took for granted. Economic necessity and educational inclination continue to attract women to careers. Such trends are viewed as intolerable by many people who grew up in a society with very different role models. In both the United States and Europe after 1970, such people expressed their protest by voting for politicians who promised to restore traditional values.

Economic Slowdown and the Search for Political Direction

The turmoil created by the challenges to authority in the 1960s was made more acute by the relatively sudden end of the unprecedented level of postwar economic growth and stability. The "thirty glorious years" came to an abrupt conclusion with huge increases in oil prices in 1973. The whole world was affected by the subsequent economic slowdown. The political consequences for Europe and the United States were profound.

Economic dissatisfaction, as well as nostalgic protest, dominated politics after 1970. Political power changed hands with increasing rapidity in the United States and Europe as one government after another failed to grapple effectively with stagflation. The re-election of President Nixon in 1972 symbolized continuing backlash against the 1960s; he defeated a Democratic nominee whose candidacy seemed to personify the revolt of blacks, youth, and women. Within two years Nixon resigned under threat of impeachment. Investigation of a burglary at the Democratic party's headquarters at the Watergate complex and of the subsequent cover-up revealed a trail of complicity leading back to the president. In 1976, Democratic nominee Jimmy Carter profited from this scandal to defeat Nixon's successor. Carter promised to restore Americans' faith in their government. But by 1980, with inflation at an annual rate of 13 percent, the voters rejected Carter's presidency and elected Republican Ronald Reagan.

In the 1980 presidential election, half the eligible voters chose not to cast their ballots. Such a turnout was evidence of widespread skepticism that, in a mass society, voting had any meaning. Polls revealed that as many as two-thirds of the U.S. electorate saw themselves as helpless victims of monied interests. In fact, campaign contributions to political action committees (PACs), formed to promote a single issue or special interest, increased tenfold in the 1970s. The temptations of these funds increased the voters' suspicion that politicians cast their votes for the highest bidder.

In Western Europe, a far higher percentage of citizens continued to vote. Often, however, they voted to punish governments they judged to have failed to restore economic health, much as Americans had judged Carter. The British electorate voted the Conservatives into power again in 1970, out in 1974, and back in again, under Margaret Thatcher, in 1979. In and out of power, the British Labour party remained divided.

Similar quarrels disrupted the German Social Democratic party, and the voters ousted it from power in 1982. A significant number of young Germans turned away from the Social Democrats to the "Green" party, which championed many 1960s causes, including protecting the environment.

Economic Slowdown in the United States

The reason for the voters' growing impatience in the 1970s lay in the worldwide economic slowdown. Its differing impact on diverse social groups polarized politics. No longer did people believe, as they had in the 1950s and 1960s, that their economies would continue to grow indefinitely. Each social group within each nation tried to cast its votes to defend its own share in a stagnant economy.

The slowdown spared no nation. Through most of the 1960s, Europeans had worried about "the American challenge." They feared that U.S.-based multinational corporations would buy up their basic industries. This proved a groundless fear, for the economic troubles that appeared at the end of the Johnson presidency were symptomatic of a deeply troubled U.S. economy.

In some ways the developing crisis of U.S. industry had been foreshadowed by the fate of Britain after World War II. Despite their burden of debt, for a long while the British attempted to maintain the appearance of a great power. At the same time, they provided the generous benefits of the guarantor state. Meanwhile, they failed to modernize industrial plants. The British share in production of the world's manufactured goods fell by half between 1960 and the mid-1970s. The growth of aggressive global competition, as well as British inefficiency, explains this outcome.

Overseas competition began to challenge U.S. industry in the 1950s. Japanese clothing sales in the U.S. retail market cost American textile workers 300,000 jobs. By the 1970s, the products of many U.S. industries no longer dominated world markets. The United States manufactured only one-fifth of the world's steel, for example, compared to nearly half of world production in 1950.

U.S. manufactured goods were at a disadvantage in world markets for interrelated reasons. From the mid-1960s onward, the rate of growth of U.S. productivity fell behind that of every other developed country except Britain. U.S. conservatives blamed wage inflation: paying people too much while expecting them to do too little. In fact, wages rose rapidly in the 1970s, though they lagged behind prices. Others blamed declining productivity on industrialists' reluctance to modernize existing U.S. plants. All too often, it was more profitable for multinational corporations to build new plants abroad where labor was cheaper.

Certainly the U.S. economy had some impressive achievements to its credit. It had found jobs for a labor force swollen by half by the baby-boom generation. The entitlement programs of the guarantor state had improved the lives of the elderly, the disabled, and some of the poor. The costs of these programs, however, increased in the 1960s and 1970s from 5 percent to 11 percent of the U.S. GNP. Taxpayers blamed such costs for the decline of their own standard of living. Increasingly, they made the guarantor state and the recipients of its benefits the scapegoats for their fears and frustrations. Less and less was heard of the generous notion of the 1960s that society had a collective responsibility for its least fortunate members.

By the 1980s, there existed two American societies: one poor, urban, and mainly black; the other relatively affluent, suburban, and mainly white. For those left behind in the shrinking central cities, the ups and downs of the economy hit much harder. A growing number of them had no job and no prospect of finding one. In 1960, almost three-quarters of black males had been either employed or seeking a job. By the early 1980s that proportion had declined to a little over one-half. The "black revolt" of the 1960s produced few economic gains. Largely because of federally enforced employment guidelines, some blacks joined the middle class. Overall, however, the gap between black and white family incomes steadily widened.

Conservatives blamed this continuing gap on the mistaken generosity of the Great Society, which supposedly made it easier to collect government benefits than to work. Others thought the origins of black poverty were more complex. The kind of job that immigrants to U.S. inner cities had historically taken was rapidly vanishing. The growing number of women in the work force took many of the low-paying jobs in the expanding service sector. The root cause of the desperate plight of most U.S. blacks was that postindustrial opportunity began deserting cities just as they moved in.

Visiting Europeans were often horrified by their glimpses of U.S. inner-city society. A stricken neighborhood like New York's South Bronx, for example, with its mile upon mile of abandoned buildings burned out by desperate landlords or tenants, reminded such visitors of the ruins of their continent in 1945.

Economic Slowdown in Europe

Europe in the 1960s had no such army of the unemployed as occupied such U.S. neighborhoods. In fact, industrial northern Europe during the boom had to import labor from less-developed southern Europe and from such countries as Turkey and Algeria to do the jobs its own citizens did not want. But by the mid-1970s, European governments were attempting to induce or coerce such "guest-workers" to go home. Europe did not long celebrate its resistance to the American challenge: its own economies soon became mired in the same stagflation as the U.S. economy—and for many of the same reasons.

The rise in OPEC oil prices in 1973 hit Europe and Japan at least as hard as the United States. It was a heavy blow to the economies of countries like France and West Germany. After 1945, they had shifted from coal to oil as their prime energy source although they had little oil of their own. After 1973, Europe responded more effectively than the United States to the need to conserve oil. The European Economic Community actually reduced its petroleum imports by 4 percent, while the United States, whose own domestic supplies had equaled demand into the late 1960s, increased its imports by a third.

Nevertheless, the inflated cost of energy contributed to the spread of stagflation in Europe, as did other factors already familiar in the U.S. economy. The rate of growth of European productivity slowed. Average European hourly wages in manufacturing, which in 1960 had everywhere been less than half the U.S. rate, matched or even surpassed U.S. wages by 1980. European governments' plans consistently emphasized the benefits of the guarantor state rather than reinvestment in plant modernization. European-based and even Japanese-based multinational companies began to locate new plants in places where taxes and wages were lower. Thus, steel made in Europe, for example, which had undercut U.S.-produced steel, was now undercut by steel produced in Brazil or India.

The effect of these developments on a country such as West Germany, where one in five jobs depended on exports, was devastating. As German industry became increasingly uncompetitive, unemployment grew, particularly among the young. Meanwhile, tax revenues fell while government expenditures tended to inflate to relieve the hardships of a stagnant economy.

To a greater or lesser extent, this combination of problems beset all the economies of the developed world by the end of the 1970s. As individuals experienced the slowdown in the form of high taxes and a living standard reduced by inflation, they tended to vote for politicians who promised to cut taxes and halt inflation by reducing the costs of the guarantor state. Moreover, as the growth of a postindustrial society changed the social composition of the electorate, a majority of voters everywhere had less and less sympathy with the unlucky poor.

Americans and Europeans who managed to escape into the service sector as the number of industrial jobs dwindled lived in a milieu much more hostile to collective social action than factory workers. The latter had often identified themselves as "us" (the union, often affiliated with the Left) against "them" (the management). Even so, one-half of the German and a third of the British working classes had usually voted for conservatives. Such a vote came even more naturally to postindustrial workers in the service sector, who tended to see themselves as middle-class competitors, not members of a group with shared goals. Nowhere did unions still represent a force for change. Dwindling in numbers and political influence, all but a few concentrated on preserving the benefits of their aging membership.

Nor were the young any longer a force for change. Facing uncertain job prospects, they had little of the enthusiasm for collective action that characterized the 1960s generation. Their college studies did little to encourage young people to think about the problems of society as a whole. The number of U.S. students majoring in the humanities—subjects that taught critical thinking about general human problems—fell by 50 percent in the 1970s. The number of graduates in subjects like business that supposedly could ensure success in a constricted job market rose correspondingly.

The faltering world economy of the 1970s thus produced an ethic of every person for himself or herself and each nation for itself. Such traditional sources of alternative vision as the Left and the young seemed unable to provide a fresh dream while the world slid haplessly into the postindustrial future.

The Triumph of Conservative Economics: Mitterrand, Thatcher, and Reagan

Nations, however, cannot indefinitely muddle along in an atmosphere of political doubt. Eventually the voters will turn to leadership that promises a real change of direction. In 1979, British voters returned the Conservatives to power under the leadership of Margaret Thatcher. In the fall of 1980 and the spring of 1981, the United States and France chose new presidents, Ronald Reagan and François Mitterrand. Each promised, by diametrically opposed programs, to resolve his or her country's economic crisis.

France Under Mitterrand

The OPEC oil shock of 1973 marked the end of three decades of rapid French economic growth, during which the standard of living virtually doubled. Still a land of picturesque backwardness in 1945, France by the 1970s had become the third producer of aerospace technology in the world. Taking for granted that such dramatic modernization would continue, the government failed to anticipate how quickly the foundations of an economy could become outmoded in the postindustrial era. As in the United States and the rest of Western Europe, it permitted wages and social services to increase at inflationary rates and failed to invest sufficiently in new technologies.

Thus when Socialist François Mitterrand became president in 1981, he inherited an economy already in decline. During his first year in office, he and his Socialist majority in parliament tried to combat stagflation by renewing economic growth. Like Léon Blum in 1936, they hoped to do this by ensuring a more

equal distribution of wealth. Like Blum, Mitterrand decreed wage hikes, reduced the workweek, and expanded paid vacations. He went further than Blum by nationalizing eleven large private companies and many banks. The Socialist hope was to stimulate the economy by expanding worker purchasing power and by confiscating for public investment the profits of large corporations. To finance compensation to these companies' former owners and to pay for enhanced guarantor-state benefits, the Mitterrand government borrowed heavily abroad.

Within a year, the discouraging results of this program proved, as in 1936–1937, that in a global economy not even a major industrial power like France could single-handedly pursue the goals of democratic socialism. Inflation rose to an annual rate of 14 percent, yet unemployment remained unacceptably high because of the worldwide slump. Meanwhile, U.S. bankers, noting its growing debt, foreclosed further borrowing by France. By the spring of 1982, the policy of trying to stimulate growth by restoring full employment and redistributing economic rewards had clearly failed.

Mitterrand then completely reversed direction. His new program stressed cutting taxes and social expenditures. His government shut down unneeded capacity in loss-making nationalized industries such as steel and shipbuilding, though this cost many Socialist voters their jobs. By the fall of 1984, this new policy had brought France's inflation rate down. But over 9 percent of the French work force was unemployed, and among the young the rate was much higher. Conservatives denounced the original inflationary program. Mitterrand's own supporters were bewildered by his new program of harsh austerity.

As in 1936–1937, when an experiment with democratic socialism ended in disillusionment, critics wondered what future the movement had. French voters for the Left—the working class, the poor, many of the young and idealistic—had danced in the streets when

Mitterrand won in 1981. Within less than a year his had become a government like any other. Even his limited effort to revive the economy by Keynesian government spending had succumbed to the continuing slowdown of the world economy. But if, in practice, democratic Socialists offered no alternative to the capitalistic system, and indeed joined its supporters in denouncing the costly inefficiency of the guarantor state, it was hard to see why anyone should vote for them instead of for conservatives like Thatcher and Reagan.

Britain Under Thatcher

For Margaret Thatcher, the stagflation of the 1970s was a symptom of what Europeans had come to call the "British disease": the combination of amateurish education and management methods, of bitterly hostile relations between capital and labor, between rich and poor, that had reduced Britain from the world's leading economy in the nineteenth century to one of the less important European economies by 1979. In Thatcher's view, decline was the result of the militant intransigence of the British labor movement in defending a wasteful guarantor state and the reluctance of the British upper classes, embodied in the Conservative party she now led, to crush that lower-class intransigence. Her own temperament inclined her, however, to the very opposite of the compromises that had characterized her predecessors. A fanatic believer in free-market economics, she relished pitiless confrontation with those she believed to be wrong. Not for nothing would she come to be called "the Iron Lady."

The general evolution of the global economy, helped her toward her goal of curing the British of what she called their "dependency culture" by smashing the guarantor state. Britain, like the other major democracies, was moving toward the postindustrial society. Manufacturing, still 70 percent unionized, was in decline while employment in the service sector, only 15 percent unionized, was growing. But Thatcher was unwilling to wait out that evolution. She set out to cripple the British unions. Her Conservative majority passed a variety of laws curtailing some of the unions' most effective tactics. Thatcher also broke strikes against government-owned companies like British Coal by simply refusing to meet strikers' demands. In 1984–1985 Thatcher refused to negotiate until she broke the strike; then, as the union had warned, she proceeded to close nearly seventy pits, throwing seventy thousand miners onto the already enormous unemployment rolls.

With British unemployment ranging up to 14 percent, it was now easier to break a strike: people lucky enough still to be working thought twice about losing the job they had. Union membership declined from over half to little over a third of the work force. Other measures further undermined working-class solidarity. The government sold off public housing at giveaway prices to tenants, for example, and offered shares in "privatized" former government-owned companies to the public. The number of British shareholders tripled from 1979 to 1988. These new working-class houseowners and stockholders now felt they had more in common with the middle class than with their former "comrades."

Such were the changes wrought under Thatcher that the theme of "the two Englands," a contrast first discerned in the grimmest days of early industrialization, revived. One England was the prosperous south, especially the booming outer London suburbs, with their expanding network of motorways connecting the gleaming new headquarters of high-tech service enterprises. The other England consisted of two parts: the north (and Wales and Scotland), once the cradle of the British industrial revolution and now its tomb, a desolate landscape of abandoned factories and empty harbors; and the inner cities, mostly, as in the United States, crumbling ghettos where black and Asian minorities faced mass unemployment and racial hostility.

To many thoughtful people, including a substantial minority of the Conservative party, this growing polarization between the two Englands seemed to threaten future political stability. To Thatcher and like-minded people, however, the idea that the government should redistribute wealth from winners to losers was exactly what was wrong not only with socialism but with the policies of all her postwar predecessors. Though she sometimes had to back off when misgivings reduced her parliamentary majority, she lost little of her determination to turn Britain into a newly competitive nation, whatever the human cost. The hope of getting richer would motivate the rich; the despair of being poor would motivate the poor.

The pattern of taxation proposed in her budget in 1988 showed how she intended to redistribute the burden of government to achieve those ends. The budget called for a 20 percent cut for the wealthiest 5 percent of taxpayers, the lowest income tax rates since 1938, before the creation of the British guarantor state, and a general reduction in the property taxes of householders. To replace those taxes based on the value of property, everyone in the country, regardless of income, would pay a flat local "community charge," thus adding some 15 million people, including the rapidly growing number living below the official poverty standard, to the tax rolls.

Public outrage at this "charge," when it was imposed in 1990, finally made Thatcher so unpopular that her own parliamentary Conservative majority turned against her. She had calculated that by forcing local governments, often controlled by the Labour party, to "charge" everyone at the same rate, she could destroy their power to spend for public purposes and thus win elections. Widespread rioting and refusal to pay showed that the public

blamed her for this regressive measure. Her colleagues forced her to resign at the end of the year.

The Labour party approached new general elections in April 1992 full of optimism. After thirteen years of Conservative rule, with Britain sunk in its worst recession since the Great Depression and an estimated 1 million homeless people living on the streets, Labour's expectation that the voters would opt for change is understandable. But it was a mistaken expectation: Labour won only 35 percent of the vote, a far cry from its 49 percent in 1951.

Labour had tried to improve its image by purging its radical Marxist wing and by downplaying its connection with Britain's dwindling unions. But Labour's program did call for increased government spending. This proposal did not trouble Labour's traditional supporters in the poverty-ridden North, where in some places two-thirds of young people could find no job. But Conservative warnings that Labour planned to drop a "tax bomb" alarmed the suburban middle classes. Despite Thatcher's unpopularity at the end of her reign, her policies had paid political dividends. They had helped to create a narrow electoral majority that voted Conservative because it feared the taxes a Labour guarantor state would impose more than it feared the disinvestment in public services and the heightened tensions between social classes that Thatcherism had produced.

The United States Under Reagan

Like Thatcher, Ronald Reagan won office by campaigning against the excessive expenditures of the guarantor state. Reagan's policies once he was in office, however, were more reminiscent of the Keynesian idea of deficit financing than Republicans cared to admit. Reagan cut taxes, especially for corporations and the very wealthy. Despite this reduction in revenue, he also called for an enormous military buildup. This combination of policies vastly increased the federal budget deficit. The Reagan administration's first years seemed to confirm the inability of governments in the postindustrial era to restrain inflation without substantial unemployment. The recession of 1981–1982 was the worst the United States had experienced since the Depression of the 1930s: up to 10 percent of Americans were unemployed.

The recovery that began at the end of 1982 carried Reagan to re-election in 1984. Many voted for him because they perceived his economic policies as being more successful than his predecessor's. Such a judgment depended on which of the twin evils of the 1970s, inflation or unemployment, the individual voter dreaded more. Consumer prices did rise less rapidly. But unemployment averaged 8.6 percent through the spring of 1984 under Reagan, compared to 6.4 percent in 1980 under Carter.

"Reaganomics" made some people "winners" and others "losers." Foreign, especially European, investors benefited, lending money at high rates to finance the U.S. deficit. Foreign workers suffered, for the European investment that might have expanded their own economies and relieved unemployment instead was flowing to the United States. The high interest rates that attracted such investment made the dollar so expensive that foreigners could not afford to buy U.S. products. These factors made those Americans who had to sell abroad—certain industries and most farmers—losers from Reaganomics.

On the other hand, the chief executive officers of large U.S. corporations were clearly winners: they voted themselves salary increases averaging 40 percent in 1983. But many employees of these companies were losers. Over a million manufacturing jobs were lost between 1979 and 1984. For the first time, white males composed less than half of the U.S. work force, outnumbered by lower-paid women. Of the new jobs created by the recovery, most were in the postindustrial service sector, which paid, on average, one-third less than industry.

Being comparatively well insulated against unemployment and benefiting from reduced inflation, members of the suburban middle class were marginal winners. Blacks and the poor in general were losers. More people lived in poverty in the 1980s than at any time since the inauguration of the Great Society programs, many of which the Reagan administration cut or discontinued.

In 1980 the Republican party had moved adroitly to exploit Americans' unhappiness with 1970s stagflation and the social changes of postindustrial society. Already the party of the nation's corporate leadership, it forged an alliance with groups opposed to such innovations as "abortion on demand." Outspending the Democrats five to one, the Republicans were able to set the tone of economic and social debate.

Reagan won re-election by a landslide in 1984 and enjoyed continuing popularity through his second term. Since television news did not attempt to explain the complexities of economics, and Americans drew most of their information from television, relatively few were aware of the warnings of many economists that much was fundamentally amiss with his administration's management of the U.S. economy.

The direst warnings, however, seemed confirmed when on October 19, 1987, the New York Stock Exchange crashed, recording the worst single day's fall of share prices in its history. In one day stocks lost almost a quarter of their value. Within a few hours, moreover, instantaneous electronic communications carried the wave of panic selling to every stock market around the globe. For months after October 19, economists and a newly anxious public wondered whether, as in 1929, collapse on Wall Street would be the prelude to a global depression. Although in the short term investors left the stock market for safer and more conservative investments, they eventually returned. In a relatively short time, the market made up its losses and continued to grow.

The root cause of the debacle was, as usual in such panics, that investors had suddenly lost confidence, though the plunge was accelerated by an innovation of the electronic age: computers programmed to sell huge blocks of stock at a given signal. The loss of confidence stemmed from investors' belated recognition that the United States had insulated itself from the global slowdown of the years since 1973 by policies that appeared to buoy its economy in the short run but might portend long-run disaster.

"Reaganomics"—the combination of tax cuts for the rich and vastly expanded military spending—created a huge hole in the federal budget that could be filled only by borrowing. By the time he left office Reagan had added more government debt than all previous U.S. presidents combined. Some critics charged that his administration had deliberately tripled the debt in order to make it impossible for his successors ever again to expand the programs of the guarantor state.

Much of this debt was owed to foreign investors. From 1948 to 1980, the balance between U.S. investments abroad and foreign investment in the United States had always been in U.S. favor. In the 1980s this balance reversed. No longer the world's largest creditor, the United States became the world's largest debtor. Moreover, foreign investors were increasingly less willing to invest in U.S. paper obligations. They sought tangible U.S. property—land, buildings, corporations—in return for the money they poured into the U.S. economy.

At the same time it was thus mortgaging its future, concerned economists pointed out, the United States in the 1980s was neglecting to maintain and upgrade the economic plant that would have to generate the wealth to pay the debt off. While the wealthy bought luxury items

such as "stretch" limousines, and Wall Street issued "junk bonds" to pay for the seizure by corporate "raiders" of valuable companies, the United States was investing less in capital equipment than any other industrialized nation except Britain. Americans were putting less money aside than anyone else, a sure sign that they feared the return of high inflation. The United States spent less for civilian research and development than its rivals, so that by 1987 almost half of U.S. patents were awarded to foreigners, compared to a third in 1977. Above all, the United States continued to run a huge trade deficit, buying more abroad, especially oil, than it sold.

Not only U.S. citizens and industry were failing to invest in the future. Government's priorities also were elsewhere. The Reagan administration fulfilled its electoral pledges to cut the costs of the guarantor state partly by such measures as closing offices at which the unemployed could seek compensation. More damagingly, the Reagan administration spent on grants to education, health, urban renewal, and job training approximately half of what it spent on military aircraft. It rejected the idea that a nation's future well-being depends at least as much on the health of its schools and cities—which lost a quarter of their federal aid—as on its air force.

And yet the guarantor state did not fade away as promised. In 1988 the federal government actually had 150,000 *more* civilian employees than when Reagan took office. Subsidies to agriculture, which now meant primarily corporate agribusinesses, nearly tripled between 1981 and 1988.

In view of the mountain of debt piled up, the Reagan years appear in retrospect as a kind of economic binge. Not everyone shared in the self-indulgences of the period, however. In actual purchasing power the incomes of the less wealthy 80 percent of U.S. families actually fell between 1977 and 1988. To keep up, both husband and wife in such families usually had to work and were still forced to resort to an unprecedented expansion of credit—"plastic"—to keep the boom in consumer goods going. Even so, for the first time since World War II, the percentage of Americans who could afford to own their own homes fell after 1980.

To those in this group who might have thought to enhance their earning power by striking, Reagan gave an unambiguous warning in 1981 by firing air traffic controllers who had illegally struck against the government. The 1980s saw many more such episodes of successful strikebreaking. By 1988 only 17 percent of the U.S. labor force was still unionized.

In reply to critics, Reagan's defenders retorted that if the guarantor state had not shrunk, it was because those who benefited from its programs had the ear of the Democratically controlled Congress. Reagan's defenders also pointed proudly to the creation of over 14 million new U.S. jobs during the Reagan years, contrasting this achievement with the failure of Western Europe to create any. Indeed, the U.S. unemployment rate was under 6 percent in mid-1988, though Europeans argued that their rates were higher because their governments had cut spending rather than run deficits and that nine out of ten of new U.S. jobs were for "temporary" employees, earning few benefits and subject to instant dismissal whenever a recession struck.

It is surprising that after such events as the crash of October 1987, Reagan lost little popularity even among those groups for whom his policies had created obvious disadvantages. Perhaps the explanation was that Americans now judged political contests not in the light of economic interest but rather on the basis of the "image" politicians projected. Reagan's experience as a film actor helped him project his jovial personality over television. But his popularity rested on more than appearances. The widespread belief in his effectiveness had rein-

vigorated a presidency tarnished by repeated disappointments.

Although Reagan described himself as a conservative, his greatest appeal was to those Americans for whom the transition to a postindustrial society represented a challenge rather than a disaster. To the suburban majority, many programs of the guarantor state now seemed increasingly irrelevant. They applauded his determination to dismantle a system of little benefit to them. They welcomed his message that, unhampered by government restraints, they could make the postindustrial age their personal success story, as earlier generations of Americans had made successes of the transition from rural to industrial America. This hope for the future was a welcome change from the political and economic pessimism of the 1970s. Moreover, Reagan's opposition to such innovations as legalized abortion seemed to suggest that the future could be won without abandoning the certainties of the past.

Economic Anxiety and the Quest for Political Alternatives

Reagan's government represented only the most prominent example of conservative resurgence in the 1980s. In much of the developed world, the dogma of the decade was the need to return to free enterprise. Conservatives everywhere proclaimed that they had finally reversed the trend to government intervention in the world's economies begun during World War I and much heightened after World War II.

The conservative public mood of the 1980s reminded many social critics of the complacent mood of the 1920s. Both were decades in which governments of the Left were, like Mitterrand's, rare, short-lived, and disappointing. Conservative leaders like Calvin Coolidge in the 1920s and Reagan in the 1980s convinced their publics that economic problems were best addressed by minimizing the role of government and leaving each individual and nation to pursue goals of enlightened selfishness, just as nineteenth-century economic liberalism had prescribed. In this "culture of contentment,"[4] the prosperous—a majority of voters though a minority of the population—remained absorbed by their own prosperity, while the less fortunate found little reason to stir from their habitual political indifference.

Yet the history of George H. W. Bush's presidency (1988–1992) showed that the complacent mood of the 1980s would not survive a worsening economy. The deepening recession of the 1990s, though not as severe as the "Reagan recession" of 1981–1982, was alarmingly different in that it seemed to threaten the economic well-being of the "contented." Even middle-class Americans began to experience economic fears and political frustrations by 1992.

The economic sluggishness of the 1970s had led to the triumphs in the 1980s of Mitterrand, Thatcher, and Reagan. Now in the 1990s, anxious voters in all of the Western democracies sometimes seemed ready to turn to new leaders or movements that might grapple more effectively with worldwide recession. What these new leaders and movements stood for was not entirely clear—and perhaps not important. It was what they were *against*—politics as usual—that attracted both formerly contented and formerly apathetic citizens on both sides of the Atlantic.

In the United States, the demand for a new politics by voters equally mistrustful of Bush and his Democratic challenger, Bill Clinton, reflected a belated recognition of the long-term decline of the nation's economy even during the years of apparent Reagan prosperity—a decline accelerated by the stubbornly persistent recession that began in 1990. The causes of the recession that devastated Bush's popularity could be found partly in the economic policies of his predecessor. Reagan's advisers had claimed that tax cuts for the wealthy would stimulate a wave of productive investment that would ultimately benefit all Americans. In fact it stimulated much unplanned waste, like the construction of new downtown office space of which a fifth still stood vacant in the 1990s. Meanwhile, the money the U.S. government needed for its vast entitlement programs and for its military buildup was borrowed, mainly from foreign lenders. The revenues collected from the middle class and poorer payers onto whom the tax burden was shifted had increasingly to be committed to paying these lenders back, to servicing a government debt growing in the 1990s at the rate of $1 billion *a day*, rather than to making investments that would strengthen the economy's productive capacity. At the same time the government's usual Keynesian weapon against recession—enhanced government spending to restart the economy—could not be used in the face of so intimidating a burden of debt.

Consumer purchases could not be expected to restart the economy because most consumers had little to spend. The rewards of the economic revival after the Reagan recession of the early 1980s had been very unequally shared. The 1980s in fact witnessed a growth in economic inequality unparalleled in U.S. history. By 1989 the wealthiest 1 percent of the population owned 37 percent of the nation's net worth, up from 31 percent in 1983. These fewer-than-a-million households owned more than the least wealthy 90 percent of the population, some 85 million families. Of course these wealthiest people lived a lifestyle very different from that of ordinary Americans. One economist characterized this as the "secession of the rich" from American society, as higher-income people withdrew to suburban strongholds protected from intrusion by an army of private security forces that well outnumbered the police.

Meanwhile, the vast majority of less fortunate Americans fared even worse in the 1980s than they had earlier. By the 1990s, many economists were reaching the sobering conclusion that the "American dream" of success through hard work from one generation to the next was becoming a less and less realistic prospect. From the end of World War II through the early 1970s, American average family income had risen by over 100 percent. But from the 1970s to the 1990s, the gain was only 9 percent, and even this was achieved only by sending additional family members out to work. The purchasing power of single breadwinners actually shrank. Part of the explanation for the failure of incomes to grow lies in the shift in postindustrial America of many millions from high-paying factory jobs to lower-paid service jobs. Yet it was not only the high school dropouts who filled many of these positions who faced dimmer job prospects in the 1980s. By the end of the decade, one in five college graduates was employed in a job in which college-level skills were neither required nor paid for.

It was not only the level of their wages that made so many Americans feel economically vulnerable. Almost 40 percent of working Americans were not covered by an employer-sponsored health-care program, and the proportion covered by a pension plan fell from 50 percent in 1980 to 40 percent in the 1990s. This lack of coverage reflected the fact that businesses were relying increasingly on "temporary" workers—almost a quarter of the U.S. work force.

All these vulnerabilities help explain the apprehension a majority of Americans felt when the economy dipped into recession in 1990. In that year the foreign lenders whose investments had kept the U.S. economy afloat had more essential uses for their money: the Japanese to restart their own now-troubled economy, the Germans to finance the recon-struction of the formerly communist sector of their country. Average Americans were in no position to take their place, for they were struggling to keep up with the bills by working longer hours, charging purchases or borrowing against the equity they held in their homes.

In this atmosphere of anxiety the familiar vicious cycle of an economic downturn quickly developed. As investment declined, earnings dwindled, and people consequently bought less. As consumption fell, businesses sought to cut costs by cutting payrolls. The chill of fear produced by these layoffs reduced business still further, forcing employers to further cuts, and so it went. In this climate industries that had already found themselves uncompetitive in the global marketplace concluded that they had no choices but to "downsize" or emigrate. General Motors, the world's largest business, "downsized." Losing half a billion dollars a month, the automaker, which had closed 19 factories since 1986, announced just before Christmas 1991 that it would close 21 of its remaining 125 plants and get rid of some 70,000 employees.

Such layoffs seemed only good business to the companies' shareholders, since reduced costs eventually implied renewed dividends. However, unprecedented features of the recession of the early 1990s alarmed many people who owned such shares. In earlier recessions, the loss of manufacturing jobs had been compensated for in part by the growth of employment in services. Now, however, the service sector was also cutting payrolls. In both manufacturing and services, moreover, businesses that were not particularly hard hit by recession were laying employees off, frankly admitting that they did not intend to rehire them when the recession ended. Worst of all, in this recession, in contrast to earlier ones, corporations were laying off blue-collar and white-collar workers in almost equal proportions. Managers, scientists, and engineers were no longer assured of a job: they constituted 40 percent of the employees laid off in 1991. IBM, having shed

A Ford engine block plant in Chihuahua, Mexico. *To American readers the logo on the workers' shirts is familiar: the quality-control slogan suspended over the line, however, is in Spanish. These Mexicans earn less than twelve percent of the wage of workers doing comparable work in Detroit.* Mark Boroff/Texas Stock

some 65,000 mainly white-collar employees between 1986 and 1991, planned to oust a further 20,000 in the 1990s.

Amid such economic contraction, the pay raises of college graduates—the managers and professionals who had best weathered the 1980s—fell below even the low rates of inflation prevailing after 1989. Economic anxiety thus was no longer limited to the people on the lowest rungs of the economic ladder.

Bush's defeat at the polls in November 1992 reflected the fact that his administration had recorded the worst economic scores of any presidency since World War II. In the early 1990s U.S. economic growth slowed to rates comparable to those of the Depression—only half the rates of the 1960s. More people—11 percent of whites and 32 percent of blacks—

met the official definition of poverty—a $14,000 income for a family of four—than at any time since Johnson had launched his Great Society programs in the mid-1960s.

It did not help Bush's image that he was perceived by many Americans as indifferent to them. Reagan in 1980 and 1984, and Bush in 1988, had defeated Democratic challengers by firmly identifying with the suburban middle class while depicting Democrats as so subservient to the inner-city poor that they encouraged crime. Under better economic circumstances, a similar campaign in 1992 might have seemed certain to assure a Bush victory, for this was the first election during which a near-majority of the U.S. population—46 percent—lived in suburbs (compared to only 23 percent in 1950).

In 1992, however, the best evidence that many even in such once "contented" groups were rejecting Bush was the startling support for the independent presidential campaign of Ross Perot. Perot was a self-made Texas billionaire, president of one of the world's largest producers of computer software. He was far from a typical leader of American industry. American industrial leadership with its "free-enterprise" slogans, he contended, had much to learn from the very different system of "organized capitalism" of Germany and Japan.

Perot won 19 percent of the vote in the presidential race of 1992. Support came not only from fellow computer tycoons but from hundreds of thousands of people of all backgrounds, all attracted by his unconventional mixture of conservative and liberal themes. The Perot phenomenon was compelling evidence of many Americans' deep concern that future generations could not expect the higher standard of living earlier ones had taken for granted, and that the old political parties were equally incapable of stopping this decline.

The End of the "Culture of Contentment"

By the mid-1990s, a dawning fear that the post-1973 global economic slowdown might preclude forever a return to the robust growth and rapidly rising living standards of the 1950s and 1960s spread throughout the Western world. As ruthless corporate downsizing, following upon decades of what Europeans were learning to call the post-1973 "crisis," spread from the United States to Europe, the choices of European voters, like those of American voters, became increasingly unpredictable. The wealthy continued to vote for the party they saw as best serving their interests. The poor, having lost confidence in all politicians, often did not vote at all. The majority in the middle continued voting for one political option and then for its

alternative, often without much confidence in either. Thus in the summer of 1996, despite his advantage in the polls, it was not certain that President Bill Clinton would be re-elected, despite some good economic news for which his administration could claim credit. The federal budget deficit had shrunk since 1992, unemployment had fallen since its peak in that year, and the stock market had reached unprecedented heights. Yet the personal experience of a majority of voters showed them that since 1992 their purchasing power had stagnated or even declined, and many were aware that the gap between their incomes and those of the wealthiest groups in society had widened. As in Europe, with the political Left in eclipse and the far Right perceived as too extreme, American voters uncommitted to either of the two parties gave their votes unenthusiastically to one and then the other, skeptical that either could confront the continuing challenges of headlong technological change and a truly global marketplace.

"New Democrat" Economics and the "Republican Revolution"

Before the presidential election of November 1992, one of Bill Clinton's closest advisers posted a sign in his campaign headquarters to remind Clinton's supporters what issue they must continue to stress to beat President Bush. It read, "It's the economy, stupid." In other words, the Bush administration had remained indifferent to economic distress, which a Clinton administration would alleviate.

The Clinton campaign had given out mixed signals as to how the new president planned to cope with the country's economic problems. As a Democrat, Clinton led the party that twice in the twentieth century had expanded the government's role in the economy—with the New Deal and the Great Society. It was the party whose goals and assumptions most closely resembled—though not very closely—those of

European parties of the Left. Its greatest twentieth-century figure, Franklin Roosevelt, had insisted that he was mobilizing government in the interests of the vast majority of ordinary Americans, stricken by the Depression, against the really powerful forces in American life, the profiteers of "business and financial monopoly," who had created during the 1920s a "government by organized money."[5] In the 1990s, however, this kind of denunciation of big business and the wealthy no longer seemed to have much resonance.

Clinton portrayed himself as a "New Democrat" mindful of how mistrustful of Washington bureaucrats and scornful of the urban poor many onetime Democratic voters had become. Thus he pledged that his administration would "end welfare as we know it." This pledge marked a partial repudiation of the guarantor state, whose taxes many middle-class Americans blamed for the stagnation of their standard of living since the 1970s. Candidate Clinton also promised to cut those taxes and to launch an all-out effort to reduce the federal deficit left over from the Reagan years—two desirable objectives it would be hard to reconcile.

Once in office, Clinton had to decide whether he was a program-building old Democrat or a deficit-reducing new Democrat. Ultimately he sided with the consensus among Wall Street financiers, corporate executives, and most economists, that the number one priority was reducing the federal deficit. In the interest of balancing the budget he championed substantial tax increases. Thus the middle classes did not get the tax cut he had promised. The reduced federal budget provided practically no funds for expanded education and other investments he had advocated.

As his party faced the voters in November 1994, Clinton could take credit for no effective initiative to reduce the public's economic anxieties. The "forgotten middle class" he had claimed to speak for still felt forgotten. Moreover, Republicans argued that Clinton was no

"new Democrat" but an old one: a high-taxing, big-spending advocate of the guarantor state. Thus the congressional elections produced a stunning reversal: the Republicans won majorities in both the Senate and the House of Representatives. Headlines proclaimed a "landslide," though in fact fewer than one-half of the eligible voters cast a ballot, and the percentage of those who did varied dramatically according to income.

Republicans could claim they now had a mandate to enact their "Contract with America." This charter for a "Republican revolution" aimed in the opposite direction from the New Deal. It reflected the conviction of Republican conservatives, who had not controlled Congress since the 1950s, that the principal cause of American economic underperformance, and the stagnation of incomes that resulted from it, was the excessive generosity of the guarantor state. Since in Republican eyes Americans were already overtaxed (though they were taxed at lower rates than those of any other developed nation), the budget could be balanced only by massive cuts in all of the guarantor state's entitlement programs. Even Medicare and Medicaid, the Great Society programs for guaranteeing health care to the elderly and the poor, now rising in cost by almost 10 percent a year, would have to be cut back.

To ensure that such politically unpopular cuts were actually carried out, the Contract with America called for a constitutional amendment mandating a balanced budget, and for an additional requirement that any proposed tax increase must be approved by three-fifths majorities in Congress—ensuring that no such increase would ever be passed.

Critics of the Contract argued that in fact some of its provisions were designed less to curb the guarantor state than to benefit the wealthy interests whose campaign contributions had financed the elections of the Contract's congressional sponsors. The powers of environmental regulatory agencies, for example, would be drastically limited and the agencies themselves downsized.

The enactment of all of the provisions of the Contract with America would indeed have constituted a "Republican revolution": the most sweeping repudiation of the guarantor state anywhere. President Clinton refused to accept some of the cuts proposed. The Republican leader of the House of Representatives, Speaker Newt Gingrich, responded with a threat of a "train wreck." By refusing to vote the necessary funds to keep the government functioning, Congress would simply shut it down, forcing Clinton to give in. As a result, twice late in 1995 the U.S. government did briefly suspend all but its most essential operations. Republican standing in the polls plunged as public opinion reacted against the recklessness of the near "train wreck" and the perceived heartlessness of some of their proposed budget cuts.

Nevertheless, two items of the Contract with America became law, effectively abolishing commitments of the guarantor state that dated back to the New Deal. Subsidies to American agriculture had begun then to rescue farmers from the Depression by supporting prices and restricting overproduction. By the 1990s, however, the program had become a national scandal. The wealthiest 2 percent of the fast-dwindling numbers of American farmers collected over one-fourth of the benefits, sometimes without planting anything. Thus there was little opposition to the Freedom to Farm Act, which mandated the phasing out of subsidies for some—though not all—crops.

The legislation that was intended to reform the federal contribution to welfare—or, as critics contended, to destroy it—was far more controversial. The law Congress passed abolished a federal commitment that dated back to 1935: the program of Aid to Families with Dependent Children (AFDC). It handed responsibility for providing such assistance to the states, each of which could design its own program, using federal grants less generous than the funds the federal government had formerly provided.

Hardly anyone pointed out that in 1935 the federal government had originally assumed responsibility for AFDC because the states had proved unequal to the task, many competing with their neighbors to provide the least assistance possible.

The Democratic Left demanded that President Clinton veto this repudiation of the New Deal and Great Society traditions. They argued that cutting welfare was prompted not by the need for cost-reduction but by a desire to punish minorities and immigrants. Many sponsors of the law did see it as a moral as well as a fiscal necessity. In their eyes the welfare programs of the guarantor state were not a response to the problem of poverty but its cause, allowing generation after generation to wallow in idleness, drug addiction, and criminal activity instead of learning the values instilled by work. To Speaker Gingrich, indeed, welfare and similar Great Society programs were part of a "thirty year experiment in destroying America. . . . in the name of some kind of bleeding-heart liberalism. . . ."

Despite the protests of some Democrats, President Clinton signed the bill into law, though it provided for none of the education or child care he had once described as essential to "end welfare as we know it." Clinton knew that he could win re-election only if he supported a law that would confirm his announcement to Congress that "the era of big government is over." Though one liberal senator warned that abolishing AFDC was only "the first step in dismantling the social contract that has been in place since at least the 1930s," its abolition was symbolic confirmation of Clinton's commitment to downsizing a federal government many Americans had come to distrust or even to fear.

The U.S. Government Under Siege

Foreign visitors were astonished at the near-unanimity with which Americans put the blame for two decades of economic disappointment on the federal government. In 1996 only one candidate for the presidential nomination, Republican Pat Buchanan, pointed the finger of blame in another direction: at the billionaire executives of multinational corporations. Their passion for downsizing and for a global free-trade system that flooded American markets with goods produced in low-wage countries, he charged, had cost millions of Americans their jobs and threatened those of many more.

Most political forecasters, noting the generally positive economic indexes of the first Clinton term, predicted the president's re-election. Yet polls continued to show a deep public mistrust of government, perhaps reflecting the fact that the "recovery" from the recession of the early 1990s had been of greater benefit to corporate executives and shareholders than to the average family. Though Ross Perot's eccentricities had reduced support for his renewed presidential candidacy, at least a third of American voters continued to hope for the emergence of a third party.

The speeches of both Perot and Buchanan sometimes hinted that the federal government was really run by mysterious forces, of whom politicians like Clinton were only tools. Others took this idea so much farther that they deemed it necessary to kill the government's representatives. In April 1995, they detonated a giant truck bomb outside federal headquarters in Oklahoma City. The explosion, the deadliest "terrorist" attack in American history, killed 169 people. Suspicion as usual was first directed at Arab organizations retaliating against American support of Israel, but investigation soon revealed that the ideas of the bombers were quite home grown.

The bombers were well acquainted with the ideas and with some members of the American "militia" movement. Members of militias were convinced that a criminal federal government directed by foreign influences—Jewish global financiers or the United Nations—was preparing to attack and disarm its own citizens. To counter this threat, militiamen met regularly in uniform to drill for armed resistance to the federal attack.

It was easy to dismiss such ideas as the paranoid delusions of a lunatic fringe. Some thoughtful commentators, however, pointed out the militias merely carried to an extreme the fear many Americans felt toward a federal government they perceived as both ineffective and oppressive. A poll taken one week after the Oklahoma City bombing revealed that four out of ten Americans believed the federal government had gotten so big and powerful as to threaten their freedom.[6]

In times of rapid economic change, people have often blamed scapegoats—persons or groups they hold responsible for misfortunes they can not otherwise explain. Historically, minorities or immigrants or foreign bankers had been cast in this role. The federal government was a more unusual villain but not a surprising one in the circumstances of the 1990s. The hosts of many radio call-in talk shows—the new political medium of the decade—daily denounced the guarantor state and all its works. Some did not shrink from regular insinuations that the president had ordered and then covered up the murder of a subordinate who knew too much. From such an insinuation to a complete distrust of government was only a step. Many Americans really did find themselves living under a "new world order" in the 1990s, though it could be more rationally explained as the consequence of global economic transformation than as the work of intrusive bureaucrats. The expanded functions of the guarantor state, however, brought the citizen into regular contact with its officials, who provided a more satisfactorily human target for resentment than the largely invisible forces of the global marketplace.

Western Europe in the 1990s: The Politics of Economic Anxiety

The impact of technological change and of a truly global economy on Western Europe in the 1990s was similar but not identical to their impact on the United States. In Europe

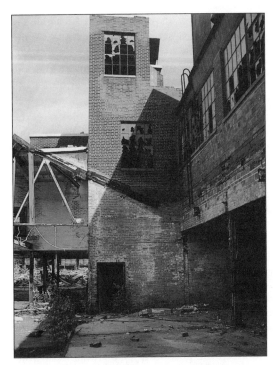

An abandoned factory in East London.
*Desolate scenes like this are to be seen everywhere
in the 1990s, from the American "Rust Belt" to
Poland—mute testimony to the downsizing of the
postindustrial age.* © *World Images News Service*

governments in power in most of Western
Europe prescribed much the same remedies as
their Republican counterparts in the United
States. Government budgets had to be balanced,
and since tax rates were already far higher than
in the United States, balance could be achieved
only by slashing the benefits provided by European guarantor states for nearly half a century.
Noting that German workers' pay and benefits
were the highest in the world, Chancellor
Helmut Kohl's government in mid-1996 decreed substantial cuts. Kohl held firm despite
the powerful trade unions, whose leaders
warned that such changes were only the first
step in a plan to drastically reduce the German
guarantor state.

Against such crackdowns as Kohl's, most of
the European parties of the Left voiced only
muted protest, though the guarantor state had
been their proudest historic creation. The fact
was that the post-1973 phase of global economic transformation had left them with no
persuasive alternative vision to oppose to the
free-trade capitalism of their conservative opponents. Historically, their role had been to insist that some of the fruits of the worldwide
boom of the 1950s and 1960s be redistributed
to working people. Now, when it was alleged
that in the post-1973 period the guarantor state
had become a costly anachronism, they found
little to say in its defense.

In Britain, for example, Tony Blair, who took
over the leadership of the Labour party in 1994,
carefully modeled its new program along the
lines that had won Clinton election in 1992.
Distancing himself like Clinton from his party's
traditional constituencies, the poor and the declining trade unions, Blair made every effort to
reassure British voters that they could trust a
Labour government not to revert to its traditional themes of class warfare. He declared that
if Labour won the May 1997 election, it would
not seek to reverse Margaret Thatcher's transformation of the British economy through privatization and restrictions on unions. Labour

unemployment rates rose much higher, to over
12 percent in France and Germany, for example. In Europe, too, it was no longer only
the blue-collar workers of declining industries
who found themselves jobless. Downsizing hit
the European middle classes in the 1990s with
a speed and extent shocking to societies that
still tended to assume that a successful managerial career would last a lifetime. In Europe,
too, the more of its workers a corporation
fired, the higher its stock rose: bad news for
employees was good news for executives and
shareholders.

Faced with an economic downturn that
some were willing to admit was the worst since
the Depression of the 1930s, the conservative

won a stunning victory, giving Tony Blair the greatest Parliamentary mandate in Labour's history.

With the Left offering, like Blair's Labour and Clinton's Democrats, only a milder dose of conservatives' economic medicine, it was left to the European far Right to give voice to the anguish of millions faced with the uncertainties of global economic change. Unlike most Americans, most Europeans probably still felt in the 1990s that the guarantor state gave good value—ranging from day care centers to minimally costly hospitalization—for the taxes it collected. The European far Right thus found its principal scapegoats not in government but in a group farther down the American list of perceived threats: nonwhite immigrants.

In Germany, bands of youths shouting "Germany for the Germans" stormed the housing the government had provided for such immigrants, some carried to Central Europe from as far away as tropical Africa by the swift currents of a globalizing economy. The youths' ostensible grievance was that immigrants took jobs that should have been reserved for the native-born. But underlying such grievances was the resentment of young people who felt they had been abandoned to economic despair by uncaring politicians of every description.

In France, economic anxiety and resentment had by 1996 made the far Right party, the National Front, a force to contend with. Though President Mitterrand remained in office until his death in 1995, he distanced himself further and further from his Socialist party, which had fallen into disrepute. In the presidential election following Mitterrand's death, its candidate lost to conservative leader Jacques Chirac, who promised to cut taxes, balance the budget, and reduce unemployment. Chirac's popularity soon plummeted, however, as he failed to accomplish any of these goals. Indeed, his government had to abandon its plans to reduce many long-standing entitlements after facing nationwide protest strikes. With both the moderate

Left and the moderate Right thus in disfavor, some observers feared disenchanted voters might turn to the National Front's leader, Jean-Marie Le Pen.

Le Pen's solution to the unemployment problem was simple: Expel France's nearly 4 million immigrants. It was they, he declared, who were responsible not only for high unemployment but for rising rates of drug abuse and violent crime—indeed, for most of the problems of France in the 1990s. In the presidential election of 1995, with nine candidates competing on the first ballot, Le Pen's share was only 6 percentage points behind Chirac's. Analyses showed that Le Pen had captured almost a third of the dwindling blue-collar workers, and many young people, one in four of whom could find no job after completing their education.

Western Economies and Politics in the 1990s

The impact of post-1973 global economic change on the lives of most people has been much more insidious than that of the Depression. Yet the general feeling that something was amiss was widespread enough in the 1990s that politicians had to address it. Certainly the world had not returned to the rapid growth, nearly full employment, and rising living standards of 1945–1973, and some people doubt that it ever will. Perhaps politicians and public alike are approaching the problems of an entirely new world, created by continuing technological change and the emergence of a truly global economy, with the slogans of the past.

In the bitter continuing debate among economists over the causes and remedies for the world's economic anxieties since the early 1970s, there seems to be agreement on only one uncontested fact: the rate of growth in productivity—output per person of private-sector employees—slowed dramatically after 1973. Slower productivity growth meant less growth in income. In the United States, the slowdown in the rate of productivity growth was unprecedented. With the exception of the Depression years, American productivity had grown at an annual rate of 3.4 percent for a century before 1973. The "thirty glorious years" after 1945 marked the climactic era of American productivity growth despite the fact that Western European and Japanese productivity had begun to grow at comparable rates, raising the standards of living in Western Europe and Japan to American levels. After 1973, however, the rate of productivity growth slowed everywhere—to 2.4 percent for the period between 1973 and the early 1990s in the United States, for example. The impact of this slowdown was dramatic: the purchasing power of U.S. wages actually fell by 12 percent, in stark contrast to its regular growth in the 1950s.

Among the many explanations offered for slowed U.S. productivity growth, some are more persuasive than others. The ballooning of the federal deficit, for example, diverting funds from wage raises and investment to pay off the government's debt, is the reason, according to economic conservatives. This argument is weakened, however, by the fact that the rate of productivity growth had already slowed long before the threefold explosion of federal debt during the Reagan years.

Though the importance of such factors is debated, there has been general agreement on the significance of heightened global competition, as all of the developed nations and many of the developing nations struggled to increase their share of the marketplace. The first postwar American trade deficit with the rest of the world, in 1971, amounted to $1.5 billion. By 1994 it had grown exponentially, to $166 billion. What this meant for the lives of everyday Americans was that by the mid-1980s, for example, almost one-third of their automobiles were foreign made.

Some economic historians maintain, however, that the enlarged dimensions of global competition are not enough to explain the slowing of productivity growth around the world, and especially in the United States, after 1973. According to their analysis, capitalism's very success in stimulating greater consumption has undermined the system of production that had long assured it unprecedented profitability. Henry Ford's assembly line had realized "economies of scale": it cost less to manufacture a huge volume of identical units like the Model T. But as consumers became less willing to accept the standardized products of the assembly line, producers' markets became "fragmented." To sell to these more choosy and less predictable customers required a different system of management and the use of new technologies, first perfected by the Japanese and adopted belatedly and often reluctantly by the Americans. The new management style emphasized a flexible system of "lean production" in smaller "batches" of more simply assembled units, using reduced inventories of components renewed "just in time" to keep from running out of them. This system used a minimum of workers, rapidly and flexibly trained in the use of new technologies like robotics, rather than the highly paid specialists of the old-style assembly line. The spread of this new system was reflected in the evolution of the American automobile market. In the mid-1950s, only 30 models, 25 manufactured in the United States and the rest in Europe, were available to American buyers. Six of these models, made by General Motors, Ford, and Chrysler, accounted for 80 percent of the sales. By the late 1980s, by contrast, the choosier consumer could pick among 140 models, including 58 made in Japan.

The post-1973 world, according to this interpretation, posed a similar challenge, of marketing for more selective and less predictable customers amid greater competition, to every industry. Faced with such markets, managers became increasingly hesitant. How much dared they invest in new plant, for example, when increased competition made its profitability so uncertain? How could they meet the costs of marketing, which had risen from a quarter to a half of the wholesale price of every item sold? The wrong managerial decision would mean failure, quickly reflected in reduced corporate earnings. In the United States such failure would be immediately punished on Wall Street. Better then for managers to keep profits up, even if that meant reduced investment in new machinery.

Thus as American capital investment declined after 1973, the rate of productivity growth, as we have seen, also slowed, eventually retarding the progress of the whole economy. Other expedients to which American industrial management resorted to keep profits up had the same effect. Downsizing was one of these. Employers also broke strikes by replacing permanent, unionized employees with lower-paid, nonunion temporary workers: Manpower, Inc., the temporary service, is now the U.S. employer with the largest payroll, dwarfing the payrolls of once-giant industries like automaking and steel. As we have seen, the combined effect of such tactics was to reduce union membership to levels not seen since before the New Deal. The year 1995 saw fewer American strikes than in any year since 1945. In Europe unions were too well established to be as directly confronted, but other managerial cost-cutting measures by the 1990s showed that European managers shared the concerns of their American counterparts.

In the decades before 1973, the skilled and high-paying jobs lost by the adoption of new management methods and technologies had been more than compensated for by the creation of new skilled and high-paying jobs: hence the continuing high rate of productivity growth. Since 1973, however, new methods like "lean production," have not sufficed to restore that high rate, though they have eliminated many jobs. In fact, since the 1970s the rate of productivity growth has fallen by half, on average, among the world's sixteen wealthiest na-

tions, compared to the rate prevailing from 1945 to 1973. Clearly, reductions in the number of employees have not compensated for the limitations on productivity growth imposed by a fragmented, uncertain, and hugely competitive global marketplace.

If the rest of the Western world's rates of productivity growth are tending to slow down to American levels, it remains to be seen whether the costs of this slowdown will be shared as unequally elsewhere as in the United States. Here, from the 1970s to the 1990s, there has been what one economic observer has called "a huge transfer of wealth from lower-skilled, middle class American workers to the owners of capital assets and a new technological aristocracy with a large element of compensation tied to stock values."[7] Whereas from 1950 to 1973 the average income of even the poorest 20 percent of American families doubled, since 1974 real wages have risen less than 10 percent. The share of the national wealth held by the richest 1 percent of American families rose from 27 percent in 1976 to 42 percent in 1992. Meanwhile, the American worker is paid, on average, less than workers in any other Western industrial country. In an international comparison of social equality—based on the ratio of the portion of national income received by the richest 10 percent of the population to the portion received by the poorest 10 percent—the United States' income distribution is far less egalitarian than Germany's, partly because the German guarantor state has regularly redistributed wealth.[8]

Despite the gravity of the social and economic issues they raise, discussion of subjects like the differences among nations in patterns of income distribution and their impact on rates of productivity growth are found in the 1990s mainly in the newspapers and journals read by the world's elites. Neither in the United States nor in Western Europe do the economic difficulties of the world since the 1970s receive thoughtful discussion in the popular media, let alone in the speeches of most politicians. The subordination of political discussion to television advertising, a practice that has now spread from the United States to Europe, partly explains this lack of serious debate. On television, difficult economic concepts like "the rate of productivity growth" are not easily reduced to the thirty-second sound bites that are said to be all that viewers can comprehend. Thus the emerging world system of the 1990s, though it affected the lives of everyone everywhere, was usually reduced in political discourse to a few clichés like "the global marketplace." More typically, incumbent politicians took credit, correctly or not, for whatever short-term positive economic developments—a month's decline in unemployment totals, for example—occurred and then blamed short-term negative developments on their opponents. Though polls revealed that voters were more concerned about economic issues than about anything else, discussion of them, especially in the United States, was often subordinated to argument over moral issues: which political party was responsible for a rise in teenage pregnancies or drug abuse, for example.

There may, however, be a more profound explanation for the absence of much serious discussion of the post-1970s global economy than the superficiality of political speechmaking. The questions of why the growth of productivity has slowed in the Western world since the 1970s and how, if at all, it can be reinvigorated may not be the subject of widespread debate because no one is certain, despite the eagerness of some to blame the guarantor state, of the answers. Faced with so uncertain a future, Europeans and Americans have responded in different ways that reflect their historical cultures. Europeans, whose long history has been one of repeated tragedies, seem resigned to accepting the inability of a quarter of their young people to find jobs as just one more of history's unavoidable calamities. Americans, who incline to perceive their history as a saga of continuous

success, tend to see the post-1973 chapter of their economic history as a temporary setback soon to be overcome by American ingenuity. A return to the prosperity of the 1950s and 1960s, many thought, could be guaranteed by another burst of American technological inventiveness, or by the encouragement of a higher net rate of saving, or by a new commitment to education, or by an energetic expansion of American sales in the world's new markets.

A few thoughtful observers wondered, however, whether in the changed circumstances of the 1990s the effectiveness of any of these solutions was certain. In a world where an article in a scientific journal can be transmitted around the world in seconds, it is hard to see how a single nation could long monopolize a technological breakthrough. Even if in the 1990s Americans were somehow to double their savings rate of the 1980s and thus revert to the level of the 1960s, it was not clear where the resulting investments should be directed in an economy that already had considerable unused capacity. Nor was it obvious that the kind of economy emerging at the end of the century would have an inordinate need for the more highly trained work force championed by some of Clinton's advisers. The American economy in the 1970s had not found jobs commensurate with their training for the baby-boom generation. As for expanding global markets for American products, most such markets were to be found in nations that were eagerly turning out their own versions of the products the United States (and Europe) had to offer.

Thus there was enough uncertainty about all the proposed remedies for slowed growth that few politicians were prepared to risk their careers by an unequivocal commitment to any of them. Moreover, the collapse of the Left everywhere had left few advocates for any remedy that would require expanding the guarantor state. In the political climate of the 1990s, few voices were to be heard proclaiming the responsibility of government to undertake tasks that private corporations would judge too risky or burdensome, like retraining the victims of downsizing or funding basic research. Any such suggestion was immediately greeted with the retort that such programs would raise everybody's taxes.

During earlier decades of the twentieth century, when people especially in the United States had feared the power of large corporations rather than the government, it had been politically acceptable as well as fiscally practical to collect more in taxes from those who had more money. As late as the 1950s, corporations had paid one-quarter of U.S. income taxes. In the 1990s, few Americans seemed to mind that corporations now paid less than 10 percent of income taxes, or that almost half of the corporations worth over $250 million doing business in the United States paid income taxes under $100,000 or even none at all.

Since the old leftist slogan "Soak the rich" was no longer to be heard even from critics of corporate leadership, it seemed unlikely at the end of the century that any government would attempt to spend its way to renewed growth at the pace of the 1950s and 1960s. Thus the global slowdown since 1973, if it did not abate of itself, would likely be addressed, if at all, by the same conservative tactic with which governments had addressed the Depression: an internationally competitive process of budget cutting that would leave more and more people at the mercy of market forces.

Such a prospect led some people to wonder whether twenty-first-century historians might eventually come to see the twentieth century in a very different light. In the 1950s and 1960s, many people had seen the guarantor state as the logical culmination to a story of continuous human progress since the American and French revolutions. But from the perspective of the year 2000, it did not appear quite as inevitable. After all, what its European critics called "wild capitalism" had flourished for a century from the Industrial Revolution to the

beginnings of the guarantor state in Bismarck's Germany. To the extent that nations shrank the guarantor state at the end of the twentieth century, the world would return to the unfettered domination by the "natural" laws of the marketplace that had subordinated the employee to the employer, and the poor to the rich, from the middle of the eighteenth century through most of the nineteenth. In such a perspective, the era of the generous guarantor state would turn out to be not the climactic stage of the human experience but a mere interlude, largely coinciding with and sustained by the global boom of the 1950s and 1960s.

Moreover, demography is now working against the guarantor state. Throughout Europe and Japan, even more than in the United States, the new century will see smaller and smaller generations of active workers paying the taxes to underwrite the benefits paid to larger and larger numbers of elderly pensioners who had once been baby boomers. Thus intergenerational tensions will likely be added to the class and racial tensions that challenge the spirit of national community on which a guarantor state must depend.

This may be too dire a forecast. In Western Europe, with its long tradition of powerful governments and its relatively recent memories of postwar economic collapse, the guarantor state is likely to be trimmed rather than abolished. And even in the United States, with its historic mistrust of government, the stalling of the Republican revolution suggests that many Americans were having second thoughts about the drastic impact of the amputations the revolutionaries were proposing.

Conclusion: Clinton and the "Third Way"

Indeed, the campaigns of the major parties for the last American presidential election of the century, in November 2000, which pitted

George W. Bush, son of the former Republican president, against Al Gore, Clinton's vice president, both seemed to point to a kind of political middle way. Neither championed the uncompromising anti-guarantor state rhetoric of Gingrich's erstwhile "Republican revolution" or the return to the guarantor state of Roosevelt and Johnson still sought by many congressional Democratic liberals.

Commentators offered several explanations for this lowering of the tone of political argument. Most importantly, from the mid-1990s onward, during Clinton's second term, many of the key performance indicators of the American economy had risen to levels not seen since before the general global downturn of the mid-1970s. Part of the reason for this economic boom could be found in the impact of continuing technological transformation, notably with the growth of the information industry. In addition, many political observers gave some credit to Clinton's skillful management of change according to a program he described as a "third way." This way of approaching the social and political consequences of economic change, was successful enough to inspire widespread imitation among the left and left-center governments that ruled most of Europe in the second half of the 1990s.

In May 2000, the U.S. Labor Department reported that the nation's unemployment rate had dropped below 4 percent for the first time in a generation. Later that year, the Census Bureau reported that American median household income had topped $40,000 for the first time in history and that the percentage of households living in poverty (defined as an income of $17,029 for a family of four) had fallen to the lowest point (11.8 percent) in over two decades. Moreover, the median income was the highest it had even been for all social groups, though it continued to vary enormously from group to group ($27,910 for African-American households, compared to $44,366 for non-Hispanic white families).

In his 1998 State of the Union speech to Congress, President Clinton had been able to proclaim that the United States was enjoying the lowest unemployment rate since 1974, the lowest inflation since 1968, the lowest number of recipients on the welfare rolls since 1971, and the smallest number of federal government employees since 1963. Where once the dollar figure of the federal government's budget deficit had included eleven zeroes, he reported, now there was "only one": the federal budget was in balance, the deficit was zero.

Clearly, the American economy at the end of the century was in a condition far superior to the one Clinton had found after his election in 1992. How much of the credit for the dramatic improvement could his administration claim, and how much had it depended on developments beyond the control of any government?

Though economists continue vigorously to debate the answer, one incontestable fact is that the rate of American productivity growth, that critical factor of economic success to which we have already referred, for the years 1996–2000, more than doubled from the rate of the years 1991–1995. Much of that increased productivity—40 percent or more—could be traced to the explosive growth of the information industry. It is all around us now in a way that could scarcely have been imagined ten or even five years ago. At the beginning of the new millenium, 59 percent of Americans have home computers, 29 percent typically log on to the Internet every day, and as many as 12 percent even have personalized web pages for their investment portfolios. So unlimited does the industry's potential seem that some young people have decided that taking a managerial job at age 20, as is possible with information's innumerable new companies, is a better guarantee of adult success that taking time for a college education. A few historians have even begun to depict the expansion of the information industry at the end of the twentieth century as constituting the foundation of a "new economy" just as revolutionary as the new economy sparked at the end of the nineteenth century by an unprecedented spate of technological innovation.

Whatever the accuracy of this comparison, there is one important difference to be noted between the 1990s and the 1890s: this time the United States enjoys a commanding lead in the race to a "new economy." Europe lags behind to an extent that fills some European analysts with alarm. There are seven times more computers linked to the Internet in the United States than there are in the European Union. In 1999–2000, the number of personal computers in the United States grew by 25 percent, compared to a growth of 4 percent in Japan and only between 2 and 3 percent in Germany and France.

Reasons for the American lead include expenditures twice as large, as a percentage of GNP, as Europe's for research and development; the availability of five times more risk capital; and the hospitality of the American information industry for foreign-born talent, who are often trained as computer scientists and engineers in the classrooms of American universities that American students seem disinclined to fill. (A quarter of the employees of the biggest information company of all, Microsoft, were not born in the United States.) By one estimate, Europe would have to increase its high-tech investment by 40 percent to have even a change of catching up with the Americans.

The inability to make such investment probably goes far toward explaining why Europe's unemployment rates remain higher, and its recovery from the recession of the early 1990s shakier, than the American recovery. The Clinton administration cannot claim all the credit for the way in which the products of "Silicon Valley," the fabled Californian center of the information industry, have transformed the American economy. Yet Clinton can claim, not entirely without merit, that his administration's policies were shaped to facilitate the transition of the American economy "from the Industrial

Age to the Information Age." These policies created a political and social environment propitious for change, a "third way" that rejected the ideas both of "those who say government is the enemy"—Reagan and Gingrich Republicans—and of "those who say government is the answer" (Democratic liberals, who never entirely trusted Clinton).

During his eight years in office, Clinton on different occasions outraged both groups and cut deals with both of them. His unwillingness to veto the harsh welfare reform bill infuriated liberals. But by taking over the Republican demand for a balanced budget and negotiating toughly with them over what to cut, he not only helped relieve the American economy of its long-standing burden of public debt but also insisted on the preservation of benefits for the working poor, like the "earned-income tax credit" that benefited some 15 million families making under $27,000 annually. His administration did not invent the Internet, but it did foster its explosive expansion after 1995 by insisting that sales over the Web not be burdened by sales taxes and that access to it should be no more costly than a local phone call.

Clinton effectively stymied the Republicans' revolution and managed to weaken them by making them look like the people responsible for the occasional paralysis of government. This tactic only deepened the visceral hatred many Republicans had for him as an upstart and a trickster. Their hatred climaxed in the attempt in 1998 when House Republicans attempted to impeach him, not for the corrupt business deals with which they originally charged him, but rather for his alleged perjury in court testimony about his sexual involvement with a young White House aide, Monica Lewinsky. These proceedings dragged on for six months with media attention focused on them to the virtual exclusion of most of the world's real problems even though the outcome was a foregone conclusion: the American Constitution requires a two-thirds majority of the Senate to convict and not a single Democratic senator voted to do so. Thus he served out his full term but left office in 2001 bearing the stigma of having endured only the second presidential impeachment in the more than two hundred years of the American republic.

Future historians, however, are likely to dwell less on the Lewinsky affair and more on the fact that Clinton's "third way" made him the first two-term Democratic president since the 1960s and enabled him to defend an admittedly diminished guarantor state against the determined onslaught of the "Republican revolution" of the mid-1990s. This feat won him the flattery of widespread imitation of his policies, not only by Britain's Labour Prime Minister Tony Blair but by most of the dozen other Left-Center governments of Western Europe in the year 2000, including those of Germany, France, and Italy.

It will be well into the twenty-first century, however, before we shall know whether Clinton's attempt to reconcile the push for "globalization" by the free play of market forces with the safeguards of the guarantor state, imitated by so many others, will prove an enduring and successful model.

Notes

1. Figures taken from David Steigerwald, *The Sixties and the End of Modern America* (New York, St. Martin's, 1995), p. 187.

2. J. Robert Wegs, *Europe Since 1945: A Concise History,* 2d ed. (New York: St. Martin's Press, 1984), p. 168.

3. Richard J. Barnet, *The Alliance: America-Europe-Japan, Makers of the Postwar World* (New York: Simon and Schuster, 1983), p. 274.

4. John Kenneth Galbraith, *The Culture of Contentment* (Boston: Houghton Mifflin, 1992).

5. Quoted in Robert Kuttner, ed., *Ticking Time Bombs: Essays from The American Prospect* (New York: New Press, 1996), p. 31.

6. CNN/USA Today/Gallup Poll, reported in the *Chicago Tribune,* April 26, 1995.

7. Felix Rohatyn, quoted in Simon Head, "The New, Ruthless Economy," *New York Review of Books,* February 29, 1996.

8. *New York Times,* October 27, 1995, and July 12, 1996; United Stations Development Programme, *Human Development Report, 1995, 1996* (New York: Oxford University Press, 1995, 1996).

Suggestions for Further Reading and Viewing

Books

Ardagh, John. *France Today* (1988).

Barnet, Richard J. *The Alliance: America-Europe-Japan, Makers of the Postwar World* (1983).

Bolter, J. David. *Turing's Man: Western Culture in the Computer Age* (1984).

Edsall, Thomas B. *The New Politics of Inequality* (1984).

Faludi, Susan. *Backlash: The Undeclared War Against Women* (1991).

Garreau, Joel. *The Nine Nations of North America* (1981).

Gilbert, James. *Another Chance: Postwar America 1945–1968* (1981).

Hacker, Andrew. *Two Nations: Black and White, Separate, Hostile, Unequal* (1992).

Head, Simon. "The New, Ruthless Economy." *New York Review of Books,* February 29, 1996.

Kavanagh, Dennis. *Thatcherism and British Politics: The End of Consensus?* 2d ed. (1990).

Lasch, Christopher. *The Culture of Narcissism: American Life in an Age of Diminishing Expectations* (1979).

Lukacs, John. *Outgrowing Democracy: A History of the United States in the Twentieth Century* (1986).

Madrick, Jeffrey. *The End of Affluence: The Causes and Consequences of America's Economic Dilemma* (1995).

Priaulx, Allan, and Stanford J. Ungar. *The Almost Revolution: France 1968* (1969).

Ranney, Austin. *Channels of Power: The Impact of Television on American Politics* (1983).

Singer, Daniel. *Is Socialism Doomed? The Meaning of Mitterrand* (1988).

Steigenwald, David. *The Sixties and the End of Modern America* (1995).

Wegs, J. Robert. *Europe Since 1945: A Concise History.* 2d ed. (1984).

Wills, Gary. "The New Revolutionaries." *New York Review of Books,* August 10, 1995.

Woloch, Nancy. *Women and the American Experience* (1984).

Films

American Dream (1990). An Oscar-winning documentary on the collapse of a strike in 1986.

Berkeley in the 1960s (1990). A documentary on the campus struggles of the Vietnam era.

CHAPTER 13

The Soviet Union, Eastern Europe, and the Collapse of Communism

THE COLLAPSE OF COMMUNISM IN EASTERN EUROPE AND THE SOVIET UNION described in the later pages of this chapter stunned the world. It had been foreseen by relatively few of the "Kremlinologists," the pundits who explained these regions to the rest of the world, and thus seemed as unpredictable as it was sudden. Yet closer attention to the ideas of those Russians who welcomed the wave of change launched by Mikhail Gorbachev in the late 1980s that swept communism away might have revealed that many thoughtful Russians, including members of the party establishment, had seen the urgent need for change as clearly as Gorbachev had.

Indeed, some of Gorbachev's most fervent supporters admitted in retrospect that Nikita Khrushchev, the Soviet leader from the mid-1950s to the mid-1960s, had begun opening the way to change, though they had not recognized this while he was still in power. Len Karpinsky, one such Gorbachev supporter, told a western interviewer that he and a friend had drunk cognac together "to celebrate Khrushchev's removal [in 1964]. We thought his impulsive half-baked decisions had become a brake on the process of reform, even a threat to that process. . . . We believed that Khrushchev had become an obstacle to the program he had initiated himself at the Twentieth Congress [of the Soviet Communist Party in 1956.] We thought he could no longer lead the process of de-Stalinization and democratization. . . . Later we realized how wrong we had been."

Such was the change of heart among Karpinksy and his friends that they decided to call Khrushchev on his seventy-fifth birthday in 1969 "when he was living in a kind of forced isolation at his country dacha." When Khrushchev came to the phone, Karpinsky remembered, he told him "speaking for our generation, I wanted him to know that we were the political children of the Twentieth Congress and of his program. That his achievements were irreversible, and that we would fight to prevent anyone from turning back the clock. . . . We wanted him to know that his life had not been in vain. . . . Khrushchev was deeply touched. He answered me very emotionally 'I have always believed this and I am very pleased that you and your relatively young generation understand the essence of the Twentieth Congress and the policies I initiated. I am so happy to hear from you in my twilight years." ' Khrushchev was the more moved, Karpinsky told his western interviewer, because "no Soviet officials called to congratulate him on his birthday, though the Queen of England . . . did."[1]

Eastern Europe and the West

Readers of our account in Chapter 11 of the era of bipolar confrontation might expect that the history of the Soviet bloc since the death of Stalin, to which we turn in this chapter, would bear little resemblance to the history of the Western world we examined in the last chapter. What could the history of the "evil empire" (as President Reagan once called it) possibly have in common with that of the democracies of Western Europe and North America? Were not the basic differences of these two kinds of society enough to explain their almost constant confrontation?

Of course there were fundamental differences in political institutions, social values, and economic systems between the two blocs. Stalin's quarter-century of dictatorship, from the late 1920s to his death in 1953, imposed on the USSR a system whose every feature flouted the values that most Americans and Western Europeans believed. Moreover, he ruthlessly replicated that system in the Eastern European countries the Soviets overran in the war against Hitler: the German Democratic Republic, Poland, Hungary, Czechoslovakia, Romania, and

Bulgaria. After Stalin, the central theme of the history of both the USSR and these satellites was the struggle of the post-Stalin Communist leadership to modify his system in order to make it more economically effective without relinquishing political control. At the end of the 1980s, Soviet Communist Party General Secretary Mikhail Gorbachev and his colleagues, the leaders of the Eastern European "People's Democracies," were still wrestling with this Stalinist legacy. Their failure to overcome it helps explain the collapse of all of their regimes by the early 1990s.

If we ask *why* Gorbachev and the Eastern Europeans felt compelled to try to reshape the Stalinist model of economics and politics, we discover that they were reacting to many of the same twentieth-century global trends—world interdependency, mass political mobilization, the dramatically accelerated and economically disruptive pace of technological change—that we have just seen at work in the West. Russian history before and under Stalin already reflected the impact of these global trends. The tsar's empire on the eve of World War I had curiously combined innovation and tradition. It was already the world's fifth-ranking industrial power, its city-dwelling intellectuals and revolutionaries aspiring to the most radical change. Yet in its rural villages, life still proceeded largely in accordance with the rhythms of peasant societies elsewhere in the world. Stalin's collectivization of agriculture, as we saw in Chapter 4, forever smashed that tradition-bound rural society. When collectivization was accomplished, at a cost of millions of lives lost to deportation and famine, the orientation of Soviet society toward rapid change could no longer be doubted. Indeed, Stalin's USSR joyfully celebrated the triumph of human technology over nature: the image of a giant dam harnessing previously untamed waters to generate electricity was one of its favorite symbols.

Stalin's government made tremendous efforts to mobilize every Soviet citizen in the struggle for economic modernization. Not that it sought each citizen's free-willed assent; dissenters, in fact, faced exile to concentration camps or execution. Yet the contribution of every individual to the USSR's collective effort was essential to demonstrate to the world a new model of society. Nothing less could realize Stalin's goal of "socialism in one country," a society built on the principle of absolute economic equality and ultimately on true communism, the abolition of private property. This society was to be developed in isolation from the contaminating influences of the hostile capitalist world. Belief in socialism and Soviet patriotism thus became synonymous, a supreme Stalinist value to replace the discredited religious values of earlier centuries.

In its attempt to ignore global interdependency, Stalinism ran counter to one of the dominant realities of the twentieth century, though in its obsession with mass mobilization and with technological development it seemed at first to be very much in step with the times. As these trends continued after 1953, however, they revealed Stalin's legacy as less and less appropriate for resolving the problems of a modern and fully developed society like the USSR.

Growing global interdependency showed the Stalinist policy of enforced isolation of the Soviet bloc to be economically damaging, once the transfer of technology from one country to another became so critical to a nation's prosperity. Decades of continuous manipulative mass mobilization, affording every citizen a vote but no choice of candidates, produced corrosive cynicism and apathy. Growing technological sophistication undermined government control of ideas: by the 1980s anyone in the USSR could start an underground opposition newspaper by getting hold of a second-hand word processor and printer, increasingly common tools of the fully developed society to which most Soviets and Eastern Europeans—and their leaders—aspired. At the same time, such disasters as the accident at the Soviet nuclear reactor at Chernobyl in April 1986, which spread radioactive fallout halfway around the world, reminded the Marxist Soviets, like their Western adversaries, of the potential dangers that lurk in humankind's continuing technological triumphs. Marxism's quarrel had never been with economic development—only with the distribution of its benefits. But in the 1980s an increasingly vocal movement of "Red Greens" appeared, ready to question whether the economic benefits expected from such vast engineering projects as damming the Leningrad estuary truly outweighed the potential environmental damage.

Thus in Eastern as in Western industrial societies, a growing unease about the global future led many people to hope for more intelligent and innovative political leadership. For such people in Eastern Europe and the USSR, the stale official rhetoric of the Stalinist past seemed irrelevant. As in the West, conservatives clung all the more tenaciously to the political and economic principles of the past as they seemed more threatened by the proponents of change. Yet as the need for change became ever more acute, the Communist party's Politburo at last faced up to it in March 1985, naming Mikhail Gorbachev as the party's general secretary—the post Stalin had held. Gorbachev soon made clear that to achieve his goal of a humane and democratic though still socialist USSR, he was as determined to reject Stalin's legacy in domestic policy as he was willing, as we saw in Chapter 11, to reverse Stalin's foreign policy of implacable suspicion of the Western democracies.

When Gorbachev looked to the immediate Soviet past for inspiration, he found few encouraging precedents. The first attempt to dismantle the Stalinist system, by Stalin's successor Nikita Khrushchev, ended in failure with his dismissal in 1964. By loosening the Soviet hold on the satellites, however, Khrushchev allowed their leaders, each in his own way, to begin reshaping his country's economic and even political system. Despite the spread of economic unorthodoxy among the satellites, in the USSR itself the years of Leonid Brezhnev's leadership, from the 1960s until his death in 1982, were an era of lost opportunities, stagnation, corruption, and disillusionment. Hardly anyone believed in Stalinist values anymore, but bureaucratic inertia kept much of the system in place while the Soviet economy drifted into ever-greater difficulties from the 1970s onward.

Gorbachev's attempts at economic and political reforms only accelerated the collapse of the Soviet Union—an event so stupendous that some historians think it marks the end of the twentieth century as 1914 marked its beginning. In the last two sections of this chapter, we shall see how the former satellites have fared since the collapse of communism, and how, after the dissolution of the Soviet Union, its largest remnant, the Russian Republic, has struggled with political deadlock, economic chaos, social disintegration, and psychic demoralization.

Stalin's Legacy

Western visitors to the countries of the former Soviet Union are sometimes surprised by the nostalgia for the Stalinist years they encounter among some of their hosts. The explanation is surely pride in and identification with the Soviet achievement of modernization under Stalin. The USSR tripled its industrial work force between 1928 and 1940, on its way to becoming not the world's fifth industrial power but ultimately the second. Under the last of the tsars, only one Russian in four could read and write. By the beginning of World War II, four out of five were literate.

The governmental system that imposed such dramatic economic and cultural changes, however, was one that nobody who had personally experienced it would want to re-create. Politically, Stalinism meant the personal dictatorship of one man who was held up as a model for virtual worship—a "cult of personality"—by a whole society. Pictures of the all-powerful, all-knowing Stalin loomed everywhere, the inspiration for the omnipresent portraits of "Big Brother" in George Orwell's novel *1984*. Economically, Stalinism meant the "command economy," in which central planners commanded from the managers of the government-owned factories ever-increasing quotas of heavy industrial goods produced with quantity, not quality, as the criterion of success. Socially, though the goal of the USSR at some unspecified future time was a society not divided into classes of differing wealth and privileges, Stalinism in practice meant a hierarchical society in which Communist party members enjoyed greater prestige and privileges than ordinary citizens, and the people holding the top 3 percent of the jobs in the party, the *nomenklatura*, had the greatest prestige and privileges of all. Under Stalin, however, even these top party members lived in an atmosphere of constant fear for their lives, for culturally, Stalinism meant "thought control"—the prevention of disloyal thinking—by the imposition of mass terror. There was no one who did not need to fear the midnight knock of the secret police at the door, the prelude to arbitrary condemnation to death or years in a concentration camp. Even the most conservative estimates conclude that some half-million party members were executed in Stalin's Great Terror of 1934–1939, which also incarcerated nearly 4 million people under atrocious conditions in the camps.

Moreover, the Stalinist system strove to have Soviet citizens internalize the norms of obedience by sanctifying as heroes people who carried that obedience to extremes other societies might find inconceivable. For example, Stalin's propagandists glorified Pavlik Morozov, whose name was to be found in textbooks, on schools and summer camps, and even on a Moscow street. Son of a peasant but a loyal Young Pioneer (member of the Communist youth movement), thirteen-year-old Pavlik in 1932 denounced his father to the authorities for hiding part of his grain harvest from the government collectors. When his father's hoarding accomplices vengefully murdered Pavlik, he became a martyr to Stalinist morality, which put loyalty to the state higher than fidelity to one's own family. In Stalinist eyes, such a code was justified by the belief that the only hope for the future of humankind lay in the survival of the USSR, the homeland of revolution, in a uniformly hostile world. Thus any act that endangered Soviet survival, even the hoarding of grain, was a crime against the future of humanity.

As we saw in Chapter 4, historians still debate whether this terrifying system was the logical outgrowth of the kind of revolution Lenin and the Bolsheviks had made in 1917. The least that can be said is that Stalin could not have created this system without eliminating the opposition, both Left and Right, of most of his old Bolshevik colleagues. The left opposition was led by Leon Trotsky, the brilliant com-

mander-in-chief of the Red Army during the civil wars that followed the revolution. Trotsky feared that if revolutionary momentum was lost, the movement would degenerate into bureaucratic dictatorship, as revolutions historically have often done. To keep up the momentum, he favored fomenting further revolution abroad and forcing through rapid industrialization at home by "squeezing" surplus capital from the peasants. A contrary view was held by the right opposition, led by Nikolai Bukharin. He had been the designer of the New Economic Policy (NEP) of 1921, which had returned small business and agriculture to private entrepreneurs. Bukharin believed the revolution's only hope lay in winning over Russia's rural majority. He rejected the gospel of centralized economic planning, fearing that it would stifle the revolution under a cumbersome and oppressive planning apparatus.

Both men paid with their lives for their disagreement with Stalin, who first aligned himself with the Right to crush the Left, then turned on the Right. Trotsky was expelled from the USSR in 1929 and murdered, on Stalin's orders, in exile in 1940. In one of the most dramatic of the "show trials" of the Great Terror, Bukharin was framed as a Nazi spy and executed in 1938. His name, like Trotsky's, disappeared from the official histories of the revolution. Only after a half-century, under Gorbachev, was Bukharin posthumously exonerated. Only then did Gorbachev allow the truth about the Stalinist chapter of communist history to be publicly told.

Khrushchev and the Limits of Reform, 1953–1964

As long as Stalin was alive, even his closest associates of the Politburo—the dozen or so men delegated by the Central Committee of the Communist party of the USSR to direct the party and through it the nation—were not safe from the fates of Trotsky and Bukharin. Not surprisingly, when he died, they all agreed that no individual should ever again concentrate so much power in his own hands. Many of them were convinced that Stalin had made disastrous mistakes: in neglecting rural Russia, for example, or in failing to channel some of the gains of the growing Soviet economy into improving the standard of living of ordinary citizens, or in entrusting Soviet science to those whose chief qualification was ideological conformity. But their motive in vowing to prevent a future dictatorship was simpler than criticism of Stalin's policies. They wanted to end the terror that had hung over their own heads and over the heads of ordinary citizens. After 1953 the USSR always had a "collective leadership," a system of shared responsibility at the top, even when one individual such as Khrushchev or Gorbachev got most of the Western headlines.

On Stalin's death the supreme authority was officially vested in three top Politburo members, including Lavrenty P. Beria, chief of the secret police. Nikita S. Khrushchev (1894–1971), who assumed one of Stalin's old posts as general secretary of the Communist party, was not a member of this trio. Yet it was he who emerged within a few years as the dominant, though not dictatorial, leader of the USSR. The first to fall in the struggle for power was Beria, the dreaded living reminder of Stalinist terror. Arrested on behalf of his colleagues by the army, he met the usual fate of Soviet political losers: execution. Beria's fall was followed by a general amnesty for political prisoners. Never again would the secret police be quite as powerful, though their prestige would rise again when Brezhnev consolidated his power after Khrushchev's fall. From 1953 to 1957 Khrushchev acquired more and more power until his rivals tried to fire him. He turned the tables on his opponents and won a crucial vote of confidence. He then proceeded to drive them from office. Unlike Stalin, whose dual posts as first secretary of the Communist party and prime

minister he now assumed, Khrushchev left his fallen enemies their lives.

Thus arrived at the summit of the Soviet hierarchy a former coal miner, still illiterate when he joined the party as a young man in 1918. Coarse, bullying, impetuous, he was nonetheless a true believer in the goals of Lenin's revolution, to which he owed everything. Though he had climbed the ranks by unquestioning devotion to the party line under Stalin, he had already startled the world in 1956 by his speech to the Twentieth Soviet Party Congress denouncing the crimes and errors of his former master. Now he hoped to rekindle faith in the goals of the revolution after the years of Stalinist darkness. He knew that this would require basic changes in Soviet direction.

In domestic as in foreign policy, Khrushchev lashed out with initiatives of all sorts. Infuriated by the poor yields of Soviet agriculture, he frankly admitted that after over a generation of collective farming the USSR stabled fewer cattle than it had in 1917. To remedy such deficiencies he championed an ambitious program to plant new strains of hybrid corn on previously uncultivated land. To improve industrial productivity, and to scatter potential centers of bureaucratic resistance to his innovations, he launched the first of many Soviet attempts to decentralize economic decision making. A man of humble origins, Khrushchev was scandalized by the emergence under a supposedly socialist government of a new privileged class: fewer than half of Moscow's university students, he discovered, came from peasant or worker families. To restore equality of opportunity, his educational reforms abolished college entrance examinations and gave priority in admissions to young people applying from factories. He also insisted that the children of white-collar families, including party members, who made up the majority of students, should have experience on the factory floor.

Khrushchev seemed of mixed mind on the issue of allowing the Soviet people greater freedom of ideas. He permitted the publication of Alexandr Solzhenitsyn's *One Day in the Life of Ivan Denisovich,* a searing depiction of life in a concentration camp. He also authorized the first exhibition of modern art the USSR had seen since Stalin imposed the style of Socialist Realism. On the other hand, his regime closed half of the USSR's remaining churches, in line with the old Marxist idea that religion for the masses was like an addictive drug.

In 1961 the party's new program confidently predicted that the USSR would make the transition to "full Communism" and equal abundance for all by 1980. By that year, Khrushchev was fond of boasting, the USSR's gross national product would surpass that of the United States. All of his boasting was in vain, however, for most of his domestic schemes went awry. After a bad harvest in 1963, he had to face the embarrassment of buying grain abroad to feed his people. Industrial decentralization seemed to produce only confusion. Educators and parents alike sabotaged his university reforms. His limited concessions to intellectual freedom frightened conservatives but failed to satisfy progressives. Meanwhile, Khrushchev's penchant for upheaval thwarted the career of many a party functionary: the membership of the Central Committee changed faster in the late 1950s than at any other time since Stalin's great purges. Even though he had named a majority among them, Khrushchev could not rally support when in 1964 the Politburo informed him he had "resigned." Ousted from power, he quickly faded from view, though at least one of his innovations survived: as he had not executed his opponents, they left him to die in peaceful retirement.

Khrushchev's chapter in Soviet history raised serious questions about the extent to which new leadership could transform the Soviet system. Khrushchev was a partial reformer, seeking to disarm the Stalinist mechanism of terror without bringing into question the rule of his party over Soviet society. Ironically, the frustration of his program suggests why Stalinists believed terror was essential to enforce change. No longer living in fear, the vast party bureaucracy—and all the other interest groups in Soviet society—simply opposed to Khrushchev's hasty initiatives the massive weight of their own inertia. The fact that they successfully thwarted him, however, did not lessen their resentment at his attempts to shake them up.

The Restive Satellites from the 1950s Through the 1980s

Among the many policies his colleagues alleged Khrushchev had bungled was his management of relations with the Eastern European satellite states. In fact, Khrushchev's "de-Stalinizing" policies toward Eastern Europe did launch the satellites toward a very different kind of communist society from the model Stalin had imposed. In this evolution, the way was led by Hungary, Poland, and for a tragically brief moment, Czechoslovakia. Despite important differences in pace and detail, developments in these countries followed a common pattern. After a bold assertion of national independence led by patriotic Communists was crushed by a Soviet invasion or the threat of one, the new and apparently servile leadership the Soviets installed proceeded, cautiously and over many years, to diverge from Soviet orthodoxy in some of the ways the rebels they replaced had demanded. This progressive dilution of the full rigors of Communist rule made it easier at the end of the 1980s, when Gorbachev declared that each country could find its own "way to socialism" without the threat of Soviet invasion, for power to be transferred relatively peacefully to non-Communist governments.

Much of the explanation for Stalin's iron rule over Eastern Europe was to be found in his conflict with Marshal Tito, the Communist leader of Yugoslavia. Tito's guerrillas had come to dominate the Yugoslavians' resistance to the

Hungarian Revolt, 1956. *Hungarian patriots crowd aboard a captured Soviet tank moving up to attack Soviet troops during the bloody street fighting in Budapest in 1956.* Erich Lessing/Art Resource, NY

Nazi invaders and had freed their country from Hitler virtually without Soviet help—a very different situation from the rest of Eastern Europe. Standing on his own ground, Tito had no intention of submitting to Stalin's postwar direction. Enraged by Tito's repeated challenges to his authority, Stalin withdrew Soviet advisers, severed economic ties, and finally expelled Yugoslavia from the international Communist movement, the Comintern. By 1949, Tito was looking to the West to counterbalance Soviet hostility. Yugoslavia, which developed its own

special brand of worker-managed economy, soon became not only the first unorthodox Communist nation but the first "nonaligned" one, setting an example of refusal to choose between East and West that many Third World nations would later follow. Such a spectacular defection was of course humiliating for the USSR. As part of his anti-Stalinist program, Khrushchev hastened to heal the breach with Tito, publicly admitting that each nation of Eastern Europe had the right to choose its own road to socialism. Such an admission sent a signal that Khrushchev did not intend, prompting others in Eastern Europe to seek comparable autonomy.

Hungary

The predictable anti-Soviet explosion came to Hungary in October 1956. Since 1949, Hungary had been a typical People's Republic, ruled by men from whom Stalin knew he could expect slavish obedience. Symbolized by its hated secret police, this regime had begun the collectivization of agriculture and the rapid development of heavy industry geared to fulfilling Soviet needs. These new factories guaranteed full employment; but in this workers' state, as in the rest of the Soviet bloc, workers had no right to strike. In the drab society of the "command economy," obedience was imposed by the usual Stalinist method: mass terror.

In 1956 the vast patriotic resentment such a regime provoked was revealed when the secret police fired on a student-led protest demonstration. The government's authority collapsed when the army, sent in to repress the rioters, instead took their side. A new multiparty government emerged, headed by Imre Nagy, a Communist but an outspoken anti-Stalinist. He requested the removal of the Soviet armed forces from Hungary. But his brand of nationalist communism was not enough by now to satisfy many of the rebels, who demanded an end to Communist rule and full national independence. Under their pressure, Nagy withdrew Hungary from the Warsaw Pact and appealed to the United Nations to defend Hungarian "neutrality." Rather than tolerate this bid for Hungarian independence, Khrushchev invaded with 150,000 troops and 2,500 tanks. After savage street fighting at a cost of thousands of lives, the Soviets reimposed the rule of a Communist presumed loyal to Moscow, János Kádár. His government condemned Imre Nagy to be hanged. The bloody lesson of 1956 was

that the Soviets had the will and the power to crush any open challenge to their domination of Eastern Europe.

The task of the Communist leaders of the region, therefore, was to find means to provide some satisfactions to their unhappy peoples without provoking the Soviets to intervene. János Kádár, in the eyes of many Hungarians no more than a traitor and Soviet agent, nevertheless understood this need for national reconciliation. In a famous speech in 1962 he declared, "Those who are not against us are with us." In other words, his government would tolerate any attitude but overt opposition. In 1968, when it launched a "New Economic Mechanism," his regime showed that it was prepared to be as unorthodox in economics as it was in politics. The new plan entrusted the cultivation of state-owned agricultural land to autonomous farmers' cooperatives. Their task, like that of Hungarian factory managers, was henceforth to earn a profit. Though it retained control of banks, transportation, and heavy industry, the government sold off small service businesses to individual entrepreneurs. Moreover, it winked at the emergence of a huge "second" economy, an under-the-table labor market in which some 70 percent of Hungarians chose to work overtime for extra money. Taking advantage of international détente in the 1970s, Kádár also encouraged capitalist investment in Hungary, including the development of joint ventures with Western-based multinational corporations. By the 1980s, Budapest worker cooperatives were selling computer software in Western markets, to which Hungary sent half of its exports.

The combination of all these departures from Marxist orthodoxy produced a distinctive Hungarian economic system, jokingly called "goulash communism" or, more meaningfully, "consumer socialism." Under this system, the standard of living for the majority was higher than in the rest of Eastern Europe. By the 1980s, one Hungarian family in three owned a car, a thirtyfold increase since the 1960s. At the same time, however, social inequality was far greater in Hungary than in the rest of the Soviet bloc: the combined income of the wealthiest 5 percent of the population was eighty times greater than the combined income of the poorest 5 percent—an odd kind of socialism indeed.

The effect of relative economic success was to legitimize, to some degree, the government of Kádár, the "traitor" of 1956. By the late 1980s, however, the partial consensus Kádár had created by such concessions was eroding. The economy lapsed into stagnation, prompting calls for further liberalization in imitation of Western economies. Gorbachev's regime promised not only more sweeping economic and political changes in the Soviet Union than Kádár had permitted in Hungary but also a relaxed Soviet grip that would enable Hungarians to restructure their government and economy as they chose. In this new atmosphere an elderly Stalinist like Kádár was an embarrassing reminder of the past: in May 1988 the Central Committee of the Hungarian Communist party ousted him in disgrace. A year later, the new leadership signaled its atonement for the repression of 1956 by ceremonially reburying Imre Nagy, Kádár's victim, who had long lain in an unmarked grave.

Such concessions came too late. In 1989, as the Berlin Wall fell and membership in the Hungarian Communist party dropped from 700,000 to 30,000, its leaders could only recognize that the game was up. They legalized rival political parties and called elections for March 1990. In these first free elections in Eastern Europe in more than four decades, the predictable winners among the twelve major parties were those that promised to safeguard democracy and complete Hungary's long transition to a free-market economy. The 1990s would reveal, however, that in Hungary as in the other former satellites, not everyone would live happily ever after the fall of communism.

Czechoslovakia

The Czech challenge to Stalinism began early in 1968 when the leaders of the Communist party, in response to demands from intellectuals for greater freedom and from workers for better pay and job conditions, forced out the Stalinist first secretary. His successor, Alexander Dubček, promised extensive reforms, including a less-centralized economy, a relaxation of censorship, and even a subordinate role for political parties other than the Communists.

Dubček intended no more—but also no less—than to create a "Czechoslovakian way to socialism," which he memorably described as "socialism with a human face." Unlike Nagy of Hungary in 1956, he would not be pushed into trying to withdraw his country from the Soviet bloc. But it made no difference. In the heady atmosphere of newly recovered freedom during the "Prague springtime," ideas far more threatening to Soviet control than his found voice. Fearing that Czechoslovakia would be "pushed off the road to socialism" whatever Dubček's intentions, the Soviets marched in a half-million Warsaw Pact troops. The suppression of "socialism with a human face" in Prague in 1968 was far less bloody than it had been in Budapest in 1956: fewer than a hundred lives were lost as the Czechs greeted the Soviet tanks only with passive resistance. By the spring of 1969, Dubček had disappeared from public life.

The regime of Dubček's successor, Gustav Husák, promptly resumed the drive for industrial production at all costs, despite ever-increasing, publicly unacknowledged evidence that the resulting pollution was doing irreparable harm to the environment. (One secret report warned that by the end of the century 60 percent of Czechoslovakia's forests would be beyond saving.) Only in the 1980s, when it felt the impact of a weakening world economy, did the Husák regime begin to talk about allowing the marketplace to determine production goals and prices. The question was whether this kind of tinkering would suffice to revive the Czech economy in the absence of political and intellectual freedom, which Husák and his successors continued to reject. When student demonstrations erupted in Prague in November 1989 on the anniversary of the repression of 1968, the police ruthlessly crushed them.

This last act of repression provoked the downfall of Czechoslovak communism. A small group of intellectuals grouped around the playwright Vaclav Havel, who had been bravely challenging the regime since 1977, formed a movement, Civic Forum, to lead continuing demonstrations by students and some workers. Though a majority of the population remained passive, the moribund Czechoslovak Communist party, knowing that it could expect no backing from Moscow, concluded that it had no choice but to bargain an end to the crisis. In December 1989 the Communists agreed to the formation of a coalition government including non-Communists. Havel, who had spent four years in Communist jails, became president of the Czechoslovak Republic. So relatively amicable and bloodless was this transition that it is remembered as the "Velvet Revolution." The 1990s would show, however, that Czechoslovakia's problems did not end with this negotiation of a Communist surrender.

Poland

History, religion, and the shape of its society combined to make Poland the most troublesome, as well as the largest, of the Soviet satellites. Polish history, which every Pole knew well, was largely a record of struggle against the German and Russian neighbors who divided Poland between themselves for over a century before World War I. Polish patriotism was nourished through such dark periods by a fervent Roman Catholicism: even under an officially atheistic regime, over 90 percent of the population was baptized into the church. Polish rural society successfully resisted Stalinist collectivization, leaving a class of stubbornly independent peasants, unique in Eastern Europe, owning three-quarters of the land. Historic patriotism, backed by a powerful Catholic church, spurred repeated and violent Polish resistance to the Soviet-imposed government. In 1956, large-scale rioting in protest against the hardships of life under the command economy brought to power Wladislaw Gomulka, a patriotic Communist imprisoned under Stalin for "nationalist deviationism." In a face-to-face confrontation, he forced Khrushchev to back down and consent to a liberalized Poland. For a time Gomulka managed to contain Polish discontent. In 1970, however, workers enraged by his announcement of 30 percent rises in food prices went on strike, occupied their factories, and forced him from office. The new leader, Edward Gierek announced a new economic policy.

The basic problem that Gierek in his turn now faced was that Polish investment had been channeled in the best Stalinist style into heavy industry, leaving few resources to be spent on modernizing agriculture to feed a rapidly growing population. Compounded by the monumental inefficiencies of a centrally managed distribution network, this policy made for scarce and expensive food. Thus consumer prices could be kept affordable to the ordinary wage earner only by maintaining government controls—in other words, by subsidizing consumers. Whenever the government ran short of money and tried to cut these subsidies by raising prices, as in 1970, there was an explosion of worker discontent.

Gierek's solution was to take advantage of the new international climate of détente to borrow heavily from Western banks. The loans would be used to make Polish industry competitive in world markets. Polish products, it was hoped, would earn enough to enable Poland to buy whatever it lacked, to raise living standards, and also to pay back the loans. A combination of factors doomed this attempt at a Polish version of consumer socialism. Agriculture still remained backward. Western loans seeped away into the hands of corrupt party bureaucrats. Meanwhile, the slump in the global economy that followed the 1973 oil embargo hit the Polish economy, newly vulnerable to world economic trends, as hard as any in the West. In this situation the government could only keep on borrowing—Polish foreign debt increased 25-fold from 1970 to the mid-1980s—while raising prices and lowering living standards to try and pay off its foreign creditors.

By August 1980, when the government announced new price increases, the workers' patience was exhausted. Meat consumption had fallen by 20 percent in four years. In a country that had been a net food exporter in the 1950s, much now had to be imported, and consumers stood in long lines to receive their meager monthly ration. Striking shipyard workers demanded a concession no Soviet bloc government had yet granted: the right to form an independent trade union. They called their unique new movement "Solidarity." For fifteen months, under the leadership of a shipyard electrician, Lech Walesa, Solidarity grew into virtually a rival Polish government to the tottering Communist regime.

This was a far more formidable challenge to the Soviets' Eastern European rule than the movements led by Nagy and Dubček. Over 200,000 Poles quit the Communist party, while 10 million, nearly a third of the population, joined the union movement. Uniting the discontent of intellectuals and peasants with that of workers, Solidarity forced more and more concessions from the government. The Soviets mobilized to invade but hesitated at the prospect of an occupation that would pin down at least 300,000 of their troops.

In the end it was the Polish army, at the orders of the new Communist party leader General Wojciech Jaruzelski, that temporarily ended Solidarity's hopes. In December 1981 he proclaimed martial law and jailed the movement's leaders. A year later he dissolved the union. Meanwhile, Jaruzelski tried to re-establish authority by promising successive doses of economic liberalization along Hungarian lines, after a period of austerity had allowed Poland to begin to pay its huge foreign debt.

In the eyes of many Poles, Jaruzelski was like the Hungarian Kádár or the Slovak Husák—a mere Soviet stooge. In fact, his situation demanded a delicate balancing act, going as far as he dared to placate the Polish people but not so far as to risk a Soviet invasion.

Under Gorbachev, however, a Soviet invasion became much less likely. The continued deterioration of the Polish economy prompted another wave of strikes in 1988. Faced with this renewed evidence of the power of the banned trade union, and encouraged by Gorbachev, General Jaruzelski decided that since he could not destroy Solidarity, he must strike a deal with it. He concluded a historic agreement with Lech Walesa to restore Solidarity's legal status and to hold free elections, though with 38 percent of the parliamentary seats "guaranteed" to Communists. This stratagem to preserve Communist control failed when many voters crossed off their ballots the names of Communist candidates running unopposed and two small parties, long subordinate to the Communists, threw their support to Solidarity. Thus Jaruzelski had no option in September 1989 but to appoint a coalition cabinet with half of its ministers belonging to Solidarity, while only four were Communists. Eastern Europe had reached a historic turning point: for the first time since the 1940s, the prime minister of a Soviet bloc country was an anti-Communist.

Stalin had once declared that trying to impose communism on Catholic Poland was like trying to saddle a cow. With the advent of one of Walesa's close associates as prime minister, more than forty years of attempts to communize Poland had proved completely futile. Yet it was not clear that the compromise between

Jaruzelski and Walesa could solve Poland's problems.

The most obvious reason for the collapse of communism, in Poland as in the rest of Eastern Europe, was that after Gorbachev became the leader of the Soviet Union in 1985, the USSR was unwilling to back up these regimes with the threat of an invasion. That threat was all that had sustained these regimes, however, because communism had proved to be such an abject economic and political failure, despite the attempts of Eastern European leaders to modify the Stalinist economic and political models.

The Stalinist economic model, we have seen, derived from the Soviet example of the 1930s: its goal was to build a heavy industrial sector—steel mills, cement plants—to meet production quotas set by central planners. Since its products were not destined for competitive world markets, inefficiently high costs of production were not a prime concern. Workers' low wages were compensated for by job security, and in any case mattered less because the economy produced little beyond the barest necessities for consumers to buy.

Such a Stalinist model from the 1930s had enabled the Soviet economy to achieve growth rates of GNP above 5 percent through the 1960s. But as we have seen in Chapter 12, the postwar decades marked a profound shift throughout much of the developed world to postindustrial economies, which emphasized the provision of high-technology products like computers for an expanding and discriminating consumer market.

For the Soviet Union and its Eastern European satellites to have followed this worldwide trend would have required a complete reversal of Stalinist economic priorities. Bureaucratic planning of the Soviet sort would have had to give way to a climate in which entrepreneurial energy could flourish. A society whose censors tolerated only the party line would have had to permit the diffusion of the information that produced technological innovation. Even to

modernize heavy industry would have required diverting scarce funds from their usual purposes of compensating for the inefficiencies of collectivized agriculture, subsidizing low consumer prices, and sustaining a costly military establishment. Such fundamental transformations proved beyond the capabilities of communist leadership, despite concessions by leaders like Kádár to deviations from the Stalinist model like "goulash communism." Thus the Soviet bloc faced the challenges of the world economy of the 1970s and 1980s with economies still geared to the priorities of the 1930s.

Moreover, as fuel costs rose and falling birth rates reduced the supply of potential workers, Eastern bloc heavy industry lost two of the advantages—cheap energy and cheap labor—that had made it productive from the 1930s to the 1960s. After 1970 the rate of growth of Soviet GNP fell almost continuously—to 2.7 percent in the early 1980s. Thus most Eastern bloc economies were not only not renewing themselves but were even failing to do well what under Stalin they had done best.

Falling rates of growth of GNP reflected the low productivity of a sullen work force that remained alienated, despite some improvement in living standards since Stalin's day. The sour joke Soviet workers told about their communist bosses, "They pretend to pay us and we pretend to work," was a succinct summation of communist economic failure that found an echo throughout most of Eastern Europe.

The glaring contrast—obvious to any thoughtful person—between communism's boasts that it had created a superior way of life and the realities of economic stagnation and consumer privation naturally produced widespread political disaffection. Police-state surveillance, periodically reinforced by Soviet invasions, made open opposition too dangerous. Most people throughout the Eastern bloc therefore resigned themselves to a hopeless political cynicism as long as the threat of Soviet repression loomed over them. When that threat disappeared after 1985, communism's record of economic failure and political disaffection doomed it to swift extinction in spite of the efforts of nationalist communists to make it more palatable to their countrymen.

The Brezhnev Decades in the USSR: Transformation and Stagnation, 1964–1982

In the Soviet Union, the later years of the rule of Khrushchev's successor Leonid Brezhnev (1906–1982) witnessed a slide similar to that of the communist regimes of Eastern Europe from economic stagnation and political disaffection into crisis. Since Brezhnev did even less than his Eastern European colleagues to arrest the slide, his successors would be faced with a daunting task of economic and political renovation. His Soviet Union barely began the transition to a postindustrial society: five years after his death, for example, there were only 100,000 computers in the USSR, a total far smaller than the 5 million sold *annually* in the United States.[2]

It was probably inevitable that the stormy innovator Khrushchev would be succeeded as Soviet leader by a lethargic conservative like Brezhnev. Imposing and conventional, he held on to power for nearly twenty years despite steadily failing health, combining Stalin's old post as general secretary of the party with the ceremonial leadership of the Soviet state.

He presided inertly over fundamental changes in Soviet life that brought the USSR in many ways much closer to the developed societies of the West than it had been in 1964. The population of Khrushchev's USSR had still been predominantly rural. In 1968, for the first time, more Soviet citizens lived in cities than in the countryside. The chief stimulus of population movement to the cities continued to be industrial development. The Soviet boom of the Khrushchev years continued until the 1970s. For a time Japan was the USSR's only rival in

annual rate of growth of GNP. The Soviets were simultaneously the world's leading producers of grain, of oil and iron ore, of steel (first surpassing the United States in 1971), and of chemical fertilizers. Continued economic growth made Brezhnev's early years a heady time for the USSR. Expanding their arms expenditures by an estimated 4 percent a year, the Soviets achieved nuclear parity with the United States and developed a navy designed to project their power around the world.

Growth seemed to provide the opportunity for the regime to satisfy the muted but unmistakable demands of the increasingly urban and sophisticated Soviet population for a higher standard of living. The Eighth Five-Year Plan (1966–1970) was the first to stress the production of consumer goods. The results produced substantial changes in Soviet lifestyles. In Khrushchev's day, three out of five Soviet families had shared both bathroom and kitchen with at least one additional family. In a little over two decades the Soviets constructed some 50 million apartments. By the 1980s, three-quarters of Moscow families had one of their own. By 1983, 83 percent of Soviet families had at least a black-and-white television set.

As in the West, the enjoyment of this standard of living required a large effort from wage earners. Not only did many male Soviet citizens work, as in the satellites, at illegal overtime jobs but almost half of Soviet women were employed outside the home. The patterns of Soviet family life thus came to resemble what we have already observed in the postindustrial West. The birth rate continued to fall, most of all among the Slavic majority of the population.

Observers of the USSR had often predicted that as the patterns of Soviet society became more like those of the West, dominated by urban, skilled, increasingly white-collar couples, Stalinist-style censorship could not be perpetuated. Brezhnev agreed with his progressive colleagues that it was desirable to satisfy consumer demand; however, he shared with conservatives an abiding mistrust of unconventional ideas. The first political trial of dissenting intellectuals since Stalin's death occurred in 1966.

Such repeated reminders that critics still had something to fear reflected both Brezhnev's chief principle of government and the source of his support. Khrushchev had hoped, probably unrealistically, to revive mass revolutionary fervor. Brezhnev had no such illusions. The Soviet masses, he believed, needed "discipline" above all. This view was widely shared among the group from which he came, the bureaucratic oligarchy of top party officials.

They were a self-perpetuating elite. Soviet sociological research revealed that over a half-century of "socialism in one country" had produced a society that offered fewer opportunities for social mobility than are found in some Western societies. The children of college-trained top party officials and factory managers were five times more likely than children from peasant or worker families to become officials and managers. They thus continued to enjoy their parents' privileges: chauffeured cars, special stores, private waiting rooms, passes that enabled them to go to the front of the long lines in which ordinary Soviets waited to buy scarce commodities.

The great danger of rule by this kind of elite is that the rulers, fearing no challenge, become concerned only with their own self-gratification. Around Brezhnev gathered an unscrupulous set of high officials who used their connections to amass tremendous wealth, sometimes simply by embezzling public funds. Meanwhile, workers in the USSR felt as powerless and manipulated as workers in capitalistic economies were supposed to feel. The legacy of Brezhnev, the socialist leader with forty foreign limousines in his collection, was a general impulse to cynical self-gratification.

In Brezhnev's second decade the Soviet economy went from dynamism to decline in the 1970s, and into crisis in the 1980s. Alarming evidence appeared in the statistics of rising infant mortality and declining longevity that the quality of Soviet life was actually beginning to decline. The government's response was to publish fewer statistics. After Brezhnev finally died in 1982, the Politburo chose to replace him with two men in succession, ages sixty-eight and seventy-two, respectively, who were both already mortally ill when they took office. Only in March 1985 did the old men of the Kremlin nerve themselves to elect to Stalin, Khrushchev, and Brezhnev's post of general secretary the youngest member of the Politburo: Mikhail Gorbachev.

From Gorbachev to Yeltsin: The Dissolution of the Soviet Union

Like Khrushchev, Gorbachev had risen from humble peasant origins to a brilliant career in the government hierarchy. Like Khrushchev, he wanted to rid Soviet society of the burden of its Stalinist history and to revive its flagging economy by a drastic reshaping of economic institutions. There were differences, however, between these two leaders that went deeper than appearances (though the elegant Gorbachev, suave master of the Western television cameras, marked a new stage in Soviet sophistication from the rumpled and belligerent Khrushchev). Gorbachev, an experienced civil servant, realized that the Soviet system as it had developed since Stalin's time was reaching a dead end, that the time for tinkering with partial economic reforms while treating Soviet citizens as passive spectators of their own national life had passed. Within a few years of taking power, he commanded the most sweeping array of economic and political changes the USSR had seen since 1917.

From the beginning, Gorbachev bluntly declared that the very future of the USSR was at stake. Though Stalin's industrialization had brought the USSR into the twentieth century, and his successors had given Soviet society some of the consumer benefits that industrialization had produced in the West, the country was no longer keeping up with the galloping pace of change. Unfavorable economic indicators—industrial productivity that lagged at half the American rate, an agricultural sector still employing almost a quarter of Soviet citizens (compared to 3 percent in the United States), declining growth rates, and food shortages—were merely symptoms of a basic failure to keep up with the technological innovations of the world marketplace.

Clearly the USSR's continuing relative isolation, with foreign trade only 5 percent of GNP, was cutting off an indispensable flow of innovation. But how, in a world market where the raw materials the USSR had to sell, like oil and natural gas, were depressed, could the Soviets earn the money to buy the technology they needed, when they also had to buy food periodically to supplement the inadequate yields of their backward agriculture sector? Certainly they could not count on selling many manufactured goods in an increasingly competitive world market as long as less than one-third of their products, by official admission, met international standards of quality. The problem was not only that Soviet factories, retooled in the 1950s and 1960s, were too antiquated to meet those standards. Workmanship was also poor, reflecting a work force with high rates of absenteeism, a rate of alcoholism three times what it had been in 1917, and a turnover of employees that in some plants amounted to 20 percent annually.

This combination of circumstances meant that the Soviet economy in the 1980s was caught in a vicious circle. With half of Soviet women already working and the birth rate rapidly falling to Western levels, the supply of cheap labor on which the USSR had long relied was dwindling. To improve productivity would require not only new technology but also greater incentives to a work force that wanted, but could not afford, sophisticated products of

the consumer society such as automobiles and VCRs. But how could the USSR afford simultaneously to keep up in the arms race with the United States, to retool its plants and improve its underdeveloped transportation network, to purchase technology overseas, and to allocate scarce resources to the production of more consumer goods? Greater investment and greater incentives—the production of more consumer goods that workers would work harder to earn—were essential to stimulate greater productivity; but while productivity remained low, the economy could not generate the resources for greater investment and more incentives.

To break this vicious circle, Gorbachev launched a veritable economic revolution he called *perestroika*, "restructuring." He insisted that it would not succeed, however, unless Soviet citizens learned to understand their relationship to the government in a new way. To foster this new understanding would require re-examining Soviet history and encouraging public discussion of controversial issues to an extent unprecedented since Lenin's time. His word for this whole process of discussion was *glasnost*, "openness."

Perestroika, approved by the party Central Committee in April 1987, undermined the Stalinist command economy. The role of the bloated planning bureaucracies in Moscow was much reduced. The manager and workers of each Soviet enterprise were henceforth responsible for its finances and could no longer depend on government subsidies to keep it going.

Likewise, consumers would have to pay the real costs of commodities: there would be no government subsidies to keep them low. One half of the service sector and 20 percent of consumer goods production would be entrusted to private enterprises; by the end of 1987, 13,000 new cooperatives and 300,000 family businesses had been created to meet this goal. In a substantial reversal of collectivization, 40 percent of agriculture was returned to individual cultivation—a predictable decision given that the small private plots permitted before perestroika, though representing only 3 percent of land farmed, produced a quarter of the Soviet crop and two-thirds of the potatoes and vegetables.

Gorbachev saw, however, that his new economic legislation would be unavailing until Soviet ways of thinking were changed. The only way to make the USSR a more productive society was to make it a more open society. As he declared in a historic speech on the seventieth anniversary of the Bolshevik Revolution: "In reorganizing our economic and political system it is our duty first of all to create a dependable and flexible mechanism for the genuine involvement of all the people."[3]

Involvement meant discussion: in the name of glasnost practically every subject once taboo in the USSR now came up for intensive discussion. Gorbachev himself set the tone in his speech by re-examining Soviet history. He stated unequivocally that Stalin's guilt in such episodes as the Great Terror and collectivization was "enormous and unforgivable." Bukharin, the architect of the NEP, which so closely resembled perestroika, now could be seen not as a traitor but as a prophet.

The leader's new "openness" set an example widely imitated. On Soviet television, citizens' panels peppered public officials with tough questions, and documentaries probed the damaging effects on Soviet society of the long, losing war in Afghanistan. Soviet environmentalists even imitated their Western counterparts by staging sit-ins to prevent the officially sanctioned destruction of historic buildings.

It is difficult for those accustomed to societies where frank discussion of controversial issues is taken for granted to imagine the stunning impact of this kind of "openness" on a society where public information, when official secrecy had permitted any, had always been given an official interpretation. Soviet intellectuals of course hailed the new freedom. The

reaction of ordinary people was probably less wholehearted. For many older people who remembered Stalin's leadership during World War II, condemnation of Stalin cast doubt on a heroic past in which they took personal pride. Others found the open discussion in the once-muzzled Soviet press disquieting. To Soviet conservatives, it seemed another symptom of social decay, like the spread of drug abuse and the inexplicable fondness of the young for clandestinely circulated tapes of rock music. Such people insisted that Russia had always needed a master—the tsar or Stalin. Freedom in Russia always led to anarchy, as during the early years of the revolution. Even Gorbachev had to admit publicly in the spring of 1988 that "there are people who think that everything is collapsing." Yet he pressed on.

To make it harder to depose him, Gorbachev instigated a fundamental democratic reshaping of the USSR's political institutions. The new Soviet constitution called for elections in the spring of 1989 to a 2,250-member National Congress of People's Deputies. Though 750 of the seats in this new parliament were to be filled with candidates chosen by various organizations like the Communist party, the other 1,500 seats were left to the democratic choice of the voters—the first "free" election in Russia since 1917.

The results not only deeply humiliated the Communist party hierarchy but convinced even skeptical foreign observers that the possibility of making real choices had shaken the Soviet citizenry out of decades of apathy. Only 25 percent of the districts were uncontested—only a few more than the 20 percent of seats in the U.S. House of Representatives that went uncontested in 1988. Even in some uncontested districts, veteran Communist leaders critical of Gorbachev went down to defeat when voters crossed their names off their ballots. Though nine out of ten of the candidates were Communist party members—no other party being legal—the contests often pitted a

Struggling to Make Ends Meet in Post-Soviet Russia. *Street markets like this one, where the poor try to sell anything they can do without, have become regular features of post-Communist society. Oleg Nikishin/Newsmakers/Copyright © 2001 Getty Images*

younger, reform-minded generation against an older one.

The political frenzy of the electoral period continued through the summer of 1989 as the proceedings of the new parliament were televised live to a record audience of 200 million stretching across the USSR's twelve time zones. Constantly clustered before their sets, Soviet viewers witnessed one unprecedented sight after another, including passionate criticism of the KGB, or secret police.

Already, however, there were signs that Gorbachev's incredibly bold historical gamble of trying to democratize the Soviet Union and liberalize its economy while still remaining faithful to the ideals of Lenin was doomed to failure. Gradually, it became evident that he could no longer control the forces of change he had unleashed. His efforts to do so brought him increasingly under a withering crossfire of criti-

cism both from those Soviet citizens who felt his reforms did not go far enough and from those who believed they had already gone much too far.

It could have been predicted that with his loosening of Moscow's authority, the many ethnic minorities within the USSR—the world's largest country—would reassert the nationalism crushed in the civil wars of 1917–1921 and begin to demand autonomy or even outright independence. Thus Gorbachev found his rule challenged everywhere from the Baltic republics of Latvia, Lithuania, and Estonia (which had been independent from 1918 until Stalin seized them in 1940) all the way to the predominantly Muslim republics along the USSR's southern Asian frontier. Every concession he offered to meet their nationalistic demands led only to further demands for more concessions, until he was faced with the stark choice of watching the

A post-Communist traffic jam in Moscow, 1995. *Ownership of private automobiles has grown exponentially since the fall of the Soviet Union. Most trips in the Russian capital can be made much more quickly by the Metro, the subway whose construction was once the proudest boast of Soviet technology. But Muscovites who can afford them clearly prefer driving their own cars, despite hours of frustrating delay and worsening air pollution. Sergei Karpuklhin/© AP-Wide World Photos*

USSR disintegrate or of trying to keep many of its restive peoples within it by force.

However, it was less and less clear that such force could be found. What had held the USSR's more than a hundred ethnic groups together had been an internationalist ideology—communism—and an omnipresent institution that embodied it—the Communist party. Probably a majority of Soviet citizens had ceased, unlike Gorbachev himself, to believe in the promises of Lenin's revolution, but the party remained the backbone of the multinational Soviet state. It was also the principal institutional obstacle to Gorbachev's reforms, however. To counter such resistance, he had launched the movement for glasnost, which discredited much of the party's past and present and had even allowed Soviet citizens to form and vote for other parties. Yet every blow he dealt to the obstructive party hierarchy not only damaged his own authority as its head but also weakened the principal institution holding the multinational state together.

None of this might have mattered if perestroika had fulfilled its promise by improving the lives of the increasingly urbanized and educated majority of the Soviet population—people who compared their standard of living not with that of earlier generations but with the Western standard glasnost showed them on their television screens. Instead, the Soviet command economy, always neglectful of consumers and already in rapid decline when Gorbachev took office, was plunged into chaos by perestroika's successive and sometimes contradictory plans for economic reform. Ironically, glasnost allowed ever louder and more indignant protests at its complete failure, which became undeniable in the spring of 1990. Meat and milk, salt and soap were all rationed; there were long lines for bread; and it became rare to find a pharmacy open, for the shelves were bare of medicines.

Gorbachev now found himself assailed on one side with demands for far more drastic economic reform and on the other side with protests from his party comrades that further upheaval risked provoking a national collapse. Such were these pressures that he appeared to be driven to one side, then to the other. Late in 1990, it appeared that he was leaning to the proponents of reaction. He backed away from a radical plan already announced for a 500-day transition to a market economy. In January 1991 he also acquiesced in a violent crackdown by Soviet troops in Lithuania, which had proclaimed its independence. Yet this lurch toward reaction did not reassure the growing anti-reform camp within the party, who were becoming convinced that if Gorbachev were not stopped, he would destroy the USSR.

By the late summer of 1991, Gorbachev seemed to have returned to the course of reform. He backed a treaty among the USSR's constituent republics that would share out among them much of the government authority wielded by Moscow. This prospect was too much for the old guard, who decided in August 1991 to snatch power back. Just a few days before the treaty was to be signed, the world learned with horror that a coup d'état had been executed in the capital of a nuclear superpower. An eight-man junta led by Gorbachev's own hand-picked vice president, prime minister, minister of the interior, and minister of defense announced that they had placed the vacationing Gorbachev on "medical leave" and concentrated all power in their own hands to save the country from disintegration.

Fortunately, these plotters had made only the sketchiest plans for their coup. Among other blunders, they failed to assure themselves of sufficient reliable troops to overcome the resistance inspired by Boris Yeltsin, the newly elected and popular head of the Russian Republic. Yeltsin dramatically mounted a tank outside the Russian parliament building to urge Moscow's citizens to resist the coup. Thousands of Muscovites did rally to defend the building from attack, while in St. Petersburg (as Leningrad had recently voted to rename itself) another gigantic rally called for resistance. It would be misleading to exaggerate the role of the Russian masses in blocking the coup: the provinces were largely indifferent to this latest turn in the distant capital's interminable and incomprehensible politics. Polls showed that as many Soviet citizens supported the coup, or were indifferent to it, as opposed it. But the show of resistance in Moscow and St. Petersburg was enough to discourage the ill-organized plotters. Within three days the coup collapsed. Its leaders fled or committed suicide. Yet the return of Gorbachev, released from house arrest, to his capital was not a triumphant one.

The effect of the botched coup was to complete the discrediting not only of the Communist party and of the Soviet Union, which the coup leaders were trying to hold together, but also of Mikhail Gorbachev, who in trying to save both had brought both to dissolution. Even the abortive threat of renewed control from Moscow persuaded the leaders of two republics, Ukraine and Byelorussia (Belarus), to follow the Baltic example by declaring their independence. In the largest republic, Russia itself, President Yeltsin, whose leadership of

Map 13.1   *The End of the Soviet Bloc in Eastern Europe*

resistance to the coup had made him a world figure overshadowing Gorbachev, suspended the Communist party and seized control of its assets.

Gorbachev, in fact, became little more than a spectator as the last act of the history of the Soviet Union was played out. Negotiating with the presidents of Ukraine and Belarus, Yeltsin cobbled together an ill-defined and loosely knit Commonwealth of Independent States to re-place the Union (Map 13.1). All of the fifteen former Soviet republics joined except the Baltic states. Thus on January 1, 1992, the Communist hammer-and-sickle flag was hauled down from

the towers of the Kremlin, to be replaced by the old Russian banner of the tsars. The Soviet Union ceased to exist, and Gorbachev, the heir of Lenin and Stalin as its president, left office forever.

He is, however, assured of a prominent place in the history books, though history's ultimate judgment upon him may well be mixed. For helping to end the Cold War, for lessening the shadow cast over humanity by the nuclear danger, and for attempting the transfor-mation of a totalitarian state into a democracy, he is likely to be counted among the truly great figures of the twentieth century. Yet many

Map 13.2 The End of the Soviet Union

citizens of the former Soviet Union remember him as the man whose advent, by destroying their party, their economic system, and eventually even their country, cast 280 million of his fellow citizens adrift into an unknown future.

Eastern Europe in the 1990s

The joyful mood that swept through Eastern Europe at the surrender under Gorbachev of Soviet dominance and Communist rule proved very short-lived. Today many in the region contemplate the present with despair and the future with apprehension (Map 13.1). While relatively few are nostalgic for the Communist era, the political and economic systems that

have emerged since it ended evoke almost as little enthusiasm. Such an outcome sometimes surprises Western observers. Surely, they feel, once rid of the one-party state and the command economy, and of a society in which only the party privileged escaped the drab norms of an enforced equality, Eastern Europe could have been expected to prosper.

Such an expectation ignores the history of the region before and after Communist rule was imposed after World War II. Only Czechoslovakia had been a functioning democracy throughout the interwar period, and even its society had been so fragmented that governments were invariably based on multiparty coalitions. After the Communist collapse, all of these countries saw a resurgence of multiple parties based on the ethnic and social divisions communism had suppressed. Parliamentary government thus became a matter of ceaseless interparty squabbling.

The most important quarrel that divided the parties of the new Eastern European democracies was over how far and how fast to go in dismantling the command economies communism bequeathed. For all their oppressive drabness, these economies had swathed a majority of Eastern Europeans in a kind of economic and social protective cocoon. The wages they paid were not high by Western standards, but government subsidies kept the prices of necessities low. Services like medical and child care were provided free of charge.

After communism's collapse, however, its triumphant opponents insisted that Eastern Europe could ensure its future prosperity only by aligning its economies with the global free market. Indeed, the new democratic governments had little choice, because the International Monetary Fund, as a condition for lending these countries funds for development and for paying off their huge Western debts, imposed on them the same policies it demanded from Third World countries. They were expected to privatize their few profitable industries and shut down the rest, to end price (but not wage) controls and consumer subsidies, and to balance their budgets even if doing so meant abolishing long-standing services like clinics and day-care centers. Moreover, these policies were to be implemented promptly, despite the fact that the whole global economy was sinking into deep recession in the early 1990s.

Hungary

Even in Hungary, where "goulash communism" had long accustomed people to a substantial private sector, the imposition of the free market came as a shock. Though Hungary received over half of the disappointingly meager investment that Western nations were willing to make in post-Communist Eastern Europe, unemployment climbed to 9 percent by the spring of 1992 as outmoded and unprofitable factories closed and privatizing entrepreneurs trimmed padded payrolls.

Hungary today is still undergoing a wrenching economic transformation, made no easier by the dramatic shift imposed on its trading patterns by the fall of the Soviet Union. Half of Hungary's trade under communism had been with the Soviet bloc countries. Today less than 15 percent of its exports find markets there. Such a drastic reorientation, superimposed on the already disruptive impact of privatization, shook Hungarian society to its foundations. For some Hungarians with capital to invest, there were rich rewards to be reaped: the Hungarian stock market became one of the "hottest" in the world. On the other hand, at the end of 1994 it was calculated that the incomes of two-thirds of the population had shrunk since 1990 and that almost one-third were living below the official poverty line. Such conditions created sufficient dissatisfaction to allow the ex-Communists to make an electoral comeback in that year. Their government responded to widespread anger at growing foreign control of Hungarian businesses by taking a less obliging attitude toward foreign investors. Finding a chillier reception, investors became less enthusiastic about putting their money into Hungary. Thus the mid-1990s found Hungary, beset by continuing high unemployment and inflation rates, and a staggering burden of foreign debt, still lingering halfway along the path to the privatization of its large industries.

The Czech Republic and Slovakia

In Czechoslovakia, regional disagreement over the speed with which economic reforms should be imposed actually broke the country in two. In the elections of June 1992, the Czech half of the country gave a plurality to a party headed by a dogmatic advocate of an immediate and complete shift to free enterprise. The Slovakian half, where industrial employment was already devastated by a two-thirds fall in exports to the former Soviet Union, voted for a Communist-backed advocate of a far more gradual transition. Unable to compromise, these two politicians agreed to dissolve Czechoslovakia on January 1, 1993. Rejected by the Slovaks in his bid for a new term as president, Vaclav Havel had already resigned in July 1992. Four years after the "Velvet Revolution," its most symbolic figure had been humiliated, and his country had fallen apart.

The Czech Republic did move rapidly to privatize its economy. Between 1989 and 1994 the proportion of the country's economic assets in private hands rose from 20 to 80 percent—more than in any other Eastern European country. One hundred thousand properties seized under Communist rule were handed back to their former owners. Small businesses were auctioned off to the highest bidder. The government issued vouchers to every citizen, enabling each to purchase shares in the new private corporations that took over industries formerly under state control. The effect of all these measures was to transform Czech life virtually overnight. Where once dull, state-run television had monopolized the airwaves, an American-owned private channel launched in 1994 swiftly attracted 70 percent of Czech viewers. The minister of health sold off most of the country's state-owned hospitals to private interests. A country where not a single roulette wheel had spun in 1989 by the mid-1990s had the highest number of gambling casinos per capita in the world.

The Czech Republic also could boast of more impressive economic accomplishments: a booming export trade, a governmental budget surplus where most nations had deficits, an official unemployment rate under 4 percent. Such statistics seemed to confirm the prescription of Western economists who had insisted that privatization was a bitter medicine better swallowed quickly, to get it over with, as in the Czech Republic, than administered slowly in fitful doses, as in Hungary. These economists did not always add that the Czechs kept their unemployment rate so low not by leaving it to the marketplace but by instituting government-financed temporary work programs and providing government subsidies to employers willing to hire recent graduates.

Poland

Poland attempted the swiftest and most sweeping shift to free enterprise in Eastern Europe. On January 1, 1990, under the inspiration of an American economist, Poland began a course of "economic shock therapy" intended to complete the transition to a free market within a year. To that end, the planners were willing to tolerate an unemployment rate of up to 50 percent for a few years as Poland halved its capacity for steel production and laid off 180,000 of its 300,000 coal miners. With the removal of price controls, the cost of electricity tripled in the first month of the plan's application, and by spring the cost of groceries had gone up 160 percent. Such economic hardship rapidly disillusioned the population with the Solidarity-backed government. In the elections of October 1991, only 40 percent of Poles exercised the right to vote that they had so recently recovered. Of those who did vote, fewer than one in five supported the parties that backed "shock therapy." During the summer of 1992, ironically, the Solidarity-backed government faced waves of strikes by the very workers whose earlier strikes had enabled Solidarity to unseat the Communists but whose real wages had fallen by a third. Polls showed that Lech Walesa, now the president, had become less popular with his fellow citizens than General Jaruzelski.

Reacting at last to popular protest, the Polish parliament voted early in 1993 to halt the privatization of state-owned industries, though fewer than 20 percent of them had yet been sold off. But this did not solve the problem of what to do with them. Closing more of them would push unemployment beyond the already alarming official rate of 13.5 percent. But keeping these economic dinosaurs going, producing inefficiently for a glutted global marketplace, would require subsidizing them, thus contributing to an annual inflation rate of 40 percent while risking the wrath of the International Monetary Fund.

The failure of successive governments to resolve this dilemma seemed late in 1993 to have disgusted many Poles with the new economics and the new democracy. Only about half of them participated in the parliamentary elections, which produced a majority for the former Communists. Much had clearly changed since Solidarity swept them from power in 1989.

Even more shocking was the defeat, late in 1995, of Lech Walesa's bid for a second presidential term by a former Communist, Alexsander Kwasniewski. Though Kwasniewski's margin of victory was small, it seemed inconceivable that the Poles, the Eastern Europeans historically most resistant to communism, should turn against the very man whose movement had restored their right to a meaningful vote only six years earlier. What could explain such a turnabout?

Part of the answer is obvious: Kwasniewski got the votes of most of those Poles hardest hit by economic shock therapy. He assembled his majority from regions where industries were collapsing as free-market economics were imposed. His victory, however, reflected more than a revolt against the harsh new economic system. His party, stemming from the old Communist party, was the best organized and financed in Poland, contrasting sharply with the many groups among whom the anti-Communists were divided. Kwasniewski profited also from a backlash against the Catholic church,

which had incautiously mistaken the fall of communism for a signal to reassert its political influence, notably by forcing the passage of a law imposing harsh penalties upon women who sought abortions.

Yet Kwasniewski's victory reflected more even than echoes of the controversies of recent Polish history. He owed many of his votes to his shrewd deployment of campaign techniques new to Poland but already familiar in the mid-1990s to much of the world. Consciously emulating American models like Bill Clinton, he established his position in the center of most issues with clever television spots designed by a French advertising man. His speeches neglected no group. He appealed to the young with the assertion that if elected he would "strengthen economic development and consolidate democracy" and to the frightened elderly poor with his pledge to "cope with the problems of unemployment."

Post-Communist Pragmatism

Kwasniewski is the Polish example of a new generation of East European politicians, Communists in their youth, who now lead much of the region. Their advent reflects above all the backlash of discontent against the hardships of the transition to a market economy. Yet these "post-Communists" are very unlike their predecessors. Having joined the Communist party when it was in power as the best way to get ahead, rather than out of any ideological conviction, they have shown a similar pragmatism in refining their appeal to the post-Communist electorate, which aspires to the benefits but not the risks of the middle-class lifestyle of Western Europe.

Ironically, there were signs in the mid-1990s that ex-Communists like Kwasniewski were poised to reap the benefits of the painful economic readjustments imposed by their anti-Communist predecessors. The latest statistics suggested that for these Eastern European "economies in transition," the worst might be over and the post-1990 trend to collapses of production and tremendous increases in unemployment and poverty might be receding. In Poland, for example, the pace of inflation slowed markedly, and the official unemployment rate declined to 12 percent, comparable to France's rate and far below that of Spain. Poland in 1995 was the first Eastern European country to regain the levels of production of the last years of Communist rule. Many economists were confident it would not be the last.

Such statistics were cited by the champions of privatization as evidence that the economic shock therapy they had recommended, though it had caused much short-term suffering, had been essential to Eastern Europe's future. Certainly the suffering had gone largely unrelieved by Western investment. The West had offered no plan to help reconstruct the devastated economies of Eastern Europe like the Marshall Plan of 1947. In fact, between 1990 and 1993, Poland, the Czech Republic, Slovakia, Hungary, Bulgaria, and Romania received less than $10 billion in direct foreign investment, compared to $15 billion that went to Singapore alone.

If indeed shock therapy was beginning to produce its heralded result of renewed Eastern European economic systems in the mid-1990s, the renewal had its troubling aspects. Though few Poles, for example, could afford the kind of Western luxuries now for sale in Warsaw's smart new shops, there were already enough of the "new rich"—shrewd entrepreneurs, the leaders of organized crime syndicates, former Communist managers quick-witted and well connected enough to profit hugely from the privatization of formerly public enterprises—to provide plenty of customers. To some thoughtful Eastern Europeans, this new ruthlessly competitive society in which the wealthy flaunted their Mercedes while the homeless camped out each night seemed an unworthy outcome of their long-awaited deliverance from dictatorship. They continued to hope for a "third way"

between the remembered oppression of communism and the rigors of unbridled capitalism.

Post-Communist leaders like Poland's Kwasniewski, taking their inspiration from the Socialist parties of Western Europe, seemed to be promising such a "third way." Ironically, however, they were calling for the adoption of a social model—the market economy tempered by the guarantor state—at just the historic moment when that model was coming under threat, as we have seen, not only in the United States but also in Western Europe. Eastern Europe has awakened from its long slumber under communism only to face the same challenges of onrushing technological innovation and the globalization of markets already posed to the rest of the world. This fact promises to make the process of post-Communist economic and political renovation doubly difficult.

Conclusion: Russia After the Fall of Communism

The collapse of communism in Eastern Europe and even in the Soviet homeland might have been anticipated—though few experts foresaw it. The dominant trends of the twentieth century, the themes of this book, all pointed toward such an eventual collapse. Growing global interdependence meant that the Soviet bloc economies could not be kept isolated. As Stalinist-style economies failed, communism's worn-out slogans could no longer rationalize authoritarian mass mobilization. Almost as soon as Gorbachev relaxed control, the new technology of television, no longer censored, carried the tidings of reform from one country to the next, toppling Communist regimes like a row of dominoes until even the one in Moscow fell.

In their place, optimistic Western observers expected the swift emergence of democratic political systems and market economies. We have already seen, however, that in Hungary, Czechoslovakia, and Poland (as in the rest of the

Soviet bloc), this transition proved not to be so easy. What would happen in the republics of the former USSR and especially in by far the largest, the Russian Republic, where communism had been entrenched so much longer?

Part of the answer depended on the political skills his career had taught Russian president Boris Yeltsin. Though only a narrow majority in the Communist-dominated Russian parliament elected Yeltsin president in May 1990, within two months he showed what he thought of the future of communism by ostentatiously quitting the party. In July 1991, he was re-elected president by popular vote, becoming the first popularly chosen leader in Russian history. To him, after the collapse of the August coup, fell the task of achieving for Russia alone what Gorbachev had failed to achieve for the USSR before it dissolved: the simultaneous creation of a democratic political system, a market economy, and a culture of civic cooperation.

On January 2, 1992, Yeltsin decreed the application to Russia of the kind of "economic shock therapy" American experts and the International Monetary Fund had persuaded Poland's government to adopt. Less than a year later, Muscovites were reciting an ironic riddle: "What has one year of capitalism achieved in Russia that seventy years of communism were unable to accomplish?" The answer was "It has made communism look good." The impact of a year of drastic reform on Russia's economy and society was indeed disastrous. Prices increased some 25-fold in 1992, pushing from 85 to 90 percent of the population below the official poverty line. Gross domestic product fell 20 percent.

It was undoubtedly Utopian to expect to transform in three or four years a country in which entrepreneurial and banking skills were practically nonexistent. Indeed, what privatization of heavy industry did occur was largely the work of the former *nomenklatura,* ex-Communist managers who simply stopped working their plants for the state and began working them for their own profit. The sight of eco-

nomic authority continuing in the same hands only accentuated public disillusionment with reform. In December 1992, the angry Russian parliament withdrew Yeltsin's authority to rule by decree and forced him to dismiss the finance minister responsible for "shock therapy." Thus began a prolonged confrontation between president and legislature, with each blaming the other for the economic debacle.

By the spring of 1993, the democratic idealism that appeared to have triumphed over communism in 1991 had faded badly. To many Russians, democracy seemed to have brought not only economic disaster but also higher rates of crime, corruption, and social inequality. In Lithuania, where the battle for democracy had also been a battle for national liberation in 1991, post-Soviet economic developments proved so devastating that in the 1993 elections, the voters threw out the Lithuanian nationalists who had proclaimed independence and replaced them with former Communists pledged to slow down the transition to a market economy.

In Russia itself, confrontation continued between Yeltsin and the Communist majority in the parliament. In October 1993, after Yeltsin issued a clearly unconstitutional decree dissolving the parliament, its supporters turned to violence in the streets, attempting to seize Moscow's principal television station. Meanwhile, the members of the parliament barricaded themselves in their meeting hall. Yeltsin's reply to these challenges was to order tanks to shell the parliament building. After a ten-hour bombardment, troops loyal to Yeltsin stormed it. Dozens of dead were recovered from the burned-out ruin. Its shattered façade loomed over Moscow as a reminder of the precariousness of Russia's new democracy.

After this showdown, polls showed that a majority of Russians now preferred a strong leader to democratic institutions. The election of a new parliament at the end of 1993, however, suggested that this preference had not worked to the benefit of Yeltsin. The voters expressed their rage not only by electing Communists but also by giving a quarter of the vote to the party of a right-wing arch-nationalist.

The division of democracy's supporters among many small parties facilitated the success of such enemies of democracy. But the vote also expressed the fury of many Russians at the devastating consequences of economic shock therapy. Statistics confirmed the instinct of many voters that their society was literally falling apart. Between 1990 and 1994, the Russian death rate rose by 40 percent as a consequence of stress-related accidents and illness, a 70 percent increase in homicides, and a tripling of suicides. Life expectancy for Russian men fell from sixty-nine years to fifty-eight, a decline unprecedented in a country at peace in the absence of famine or fatal epidemic disease.

The long-suffering Russian public had also to worry about their sons, drafted into the army to fight an unpopular and perhaps unwinnable war in Chechnya. This region far south of central Russia in the Caucasus Mountains, largely populated by Muslims, had been included in the Russian Federation after the breakup of the Soviet Union. Rather than submit to this new form of Russian domination, Chechnya declared its independence in 1991. After an economic blockade failed to force it to knuckle under, Yeltsin launched a full-scale invasion at the end of 1994. Despite a series of short-lived truces, the war dragged on with the outcome still in doubt. Chechnyans demonstrated, as the Vietnamese and the Afghans had done, how hard it is for a great power, even equipped with the most modern weapons, to overcome determined guerrillas defending the independence of their country.

The political consequences were evident in the results of new parliamentary elections at the end of 1995. Among the forty-three parties competing for votes, the one most closely associated with Yeltsin, who had not built a party of his own, got fewer than 10 percent of the votes. The party led by the chief architect of economic shock therapy got only 7 percent. The Communists emerged as clear winners, holding

one-third of the seats in the lower house of parliament. Yeltsin could no longer simply defy them. He dismissed those of his ministers who were ardent champions of economic shock therapy.

As a new presidential election loomed in the summer of 1996, Western leaders like U.S. President Clinton who had invested their prestige in a commitment to Yeltsin worried that he might lose. Polls showed that the tremendous popularity he had enjoyed in 1991 had virtually vanished. Moreover, he faced a formidable challenger in the Communist presidential candidate, Gennadi Zyuganov.

Zyuganov maintained a moderate tone, never uttering the old Communist slogans about the dictatorship of the proletariat. Nevertheless, the Communist platform on which he ran promised the exact opposite of most of Yeltsin's policies since 1991. A Communist victory would bring a return to guaranteed employment and free education and health care. Government subsidies, protective tariffs, and a return to strict tax collection would restart the Russian economy and thus make loans from the International Monetary Fund unnecessary. The turn to free markets would be stretched out over decades and foreign programming would be restricted to 20 percent of the total broadcast time of Russia's television channels.

This last promise reflected Zyuganov's effort to appeal to the cultural as well as the economic resentments Russians had come to feel since 1991. He revived the old Slavophile argument with which Russians had resisted the threats and temptations of the West over a century and a half: Russia was a unique civilization that had nothing to learn and everything to fear from Western ideas. In taking this line, Zyuganov was not just echoing the conviction of half of the Russian population, according to the polls, that Western economic advice had been deliberately designed to weaken Russia. He was also appealing to Russians horrified by the alien institutions Western contacts had brought to Russia: stock exchanges, striptease clubs, hamburger joints. Thus he bid for the support both of those devastated by economic disaster and of those humiliated by the collapse of Russian values since 1991.

In Russia as in many countries elections are a two-stage process. If no candidate wins a majority on the first round, the two with the highest totals face one another in a runoff. In the first round of the presidential election in the summer of 1996, Yeltsin and Zyuganov finished virtually neck-and-neck. In general, elderly and rural voters supported the Communist, and city dwellers voted for Yeltsin or another non-Communist. Significantly, three-quarters of the age groups under thirty-five voted against Zyuganov. Thus on the second round, Russia's voters had a clear-cut and fateful choice: Continue with Yeltsin, a man whom most Russians now despised, or revert to a remodeled communism. Polls showed that almost half of Russia's voters, like voters in Eastern Europe, wished that they had a third alternative. Yeltsin himself had never clearly articulated a new political ideal to take the place of communism. Still, faced with the choice of a lesser evil, a surprising majority of Russian voters chose Yeltsin. Bad as he was, the alternative—a return to the past—was even worse.

In this contest, Yeltsin had enjoyed a number of advantages. Television was blatantly biased in his favor. His government showered voters with all sorts of gifts. The International Monetary Fund made much of this electoral generosity possible by floating a loan for Russia at just the right moment. Yeltsin also got the unlimited support of the powerful economic interests, ranging from corporations to criminal gangs, that had been enriched by privatization. Zyuganov, on the other hand, faced the perhaps impossible task of sounding Communist enough to reassure his electoral base, but not too Communist to win over uncommitted voters.

Whatever their doubts about the winner, most Western observers of Russia heaved a sigh of relief at Yeltsin's victory. It marked the first time in Russian history that a decisive contest for political power had been carried through without violence.

Yet Yeltsin's re-election, applauded though it was by Western leaders as a triumph for democracy and free markets, hardly signaled an improvement in Russia's dismal post-Communist fortunes. His frequent disappearances into hospitals as his health continued to fail, like his occasional public antics while drunk, did little to heighten his prestige. Moreover, he continued to preside after 1996 over the systematic looting of the Russian economy by a small group of fabulously wealthy "oligarchs," powerful businessmen who used their political connections to build vast financial empires often capped by the powerful new television stations the advent of democracy had produced. Those economic institutions the oligarchs did not control fell into the hands of the rapidly growing Russian Mafia, who by the end of the century were estimated to control a third of the country's financial institutions. In the 1990s, oligarchs and the Mafia together probably shipped more Russian capital out of the country to offshore havens or Swiss banks than international lenders and increasingly wary foreign investors shipped in.

Meanwhile the vast majority of ordinary Russians faced a daily struggle for survival. The collapse of the ruble in 1998 hit not only Western investors, who lost billions, but millions of Russians whose few remaining savings, if any, were again devalued. By the end of the decade, Russia's gross domestic product had fallen to half what it had been at the beginning—a fall twice as large as the one the United States had witnessed during the Depression of the 1930s.

After such disasters, Yeltsin's decision to leave office early on the last day of 1999 was readily accepted by most Russians. He named as his successor Vladimir V. Putin, a choice the Russian voters confirmed in a new presidential election in the spring of 2000. Putin, one of whose first presidential acts was to give Yeltsin a pardon in advance for any crimes for which

Russian President Vladimir Putin visits a judo class during a state visit to Japan in 2000. *As his costume suggests, the former KGB agent is himself a champion of the martial arts.* Sovfoto/Eastfoto

he might be indicted, had already been setting policy in Yeltsin's shadow for many months. In addition, he was widely admired for his hard-line renewal of the war against the rebels in Chechnya. Thus supreme power in Russia passed from Yeltsin, the blustering democrat who had helped thwart the attempted coup of 1991, to a steely-eyed and close-mouthed former secret policeman, who had served for sixteen years in the KGB before the collapse of the Soviet Union.

It is still too early to be certain in what direction Putin intends to try to take Russia. Clearly many long-suffering Russians hope that he will prove the tough master they believe Russia has always needed to check its recurrent slides into anarchy. His first acts a president, such as curbing the powers of the local governors of Russia's eighty-nine regions or setting prosecutors on the trail of some of the most notorious oligarchs, media moguls whose rivalries were rumored sometimes to extend to as-

sassination, seemed to confirm this harsh image. His economic program shows little sympathy for the plight of ordinary Russians. It calls for continuing to slash consumer subsidies, curbing already wretchedly inadequate pensions, and imposing a regressive 13 percent flat tax on everyone. His new labor law would permit the imposition of twelve-hour days upon workers. Clearly, though the process of privatization that the West had imposed upon Russia had proved spectacularly corrupt, Putin has no intention of attempting to reverse, or even delay it. His clashes with the oligarchs are probably intended merely to make clear to them who is boss, rather than to express a generalized disapproval of the changes they have brought to Russia's economy. Privately, he is said to favor setting presidential terms at seven years, which would provide him a freedom from interference as close to the one that tsars enjoyed as the twenty-first century is likely to permit.

Putin presides over a nation that in the last decades of the twentieth century suffered a loss of power and prestige without parallel in the modern era. Once Russian and American nuclear submarines shadowed one another throughout the world's ocean depths. But in the autumn of 2000, the Russian navy could not muster the technology to save the sailors trapped on the bottom in the *Kursk,* a supposedly top-of-the-line submarine sunk by an unexplained explosion during a rare foray out of port. Perhaps the failure is not surprising, given that the Russian defense budget today is equal to about one-seventh of the American one.

Similar evidence of humiliating collapse is to be found on every hand. From the rostrum of the Russian parliament, for example, a Nobel Prize-winning scientist revealed that Russia, the nation that once dueled the United States in space, was budgeting less money for basic research in all the sciences than it would cost to build a apartment building in Moscow to house the members of parliament, Failure seemed total, on all fronts. Russia, the country that for most of the twentieth century claimed to be on the way to creating a more just society—a model of socialism—now ranks behind Colombia, that nation of drug lords and landless peasants, in the world's "inequality index"—the measure of how evenly each society distributes its wealth among its people.

Given the calamitous decline of the last decade, it is easy to understand why much of the rest of the world has lost interest in Russia—to the extent that some question whether American universities need bother to teach Russian. Yet we cannot afford to dismiss Russia, if for no other reason than because it still has some seven thousand active nuclear missiles that could reach the United States in an hour and another five thousand tactical nuclear weapons that could easily be "privatized" by a few of the long-unpaid soldiers who still guard them and sold to the highest bidder. The technological safeguards developed to prevent the mistaken launch of these weapons continue

slowly to deteriorate, like everything else in Russia. The Cold War has become merely a memory, and not even that for the generation that has reached adulthood in the last ten years. But many of the weapons that were emplaced to fight it are still there, scattered among a population many of whom still feel its fears and resentments, now magnified by continuing misfortune.

Notes

1. Quotations taken from Stephen F. Cohen and Katrina Vanden Heuvel, *Voices of Glasnost: Interviews with Gorbachev's Reformers* (New York: 1989), pp. 289–290.

2. Paul Kennedy, *Preparing for the Twenty-First Century* (New York: Random House, 1993), p. 247.

3. *New York Times,* November 11, 1987.

Suggestions for Further Reading

Bialer, Seweryn. *The Soviet Paradox: External Expansion, Internal Decline* (1986).

Cohen, Stephen F. *Failed Crusade: America and the Tragedy of Post-Communist Russia* (2000).

Colton, Timothy J., and Robert Logvol, eds. *After the Soviet Union* (1992).

Freeland, Chrystia. *Sale of the Century: Russia's Wild Ride from Communism to Capitalism* (2000).

Garton Ash, Timothy. *The Magic Lantern: The Revolution of '89 Witnessed in Warsaw, Budapest, Berlin and Prague* (1990).

"'Neo-Pagan' Poland." *New York Review of Books,* January 11, 1995.

Gwertzman, Bernard, and Michael T. Kaufman, eds. *The Decline and Fall of the Soviet Empire* (1992).

Kaiser, Robert G. *Why Gorbachev Happened* (1992).

Kerblay, Basile. *Modern Soviet Society* (1983).

Randolph, Eleanor. *Waking the Tempests: Ordinary Life in the New Russia* (1996).

Remnick, David. "Hammer, Sickle, and Book." *New York Review of Books,* May 23, 1996.

PART FIVE

Independence for the Developing Countries?

CHAPTER 14

Latin America: Necolonial Authoritarianism or Democracy and Development?

IF THE FOUR BRAZILIAN FISHERMEN, WHOSE EPIC VOYAGE TO RIO WAS DESCRIBED in Chapter 7, were alive today, they might long since have moved permanently to a big Brazilian city to seek opportunity. If so, their descendants would most likely now be caught in a new life of poverty and disadvantage. Such was Leandro Dias, age 25 in 2000, a handsome Afro-Brazilian imprisoned in São Paulo's Carandiru Prison for murder.

The urban hearts of one of the world's most inegalitarian societies, Brazil's big cities have turned into places where drugs and crime are the only route to a better life that many poor people can find. The world's third largest city with 17 million people, São Paulo has gleaming skyscrapers, to which executives commute by helicopter, flying over shantytowns (*favelas*) where 20 percent of the city's population live in shabby houses with raw sewage running into the streets. As Dr. Varella, the prison doctor, puts it, this is a society that "produces bandits much faster than it can produce prisons. The main reasons are inequality, police corruption and impunity. Of every 30 violent crimes in the city, one is brought to justice. The situation is out of control." Col. José Vicente, former security chief, adds a different perspective: the 1940s penal code does not recognize modern forms of evidence like videos; justice is slow, there are both military and civilian police, "so in most situations, you have two chiefs, two cars, two bureaucracies, and no results."

The world's largest prison, Carandiru occupies a large tract of the central city. It was built to house 5,000 prisoners but now holds 7,200, with 15 to a cell. Some 15 percent of them are H.I.V. positive, many have tuberculosis or other infectious diseases. Perhaps 90 percent of them enter prison on drugs. Underpaid prison employees are known to sell crack for a dollar a dose, and drug-related violence is common. Medical attention consists of a doctor who makes weekly visits. For Leandro, confinement there meant "descent into a very dark place."

How did he land there? During his early years in Brasilândia, a poor neighborhood, things were "all right" until he was fifteen. Then his aunt killed his father, to whom he was close. The sometimes violent father may have struck her first. Leandro had to leave school to support his mother, and it was not long before he began to get into trouble. Soon he was committing armed robberies. "How else was I going to have a nice car, nice clothes?" His mother Fátima moved the family to the country in 1994 to get him away from urban temptations. Getting into an argument there over a trivial matter, he flew into a rage and killed a man.

Captured, tried, and sentenced to twenty-three years in prison, Leandro landed in Carandiru. Seeking oblivion in crack, he would ask his mother at each visit to bring him money to pay his debts to suppliers, who might kill him otherwise. Finally, in 1996, he heeded her pleas and quit. Becoming a model prisoner, he turned to religion. He became leader of a group of prisoners doing production work for a local company, earning one day off his sentence for every three days worked. Meeting another prisoner's sister-in-law who had come to visit, he began a relationship with her and during an "intimate visit" in his cell, which prison regulations allow once every two weeks, fathered a daughter by her, one of five children that she has borne to different men. Describing his daughter, Sabrina, as his "hope," Leandro dreams of taking his family to a "quiet place"—not São Paulo. First, he has to survive another fifteen years in prison, where some other prisoners are not as admiring of his turnaround as are Fátima, his mother, or Ana Celia, the mother of his child. As for Aunt Jane, who killed his father, her comment now is "nobody's conscience can be entirely at peace in a country with this many problems."[1]

Continental Overview

Latin America's political and economic history since 1945 includes three periods, shaped partly by global and partly by regional factors. The trends toward industrialization and populist mass mobilization begun in the 1930s continued through the 1960s. Partly a reaction against Cuba's 1959 revolution, the region then relapsed into military authoritarianism and economic neocolonialism, worsened by changed conditions in the world economy after 1973. In the 1980s, elected civilian governments reappeared with market-oriented economic policies, an adjustment to the post-Cold War era and increasing globalization.

Living through these shifts, Latin Americans had difficulty escaping political and economic subordination at either the national or for many—like the young Brazilian just discussed—the individual level. Even revolution offered no sure escape from dependency and underdevelopment, as Cuba's fate proved. An overview of the region, followed by closer looks at Argentina, Brazil, Mexico, and Cuba, will illustrate these points.

Mounting Social Pressures

While social conditions there are better on the whole than in other developing regions, Latin America remains a place of rampant inequity in gender, class, and race. The hacienda system and debt peonage survive in some places. Only six Latin American countries—Ecuador, Brazil, Uruguay, Cuba, El Salvador, and the Domincan Republic—had given women the vote before 1945; Argentina did in 1947, Mexico in 1953, others even later. Whole native American ethnic groups have been eliminated in Brazil and Guatemala.

Atop the old lack of social integration, new problems have also appeared. Mass mobilizers have discovered that the class structure of most Latin American societies has become more complex. The old pattern was made up of landlords and peasants, with rudimentary urban middle and working classes. But by 1945, many countries had a social structure more like that of industrial societies, in part because of rapid population growth.

Chapter 1 introduced the twentieth-century population explosion, concentrated in the developing countries, where many poor people still believed that they needed to have large families. In the past, more hands meant more income, and many offspring were the parents' only security in old age, given high infant mortality and limited public services. In the middle decades of the twentieth century, death rates began to decline, but birth rates did not immediately adjust. A population explosion resulted.

Governments began to recognize this as a problem in the 1960s and 1970s. With changing policies and attitudes, birth rates began to drop. Still, because fast-growing populations are very youthful ones, many of whose members' childbearing years still lie in the future, growth in numbers could not stop quickly. By the mid-1980s, the world seemed divided between slow-growth regions with population growth rates under 1.0 percent a year and fast-growth regions with rates near or above 2.0 percent a year. All comparatively affluent, the slow-growth regions were Western and Eastern Europe, North America, East Asia, Australia, and New Zealand. The fast-growing regions were all poor and less developed, including Latin America. Between the 1980s and 1990s, population growth rates in selected countries fell from 3.5 to 2.0 percent in Mexico, from 3.1 to 1.6 percent in Brazil, and from 2.5 to 1.5 percent in Argentina. By 2000, growth rates for almost all of Latin America except some of the poorest places (Nicaragua, Guatemala) were at or below 2 percent. The winding down of the demographic explosion left behind a young population that would have a high ratio of productive to dependent members—good economic news—and that would continue to produce

Rio de Janeiro: The "hills" versus the "asphalt." *While the affluent enjoy the paved streets and high rises in the distance, shanty dwellers crowd onto slopes so steep that mudslides cause some houses to collapse. Drug traffickers built this playground, which they use to watch out for state troopers. Carlos Hungria/© AP-Wide World Photos*

children in large numbers—less-good demographic news. For example, Mexico's population quintupled, from 20 million in 1940 to 100 million in 2000, and at current rates it will not stop growing until 2045 at about 150 million.

As Latin America's population grew to 518 million in 2000, serious social problems prevailed, although the slowing of growth alleviated some. For example, Latin America went from being the world's largest grain exporter in the 1930s to being an importer. Most countries' infant mortality rates, while falling, still remained high in 2000: 7 per thousand live births

in Cuba (as good as the United States), but 19 in Argentina, 32 in Mexico, 38 in Brazil, and 103 in Haiti. With rapid population growth, after 1945 both Brazil and Mexico experienced growth in the actual numbers of illiterates in the population, even as the percentage of illiteracy declined. Educating fast-growing populations also proved difficult. In the late 1990s, enrollment rates for all of Latin America and the Caribbean stood over 90 percent at the primary level but only 33 percent at the high school level. One of the hardest problems was creating jobs. In the 1990s, Mexico's expanding economy created

0.9 to 1.0 million jobs a year, leaving 300,000 people unemployed. Many of them sought work, legally or illegally, in the United States, which by 1990 had the fourth largest Spanish-speaking population (22 million) of any country in the Western Hemisphere.

Economic change channeled burgeoning Third World populations into the largest cities. Since about the 1960s, these have grown much faster than their national populations. Some have become bigger than any cities in affluent countries. As in São Paulo, superurbanization overloads every urban facility and leaves the center ringed with shantytowns, known as *villas miserias* ("poverty-villes") in Argentina. Mexico City grew from 8 million inhabitants in 1970 to perhaps 15.6 million in 1995 and was predicted to become the world's biggest city, with over 30 million, by 2025.

Comparatively, social conditions in Latin America do appear better than in most other developing regions. In terms of the human development index (HDI),* which takes into account life expectancy, adult literacy, educational enrollment rates, and real incomes, all the countries of Latin America and the Caribbean have a combined 1998 score (0.758), closer to the scores of East Asia excluding China (0.849) or of the industrial countries of Europe and North America (0.920) than to those of sub-Saharan Africa (0.464) or South Asia (0.560). Individual country scores, however, are as far apart as Chile's 0.851 and Haiti's 0.440. The country scores, moreover, mask wide disparities by ethnicity, gender, and class. Even if population growth has slowed and Latin America's developmental problems are not as severe as those of

other developing regions, these figures bring us back to the point where this section began. Latin American societies suffer serious developmental problems and inequities.

The Uncertain Course of Economic Development

The Latin American countries' economic and social problems are clearly inseparable. The national economies vary widely. Large and comparatively industrialized, Argentina, Brazil, and Mexico had exports valued respectively at $31, $59, and $130 billion in 1998. In contrast, the exports of the Central American countries (Panama, Costa Rica, Nicaragua, Honduras, El Salvador, and Guatemala) ranged between $0.9 billion for Nicaragua and $4.5 billion for Costa Rica in 1997. That Latin American economies still have common problems, however, is clear from regionwide debate over development strategies.

The debate focuses on two questions that all industrializing economies face: where the resources for industrialization will come from and how to use them. One answer is to extract resources from agriculture. Other sources are external: foreign investment or profits from foreign trade. Another possibility is to extract capital by holding down workers' wages. The success of any of these strategies depends in part on the strength of those who accumulate capital—industrialists, landlords, the state—in relation to those with whom they must deal, at home and abroad. Another question is the goal of industrialization: what industries to create and for what market.

The larger Latin American countries, as noted in Chapter 7, began to answer these questions by the 1930s with a strategy aimed first at local production of formerly imported goods, then at heavy industry. The market for import substitution was by definition internal, and various devices, such as high import duties, were

---

*The Human Development Index (HDI), published annually by the United Nations Development Programs in the tables at the back of the *Human Development Report,* is a statistic that ranges between 0 and 1. Values above 0.800 are in the "high" range. Values from 0.799 down to 0.500 are "medium." Values of 0.499 or less are "low." The remaining chapters of this book will also refer to the HDI.

used to protect it. Exerting leadership by founding state enterprises or providing facilities such as credit, governments expanded in power and size as their economic role grew. Capital came from agriculture, to some extent. But only Mexico attempted any basic restructuring of agriculture, whose workings historically emphasized the landlords' dominance over the peasantry more than economic productivity. The usual failure to couple import substitution with agrarian reform undercut industrialization by restricting the productivity of agriculture, the size of the internal market, and the development of a skilled labor force.

Import-substitution industrialization predominated through the 1960s. But by then the policy had reached its limits. After a first "easy" phase that satisfied domestic demand for simple consumer goods, import substitution meant moving into industries that required greater capital and more advanced technology, that produced proportionally fewer jobs, and that could produce efficiently only for large markets.

Rapid technological advance compounded these problems. It was one thing to conquer heavy industry symbolically by building a steel mill, another to become self-sufficient in machine tools or chemicals, or later to master the quite different requirements of the information technologies. Without such self-sufficiency—something small countries could not aspire to—import substitution merely shifted the frontier of import dependency from the finished product to the machines or parts used to make it. Protectionist policies did not overcome these problems but merely led multinational firms to penetrate the protected economies by creating local subsidiaries.

The exhaustion of the import-substitution strategy became a major factor in opening a new period in the 1960s. The following decades displayed two distinct approaches to economic development. The less common, socialist policy sought development through radical structural change in society and economy, including agrarian reform and attempts to sever external dependency relations. Countries that attempted this approach include Castro's Cuba (1959 to the present), Chile under Allende (1970–1973), and Nicaragua under the Sandinistas (1979–1990). Only in Cuba did this approach become established for long. Even Castro changed only the form of dependency, as Cuba's hardship after the collapse of its Soviet patron showed. Like most of the 190-odd countries in today's world, Cuba may simply lack the potential to rise above a subordinate place in the world economy.

The more common economic policy after 1960 was neocolonial or neoliberal. In crude form, this recalls the nineteenth-century "liberal" view of Latin America as an agrarian region whose role was to export agricultural and mineral products and import industrial ones. In the up-to-date view of finance technocrats, the policy seeks development largely through foreign investment, accepting the restrictions, including drastic squeezing of wages, that foreign investors and lenders like the International Monetary Fund (IMF) demand to secure their investment.*

Brazil's experience showed that this approach can produce gains. Brazil even became an exporter of advanced industrial products, but Brazil's growth proved uneven and worsened existing inequalities. There, as in other relatively industrialized countries, neoliberalism passed through two stages. Direct investment by multinational corporations

---

*The International Monetary Fund is a UN agency created to aid member states in temporary balance-of-payment difficulties. Originally the IMF conditioned its aid on "stabilization" programs to respond to specific crises. Later, IMF emphasis shifted to "structural readjustment" programs to restructure developing economies along free-market lines. The IMF has recently begun to emphasize debt relief and human development, but remains much criticized for its policies' impact on poor countries.

characterized the first. Direct government borrowing from large international banks typified the second. The result of both phases was that foreign investment in Latin America, having fallen during the Depression, rose again sharply after 1960.

Both phases had important costs. Industrialization through direct foreign investment worsened balance-of-payments problems because money left the country to cover profits and royalties. The capital that multinational firms took out of Latin America probably exceeded their investments greatly. For example, Brazilian statistics record a total capital inflow for the period 1947–1960 of $1.8 billion but a total outflow of $3.5 billion. Latin American governments attempted to limit these outflows, but multinational firms defeated these efforts by working with the historically foreign-oriented local elites. In the military-dominated Argentina of the 1960s, for example, 143 retired military commanders held 177 positions in the largest and mostly foreign-controlled firms.

The foreign-debt approach to capital accumulation seemed to solve some of these problems but ultimately made them worse. Government borrowing brought capital into Latin American countries under the guise of national control, and it enabled the governments to enlarge their role as investors or lenders. Yet if direct investment by foreign firms required remittances abroad to cover profits and fees, government borrowing required larger foreign remittances to cover principal and interest.

Before the foreign-debt approach had gone far, global economic interdependency tightened abruptly as a result of the revolutionary oil price increases imposed by the Organization of Petroleum Exporting Countries (OPEC), which includes Venezuela, Nigeria, and Indonesia though most members are in the Middle East. The first increases almost quadrupled the price of oil on the world market, from $2.70 per barrel in 1973 to $9.76 in 1976. Further increases in 1979 led to a price of $33.47 per barrel in 1982.

No part of the world felt these price increases more than developing countries that had to import oil. By 1979, various factors— conservation, shifts to alternative energy sources, and recession—had reduced world oil consumption. Price drops followed in the 1980s. Then even oil-producing countries began to suffer—a fact suggesting that, despite their sudden wealth, they were not really different from other economies dependent on a single export commodity.

Partly because of double-digit U.S. interest rates provoked by the financial crisis of the early 1980s, Latin American foreign debt shot up, reaching $418 billion by 1990. Latin America transferred over $200 billion in payments to industrialized nations in the 1980s, and economic output per capita declined nearly 10 percent for the decade. In 1990, Brazil, Mexico, and Argentina—at $116, $97, and $61 billion respectively—had the second-, third-, and fifth-largest foreign debts among the world's nations. For Latin America as a whole, external debt was three times more than exports by 1987.

The huge debt buildup suggested that the neoliberal development strategy had reached an impasse, as import substitution had by the 1960s. As of 1992, crisis symptoms for the region included a net outflow of funds for debt service, average annual inflation rates high in triple digits, decline in real wages, and a near doubling—to 62 percent—in the percentage of households that could not provide for their basic needs. Between 1960 and 1990, the income distribution, as measured by the share of national income received by the poorest 20 percent of the population, had become more inequitable for all of Latin America except Colombia, Costa Rica, and Uruguay. In two-thirds of Latin American and Caribbean countries, per capita incomes were lower in the mid-1990s than in earlier decades. How would Latin America develop economically if over half its households lacked the food and clothing needed for the adults to work effectively or for the children to learn in school?

Responding to the global trend, Latin American policymakers reacted to the debt crisis of the 1980s by starting to move away from regulated economic systems and liberalize their economies through *privatization:* selling government-controlled companies to private interests. Brazil had over 400 government-owned companies; Mexico had over 1,100. Shifting these to the private sector, where survival depended on making a profit, might increase competition and productivity—or, as in Mexico, it might provide opportunities for inexplicable enrichment to those close to power. Latin American politicians also began to shift policy toward export-led growth and—in reaction to external changes such as European integration—to create free-trade agreements or common markets with other countries. From Mercosur, the "southern market" uniting Argentina, Brazil, Paraguay, and Uruguay, to the North American Free Trade Agreement (NAFTA), which would link Mexico to the United States and Canada, enough such agreements were proposed to blanket the hemisphere. The most daring such strategy, Mexico's commitment to NAFTA, has been interpreted as an attempted leap from the ranks of the underdeveloped into those of the highly developed nations. By 1999, Argentine proposals to adopt the U.S. dollar as the official currency even raised the question of whether the entire western hemisphere might acquire a common currency, analogous to the euro.

Until such policy changes do produce significant benefits, the region's most painful economic policy choice would seem to lie in deciding how to respond to the demands of international lending agencies. Restoring Latin American nations' creditworthiness implicitly requires either politically intolerable sacrifices from consumers or higher export profits to cover debt repayment—as if debt-service obligations left capital to invest in promoting exports. In fact, however, Latin American elites of the 1990s seemed not to hesitate over this choice, but rather exercised their historical option to cooperate with foreign interests and enrich themselves at the detriment of their fellow nationals.

Perhaps nothing is more indicative of Latin America's chances for balanced economic development than a comparison with East Asia. As Chapter 17 will show, Latin America was much slower than East Asia to move beyond import substitution industrialization. Latin America also suffers starker social inequalities, as reflected in educational levels, income distributions, and access to resources, starting with the unreformed land tenure systems in most Latin American countries. There is no way to bypass these problems and achieve prosperity for more than the few.

Political Reflections of Socioeconomic Stress

Post-1945 political development followed from the region's social and economic history. Each of the three major economic policies—import substitution, socialism, and neoliberalism—was associated with a particular type of politics and with particular social groups. Since the 1930s, for example, the import-substitution strategy was associated with corporatist mass mobilizers, of whom Perón and Vargas still played leading roles after 1945.

Radical leftist policies appealed to frustrated nationalists and the disadvantaged. Many radicals were communists, and a larger number held some ideas inspired by Marx, Mao, or Ché Guevara, who figures in the discussion on Cuba later in this chapter. Yet the communists were not united, and not all radicals were communists, as Roman Catholic political activism shows.

Radicals dominated the course of change in only a few places, chiefly Cuba. Cuba's efforts to export its revolution in the 1960s proved unsuccessful. However, the Cuban experience exerted a pervasive influence on Latin American politics. Leftists everywhere saw in it signs that revolution could succeed in Latin America despite U.S. opposition. Rightists took fright from Cuba's revolution, which toppled old elites and transformed socioeconomic relations in a way that earlier Latin American "revolutions" had not. Castro's triumph not only excited leftist hopes but also helped provoke rightist repression under the military dictatorships of the next quarter-century. Worsened economic conditions after 1973 played into military authoritarians' hands, confirming the secular radicals' eclipse.

Called by Pope John XXIII to serve the poor, Catholics also moved leftward in the 1960s. Religious thinkers developed a liberation theology demanding social justice. The new theology had great impact, especially through the Christian Base Communities. Known as "CEBs" in Spanish or Portuguese, these are activist groups, led by clergy or lay delegates, who teach the poor to read the Gospel as a guide to social action. By defining the people as the church, CEBs inverted hierarchical authority and the old alliance between the church and the elites. More recently, Pope John Paul II, steeled in the struggle against communism in Poland, has reined in the left-leaning clergy. Latin America's religious map has also became more complex, as the increasingly urbanized poor began gravitating toward Protestant Pentecostalism rather than Catholicism. Yet liberation theology had made its mark. From Brazil to Mexico, leaders formed in CEBs headed unionization or political efforts, even when CEBs, as such, played no part. Morally, liberation theologians stood against militarism and repression. In northeastern Brazil, home to the four fisherman whose journey by raft opened Chapter 7, Archbishop Helder Câmara was known for saying: "When I fed the poor, they called me a saint. When I asked, 'Why are they poor?' they called me a Communist."

Neoliberal authoritarianism, which became so conspicuous in the 1960s and 1970s, appealed to conservatives, especially military leaders. Not all Latin American military officers are conservative. But the shift to neoliberal policies coincided with the military installation of repressive regimes in Brazil, Chile, Bolivia, Uruguay, Paraguay, and Argentina. The only large Latin American country to escape military domination—for reasons that will merit further comment—was Mexico.

After 1980, the trend reversed, and civilian rule had replaced military government in eighteen Latin American countries by 1995. Partly because of economic crisis, the share of gross domestic product (GDP)* spent on defense rose between 1985 and 1995 from 0.7 to 1.0 percent in Mexico, 0.8 to 1.7 percent in Brazil, while falling from 3.8 to 1.7 percent in Argentina, 4.0 to 3.8 percent in Chile, and 9.6 to perhaps 5.0 percent in Cuba. Low all along by world standards except in Cuba, these rates show that most Latin American armies faced few external security threats. Costa Rica, Haiti, and Panama in fact abolished their military forces, keeping only police. Yet nowhere was democracy complete. In most places, the military retained extensive power or even a policy veto. Human rights remained in jeopardy. Soviet collapse had discredited the Left, and social reform lacked effective advocates.

Perhaps the key question was why narrow-based authoritarian regimes ever emerged in defiance of the global twentieth-century trend

---

Gross domestic product (GDP) and *gross national product (GNP)* are two ways of measuring economic productivity. GNP is the total market value of all final goods and services produced in a country during a year, including income earned abroad by citizens of the country but excluding income earned inside the country by foreigners. GDP is the same measure but without allowance for earnings paid abroad or received from abroad. Only "final goods and services" are considered, because inclusion of intermediate products (like hides used to make shoes) would lead to double counting.

toward mass mobilization, albeit usually in an authoritarian mode in the developing world. To explain this, some analysts focused on neo-liberal economic policy, arguing that only a repressive government could restrain working-class demands, which populist leaders had mobilized, and impose the sacrifices needed to stabilize the economy and attract foreign investment. Others pointed to the impact of Cuba's revolution, which had incited leftist activism and rightist repression all over the region. Another explanation not unrelated to the others emphasized U.S.–Latin American relations.

U.S.–Latin American Relations, with a Chilean Example

At the end of World War II, U.S. influence in Latin America was at a high point. The United States capitalized on its influence by persuading most Latin American governments to sever relations with the Soviet Union, ban local communist parties, accept a collective security agreement (the Rio Pact, 1947), and join the Organization of American States (1948). After the communist victory in China and the Korean War (1950–1953), the United States saw its struggle with communism as a global one. As a result, the United States concluded defense assistance agreements with ten Latin American nations during 1952–1954, with important results. Latin American military elites acquired U.S. equipment, far beyond what their governments could have bought them, and trained jointly with U.S. forces. Thus these elites acquired greater prominence in their own countries than they would otherwise have possessed and became identified with the U.S. military.

Under different U.S. presidents, policy toward Latin America shifted, but the military emphasis persisted. Truman (1945–1953) tried to balance the military policy with the Point Four Program, which offered technical assistance to developing countries. Eisenhower (1953–1961) mostly abandoned economic aid

in favor of free enterprise. Faced with the Cuban Revolution and Soviet penetration of the Western Hemisphere, Kennedy (1961–1963) shifted again, producing the Alliance for Progress. One part of it aimed at social and economic development. Latin American nations were to submit development plans covering topics such as agrarian and tax reforms, and the United States was to help finance the plans. Such development would help prevent more Cubas. But rapid development itself could create social stress that might lead to revolution. Working through the Alliance, the United States tried to prevent revolution through counterinsurgency, a policy that it also applied in Vietnam (see Chapter 11). The concept combined military and "civic action" in such fields as public works and health care and was to be carried out by military forces working to cement the people's loyalty to the existing governments.

Latin America may have seemed more promising for counterinsurgency than war-torn Vietnam, but the Alliance for Progress failed. Hindsight shows that it was unrealistic to expect freely elected Latin American governments to achieve economic growth and social reform at the same time. The Alliance's key economic assumption—that industrial development in Latin America could "take off" as it had earlier in Britain or the United States—erred in ignoring Latin America's dependency. Indeed, the Alliance reinforced dependency. Much of the aid took the form of loans, with requirements to spend the funds on U.S. goods. Also serious were the results of entrusting "civic action" to the military. Latin American officers felt it was insulting to employ soldiers in manual labor like road building. The meaning they drew from counterinsurgency was that only military regimes could both push hard for economic development and control the stress it placed on workers and peasants. So viewed, the Alliance furthered the militarization of politics in the 1960s.

Kennedy's successor in Washington, Lyndon Johnson (1963-1969), abandoned the development side of the Alliance but not the military side. Reacting to events in Vietnam, the Nixon administration (1969-1974) declared that the United States could not keep peace all over the world; it shifted attention to regimes that could play the role of peacekeeper in their own regions—in Latin America, the military regimes. Despite the Carter focus (1977-1981) on human rights, no fundamental revision of the military emphasis appeared in U.S. policy before the late 1980s.

The Chilean experience of the 1970s provides the most memorable example of the military-oriented U.S. policy. Chile's economy had long been dominated by U.S. interests, especially in copper mining, and by a small local elite with interests in land, industry, and finance. As rapid population growth and urbanization began to strain Chilean society, it became clear that those interests could no longer control political mobilization. By the late 1950s, the country had acquired a range of political parties, from "Conservatives" and "Liberals" on the right to socialists and communists on the left. In the 1964 presidential election, the Right temporarily checked the radicalizing trend by joining with the left-moderate Christian Democrats to elect their candidate, Eduardo Frei, and beat the left coalition's Salvador Allende.

Frei's presidency was not a success. He accepted aid under the Alliance for Progress and opened Chile increasingly to foreign investment, so deepening dependency. His centrist positions on issues like land reform and nationalization provoked controversy. His Christian Democratic party competed with leftists to mobilize the populace, with sharp political polarization as the result. In the 1970 election, this polarization blocked formation of a broad coalition like the one that had won in 1964. Rightist, centrist, and leftist candidates ran. The leftist candidate, Salvador Allende, won, but with only 36 percent of the vote. The election went to the

Congress, which approved Allende. A second Marxist government had come to power in Latin America, this one freely elected, but only by a narrow margin.

Allende's program called for a peaceful transition to socialism. Recalling European social democrats' failed hopes of the 1930s (see Chapter 5), this was a tall order for a narrowly elected Third World government that had to operate in the Western Hemisphere under U.S. scrutiny. Allende began by freezing prices and raising wages to redistribute income. He next sought complete nationalization of the copper companies. Nationalization then extended into other sectors, affecting both Chilean and foreign-owned firms. Allende also pushed ahead with land reform and by the end of 1972 had liquidated the large estates. In these measures, Allende tried to proceed by legal means, but left-wing radicals often forced his hand. Nationalization had soon gone so far that the government could not have compensated foreign firms if it had wanted to.

Opposition to Allende gradually mounted so as to block any peaceful transition to socialism. By late 1972, agricultural production and copper prices had fallen. Inflation was getting out of control. Radicals demanded faster change, while conservatives—who still controlled much of the media, the Congress, the bureaucracy, the officer corps, and the church—organized actions such as a massive strike in the fall of 1972. The U.S. government and U.S. firms with interests in Chile did everything possible to thwart Allende. The Nixon administration took steps to halt loans and private investment, and the CIA spent $8 million in three years—as later revealed in Senate testimony—to undermine the economy. Only to the Chilean military did U.S. aid continue. As the crisis mounted, Allende made concessions to his opponents but could not save the situation. In September 1973, military officers mounted a coup that left Allende dead and the Left crushed.

"Widen the agrarian reform! The nation is stronger than the big landowners." *So proclaimed the banners of peasants and workers demonstrating for Allende shortly before his overthrow, September 1973. Ojeda/Magnum Photos*

At the head of the new regime stood General Augusto Pinochet, an alumnus of the School of the Americas, founded by the U.S. Army to train Latin American officers. One of Latin America's most repressive and durable military regimes, Pinochet's survived long after civilian government resumed in Argentina (1983) and Brazil (1985). He could not have lasted so long if Allende's socialism had not frightened Chile's middle class into accepting from Pinochet even policies that undermined business and industry. He abolished political parties and suspended the constitution, with its guaranteed rights. Then he set out to reduce the state in size, shift government services into the private sector, es-

tablish a free-market economy, and ban the Left from politics. He turned economic policy over to technocrats who fulfilled the neoliberal program to the fullest. Import duties fell from 100 percent to 10 percent, depriving much Chilean industry of protection it needed to survive but—more important to Pinochet—attracting foreign investment and weakening the working class through job loss. To further undermine labor, unionization was limited to "factory unions," whose members all worked for the same firm. Privatization went so far that even schools and social security were privatized. Pinochet had the common rightist goal of shrinking the state. His purpose, however, was not greater freedom, for he also had the radically authoritarian goal of increasing the state's control by shrinking the society's potential for opposition even more. Pinochet sought to ensure his position through the constitution of 1980, which named him president until 1989 and empowered the armed service commanders to reappoint him after that.

What Allende could have achieved if he had not faced foreign intervention remains unclear: scholars debate the extent to which U.S. interference, internal opposition, or his own mistakes caused his fall. Pinochet, in contrast, had time to make his impact quite clear. His brutally conservative economic policies lowered inflation from 500 percent a year in 1973 to 20 or 30 percent a year in the mid-1980s, diversified exports until copper accounted for less than half of export value, privatized most of the five hundred firms that the state had owned in 1973, and achieved economic growth of 7 percent a year in the late 1970s. But they also bankrupted much of agriculture and industry, worsened rural landlessness, and reduced workers' wages and social services. His efforts to destroy political parties and the labor movement never succeeded, and anti-government protests resumed in 1983. Progressive church leaders embarrassed Pinochet by documenting his human rights abuses.

When he mistakenly gave them a chance, Chileans voted against Pinochet, electing as president a Christian Democrat, Patricio Aylwin in 1989. Pinochet ceded the presidency in 1990 but was constitutionally entitled to remain army commander-in-chief until 1998 and senator for life after that. In his old age, however, he faced legal proceedings at home and abroad for his human rights violations. When Chileans voted for president in January 2000, narrowly electing Ricardo Lagos, a social democrat once close to Allende, over a conservative who used to support Pinochet, lessons remained to ponder about the impact of such brutal policies on a developing country and about the part U.S. policy had played in Chile's travails.

The Shark and the Sardines

Chile's experience illustrates not only problems of relations with the United States but also the other Latin American themes discussed earlier. These problems began with the addition of runaway population growth and superurbanization to the old social inequalities. Such problems overtaxed the capabilities of governments that aimed at both political mobilization and economic development. By the 1960s, the characteristic economic strategy of these governments, based on import substitution, was exhausted. This fact, and the fears touched off by the Cuban Revolution, then launched a trend toward military-authoritarian regimes. They pursued neoliberal economic policies more favorable to the foreign interests that supported them than to the local populace. Chile's experience was unusual in that the radical alternative briefly triumphed with Allende, between the Christian Democrat Frei and the military dictator Pinochet.

Pursuing the perceived interests of their nation, U.S. policymakers through the 1980s favored stability and a secure climate for investment and thus normally disregarded the political environment that Latin American rulers created for their citizens. In this way, U.S. policy contributed to the resurgence of militarism more than most U.S. citizens realize. Indeed, the average U.S citizen has little grasp of why former Guatemalan president Juan Arévalo (in office 1945–1950) described U.S.–Latin American relations in terms of "the shark and the sardines." Some Latin American countries are bigger than sardines, but U.S. leaders know what Arévalo meant.[2]

After the oil price increases of 1973 and 1979, economic pressures exposed the military regimes of Latin America to new difficulties. By the 1980s, it appeared that those regimes had not permanently thwarted the characteristic twentieth-century demands for mass political mobilization and economic development to benefit the people. To replace those regimes with more democratic ones would not be easy, considering how many parties and other institutions the military had destroyed. Partly because of the economic regressiveness of the military regimes, Latin America—while better off in social conditions than most other developing regions—still had no country that had risen to more than an intermediate position in the global pattern of economic relations, although Mexico stood poised to bid, through NAFTA, for economic integration with the United States and Canada.

Argentina: The Perils of Authoritarianism, with Charisma and Without

While Perón's influence gave a distinctive stamp to its post-1945 history, Argentina passed through the same phases noted elsewhere: the relatively democratic, development-oriented regimes of Perón (1946–1955) and his Radical successors (1958–1966), a period of military authoritarianism (1966–1983), and a return to civilian government (since 1983). Throughout, several factors proved especially important. Perón was better at mobilizing the people than at charting political and economic policy. The military not only had means to exert force but were politically assertive; their control of government firms that manufactured military supplies also gave them economic influence. Argentina suffered acutely from lack of political consensus. Peronists, middle-class Radicals, the military, the Left—all had splits and conflicts that made orderly political life difficult. But the most important problem was the economy. Despite progress in industry, almost all of Argentina's foreign exchange still came from agricultural exports, but Argentina's share of

world trade was shrinking. By the 1980s, the once "amazing Argentine" had become one more underdeveloped, unstable Latin American country.

Toward Democracy and Development?

Chapter 7 followed Perón's rise and his election to the presidency in 1946. As president, he aimed economically at industrialization through import substitution and politically at corporatist mobilization. This he set out to achieve by broadening his constituency into a labor-management-military alliance and redistributing income to his followers. To support industrialization, he enacted a Five-Year Plan and created a foreign trade organization, IAPI (Instituto Argentino de Promoción del Intercambio). IAPI was to monopolize the marketing of agricultural exports, and its profits were to go for industrialization. To reduce foreigners' economic role, Perón nationalized foreign-dominated enterprises, including railroads and the central bank, using wartime export earnings to compensate the owners. In 1947 he paid off the foreign debt. Perón's policies made Argentina almost self-sufficient in consumer goods by 1955, although there was still little heavy industry.

Perón's populism was strong, but his economic ideas were weak. They were inflationary: living costs at Buenos Aires rose some 700 percent from 1943 to 1955. Enlarged to provide new services, the government was one of the world's costliest. Despite his populism, the high taxes required to support the government were mostly indirect, hitting the poor hardest. By substituting bureaucratic inefficiencies for the spur of competition, nationalization also made firms less productive. As an intermediary between Argentine producers and world markets in which it lacked power to influence prices, IAPI could make a profit only by buying Argentina's grain and livestock at below-market

Juan and Eva Perón at his presidential inauguration in 1952. *To many Argentines, this charismatic pair symbolized the opening of an era of mass politics.* *UPI/© Bettmann-CORBIS*

prices, thus reducing incentives for Argentinians to produce and invest. Since Argentina still relied on agricultural exports to earn foreign currency, Perón was killing the goose that laid the golden eggs.

For some time, most Argentines probably believed conditions were getting better. Industrialists and the urban middle class were pleased by patronage in the bureaucracy and the enlargement of the market for their goods as working-class living standards rose. The military liked industrialization and the salary increases and equipment they received. Given the vote in 1947 largely through the efforts of Eva Duarte Perón, women voted heavily for her husband. Thanks to the strong export market of the early postwar years, Perón was able to gratify labor with steady increases in purchasing power through 1949—another factor that

helped diminish agricultural exports, because consumption grew at home. The flow of new benefits, such as improved health care, continued. Until her death in 1952, Eva Perón dispensed many of the benefits through her Eva Perón Foundation. "Evita" became a cult figure to many Argentinians, and her mystique has become the stuff of theater and film. Conflicting interpretations of her and her husband have arisen, however, including allegations that they used their power for personal enrichment.

Nationalism and populism on such scale are enough to explain Argentinians' lasting love for the Peróns. In 1949, he secured a new constitution that embodied his principles and authorized presidential re-election to consecutive terms. Although military objections to the possibility of a female commander-in-chief blocked Eva's vice-presidential candidacy, Juan

Perón won the much-manipulated election of 1952. Yet conditions were turning against him.

Populism without economic realism could not last. Income redistribution and expanded government spending depended on postwar boom conditions. After 1948, recession, bad harvests, and keener competition in export markets led to balance-of-payment deficits. Industrial output and real wages were falling by the early 1950s. Perón never coped successfully with this change, nor have his successors ever overcome the resulting combination of economic stagnation and political instability.

Perón's political alliance began to crumble, and he turned to erratic measures that led to his fall. Re-elected in 1952, he launched a new Five-Year Plan that departed from the first by calling for a two-year wage freeze and giving incentives to agriculture and foreign investment. As if to mask these changes, he tightened political discipline among his followers, became increasingly dictatorial (though he never eliminated all opposition), and emphasized the "Justicialist" ideology that he had made up to explain his policies. Still, the complaints grew. Church-state tensions rose to the point of bloody violence by 1955. The pope excommunicated him, and the military abandoned him. Facing a military conspiracy in September 1955, he fled without a fight. For the next eighteen years, Perón overshadowed Argentine politics from afar, while his followers, though divided, remained a major force inside the country.

After Perón's fall, the military attempted to rule. As yet, however, they had no effective policy beyond the wish to root out Peronism. Their attempts to break the unions, end Perón's consumer subsidies, and deregulate the economy caused the exiled leader's popularity and that of his now-outlawed party to rise again. Politics became so fractious, and the economy so unstable, that the military soon decided to withdraw into the background and permit a return to electoral politics. The largest legal party was the Radicals, who had last ruled Argentina before the Depression. By promising to relegalize the outlawed Peronists in return for votes, Arturo Frondizi, the candidate of one of two Radical factions, won the 1958 election and became president.

Civilian presidents from the Radical party—actually not radical but middle-class moderates—governed Argentina for the next eight years. Their rule forms a second stage in the postwar trend toward mass political participation and economic development. Frondizi's key problems as president were to cope with Perón's legacy of economic deterioration and political instability. Economically, Frondizi seemed ready to try anything to revive the economy—from a large initial wage increase for labor, to foreign borrowing, deals with foreign oil companies, and government personnel cuts. But his policies failed to reverse inflation and unemployment. Partly for this reason, Frondizi's political support eroded so much that thirty-five coup attempts occurred against his presidency. When he followed through on his deal with the Peronists and again allowed them to participate directly in elections, the armed forces overthrew him. Civilian government resumed indecisively under the rival Radical faction in 1963, but another military coup toppled it in 1966. The middle-class Radicals had again failed to rule Latin America's most middle-class country, and the problems stemming from Perón's combination of populism and economic unrealism persisted.

Neocolonial Militarism in Argentina

The new military government of 1966 dismantled the fragile institutions of Argentina's modern political life by closing Congress, suppressing political parties and the labor movement, purging the universities, and ruling through an alliance of military commanders, technocrats, and foreign investors. Its economic program featured a two-year wage freeze, elimination of all restrictions on profit remittances by foreign firms, and devaluation. Devaluation produced dramatic effects, making it harder for Argentine firms to import machinery or new technology and easier for foreign firms to buy them out. Foreign dominance of Argentine industry increased markedly.

Military rule could not make Argentines take such medicine quietly. In 1969, troops fired on a labor demonstration in Córdoba, center of the automobile industry, and violence spread to other cities, opening a period of urban guerrilla activism. Numerous guerrilla groups emerged, such as the People's Revolutionary Army (ERP in Spanish) and the left-Peronist Montoneros. The revolutionary danger that some officers had mistakenly thought they saw in the masses in the 1940s was becoming a reality. Some radical movements were Marxist, but the roots of others lay in Perón's populism. His policies, and military reactions to them, had created the peril they were meant to thwart.

As violence grew—with attacks on government installations, kidnappings of foreign businessmen, the killing of a former president, and brutal retaliation—Argentina drifted toward civil war. Military leaders finally struck a deal with the exiled Perón, hoping that his magic could still restore order. He returned to become president again, at age seventy-seven. This time, his wife, Isabel, was his vice president. They were elected in September 1973 with 62 percent of the vote.

From exile, Perón had made statements to encourage both Left and Right. His one goal was to regain power. In office, he cracked down on the Left—the military commanders who let him return had not misjudged him. Perón died in 1974, and his wife succeeded him but was unable to control events. The crackdown on the Left intensified, as right-wing death squads, thought to be linked to one of her advisers, mounted a counterterror. When the economy went out of control, the army removed her from office in 1976, and military

rule resumed. The generals who had seized power meant to change Argentine politics permanently. Their biggest problems were the Left and the economy.

The generals expanded the struggle with the Left into a "dirty war," in which both sides made fatal mistakes. The Left blundered from the start in bypassing mass mobilization and organization to launch military action against the regime. If leftists had first been able to win control of the labor movement from right-wing Peronists, for example, things might have ended differently. The regime's mistake was to overreact, terrorizing the nation indiscriminately in order to quell guerrilla movements with perhaps only ten thousand members. By the time the military won, ten thousand people—if not several times more—had "disappeared," tortured and in many cases pushed from helicopters to die in the sea. Many *desaparecidos* (those who have "disappeared") were university students or former students, middle class in origin, whose interest in radical ideas was an understandable reaction to a military regime that offered them so little. The desaparecidos' memory—publicized by a movement that their mothers created—still haunts Argentine consciences.

Economically, the military rulers introduced predictable policies. Favoring the agrarian side of the economy rather than the industrial, they sold off state enterprises and tightened credit. Real interest rates rocketed to 20 to 40 percent. Workers' living standards plummeted. The industrial working class actually shrank by a quarter from 1975 to 1980. These brutal policies slowed inflation and produced a positive payments balance until the 1981 recession sent the economy reeling and added massive foreign debt to the military rulers' economic legacy.

In the spring of 1982, the troubled regime attempted the classic maneuver of rousing patriotic support through a popular war, fought over the Falkland Islands, known as the Malvinas in Spanish. About three hundred miles off the coast, the islands were ruled by Britain but claimed by Argentina. Argentina's defeat disgraced the military regime, which then had no choice but to step aside and call presidential elections for October 1983.

Again Toward Democracy and Development?

The winner, in an upset of the Peronist candidate, was Raúl Alfonsín, a Radical and human rights activist. His victory roused excitement in Argentina and abroad. For Latin America, it seemed to signal a new turn toward democracy and economic development in the national interest.

Alfonsín faced huge tasks. The "dirty war" had left a vast backlog of rights violations to prosecute. In addition, the legacy of Perón's economic and political policies—combining state-dominated industry and a weakened agricultural sector with a highly politicized society—would have assured low economic growth and high political conflict even without the foreign debt piled up under the military. To dismantle state corporatism and make the economy internationally competitive seemed urgent. Could this be done in a country edgy over the trials of military figures from the fallen regime, where Peronists remained powerful and international lenders demanded austerity as a condition for debt rescheduling?

By the May 1989 presidential election, the economic situation had worsened to the point of food riots and looting. The flamboyant Peronist candidate, Carlos Saúl Menem, won. Alfonsín dejectedly resigned before his term ended, and Peronists came to power for the first time without Perón himself. Facing both economic disruption and rightist military revolts, Menem had to sacrifice ideology to seek foreign investment, raise the efficiency of tax collection, privatize government firms, weaken unions, cut military spending, and even relax prosecution of rights violations under military rule. After shrinking by 25 percent in the 1980s, the economy began to grow again, at a yearly average of 5.3 percent from 1990 through 1998. Menem managed to win re-election in 1995. In 2000 he was succeeded by Fernando de la Rúa, and Argentina proved that economic reform was possible under democracy, without the repression that Pinochet had inflicted on Chile.

Argentina's fifty-year slide into underdevelopment and instability spotlighted the difficulty of combining economic growth with social justice in a developing country. Perón's first presidency tested the possibilities of populist corporatism coupled with state-led industrialization. His military successors tested those of authoritarianism and economic neoliberalism. Alfonsín and Menem again faced the problem of achieving both democracy and development with the complications added by their predecessors' mistakes and the tightening of global interdependence.

Brazil: Political and Economic Vacillations

Events in Brazil after 1945 paralleled those in Argentina but with significant differences. Here, too, the later years of the import-substitution phase were dominated first by a prewar populist leader, Getúlio Vargas (1951–1954), and then by two presidents who aimed, not very successfully, at nationalist economic development and political mobilization: Juscelino Kubitschek (1956–1961) and João Goulart (1961–1964). As in Argentina, the military wielded considerable influence, seizing power in the mid-1960s and introducing neoliberal policies. In Brazil, civilian rule resumed in 1985. Differences between the two countries included the existence of a sizable peasantry in Brazil. This fact prompted both an attempt at political mobilization in the countryside in the early 1960s and ongoing social tensions after its failure. Ultimately,

Brazil's most distinctive trait is that it is one of Latin America's—indeed the world's—most inequitable societies.

The Second Republic

The postwar part of Brazil's import-substitution phase coincided with its Second Republic (1946–1964). In reaction against Vargas's New State, the new constitution adopted in 1946 reduced the powers of the presidency, separated the three branches of government more effectively, and extended the vote to all but military enlisted men and illiterates (the latter still accounted for nearly 60 percent of the population). Political parties, which Vargas had banned, formed in 1945 and helped to democratize the country over the next twenty years. Until 1950, the presidency remained in the hands of one of the generals who had overthrown Vargas in 1945. His regime wasted on imported luxuries the foreign exchange accumulated during the war. In the elections of 1950, Vargas ran for president with a program emphasizing industrialization. A coalition of labor, industry, and the middle class supported him.

Resuming the presidency at age sixty-eight, Vargas concentrated on the economy. Faced with deficits and inflation, he charted a middle-of-the-road policy that aimed to attract foreign investment but also had nationalist components. Vargas proposed to limit foreign companies' profit remittances and form a mixed public-private corporation, Petrobrás, to monopolize the petroleum industry. Like other middle-of-the-road programs, this one attracted opposition from both Left and Right—and from the United States.

As inflation and the foreign trade deficit continued to worsen, Vargas faced a cabinet crisis and other troubles in 1954. His finance minister called for a stabilization program, while his labor minister, the future president João Goulart, demanded wage increases. Evidence of financial scandal also came to light. Then an attempt to assassinate an opposition journalist was traced to Vargas's security chief. Even though he had acted without Vargas's knowledge, the military demanded Vargas's resignation. His response was sensational: suicide.

Brazil's next elected president, Kubitschek, came to power in 1955 despite much maneuvering by officers and politicians. He committed the country to an inflationary development strategy summed up in his slogan "Fifty years' progress in five." From 1957 to 1961, the economy grew at the remarkable average annual rate of 7 percent. By the time Kubitschek left office in 1960, Brazil's heavy industry supplied half of the country's needs, from machine tools to mining equipment. By 1962, Brazil was the world's seventh-biggest auto manufacturer. There were also vast public works projects. New dams supplied electrical power. The most spectacular innovation was the new capital city in the interior, Brasília, built in three years at huge cost. The new capital, with the highway network leading to it, was meant to create a new sense of national unity.

Yet a reckoning had to come. Kubitschek's policies favored profits over wages, and he courted foreign capital by offering incentives not available to Brazilian enterprises. Foreign interests soon controlled half of Brazil's large corporations. The foreign debt shot up to $2.7 billion in 1961, a level that already required more than half of export earnings for debt service. Refusing demands to stabilize the economy, Kubitschek let inflation continue. As a result, the value of the currency, and Brazil's export earnings, fell drastically. Unrest spread through the country. In the northeast, Peasant Leagues formed, denounced by landowners as communist. Kubitschek's nationalist development strategy was proving no sounder than Perón's.

Kubitschek's successors faced crisis conditions. His immediate successor resigned after seven months. The next, Goulart, faced a congressional attempt to check his populism by amending the constitution to reduce his powers. Goulart regained full powers in 1963 but was less successful in economics. One dubious success was a law regulating foreign investment and limiting annual profit remittances to no more than 10 percent of the capital invested. The law almost halted foreign investment, creating a capital shortage that forced a return to Kubitschek's inflationary method of expanding the money supply. The currency collapsed again. Arguing that inflation and development went together, Goulart did nothing, and his moderate support began to evaporate.

Goulart responded to his difficulties by moving to the left. Unable to get Congress to pass a program to reform taxes and expropriate large estates, he presented more radical proposals: immediate expropriation of certain types of landholdings, periodic wage adjustments, votes for illiterates and enlisted men, legalization of the Communist party. He began to enact some of these measures by decree. His support for political activism in unaccustomed places—among the peasantry and in the army's enlisted ranks—panicked moderates and conservatives. Civilian opponents of the regime called for military intervention. Faced with rebellion in the ranks, the military commanders swung into action, forcing Goulart to leave Brazil in April 1964. Having recently weathered Castro's rise and the Cuban missile crisis, the United States approved the coup in advance and sent a naval force to stand by offshore.

Goulart's policies were mistakes in many ways. He failed to tackle inflation and further politicized the military. Yet his was the only Brazilian government that has yet tried to complete political mobilization by carrying it into the countryside.

Military Rule and Growth Without Development

Goulart's fall opened a twenty-year period of military rule. The 1964 coup ended the Second Republic, and a dictatorship took form under new constitutions in 1967 and 1969. All Brazilians could be deprived of their rights, as three former presidents were, and the generals replaced the old political parties with two new ones they created. Thereafter, the problems facing the military resembled those in Argentina: the Left, the economy, and eventually demands to restore civilian rule.

Dissatisfaction with the new regime found expression throughout Brazilian culture, from popular songs to guerrilla attacks. By the late 1960s, moderates demanded a return to civilian government; the Left demanded social revolution. Student groups began to riot, and a Mothers' Union formed to protest the violent treatment the students received. Urban guerrillas began action on the far left, government-linked death squads on the right.

Brazil's military government soon mastered state terrorism sufficiently to offer itself as a model to other Latin American countries—such as Chile and Argentina—threatened by "subversion." Brazil's radical Left had suffered enough by 1973 that it could no longer threaten the regime. Yet rights violations continued. Among the most vocal critics were activist churchmen, such as Archbishop Helder Câmara.

Economically, the most important feature of the military period was the so-called Brazilian miracle. Seeking to slow inflation and boost investment, the military governments pursued a blatantly neoliberal, foreign-oriented strategy. Foreign investment grew so much that foreigners fully controlled the tire and auto industries and were nearly as dominant in others. Though unbalanced, Brazil's economic growth averaged around 10 percent a year between 1969 and 1974. During this "miraculous" period, industrial products first surpassed coffee among Brazil's exports.

This change meant neither an end to dependency for Brazil nor anything miraculous for most Brazilians. As multinational corporations tightened their grip on the economy, their profit remittances often exceeded their investments in Brazil eight or ten times over. Agriculture, still dominated by huge, inefficient estates, "modernized" by producing more for export and less for Brazil's soaring population—soybeans rather than black beans. Shortsighted attempts to develop the interior expanded into extensive cutting of the Amazon rain forest, producing lasting ecological damage for short-term economic gain. Inequalities among regions and social classes widened. Brazil's income distribution became exceptionally unequal by Latin American, indeed by global, standards. Between 1960 and 1990, the top 10 percent of the population's share of national income grew steadily from 40 to 53 percent, while the lowest 10 percent of the population's share fell by over half, from 1.5 to 0.7 percent.

The OPEC oil price increases destroyed Brazil's "miracle." The military government raised gasoline prices to reflect the 1973-1974 quadrupling of oil prices but let later price increases fall behind the inflation rate, gambling that the increases were temporary. Economic growth continued in Brazil through 1978, but the major oil price hike in 1979 exposed the government's strategy error. Oil imports began to consume most of export earnings. Petrobrás stepped up exploration, and Brazil's oil production reached a half-million barrels a day by 1984. The shift to other forms of energy also progressed, and Brazil soon led the world in using alcohol derived from sugar cane as a fuel. Still, inflation slipped out of control, and the foreign debt soared, especially after U.S. interest rates rose to unprecedented heights in the early 1980s.

The results gravely threatened Brazil and the international banking system as well. Brazil's economic growth did continue, lopsidedly. The arms industry began exporting to such countries as Libya; the microcomputer industry became the world's third largest after the United States' and Japan's; and Brazil exported steel to the United States. Yet most Brazilians'

fortunes had worsened. By the early 1980s, middle-class cooperation with the military waned, and pressures to return to civilian rule mounted.

A Masquerade of Democracy

In 1982, when Brazil held the first direct elections since 1965 for state governors, many opponents of the regime won. The victories strengthened the opposition, and the military began preparing for the election of a civilian president. This occurred in 1985, but the military retained enough power to make civilian control questionable. Generals held six cabinet posts, and the military controlled both its own nuclear program, separate from the civilian one, and the National Information Service, an intelligence agency with powers unequaled in democratic states. The new civilian president promised a new constitution, but he died three months after election, leaving fulfillment of the promise to his vice president and successor, José Sarney (1985-1990).

Despite talk of change, Sarney achieved little, though the military at least remained in the shadows. Inflation was back at 1,500 percent in 1990, after a decade with almost no gain in production per capita. Brazil's industry had developed to the point that it could export jet planes to the United States, as well as steel. Yet Brazil had defaulted on interest payments to foreign banks in 1987 and stood second only to the United States in the size of its foreign debt. Drafting began on a new constitution to institutionalize civilian rule. Yet corruption and threats of force poisoned the atmosphere, as Sarney and the military proved in 1988 by openly using treasury funds and coup threats to influence the terms of the new constitution.

Begun on that cynical note, the 1989 presidential campaign brought in the younger Fernando Collor de Mello. His campaign promises of honest, efficient government attracted voters but were soon forgotten. In 1992, a massive

Landlessness in Brazil. *A provision of the current constitution provides for expropriation of idle land. But when some landless Brazilians tried to claim unused land in the northern state of Pará in 1996, this is how they ended up.*
O Liberal de Pará, Ary Sousa/© AP-Wide World Photos

corruption scandal broke open, and Brazil became the first nation in Latin America to impeach a president.

By 1995, things were back on the neoliberal track to the point that President Fernando Cardoso (1995–) was trying to amend the 1988 constitution to open Brazil further to foreign investment and even abolish legal distinctions between foreign and Brazilian corporations. By then, Brazil was one of the world's ten most industrialized nations. But this was still growth without development. The government itself estimated in the 1980s that 60 percent of the population was malnourished, and the armed forces annually rejected 45 percent of con-

scripts for physical deficiencies. With 26 percent of the world's cultivable land, Brazil could not feed itself, primarily because 1 percent of the population still controlled 45 percent of the arable land in vast estates, using their political power to thwart land reform. The landless rural poor flocked to the urban shantytowns looking for work, and often from there to the Amazon, where their search for land accelerated the cutting of the tropical forest or ended in bloody clashes between squatters and landlords' private armies. Virtual slaves, some estate workers still labored under conditions of debt servitude, receiving no money at all but having to charge their food at a company store where their purchases were debited, at unstated prices, against their earnings. As we have seen, social violence veered out of control in large cities like São Paulo.

Outsiders naively admired Brazil for its music and festive carnivals. Behind its mask of democracy, however, Brazil remained—even as its elites renegotiated the (for them) lucrative conditions of dependency in the age of global capitalism—riddled with violence along lines of race, class, and gender. If Brazil was the land of the future, was this Latin America's future in the era of globalization?

Mexico: Drifting Away from the Revolutionary Legacy

Mexico, too, moved through a series of phases—mass mobilization, then neoliberal authoritarianism followed by an opening to the world economy—with modifications that reflect its exceptional history before World War II. After a high point of reform under Lázaro Cárdenas, Mexico moved to the right rather than to the left, though a populist reprise occurred in the late 1950s and early 1960s. Thereafter, the single dominant party remained more strongly institutionalized and broadly based than any other in Latin America. Because it had a degree of control over the military that other Latin American countries could only envy, the renewed rightward move toward authoritarianism and neoliberalism occurred under party auspices, without military rule. By the 1980s, Mexico's distinctive party-state combination remained more firmly established than the military regimes then reaching their ends in Argentina and Brazil, and Mexico had also become a major oil exporter. Rapid growth of oil exports, however, had upset the balance among economic sectors; and the trend toward democratization in Latin America took the form of new challenges to the single party. In the 1990s, it tried to tighten its grip on power and extend its

outward-oriented development policy into a high-stakes bid for free trade with the United States and Canada. However, corruption and economic crisis jeopardized these efforts spectacularly. The 1997 election finally ended its seventy-year political monopoly.

The Single-Party Regime

For decades, Mexico's relative political stability was largely due to its system of one-party rule. As noted in Chapter 7, President Lázaro Cárdenas (1934–1940) reorganized the official party along corporatist lines, with separate agrarian, labor, military, and "popular" (essentially middle-class) sectors. In this way he mobilized both workers and peasants but kept them separate. In 1945 the party was again reorganized as the Institutional Revolutionary party (PRI in Spanish), the name it still retains, with peasant, labor, and "popular" (middle-class) sectors.

Good organization enabled the one-party regime to endure. The party had firm control of both organized labor and the countryside. Party governance remained highly centralized in Mexico City. As usual in one-party systems, political interest focused more on nominations, an in-party matter, than on elections. Government and party interpenetrated each other so deeply that they became virtually indistinguishable. Because the state controlled many enterprises, the state-party symbiosis extended into the economy as well. The president had vast powers over this combine. For example, he originated the budget and most legislation, which the Congress merely rubber-stamped, and he chose the candidate to succeed him.

Opponents rightly accused the PRI of corruption, repression, and election rigging. Indeed, the candidate with the most votes would win only if the government so allowed. Such methods helped the PRI maintain control, especially in rural areas with long histories of authoritarian rule. The PRI had also co-opted a broad range of opinion that might otherwise have fed opposition movements. It had inherited the rhetoric and symbolism of Mexico's revolution. Even opposition parties came under PRI patronage, once the government, responding to criticism of one-party rule, began to guarantee them representation in the Chamber of Deputies. The Institutional Revolutionary party was not revolutionary, but it was institutionalized.

Emerging from party leadership to head such a strong party-state combine, Mexico's recent presidents mostly made no profound mark as individuals, but there have been differences among them. Miguel Alemán (1946-1952), the PRI's first civilian candidate, reduced military expenditure to 7 percent of the budget, down from 30 percent in 1930 and 70 percent in 1917. Mexico thus escaped the military-dominated politics that still bedeviled most of Latin America. Adolfo López Mateos (1958-1964) came closest to the Alliance for Progress ideal. He revived land distribution by giving out more land than any president since Cárdenas. He also expanded social services, introduced profit sharing for workers, and began the system of assuring congressional representation to small parties.

The presidency of Gustavo Díaz Ordaz (1964-1970) began the shift back to the right then underway elsewhere in Latin America. The worst smirch on his record came in 1968, as the government prepared to host the Olympic Games—the first time a developing country got to show off its achievements in that way. Amid preparations for the games, anti-government demonstrations began. As in other countries in the 1960s, students played a leading role, though up to 400,000 sympathizers would turn out to demonstrate with them. The government's response showed how much it had abandoned revolutionary populism. The climax came on October 2, when troops killed several hundred demonstrators and jailed two thousand. The Olympic Games went off without a hitch, and the guerrilla violence that followed

was squelched by the early 1970s; but whatever else he did, Díaz Ordaz was remembered for the violence. Later presidents have never regained López Mateos's populist stance, and economic problems have preoccupied them increasingly.

Economic Issues to the Forefront

Stimulated by wartime demand for labor and raw materials in the United States, Mexico's economic growth remained rapid through the 1960s. By then, Mexico was nearly self-sufficient in consumer goods and was developing heavy industry. A major problem, until the mid-1950s, was inflation, especially for rural and urban workers, whose wages did not keep pace.

To deal with this problem, the government devalued the peso in 1954 and adopted a "hard-money" strategy. Mexico's ability to maintain a fixed exchange rate, while allowing unrestricted exchange of the peso against the U.S. dollar or other currencies, became a treasured symbol of development—one that few Third World countries could match. The 1954 devaluation made Mexican exports cheaper and Mexico itself cheaper for foreign tourists. Devaluation also stimulated foreign investment. In dollars of constant value, such investment in Mexico in 1940 was still only one-third what it had been in 1911. Although economic nationalism remained an official priority, the hard-money policy began a reversal of a trend that vastly increased foreign—mostly U.S.—investment over the next twenty years, creating the usual problems about profit remittances. Eventually, Mexico tried to limit these dangers. The government borrowed in order to expand its role as investor and lender. It also limited foreign ownership to a 49 percent share of any company. These measures did not solve Mexico's economic problems, however. Government borrowing started Mexico's fantastic debt accumulation, and the limit on foreign ownership left many opportunities for elite Mexicans to cooperate with foreign interests, as they always had.

The 1954 hard-money strategy reduced inflation but led to new problems in the early 1960s. Mexico's population growth had begun to cause alarm in the late 1950s. Urbanization accelerated, partly because a mechanized "new hacienda" was emerging in the countryside. As in other developing countries, many urban migrants could not find factory jobs and had to scratch out a living as bootblacks, street vendors, or servants. The government had long had programs to restrict the costs of goods and services to the poor. In the 1960s and 1970s, those programs had to be expanded. When population growth outstripped domestic food production and necessitated imports, the costs of the programs became prohibitive. This problem compounded the effects of rising oil prices. Inflation resumed, the 1954 exchange rate became untenable, and the government finally had to devalue the peso twice in one month in 1976.

Soon after, the world learned that Mexico was a major oil power. Discoveries raised its proven oil reserves to 49 billion barrels by 1984, ranking Mexico fourth in the world after Saudi Arabia, Kuwait, and the Soviet Union (with 169, 90, and 63 billion barrels, respectively, at that date). Iran's experience had shown that rapid growth of oil income could produce undesirable effects in a populous country with a complex economy. Mexico, which was not a member of OPEC, therefore set out to increase production only gradually. Even so, Mexico's petroleum earnings grew more than 25-fold from 1976 to 1981, when they reached $13 billion, indeed making Mexico dependent on oil exports.

The oil price slump after 1981 led to increased foreign borrowing that made Mexico one of the world's most indebted nations. Growth continued but only spottily. Foreign firms kept opening assembly plants in Mexico to profit from low wage rates. Japan, too, used this method to penetrate the U.S. market (Japan was also eager for Mexican oil, since Mexico looked like a surer source than the Persian Gulf). Mexico's government searched for ways to reinvigorate the economy—for example, by selling state-owned companies. The catastrophic Mexico City earthquake of 1985, causing eight thousand deaths and $4 billion in damages, wiped out the gains of government policy up to that point, however. Then, the Mexican stock market crashed in October 1987, shortly before the New York exchange did. After that, the Mexican government had to adopt a severe IMF-approved austerity program. It dropped the peso below 2,000 to the U.S. dollar (less than one-tenth the peso's 1984 value), raised prices of subsidized goods and services, and installed wage and price controls. As part of the deal, Mexico also had to begin lowering its tariffs and promoting exports, abandoning import substitution. By the 1988 presidential election, real wages had fallen 40 percent in six years.

Reactions to this situation became clear in the election. Not surprisingly, victory went to the PRI candidate, Carlos Salinas de Gortari, who as budget and planning minister had initiated the 1980s austerity policy. For the first time, however, the PRI faced opposition from the Left and Right. The most exciting candidate was the leader of a breakaway PRI faction, Cuauhtémoc Cárdenas, Lázaro's son. Named for the last Aztec ruler (father Lázaro Cárdenas was proud of his mixed ancestry), Cuauhtémoc Cárdenas campaigned on a populist, nationalist platform, reasserting the revolutionary legacy. Salinas won with only 50.3 percent of the vote; Cárdenas got 31.1 percent. Given the PRI's history of winning all races and the government's control of the vote count, Cárdenas's followers thought him the moral victor. Over the next several years, opposition candidates did win several state governorships.

Abandoning the Revolutionary Legacy

Seeking to adjust Mexico to the post–Cold War era, Salinas systematically broke with Mexico's revolutionary tradition. Politically, he improved relations between the government and the Catholic church. He reformed the electoral law and the inner workings of PRI, making some concessions to the opposition on the right but not the left. Harassment of Cárdenas and his followers, and growing charges of torture and other human rights violations, raised questions about whether the reforms were supposed to make Mexico more democratic or merely tighten its existing system.

Economically, Salinas showed his biases as a conservative economist. He lowered trade barriers, attacked organized labor and the *ejido* (the communal land-tenure system sanctified in the 1917 constitution), privatized nearly all the public enterprises, allowed foreigners to own minority stakes in agricultural enterprises, and daringly proposed a free-trade agreement with the United States. This idea blossomed into the North American Free Trade Agreement among Mexico, the United States, and Canada (1993). The treaty would not create a common market for the movement of workers, but it would eliminate most customs duties, entitle investors from each country to the same treatment as nationals in the other countries, ensure free exchange or transfer of currencies, and protect investors against expropriation.

Only the most publicized of many regional integration projects in Latin America, NAFTA excited all the hopes and fears awakened by the tightening of global integration in the 1990s. U.S. workers reacted with fear of losing more jobs. Some Mexican analysts—echoing sentiments that the revolutionaries of 1910 would have understood fully—argued that free-trade agreements by nature furthered U.S. dominance. Far from advancing Mexico's overall de-velopment, the treaty, so viewed, would lead to further exploitation of Mexican workers and further environmental degradation through nonenforcement of Mexican law.

If Carlos Salinas meant to move Mexico beyond its revolutionary legacy, the problem was what to put in place of it. The biggest problem was PRI itself. It suffered internal divisions and lost power in seveal states. When the party's candidate to succeed Salinas was murdered in 1994, the PRI's alternate candidate, Ernesto Zedillo, was elected. His presidency proved unsettling to many Mexicans, however, partly because his more democratic style left freer rein to other politicians who were no democrats themselves. Scandal also dramatized the decrepitude of the PRI machine. Mexico's presidents had normally enriched themselves before leaving office. With Salinas' privatizations and the growth of foreign investment, large fortunes had mushroomed, none more suspect than his brother Raúl's, estimated at $300 million, most of it stashed abroad. By 1996, Raúl Salinas was in prison, and ex-president Carlos Salinas was living abroad. To make matters worse, under Salinas Colombian drug traffickers transferred a large part of their transhipping and money laundering to Mexico—with official collusion, some critics thought.

Ultimately, one price for burying the revolution was political violence. Political assassinations, kidnappings, and drug-related violence increased. Antigovernment revolts also broke out in the southern states of Mexico, Guerrero, Oaxaca, and Chiapas. The "Zapatista Army of National Liberation" in Chiapas, under its masked leader Subcommander Marcos, asserted the still-unmet grievances of the Maya people. But it did so in a way that looked far beyond the narrow horizons of the revolutionary caudillo Emiliano Zapata (see Chapter 7). Faced with the armed might of the Mexican military, the Zapatistas of the 1990s and their charismatic Subcommander Marcos (reportedly a former university professor) turned their muddy, snake-infested villages into tourist destinations for chic leftists and media moguls from abroad, promoting "Zapatourism," international conferences, and media coverage not only to attract support but also to keep the Mexican army at bay. For native American rebels in a backward province to turn their movement into a virtual theme park signaled how integrated the world had become in the age of the information technologies.

Not only the micropolitics of the local but also national elections expressed dissatisfaction with the status quo. In 1997, Mexican voters took advantage of a new, independent electoral system introduced by PRI President Zedillo and ended seven decades of PRI rule. The pro-business National Action Party (PAN in Spanish) won the governorships of seven out of thirty-one states, including all the largest and wealthiest. Cuauhtémoc Cárdenas, from the left-of-center Party of the Democratic Revolution (PDR in Spanish), won the mayorship of Mexico City by a landslide. With the PDR winning 26 percent of the national vote and the PAN winning 27 percent, the PRI also lost control of the Chamber of Deputies, the lower legislative house. In 2000, PAN candidate and businessman-turned-politician Vicente Fox won the presidency with ambitious goals for privatization, governmental restructuring, and tax reform, but without the legislative majorities needed to ensure passage of his measures.

Cuba: Social Revolution Without an End to Dependency

The small countries of Central America and the Caribbean (Map 14.1) have experienced many of the common Latin American problems—single-crop export economies, caudillo (strongman) politics, U.S. intervention—with special sharpness, without matching the developmental successes of their larger neighbors. Yet Cuba achieved Latin America's most successful social revolution to date. In the world of superpower bipolarity, Cuba's revolution showed that dependency could be altered, if not escaped. How solid was Cuba's achievement?

Whence the Cuban Revolution?

By the nineteenth century, Cuba had discovered its vocation as a producer of cane sugar and, secondarily, tobacco. A slave-based plantation economy grew up, and by 1860 Cuba produced almost one-third of the world's sugar.

Cuba's landowners did not rebel against Spanish rule in the 1810s and 1820s, when most of Latin America did. But Cubans of a half-century later resented Spanish domination and had economic ties to the United States more than to Spain. A first rebellion (1868–1878) ended without independence from Spain. Another rebellion broke out in 1895, and U.S. intervention forced Spain to concede Cuba's independence in 1898. Cuban revolutionaries opposed the U.S. role. What followed after "independence" showed why.

Cuba became independent under U.S. occupation. Americans wanted independent Cuba to favor U.S. interests. They seemed not to realize that their wishes might infringe on the "independence." The first U.S. act was to disband the rebel forces. Improvements in public works and sanitation followed—most notably, the elimination of yellow fever, made possible by a Cuban doctor's discovery that mosquitoes carry the disease. The United States encouraged Cubans to draft a new constitution (1901), then forced them to add the Platt Amendment, which gave Washington extensive rights, hence the U.S. naval base at Guantánamo Bay. Cuba was really a U.S. protectorate.

Economically, the protectorate meant an increase in U.S. investment, from $50 million in 1896 to $1.5 billion in 1929. Cuba was more than ever a colonial economy, vulnerable to

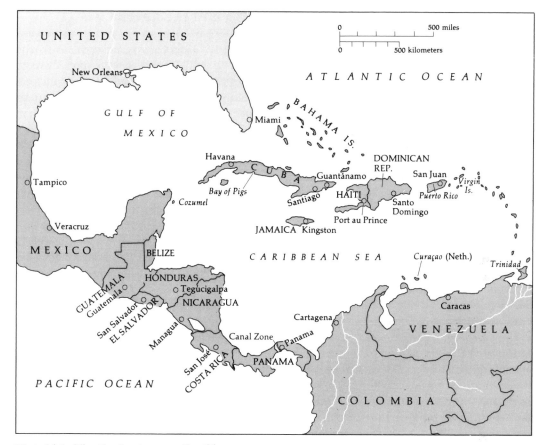

Map 14.1 The Contemporary Caribbean

variations in the size and price of the sugar harvest. Export earnings in 1932, for example, were less than one-fifth of 1924's. During the Depression, U.S. investment, at least in sugar, began to decline, and by the late 1950s Cubans owned more than 60 percent of the industry, up from 22 percent in 1939. Cuba remained tied to the United States through special trade arrangements, however. From 1934 to 1960, a quota system gave Cuba a set share of the U.S. sugar market at prices above world market prices. In exchange, Cuba had to accept U.S. manufactures.

Cuba's dependence on sugar had major political and social effects. Just as the technol-ogy and capital requirements of sugar mill-ing led to a concentration of ownership, the requirements of cane cultivation affected the people. Sugar cane is harvested annually but needs replanting only after five to twenty-five years. Laborers therefore get work dur-ing the three-month harvest season and have little or no work the rest of the year. Un-able to buy or rent land because of concen-trated ownership, and often kept in place by debt servitude, the rural poor faced a bleak outlook.

Most rural Cubans were not peasants, whose normal goal is to acquire land, but work-ers, whose main concern is wages, and they were in touch with their urban counterparts. By the 1930s, there was much migration from countryside to urban slums. Partly because of improved public health, the population also grew rapidly, more than doubling between 1899 and 1931, to almost 4 million. By 1950, almost 40 percent of Cubans lived in cities, mostly in extreme poverty. Cuba's workers, rural and urban, were ready for political mobilization. Who would lead them?

As elsewhere in Latin America, the Depression provoked political change, but only briefly did this seem to answer the question just posed. The Depression led to the toppling of the brutal regime of Gerardo Machado (1925–1933). What emerged at his fall was an alliance of army sergeants, radical students, and Ramón Grau San Martín, who took over the civilian side of government.

At first, major change appeared to be underway. Grau proclaimed a socialist revolution and abrogated the Platt Amendment. His government produced much social legislation— the eight-hour workday, creation of a labor department, votes for women. But it antagonized Washington by suspending loan payments and seizing sugar mills. Then the United States encouraged Fulgencio Batista, one of the sergeants in the governing coalition, to overthrow Grau. Washington was ready to give up the Platt Amendment by treaty in 1934 and was backing away from interventionism. But it had no hesitation in preferring a dictatorship that would collaborate with U.S. interests to a democratic or populist regime that was economically nationalistic—especially if it talked of socialism. If anything, backing away from interventionism heightened the U.S. "need" for cooperative strongmen such as Batista.

Batista dominated Cuban politics through 1958. Sometimes he was the president. Sometimes others were his puppet presidents. Throughout the period, corruption, violence, and cynicism marked political life.

Castro and the Revolution

Born in 1927, Fidel Castro grew up in the Batista era. While studying law, he became active in student politics. He mounted his first attack on the Batista regime on July 26, 1953, with an unsuccessful assault on a provincial army barracks. Fidel and his more radical brother, Raúl, survived but were sent to prison. Amnestied in 1955, Fidel fled to Mexico to plan a comeback. With him were Raúl and a young Argentine who would become a great martyr of the revolutionary Left, Ernesto "Ché" Guevara. In December 1956, Fidel set sail with eighty-one others to land in Cuba. Barely a dozen—including Fidel, Raúl, and Ché—survived the landing, fleeing into the Sierra Maestra to regroup.

The ensuing struggle proved Batista to be his own worst enemy. His brutality alienated people, while Castro's guerrillas, like the Chinese communists of the 1930s, learned to operate among them without alienating them. When Batista mounted a "liquidation campaign" into the Sierra Maestra, it failed, and he fled. Castro's rebels, about three thousand strong, entered Havana at the beginning of 1959.

It took two more years to consolidate the revolution and define its course. In 1959, an initial episode of collegial rule ended with Castro in sole charge. An agrarian reform law expropriated farmland holdings over a thousand acres and forbade foreigners to own agricultural land. Castro visited the United States twice. Not yet having identified his regime with communism, he presented himself as a reformer. Yet the land reform law and Cuban refugees' accusations made it hard to win goodwill. U.S.-backed anti-Castro operations by Cuban refugees began almost immediately.

In 1960, several major changes helped define Cuba's course. First, when U.S.-owned oil refineries reacted to a Cuban-Soviet deal to trade sugar for crude oil by refusing to process the oil, Castro nationalized the refineries. The

United States then embargoed exports to Cuba and suspended the sugar quota. At that, Castro nationalized other U.S.-owned enterprises. He also began organizing an authoritarian mass-mobilizing regime based on the army, the militia, local citizen groups known as Committees for the Defense of the Revolution, and controls over the press and most other organizations. Finally, he introduced an egalitarian social and economic policy, freezing prices, increasing wages, and launching a literacy campaign that halved the already low illiteracy rate (25 percent) in one year. In response, the United States severed diplomatic relations and, through the CIA, supported an abortive invasion by Cuban exiles at the Bay of Pigs (April 1961). The Soviet attempt to exploit this failure by placing missiles on the island led to the Cuban missile crisis of 1962, which ended with withdrawal of the missiles and a tacit U.S. promise not to invade Cuba.

In December 1961, Castro announced for the first time that he was a Marxist-Leninist. The statement proved epoch-making for several reasons. It shifted Cuba's dependency from the United States to the Soviet Union. The choice of the Soviet model also facilitated what Castro perhaps most wanted: consolidation of his personal power. For other Third World countries, finally, here was something new on the left. Instead of the complex developmental processes of Marxism-Leninism or Maoism, Castro had shown that one could overthrow a government, simply announce that one was a Communist, and so perhaps transform one's country's position in the world. U.S. and local opposition made the pattern hard to repeat in Latin America. Farther afield, in Africa, it found numerous imitators.

With its Marxist character set, Cuba experimented through the 1960s to define its policies. A second agrarian reform law (1963) made state farms the dominant form of cultivation. By 1965, Castro had formed his revolutionary elite into a new Cuban Communist party. Meanwhile,

debate raged over what to do about dependence on sugar. Ché Guevara dominated the debate at first with his Four-Year Plan for diversification and light industrialization, but its results fell short of target. The emphasis reverted to sugar, with Castro predicting that the 1970 harvest would reach a record 10 million tons.

Guevara then came out with an "idealist" strategy for reaching the new goal. His ideas recalled some of Mao Zedong's in China. Guevara argued for a clean break with capitalism, elimination of the market, and creation of a "new Cuban" whose heightened political consciousness would satisfy him or her with moral rather than material incentives. In this view, consolidating the revolution in Cuba also required promoting it elsewhere—whence the international guerrilla strategy that led Ché to his death in Bolivia in 1967. Not everyone agreed with Guevara. Some Cuban leaders advocated greater pragmatism, and the Soviet Union had little use for Guevara's claims to international revolutionary leadership. Castro began to back away from Ché's view in international affairs in 1968 but held to it in domestic policy until 1970, when the cane harvest reached 8.5 million tons—a record but short of the goal of 10 million.

Facing the need for change, Castro made a dramatic speech, taking blame for the failure to meet the goal and offering to resign. The crowd shouted "no." Castro stayed in power but changed policy. With the adoption of newer techniques of economic planning and the reintroduction of material incentives, economic growth rose to over 10 percent a year from 1971 to 1975.

Other measures of the 1970s showed a new concern to expand political participation in ways compatible with the regime's character. Castro broadened the social bases of the labor movement and Communist party. The party held its first congress in December 1975. The new constitution of 1976 set up a system of

Assemblies of Popular Power, with the directly elected members of the municipal assemblies electing members of the provincial assemblies and the national assembly. Cubans still could not form political organizations at will, and many elections were not by secret ballot. But opportunities for discussion of issues and political mobilization had increased. An official Cuban Women's Federation came into being, and a Family Code (1976) mandated equal division of household tasks—a departure from *machismo,* on paper at least.

The policy shift of the 1970s affected international relations. Other Latin American nations resumed diplomatic relations with Cuba, and demands to do so grew in the United States. The main obstacles, for U.S. officials, were human rights and Cuba's interventions in Africa and elsewhere in the Caribbean. An accord of December 1988 removed one troublesome issue by requiring Cuba to withdraw its troops from Angola, where Cuba had supported the Marxist government since 1975 against both U.S.-backed guerrillas and South African forces based in Namibia (see Chapter 15).

Cuba's was Latin America's most successful social revolution. However, its accomplishments depended on annual subsidies of $3 to $5 billion from the Soviet Union. In the late 1980s, over 80 percent of Cuba's foreign trade, imports and exports, had been with socialist countries. Soviet collapse mortally threatened Castro. With the United States tightening its trade embargo and sugar prices in decline, Cuba's imports shrank by at least three-fourths between about 1989 and 1993, while the whole Cuban economy shrank by 50 percent. As oil imports shrank to the point where oxcarts replaced motor vehicles, Cubans watched their revolutionary gains erode.

In the limited room for maneuver that remained, Castro attempted to make adjustments and also maintained the high levels of repression that had long squelched dissent on the island (the fact that so many of his opponents

fled the island had helped to keep him in power). Reforms were made to allow direct elections to the provincial and national Assemblies of Popular Power, remove atheism from the constitution, guarantee foreign investments against nationalization, and add the thought of the nineteenth-century nationalist José Martí, to that of Marx, Engels, and Lenin as guiding principles—thus creating an escape hatch through which socialism might be sacrificed to national interest. In 1993, Castro legalized the use of U.S. dollars in Cuba, as well as limited self-employment and free markets. By the mid-1990s, the economy had begun to grow again, partly thanks to tourism and foreign investment. The party plenum of March 1996 nonetheless reasserted the party's political control, and economic deterioration caused a new surge in illegal immigration to the United States as the 1990s ended.

Economically, Cuba's record looked bleak. Cuba had escaped dependency on the United States only at the cost of dependency on the Soviet Union. The fact that the world economy is capitalist overall had helped provoke Soviet collapse, and Cuba had to face the same fact. Nothing made communist Cuba's failure in economic development more visible than the island's stock of cars, which still consisted of pre-1959 U.S. models plus some Soviet Ladas. Still, most Cubans—the workers who had fared so badly before 1959—would look back on the revolution as an improvement. Economic growth had been puny, but the distribution of resources had become egalitarian. Illiteracy had almost vanished. The creation of a comprehensive school system had given many Cubans new power to shape their lives. The regime had done more for women than any other in Latin America. Over forty years, improvements in public health had increased life expectancy from sixty-three to seventy-six years, and infant mortality had fallen to the U.S. level. These improvements in quality of life exceeded those of Latin American countries with far stronger economic

"Socialism or Death!" *So proclaimed this billboard at Guantánamo in the early 1990s. The Cuban child in front of it does not seem sure what the future holds.* © *Martin Sugarman/Sugarman Productions*

growth records. Allowed no dissent, Cuba's 11 million people would have to hope that the changes of the 1990s would not wipe out these gains.

Conclusion: Development or Disappointment?

In the fifty years following 1945, Latin America experienced three historical phases. Import-substitution industrialization and democratizing mass mobilization set the trend through the early 1960s. The weakness of democratic institutions, the exhaustion of import substitution, the political stresses of the 1960s, and the military emphasis of U.S. policy then led to a turn toward military authoritarianism and economic neoliberalism. With the 1980s came a trend back toward civilian rule. Political democratization was not usually accompanied, however, by economic development in the interest of the people. Instead, the demands of the debt crisis brought into the limelight—not the generals—but the civilian technocrats who had shaped the military governments' neoliberal economic programs.

The experiences of specific countries introduced variations into the regional pattern. Some countries were too small to experience each developmental phase fully or, for that matter, to function effectively as nation-states. Cuba, for example, overturned old-fashioned caudillo rule only when it took a revolutionary turn to the left, but still could not escape dependency. Some larger states also introduced variations into the pattern of phases, while following it more fully. Mexico and Brazil became highly enough industrialized that they could be regarded as mid-size industrial powers. Mexico also became a major petroleum producer and then, with its daring bid to join NAFTA, a major exporter of industrial goods.

In today's world, no country escapes dependency on others. For that matter, for all their efforts to protect themselves with free-trade agreements and regional blocs, the sovereignty of nation-states has declined in many ways. In this context, the crux of the Latin American countries' problems lies in coping with their growing populations' needs while trying to profit from participation in a capitalist world economy in which none of these nations holds a leading position. A long history of internal and external colonialism has helped shape this problem, but the rapid social and economic changes of the late twentieth century made solving it more difficult than ever before. If Latin America's record has been this disappointing, have other parts of the developing world fared better?

Notes

1. Roger Cohen, "A Young Brazilian Killer's Fear and Hope in 'a Very Dark Place.'" *"New York Times,* April 29, 2000, p. A6.
2. Juan-Jose Arévalo, *The Shark and the Sardines,* trans. June Cobb and Raúl Osegueda (New York: Stuart L. Stuart, 1961).

Suggestions for Further Reading

Books

Bethell, Leslie, ed. *Cuba: A Short History* (1993).

Gleijeses, Piero. *Shattered Hope: The Guatemalan Revolution and the United States, 1944-1954* (1991).

Guevara, Ché. *Guerrilla Warfare.* With an introduction and case studies by Brian Loveman and Thomas M. Davies, Jr. (1985).

Horowitz, Irving Louis, ed. *Cuban Communism.* 6th ed. (1987).

Keen, Benjamin, and Keith Hayes. *A History of Latin America.* 6th ed. (2000).

LaFeber, Walter. *Inevitable Revolutions: The United States in Central America.* 2d ed. (1993).

Levine, Robert, and José Carlos Sebe Bom Meihy. *The Unedited Diaries of Carolina Maria de Jesus* (1999).

——. *The History of Brazil* (1999).

Loveman, Brian. *Chile: The Legacy of Hispanic Capitalism.* 2d ed. (1988).

Meyer, Michael C., William L. Sherman, and Susan M. Deeds. *The Course of Mexican History.* 6th ed. (1999).

Nugent, Daniel, ed. *Rural Revolt in Mexico: U.S. Intervention and the Domain of Subaltern Politics* (1998).

Puig, Manuel. *Kiss of the Spider Woman.* Translated by Thomas Colchie (1980).

Rock, David. *Argentina, 1516-1987* (1987).

——. *Authoritarian Argentina* (1993).

Skidmore, Thomas E. *Brazil: Five Cultures of Change* (1999).

Skidmore, Thomas E., and Peter H. Smith. *Modern Latin America.* 4th ed. (1997).

Waisman, Carlos. *Reversal of Development in Argentina* (1987).

Newsletters and Periodicals

Latin American Weekly Report.

Latin American Regional Reports.

CHAPTER 15

Sub-Saharan Africa:
Decay or Development?

NO JEWEL REFLECTS LIGHT LIKE A DIAMOND OF THE FINEST COLOR, CLARITY, AND cut. Among the hardest of gems, diamonds symbolize permanency. Because their price and supply are manipulated by a powerful cartel founded in South Africa over a century ago, they concentrate more value in less matter than almost anything else. Astute advertising has spun romance from their pricey sparkle. Diamonds are the stuff of global economic exchanges with a retail value of $50 billion a year. Most diamonds are mined in Africa, and the finest come from Namibia, Angola, and Sierra Leone. Most stones are marketed by a firm based in South Africa, cut and polished in Antwerp (Belgium), and hoarded in London, whence they are carefully released onto the world market. They are worn by the affluent everywhere, but more than half of all diamond jewelry is sold in the United States.

As with most minerals, glamor and romance are not often in evidence where diamonds are mined. One morning in 2000, Mati Balemo, a poor young Congolese, traveled three hours to a stream where he prospected for diamonds. After an hour of sifting mud, he saw something. Putting it into his mouth to clean it, he found that he had a diamond that he might be able to sell for $20. The other prospectors clapped. A soldier, who had been sitting on the bank with an automatic weapon, came over, took the diamond, and put it in his pocket. The man with the gun got the diamond. The man with the most diamonds gets the most guns.

The impact of diamond mining on African societies is not always bad, although it has become increasingly so in most places. In Botswana (see Map 15.3), diamonds were only discovered in 1969, three years after the country gained independence. The government and the De Beers conglomerate of South Africa equally controlled an industry that employed nearly a fourth of Botswana's population and produced nearly two-thirds of its national income. Ethnically homogeneous, the country benefited from a history of democratic decision-making and a government that invested in infrastructure, education, and health care. The result was a 1998 Human Development Index (HDI) of 0.593, compared to 0.464 for all sub-Saharan Africa.

Few African countries were blessed with leaders of equal vision. The post–Cold War decline in the readiness of outside powers to bankroll local conflicts magnified the importance of diamonds, oil, and other natural resources in financing governments and rebels alike. The government of Angola, formerly backed by Cuba and the Soviet Union, long faced the rebellion of UNITA (a Portuguese acronym for the Union for the Total Independence of Angola), which the United States and white-ruled South Africa supported. By the late 1990s, UNITA had adapted to its loss of foreign support by seizing Angola's richest diamond fields in the Cuango River valley. UNITA leader Jonas Savimbi became a major purchaser of armaments, mostly Bulgarian, using bags of diamonds worth millions of dollars apiece to bargain with his suppliers. When he threatened the capital, Luanda, in 1999, the government could only defend itself because it had bought weapons with most of the $900 million dollars that western oil companies had paid it for offshore drilling rights. Angola's 1998 HDI score was only 0.405, below the 0.464 recorded for all sub-Saharan Africa. The paradox of misery and civil war amid the makings of prosperity was not unique to Angola.

In West Africa, Sierra Leone, like its neighbor Liberia, was originally founded as a refuge for freed slaves. By 2000, Sierra Leone was a nation in name only, with an elected but powerless government, and a rebel force, the Revolutionary United Front (RUF), in control of the diamond fields. RUF leader Foday Sankoh was a former corporal with a grade-school education and no ability to articulate a political program. A friend of Liberian strongman Charles Taylor, with whom he had trained in Libya, Sankoh bankrolled and armed the RUF by diverting much of Sierra Leone's diamond exports through Liberia, whose sales on the world market far exceeded its own production. After a campaign of terror in which his men chopped off the hands and feet of many Sierra Leoneans, Sankoh failed to take Freetown, the capital, but signed a peace deal that amnestied his rebels and made him chairman of the government agency that was supposed to control diamond mining. After the RUF's capture of some five hundred peacekeepers brought UN efforts to bring order to Sierra Leone nearly to collapse, the British sent in troops. Sierra Leoneans received them with relief, and some asked, "Will you come back and recolonize?" Well might they ask. Sierra Leone's 1998 HDI of 0.252 ranked dead last among 174 nations with reported scores.

The rarity and romance of diamonds, artificially created by restrictive marketing, contrast shockingly with realities like these. In an underdeveloped region whose economic fortunes still depend largely on mineral exports, similar stories of squandered opportunities can be told about less glamorous commodities like oil. Why have African societies' fortunes declined in so many cases since independence? Why do not more of their leaders show the vision and public spirit found in Botswana? Why do the economic linkages that bring resources, even luxuries, to other parts of the world bring death and degradation to Africans? What ought those who benefit from such linkages do in response to Africa's troubles?[1]

Continental Overview: The Underdeveloped World par Excellence

Since 1945, sub-Saharan Africa has passed through three periods. Their dates resemble those in Latin America and reflect changes in the wider world. Yet much of what marks each period is African in origin. The years from 1945 to 1960 were the twilight of colonialism. The years from 1960 to about 1990 were ones of formal independence, incomplete mass mobilization, state-dominated economic policy, and ongoing dependency, coupled with conflicts that resulted from either the Cold War or, in South Africa, apartheid. Since 1990, the post–Cold War period has meant the retreat of Africa's Marxist-inspired movements, South Africa's shift to majority rule, and new demands for democratization and development everywhere. To the optimist, if decolonization served as Africa's first "revolution," democratization

promises to be its second.[2] Yet Africa's record disappoints most Africans. Much of the trouble stems from demographic and environmental problems that began to become apparent only after 1960, and from tardiness in realizing that economic development requires human development. A look at Africa overall and at the two countries with the continent's largest national economies, Nigeria and South Africa, will illustrate these problems.

Today as throughout history, Africans display great creativity. Some achievements are those of outstanding individuals, like Desmond Tutu, Anglican bishop of Johannesburg and winner of the 1984 Nobel Peace Prize, or Wole Soyinka, Nigerian novelist, winner of the 1986 Nobel Prize for Literature. Sometimes the achievements are those of ordinary people working together, such as the thousands of Kenyan women's groups that formed the Greenbelt Movement to halt deforestation through tree planting and use of improved cookstoves, or the

West African Naam Movement that mobilized local self-help traditions for soil and water conservation projects—two initiatives in the realm of survival technologies (see Chapter 1). The greatest challenge facing Africa is to mobilize such energies on a large enough scale to achieve development and equity while also maintaining a viable relationship between human societies and their natural habitat. This is a key problem the world over, but Africa's poverty and hardship bring it into sharp focus.

The Spread of Independence

Europeans took control of sub-Saharan Africa abruptly, at a time when their economies were the world's strongest. The costs of taking control in the nineteenth century were relatively low. By 1945, conditions had changed so much, and wartime experiences had so stimulated African nationalism, that colonial rule ended even more suddenly than it had begun. The largest colonial powers, Britain and France, prepared for the transition. Britain passed colonial development acts in 1940 and 1945; France provided larger amounts of aid after the war. Among smaller colonial powers, Belgium did not anticipate the end, and Portugal tried to hold on. Still, decolonization worked its way across the continent, leaving over fifty independent countries, most of which gained independence in the early 1960s (Map 15.1). Events soon proved how unprepared those countries were to face their demographic, economic, and political problems. As Nigerian novelist Chinua Achebe said of his generation, they had to become the "*parents* of Nigeria," not its children.[3]

The decolonization of sub-Saharan Africa began in 1956, when the Sudan, nominally under joint Anglo-Egyptian rule, won independence as a byproduct of the Egyptian revolution of 1952. The next countries to become independent were in West Africa, starting with Ghana (1957, formerly the Gold Coast) under the leadership of Kwame Nkrumah. Of Britain's

other West African colonies, Nigeria became independent in 1960, Sierra Leone in 1961, and Gambia in 1965.

By then, French Africa also had won independence. France was preoccupied with colonial struggles in Indochina (1946–1954) and in Algeria (1954–1962). Political repercussions of the Algerian conflict led to the toppling of France's Fourth Republic in 1958 and the advent of the Fifth. President de Gaulle then provided leadership for decolonization, eventually in Algeria (1962) and immediately in France's other colonies, to which he offered a range of options. Guinea, under Sékou Touré, chose immediate independence in 1958. By the early 1960s, fourteen former French colonies had become independent, most as republics within a new French community.

In the Belgian Congo (later Zaire and now the Democratic Republic of Congo), the Belgians did not foresee that they could not hold on indefinitely. When rising nationalist opposition challenged their control, they abruptly granted independence in 1960. Civil war broke out, as Katanga (now Shaba) Province, with rich copper mines, attempted to secede. By the time order was restored, the country lay under the dictatorship of General Joseph Mobutu (president, 1965–1997) after one of many postindependence military takeovers.

White settler communities hindered decolonization in parts of eastern and southern Africa. In Kenya, whites held much of the best land, and the Kikuyu people had inadequate land to support themselves. This pressure produced the Mau Mau rebellion of 1952–1956, which the British repressed with thousands of

Map 15.1 Political Independence in Africa and Asia. *The following countries became independent in stages: Egypt in 1922, 1936, 1954; Iraq in 1932, 1947; and Lebanon and Syria in 1941–1945.*

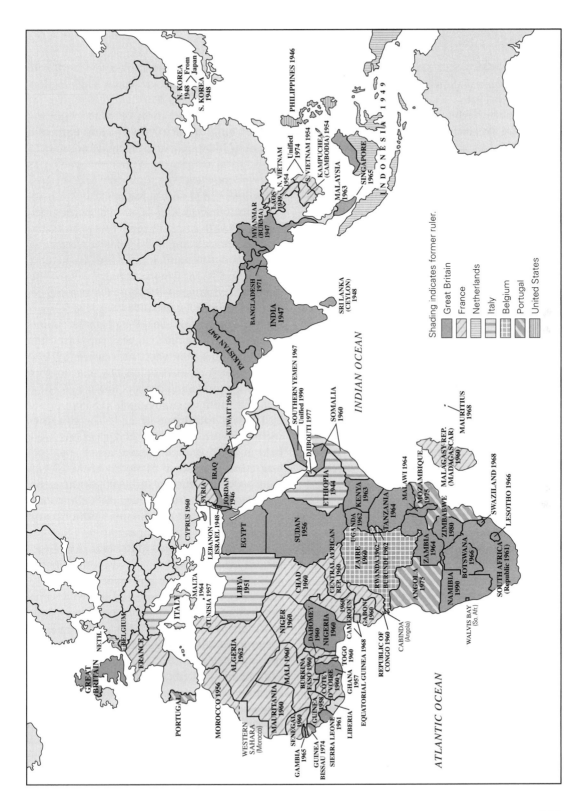

N. KOREA 1948 From Japan 1948
S. KOREA 1948

PHILIPPINES 1946

Unified 1974
S. VIETNAM 1954 N. VIETNAM
LAOS 1949
KAMPUCHEA (CAMBODIA) 1954
MALAYSIA 1963
SINGAPORE 1965
I N D O N E S I A 1 9 4 9

MYANMAR (BURMA) 1947

SRI LANKA (CEYLON) 1948

BANGLADESH 1971
INDIA 1947

PAKISTAN 1947

INDIAN OCEAN

SOUTHERN YEMEN 1967 Unified 1990
DJIBOUTI 1977
SOMALIA 1960

KUWAIT 1961

CYPRUS 1960
LEBANON 1948
ISRAEL 1948
JORDAN 1946
SYRIA
IRAQ

MALTA 1964
TUNISIA 1957

ITALY

MAURITIUS 1968

MALAGASY REP. (MADAGASCAR) 1960

SWAZILAND 1968
LESOTHO 1966

MALAWI 1964
MOZAMBIQUE 1975
ZIMBABWE 1980
ETHIOPIA 1944
KENYA 1963
TANZANIA 1964
ZAMBIA 1964
BOTSWANA 1966
NAMIBIA 1990
SOUTH AFRICA (Republic 1961)
ANGOLA 1975
UGANDA 1962
ZAIRE 1960
RWANDA 1962
BURUNDI 1962

EGYPT
SUDAN 1956
CENTRAL AFRICAN REP. 1960

CHAD 1960

LIBYA 1951

NIGER 1960
CAMEROUN 1960
GABON 1960
REPUBLIC OF CONGO 1960
CABINDA (Angola)

WALVIS BAY (So. Afr.)

ALGERIA 1962

MOROCCO 1956

MAURITANIA 1960
MALI 1960
BURKINA FASO 1960
NIGERIA 1960
DAHOMEY 1960
TOGO 1960
GHANA 1957
CÔTE D'IVOIRE 1960
GUINEA 1958
EQUATORIAL GUINEA 1968
LIBERIA
SIERRA LEONE 1961
GUINEA BISSAU 1974
SENEGAL 1960
GAMBIA 1965

WESTERN SAHARA (Morocco)

PORTUGAL

GREAT BRITAIN
FRANCE
BELGIUM
NETH.

ATLANTIC OCEAN

Shading indicates former ruler.
Great Britain
France
Netherlands
Italy
Belgium
Portugal
United States

Kenyan casualties. Still, Kenya, Tanganyika, and Uganda became independent under black rule in the early 1960s. Becoming independent in 1963, the island nation of Zanzibar joined Tanganyika on the mainland to form Tanzania in 1964. A key factor in the smooth transition to black rule was the care taken by leaders such as Kenya's Jomo Kenyatta and Tanzania's Julius Nyerere to reassure whites that the change would not hurt them. A generation later, land hunger would jeopardize such promises.

Farther south, the British tried to form a federation of Northern and Southern Rhodesia and Nyasaland, all economically interdependent. By the early 1960s, the British had decided on independence on the basis of one person, one vote. This decision broke the federation, for the two Rhodesias' whites feared black domination. In 1964, Nyasaland became independent as Malawi, and Northern Rhodesia—despite white opposition—became independent under black rule as Zambia. Southern Rhodesia's whites, who formed 7 percent of the population, against 3 percent in Northern Rhodesia, tried to preserve their dominance with a unilateral declaration of independence (1965). International opinion opposed the move, as did nationalist movements based among the Shona (Zimbabwe African Nationalist Union, ZANU) and the Ndebele peoples (Zimbabwe African People's Union, ZAPU). The white regime held out until 1980, when it too yielded. A black majority government, headed by ZANU leader Robert Mugabe, took power and Africanized the name of the country as Zimbabwe. Though a professed Marxist, Mugabe reassured whites, whose economic roles remained crucial. By 2000, as the aging Mugabe clung to power, white landowners were attacked in Zimbabwe, too.

Portugal's resistance delayed its colonies' independence. In Angola, where violent outbreaks began in 1961, the independence movement divided into several parties. Nationalist violence broke out in 1962 in Portuguese Guinea (now Guinea-Bissau), and in 1964 in Mozambique, where there was a single nationalist party (FRELIMO, Portuguese acronym for Mozambican Liberation Front). Fighting dragged on into the 1970s, draining Portugal's economy. Independence finally came in 1975 when an army mutiny overthrew Portugal's government. FRELIMO took over and set up a government in Mozambique.

Meanwhile in Angola, several parties vied for power with foreign support. As a Soviet ally, Cuba supported Angola's Marxist government. The United States and South Africa backed the opposing UNITA (Union for the Total Independence of Angola). South Africa also still occupied Namibia in defiance of a UN Security Council resolution demanding Namibia's independence. In response, Angola supported the Namibian independence movement SWAPO (Southwest African People's Organization). In 1988 the intervening powers finally agreed on Cuban withdrawal from Angola. U.S. support for UNITA was withdrawn in 1990. The two sides were forced to negotiate and elections were held in 1992, though Angola lapsed into civil war again afterward, as noted above. When South Africa withdrew in 1990, Namibia became the last African country to become independent, except for Eritrea, which won independence from Ethiopia in 1993.

As Africa achieved independence under majority rule, a number of common problems stood out. Despite the artificiality of the colonial boundaries, they generally survived as national borders. Within them, however, ethnic heterogeneity and other issues hindered national integration. By 2000, some nations had become divided—Ethiopia, Somalia—and others—Congo—faced that danger.

Independence meant, too, that the nationalist leaders inherited their former rulers' administrative systems. Because this colonial apparatus was inadequately developed for governing independent nations, the heads of the newly independent states found themselves in charge of "weak" or "soft" states, with limited capacity to make and implement policy. All African states began to "harden" institutionally, once elites with vested interests in clinging to power turned from leaders of nationalist opposition movements into rulers of independent countries. Yet crises like the AIDS epidemic revealed their unreadiness to cope with major policy problems. The low level of education, elite-mass gaps in political awareness, and the authoritarian nature of preindependence political mobilization (noted in Chapter 8) meant that most of those who had supported the cause were not yet prepared to assert themselves as citizens—a fact with important consequences for African political development. In economics, finally, independence did not mean that international economic interests surrendered. Africa's independent but underdeveloped states had to connect with the capitalist world economy as best they could. Africa's neocolonial dependency resulted from this fact.

Africa's Population Explosion

Population growth was one of the greatest problems the new states faced. Africa's population problems resembled those of Asia or Latin America but produced graver social and economic effects. African population data are unreliable, partly because census taking can raise political tensions if it shows that the balance among rival ethnic groups has changed. But available estimates indicate that Africa had about 224 million people in 1954 and 800 million in 2000, when Africa's rulers led populations that had more than tripled since independence.

Africa's population growth raised many problems. One was large-scale migration, both from rural to urban areas and across national borders. Many migrants were refugees fleeing famine or war, like the million Hutus who flooded into Zaire in 1994 when the Tutsis took control of Rwanda. Rural-to-urban migration

grew rapidly, so much that while Africa's population doubled every twenty years, its urban population doubled every ten years. In 1993, no African city was as large as Latin America's biggest, though Cairo (Egypt) had 14.5 million people. A dozen African cities, from Casablanca (Morocco) to Addis Ababa (Ethiopia) to Cape Town (South Africa) had passed the million mark. At 1990 rates of growth, Africa would have twenty-five cities of over 5 million people by 2025, but Latin America would have only fifteen. By 1996, Lagos (Nigeria) had passed 6 million, attaining levels of poverty and congestion that resulted in violence and insecurity not found in other Nigerian cities.

Headcounts alone scarcely suggested the consequences of explosive population growth. In the cities, for example, sanitation and transportation facilities dating largely from the colonial period were totally overwhelmed by urban migration. Urban or rural, the quality of life was poor by many indicators. In 2000 Africa combined the highest birth rate of any continent (38 per thousand) with the lowest life expectancy (51 years for males, 53 for females). The infant mortality rate was 88 per thousand in 2000, compared with 9 per thousand for Europe and 7 for North America.

Rapid growth meant, too, that much of Africa's populace was very young: 43 percent of Africans were under age fifteen in 2000. As a result, many problems clustered around youth-related issues: inadequate schools, too few jobs for graduates, distinctive forms of political activism, crime, or violence. But the biggest demographic problem of extremely young populations is that so many members of them have yet to enter their reproductive years. Whatever efforts are made to stem population increase, such a young population will keep growing for years unless other factors intervene.

The problems of a fast-growing, young, and disadvantaged population are bound to affect women particularly. Africa and South Asia

Hutu refugees fleeing Rwanda. *Population densities and growth rates among Africa's highest have given rise to genocidal conflict among the Hutu and Tutsi peoples of Rwanda and Burundi. Sayyid Azim/© AP-Wide World Photos*

together make up the zone where, by some indicators, women's status is the lowest in the world. International attention has focused recently on female genital mutilation, a custom practiced in various forms in parts of Africa. Indeed, the practice dramatized African women's dependency. Yet, as women's activists pointed out, focusing on this issue, however justified, obscured many other problems. As of 2000, sub-Saharan Africa's adult literacy rate stood at 50 percent for females, compared to 66 percent for males; 52 percent of females of the appropriate ages were enrolled in elementary school, compared to 61 percent of males;

and females received one-third of earned income, compared to two-thirds for males. Poverty perpetuated high fertility, as women sought help from child labor and security in old age and as gender bias in education and employment reduced women's choices. Women still did most of the agricultural labor, were responsible for feeding most of the population, and with their children formed most of Africa's refugee populations.

At times, it has seemed that Africa's population growth could not go on without encountering ecological or epidemiological limits. Sub-Saharan Africa has experienced several waves of drought and famine since the early 1970s. In the 1980s, starvation threatened almost half of Africa's countries. In the early 1990s, the worst drought in fifty years threatened 40 million people in eastern and southern Africa. In 2000, Ethiopia again suffered drought and famine, while its leaders had their minds on a costly border war with Eritrea. At least in part, these droughts resulted from population growth. Increased cutting of firewood and over-extension of cultivation have reduced moisture retention in the soil, accelerating runoff and soil erosion. These changes have disrupted climatic patterns that used to assure rainfall, leading to perhaps irreversible environmental degradation in some places. At the same time, the fact that half of Africa's population lacked safe water or sanitation as of 1997, while millions of Africans were refugees or displaced persons, did nothing to reduce vulnerability to famine and disease. By 1997, malaria and tuberculosis were more widespread in sub-Saharan Africa than in any other large region. By 2000, out of 34 million people worldwide who had AIDS or HIV, 24 million were African. Sixteen African countries had HIV infection rates above 10 percent, and AIDS deaths had devastating impacts on family life, education, and economic production.

Like other parts of the world, sub-Saharan Africa has experienced some improvements in social conditions in recent years. Between 1970 and 1997, life expectancy rose from 44 to 50 years, and infant mortality fell from 105 per thousand live births to 94. The spread of at least elementary education has done much to strengthen demand for democratization in the 1990s. Yet social conditions remain more depressed in sub-Saharan Africa than in any other major world region. In calculating the human development index (HDI, introduced in Chapter 14), as we have seen, sub-Saharan Africa emerged with the lowest combined score— 0.464 in 1998—for any major region, and some countries' scores were lower than that.

Economic Development in Reverse?

Rapid population growth has produced major economic and ecological consequences. As late as 1970, Africa essentially fed itself. Between 1970 and 1997, however, sub-Saharan Africa's food production per capita declined slightly, ending with a daily calorie supply per person barely over 2,200, compared to 2,600 for all developing countries. Calculated in terms of purchasing power, sub-Saharan Africa's real GDP per person increased from $990 in 1960 to $1,530 in 1997. In 1960, Arabs, South Asians, and East Asians had been less well off by the same measure; by 1993, however, they were much better off. Losing ground, Africa had become the underdeveloped world par excellence.

Achieving independence only late in the world economy's 1945–1973 growth phase, most African countries performed poorly in economic development for many reasons. Some problems were legacies of imperialism. National borders had been drawn by outsiders, whose interest in development did not go past resource extraction. Multinational firms continued this function for independent governments that often had no initial choice but to rely on them. Decolonization, then, was more a political than an economic event. Most sub-Saharan countries also remained dependent on one or a few agricultural or mineral products for most of their export earnings. Economically as well as ethnically, most African countries lacked the makings of viable nations. Many were too small: in 1998, the total GNP of Africa's ten smallest nations was still less than that of Luxembourg, one of Europe's smallest countries. Communication and transportation networks, too, reflected colonial needs. Still faced, nearly four decades after independence, with huge costs for routing telephone calls among African countries through Paris and London, African governments finally formed an organization to launch a communications satellite in 1997.

Heads of Africa's newly independent states faced urgent needs to build up their nations and fulfill their peoples' hopes for development. Where colonial regimes had pursued limited goals with conservative financing, independent African rulers pursued ambitious developmental goals with deficit financing. Following then-current ideas about development, they expanded the governmental role in the economy, prioritizing industrial development and controlling agriculture by using marketing boards to monopolize exports. Lack of qualified personnel to fill needed positions in government and the economy magnified the impact of the policy switch. Industry seldom progressed beyond light import substitution and—if not still foreign controlled—tended to be ineptly run in the public sector. Atop the ecological difficulties noted earlier, the lack of incentives to African farmers largely explains why food production grew only 2 percent a year between 1960 and 1990, while population growth averaged 3 percent. African agriculture also suffered because the kind of international research that produced a "green revolution" in wheat and rice, which are leading crops in other developing regions, was not devoted to the root crops like cassava, or to the grains like maize, millet, and sorghum, that Africa produces.

Independent Africa's leaders were not always up to the challenges of economic policy-making. Many of them degenerated into "kleptocrats" (robber-rulers), like Zaire's Mobutu, who acquired vast properties in Belgium but found his own country so unpleasant that he disdained to stay there, unless on his yacht in the Zaire River. Forms of corruption rooted in the impact of kinship ties on politics—a subject discussed below—drained capital from productive use. Military spending, which grew for all sub-Saharan Africa from 0.7 percent of GDP in 1960 to 2.9 percent in 1994, was a further drain. Since only a few sub-Saharan countries—Angola, Gabon, Nigeria, Cameroon—had oil to export, the 1970s oil price rises also helped depress economic performance overall. Nigeria's misuse of its oil resources (see below) showed that they alone were no key to development.

Dependence on agro-mineral exports—whether petroleum or peanuts—still left African economies exposed to unpredictable price swings. The resulting fluctuations in national revenue did a lot to plunge Africa into debt. Sub-Saharan Africa's external debt had risen to more than $230 billion by 1998, compared to a collective GDP of $317 billion.

By then, African governments faced mounting demands, from both within and without, not only to democratize but also to reorient economic policy. The demand from international financial agencies like the IMF and World Bank was for structural adjustment, including privatization, devaluation, and removal of governmental subsidies or other controls on the economy. Many Africans criticized such demands as hard on the poor. Advocates of the policy retorted that the old policies had failed and had been biased in favor of the urban population, while most of the poor were in the countryside. Many Africans agreed that there was need to restore market forces, although government still had a role to play in regulating the economy.

Growing recognition that economic development depended on human development also shaped demands for policy change. An unhealthy, unschooled, unskilled populace was increasingly seen as both cause and consequence of underdevelopment. Countries with high rankings in literacy, life expectancy, health care, and nutrition also achieved faster economic growth. Improvements in women's status were the key to improvement in many of these variables. Research showed, too, that famine results not so much from lack of food as from poverty, breakdown in normal socio-economic mechanisms by which people acquire food, and irresponsible government.

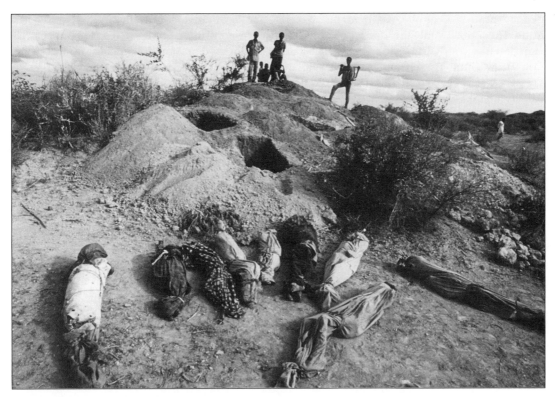

Starvation victims await burial, Somalia, 1992. *The bodies are shrouded in sacks from food shipments that arrived too late for them.* © *1992 Christopher Morris/Black Star*

Since the late 1980s, signs of improvement in economic performance have appeared. Agricultural output has risen. Farmers in several countries have developed specialized exports—from cut flowers to runner beans—for the European market. Debt relief and human development gained importance as international policy goals in the post–Cold War era.

Below, we shall consider Africa's two largest economies. Nigeria's $43 billion and South Africa's $131 billion in GDP accounted for 52 percent of sub-Saharan Africa's 1999 GDP of $333 billion. Here, to illustrate some of the obstacles to democracy and development, we shall also consider Somalia, a less-favored case.

Anarchy and mass starvation in Somalia gripped world attention in 1992. Somalia lies at the Horn of Africa, a landmass, vaguely horn shaped, that projects into the Indian Ocean just south of where the Red Sea opens into it. Somalia and nearby regions (Djibouti and Ethiopia's Ogaden Province) are home to the Somali people, divided into numerous clans. Somalia is arid, and many Somalis depend on camel nomadism for subsistence. Not surprisingly given the nearness of Islam's Arabian homeland, most Somalis are Muslims.

Nineteenth-century European rulers divided the Somali lands. The French took Djibouti, one of East Africa's best ports, and surrounding countryside; Djibouti became independent in 1977 as one of Africa's micro-nations. The British took the north side of the Horn (1884), the Italians took the south side (1889), and Ethiopia seized Ogaden Province (1890s). When the British and Italian colonies gained independence in 1960, they merged to form Somalia.

Independent Somalia's history has been grim. A military coup soon toppled its civilian president, installing dictator Siad Barre (1969–1991). Hallmarks of his regime included rights violations, abuse of power, economic mismanagement, and failure in political institution building. At different stages in their policy toward Somalia and Ethiopia, both the United States and the Soviet Union, as well as various Arab regimes, supplied weapons to the Somalis. When rebels chased Barre from the capital, Mogadishu, no new government emerged. Rival clan-based factions looted government armories and turned on one another. Civil war splintered the country. Common consumption of *qat* or *khat,* a mild narcotic, made trigger fingers itch, aggravating the violence. Fighting spread into Somalia's farming areas by March 1992, worsening famine conditions. Two-thirds of Somalia's 6 million people faced starvation.

A food-importing country in the best of times, Somalia could not cope with mounting violence, devastation of its farmlands, and the worst drought in a half-century. By the fall of 1992, one-sixth of the country's population had fled to other countries. Despite massive international relief efforts, thousands of Somalis died each day, often because fighting prevented distribution of food.

Somalia also tested what international action could do to alleviate such crises. To operate, relief agencies had to endure having part of their food supplies stolen or else pay for protection, which cost the International Red Cross nearly $50,000 a month. The United Nations sent in troops, but the lack of a government for them to cooperate with frustrated their humanitarian mission, raising serious questions

about whether the UN should be empowered to respond more aggressively to local crises. U.S. Marines were sent to Somalia in December 1992, only to be withdrawn later after the failure of what was supposed to be a humanitarian mission. The Somali warlord who had bested the UN and the United States, Brigadier General Muhammad Farah Aidid, himself became a casualty of the ongoing civil war in July 1996. By 2000, both the northeast and the northwest had seceded. Efforts to retrain the militias for peacetime police work and create institutions for a new government confronted the warlords' refusal to cooperate.

Somalia's problems were unique only in degree. Clearly, few sub-Saharan countries—except South Africa—had excelled the economies of Latin America in development. Somalia's fate also showed how closely economic development depends on political stability.

Political Evolution: Common Phases and Themes

From independence until the 1990s, African governments tended to pass through a series of phases marked by common themes: lack of restraint on government power, ineffective administration, a narrow range of ideological choices, ethnic tension, corruption, human rights violations, and common problems in relations with the outside world. Not until the end of the Cold War era did a shift of trend—toward democratization—appear.

In former British colonies, the postindependence phases commonly began with an independent government headed by a prime minister responsible to the legislature. As in Britain, if the prime minister could not muster a parliamentary majority on a key vote, the government fell from office. These countries generally became independent as members of the British Commonwealth.

Most countries that began with a prime minister soon changed to a government headed by a president. Former French colonies began their independent life with this phase. This system offered two advantages: the president's tenure in office did not depend on the ability to command a parliamentary majority, and the constitution could define presidential powers extremely broadly—more so than in the United States, for example. Blazing the trail into this second phase, Ghana's new constitution of 1960, which was soon imitated elsewhere, gave president Kwame Nkrumah virtually dictatorial powers. Such concentration of power no doubt seemed like a necessity to leaders faced with massive problems of nation building.

The next phase, in countries that had more than one party to start with, was to abolish all parties other than the one in power. Nkrumah did this in 1964 by making his Convention People's party the sole legal one. Most other African countries followed suit. We shall offer an explanation of this practice in discussing the impact of regionalism and ethnicity on politics.

In the fourth phase in postindependence politics, a military dictatorship replaced the civilian presidency. In some countries, as in Ghana after the military overthrew Nkrumah in 1966, power shifted back and forth between military and civilians several times. However, the general trend was toward military rule. The number of military governments rose from two in 1963 to twenty-four in 1984. Several factors reinforced this trend. Colonial rule was imposed by force and often carried out by military officers. Independent Africa's coup-makers were European-trained officers. They had little difficulty seizing control of weakly institutionalized governments that had no firm tradition of military subordination to civilian authority.

Access to power politicized the military more and more. Over time, the coups tended to be the work of younger men of lower rank overturning generals or colonels. Lieutenant Jerry Rawlings, in his early thirties, led two successful coups in Ghana in 1979 and 1981. Before reaching the age of thirty, Sergeant Samuel

K. Doe led the 1980 coup that overthrew Africa's oldest republican government, that of Liberia.

By 1990, however, the fading of the Cold War and the growth of European integration seemed to provoke a shift of trend, as in Latin America. New demands arose for civilian rule, multiparty democracy, human rights, gender equality, and sustainable development. The spread of at least basic education stimulated these demands. So did outside pressures. For example, France tied its aid to democratization and development from 1990 on. U.S. president Clinton sent similar messages in his contacts with African leaders. The 1994 shift to majority rule in South Africa no doubt strengthened the trend. By 1996, twenty-seven multiparty elections had been held in Africa (in twenty-one cases for the first time); and opposition parties had been legalized in thirty-one countries.[4] The future of democracy in Africa was not assured. Most West African countries, for example, had "civilian" presidents who were no more than recycled military rulers. But at last Africa was moving beyond the authoritarian mobilization phase, where charismatic leaders could rouse the people with speeches and promises, but could not be held accountable by the people.

One notable feature of the change was the proliferation of international organizations. The Organization of African Unity (OAU), founded in 1963, had long since degenerated into a dictators' club. Over time, the emphasis shifted more toward organizations to promote specific regional or developmental goals. Such were the Economic Community of West Africa (ECOWAS), the Inter-African Union of Human Rights, or the biennial Franco-African summits. Other organizations pursuing economic priorities included the West African Monetary Union (UMOA in French), whose member states retain a common currency linked to the French franc, or the Southern African Development Community (SADC), whose member states aspired to make of it a regional common market.

In each phase of their postindependence political development, most African governments showed limited political or administrative capacity. Scarcely unique to Africa, this trait of underdevelopment manifested itself in many ways. Governments seemed unable to conduct impartial elections or censuses; to implement effective family planning, AIDS-prevention, or agricultural development programs; or to adopt more than rudimentary forms of revenue collection, such as the compulsory marketing boards that served essentially to tax exports. In most African countries, the excessive size of the public sector and the lavish perquisites that it inherited from colonial days both reflected and compounded governmental inefficiency. On the positive side, it is worth noting that few African regimes have been as repressive as some found on other continents. Only a couple of other African regimes—like that of Jean-Bedel Bokassa in the Central African Republic—have rivaled the violence of Uganda's Idi Amin, who killed over a hundred thousand Ugandans before his fall in 1979.

As independence spread, African leaders expounded ideologies intended to promote socioeconomic development and, in the process, to consolidate the power of the governments they headed. Often, the ideologies were socialist in one of two senses.

The first was an African populist socialism that had little to do with Marx. Instead it reflected the desire for a development program expressly suited for Africa. Formative influences on populist socialism included the communalistic heritage of African societies, Pan-Africanism, and the idealization of African identity (*négritude*) by writers such as Aimé Césaire, a French-speaking West Indian of African ancestry, and Léopold Senghor, president of Senegal (1960–1980) and an internationally known French-language poet. Their notion of négritude had counterparts in Nkrumah's idea of "African personality" and in a widespread concern for

authenticity that led, for example, to many name changes. The Congo became Zaire, Leopoldville became Kinshasa, and Joseph-Désiré Mobutu became Mobutu Sese Seko. Sometimes dismissed as "tinsel modernization," such Africanization was a needed adjustment to a new order, much as the re-evaluation of blackness in the United States was an adaptation to the conditions created by the civil rights movement. Julius Nyerere of Tanzania developed one of the most widely admired populist socialisms with his concept of *ujamaa*, or kinship communalism. Tanzania took populism seriously, by trying to redirect education away from the elitism of the colonial system, for example, and by stressing agrarian change. The attempt to create village cooperatives was not highly successful, partly for reasons beyond Nyerere's control (like the agricultural crisis conditions of the 1970s); but such recognition that development depended on structural change in the rural sector has been all too rare in developing countries.

Largely inspired by Cuban example, the other type of African socialism has been called Afro-Marxism. Contrary to Marxist-Leninist assumptions, Cuba first had its revolution, and then Castro announced that he was a Marxist-Leninist and used this identification to alter Cuba's external dependency ties. Starting in Congo-Brazzaville in 1968–1969, similar phenomena appeared in Africa, as military rulers simply announced the advent of "Marxism" in various countries: Somalia (1970), Benin (1974), Madagascar and Ethiopia (1975–1976), Mozambique and Angola (1977).

Afro-Marxist regimes were Marxist-Leninist mostly in trying—like Cuba—to use this identification to improve external dependency relations. They also took a Leninist view of the party as an elite vanguard, in contrast to the populist-socialist regimes' mass movements. Otherwise, most Afro-Marxist regimes pursued few Marxist policies. Except for Ethiopia, most steered clear of agricultural collectivization. Afro-Marxist regimes typically created a state-controlled sector and nationalized foreign interests regarded as vestiges of colonialism. But almost all of them tried to attract Western investment. Angola long depended on Gulf Oil, a dominant firm in the international oil industry, for almost all its government revenue and foreign exchange and used Cuban troops to guard Gulf's operations.

The scant economic rewards of pro-Soviet policies took most of the Marxism out of Afro-Marxism, even before the Soviet Union fell apart. In the long run, Afro-Marxists could not escape the capitalist nature of the world economy anymore than could Cuba or the Soviet Union. By the 1990s, Africans scanned their past for indigenous bases not for socialism but for democracy.

All the while, pre-existing sociopolitical realities did as much to govern political behavior as did ideology. Preindependence political parties and movements had been mostly regional in scope, rather than national, and represented one or a few, but not all, of the peoples living in the country. The hasty organization of postindependence political life according to imported models meant giving power to one of these parties, or perhaps to a coalition, and casting the others in the role of opposition. We shall see how this worked out in Nigeria, but there are many other examples.

Liberal democracies assume that all citizens are equal as voters—one person, one vote—and that the political parties succeed each other in office. The parties differ on policy and political philosophy but are all loyal to the political system, so that those out of office form a "loyal opposition." But what happens if voters' and parties' primary loyalty is not to the nation and its constitution but to their own ethnic groups, clans, or regions? Then there can be no loyal opposition, and the political victory of any party means that a single sectional interest has captured the entire government. Somalia's anarchy offers an extreme example of what can follow. In Zimbabwe, the importance of ethnic identifications helps explain why Robert Mugabe's ZANU government, based among the Shona people, was at first more lenient to whites than to Joshua Nkomo's ZAPU movement: ZAPU represented the Ndebele minority, who were potential rivals, as the whites no longer were, for control of the country. In countries like Zimbabwe that have two main ethnic groups, some experts thought that a single-party regime actually served a useful purpose if it included members of both groups. Zimbabwe acquired a single party in 1987, at the cost of expanding government services, so that Nkomo followers could receive patronage plums without Mugabe followers losing theirs. Yet by 2000 Zimbabweans, too, demanded democratization, and a Movement for Democratic Change (MDC) had emerged. Despite a campaign of violence against the MDC and the white farmers, whose land unemployed Zimbabweans now coveted, voters rejected Mugabe's attempt to increase his presidential powers and gave a third of the parliamentary seats to the MDC.

More than ethnic tension lay behind African intolerance of opposition. Many Africans have pointed out that decision making in kinship societies was historically by discussion among the elders. The goal was to reach consensus, after which no one would be allowed to oppose the group decision. Discussion progressively worked out disagreement until the decision could be regarded as unanimous. In the past, this kind of decision making was not unique to Africa but characterized kinship societies in many places, including rural prerevolutionary Russia and the Middle East. Analysts cited this tradition of decision making as a reason for intolerance of political opposition. In Africa, such thinking went so far that the secret ballot, seen in the United States as a vital safeguard of democracy, may be seen as "un-African." Kenyans, for example, have voted by "queuing" or "open voting": voters lined up behind the picture of their candidate. If elections by secret ballot had been marred by corruption and violence, was this method less manipulable?

In Africa, again as in many parts of the world, kinship and ethnicity also helped shape certain forms of political corruption. Indeed, behavior that appeared corrupt to outsiders might not seem so to Africans. Historically, kinship societies typically held much property in common, and a major leadership function was to distribute the group's resources among its members. Such leaders headed great households, supported many dependents, and dispensed much hospitality. They seldom distinguished between personal and public property.

Given this outlook, postindependence politics turned into a contest among parties based in specific regions or ethnic groups to control the whole country and parcel out its benefits as if they were those of the group's ancestral lands. Politicians saw no distinction between public funds and personal compensation. At best, it would take time for behavior to adjust to a situation that called for new standards. Meanwhile, politics degenerated into runaway patronage, misuse of public funds, and manipulation of political power for private enrichment. For example, after a Nigerian military coup of 1983, it was reported that an official of the fallen government had a house in England with a gold bathtub appraised at $5 million. Nigeria's corruption under head of state Sani Abacha (1993–1998) topped that. To make matters worse, as Chinua Achebe pointed out in his novel *A Man of the People* (1966), anyone who attacked corrupt leaders would be suspected of wanting to take power and follow their example.

To move beyond local loyalties to national and regional integration has so far been the chief obstacle to African nation building. So far, ethnic and local interests have prevailed. In

Nigeria's and South Africa's 1999 elections, for example, traditional chiefs and kings still played key roles in grassroots voter mobilization. The success of democratization will depend critically on the achievement of new consensus about how to accommodate regional and ethnic diversity within the national framework.

Africa and Outside Powers

No outside power has had as much influence in independent Africa as the United States has had in Latin America. However, no survey of African affairs in a time of tightening globalization can be complete without a look at international relations.

Both Britain and France tried to maintain connections with former colonies. Britain did so through the Commonwealth of Nations. After de Gaulle's French Community (1958) dissolved in 1961, France relied on cooperation agreements and succeeded, more than Britain did, in retaining functions it had performed before 1960. After France joined the European Economic Community (EEC), France's former colonies' special economic relations with France were extended into analogous relations with the entire EEC. France remained the largest aid donor to sub-Saharan Africa, and its Franco-African summits brought together leaders from many states. France still regarded its former colonies as its sphere of influence and carried out a number of military interventions in Africa, policies that Africans increasingly criticized in the 1990s. Britain retained former positions less well than France, but British interests could still be imposing. In 1980, about half the $25 billion in foreign investment in South Africa was British.

Superpower rivalries also had an impact. Seeing the African independence movements of the 1950s and 1960s as a chance to advance its influence, the Soviet Union provided some of them with arms and military assistance. More intense Soviet involvement followed the rise of

Afro-Marxist regimes in Ethiopia, Angola, and Mozambique. But in the long run, Africa had low priority in Soviet policy. African populist-socialist leaders either dissatisfied the Soviets ideologically or became dissatisfied with Soviet aid. The USSR served as Africa's chief source of weapons but demanded payment in hard currency. By the 1980s African leaders no longer found the Soviet system credible as a developmental model. Racial discrimination against African students in the USSR heightened resentments, and unpleasant experiences with "socialist imperialists" helped prepare African leaders to change policies in the 1990s.

If Soviet interest in Africa developed tardily and thinly, U.S. policy at first went little beyond advocating an end to colonialism. After independence, the United States still assumed that the former colonial powers would be those most active in African affairs. Gradually, however, the United States became more forward in pursuing certain interests: ensuring access to minerals and a stable investment environment, preventing the Soviets from acquiring strategic advantages, and protecting the shipping lanes around the Cape of Good Hope so as to ensure oil imports. Gradually, too, the United States took more interest in some of Africa's trouble spots—for example, joining in British efforts of the late 1970s to achieve a settlement in Rhodesia or propping up the Mobutu regime in Zaire in order to ensure access to the country's minerals. In the long run, the thorniest policy problem was to define a policy toward South Africa that could both satisfy U.S. business interests and show Africans that the United States opposed apartheid with more than words.

By reinforcing incentives for economic and political liberalization and integration, the end of the Cold War marked a turning point in Africa's international, as well as its domestic, politics. The connection, discussed above, between diamond mining and armed conflict shows, however, that the consequences were not all benign.

Nigeria: Independence plus Oil Dependency

Home to one in six sub-Saharan Africans, Nigeria is Africa's most populous country and potentially one of its wealthiest. Yet it shares such problems of its neighbors as ethnic factionalism and military rule. Nigeria's experience shows what obstacles even an oil-rich nation may face in political and economic development.

Rise and Fall of the First Republic

By the end of World War II, several rival nationalist movements had emerged in Nigeria, and experiences of the war years had raised political expectations. The British had not yet taken additional steps to broaden political participation, however, and they had only begun to emphasize social and economic development. After the war, change accelerated on all fronts.

The economy quickened dramatically. From 1947 to 1958, government revenue rose from 14 million British pounds to 58 million, while the amount of money in circulation rose from 23 million to 55 million pounds. Over the same period, exports tripled, from 44 to 136 million British pounds in value, while imports quintupled, from 33 to 167 million. The shift from a positive to a negative foreign trade balance worried economists but was associated with rapid growth of investment. The basis of the economy remained colonial exports, 85 percent agricultural and the rest mineral. Government marketing boards bought and marketed the agricultural goods, and industrialization was only starting. But the government made efforts at diversification, including oil exploration. Small-scale oil exports began by 1960.

These economic changes affected Nigerians profoundly. In particular, the growth of the economy and the approach of independence increased the need for educated Nigerians. The colonial government expanded education greatly, especially at the secondary level. Many

Nigerians received scholarships to study abroad, and in 1948 the University College of Ibadan opened. Still, the numbers of graduates remained far short of need. Education became a political issue, too, for many nationalists preferred to emphasize universal lower-level education, even at the cost of limiting expansion at higher levels. And the spread of education had economic effects. Rural youngsters with primary schooling, especially boys, no longer wanted to work on farms as their parents did. Instead they flocked to the cities seeking jobs as clerks and thus launching the superurbanization of Lagos.

Amid these economic and social changes, preparations for independence advanced. Nigeria received new constitutions in 1947, 1951, and 1954. The result was a federal system of government, headed by a prime minister, with an elected federal legislature and three self-governing regions: Northern, Eastern, and Western (Map 15.2). With modifications, the 1954 constitution remained in force until 1966. Meanwhile, important new issues emerged.

The most troublesome point was ethnic and regional tension. The three regions were dominated by the Hausa-Fulani (Northern), Yoruba (Western), and Ibo peoples (Eastern). The Northern Region was larger and more populous than the other two combined. Before long, the strongest national movement, the National Council of Nigeria and the Cameroons (NCNC), broke apart into ethnically based parties. Founded in 1944 by the Ibo leader Nnamdi Azikiwe, the NCNC initially had Yoruba and Ibo support, but relations between the two groups soon became strained. The northern Muslims also formed a political organization. They feared

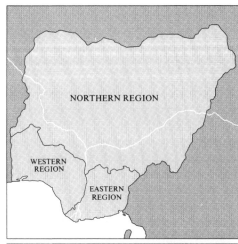

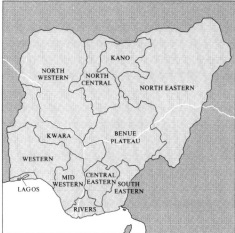

Map 15.2 Nigeria's Three Regions (1960), Nineteen States (1976), and Thirty-Six States (1998). ▶

that southerners, who had been quicker to seek Western education, would gain political dominance after independence. Soon there were three regional parties based on specific ethnic groups: the Northern Peoples Congress (NPC, Hausa-Fulani), the Action Group (AG) in the Yoruba Western Region, and the NCNC. The NCNC was basically an Ibo party centered in the Eastern Region, though the presence of many Ibo migrants in other parts of the country gave it followers elsewhere and made its outlook less regional than the other parties'. Small ethnic groups began to demand increases in the number of regions so that they could acquire local dominance.

Despite such problems, Nigeria moved toward independence more by negotiation than by violence. The first federal general election (1954) produced a coalition government combining the Northern Peoples Congress and the National Council of Nigeria and the Cameroons. The NPC leader in the House, Abubakar Tafawa Balewa, a northern Muslim from a small ethnic group, became the first federal prime minister. The three regions became self-governing between 1957 and 1959, and the country became independent in 1960 under a government headed by Balewa. Azikiwe assumed the mostly ceremonial role of governor-general, or president, after the change to a republic in 1963.

Nigeria's parliamentary government lasted only until January 1966 before falling to a military coup. Until then, Nigeria never abandoned multiparty for single-party rule. In that, Nigeria differed from many African nations. Yet by 1966, several factors had discredited the republic. One factor was most politicians' corruption and lack of concern for their constituents in a time of rising prices and widening income inequality. The government also failed to respect constitutional requirements, especially in high-handed acts directed at the Western region and the Western-based Action Group, then an opposition party. A third problem was regional imbalance. This became a chronic problem, affecting even census taking, which Nigeria's combination of a multiethnic society and a federal political system made a very touchy issue. After the last preindependence census in 1952–1953, Nigeria's next three censuses produced results that were contested or officially disavowed. Problems like these pushed Nigeria toward chaos.

From the Biafran Civil War Through the Oil Boom and Bust

After the overthrow of Nigeria's First Republic in January 1966, civilian rule was not restored for thirteen years. Two military coups occurred early in 1966, largely Ibo backed. A new constitution, rushed through after the second coup, abolished the three regions, creating a unitary rather than a federal state. By now, Nigerians had noticed the prominence of Ibo among the coup-makers but not among the victims. Further, Nigerians saw the abolition of federalism as an attempt to gain power for the Ibo, who had a larger educated elite and were more widely dispersed nationally than other ethnic groups.

July 1966 therefore witnessed a third coup, which installed a government under a northern officer from a small ethnic group, Lieutenant-Colonel Yakubu Gowon. Discussion of return to civilian rule continued. But massacres of the Ibo also occurred. The Eastern Region refused to recognize the Gowon government, thousands of Ibo began returning from other parts of the country, and secession seemed likely. In May 1967, Gowon tried to defuse the issue by dividing Nigeria into twelve states, in place of the former regions, so appealing to the interests of small ethnic groups in the east as elsewhere. Three days later the Eastern Region declared its independence as the Republic of Biafra. This was a major challenge: most of Nigeria's oil was in the east, though not in Ibo territory proper.

In the ensuing civil war, Biafrans, supported by multinational oil companies, succeeded at first. Nigerian forces soon turned the tide, however, reducing Biafran resistance village by village. The war roused much outside interest, partly because the Biafran government claimed, and overseas sympathizers believed, that the Nigerian forces intended genocide. When the Biafrans capitulated in January 1970, the Gowon regime responded with a magnanimous call for reconciliation, and the former rebels were reintegrated into the nation in much that spirit.

With the civil war past, Nigeria entered a new period of opportunity, though military rule proved hard to end. Even the war years brought some gains. The new states became established relatively smoothly, and the wartime foreign exchange shortage stimulated import substitution. By the early 1970s, Nigeria was becoming self-sufficient in consumer goods such as textiles, footwear, beverages, and soap. Foreign automobile firms had opened assembly plants in the country, and the government was pressuring them to use Nigerian-made parts. As elsewhere in Africa, "indigenization" decrees were used to force sale of foreign-owned firms, wholly or partly, to Nigerians.

What drove economic change, however, was Nigeria's emergence as a major oil exporter. The value of Nigeria's exports increased fortyfold between 1960 and 1980. At the start of that period, agricultural goods and tin represented 84 percent of exports. By its end, their share had fallen to 3 percent, and petroleum had shot from 3 to 96 percent of exports.

Such changes predictably created economic and social stress. Agricultural exports declined not only proportionally but also in absolute amount, largely because the agricultural marketing boards deprived producers of incentives to produce. This was one cause of the labor shift out of agriculture. But the petroleum sector could not absorb all the available workers. It produced too few jobs—perhaps only twenty thousand by 1980. Rapid urbanization also meant the need to reorient agriculture from export crops to foodstuffs for domestic consumers. Neither the declining rural population nor the government responded to this need effectively.

The major growth of Nigeria's oil exports coincided almost exactly with the price rises engineered by OPEC, which Nigeria joined in 1971. But the Gowon government failed to use its gains wisely. Since oil revenue went to the central government, increasing its power in relation to the states, the key problem was its incapacity to manage and redistribute the benefits. The growth of oil revenue seriously overstrained the country's supply of qualified technical and managerial talent. The fact that many Nigerians still lack running water, modern sewerage, or even a regular fuel supply indicates the grave consequences of this problem.

Leadership was clearly part of Nigeria's problem. After the Biafran war, Nigerians expected a return to civilian rule. Instead, Gowon announced that the change would take six more years, during which he would implement a nine-point program, including a development plan, a census, and organization of national political parties. Gowon's increasingly inept military regime had little success with all this. The 1973 census became the third since 1962 to yield politically unacceptable results. As dissatisfaction grew, Gowon kept postponing civilian rule until he fell to another military coup in 1975.

The new regime, led from 1975 to 1979 by Major General Olusegun Obasanjo, made a strong start. It set a date (October 1, 1979) to restore civilian rule and called for preparatory steps, such as deciding whether to create new states and drafting a new constitution. By 1976, the number of states had grown to nineteen (see Map 15.2). Along U.S. lines, the new constitution prescribed a popularly elected president, a bicameral federal legislature, and elected state governors and assemblies. A federal commission was to monitor formation of truly national, not regional, parties. Of some fifty attempts, only five new parties passed commission scrutiny. In

1979, the country's 48 million voters elected Shehu Shagari of the Northern-based National party of Nigeria (NPN) as president of Nigeria's Second Republic.

Shagari began with important assets. The U.S.-style presidency and federal system strengthened the central government in relation to the states, as did oil revenues. But other problems remained unsolved. The new parties still proved too responsive to regional interests. Shagari's NPN was little more than a Northern party that agreed to rotate people from other parts of the country in leadership positions. To heighten the problem, the tendency toward single-party dominance, familiar all across Africa since the 1960s, now asserted itself in Nigeria too. When Shagari won re-election in 1983, voting patterns showed blatant manipulation: the list of voters proved to contain 65 million names, although Nigerians of voting age were probably not two-thirds that numerous.

Economic problems worsened the political ones. Annual oil earnings peaked at $25 billion in 1981 but fell to a fraction of that in the late 1980s. The foreign debt rose correspondingly to $25 billion. Austerity measures had to be imposed as early as 1982, especially because Nigeria had lost agricultural self-sufficiency and had to import basics like sugar and rice.

The Second Republic fell to a military coup in 1983, followed by another that brought to power Ibrahim Babangida (1985–1993). He completed Nigeria's economic transition away from policies aimed at providing basic human needs and toward export-oriented strategies. Playing to Nigerian patriotism, he refused to accept IMF terms for the economy, yet he implemented the same kind of structural adjustment program. That reduced the practical difference of not cooperating with the IMF to inflicting the pain of structural adjustments on ordinary Nigerians without getting the benefit of an IMF loan. His plan devalued the currency, raised the price of imports, abolished commodity marketing boards to restore agricultural producers'

incentives, and aimed to privatize government firms. The resulting disaster provoked widespread protest and increased state violence. Prices increased tenfold, and the foreign debt rose to an unmanageable $30 billion.

Politically, Babangida proposed a five-year, phased return to civilian rule. A new constitution was drafted, in 1991 the number of states was raised to thirty, and the capital was moved from Lagos to Abuja, a central, more neutral location (see Map 15.2). By not collecting the religious or ethnic data that had made earlier attempts controversial, the government managed to carry out a census in 1991. It yielded a total of 89 million, nearly 20 million less than earlier estimates inflated by ethnic and religious interests. Babangida thoroughly manipulated the supposed return to civilian rule, however, attempting to set up the 1993 presidential election so as to produce no clear result. When the popular Chief Moshood Abiola won 58 percent of the vote anyway, Banbangida annulled the election. A successful businessman who could probably have managed the economy better, Abiola landed in prison.

Nigeria plunged into five more years of crisis, dominated by Babangida's deputy and successor, General Sani Abacha (1993–1998). He created a kleptocratic, one-man regime, repressive but without effective policies. Economic decline reached the point where oil accounted for over 90 percent of export earnings. Yet Nigeria's oil resources produced no benefits for most Nigerians, least of all the half-million Ogoni people of the Niger Delta, who actually lived on the land from which most of the oil was extracted and endured the resulting pollution and environmental degradation. Abacha's response to their protests was to have their leading writer, Ken Saro-Wiwa, and eight others summarily tried and executed in 1995. The British Commonwealth and European Union retaliated with sanctions, reducing Nigeria to pariah status. By 1998, Nigeria was the world's sixth-largest producer of oil but also the thirteenth poorest nation. It was reduced to importing basics like soap and toothpaste and failed to supply its own gas stations with gasoline, but it was ruled by a man who had amassed $3 billion during four years in power.

What really prepared Nigeria's return to civilian government was Abacha's sudden death in June 1998. Many Nigerians thought that Abiola, winner of the 1993 elections but in prison since then, should become president. But he died of a heart attack in July 1998 while still in prison. Leadership in Nigeria's return to civilian rule passed to Olusegun Obasanjo, a former general and chief of state (1976–1979), now a convert to democracy and elder statesman. Obasanjo had also been imprisoned by Abacha. Decisively winning the February 1999 election, he promised far-reaching reforms and a "detribalized" administration, bringing members of different ethnic groups into office. However, he faced trouble on every front. After sixteen years of military rule, few Nigerians were ready to serve honestly as senators and representatives. The corruption of the 1990s had also left Nigeria a center of drug-trafficking and organized crime. The end of military oppression allowed ethnic and religious cleavages freer expression. Several northern states announced that they would introduce Islamic law. Violence among different ethnic and religious groups began to rise, provoking flight, self-segregation, and talk of secession in several regions. Still strongly state-controlled, the economy remained stagnant. In words from songs of its truly most popular public figure, Afrobeat singer Fela Anikulapo-Kuti, Nigeria, too long ruled by "animals in human skins," would remain a land of "suffering and smiling."

South Africa: Inequality, Exploitation, Isolation

Until 1948, South Africa's history had been that of two struggles—one between British and Afri-

kaners for political power, the other between whites and Africans for control of land and labor (see Chapter 8). The introduction of apartheid in 1948 under the Afrikaner-dominated Nationalist party, which remained in power for nearly half a century, marked the victory of the whites, especially the Afrikaners. With the old dual struggle settled, South Africa embarked on a period of prolonged economic growth, but its political system became more exclusionary than ever. The result was a new struggle that pitted Africans vying for political as well as economic power against the ruling white minority. Not until 1994, long after white rule had collapsed everywhere else in Africa, did South Africa's isolation and bizarre internal contradictions force it too to risk change by accepting majority rule.

White Domination, Economic and Political

Into the 1980s, growth and inequality became more than ever the dominant traits of South Africa's economy. Minerals remained basic to its prosperity. South Africa ranked first in the world in reserves of gold, platinum, chrome, manganese, and vanadium. The country ranked second in reserves of diamonds, and between third and eighth in antimony, asbestos, coal, lead, nickel, phosphate, silver, titanium, and perhaps uranium. The land produced a sizable agricultural surplus for export, at the price of malnourishment for millions of Africans in the black reserves. By 1965 the country was virtually self-sufficient in heavy industry, and manufactured goods accounted for 40 percent of exports. As before World War II, the state controlled key industries, particularly in energy, one field where South Africa had resource shortages. With no known petroleum resources, the government founded SASOL (South African Coal, Oil and Gas Corporation) in the 1950s to manufacture oil from coal. After the Iranian Revolution of 1979 deprived South Africa of its one regular source of oil, efforts began to expand SASOL's production. South Africa also developed nuclear power and began exploring for offshore petroleum.

Another resource essential for South Africa's economic growth was nonwhite labor, exploited through bad working conditions and grossly unequal pay. In 1984, the average salary for whites was almost four times that for Africans. African living standards were especially bad in the black homelands, which reserved 13 percent of the land for over 70 percent of the population. South Africa's exploitation of blacks did not stop at its borders. The mines had long employed migrants from as far north as Zambia (see Map 15.1). This practice increased the supply, and lowered the price, of black labor in South Africa. It also helped ensure South Africa's regional dominance.

Exploitative but resource rich, the South African economy grew at an average annual rate of nearly 7 percent from 1910 to 1974, an astonishing record. The OPEC oil price increases and other factors then caused a crisis. When the United States stopped buying and selling gold at a fixed $35 per ounce in 1971, however, the world price soared, reaching an all-time high of $875 an ounce in January 1980. Despite wide fluctuations, gold price increases of such an order for a time helped pull South Africa back out of recession. But drought and commodity price declines caused a new downturn by 1983. From 1984 on, the costs of virtual black rebellion at home and trade sanctions abroad—South Africa's coal exports fell by 40 percent in the first half of 1987—created new pressures that left South Africa scrambling for solutions. The government privatized even key state firms like SASOL, the oil-from-coal concern, and planned to create new indirect taxes to raise revenue from those too poor to pay income tax. Meanwhile, growing labor militancy highlighted the contradiction inherent in trying to separate economically interdependent races, especially in a complex economy where

growth required placing nonwhites in more and better jobs.

In politics, South Africa remained formally a parliamentary democracy. Yet changes over time greatly eroded resemblances to the original British model. From 1948 until 1994, for example, the Afrikaner-dominated National party always controlled the government. Single-party rule signaled the Afrikaners' political triumph over the English-speaking South Africans. In 1961, when the country declared itself a republic and severed ties with the British Commonwealth, British influence further diminished.

The character and policies of selected prime ministers reinforced this trend. With the Nationalist party victory in 1948, Prime Minister D. F. Malan (1948–1954) formed the first government to consist of Afrikaners only. Its legislation systematized racial separation (apartheid). The consistency of the governments from then on derived not just from the party but from a larger complex of Afrikaner interest groups. The most important was the Afrikaner Broederbond (Brotherhood, founded 1918). Under National party rule, all prime ministers and virtually all Afrikaners in public life were members of this secret society, whose members largely formulated the apartheid idea. The triumph of such interests meant a shift from British-style restraint toward Afrikaner authoritarianism—a shift abetted by English-speaking South Africans' belief in white supremacy, if not always in Afrikaner methods.

Prime Minister Hendrik Verwoerd (1958–1966) reflected this shift. A former Nazi sympathizer, he fulfilled the Afrikaner dream of a republic without links to Britain. At the same time his policy of separate development aimed at transforming the native reserves into homelands that would become "independent," theoretically quite separate from the white republic.

The first prime minister to react significantly to the collapse of white rule in neighboring countries was P. W. Botha (1978–1984). But his new constitution (1984) still made only limited political concessions to coloreds (persons of mixed race) and Asians and none at all to Africans. By then, such limited concessions were clearly inadequate responses to the forces they were meant to contain.

Apartheid in Action

Over time, South African racial policy became minutely regulated and rigidified. The bases for apartheid long predated 1948. The Native Land Act of 1913 created the Native Reserves, the Native Urban Areas Act of 1923 segregated black residents of towns, and the Native Representation Act of 1936 removed Africans from the common voter rolls in Cape Province. From 1948 on, discriminatory laws proliferated.

By 1960 they had transformed South Africa into a racially based caste society. The purpose was to separate racial categories—white, colored, Asian, African—in every way possible and to deny political participation to the nonwhite categories, all three of which are known in South Africa as "black." Apartheid was to ensure white minority control by "dividing and ruling" and by maximizing inequality. Africans were not even supposed to reside permanently except in small parts of the country set aside for their various ethnic groups, whose differences were emphasized to fragment the African majority. Africans were to go elsewhere only as temporary migrant workers. They had to carry passes, so that their movements could be controlled, and they could hold only jobs not reserved for whites. First set up for the mining industry, the system assumed that migrant workers were bachelors who did not need a "family" wage. Wages were further depressed by bringing in workers from other countries, as noted. Since jobs for Africans—including industrial and domestic jobs, as well as those in mining—were mostly remote from the places where they were supposed to reside, the impact of such labor conditions on African family life was dras-

tic, through either long-term family separation or extremely long daily commuting times, in addition to inadequate pay. In fact, because most jobs for Africans were in cities, it proved impossible for the government to make all Africans live in rural reserves. The main response to this was the creation of segregated "townships," like Soweto, in which Africans who worked in the cities had to live, far from their jobs.

Bad working and living conditions indicated the dehumanizing intent of apartheid but did not show its full extent. Under the Promotion of Self Government Act (1959), the many native reserves were consolidated into ten tribal homelands, or bantustans. The consolidation was only administrative, for the homelands still consisted of scattered pieces of land. Still, Prime Minister Verwoerd, mastermind of the policy, argued that just as whites could find fulfillment only in a state they controlled, "separate development" was the key to fulfillment for each African ethnic group. The ultimate fulfillment was to be the homelands' "independence," which would provide the excuse to deprive homeland residents of South African citizenship.

In 1976, South Africa began giving "independence" to some homelands. No other nation recognized them as independent nations, however, and some ethnic groups refused to accept this status. Set aside for the Ndebele, an ethnic group that historically had no home in South Africa, the "homeland" KwaNdebele was in fact a dumping ground for ethnically mixed elements ejected from the cities under the pass system. Nowhere did the government's concern for ethnic fulfillment extend to economic development or good government. In fact, part of the government's strategy was to bring ruthless people to power within the impoverished homelands, then watch the residents divide into warring bands as henchmen, or opponents, of their government-backed "leaders."

As the homeland policy developed, segregation and inequality worsened in countless other ways. Not only was education segregated at all levels, but the requirement that African children be educated in their various ethnic languages for the first eight years played up ethnic differences and left the children unprepared for secondary or higher education in English or Afrikaans. Other laws were designed to protect racial barriers by prohibiting mixed marriages (1949) and interracial sex outside marriage (1957), or by requiring people over sixteen to carry an identity card specifying their race (1950). The Suppression of Communism Act (1950) defined communism as practically any attempt to change the status quo. What whites lacked in numbers, they sought to make up through socioeconomic advantage, control of the state, and unrestrained use of the state's coercive power.

As prime minister (1978–1984) and then president (1984–1989), P. W. Botha reacted to the erosion of white power elsewhere in Africa by readjusting foreign and domestic policy. In addition to neighboring countries' economic dependency, long since effected by employing migrant miners, Botha sought to achieve a regional dominance not unlike that of the United States over Central America. For this purpose, South Africa fought its opponents on neighboring states' territory and supported movements hostile to unfriendly regimes in those states. South Africa invaded Angola repeatedly after 1975 and supported an opposition movement, UNITA, against the Cuban-backed Angolan government. To undermine the Afro-Marxist government of neighboring Mozambique, South Africa also supported the so-called Mozambican National Resistance Movement (RENAMO in Portuguese), in origin not a nationalist movement but a mercenary force that ravaged the country until an internationally brokered cease-fire in 1992. Diplomatically, Botha sought agreements that would keep opponents of the regime, particularly the African National Congress, from operating out of neighboring countries. Namibia, controlled by South Africa since

the end of World War I, remained a special case. As part of a U.S.-mediated attempt to end the Angolan civil war, however, South Africa finally agreed for Namibia to become independent in 1990. The apparent motive was to spare South Africa's white minority the costs and casualties of armed intervention.

Internally, Botha made certain concessions to nonwhites. For the African majority, concessions were mostly limited to the field of labor relations. African and mixed labor unions received official recognition (1979). As the need for skilled labor grew, Botha also gave Africans some recognition as permanent residents of urban areas by letting them buy their own houses—but not the land—in the townships. Since the 1960s, a system of local councils had existed in nonwhite areas. Yet administering and policing the townships remained insoluble problems, for institutionalizing these services would mean admitting what the homeland policy denied: that Africans' urban presence was legitimate.

The two other nonwhite communities, the coloreds and Asians, represented about 9 and 3 percent, respectively, of the estimated 1988 population of 35 million, compared to about 15 and 73 percent for whites and Africans. Botha's 1984 constitution made political concessions to the two smaller groups. Creating separate elected national assemblies for each of them as well as for the whites, the constitution created a complicated governmental system, in which an extremely powerful executive president replaced the prime minister. The official reason for not making such concessions to Africans was that they had political institutions in the homelands. Taking another step away from British parliamentarism but offering the African majority nothing, the 1984 constitution intensified African opposition to white rule.

In the long run, the African majority's response to these maneuvers would be the most important one, but it was not the only consequence Botha had to consider. The 1984 constitution and African opposition to it raised international awareness of South African racism to new levels, symbolized by the economic sanctions that European and North American governments imposed on South Africa and by mounting demands for multinational firms to disinvest from South Africa and stop doing business there. Inside South Africa, controversy racked the white minority. Ultra-rightists assailed the Botha government for making concessions to nonwhites. Moderates, including business people concerned about international sanctions and about how the systematic impoverishment of three-quarters of the population limited the market for consumer goods, advocated further change. Some analysts argued that apartheid's costs would kill it, if nothing else did. Aside from the costs of military intervention abroad and repression at home, the 1984 constitution increased the number of cabinet members and members of parliament many times over, while civil service payrolls grew to one-third of government spending. Such issues are worth keeping in mind as we examine black African opposition to apartheid and the end of white rule.

African Responses to Apartheid

Black South Africans' radicalization was already beginning during World War II. In the African National Congress (ANC), young intellectuals, such as Oliver Tambo and Nelson Mandela, grew dissatisfied with older leaders and formed a new pressure group, the ANC Youth League. They won control of the ANC in 1949 and pushed through a program of strikes, civil disobedience, and noncooperation. During the 1950s, the ANC still emphasized civil disobedience campaigns in collaboration with Indian, colored, and liberal white organizations. This phase culminated at a Congress of the People that adopted the Freedom Charter (1955). Asserting that South Africa's people, black and white, were "equal, countrymen and

brothers," and would work together for democratic change, the charter lastingly defined ANC ideology.

Reactions to the Congress of the People opened a new phase in the history of the African opposition. The government responded by passing more repressive laws and arresting 156 people, including leaders of the congress. They were charged with conspiring to overthrow the state and replace it with a communist one. All the defendants were later released, but not until 1961 in some cases.

Meanwhile, African activists began to differ about nonviolence and cooperation with other racial groups. One group wanted a purely African movement that would use any means to ensure majority rule. It broke from the ANC and formed the Pan-Africanist Congress (PAC) in 1959. Seeking to retain leadership, the ANC planned a civil disobedience campaign against the pass system for late March 1960. But the PAC launched a similar campaign a few days earlier. At Sharpeville, near Johannesburg, the police shot at the demonstrators, killing 67 and wounding almost 200. When demonstrations ensued, the government mobilized the armed forces, outlawed both ANC and PAC, and jailed some 18,000 Africans, with much violence. With both ANC and PAC forced underground, even men like Tambo and Mandela concluded that nonviolence—after the response it got at the Sharpeville massacre—would not work for their movement.

The ANC then organized an underground group, Umkhonto we Sizwe (Spear of the Nation), which carried out its first act of sabotage in December 1961. The group's first commander, Nelson Mandela, was captured in 1962 and given a life sentence. Repeatedly offered freedom if he would renounce violence, Mandela's steadfast refusals made him South Africa's most revered leader. By 1963, all ANC leaders but Tambo, who had gone abroad to found an exile branch, had been captured. For the remainder of the 1960s, the government managed to repress other anti-regime organizations as well.

When black activism resurfaced inside the country, it focused at first on issues arising from segregation in education. Influenced by the U.S civil rights movement, a black consciousness movement emerged to challenge the white liberals' idea of integrating blacks into white society. The movement's slogan became "Black man, you're on your own." The government began cracking down in 1973. In 1976 the attempt to impose Afrikaans as a language of instruction in the Soweto schools brought out thousands of children to demonstrate. When the police shot a student, protests swept the land. The government response left 575 dead, of whom only 5 were white and 134 were younger than eighteen. Ruthless repression led many activists to join ANC forces abroad. Inside South Africa, anti-regime organizations continued to form, such as the Soweto Civic Association and the Azanian People's Organization (AZAPO). Defiance spread among all three subordinate castes.

In the period between the Soweto uprising and the 1984 constitution, the struggle proceeded both inside and outside South Africa. Inside, Africans had some leaders who still emphasized nonviolence, such as Desmond Tutu, Anglican bishop of Johannesburg. Among resistance groups, the most important event inside the country in this period was the creation of the United Democratic Front (UDF, 1983), an umbrella organization that combined hundreds of groups with some 1.5 million members. The UDF shared the ANC commitment to interracial collaboration and was therefore opposed by groups like PAC and AZAPO, which rejected white participation.

Externally, the exile branch of the ANC remained the main opposition force after Soweto. In the early 1980s, it conducted military operations from foreign bases, bombing South Africa's main oil-from-coal plant (1980), a new nuclear plant (1982), and South African air force headquarters (1983). As at Sharpeville in 1960,

the government responded disproportionately to such acts.

The ANC's actions paled, however, compared to the violence inside South Africa after September 1984. Sparked both by attempts to increase rents on government-owned township houses and by the new constitution, disturbances occurred all over the country in a way that made them harder to control than earlier, localized incidents. From abroad, the ANC had long called for making the townships ungovernable. This now happened in townships and homelands alike, but the ANC was only the symbol of resistance, not its organizer.

In South Africa, too, political mobilization was rising to a new level. Africans, and eventually other nonwhites, challenged every aspect of repression. In the townships, Africans who had collaborated with the authorities by assuming leadership roles or, still worse, by serving as police informers faced summary execution by the "necklace"—an old tire placed around the neck, filled with gasoline, and set afire. Where competing political groups faced one another, violence became especially common, all the more when criminals took advantage of disorder to mask their own acts. Such was the "black-on-black" violence that the government cynically publicized, as if its own kind of "law and order" had nothing to do with what was happening. In the homelands, conflict raged between the corrupt and repressive government-backed leaders and their henchmen, on the one hand, and the young "comrades" who opposed them, on the other. There, too, the "necklace" became familiar. Even children took part in resistance through school boycotts organized by activist groups. The resistance asserted itself economically, not only through rent strikes, which cost the government hundreds of millions of dollars, but also through boycotts of white businesses and through actions like the mineworkers' strike of August 1987, which caused over $50 million in production losses to the country's largest gold-mining company.

Nelson Mandela *addresses a crowd of a hundred thousand people in Soweto, February 1990, shortly after his release from prison. The African National Congress elected Mandela its president in 1991. He was elected president of South Africa in 1994.*
© *AP-Wide World Photos*

Faced with such problems, the government declared a state of emergency (June 1986), detained tens of thousands of people without even allowing their names to be published, and banned all political activity by the UDF, African labor organizations, and other groups.

Toward Majority Rule

As South Africa approached mass political mobilization of a sort incompatible with survival of the existing order, signs of readiness for accommodation began to appear. P. W. Botha resigned from the presidency in August 1989. In 1990, his successor, F. W. de Klerk, lifted the ban on the ANC and—needing someone of stature to negotiate with—freed Nelson Mandela from prison. At this, the UDF disbanded and urged its affiliates to support the ANC.

These events launched a restructuring that depended on the two leaders' ability to work together and maintain their positions as leaders of the country's whites and blacks. With militant whites to de Klerk's right and many forces at work among the African population—most notably the Inkatha Freedom party, whose agenda combined Zulu ethnic reassertion and economic ideas to the right of the ANC's—success was not assured. De Klerk's government abolished apartheid in 1991, and foreign governments began lifting the sanctions they had imposed. Having announced suspension of the armed struggle in 1990, the ANC held a national conference in July 1991. Electing Mandela its president and bringing members of a younger generation into other leadership positions, the conference looked like a step toward turning the ANC into a political party. The government agreed with the ANC and Inkatha to open negotiations for a new constitution, and the Convention for a Democratic South Africa (CODESA) began meeting in December 1991. In March 1992, nearly 70 percent of the white electorate voted to end minority rule. Optimists predicted the formation within months of a multiracial interim government.

Progress was not so swift, however. Racial violence, abuses, and insubordination among government security forces, disclosures of corruption in homeland administration, and a deteriorating economy weakened de Klerk's position. The ANC had to face internal scandals, ongoing violence in homelands and townships, and opposition from both the Left and Inkatha. Yet by February 1993, the government and the ANC had agreed that white rule would end in April 1994 with the election of a new parliament, which would serve for five years and write a new constitution. Black South Afri-

Black South Africans get the vote, 1994. *Nothing better symbolizes the spreading, global demands for democratization than the orderly line of people waiting to cast their ballots at Soweto. Denis Farrell/© AP-Wide World Photos*

cans would get to vote in the 1994 election, and minority parties—which would thenceforth include the Nationalist party—would be eligible to participate in the interim government of the next five years. The ANC emerged from the 1994 elections with a clear majority, Mandela as president, and de Klerk as one of two deputy presidents. With the adoption in 1996 of the new constitution, including an extensive bill of rights, South Africa officially completed one of the world's most difficult democratization processes.

South Africa's future prospects were not unclouded, however. De Klerk and other members of his National party withdrew from the government and went into opposition over dis-

agreements about the constitution and the economy. The Zulu Inkatha party also criticized the constitution for imposing unitary rule on a complex society, despite the fact that the nine new provinces were largely drawn along ethnic lines (see Map 15.3). Such political tensions undermined confidence in financial markets, leading to sharp declines in exchange rates and in the stock and bond markets. Chronic violence in KwaZulu-Natal Province cost sixteen hundred lives in the first half of 1996. The Truth and Reconciliation Commission, set up under Archbishop Tutu to come to terms with South Africa's recent brutal history, faced the difficult task of steering between white demands for amnesia and black demands for vengeance,

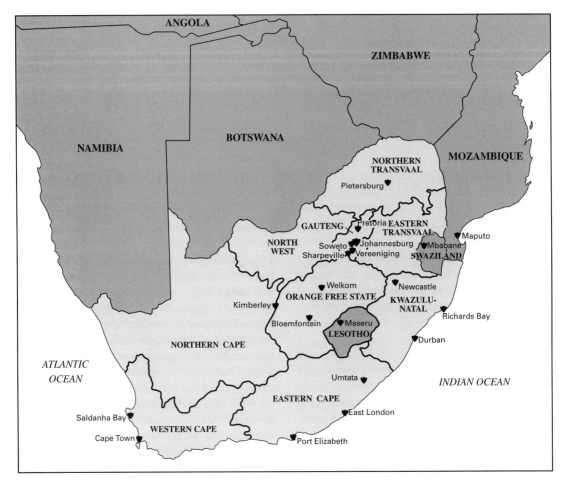

Map 15.3 South Africa's Postapartheid Provinces

while the new government lacked the means to offer meaningful reparations to victims of the past.

By the time of South Africa's second postapartheid election in 1999, majority rule had solved some problems, but other problems had worsened. Retiring from office at the age of eighty, Mandela retained the mantle of elder statesmen. Former deputy president Thabo Mbeki was elected to succeed him, and the ANC won nearly a two-thirds majority. Lacking Mandela's charisma but methodical and trained in

economics, Mbeki turned his attention from reconciliation, which had occupied Mandela, to rebuilding. Five years of majority rule had given South Africa a liberal constitution, a revamped legal system and five hundred new laws, more than half a million new housing units, electric and telephone lines extending even across the shanty towns, while clean water, health care, and school feeding programs had benefited millions. Economically, however, South Africa was still "two nations," as Mbeki said. With the opening of its formerly isolated and protected economy to global competition, South Africa had lost a half million jobs, and unemployment rates among Africans stood as high as 40 percent, compared to 4 percent for whites. Crime rates remained among the highest in the world. Most menacing of all, South Africa had acquired one of the fastest-rising AIDS infection rates in the world. The government had faltered in developing effective policies to combat it, and Mbeki himself had attracted international criticism for his confusing statements about the link between HIV and AIDS. Africa's major power, with a population over 40 million and a GNP of roughly $120 billion, majority-ruled South Africa still struggled to realize prosperity for more than the few.

Conclusion: Moving Beyond Change Without Development?

Africa was the last of the continents to be integrated into the European-dominated global pattern of the pre-1914 era and the last to be formally decolonized. Mostly becoming independent in the 1960s, just as the Third World population explosion was emerging as a policy problem that could no longer be ignored, Africa's nations remained impoverished despite their natural resources, disunited, plagued by corruption, and politically unable to resist military authoritarianism. The oil-related stresses of the 1970s and 1980s seriously affected all African countries, including the few that had oil to export. By the late 1980s, the same pressures for democratization were at work in Africa as in Latin America. Caught between foreign debt, the ecological and socioeconomic consequences of the demographic explosion, and the ravages of AIDS, African nations had difficulty responding to the new trend. Optimistic observers pointed out, however, that South Africa was not the only African country to respond positively. A number of conflicts that had echoed the Cold

War, had ended. More widely still, with the spread of at least elementary education, the era of authoritarian mobilization behind small cadres of nationalist leaders had ended. Demand for democratization had begun to acquire a broader human base, even as the claims of ethnic and regional particularism continued to make themselves heard. African societies that could build on this momentum to achieve greater success in national integration and human development might be able to move beyond Nigeria's corruption or Somalia's chaos to achieve a "second revolution" of democratization and improve their relative position in the era of globalization. As one Nigerian voter put it in February 1999, "Globally, things are going democratically. We want to join the globe." [5]

Notes

1. Blaine Harden, "Africa's Gems: Warfare's Best Friend," *New York Times,* April 6, 2000, pp. A1, A10–A11; Robert Black, "Diamonds Lie Behind Africa Bloodshed," *Wall Street Journal,* May 12, 2000, pp. A14, A16.

2. Stephen McCarthy, *Africa: The Challenge of Transformation* (London: I. B. Tauris, 1994), pp. 97, 118–119, 195.

3. Quoted ibid., p. 197.

4. United Nations Development Program, *Human Development Report 1996* (New York: Oxford University Press, 1996), p. 23.

5. Statement of Ndubuisi Ebubeogu, a shipping worker, at polls in Ajengule, a Lagos slum, as quoted in Norimitsu Onishi, "Nigerians Vote, with High Hopes for Civilian Rule," *New York Times,* February 28, 1999, p. 1.

Suggestions for Further Reading

Books

Achebe, Chinua. *A Man of the People* (1966).

Crowder, Michael. *The Story of Nigeria* (1978).

Davidson, Basil. *Modern Africa: A Social and Political History.* 3d ed. (1994).

Falola, Toyin. *The History of Nigeria* (1999).

Fieldhouse, D. K. *Black Africa, 1945–1980: Economic Decolonization and Arrested Development* (1986).

Mazrui, Ali. *The Africans: A Triple Heritage* (1986).

McCarthy, Stephen. *Africa: The Challenge of Transformation* (1994).

Oliver, Roland, and Anthony Atmore. *Africa Since 1800.* 4th ed. (1994).

Thompson, Leonard. *A History of South Africa.* Rev. ed. (1995).

United Nations Development Program. *Human Development Report 2000: Human Development and Human Rights* (2000).

World Bank. *World Development Report 2000/2001: Attacking Poverty* (2000).

Newspapers and Periodicals

Africa Report.

Africa Research Bulletin.

Jeune Afrique (*Young Africa,* French-language weekly published in Paris).

CHAPTER | 16

The Middle East and North Africa Since World War II

"*WE ARE ALL WELL . . . BUT FOR THE LOSSES WE SUFFERED DURING THE EARTHQUAKE,* seven all together . . . both from my husband's and my family. . . . Now while Turkey is trying to heal the wounds, so are we personally. . . ."

"[T]here was an earthquake a month ago, and we are struggling with the grief. I used to live in Adapazari, which is close to the epicenter, but one month before the earthquake, I moved to Ankara with my family. . . . We were thus not right in the earthquake. . . . We only lost three of our relatives, thank God. . . . After it, my father's heart trouble got worse . . . , but he is better now. . . .[1]

On August 17, 1999, an earthquake measuring 7.4 on the Richter scale shook Izmit on the Marmara coast, east of Istanbul in a region that houses one-third of both Turkey's population and its economic production. Hundreds of aftershocks followed. Earthquakes struck again in September and November, the last nearly as severe as that in August. In comparison, the 1995 earthquake at Kobe, Japan (see Chapter 17), measured 7.2 on the Richter scale; San Francisco's of 1906 measured 8.3. Izmit's August quake left over 10,000 dead and a half-million homeless.

Major earthquakes shake more than the ground. Here, the government failed to respond quickly. For reasons a thousand years old, Turks have great respect for state authority, and phrases like *devlet baba* ("father state") or *devlet ana* ("mother state") are not unheard. When no rescue teams appeared the first day and when the first to come were foreign, survivors asked *devlet nerede* ("where is the state")? The crisis made old nationalist formulas look foolish. The Minister of Health, Osman Durmush of the far-right National Action Party (MHP in Turkish), insisted that Turkey did not need foreign help, especially not from Greece, Armenia, or the U.S. Navy. He also opposed Turkish non-governmental groups, like the volunteer AKÜT rescue team, who played an international role in the earthquake story before it ended. Even the Turkish army did not show up quickly. "We died twice," a newspaper wrote, once from the quake, once from lack of help. Some of the worst aftershocks were political.

Others were socioeconomic. Urban Turks are apartment dwellers, and towns around Izmit had recently begun to sprout high-rise buildings. One building crumbled; the next remained standing. Contractors whose buildings failed became targets of rage; at least one fled the country. Turkey has advanced earthquake engineers; their buildings stood. For those who lost home and family, the crisis became a test of self-help and fledgling nongovernmental groups. People dug for loved ones. Cell phones aided coordination. Television provided continuous coverage. Volunteers trying to come help snarl the roads. Turkey's secularist authorities feared that Islamic groups would win followers by aiding the victims. Yet the Islamic response proved unexpectedly weak; a leadership struggle had tied up the Islamic political party. Meanwhile, Turkey's largest oil refinery, blazing out of control near Izmit, symbolized economic losses of $20 billion, 10 percent of 1999 GDP.

Some international aftershocks proved beneficial. Aid poured in from North America, Europe, the Arab world, Israel, even Armenia. Greek sympathy and aid were especially spontaneous, including funds, blood, relief workers, and supplies. Reasons for strong sympathy, despite political differences, became clear when earthquakes struck Athens in September. Then the Turks were the first foreign rescuers to arrive, notably the gallant AKÜT team, who used sophisticated sensors to locate survivors and gave a souvenir hardhat to Greece's president before leaving. "Seismic diplomacy," some said. Spatially, the August earthquake pushed Turkey four feet closer to Europe; politically and psychologically, the move was greater.

The earthquakes even had global implications. Geologically, the North Anatolian fault is a near twin to California's San Andreas fault. U.S. seismologists were keen to study it. Since 1939, a dozen quakes have occurred on the North Anatolian fault from east to west, ever closer to Istanbul. Its 12 million people suffered losses in 1999 and feared future quakes even nearer to them. Population concentration near a fault line was another similarity to California—and to Greece, Egypt, Mexico, Japan, and other places. Turkey was not the only place where explosive population growth and even faster urbanization interacted with human struggles to tame the forces of nature, creating potentials for disasters at once natural and human.

Regional Overview: The Search for Independence and Integration

In the Middle East and North Africa, the major post-1945 periods have been clearly marked, and not only in economic terms. Between 1945 and the early 1970s, foreign-ruled countries won independence; and a process of radicalization, touched off in the Arab world by the 1948 war and the creation of the state of Israel, brought Arab socialists to power in several states. During this period, Middle Eastern oil literally helped fuel the post-1945 global economic boom. Yet the price of oil did not rise correspondingly—a fact that angered oil-producing countries.

Several factors—the OPEC-engineered rise in oil prices being the most obvious—opened a new period around 1973. The 1967 Arab-Israeli war discredited "radical" Arab leaders and their ideal of Arab unity, much as the 1948 war had discredited liberal nationalists. Loss of faith in imported ideologies drew attention to the region's indigenous belief system, Islam, which advocates had promoted all along as the answer to society's ills. Transforming economic relations between the Middle East and the outside world, the oil price rises also yielded new wealth to support Islamic priorities. Yet the fear, touched off by the 1979 Iranian revolution, that Islamic revolution would spread proved exaggerated: not all Islamists spoke with one voice.

After the price of oil fell again in the 1980s, it emerged that Middle Eastern societies still had major shortfalls in political and socioeconomic development. Here, as elsewhere, the 1990s looked like the start of a new period marked by peacemaking—at least by decline in external support for conflict in the region—and by demands for democratization and human development. While the situations of individual countries varied markedly, however, this remained a region where multiple stresses—ecological, economic, political—clouded future prospects. A comparative overview, followed by closer looks at Turkey, Iran, Egypt, and Israel, will illustrate these points.

Entering the Age of the Mass Society

By the 1945–1973 period, the Middle East had entered the age of the mass society, first of all in demographic terms. The region's total population rose from 80 million in 1930 to 419 million in 2000. This population was, however, very unequally distributed among countries. The three most populous countries by far—Iran, Egypt, and Turkey—had populations of 21, 26, and 28 million in 1960; by 2000, all three had populations of 65 to 68 million. As of 2000, the region's only other countries with as many as 20 million people were Algeria (32 million), Sudan (30 million), Morocco (29 million), Iraq (23 million), and Saudi Arabia (22 million). Almost all the rest had populations under 10 million. Israel had 6.2 million. One of the region's most striking traits was that its population and its oil were mostly concentrated in different countries.

Partly for this reason, the entire region's rank in the Human Development Index (HDI)—a statistic combining measures of life

Female genital mutilation and women's dependency. *More an African than an Islamic custom, female circumcision occurs in Egypt and some nearby countries. This Egyptian poster denounces the practice as "a wrong that time cannot efface"; however, a government attempt to ban it has been overturned in court.* Barry Iverson

expectancy, literacy, education, and income—stood in the "medium" range, higher than the values for sub-Saharan Africa or South Asia but lower than Latin America. Israel and a handful of the small Gulf states ranked among high HDI countries, Israel having the highest values for all components of the index. Countries in the upper half of the medium-HDI range in 1998 included Saudi Arabia, Turkey, Oman, Jordan, Iran, Tunisia, Algeria, and Syria. Countries in the lower half included Egypt and Iraq. Sudan and

Yemen ranked as low HDI countries. Where data existed to recalculate the same index for women separately, the scores fell for all Islamic countries except Turkey, whose unusual record in gender relations was already noted in Chapter 9.[2]

Almost all these countries have made major gains in human development. For example, the birth rate for the region fell from around 40 per thousand in 1986 to 28 per thousand in 2000. Most of these countries achieved majority literacy after 1945. Bahrain, Qatar, Lebanon, and Turkey achieved literacy rates above 80 percent. Within countries, however, sharp disparities by gender, class, and region persisted. As in other developing lands, the largest cities grew much faster than the nations they dominated, becoming congested, stressful environments as they did. While Turkey's, Iran's, and Egypt's national populations each more than quadrupled between 1930 and 1996, Istanbul's population grew at least tenfold, from 700,000 to 8 to 12 million; Cairo's grew over tenfold, from 1.2 million to 14.5 million; and Tehran's grew more than thirteenfold, from half a million to about 7 million.

Perhaps what most clearly proved unevenness in human development was that even the oil producers of the Arabian peninsula ranked high only in income and otherwise resembled underdeveloped societies. In 2000 Saudi Arabia still had a birth rate of 35 per thousand, and 1997 secondary school enrollment rates of 65 percent for males—only 53 percent for females. Israel, while far from the region's highest-income country, best balanced social and economic development.

Today, it seems increasingly clear that social and economic development goes together with political development, and that the kind of disparities seen in most Middle Eastern societies point to shortcomings in mass mobilization in the political sense—specifically, in democratization.

Economics: Oil and Development?

In the 1950s and 1960s, experts surveying Middle Eastern potentials for economic development normally pointed to Turkey as the country with the best prospects in the region. It was not a petroleum producer but had the best resource mix otherwise. In the 1970s, the oil price rise shifted attention to the oil producers. By the late 1980s, however, falling oil prices and signs of economic trouble in even the largest producer, Saudi Arabia, had again altered perceptions. Turkey again attracted notice as the region's most successful Muslim country in economic development. Yet Turkey's uneven performance and its failure to rise out of the upper ranks of lower middle-income countries suggested lingering developmental problems regionwide.

Because it played a major part, both in the political shift of emphasis from Pan-Arabism to Islamic unity and in the world economy, the transformation of the petroleum industry is important to understand. In the post-1945 economic history of all Asia, the 1970s OPEC oil boom is second in importance only to Japan's growth and East Asia's subsequent economic upsurge. Yet the situations of Japan and the OPEC countries, most of which are in the Middle East, differed sharply. Japan developed one of the leading industrial economies, whereas the oil-exporting countries experienced a huge export boom based on one commodity. In the Middle East, the results were not equitably distributed: some countries—including two of the most populous, Egypt and Turkey—were not major oil producers. Because oil is a nonrenewable resource, even the exporters' future depended on how long the high income continued and how well it was invested for development.

The earlier history of the Middle East's oil industry throws added light on the OPEC experience. International firms, acting under concessions from local governments, started exporting Middle Eastern oil before 1914. At first, demand was low, and the host governments got only about 25 cents per barrel in royalties. Significant change came after 1945. The Marshall Plan for European reconstruction assumed the availability of cheap Middle Eastern oil, a major resource of the global economic surge of 1945–1973; and that assumption gave the oil states potential leverage over the oil companies. The oil states soon won agreements for equal profit sharing, and Iran made the first attempt at nationalization in 1951. It failed, partly because the other producers lacked organization and failed to support Iran. With the companies still controlling the industry, the real (inflation-adjusted) price of oil actually fell, even as the Western economies' oil consumption rapidly grew.

In 1960, Iraq, Saudi Arabia, Iran, Kuwait, and Venezuela—then the one major Latin America producer—formed the Organization of Petroleum Exporting Countries (OPEC) as a means for joint action to improve prices. In 1973, the cartel's membership also included Algeria, Libya, Qatar, the United Arab Emirates, Ecuador, Gabon, Nigeria, and Indonesia; and Libya, Iraq, and Iran had successfully nationalized their oil industries.

The 1973 Arab-Israeli war brought the biggest shift in economic relations between the Middle East and the outside world in the five centuries since Europe's overseas expansion began. The war governed the timing, but the underlying causes were OPEC's determination to control production and pricing and the fact that U.S. oil consumption was growing while U.S. production had begun to drop. Imports accounted for 36 percent of U.S. oil use in 1973, 48 percent in 1977. With Europe highly dependent on OPEC oil and Japan yet more so, growing U.S. demand gave OPEC leverage to raise prices at will. Angry over Israeli retention of lands taken in 1967 and over U.S. aid to Israel in the

1973 war, Arab oil states also cut production, embargoing nations friendly to Israel.

The five-month-long embargo, the quadrupling of prices in 1973–1974, and another doubling or more triggered by the 1979 Iranian revolution jolted the world economy, creating an unprecedented new flow of wealth. OPEC's combined oil revenues rose from $22.5 billion in 1973 to $272 billion in 1980.

By then, rising prices had caused global oil consumption to fall. Soon prices fell, too. Plunged into the worst recession since 1929, the industrial nations grew serious about conserving energy, developing non-OPEC oil sources (such as Mexico and Alaska's North Slope), and to a degree shifting to other forms of energy (see Chapter 18). Predictably, because oil was a depletable, nonrenewable resource, scarcity and high prices would in time return. By 2000, oil prices had risen again to the dollar levels seen around 1980, although real 2000 oil prices were about half as high in inflation-adjusted terms.

Today, the Middle Eastern oil exporters' prospects look no surer than those of their oilless neighbors. As in Mexico and Nigeria, Iran's experience illustrates that the impact of oil wealth on a highly populous country, with complex economic and social structures, is likely to prove especially upsetting. In contrast, a country that lacks petroleum but has a diversity of resources to support industrialization, especially if it can also feed its population, may fare better—especially if that country has ample water, which Turkey alone has in the Middle East. Even a small country that lacks natural resources but has an educated and motivated population and development-oriented policies can, like Israel, outperform its larger neighbors.

Politics and Cultural Reassertion

Before 1945, European imperialism had redrawn the political map of the Middle East, somewhat as in Africa, creating new political subdivisions at odds with Islamic ideals of unity (see Map 16.1). Imperialism and local reactions to it had, as well, introduced major themes of nineteenth-century thought, including classical liberalism and nationalism. Nationalist movements had grown up to mobilize support and seek independence within the new boundaries. As in many other regions, the lack of an indigenous democratic heritage and the gap between the nationalist leaders' ideas and those of the masses gave an authoritarian cast to nationalist political mobilization. The majority was often more responsive to Islamist urgings that the right priority was to unite Muslims and revitalize Islam. Yet as long as different outside powers controlled or threatened different parts of the Islamic world, the Islamists' goal of unity seemed utopian and less practical than the liberals' nationalism.

Had more Middle Eastern countries been independent, the inadequacy of the nationalist's old-fashioned liberalism as a response to the masses' needs might have been exposed during the Depression, provoking a change of leadership, as in Latin America. Turkey, which was independent then, averted this fate when its liberal nationalist leadership responded to the Depression with a new state-led economic development policy (see Chapter 9). In most other Middle Eastern countries, continuing foreign control masked the liberal nationalists' lack of ideas about development. Such countries reached 1945 with growing, unmet needs for social change.

The years from 1945 to 1973 therefore brought many changes. Politically, while Turkey and Iran continued to develop on bases laid between the world wars, this was the period when most Arab countries became independent, largely within boundaries traced by Europeans. Just as the Arabs' liberal nationalists neared triumph, however, the emergence of the state of Israel on territory that most Arabs regarded as rightfully the Palestinians', and the failure of five Arab countries who fought in

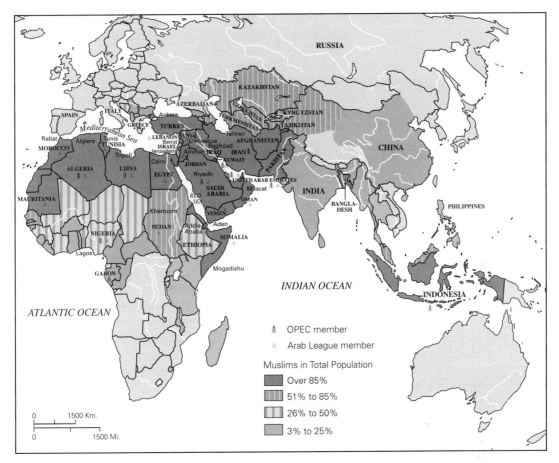

Map 16.1 The Islamic World

1948 to block this development, discredited the old leaders, provoking widespread radicalization. Conservative regimes survived in some Arab countries, including Saudi Arabia, Jordan, and Kuwait. But in Egypt, Syria, and later Iraq, liberal nationalists fell, and "radical" Arab socialist regimes came to power. Egypt's Gamal Abdel Nasser became the charismatic Arab leader until his death in 1970.

Arab socialism amounted to a variable set of development programs, rather like Africa's populist socialisms. The emphasis on socio-economic development, differentiating Arab social-

ism from the earlier liberal nationalism, was meant to compensate for the liberals' greatest failing. Rather as in Mao's China, too, Marxian class conflict was rejected in favor of solidarity among classes in opposition to foreign imperialists. Moreover, as Arab socialists came to power in various countries, particularly Egypt, Syria, and Iraq, they began to see this solidarity in terms not of existing boundaries but of Arab unity (pan-Arabism). A natural idea for countries that shared language and culture but had been divided by outsiders, Arab unity nonetheless proved a frustrating goal. One reason for this was rivalry among Arab leaders: those of other countries did not want to play second fiddle to Nasser, a fact suggesting the "hardening" of the newly independent state structures here as in Africa. Another reason was that not all Arab regimes were socialist: Arab politics had become polarized between socialist and conservative regimes. The result was an Arab "cold war," which during the Yemeni civil war of 1962–1967 became a war by proxy between Egypt and Saudi Arabia. The final obstacle to Arab unity was the geographical location of the state of Israel—in effect, a barrier between Egypt and the Arab states of Southwest Asia (see Maps 16.1 and 16.2). The higher expectations rose about Arab unity—especially in the sense of mergers among countries—the higher rose Arab resentment of Israel and Israeli anxiety about Arab plans. This trend climaxed in the Six-Day War of 1967, a second "disaster" for the Arabs (like 1948), which discredited Arab radicalism and touched off profound soul-searching in the Arab world.

The outlines of a new political configuration began to appear by 1973. As if the region had finally overcome a cultural "hangover" from imperialism, imported ideologies—liberal or socialist—lost appeal. Why, moreover, prioritize the unity of Arabs alone? Why not a wider, perhaps looser, unity, which would avoid the pitfalls of Arab-socialist attempts at political mergers? With the new oil wealth, surely the unity to pursue was the largest: Islamic unity. At last, circumstances favored the Islamic revitalization and unity that religious activists had championed all along. The end of the Cold War and of hopes that socialist rhetoric could win international backing in regional conflicts helped confirm this trend.

This did not mean that Islamic unity would sweep all before it. Again, the persistence of the region's nation-states meant that unity generally took the form of Islamic internationalism, expressed, for example, in the proliferation of international Islamic organizations. Predictably,

within one of the world's largest religious communities, there were numerous traditions and many voices. The fears, aroused in the outside world by the Iranian revolution of 1979, that a wave of Islamic Revolution threatened the world, proved as unfounded as similar fears once had proven about "world communism."

By 2000, Islamic activists controlled governments in only a few places: Iran, Sudan, and Afghanistan. For a year (1996–1997), Turkey, too, had an elected Islamist prime minister in a coalition government, although the continuing strength of the country's secularists made this a far-from-revolutionary change. Islamic movements were active in many places where they did not rule. The international media most noticed those that engaged in violence, like Hamas in Palestine or the Islamic Group (al-Gama'a al-Islamiyya, led by Shaykh Umar Abd al-Rahman) in Egypt.

As Shaykh Umar and his followers illustrated, the environmental, socioeconomic, and political stress under which most Muslims lived did much to explain the radicals' rise—which is not to justify their acts. Mentor of the radicals who assassinated Egyptian president Anwar al-Sadat in 1981 in retaliatiation for his peacemaking with Israel, his westernization, and the inequity of his regime, Shaykh Umar reappeared in Pakistan in the 1980s to spur on young Arab recruits to the U.S.-backed cause of helping the Afghans repel the Soviet invaders of their country. Soviet withdrawal left these Arab "Afghans" used to armed violence but idled and feeling that they had been used as pawns of U.S. policy. Not surprisingly, in the 1990s world of space-time compression and cultural clashes, Arab "Afghans" quickly resurfaced in Arab countries, attacking the regime in Egypt, and even in the United States, where Shaykh Umar and others were convicted for roles in the 1993 bombing of the World Trade Center in Manhattan and other acts. Later incidents like the bombing of a U.S. Navy ship in Aden (Yemen) in 2000 proved that terrorists were still at work.

Far larger numbers of Muslims responded more quietly to the appeal of Islamic revivalism as a way to reintegrate their lives. Many such people condemned radical activism as an abuse of religion. Political scientists noticed signs that electoral office moderated the demands of Islamic activists in countries like Jordan and Turkey. Dreams of unity had prepared radical Islamists ill, as well, for assertions of difference within the Islamic fold—for example, by sectarian Muslim minorities, such as Turkey's Alevis, or by educated Muslim women attacking the male monopoly over studying and interpreting Islam. Finally, just as Islamic activists operated throughout the periods of liberal nationalist and Arab socialist ascendancy, so secularists continued to operate in the midst of Islamic resurgence, still controlling most governments in the Middle East and North Africa in 2000. The fact that rightists, secular and religious, had also played enlarged, sometimes dominant, roles in Israeli politics since the late 1970s proved a reminder, finally, that the Islamic resurgence was not the only one in the 1990s world of identity politics.

To better understand the social, political, and economic issues discussed so far, we shall now consider Turkey, regional success in political and economic development; Iran, major oil exporter and scene of an Islamic revolution; Egypt, biggest Arab nation yet one of the poorest; and finally Israel, Jewish state and major factor in recent Middle Eastern history.

Turkey: Democratization and Development

Independent and decisively led before 1945, Turkey developed in major new ways thereafter. It strengthened its pro-Western orientation, joining NATO in 1952 and becoming an associate member of the European Economic Community (EEC) in 1964—acts that distanced Turkey from other Middle Eastern countries despite its manifold ties to the region. The stresses that beset populous, oilless developing countries in the 1970s threatened Turkey gravely. In the 1980s, however, Turkey reaffirmed its democratic emphasis while changing economic policy, moving beyond import substitution to export-oriented industrialization. By the 1990s, Turkey had become the region's most successful Muslim country in democratization and development. Yet economically it lagged behind some Asian countries—like South Korea—that it once excelled; and ongoing political mobilization had strengthened voices of ethnic and religious diversity that did not all support the established order.

From Single-Party to Multiparty Politics

Turkey's experience during World War II defined starting points for postwar development. Learning from the Ottomans' mistake in entering World War I, Turkey remained neutral. It thus escaped the costs of war and possible defeat yet had to pay for full mobilization to defend its neutrality in case of need. With the drafting of large numbers of men and requisitioning of farm animals, GDP fell nearly 40 percent during the war. Unwise economic policies, including forced sale of agricultural goods at low prices and a capital levy that discriminated against minorities, worsened matters. Yet Turkey amassed foreign exchange; and some commercial and agricultural interests profited from wartime inflation and goods shortages.

Turkey came through the war under the presidency of Atatürk's deputy and successor, Ismet Inönü, and still with only one party, the Republican People's party (RPP; see Chapter 9). Yet Atatürk had strongly believed in liberal politics. Wartime socioeconomic stress had created new demands for liberalization, and Inönü responded in 1946 by letting new parties form. The main beneficiary of this change was an alliance of businessmen and landowners, enriched by the war, who formed the Democrat party (DP) and beat the RPP in the 1950 elections. For an opposition party to win power from the ruling party in a developing country was almost unheard of, and the event was widely hailed as a triumph for democracy.

Foreign policy reinforced this trend. At war's end, Turkey faced Soviet demands for territory in the east and concessions concerning passage through the straits that flow from the Black Sea past Istanbul to the Aegean Sea. Turkey resisted these demands alone at first and then, from 1947–1948 on, with U.S. aid. Turkey confirmed its pro-Western orientation by fighting in Korea and joining NATO in 1952. Turkey would not experiment in "socialism," as some Arab states did in the Nasser years.

With Adnan Menderes as prime minister and party leader, the DP ruled Turkey for a decade (1950–1960). It did not chart a radically new course. Politics was dominated by the unfamiliarity of the multiparty system and by the Democrats' tense reactions to their RPP opponents, especially the prestigious Inönü. With rapid population growth and faster urbanization, the commercial-agrarian interests that had formed the DP made government more responsive to the voters and established closer links between Ankara and the towns and villages. The DP relaxed some of Atatürk's secularizing policies, and conservative rural voters liked that. Yet the Democrats did not abandon secularism.

Economically, too, the Democrats shifted emphasis more than changed policy. They favored private enterprise, agriculture, and consumers but did little to shrink the state sector. Although the country was officially committed to import-substitution industrialization, some of the most important change came in agriculture. Until the late 1950s, Turkey's land supply still exceeded demand. The RPP had used a 1946 land reform law mainly to distribute state land and divide communal pastures. Menderes continued this process; but increasingly, agricul-

tural growth depended on productivity gains, chiefly caused by introducing tractors. Smallholders who could not afford tractors benefited by making crop-sharing deals with tractor owners. As rural-to-urban migration accelerated, land distribution and mechanization boosted productivity to compensate for the population shift.

Benefiting at first from foreign exchange acquired during World War II and a boom during the Korean War (1950–1953), the DP opted for consumer-oriented policies, including liberalization of imports, that sparked inflation. The DP remained popular at the polls through the 1954 election. By the 1957 election, however, inflation and DP intolerance of opposition had eroded voter support. Menderes's problems worsened when growing foreign debt forced him to accept a World Bank stabilization program in 1958. Inflation hit salaried officials and the military severely. Thinking of themselves as guardians of the republic and seeing Inönü— their revered former leader—reviled as RPP head, a group of military commanders overthrew the Menderes regime in a coup on May 27, 1960.

Political scientists regard Turkey's 1960 coup as differing significantly from most military coups discussed in this book. Unlike poorly institutionalized postcolonial regimes where military intervention in politics reflects lack of consensus about governmental norms, the Turkish republic was a strongly consolidated state, heir to the centuries-old tradition of the Ottoman Empire. Identifying with Atatürk, the charismatic leader of the national independence struggle who had taken care to set aside his uniform and reappear in civilian dress as the republic's first president, Turkey's career officers were well versed in democratic norms—including civilian control of the military—which their experience in NATO had reinforced. However, Atatürk had also charged the military to defend the republic. When the commanders thought civilian government had faltered, they would act to correct its course. This happened in 1960 and twice later.

The 1960 coup-makers quickly showed that they did not mean to rule permanently. They not only banned all political parties but also appointed a group of professors to write a new constitution. They thought the 1924 constitution did not provide the checks and balances needed for new conditions. The 1961 constitution expanded the role of the judiciary, added a second legislative house (the Senate, as a check on the Grand National Assembly), slightly strengthened the presidency, and guaranteed many freedoms, giving autonomy to universities and media and the right to strike to unions.

In force until 1980, the 1961 constitution solved some problems but gave rise to others. In the 1960s, demographic growth—especially the fact that much of Turkey's population was very young—gave mass political mobilization new meanings. Favorable economic conditions surely made these political problems more bearable. With economic planning entrusted to a State Planning Organization created in 1960, GDP grew at an annual average rate of 6.4 percent, more than enough to keep up with population. From 1962 on, the migration of Turkish workers to Germany also provided a new source of hard currency through their remittances. Turkey had its share of the worldwide youth radicalism of the 1960s. Yet Turkey still had two major parties: the RPP, now repositioned as a left-of-center social democratic party, and the Justice party (JP), successor of the now-abolished Democrats. The two ruled jointly in coalition until 1965, after which the JP, under Süleyman Demirel, ruled for the rest of the decade.

Turkey's political problems came not from the big center parties but from the rise of new, extremist groups not committed to the constitution. By 1970, the far Right had divided into a secular ultranationalist National Action party and a religious National Order (later National Salvation) party headed by Necmettin Erbakan; Erbakan's party has since been abolished several times but relaunched under new names: National Salvation (*Milli Selamet*), Prosperity (*Refah*), Virtue (*Fazilet*). The Left had produced a Confederation of Revolutionary Workers' Unions and a Turkish Workers' party. Leftist and rightist groups also formed among university students. Much political extremism expressed reactions to rapid social and economic change, reactions that could be more freely voiced under the 1961 constitution. The situation became volatile when violence broke out in the universities, whose new autonomy prevented effective police response.

Mounting violence led the military to intervene again in March 1971. This time, they did not suspend the constitution or civilian rule, but they installed civilian governments and forced them to take their advice. The Workers' party was abolished, the constitution was amended to limit freedoms, and martial law was declared in some provinces. Having tried to correct the trend of political development, the army withdrew again from politics in 1973.

Crisis and Reorientation

Later in the 1970s, Turkey's economic situation deteriorated badly, as did its political situation, despite civilian rule. The effects of the oil price increases were compounded by drops in remittances from the half-million Turkish workers in Europe, where economic activity also slowed. By 1978, the foreign debt had grown alarmingly, and Turkey had to accept an IMF stabilization program. The 1979 oil price increase caused further contraction and inflation in double digits.

Under such conditions, politics became even less stable than in the 1960s, again because of extremist activism. Through the 1970s, a large majority of Turks voted for one of the large parties, either the center-left RPP or the center-right JP. Yet most governments combined one of these with smaller, extreme parties. This pattern magnified the small parties' influence and enabled them to demand concessions. Politics became polarized. Worse yet, ministers tried to "colonize" the ministries they headed by filling them with like-minded officials. Spreading into the police forces, this practice jeopardized their ability to keep order.

Threats to law and order also became more serious than in the 1960s. The late 1970s witnessed violence among students and workers, between Islamic sects (the Sunni majority and the Alevi minority), and between the Turkish armed forces and the Kurds (mostly Sunni Muslims speaking a language related to Persian, Kurds historically lived in southeastern Turkey and adjacent parts of Iran, Iraq, and Syria). Prominent figures were assassinated. Islamic revivalism created tensions throughout Turkish society, jeopardizing the Alevi minority and angering secularists, notably the military elite, ever mindful that they guarded Atatürk's legacy. Emboldened by the Iranian Revolution of 1979, Necmettin Erbakan's National Salvation party even called for the restoration of Islamic law.

Deciding that the civilian politicians could no longer cope, the military intervened a third time in 1980, more decisively than in 1971 and with wide support. They mounted security operations to halt political violence. They kept an economic stabilization program started by Turgut Özal, head of the State Planning Organization in the precoup government. With IMF traits like devaluation, rises in subsidized prices, public sector cuts, and restrictions on labor, this program also had a truly far-reaching goal: to replace protectionist import substitution, pursued since Atatürk, with a promarket orientation. The generals meant to restore democracy, but under a new constitution designed to solve problems faced under that of 1961; they also banned the old parties and many of the old politicians.

The new constitution of 1982 provided for a strong president who could appoint the prime minister, dismiss parliament, and declare a state of emergency. It restored a single-chamber parliament on the ground that Turkey did not need bicameralism; limited the rights granted in 1961, chiefly by forbidding their use to undermine the constitution; and—to limit small-party influence—denied parliamentary representation to any party receiving under 10 percent of the vote. Elections resumed with all new parties in 1983, and the winner was neither of two parties the military preferred but the Motherland party (MP) of Turgut Özal, the technocrat in charge of the economic program. It had restored growth in per capita GDP and—remarkably—produced double-digit growth in exports.

Continuing in this vein, Turkey, which had pioneered import substitution and public sector expansion in the 1930s, became one of the most successful developing countries in shifting to export-led growth in the 1980s. The policy widened inequality, producing losers, especially workers, as well as gainers. It also failed in some ways—for example, by doing little to shrink either the public sector or inflation. Yet the extent of change became clear from the fact that while agromineral products had made up more than 90 percent of Turkey's exports in the early 1960s, by 1990 manufactures accounted for over 75 percent. Between those dates, too, the value of Turkey's exports had grown thirty times over, to about $12 billion, and their destinations had become more diverse. Turkey was one of few Middle Eastern countries where per capita incomes were higher in the mid-1990s than ever before.

Prime Minister Özal dominated Turkish politics through the 1980s, securing election as president in 1989. Yet with time, criticism mounted and support declined. After the ban on old politicians ended in 1987, new parties appeared, much like the old ones. Ending Özal's power, though he remained president, the October 1991 elections led to the formation of a coalition government under Süleyman

Demirel of the True Path party (a remake of the JP).

Turkey Since 1990

At Özal's death in 1993, Demirel became president. Tansu Çiller, former minister for the economy, became prime minister, making Turkey the first Middle Eastern Muslim country with a woman prime minister. The signs of change did not point all one way, however. In the 1995 elections, the Islamist party, then known as the Prosperity party, won 21 percent of the vote, electing mayors in Istanbul and Ankara. Its leader, Necmettin Erbakan, was able to make a surprising power-sharing deal with Çiller in 1996: he, becoming Turkey's first Islamist prime minister, and she, its first woman prime minister, would each hold that office for two years in rotation. The Prosperity party had outshown its rivals in grassroots organizing, much of it by women, and in providing effective services where it gained power. The left half of the political spectrum had nearly died, thanks to disunity and lack of new ideas for the post–Cold War era.

New in office, some Islamists made blunders that antagonized their secularist opponents. Erbakan's diplomatic ventures to Iran and Libya exposed the naiveté of his vision of Islamic brotherhood. The mayor of Sincan, near Ankara, held a "Jerusalem night," with local young people in the role of Hamas militants (see below) and a provocative speech by the Iranian ambassador. The military reacted by turning the February 1997 National Security Council meeting into a veiled coup and presenting twenty demands for secularist policies. Erbakan tried to stall and was forced to resign in June 1997; his party was again abolished, reappearing as the Virtue party. With Çiller also under attack for corruption, her party's National Assembly members began defecting to other parties. From Erbakan's resignation until the next general election in April 1999, Turkey was

ruled by coalition governments headed first by Mesut Yilmaz of the Motherland party and then Bülent Ecevit of the Democratic Left party.

Voting again in 1999, Turks rewarded success and punished failure. After a remarkable year as prime minister, Ecevit made the best showing; his Democratic Left party gained 22 percent of the vote. Showing that Islamists had no lock on the Right, voters gave the Virtue party only 15 percent, compared to the Islamists' 21 percent in 1995. In contrast, the chauvinist National Action party, which had not reached the 10 percent minimum required to send representatives to the National Assembly in 1995, won 18 percent of the vote under the new leadership of Devlet Bahçeli. Known for their mutual animosity, both Çiller and Yilmaz lost most of their supporters. The Republican People's party, Atatürk's own party, failed to get 10 percent and for the first time had no representation in the assembly. The new government was a left-right coalition of Ecevit's Democratic Left and Bahçeli's National Action. Surprisingly for such a combination, over the next year it proved effective, passing a large volume of legislation and benefiting from economic improvement. Possibly more important as an indicator of Turkey's political development was the change in the presidency, which is limited to one term. To succeed Demirel, in 2000 the National Assembly elected Ahmet Necdet Sezer, former chief justice of the Constitutional Court. Uncorrupted champion of the rule of law, Sezer soon became Turkey's most trusted political figure.

Factors shaping these political changes included major failings but also great successes. Ongoing revelations raised questions about links between top politicians, organized crime, and political violence. The police and the courts rarely brought those implicated to justice, although they were quick to crack down on Islamists, Kurdish nationalists, and dissident intellectuals. The military high command maintained its guard as bulwark of the secular

Compromise or contradiction, 1996. *Mr. Erbakan, an Islamist, forms a coalition government with Ms. Çiller (pronounce CHILL-lehr), who had become Turkey's first woman prime minister in 1993. A year later, secularist opposition from the military, forced Erbakan to resign, while corruption charges plagued Çiller. SIPA Press*

republic, even as the public shifted its respect to the civilian authority newly embodied by President Sezer. Finally, the earthquakes of 1997 not only toppled buildings but also shook the prestige of revered state institutions that failed to respond effectively.

Still, few countries benefited from the 1990s more than Turkey. The collapse of the Soviet Union weakened its oldest, biggest enemy and radically changed foreign policy vistas. Now not only were there 3 million diaspora Turks in Europe, but there was also the exhilarating vista of five new, post-Soviet Turkic republics—Azerbaijan, Kazakstan, Kyrgyzstan, Turkmenistan, and Uzbekistan—whose peoples

spoke Turkic languages. In 1998, after fourteen years of separatist rebellion by the Kurdish Worker's party (PKK) in southeastern Anatolia, the Ecevit government pressured Syria to expel PKK leader Abdullah Öcalan, subsequently captured him in Nairobi (Kenya), tried him, and condemned him for treason, although appeals would continue for years. This triumph largely explains both Ecevit's victory and rightist voters' swing from Islamists to nationalists in the 1999 election. In custody, Öcalan astonishingly turned cooperative, calling on the PKK to cease hostile operations and withdraw from Turkey. The Turkish military did not take these calls at face value, given the danger of PKK operations from adjoining countries. As a peaceful approach to transforming the Southeast, the government had long since launched a vast Southeast Anatolia Project (GAP in Turkish, Anatolia being the Asian part of Turkey), designed to develop irrigation and hydropower by building dams on the Tigris and Euphrates Rivers, which both rise in this region (see Map 9.2). While this region drastically needed development, most Kurds had in fact moved to more prosperous parts of the country. Surveys showed that they wanted political and cultural expression, but that few wanted an independent Kurdistan, which Syria, Iraq, Iran, and Turkey would all oppose. Economically, despite slow progress in privatization and inflation control, Turkey's GDP grew an average of 4 to 5 percent a year from 1980 to 1998. At $200 billion, Turkey's 1999 GDP exceeded Russia's.

No indicator of how Turkey was doing wavered up and down more than its relations with the European Union (EU). Turkey had become an associate member in 1964, and Prime Minister Özal had applied for membership in 1987. In 1996, a Turkey-EU Customs Union was approved. Yet in 1997, when the EU began "enlargement talks" with East European countries and even Cyprus, Turkey was left out. In 1999, the year of "earthquake diplomacy," Turkey was finally invited to become an official candidate. However, a successful response to this invitation would require far greater changes than would have been needed, say, to join a mere free-trade agreement, the way Mexico joined NAFTA. The Turkish public had still to consider most of these issues when the EU issued its "partnership" criteria in November 2000. These required reforms in human rights, cultural freedoms, maintaining the moratorium on the death penalty, tightening civilian control over the military, and a comprehensive settlement of the Cyprus problem, all within set time frames. People like President Sezer and much of the business and intellectual elite seemed ready for such changes; ultranationalists and Islamists

would have trouble with them. For the Turks, living in a land where geography and culture reacted in unique ways with the forces of globalization and the politics of identity and difference, the invitation to join the EU was a challenge to take further steps on the westward path that the Turkish Republic had followed since its foundation.

Iran in Revolution: Turban Against Crown and Necktie

Through the 1970s, Iran remained an authoritarian monarchy. Few such regimes survived elsewhere, but Iran seemed stable because of its oil wealth. Indeed, Iran played a leading role in raising oil prices in the 1970s. The revolution of 1979 revealed a mortal antagonism between Iranian Islam and the secular-national monarchy, however. Alarmists saw the shah's fall as the start of a wave of Islamic revolution. In fact, Iran's revolution was too rooted in Iranian conditions to be widely exportable. Still, it raises important questions for the comparative study of revolution and its outcomes.

The Regime of Crown and Necktie

When the British and Soviets occupied Iran in 1941 to use it as a supply route to the USSR, Reza Shah (r. 1925–1941) abdicated in favor of his son, Muhammad Reza (r. 1941–1979). It took the new shah a long time to build up the power he later wielded. First, Iran had to wait out World War II and—with luck and U.S. help—evade Soviet efforts to divide the country and gain access to Iranian oil. Then, since Iran was formally a parliamentary monarchy under the 1906 constitution and politicians had seized the initiative after Reza Shah's abdication, the young shah had to regain political initiative from parliament. A parliament-led effort to nationalize the oil industry, which the Anglo-Iranian Oil Company (AIOC) controlled, gave him his chance.

To the British and their U.S. allies, the crisis offered a choice like many in U.S.-Latin American relations. Nationalization was highly popular in Iran and made its champion, Prime Minister Muhammad Mosaddeq, a hero. Britain and the United States might have chosen to foster democracy in Iran by seeking accommodation, though at some cost to their economic interests. Or they could defend those interests and attack the parliamentary government that challenged them. Britain and the United States chose the latter course. Iranians never forgot the CIA-backed coup that toppled Mosaddeq in 1953.

The Western democratic powers then helped the shah form the undemocratic, pro-Western regime they preferred. AIOC (later British Petroleum, BP) and other foreign oil interests worked out a new agreement. One new prop for the monarchy was the Plan Organization. It took charge of economic development, although its taste for vast projects, the privileges it gave foreigners, and corruption kept the agency from doing much for Iranians. Rising from $34 million in 1954 to $358 million in 1960, oil revenues kept the shah afloat. He also increased his security apparatus, including both the U.S.-equipped military and the secret police, known by the Persian acronym SAVAK. Formed with aid from the CIA and the Israeli intelligence agency Mossad, SAVAK targeted the shah's Iranian opponents. Its abuses helped provoke the 1979 revolution. But the shah used the carrot as well as the stick: he expanded government payrolls until Iran had over 300,000 civil servants and 400,000 military.

Pro-Western foreign policy, planned economic growth, the security forces, patronage—these were the props of the throne. For most Iranians, the shah allowed no political participation. The parliament survived, but the government manipulated elections, chose all candidates, and reorganized "parties" at will. Pushed

by U.S. President John F. Kennedy's administration to consolidate the people's loyalties, the shah enacted a "Shah-People Revolution," including land reform, women's suffrage, and a literacy campaign. Because the parliament, many of whose members were big landowners, opposed these policies, the shah suspended parliament in 1961 and ruled by decree. Religious leaders also opposed the shah, objecting not so much to specific policies as to his secularism and dictatorial ways. The shah exiled his sharpest religious critic, Ayatollah Ruhollah Khomeini, in 1964.

The outcome of land reform told a lot about the shah's goals. The first phase (1962–1963) bore some of the Kennedy imprint seen in Latin America's Alliance for Progress. In this phase, landlords who owned more than one village had to sell their land to the state for resale to their sharecroppers. Later phases, truer to the shah's outlook, asserted central government authority more strongly in the villages, preserved landlord rights, and shifted emphasis to capitalist mechanization of agriculture rather than land reform. Ultimately, 92 percent of Iran's sharecroppers received some land. But wage laborers, a large part of the rural population, got none. Even those who got land ended up more dependent on the government. In the past they could blame the landlords for their troubles. Now they blamed the shah.

For years, oil wealth hid the failures of the Shah-People Revolution, at least from foreigners. Iran, the most populous Middle Eastern oil state, took the lead in quadrupling oil prices in 1973. Its oil revenues shot from $5 billion in 1973–1974 to $20 billion in 1975–1976, staying at that level through 1979. Iran's population doubled in twenty years, reaching 41 million by 1982, but real GNP increased more than tenfold between 1963 and 1978.

For most Iranians this growth was destructive. Agriculture represented 27 percent of GNP in 1963 but only 9 percent in 1978, while the contribution of manufacturing barely kept up with growth in GNP, staying at 13 percent. Industrial growth did not compensate for rural decline. Only government and the petroleum sector grew. The latter accounted for one-third to one-half of GNP through most of the 1970s but employed less than 1 percent of labor. Such unbalanced growth had high human costs. People poured into the ill-equipped cities—Tehran, for example, had no modern sewers. Iran's income distribution was one of the world's most unequal; the population growth rate was one of the world's highest. Conspicuous consumption and corruption flourished in high places, while the majority struggled with high inflation. How could they express their grievances?

Since 1925, the Pahlevi shahs had modernized Iran in many ways but denied mass political participation by attacking other power centers, including liberal democrats like Mosaddeq, the Left, and even the religious leadership (the *ulama*). Power became so concentrated in the shah's hands that the only way to change government policy was to overthow him.

The only "political" force strong enough to lead a revolution was the ulama, the only organized group of national scope. While Turkey was developing national political parties, the shah had thwarted that kind of development in Iran. But he could not get rid of the ulama, who numbered about ninety thousand in 1979 and lived in every city and town, though in few villages. These men were custodians of the belief system that mattered to Iranians in a way that the shah's secular nationalism did not.

The fact that Iran was the only country officially committed to the Shii branch of Islam, as opposed to the majority Sunni branch, proved highly significant. Shii ideas of authority, as developed in Iran, made it hard to justify a state that does not conform to strict Shii ideals. Iranian Shiism emphasized the believer's duty to defer not to the shah but to the experts in Islamic law, the most senior of whom are known by the title *ayatollah*. In a radical departure that some learned Iranian ulama disap-

proved, Ayatollah Khomeini argued that the ulama should not just teach and advise but should seize executive power. Unable to win over the ulama, the shah had attacked them. But they were Iran's mass mobilizers, not he.

The Turbaned Regime

What launched Iran's revolution was socioeconomic stress coupled with the shah's wavering in reaction to criticism—by U.S. president Jimmy Carter among others—of his rights violations. The wavering between concession and repression led to a series of bloody riots. All political forces—religious conservatives, liberal democrats, leftists both secular and Islamic—united, and the shah's support vanished. As millions shouted, "Death to the shah, death to America," mass political mobilization became a fact. The shah fled, and Khomeini returned from exile on February 1, 1979.

How successful was Iran's revolution? Chapter 4 argued that in an inequitable society, revolution must change more than politics. It must also alter socioeconomic relations and redistribute power and wealth. The most profound revolutions transform culture, too. For a dependent country, successful revolution means breaking external dependency relations. To do all this requires decisive leadership, a coherent ideology, and a well-organized movement.

Iran's revolution met these criteria more fully than any other since Cuba's. The comparison of Islamic Iran with communist Cuba may seem paradoxical. Chapter 6 pointed out, however, that fascists of the 1930s saw themselves as revolutionaries from the right. Iran's revolution compares to fascism in that sense. Perhaps Cuba and Iran were equally revolutionary, but in ideologically opposite senses. The Cuban comparison is also relevant in another way: a revolution may better many people's lives without producing high levels of development. In this regard, Iran perhaps did less well than Cuba.

Political mobilization and the revolution against western-style modernity converge in Khomeini's Iran. *Weapons training for women clad in the enveloping black chador. Gaumy/Magnum Photos*

In Iran, the united front that toppled the shah did not last. By 1983, Khomeini and associates had suppressed the Left, the liberals, and the dissident ulama. To consolidate its power, the regime built new institutions and Islamicized old ones. It purged thousands of the shah's officials. The 1979 constitution provided for a parliament and president but subordinated them to a senior expert in religious law (or, in some cases, a council of experts). The regime organized its followers into an Islamic Republican party, which monopolized parliament. The regime created organizations to mobilize and regiment the populace. Suspicion of military forces patronized by the shah led to creation of

a Revolutionary Guard, which rivaled the regular military. Islamic courts enforced religious law. Khomeini attached special importance to the prayer leaders of the large mosques, where Muslims congregate for the Friday noon prayer followed by a sermon. No one knew better than he how to exploit the sermons politically. By 1983 he had organized the prayer leaders under a national agency. By 1987 they controlled political mobilization so fully that the Islamic Republican party was abolished: religion had reabsorbed politics.

Nor did Khomeini neglect thought control. A Ministry of Islamic Guidance took charge of propaganda. Islamic societies appeared in all important organizations to ensure conformity. Vigilante groups did likewise in the streets. For example, the Sisters of Zaynab stalked women violating the Islamic dress code. Education underwent strict Islamicization. Religious functionaries serving in military units indoctrinated the troops. Internal intelligence agencies, more feared than the shah's, reappeared. Thus political revolution shaded into social and cultural upheaval. Many Iranians approved, agreeing with Khomeini that secularism and Westernization had been a sickness.

Had Iran experienced social revolution—a basic reallocation of wealth and power, usually signaled by violent class conflict? If so, it was not in terms that Marx would recognize: the classes that had won and lost were defined in cultural, more than economic, terms. To state things in symbolic terms that Iranians used, the "turbans" had toppled the "crown" and the "neckties."

Iran's uneven economic record showed how much its revolution differed from commonly cited models of social revolution: the French, Russian, or Chinese cases of 1789, 1917, and 1949. A saying of Khomeini's—that people do not make revolutions over the price of watermelons—suggests his thinking. For example, despite the shah's failed land reform and the land seizures that began after his fall, the new regime wavered on land reform. In 1986 parliament finally passed a law ratifying land seizures prior to a date in 1981. This was hardly a radical act for a government that blamed the shah for Iran's loss of agricultural self-sufficiency and still faced rising food imports.

Nor did business and industry prosper. The government controlled 80 percent of the economy through the 1980s. By 1989, inflation was out of control, and officials admitted that expanding the state's economic role had been a mistake. With population growth near 4 percent a year, Iran still suffered many ills of the 1970s: low productivity, inflation, superurbanization,

joblessness, housing shortages. Perhaps Khomeini lagged even Castro economically.

Where Khomeini excelled Castro was in cultural revolution, noted above, and in severing external dependency. Iran quickly showed its zeal to break external bonds—notably, with the detention of the U.S. embassy hostages (1979–1981). Iran's economic problems partly resulted from this zeal. Iran paid off its foreign debt. To balance the budget, it cut spending between 1979 and 1983 by 18 percent of GDP, more than the IMF would have asked from a debtor country. To Khomeini, the Iran-Iraq War (1980–1988), started by Iraq, was a war of the worlds, pitting secular Arab socialism against Iran and Islam. Both were oil states, but Iran's population was three times Iraq's and should seemingly have prevailed, especially given Khomeini's use of the Shii mystique of martyrdom to incite young Iranians to suicidal bravery. In 1988, however, Khomeini accepted a UN ceasefire. Scrupling at nothing, not even chemical weapons, Iraq had held out.

Khomeini's international goal was not just to defeat Iraq or defy the U.S. and Soviet "great Satans" but to export Iran's revolution. Differences of doctrine confined its exportability to Shii minorities in other countries with weak or favorably inclined governments (mainly Lebanon or Syria). Still, he exhorted Iranians to persist and create a universal Islamic state.

The mass grief at Khomeini's funeral, as hundreds of thousands struggled to touch his shrouded body, expressed his hold on the masses and Iran's insecurity without him. Leadership passed to his ulama associates with little disorder. Thereafter, two major tendencies competed in politics. Pragmatists like President Ali-Akbar Hashemi-Rafsanjani favored freeing the economy, inviting foreign investment, luring back educated Iranians who had fled, and normalizing relations with other countries. Doctrinaire figures like Khomeini's successor as senior religious leader, Ayatollah Ali Khamenei, favored centralized economic control and strictly Islamic domestic and foreign policies.

Iranian politics of the mid-1990s—an ongoing factional feud—showed that the revolution had ended without stability being achieved. Population growth, a major prerevolutionary worry, remained high until the end of the decade, while GDP per person had still not regained 1970s levels. A U.S-imposed trade embargo, high inflation, high unemployment, and dependence on oil for nearly all export earnings in a time of falling oil prices, did not help. Khomeini said Iranians do not make revolution over watermelons, yet a Tehran shantytown rioted over bus fares in 1996.

By the late 1990s the fading revolution yielded signs that even the Islamic Republic would, in its way, join the democratizing trend of the times. Symbolic of this trend was the rise of Muhammad Khatami, a man with both Islamic and western education, both religious and populist credentials, who won nearly 70 percent of the 30 million votes cast in the 1997 presidential election. The 1999 election of 270,000 municipal councillors—Iran's first elected local governments ever—again drew high turnout and put reformists in charge of most cities. The February 2000 parliamentary election drew 80 percent voter turnout, giving victory to the democratizing forces and defeat even to Rafsanjani and his politically prominent daughter Faezeh—former progressives, now merely centrists. In parliament, the conservatives—the political groups originally linked to Khomeini—were reduced to a minority opposition. Equipped with an Islamic version of a parliamentary, presidential government by the 1979 constitution, Iran, too, now had contested elections and turnover in elected office.

Still, conservatives wielded great power, directly through the religious offices to which the constitution gave highest power, and indirectly through the courts and security forces, which they used to counterattack the progressives. Ayatollah Ali Khamenei, the top religious authority, did begin to gain added respect as an arbiter who did not automatically side with religious conservatives. Yet, elections or no elections, Iranian politics continued to be the factional tug-of-war that had come into view after Khomeini's death. In a country without a tradition of open politics, the conservatives showed their strength in the way they used the courts—all of them religious—to go after Khatami's supporters and shut down newspapers. Likewise, security forces were implicated in the murder of progressive intellectuals. What worked in internal politics could also influence foreign policy. The trial of thirteen Iranian Jews and eight Muslims accused of spying for Israel in 1999 was widely viewed in Iran as using the courts to embarrass Khatami and undermine his attempts to reduce Iran's diplomatic isolation. After more than a year, no one was executed, a few were acquitted, and the others' sentences were reduced on appeal. One reassuring thing about Iranian politics was that conservatives and progressives alike agreed on civilian control of the military, pointing at both Pakistan and Turkey as object lessons.

Religious conservatives remained powerful, but a democratizing, normalizing trend was gaining ground. One straw in the wind in 1998: on the anniversary of the 1979 seizure of the U.S. Embassy, pro-reform university students invited the former hostages to visit as guests of the Iranian people.

Egypt: The Struggle to Escape Poverty

Egypt is the most populous Arabic-speaking country and one of the most influential, yet paradoxically also one of the poorest. After 1945, it probably exerted its greatest influence as a center of Pan-Arab socialism, under Gamal Abdel Nasser (properly 'Abd al-Nasir, 1952–1970). After him, Egypt's policy orientation shifted again. What governs the shifts is Egypt's poverty?

Nasser and Arab Socialism

Egypt's wartime troubles, noted in Chapter 9, discredited its liberal nationalist leadership and its parliamentary institutions. Especially after the defeat in the 1948 Palestine war, Egyptians looked for new alternatives. The Muslim Brethren, an Islamic activist group founded in 1928, grew more militant. But it was a group of young officers, including Nasser and Anwar al-Sadat, who overthrew the government in a bloodless coup on July 23, 1952. Installing an older officer, General Muhammad Nagib, as figurehead leader, they stayed in the background as the Revolutionary Command Council (RCC).

The events of July 1952 were no real revolution. The officers took power without a clear program or mass following. Nasser's policymaking remained largely improvisational. Yet he had some clear goals: independence, and social justice for people like his postal-worker father, rather than privilege for Egypt's elites and the British. From these goals, important changes followed.

The first few years were a time of consolidation. The RCC abolished the monarchy and the old parties. The most difficult problem turned out to be the Muslim Brethren, a vast movement. It was outlawed and forced underground. When some Muslim Brethren tried to assassinate Nasser, he seized his chance to implicate Nagib, who had begun reaching for real power. Nagib's ouster left Nasser in charge, though he did not take the title "president" until 1956. The power struggle led to the first attempt to organize mass support. Called the Liberation Rally, this was actually an organization to rally support for the regime—the first of several experiments in authoritarian mobilization. Meanwhile, needing to control the bureaucracy, the RCC appointed its members to head various ministries, but with little coordination. The resulting "bureaucratic feudalism" proved unwise for a regime that would greatly expand government's role in the name of "socialism."

The one revolutionary idea of these years was the 1952 land reform. This limited the land one person could own to 200 acres. Large estates were to be redistributed to peasants in 2- to 5-acre units. Later laws lowered the ownership limit to 50 acres per person, or 100 acres per nuclear family. In the 2.4 percent of Egypt's land that is cultivable, the amount of land held in estates of over 50 acres thus shrank to one-sixth, while the proportion of land held by owners of 5 acres or less rose from one-third to one-half. The power of the old elite had been undermined.

In 1955, Nasser entered a new phase that made him the hero of Arab nationalism. Invited to a conference of Afro-Asian leaders in Bandung, Indonesia, he met Yugoslavia's Tito, India's Nehru, and China's Zhou Enlai, who introduced him to the idea of nonalignment. The next September, Nasser applied this lesson by making an arms agreement with Czechoslovakia. Until then, the United States, Britain, and France had monopolized supplying arms to both sides in the Arab-Israeli conflict. The Czech arms deal brought Egypt Soviet weapons and made it impossible for the Western powers to limit the scope of the Arab-Israeli conflict, launched a strong Soviet-Arab involvement, and started the Middle Eastern arms race.

Rapid changes followed. A new Egyptian constitution introduced a strong presidential system in 1956 to replace the parliamentary form of government in which a prime minister headed the cabinet. The constitution also committed the state to economic planning and social welfare. And it played up Egypt's Arab identity—a point that acquired new value now that most Arab lands were independent and Egypt was bidding for leadership among them. A new effort at mass mobilization, the National Union, replaced the Liberation Rally.

The cutting edge of policy remained international, given the need to seek resources with which to alleviate Egypt's poverty. The arms deal raised Nasser's prestige in the Arab world. British and U.S. offers to help finance a high dam on the Nile at Aswan—needed for year-round irrigation, multiple cropping, and electric power generation—seemed to prove that nonalignment did produce gains from both superpowers. But the United States and Britain soon withdrew their offers, resenting Nasser's diplomatic independence. He retaliated by nationalizing the Suez Canal, which was owned by foreign interests, mostly British and French. This move united France, Britain, and Israel, which was disturbed by Nasser's rise and by Palestinian raids coming from the Gaza Strip. In the Suez War of 1956, Israel invaded Sinai; Britain and France sent troops to take the canal. Fearing a diplomatic crisis just before a presidential election, the United States joined the Soviet Union in condemning the attack.

Only foreign intervention stopped Israel from taking Sinai. Yet Nasser emerged looking like a hero to the Arabs. Inside Egypt, he began nationalizing foreign firms and, by 1960, Egyptian ones, too. The best proof of his new standing was the union of Egypt and Syria in 1958, at Syria's request, to form the United Arab Republic (UAR). At that, the idea of Arab unity took on the meaning of fusion into a single state. Becoming a virtual colony, however, the Syrians soon regretted the union, which collapsed in 1961.

The UAR's demise touched off a search for explanations that had a radicalizing effect, pushing Nasser into a new phase of Arab "socialism"—a populist ideology evolved from the land reform, the military link to the USSR, and the nationalization ("socialization") of much of the economy. The National Charter (1962) attempted to spell out how Egypt was to combine Islam, Arab nationalism, and socialism. The charter defined yet another movement for mass mobilization, the Arab Socialist Union (ASU).

The regime also greatly expanded its welfare policies, providing many new services and subsidies to the public.

Some Egyptians hailed these changes as a "socialist revolution," but neither term applied. Expanding state control of the economy, just as Egypt moved beyond import substitution into heavy industry, proved counterproductive. The lack of coordination that resulted from "bureaucratic feudalism" meant the government could not efficiently direct industrialization. In 1963 Nasser also guaranteed university entrance, without cost, to every secondary school graduate; in 1964 he guaranteed employment to every university graduate. These well-meant measures overwhelmed both the universities and the bureaucracy, which became a vastly expanded employer of last resort. As in Perón's Argentina, "socialism" in Nasser's Egypt combined populism with authoritarian mass mobilization but not economic realism.

After the UAR broke up, moreover, Nasser had to work to maintain his Pan-Arab leadership. In 1962 he sent Egyptian troops into a civil war in Yemen, antagonizing Saudi Arabia, which backed the other side and had close relations with the United States. A physical barrier to Arab unity because of its location, Israel, too, remained a chronic worry.

In 1967, Nasser moved the Israeli question abruptly to the fore. In May, reacting to a Soviet report that Israel intended to attack Syria, he began calling up reserves and moving forces into Sinai. He negotiated the removal of a UN buffer force stationed there after the 1956 war. Past that point, the flow of events seemed to sweep Nasser away. By the end of May, he had closed the Gulf of Aqaba, Israel's only access by sea to the southern port of Eilat. Verbally raising the stakes, he declared that the real issue was Palestinian rights. The Arab countries excitedly promised Egypt military support, while diplomatic efforts to restore calm proved fruitless. Thus threatened, Israel attacked on June 5, 1967. Egypt lost most of its bombers the first day. By the end of the sixth day, Israel controlled Sinai, the Golan Heights, the West Bank of the Jordan, and old Jerusalem.

With this catastrophe, Nasser's career entered its final phase (1967–1970). In a moving speech, he announced his resignation. Unable to face defeat without their charismatic leader, Egyptians demonstrated in the streets, forcing him to stay on. Nasser's last years were hard, but his sudden death in 1970 aroused even more emotion than his resignation attempt of 1967. Still, the day of Arab socialism had passed.

Sadat's Opening to the West

Nasser's vice president, Anwar al-Sadat, now became Egypt's leader. One of the 1952 conspirators, he was little known. Yet he soon outmaneuvered strong opposition to prove he was in control. He then opened an era of dramatic change by breaking with the USSR and expelling Soviet advisers in 1972. Egyptians were fed up with Soviet meddling. Strangely, the Soviets—worried about losing influence—reacted at first by increasing military aid.

Sadat's next surprise was to attack Israel. The 1967 defeat had been so disastrous, he thought, that something must be done to restore Arab self-respect. He also wanted to regain Sinai. To achieve these goals, he avoided mistakes that Nasser had made in 1967. Instead of planning for war in a fanfare of publicity and letting Israel take the initiative, Sadat planned secretly, taking only Syria into confidence. On October 6, 1973, a difficult cross-water attack against Israeli fortifications along the Suez Canal and a simultaneous Syrian attack in the Golan Heights painfully surprised the Israelis. In this, the war succeeded from the Arab viewpoint, even though Israel would eventually have achieved another lopsided victory had not U.S. secretary of state Henry Kissinger intervened. Drawing another lesson from 1967, Kissinger foresaw that an early ceasefire might shift the momentum from war to peacemaking. He did

manage to win some gains in "step-by-step" diplomacy before it bogged down, as had all previous approaches. Meanwhile in Egypt, Sadat became the "hero of the crossing" (of the Suez Canal).

Sadat's next dramatic stroke was to open Egypt to the West. Egypt's 1973 population of 35 million had grown more than 50 percent since 1952, and Nasser's "socialist" approach to development had failed. Breaking with Soviet-oriented policy, Sadat envisaged a return to liberalism. He made some experiments with broader freedoms and multiparty politics. Economically, he fostered the private sector and tried to lure foreign investment.

Economically, he had slight success. By the end of 1979, the government had approved foreign investment ventures worth $3.6 billion. But the projects were clustered in tourism and finance. Many never got off the ground because of bureaucratic red tape or the inadequacy of Cairo's communications and transportation systems. Egypt's economic situation would have become quite desperate but for recovery of the Sinai oil fields, tourism, tolls from the reopened Suez Canal, and the emigration of workers and professional people to work in Arab oil states. The most threatening fact was that population growth was ending Egypt's age-old ability to produce an agricultural surplus.

After 1945, Egypt ceased to be self-sufficient in one foodstuff after another, despite the Aswan Dam (completed 1971). Egypt's response was to subsidize poor consumers—if necessary, by selling imported food for less than it cost to import. With the rapid OPEC-era inflation, all Egyptian public expenditure shot up, but the proportion of it devoted to subsidies rose faster, from under 10 percent in 1970 to almost 60 percent in 1980. As balance-of-payments problems worsened, the government turned to international lending agencies. They demanded an end to subsidies. An attempt to end several subsidies in January 1977 provoked serious riots. "Hero of the crossing, where is our breakfast?" the crowds cried. It was time for another dramatic act.

In November, Sadat made a startling trip to Jerusalem to seek peace, from which he hoped Egypt would gain economic relief. Speaking to the Israeli Knesset (parliament), he made clear that his conditions included evacuating the territories Israel had taken in 1967 and creating a Palestinian state. He repeated these terms in the negotiations, mediated by President Carter, that led to the Camp David accords of September 1978 and the Egyptian-Israeli Peace Treaty of March 1979. The treaty set up diplomatic and trade relations between the two countries, allowed Israeli ships to use the Suez Canal, and required Israel to return Sinai to Egypt in stages. Yet Israel went on taking tough stands about other occupied territories and the Palestinians.

Feeling that Sadat had made a separate peace and sacrificed the Palestinians, most Arab states broke with Egypt and tried to isolate it. Inside Egypt, the economic benefits sought from peace failed to materialize. Religious radicals grew angry that Sadat, who had made hollow efforts to project a pious image and had tried to use Islamists as a counter against the Left, had made peace with Israel while failing to fulfill Islamist objectives. Some saw violence as the only way to change such a state. The result was Sadat's assassination in 1981 on the anniversary of the October War. Lamented in the West, his death roused few regrets in the Arab world.

Mubarak: State, Religion, and Society

Two decades later, Sadat's drabber successor, Husni Mubarak, still held power. He made no dramatic shifts like Nasser's opening to the Soviets or Sadat's to the West. Instead, he worked to regain acceptance for Egypt from other Arab states and to maintain vital U.S. aid—Egypt's reward for making peace with Israel and joining in the 1991 Persian Gulf War against Iraq.

Egypt's poverty and internal conflict contrasted starkly with its leading role in the Arab world. With a history of authoritarian political mobilization at best, the government struggled to contain the Islamists—not just radicals but also the more moderate Muslim Brotherhood. Despite talk of democratization, the government restricted even secular parties other than the ruling National Democratic party. Consequently, the November 1995 parliamentary election, the most rigged and violent since multiparty elections resumed in 1984, produced the biggest progovernment majority: 416 out of 444 seats. Before the 1999 referendum to approve Mubarak's fourth term as president, prominent Egyptians were induced to rush forward and pledge their allegiance in the sanctified form used for early Islamic caliphs (*bay'a*). Still, demand grew for democracy and concessions to civil society—groups and activities not controlled by government. In contrast to the military courts' scenes of show trials under martial law (in force ever since Sadat's assassination in 1981), Egypt's higher courts also began to assert their independence. Insisting that no Egyptian election since 1978 had been legal because none had been monitored by judges as the law required, they successfully demanded judicial monitoring of the November 2000 parliamentary election. That restricted voter intimidation inside the voting places, if not outside. As a result, the official party was left to agonize about why it received "only" 80 percent of the vote and some of its leaders tasted defeat. As Mubarak aged in power, Egyptians recalled Sadat's last phase. Prominent sociologist Saadeddin Ibrahim, arrested on far-fetched charges about his research on Egyptian voting behavior, coined a comical word for the government: "republarchy" (*gumlukiyya* in Egyptian Arabic, splicing *gumhuriyya* with *mulukiyya*, "republic" with "monarchy").

Increasingly out of step with the global trend toward democratization, the Mubarak government still showed the centralization of

Islamic militants on trial in Egypt, April 1992. *Brandishing religious books and showing contempt for the court, followers of Shaykh Umar Abd al-Rahman stand trial. Seven of the forty-nine defendants were condemned and hanged.*
© *Frederic Neema/CORBIS-SYGMA*

power and the zealously defended autonomy from society that had characterized many developing countries in the post-1945 period. Many factors made it hard to change this pattern in Egypt.

Economically, the regime faced the thankless task of trying to cope with Egypt's poverty while dismantling the Nasser-style barriers that had previously protected Egyptians from the world market. For powerful Egyptians close to the regime privatization meant "crony capitalism." To the poor, the 1990s brought cuts in price subsidies, the end of guaranteed employment for graduates, many bankruptcies, and an end to agrarian rent controls. For 6 million Egyptians who were agricultural tenants or their dependents, this negated the land reform

of 1952. For Egyptians in general, however, gains from consolidation of tiny landholdings and more market-oriented crop selection could be worth billions a year. Such a change of agrarian policy was hard to resist for a country that earned most of its foreign currency from tourism and that had only recently discovered exportable amounts of natural gas. The need for Egyptian leaders to manage their relations with the outside world so as to generate resources to apply to internal problems had not diminished.

Agrarian unrest was only one of Egypt's social problems. After a government program to reduce the birth rate succeeded with the help of non-governmental organizations, the 1994 UN Conference on Population and Development was allowed to convene in Egypt. That heightened private organizations' demands for legal recognition and attracted international attention to women's issues, including female genital cutting (circumcision). Yet fifty years of dictatorship had left Egyptians with so little respect for the state's laws that subsequent attempts to enact legislation about either private associations or gender and family foundered in controversy. Separately, Muslim-Christian conflict also flared up, notably in Coptic-majority rural locales. The consequences were worsened by police incompetence and brutality and by efforts of some overseas Copts and foreign governments to pressure Cairo to stop "persecuting" Copts, when in fact the issues seemed to be more local ones with agrarian and familial roots.

Vastly greater conflict arose over Islamic activism. There were many reasons for the emergence of new groups more radical than the supposedly nonviolent Muslim Brotherhood. With 68 million Egyptians trying to feed themselves off a cultivable area (the banks of the Nile and its delta) no bigger than New Jersey, land hunger engendered activism, with resentment of rural Copts being one of its consequences. Unemployment and the lure of higher wages had led many Egyptians to migrate to other Arab countries, where some of them fell under radical Islamist influences. Egypt's "Afghans," veterans of the conflict in Afghanistan, also promoted radicalization, as noted. Cairo's inadequate infrastructure and housing shortages, which made it difficult for many young people to marry, were major stress factors. The number of violent militants, never large, was estimated at 3,000 in 1995. By the late 1990s, they had encountered such reverses that the jailed leaders of the Muslim Group (al-Gama'a al-Islamiyya, including Shaykh Umar Abd al-Rahman from his U.S. prison) told their followers to cease armed struggle. Yet dissident factions still struck, notably at Luxor in November 1997, killing 58 tourists and 4 Egyptians before dying themselves. Closer to the mainstream, the Mus-

lim Brotherhood, after much success in expanding its influence by competing for office in Egypt's professional syndicates, met so much official resistance that it stopped all public activities in 1996. With many radicals executed, exiled, or imprisoned, and with milder Islamists biding their time, the government appeared to have won by the late 1990s, but only insecurely. Now, Egyptians both secular and religious wanted greater freedom.

Israel: The Search for Security

The Zionist movement that created the state of Israel is unique in the history of nationalism. The movement claimed the Jews' ancient homeland yet emerged elsewhere, among Jewish communities scattered across Europe. The land the Zionists claimed had a long-established people who developed their own nationalism as Palestinians, opposing Zionism. These facts help explain the resultant conflict over nationalist goals. Interference by outside powers worsened the conflict.

Israel Under the Labor Party, 1948–1977

After World War II, Britain faced urgent demands for massive immigration of European Jews to Palestine. Sensing that it could not grant these demands and preserve influence in the Arab world, Britain announced in 1947 that it would turn its mandate over to the United Nations, which adopted a complex partition plan (Map 16.2). Civil war broke out between Jews and Arabs, with atrocities by both sides, and Arab refugees began to flee.

When the British withdrew on May 14, 1948, the Zionists proclaimed Israel's independence. The proclamation announced Israel's openness to Jewish immigrants from all over the world and the equality of all citizens regardless of religion, race, or sex. The proclamation offered peace to neighboring states and called

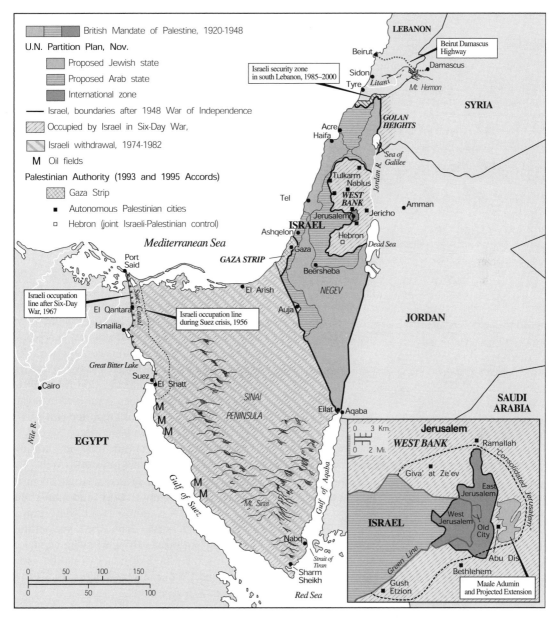

Map 16.2 Israel and Neighboring Countries, *including lands subject to negotiation and areas under Palestinian autonomy.*

on Arabs inside Israel to participate as equal citizens in developing the state. Fulfilling all parts of this vision would not be easy.

Egypt, Jordan, Lebanon, Iraq, and Syria responded to Israel's declaration of independence by invading. With the Holocaust fresh

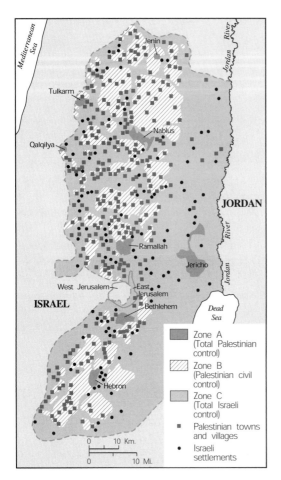

Map 16.3 *The West Bank and Jerusalem*
under the Oslo II accord (1995).

Legend:
- Zone A (Total Palestinian control)
- Zone B (Palestinian civil control)
- Zone C (Total Israeli control)
- ▪ Palestinian towns and villages
- • Israeli settlements

had a Jewish majority: 650,000 Jews alongside 165,000 Arabs. About 750,000 Arabs had fled, mostly to the refugee life that fueled later Palestinian militancy.

From 1948 to 1977, the Labor party (Mapai) ruled Israel. Founded by a 1929 merger among socialists, the party resembled European social democrats. Its leaders were mostly eastern Europeans who had migrated to Palestine before World War I. The party dominated Israel's labor federation, the Histadrut, and had close ties to an important type of collective agricultural settlement, the kibbutz. Kibbutz members played key roles in agriculture and politics, though they formed only 5 percent of the population in 1948 and less since.

The Labor leaders' European origins and socialist ideas set the tone for the new state, but its population quickly changed. Mass immigration doubled the Jewish population in three years, first with European Holocaust survivors, then with Jews from Islamic lands where the new Arab-Israeli conflict was destroying historical intercommunal accommodation. After 1951, immigration declined but continued in small waves. Every Jew's right of migration (*aliya*) to Israel was a basic Zionist principle.

Questions arose about relations among Jews, as well as between Jews and Arabs. By 1951, Jews of African or Asian origin formed one-third of Israel's Jewish population, and their rate of increase was almost twice the Europeans'. Labor leaders like David Ben-Gurion and Golda Meir had only so long to assimilate later immigrants, it seemed, or Israel would become "orientalized." When Labor fell in 1977, this seemed to be happening.

A key Zionist goal was always economic: to create a self-sustaining Jewish community that could become a viable state. After 1948, massive immigration demanded further development, which began slowly but made great progress through the 1970s. With little water or other resources, Israel faced huge obstacles to

in mind, and with little territory and few forces, Israelis saw this as a life-or-death struggle against a much larger foe. In fact, most Arab states were not fully independent, they lacked unity of command, and they did not field as many soldiers as the Israelis. For the Arabs, this first test of a dawning era of independence ended as "the disaster." Israel won but got only UN-mediated armistices, without peace treaties or recognition from neighboring states. For the first time since antiquity, however, the country growth. Zionist goals required high welfare spending to attract and retain immigrants. The Arab countries boycotted Israel economically, and the lack of real peace kept defense spending high. By 1967, Israel and its Arab neighbors spent more of their GNP on defense (11 percent in Israel) than any other countries except the Soviet Union.

Israel's development also benefited, however, from unusual positive factors. For its citizens, developing Israel was a life-or-death matter. They brought to the country high educational levels. Israel's schools became better, its irrigated countryside greener, and its industry more advanced than those of surrounding countries. Israel enjoyed high investment. From 1950 through 1973, annual capital investment averaged 25 percent of GNP—a rate rarely matched elsewhere. Most capital came from U.S. aid or loans, German reparations, support from Jews abroad, or funds brought by immigrants. For its first quarter-century, Israel achieved an average annual growth rate of 10 percent, slightly higher than Japan's.

In politics, strong consensus about defense, and Labor's hold on power through 1977, created an apparent simplicity. Yet Israeli politics was complex. Among twenty or more parties, three groups stood out. On the left was a group ranging from social democratic to Marxist, dominated by the Labor party. On the right stood a group of staunchly nationalist parties, the best known being Menachem Begin's Freedom (Herut) party. It took a militant stand on unification of the historical land of Israel. While Labor would have accepted diplomatic recognition from the Arabs within the 1949 armistice lines, Herut continued to demand a "Greater Israel" including the kingdom of Jordan as well as the West Bank (biblical Judea and Samaria). The third group consisted of religious parties that wished Israel to be run according to Jewish law. No party ever had a majority, and Israel always had coalition governments. Ready to

trade votes on other issues for support on religious ones, the religious parties were often coalition partners, gaining much influence as a result.

The high point of Labor's years in power was the victory in the Six-Day War of 1967, which gave Israel control of Sinai, the Golan Heights, the Gaza Strip, the West Bank, and the Old City of Jerusalem. Victory strengthened Israel strategically, tripling the amount of land under its control but shortening its land borders by 25 percent. The war also generated enough support from abroad to ignite an economic boom that lasted into the early 1970s. Yet the Arabs still refused to make a peace treaty that recognized Israel's right to exist. Later, Israelis realized that such bitter defeat could not make the Arabs compromise. But Israel did not grasp this lesson immediately, and the triumphal mood of 1967 opened the way for the surprise of 1973.

The chief question to emerge from the 1967 war was that of the occupied territories. Sinai meant the least to Israel. The Golan Heights seemed vital for security. The West Bank meant more, at least to rightists and religious conservatives to whom this was ancient Judea and Samaria. Old Jerusalem meant most of all. Territorial issues soon eroded the consensus on defense. Some Israelis thought it in their interest to trade land for diplomatic recognition. To hold territories with a large Arab majority could create a demographic danger, given the high Arab birth rate. Other Israelis rejected this argument, holding that the occupied land provided a buffer that could be consolidated by Jewish settlement, especially in places identified with biblical Israel. This view worked its way into policy in the 1970s. Many Israelis became used to a new status quo in which Arabs from the territories would never participate fully in Israeli life, whatever their numbers, because they had not been granted citizenship. Other Israelis protested that retaining the territories on such a basis would make Israel another South Africa.

Meanwhile, Palestinians in the territories and surrounding states grew in militancy. After the 1967 war, Palestinians in exile concluded they would have to regain their homeland by their own efforts, not await help from Arab governments. The most important Palestinian organization was al-Fatah (Movement for the Liberation of Palestine), headed by Yasir Arafat, who also became the leader in 1968 of the Palestine Liberation Organization (PLO), the Palestinian umbrella organization. Though sympathizing with the Palestinians, Arab governments could not allow guerrillas to operate from bases in their territory without inviting Israeli reprisals. After 1971, Lebanon—least resolute of the Arab states because of its religiously fragmented society—was the only country adjoining Israel in which Palestinians could operate at all freely. Their increased activism was probably the strongest expression of the global wave of guerrilla violence in the late 1960s. Israelis saw Palestinians' efforts to regain their homeland as terrorism and viewed Israel's larger-scaled retaliatory attacks as legitimate self-defense.

With Palestinian militancy as a backdrop, the October War of 1973 marked the beginning of the end of unbroken Labor rule. Sadat's successful surprise attack raised questions about Israeli military intelligence and preparedness. An official inquiry led Prime Minister Golda Meir and Defense Minister Moshe Dayan to resign. The next Labor government, under Yitzhak Rabin, was tainted by scandal. Economic woes included defense spending still above 30 percent of GNP after the war, high inflation, and swelling foreign debt. The OPEC shock also weakened diplomatic support. The UN and over a hundred nations recognized the PLO. Inside Israel, Jews of Afro-Asian origin began to outnumber Europeans in the 1970s. "Oriental" Jews remembered past inequities and found

Menachem Begin's simple Greater Israel theme more meaningful than Labor party theory.

Israel's Move to the Right

The May 1977 election consequently opened a new period. The winner was the Likud (Unity) bloc, formed around Ariel Sharon, hero of the 1973 war. The bloc included Begin's Herut party, and Begin became prime minister.

Begin stressed the Greater Israel idea. In a peacemaking effort started by Egyptian president Sadat and mediated by U.S. president Carter, Begin joined in concluding the Camp David accords (September 1978) and the Egyptian-Israeli treaty (March 1979)—Israel's first with an Arab state. These agreements led to the return of Sinai to Egypt, a concession that did not detract from the Greater Israel idea. As for the West Bank, Begin agreed at Camp David to negotiate autonomy for its people. But he developed an autonomy plan that offered Arabs no more than they already had: Israeli military control and sovereignty, with continued freedom for Israelis to settle. By 1982 the state controlled more than half the land on the West Bank and was making it available to build planned communities. Soon so many Israelis would own property there that returning the region to Arab control might be unthinkable.

The situation in the territories worsened, but the greatest blows to the Arabs came in Lebanon. Having invaded south Lebanon in 1978, Israel invaded again in June 1982, pushing as far as Beirut. Defense Minister Sharon seemingly convinced his government that invading would both protect northern Israel from guerrilla attack and thwart militancy in the territories by smashing the PLO center in Beirut. The PLO headquarters was forced out of Lebanon in August 1982, and a rebellion within al-Fatah challenged Arafat again a year later.

However, the Lebanese invasion also handed Israel its first defeat. It took Israel three years to disengage from Lebanon. Israel suffered many casualties, and some soldiers refused orders to serve. More upsetting were the massacres in September 1982 that the militia of the Maronite Christian Phalange perpetrated in two Palestinian refugee camps in West Beirut, an area under Israeli military control. Israeli commanders claimed not to have known that hundreds of civilians were being massacred, but Israelis with long memories of the Holocaust were horrified. An official inquiry censured those responsible, including Begin and Sharon. Meanwhile, focused on territorial issues, Begin had neglected hard economics. Worsened by the settlement policy and the Lebanese invasion, the inflation rate reached triple digits in 1984.

Begin withdrew from politics in 1983, and the 1984 general election reflected Israel's problems. Neither Labor nor Likud got enough votes to form a coalition. The result was a national unity government combining both, with Labor's Shimon Peres as prime minister for two years, followed by Likud's Yitzhak Shamir for two years. Israel withdrew from Lebanon in 1985, unable to leave behind anything to secure its interests, other than a border zone manned by the Israeli-backed South Lebanon army. Withdrawal helped stabilize the economy, but a new stage in Palestinian resistance soon threatened this gain.

The Palestinian Uprising

Beginning in December 1987 when a traffic accident provoked riots in the Gaza Strip and the West Bank, the *intifada* (the "throwing off" of Israeli rule) opened a new era in Palestinian nationalism. Now, Palestinians living under Israeli rule took the initiative. They created an underground Unified National Command (UNC). Linked to the PLO outside, the UNC combined representatives from nationalist and Islamic movements in the territories. Israeli security could not root out the UNC. It kept itself invisible, except for the directives it published. If one of its members was caught, the movement that member represented simply appointed a replacement. The uprising included many forms of action: stones thrown at Israeli forces; street barricades; mass resignations by Palestinian policemen; demonstrations by men, women, and children; boycotts of Israeli goods; refusal to pay taxes; strikes by Palestinians working inside Israel; and school closings. A major goal was to create an alternative infrastructure with its own schools, medical services, and even intifada gardens. The UNC having forbidden use of firearms, the intifada remained largely nonviolent for several years. Israeli security forces faced the nerve-racking task of policing an occupied country where, as often as not, the stonethrowers were not guerrillas but schoolgirls.

Not enough to win Palestinian independence, the uprising led to important changes. For Palestinians, it meant political mobilization more thorough than any yet seen in Arab lands. For Israel's economy, which had profited from the occupation by $1 billion a year, the uprising turned profit into loss. Like the Lebanese invasion, the uprising led some Israelis to refuse military service. It also affected Israel's election of November 1988, which produced another Likud-Labor stalemate and a unity government under Yitzhak Shamir.

The uprising affected international relations, too. In November 1988, the Palestine National Council (the Palestinian parliament in exile, a PLO agency) reacted symbolically to the uprising by declaring the West Bank and Gaza an independent Palestinian state. In December 1988, Arafat, addressing the United Nations in Geneva, condemned terrorism and called on Israel to join in peace talks. In a startling shift, the U.S. State Department accused Israel of human rights violations in response to the uprising. Also accepting that the PLO had renounced terrorism and recognized Israel's right to exist, the United States agreed to negotiate with the PLO. Much of U.S. and Israeli opinion was ready to support this move, even if the Shamir government was not.

Peacemaking Versus Identity Politics

The Likud-Labor coalition broke down over this issue in 1990. Labor failed to form a new coalition, and the next government was a coalition of Likud and the far Right. By then, however, the world was changing in ways that made Likud's seeming victory deceptive. The end of the Cold War implicitly lessened Israel's strategic importance as a U.S. ally in the Middle East—a trend highlighted in the Gulf War when several Arab states became U.S. allies but Israel remained nonbelligerent. The migration of hundreds of thousands of Soviet Jews to Israel raised hopes of changing the Arab-Israeli demographic balance and strengthening Israeli conservatives' resistance to compromise. Yet the Likud government had to face the costs of absorbing the immigrants, on top of other expenses, including settlement building in occupied territories. The attempt to secure added U.S. support for immigrant absorption provoked severe strain in U.S.-Israeli relations, with the Bush administration refusing further assistance as long as the settlements continued.

Changes in international relations also affected the intifada profoundly. Because the PLO backed Iraq in the 1991 Gulf War, Iraqi defeat destroyed much of the Palestinians' financial support. The Gulf states, formerly major donors, cut off aid to the PLO, forcing it to reduce its operations in the territories. Palestinians who had worked in the Gulf states became unwelcome; their loss of jobs reduced remittances to the territories by three-fourths. Likewise, the collapse of European communism also deprived the Palestinians of support and created a political situation where many Arab states,

which before had all given at least verbal support to the Palestinians, tried to reposition themselves in relation to the United States. All these factors undermined the intifada. Techniques Israel developed to control it—including mass arrests and deportations—furthered this trend.

Yet as this occurred, U.S. cooperation with Arab states in the Gulf War created new impetus to settle the Arab-Israeli conflict through negotiations, starting at Madrid in October 1991. For supporting Iraq, the PLO was barred from direct participation, and Palestinian representatives were chosen directly from the territories, one of them being Dr. Hanan Ashrawi. She, in particular, presented the Palestinian cause in a humane, reasonable way that compared favorably with those of both PLO and Likud leaders.

With the appropriateness of Likud policy challenged by both the need to negotiate and the costs of absorbing Soviet immigrants while still building settlements, Israel's 1992 election produced the biggest upset since that of 1977. Many Israelis blamed the Greater Israel idea for the mounting Palestinian violence. Support for Likud among Israelis of Afro-Asian origin weakened because of a feeling that Arab-Israeli peace would bring economic gains. Russian immigrants, whom analysts expected to support Likud out of anti-socialist bias, voted for Labor to punish Likud for not providing housing and jobs. Fast becoming Israel's largest ethnic subgroup, the secular-minded Russians also threatened the religious parties' power. The result was Likud's defeat and a new coalition led by Labor with Yitzhak Rabin as prime minister.

Labor's return to power produced major change. Rabin did not stop settlement in the territories, but he did stop building new settlements, while continuing work on existing ones. This change sufficed to regain the U.S. financial support for immigrant absorption that had been denied to Shamir. Rabin had long supported giving up some of the territories while keeping strategic parts. The negotiations begun at Madrid made so little progress, however, that the Palestinians began to oppose both them and the West Bank leaders who participated in them.

Violence mounted, both in the territories and inside Israel, a major factor being the growth of the militant Islamic movements, Hamas and Islamic Jihad, both backed financially by Muslims abroad. Rabin responded in December 1992 by trying to expel 415 suspected activists into Lebanon, which refused to accept them, and by closing the territories in March 1993. The closure made it impossible for most Palestinians who worked inside Israel to get to their jobs, and it denied Palestinians access to East Jerusalem. To Israelis, it demonstrated both Rabin's toughness on security and the possibility of separating Israel from the territories. Settler activists threatened violence if Israel withdrew from the territories, but their attempts to win support drew little response.

Rabin had argued that agreement with the Palestinians was the key to peace with the Arab states. In 1993 events moved dramatically in that direction. Israel's main incentive was to strengthen the secular nationalists of the PLO, as opposed to Islamic activists like Hamas, who opposed negotiation. After months of negotiation, the PLO recognized Israel's right to exist and renounced violence; Israel responded by recognizing the PLO as the Palestinians' representative. This exchange opened the way for Rabin and Arafat to meet in Washington in September 1993 and conclude a historic Israeli-PLO peace accord. It provided for a five-year period of limited Palestinian autonomy, starting in the Gaza Strip and the West Bank town of Jericho. The agreement called for withdrawal of Israeli security forces, Palestinian responsibility for municipal administration and police, Israeli protection for remaining Israeli settlers, joint Israeli-Palestinian cooperation for economic development in the territories, and further negotiations within three years for a permanent

agreement. A second Palestinian-Israeli agreement in October 1995 gave the Palestinians direct control of six main West Bank towns, partial control of Hebron, civil authority over 440 West Bank villages, and executive and legislative authority, the last exercised through an eighty-eight member Palestinian Legislative Council. Even so, Israel retained control of 73 percent of the West Bank, and the Palestinians had full control only in the towns, amounting to about 4 percent of the area. Negotiated with Norwegian mediation, the 1993 and 1995 agreements are often referred to as Oslo I and II. Israel also concluded a peace treaty with Jordan in October 1994. Diplomatic relations with Morocco and Tunisia, and trade relations with the small Gulf states, also were established.

Scholars debated whether Oslo I and II marked steps toward Palestinian sovereignty. In the 1990s world of identity politics, the agreements dissatisfied people on both sides. Hamas and Islamic Jihad launched suicide bombings intended to destroy both the PLO and the Labor government. Some Israeli rightists also reacted violently, as when settlers massacred Palestinians in Hebron in 1994 and 1997 or when a religiously conservative intifada veteran assassinated Prime Minister Rabin in 1995. In the 1996 and 1999 elections, that office passed to Benjamin Netanyahu (Likud) and then Ehud Barak (Labor). Both headed fractious coalition governments that did not last long, yet showed continuity in resisting concessions to Palestinians but not to Israeli settlers in occupied territories. U.S. attempts at peacemaking resumed on Israeli terms at the end of the Clinton presidency, but the gap between Israeli and Palestinian positions remained unbridgeable. Barak's aim was to separate Israelis and Palestinians and to maintain four "red lines": no return of Palestinian refugees to Israel, no return to 1967 borders, no "foreign armies" west of the Jordan, and Jerusalem as Israel's capital. The Palestinians officially demanded the right of all Palestinian refugees to return or receive compensation, Israel's com-

لن يكتمل حلمي...
إلا بك ياقدس

"My dream will never be fulfilled without you, oh Jerusalem." *Arafat proclaims on a Gaza billboard. Because Israelis feel the same way, the status of Jerusalem is the most difficult item on the peace agenda. Meanwhile, this donkey cart scene dramatizes Palestinian needs for economic development.* Barry Iverson

plete withdrawal to the 1967 borders, removal of all Israeli settlements from occupied territory, and East Jerusalem as the capital of their state. Release of some 1,650 Palestinians held in Israeli prisons was another issue. (The Palestinian positions on refugee rights and borders were supported by UN Resolutions 194, 242, and 338; since 1947, Jerusalem has the status in international law of an international zone under UN jurisdiction. See Map 16.2.)

Part of the challenge the Palestinians faced was that Israel was vastly stronger militarily, diplomatically, and economically. Arafat had returned to Gaza in 1994 to head what became known as the Palestinian Authority, which had limited powers over the Gaza Strip and parts of the West Bank, separated territories between

which Israeli controls made it impossible for most Palestinians to travel. While by 2000 Israelis enjoyed the highest per capita income ($18,000) of any Mediterranean country after France and Italy, nearly half the Palestinians lived on $2 a day or less. With democratic Palestinian institutions still undeveloped, Arafat, aging and infirm, ruled by decree and patronage, even as younger Palestinians demanded rule of law. Dependent in many ways on Israel, the Palestinian Authority was in a weak position to resist the expansion of Jewish settlements, including the encirclement of East Jerusalem or the division of the West Bank into separated Palestinian cantons ("bantustans"). Palestinians concluded that the Israelis negotiated only among themselves and then, often with U.S.

"mediation," asked them to "compromise." Polls showed a majority of Israelis as favoring peace and further territorial concessions (only not about Jerusalem), while also accepting the likelihood of Palestinian statehood. Still Netanyahu and Barak took a hard line. The outbreak of the *intifada* in 1987 had shown how easily conflict could flare up in such a situation.

In September 2000, it happened again. Ariel Sharon, champion of settlements in the occupied territories, commander of the 1982 invasion of Lebanon, and then trying for a political comeback, made a provocative visit to the Muslim holy places atop the Temple Mount in Old Jerusalem. In incidents following Muslim Friday prayers the next day, the police killed seven Palestinians and wounded over two hundred. Television relayed to the whole world the death of a young Palestinian boy, caught with his father in army gunfire in Gaza. So began a new *intifada*. This time, it spread to Israel's Arab citizens, those living inside Israel proper. In the territories, Palestinians attacked settlements, especially outposts deep in Palestinian territory, and managed to take at least one settlement in Nablus. Inside Israel, Jews reacted by attacking Palestinians in several cities. An Israeli peace activist described events at Nazareth as an anti-Arab "pogrom." Unlike that of 1987, this *intifada* also united both the Palestinian nationalists and Islamists as the Palestinian National and Islamic Forces (PNIF). Israel retaliated overwhelmingly to close the territories, squeeze them economically, and subdue them militarily. In November, after the shelling of a settler schoolbus, the Israelis attacked Gaza city with tanks, gunboats, and helicopters.

Seven years after Oslo I, the Palestinian territories were still under military occupation. Armed force might defeat them but could not win peace from them. When the erosion of his coalition forced Barak to call new elections in 2001, Israeli voters, given a new chance to express their wishes about one of the most difficult problems in today's world of interde-

pendence and contested identifies, chose Ariel Sharon as prime minister.

Conclusion

During successive phases of post-1945 global history, the history of the Middle East and North Africa illustrates all the major themes of this book. The global tightening of interrelatedness shows in Turkey's links with NATO and the European Union, the Nasser-era experiments in Arab unity, and the more inclusive Islamic internationalism. Economically, the oil industry and its post-1973 transformation best illustrate the region's ties to the global economy. Questions of identity and difference, too, have become critical in each country surveyed. Examples include Turkey's secularists and Islamists, its Kurdish and Alevi minorities; Iran's questions about its postrevolutionary future; Egypt's tensions between the state and Islamic radicals; Israel's leftists and settler militants; and the secular nationalism of the PLO and the Islamic activism of Hamas; as well as the larger Zionist-Palestinian opposition. The theme of the mass society appears throughout the region in every sense from demographic growth and superurbanization to tensions between authoritarian mobilization and demands for democratization. In an arid, underdeveloped region, technology-related issues recur in questions of development strategy, resource shortages, and vulnerability—compounded by population growth—to natural catastrophes like Turkey's earthquakes of 1997. The era of globalization will open new vistas but also bring new challenges to all Middle Eastern societies.

Notes

1. E-mail messages, quoted by permission, from Baysan Bayar, whose late husband was from Adapazari (dated Ankara, October 10, 1999), and from Gülcan Yeröz, an undergraduate in Ankara (Sep-

tember 20, 1999; she says "Hi!"—*Merhaba!*—to all students who read this book).

2. United Nations Development Program, *Human Development Report 2000* (New York: Oxford University Press, 2000), tables 1, 2.

Suggestions for Further Reading

Abu-Lughod, Lila, ed. *Remaking Women: Feminism and Modernity in the Middle East* (1998).

Ahmad, Feroz. *The Making of Modern Turkey* (1993).

Arjomand, Said. *The Turban for the Crown: The Islamic Revolution in Iran* (1988).

Bakhash, Shaul. *The Reign of the Ayatollahs: Iran and the Islamic Revolution.* Rev. ed. (1990).

Cleveland, William L. *A History of the Modern Middle East* (1994).

Dowty, Alan. *The Jewish State: A Century Later* (1998).

Eickelman, Dale F., and James Piscatori. *Muslim Politics* (1996).

Hansen, Bent. *The Political Economy of Poverty, Equity, and Growth: Egypt and Turkey* (1991).

Hourani, Albert. *A History of the Arab Peoples* (1991).

Middle East International (London).

Middle East Report (New York).

Smith, Charles D. *Palestine and the Arab-Israeli Conflict.* 4th ed. (2001).

Zürcher, Erik J. *Turkey: A Modern History* (1998).

CHAPTER 17

Asian Resurgence

IN APRIL 1999, OVER TEN THOUSAND CHINESE GATHERED SILENTLY IN BEIJING outside the compound that houses China's leaders. It was the largest demonstration since the Tienanmen Square massacres of 1989. But this was different. Ordinary people, often older, appeared out of nowhere, with no visible organization, no slogans, no banners. They spent the day meditating or slowly doing exercises. They were practitioners of Falun Dafa,

"Falun Dafa is good," proclaimed this demonstrator on Tienanmen Square, 2001. *She was quickly arrested. Falun Dafa is an "evil cult," proclaims China's government.* Greg Baker/© AP-Wide World Photos

a spiritual movement inspired by Buddhism and *qigong,* a kind of physical and moral self-help program. They sought official recognition of Falun Dafa. As they dispersed that night, group leaders announced that high officials had promised to meet with them.

Things were not to be so easy. Founded in 1992, the movement already had 70 million members by government estimate, more than the Communist party's 55 million. Founder Li Hongzhi's most influential book, published in 1996, had sold nearly a million copies before being banned. Exiled in 1998, he lived in New York. Books, audio and video tapes, and many websites spread his message around the world. Inside China, post-Mao materialism had left many Chinese spiritually starved, and rising health care costs heightened the appeal of *qigong* movements that promised physical as well as spiritual benefits. The Beijing demonstration followed incidents in the city of Tianjin. There a magazine had attacked Falun Dafa, and followers who had surrounded the magazine's offices had been arrested. Activists tried to avoid official wrath by insisting that this was not a religion and had no organization. Yet they attributed supernatural powers to Master Li and held that he, not the party, had the answers for making China a better place.

Any Chinese government had to worry about such a movement. Sects and secret societies had triggered civil unrest in earlier times. In the nineteenth century, the Taiping movement ruled a large region for over a decade, and government efforts to regain control left millions dead. Now Falun Dafa was spreading rapidly. For the party, any national movement was a threat. The many officials and party members attracted to the movement heightened this concern. Officially recognizing five religions and tolerating other *qigong* groups, the government therefore outlawed Falun Dafa in July 1999, comparing it to American cults that had ended in mass death, and denouncing Li as a charlatan. The government arrested followers and staged show trials. The trials ended with long jail sentences, especially for party members who had joined the movement. Hundreds of other practitioners were sent without trial to labor camps for "re-education." Thousands of activists responded by converging on Beijing to demonstrate or even, in a few cases, to die fiery deaths by dousing themselves with gasoline and setting themselves alight in Tienanmen Square.

Some of the worst excesses against Falun Dafa occurred at Weifang in Shandong Province. When the show trials provoked demonstrations in Beijing, the government announced that local officials who did not stop demonstrators coming from their locales would be held responsible. It had been easy to go from Weifang, only three hundred miles from Beijing, to demonstrate. However, Shandong Province Governor Wu Guangzheng, unlike most province governors, was a member of the Communist party's Politburo in Beijing. When it discussed the protests, all eyes turned to him. He passed the pressure down the chain of command. Soon Shandong police were operating out of the province office in Beijing, arresting protestors from their province and bringing them back before their arrests could be noted in the capital. In Shandong, local administrators were illegally fined for every Falun Dafa practitioner from their district who went to Beijing. They passed the fines on down to the policemen who punished the offenders. Facing fines that could wipe out their meager salaries, policemen pressed detainees for money and even tortured them to death, if they did not pay. Some detainees had lost their jobs because of Falun Dafa and could not pay. To pass responsibility down the hierarchy was an ancient Chinese method of enforcing central orders; here its worst potentials for abuse materialized.

Sixty-five years after the Long March had proven communism the most effective mass-mobilizing force in China, an apolitical movement that appeared harmless to people outside China had mobilized more people than the party. Together with Cuba, Vietnam, and North Korea, China remained the last officially communist country in the world. Yet for how much longer? And what did the story of Falun Dafa foretell about the future of mass mobilization in the era of globalization and identity politics?

South and East Asia: From Decolonization to Reassertion

After 1945, the Third World's most dynamic efforts at national development occurred in Asia. In South Asia, India, now home to one-sixth of humanity, became the largest democracy; but stark inequity undercut its developmental achievement. In East Asia, China, with nearly one-fifth of the world's people, emerged from one of history's most drastic revolutions to launch an economic transformation of epic scale. Japan, all but destroyed in World War II, re-emerged as the world's second-largest national economy (a title now challenged by China), effectively a part of the West. A number of other Asian countries emerged from underdevelopment to join the world's high-growth economies. Some experts foresee an East Asian economic complex able to rival or excel Europe and the United States. These Asian superlatives imply this chapter's agenda.

Long home to the world's most brilliant civilizations, Asia has produced the greatest contemporary challenges to Western dominance. The conclusion of Chapter 9 compared major Asian countries in order to identify factors that aided them in adapting to twentieth-century conditions of tightening global integration, accelerating change, mass mobilization, and technological change. After 1945, similar factors again proved critical: facility in mastering new ideas; consensus about national identity and the organization of political life; responsiveness to the demands of mass mobilization (in both political and socioeconomic terms); and development of economic growth strategies capable of meeting the people's needs and bettering the country's economic place in the world. Here, to prepare for discussion of specific countries since 1945, basic points of regionwide significance merit notice: decolonization, population trends, economic development, and cultural reassertion.

Decolonization in South and East Asia

Weakened by two world wars and the Depression, challenged by Asian nationalism and economic development efforts, Western dominance collapsed in Asia in the 1940s and 1950s, except in outposts such as Britain's Hong Kong. Decolonization began during World War II. Japan seized many European colonies—French Indochina (now Vietnam, Cambodia, and Laos), Burma, Malaya, the Dutch East Indies (now Indonesia), and other Pacific islands—as well as the U.S.-controlled Philippines. To this day, many Japanese regard themselves as liberators of these countries—a view not widely shared in the countries in question. Japan also had or took control of much territory—Taiwan, Korea, Manchuria, parts of China—that had not been under European control. After 1945, former colonial powers' attempts to regain control of some

countries, such as Indochina and the Dutch East Indies, proved short-lived. The Philippines gained independence from the United States in 1946. In 1947 the British lost Burma, India, and Pakistan (including East Pakistan, which became independent as Bangladesh in 1971). Map 15.1 shows Asian as well as African independence dates; see also Map 17.1 on South and East Asia on p. 471.

As the wartime U.S.-British-Soviet alliance broke up, it seemed for a time that Stalin's effort to create a defensive perimeter for the Soviet Union would extend from eastern and southeastern Europe, across the Middle East—where Turkey and Iran resisted Soviet pressure only with U.S. support—and across the rest of Asia, too. In East Asia, while Japan remained under U.S. occupation (1945-1952), Mao's Communists triumphed in mainland China, creating the People's Republic of China in 1949; Chiang Kai-shek's Nationalists withdrew to the island of Taiwan and set up the rival Republic of China. Like Germany, Korea and Indochina were divided between communist and noncommunist regimes. Outsiders took a long time to grasp that Chinese and Vietnamese communists were nationalists, not Soviet puppets. The later Soviet invasion of Afghanistan (1979-1989) was a throwback to Soviet policy of these years.

Except in China, Indochina, and North Korea, however, Asian nationalists mostly kept a distance from Marxism and, in some countries, reacted against it by making policy choices that stimulated extraordinary economic development. Also in reaction to the Cold War view of the world as divided between the "Free World" (the United States and Western Europe) and the "Communist Bloc," India, especially, took a leading role in promoting nonalignment, or solidarity within the "Third World" of Asian, African, and Latin American nations, whose interests differed from those of both superpowers.

Population Growth, Superurbanization, and Human Development

Decolonization meant formal political independence but, as usual, not necessarily development. The postcolonial regimes' prime goal was economic development or, for Japan, reconstruction. Communist takeovers in several countries heightened the urgency of this need. The question was how to rebuild and develop economically while also facing the problems, starting with explosive population growth and even faster urbanization, that blocked development in other regions.

Asian societies' responses to their demographic needs have varied more widely than those in any other developing region. India's population growth rate began to exceed the developed countries' in 1941, when India had 319 million people. The figures for India (no longer including Pakistan or Bangladesh) rose to 435 million in 1960 and 1.0 billion in 2000. What is now Pakistan (West Pakistan from 1947 to 1971) rose from about 25 million in 1947 to 151 million in 2000. Between 1947 and 2000, the population of Bangladesh (what had been East Pakistan from 1947 until independence in 1971) grew from about 50 million people to 128 million. Bangladesh is the most densely populated of the world's poorest countries.

To the east, China's population rose from 600 million in 1947 to 1.3 billion in 2000. China's increase rate—now 0.9 percent yearly, closer to the rates of affluent lands—shows how an authoritarian government can use pressure to slow population growth. Japan's population, which rose from 72 million in 1945 to 127 million in 2000, has fallen to a truly low growth rate: 0.2 percent. Southeast Asia includes others of the most populous nations. Indonesia rose from an estimated 77.2 million in 1955 to 212 million in 2000, becoming the world's fourth most populous nation. In 2000, both Vietnam (79 million) and the Philippines (80 million) were more populous than any West European country but Germany (82 million).

As in other developing countries, the largest cities grew faster than the nations they belonged to. As of 1995, Dhaka (Bangladesh) had a population of 8 million; Karachi (Pakistan) had 10 million; Jakarta (Indonesia) had 11.5 million; Seoul (Korea) had 11.6 million; Bombay (now Mumbai, India) and Shanghai (China's largest city) each had 15 million; and metropolitan Tokyo had 30 million living within a fifty-kilometer radius. China's Beijing and Shanghai, Indonesia's Jakarta, Pakistan's Karachi, and India's Mumbai, Delhi, and Calcutta were all expected to grow to between 20 and 30 million by 2025. At 1.4 percent a year in 1990–1995, metropolitan Tokyo's growth rate was still several times higher than Japan's national population growth rate. One of the few traits Japan still shared with poor countries (and some other affluent ones) was its biggest city's dominance compared to the nation's other cities—a problem that inspired many plans for decentralization but little action.

Wide variations in Asian responses to the challenges of demographic growth appear as soon as we look past raw numbers to a measure like the Human Development Index, which as noted in Chapters 14–16, combines life expectancy, adult literacy, educational enrollment rates, and real incomes. Here South Asia's level of achievement barely excelled sub-Saharan Africa's; India particularly neglected elementary education, health care, and women's welfare. East Asia outperformed South Asia by a wide margin. Excluding China, the rest of East Asia nearly attained the level of the world's most highly industrialized economies. This contrast between South and East Asia indicates a major fork in developmental paths, as a discussion of economic strategies will further clarify.

Divergent Economic Strategies

In a way unlike the post-1945 economic history of Latin America or sub-Saharan Africa, South and East Asian nations have followed divergent developmental paths. One of the important tasks of this chapter will be to explore these differences, which this section serves to introduce.

South Asia—a region dominated by India but also including Pakistan, Bangladesh, and Sri Lanka—avoided the Latin American and sub-Saharan African fate of economic shrinkage during the 1980s and early 1990s. Still, South Asia's growth in GNP per person, averaging fractionally more than 2 percent per year for 1965–1993, was nearly a full percentage point below the average for all developing countries in the same period. In a country of such ethnic, religious, and regional diversity as India, there were wide variations. The southern state of Kerala, despite low economic growth, excelled China's development by many social indicators. While the ratio of females to males had declined for all India throughout the twentieth century, the status of women—especially widows—was particularly wretched in the populous states of the north. For India as a whole, two factors, in particular, seemed to explain the poor performance. One, already familiar, was the structural inegalitarianism of Hindu society. The other was independent India's commitment to the Third World "socialism" of protectionist import substitution and heavy regulation of the economy—a policy not abandoned until the 1990s, although its limits had become visible in Third World countries from the 1960s on.

Further east, while Southeast Asia's annual growth in GNP per person roughly matched that for all developing countries between 1965 and 1993, that for East Asia was much faster—from 1980 to 1993, at 8.2 percent a year, more than twice as fast. China—by far the region's most populous country—lagged the rest of East Asia under Mao but later excelled the rest in per

capita GNP growth. Major reasons for East Asia's astonishing record start with the fact that Japan was already highly developed before World War II. Despite wartime destruction, it had an exceptional base to resume from after 1945. China, after exceptional efforts in raising the level of the masses under Mao, adopted market-oriented development policies after 1979. Several other East and Southeast Asian economies—starting with Hong Kong, Singapore, Taiwan, and South Korea—also achieved high rates of growth from the 1960s on. Differing in many ways, they share with Japan a number of growth-conducive traits, which the last section of this chapter will examine.

Together with that of the affluent countries of Europe and North America, East Asia's economic record also raises important growth-related questions. Affluent but resource-poor, Japan already consumes—in some cases even more than other rich countries—disproportionate shares of global resources. China is also resource-poor but nearly ten times as populous. If its growth led to comparable consumption levels, it would place unsustainable burdens on the world economy. China's recent upsurge thus raises resource questions of global significance, to which we shall return in considering ecological issues in Chapter 18.

Cultural Reassertion

Underlying Asian societies' drives for independence and development was a push for cultural decolonization, or—stated positively—cultural reassertion. India's democracy, for example, underwent marked shifts, from Nehru's liberal democratic socialism, to his daughter Indira Gandhi's authoritarianism, and perhaps back toward a liberalism farther from the British model under her son Rajiv Gandhi. Tensions between the Hindu majority and the Sikh religious minority, culminating in Indira Gandhi's assassination, and still more the Hindu-Muslim violence of the 1990s, proved the resurgence of

Identity politics in Japan. *Prime minister Nakasone's 1985 official visit to the Yasukuni shrine, where Japan's war dead are honored, raised questions about the constitutional separation of religion and state and about attitudes toward Japan's war record.* Koji Sasahara/© AP-Wide World Photos

religious politics in India, subjecting its democracy to new strains.

In East Asia, Mao's thought always had a strong nationalist dimension, and policy under Deng Xiaoping, in retreating from Mao's excesses, not only moved farther away from Marxism-Leninism but also showed greater tolerance for traditional Chinese culture. In Japan, finally, not only has the country's economic development gained from traditional Japanese traits and work habits, but historical worldviews have reasserted themselves in a revival of Japanese nationalism. Prime Minister Yasuhiro Nakasone (1983–1988) expressed this in ways foreigners found alarming, such as a speech praising Japan as a "monoracial state." Prime Minister Yoshiro Mori (2000–2001) referred to Japan as a "divine country with an emperor at

its center." Japan's cultural insularity and the fact that the Japanese were not forced after 1945 to examine their war record as the Germans were have left as one of their costs a lingering identity crisis expressed in wavering between openness to the outside world, on the one hand, and virulent insistence on Japanese uniqueness, on the other.

Renewed interest in traditional belief systems had become a global phenomenon by the 1970s. In former colonial lands, this renewal signified political, economic, and finally cultural decompression from the stresses of European dominance. Nowhere has this phenomenon been more marked than in Asia, especially in those societies that are most directly heirs of the most influential Asian civilizations of the past. To illustrate this point, we shall consider

India, China, Japan, and—more briefly—the other high-growth Asian economies.

India: Development Amid Underdevelopment

To study South and East Asia requires expanding the scale of analysis to accommodate the world's most populous nations. India is the second most populous, with 1.0 billion of the world's 6.1 billion people in 2000, surpassed only by the People's Republic of China, with 1.3 billion. Both countries are historical centers of empire, with strong governmental traditions. Both changed greatly after 1945. Yet the two also differ sharply. India became the world's largest democracy, shaped without revolution; China remained politically authoritarian. India's democracy, coexisting with the Hindu caste system and tremendous linguistic and religious diversities, tolerated inequalities that China did not. Yet India developed remarkably in some ways, with less loss of life than in China. By the 1990s, new challenges to Indian inequality had emerged, while China had begun to liberalize economically, but not politically. India, in sum, has combined traits of both development and underdevelopment. An examination of India's history during the premierships of Jawaharlal Nehru (1947-1964), his daughter Indira Gandhi (1966-1977, 1980-1984), her son Rajiv Gandhi (1984-1991), and his successors will shed light on this paradoxical record.

India Under Nehru

The evolutionary character of Indian nationalism (see Chapters 4 and 9) found expression in the Congress party's character as mostly a coalition of elites: merchants, professionals, and landowners. To gain influence at the grassroots, members used traditional relationships based on caste, clientage, or kinship to mobilize support. With partial exceptions—chiefly Mahatma

Gandhi's attempts to improve Untouchables' and women's status—the party accommodated, rather than transformed, traditional social relations. Yet economic development formed a major goal, particularly for Nehru and other left-wing reformist socialists. The key question was whether the party could combine development with its accommodative approach to political mobilization.

In the way of doing so stood huge obstacles to social integration, even after the 1947 partition had created a separate Muslim state: Pakistan, with territories in both west and east (Bengal). Some 10 million people had fled, suffering a million fatalities while trying to get to the "right" side of the partition lines. Separatist violence also occurred among the religious and linguistic minorities, such as the Sikhs of the Punjab and the speakers of Dravidian languages in the south. Not all the 570 princely states wanted to accept control by the nation in which their territories lay. India used force to gain control over some and fought Pakistan over Kashmir, which was partitioned. Socioeconomic inequality, reinforced by caste, remained stark. The average Indian was one of the worst-fed, most unhealthy people on Earth, with a life expectancy of only thirty-two years. The population reached 360 million by 1950 and was growing fast enough to offset gains in food production.

With Nehru (1889-1964) as prime minister, India began organizing its national life. It had political assets few postcolonial nations could match: a respected parliament; a political party with a national organization and quality leadership; and professional, nonpoliticized military and civil services. Over half the articles of the 1950 constitution came from the 1935 Government of India Act, a familiar source. Federalism helped accommodate India's social complexity through power sharing between central and state governments. The constitution also proclaimed equality and abolished untouchability—on paper. Memories of religious conflict strengthened initial consensus in favor of secularism and social democracy. Compared to Pakistan's military politics, India's enduring, if imperfect, democracy shows how much more it inherited from pre-1947 state-building efforts in the subcontinent.

Nehru retained power for life. One weakness of India's democracy was, in fact, the Congress party's preponderance and the personalization of leadership within it, from Mahatma Gandhi on. Most other parties were not national but represented linguistic or religious minorities. Nehru also acted as foreign minister, gaining an international reputation as a proponent of nonalignment. Along with India's size, especially as compared to its South Asian neighbors, nonalignment helped India emerge from dependency much more than most Third World countries could.

The Nehru government tackled India's developmental problems with a mixture of reformist socialism, Gandhian idealization of village society, and tolerance for private enterprise. World War II had stimulated industrialization. At least after the disastrous Bengal famine of 1943, the British had also pushed agricultural development. Nehru attempted to build on this base through centralized planning and state control of major industry. He introduced five-year plans for 1951-1956, 1956-1961, and 1961-1966. Benefiting from foreign aid, the plans produced modest results.

In agriculture, land reform eliminated some abuses, such as large-scale absentee landlordism. Yet landowners wielded enough influence that only part of the land was distributed, and the reform did little for the landless quarter of India's rural households. But the reform made another third of them into "bullock capitalists," so called after their draft animals. With 2.5 to 15 acres each, these small farmers held over half of India's farmland by 1972. The government also promoted technical modernization of agriculture and mobilized villagers politically to participate in development

through over 200,000 elected local councils (*panchayats*). Community Development and Rural Extension programs helped villagers reclaim land, dig wells, and obtain fertilizer or improved seed.

The later 1960s brought major gains in food production thanks to a strategy known internationally as the "green revolution," requiring improved seed, irrigation, and heavy use of chemical fertilizer. The strategy was costly; it was vulnerable to increases in the cost of petroleum, needed to make fertilizer; and inadequate water supplies excluded use of the new seed in many places. The "green revolution" thus heightened rural inequality, causing divergent trends in the politicization of "bullock capitalists," who could afford the new techniques, and poor peasants, who could not. From the 1970s on, the government faced serious political tensions for this reason.

The Nehru years saw gains in industry, too. In the 1960s, import substitution neared completion, thanks to high protectionism. The push for self-sufficiency, even where India could not produce efficiently, proved costly, though—like nonalignment—it diminished dependency. Nehru's socialism shaped India's economy by making government a third economic "actor," along with labor and capital. The private sector included huge industrial empires but lacked autonomy, thanks to regulation and the low prestige of entrepreneurship. To cite one sign of uneven development, by 1966 India produced 7 million tons of steel but—too underdeveloped to use it—exported much of it to Japan. India's industrialization suffered from the Third World problem that only a small part of the populace had enough income to buy many industrial products. Yet in India, that small percentage amounted to a market the size of France.

Intended goals of social reform under Nehru included women's rights and education. The constitution gave women the vote. By the late 1950s almost half of the eligible women did vote. Laws on marriage and inheritance revolutionized women's social status—on paper. Some elite women took part in public life, but tokenism prevailed for both women and *dalit*s (former Untouchables). Most Indian women were too uneducated or isolated to take advantage of the laws. Indian women's hardships led to one of the highest rates of female suicide in the world. Inequities permeated education, too. Higher education expanded greatly under Nehru, especially in technical fields—a fact significant for India's economic future. Simultaneously, literacy rose, but no higher than 28 percent in 1961 for the whole population and barely half that for women. The costs of such inequity would grow with time.

India Under Indira Gandhi

Nehru's death in 1964 opened a succession struggle between the right and left wings of the Congress party. The Left's leader, Indira Gandhi (unrelated to Mahatma Gandhi), emerged in 1966 as the winner, partly because party leaders thought they could manage her. They were wrong. Within three years, voter support for the Congress party, especially its right wing, eroded. But Mrs. Gandhi became a popular leader; when Congress tried to "expel" her in 1969, she split the party. Most members followed her into the new Congress-R, or Requisition, party and the left-wing coalition that she built around it.

Prime Minister Gandhi faced major challenges, both in development policy and in holding together her complex country; yet growth continued with some significant results. The fourth and fifth five-year plans (1969–1974, 1974–1979) produced important gains, although rising prices for oil and grain imports increased India's trade deficits. Land reform initiatives failed, but the "green revolution" raised food grain production to 100 million tons in 1968–1969. By then, the average Indian's daily food consumption exceeded 2,100 calories, and life expectancy stood at fifty-one years. The government invested increasingly in family planning, although gains in life expectancy offset the program's impact on total population during the 1970s. Industry reached the point where, by 1975–1976, it produced half of India's exports, even though Mrs. Gandhi's increasingly socialist emphasis led to bank nationalizations and greater controls over private business. An underground nuclear test in 1974 and the beginning of satellite television transmission a few years later showed what India's scientists and engineers could do.

Mrs. Gandhi's political dominance grew with time. In the 1971 general election, her branch of the Congress party won two-thirds of the seats in the lower legislative house, while the Congress Opposition won only a handful. When Bangladesh broke from Pakistan in 1971 to form a separate state, the crisis that followed also redounded to her credit. India supported the seceders and won the ensuing war with Pakistan. Pakistan's breakup into two nations increased India's regional dominance. The Sino-Soviet split and the long-standing India-Pakistan hostility also helped move Mrs. Gandhi's regime farther to the left. By the early 1970s, Pakistan and the United States were cultivating China, while India and the Soviet Union had become allies.

Victory against Pakistan gave Mrs. Gandhi momentum to carry through more socializing measures, but economic stress created new challenges to her power from 1973 on. Students and workers demonstrated to protest inflation and corruption. By 1975, a coalition of anti-Congress parties, the People's Front (Janata Morcha), had formed, and anti-government violence was occurring. Mrs. Gandhi found herself in court facing charges of campaign abuses. She retaliated in 1975 by arresting her leading opponents and declaring a state of emergency. She announced a Twenty-Point Program, including social and economic promises significant for the rural poor. Some Indians thought the emergency provided the strong rule needed to restrain corruption and slow inflation. Any such benefits, felt briefly in the cities, did not extend to the countryside.

India was suffering from domination not by one party but by one person, Mrs. Gandhi. Her son Sanjay (1947–1980) also emerged in this period as a powerful figure and her presumed successor. He was largely responsible for the abuse of the population policy that led, during the emergency, to the involuntary sterilization of millions of Indian men, mostly from lower castes. When Mrs. Gandhi terminated the emergency and called for general elections in 1977, 200 million voters showed what they thought by ending thirty years of Congress party rule and giving a parliamentary majority to the Janata opposition.

Prime Minister Morarji Desai's Janata government (1977–1980) proved but an interlude, marked by economic instability and unrest. Mrs. Gandhi won re-election to parliament within a year. When the Janata government jailed her briefly, she became a martyr. The 1980 election gave her party, now known as Congress-I (for Indira), a two-thirds majority in the lower house and swept her back into office.

During her second premiership (1980–1984), India's combined problems and achievements became more paradoxical than ever. Although the population had doubled since 1947 to over 700 million, India achieved self-sufficiency in food grains in 1978—a precarious achievement. Aside from whether Indian production could keep up with population growth, this was the self-sufficiency of limited demand. Poverty still doomed one-third of the population to chronic hunger, and agricultural modernization depended on strategies beyond the means of most farmers. Moreover, exploitation of the land could not intensify forever without environmental degradation. After tripling between 1965 and 1985, India's grain harvest did level out. By then, the geographic unevenness of agricultural development had raised political tensions, too. The Punjab, where wheat produc-

tion had tripled in the 1960s, happened to be the center of the Sikhs, a discontented religious minority (2 percent of the population).

Achievements in industry and technology were similarly paradoxical. Partly because of its educational elitism, India in the 1980s was home to the world's third-largest scientific community and to half the world's illiterates. India sent up its first communications satellite with an Indian-made launch vehicle in 1980 and opened its first microelectronics plant to produce silicon chips in 1984. Enthusiasts boasted that India would become a colossus of industry and technology. Critics worried not only about India's gross inequities of caste and gender but also about government control of the economy. From 1960 to 1980, the public sector share of GDP had risen from 10 to 21 percent, an increase bound to depress future productivity.

Politically, Mrs. Gandhi faced severe tests. Increasingly, Indians wanted political power and better lives. Women and dalits campaigned more militantly against their worsening lots. The world learned with horror that many Indian women mysteriously died in kitchen fires, freeing their husbands to remarry and gain a new dowry. (South Asia is the only major world region where men's life expectancy normally exceeds women's.) Prosperity emboldened "bullock capitalists," from the "backward classes" (lower castes), to demand for their children educational and occupational opportunities monopolized by higher castes. Tensions in outlying provinces raised fears of secessions like that of Bangladesh. In 1983, the government was sharply criticized for its handling of Muslim-Hindu violence in the state of Assam—the worst communal violence since 1947. In 1984, facing a Sikh autonomy movement in the Punjab, the government sent troops into the main Sikh temple at Amritsar.

Having described her father as "a saint" lacking "the necessary ruthlessness" for politics, Mrs. Gandhi tried to show her toughness. Nehru had coached his ministers in democratic norms and insisted on nonpolitical professionalism among officials. Throwing such caution to the winds, she risked politicizing the army by using it to police or administer strife-torn regions. She politicized the civil service by demanding personal loyalty, openly disdained parliament, crowded out rivals from her Congress-I party, and bribed opposition leaders to desert their parties. In opposition-controlled states, she declared "president's rule" so that she could replace elected state officials with rule from New Delhi. Challenged by Indians' mounting political demands, she did much to undermine democracy, until Sikh assassins felled her in 1984, a few months after she had sent troops into their Golden Temple at Amritsar.

Democracy Restructured?

The dynastic theme in South Asian politics reasserted itself as her son Rajiv Gandhi succeeded her. He attracted initial support by showing understanding of the need for power sharing and consultation. In 1985, he concluded an agreement with moderate Sikhs, one of several cases where he conciliated groups his mother had antagonized. A figure with whom India's technocrats and managers could identify, he represented a growing sentiment that the state's economic role had become a source of inefficiency, rather than a key to development. Yet with time, many Indians decided he had betrayed their hopes. The middle class thought economic liberalization had not gone far enough. Peasants resented unfulfilled pledges to end corruption in the villages. Indeed, corruption seemed to reach the very top: charges that Gandhi had taken big bribes from a Swedish arms firm led to his defeat in the 1989 elections. Campaigning to make a comeback two years later, he met his mother's fate—assassination—at the hands of militant Tamils, who dominate the southern state of Tamil Nadu and also form a minority in Sri Lanka, where Indian intervention in a civil war between

Tamils and the dominant Sinhalese had caused much bitterness.

After Rajiv Gandhi's death, the Congress party government of Prime Minister P. V. Narasimha Rao (1991–1996) faced mounting challenges, partly as a result of India's ongoing economic development. Annual growth in GDP, having averaged 3.6 percent from 1965 to 1980, accelerated to 5.3 percent between 1980 and 1990, then dipped, but regained that level by the mid-1990s. The results were felt widely enough that the urban middle class grew to over 100 million people. During the 1980s, food consumption grew almost twice as fast as population, and production of consumer goods grew even faster. India's financial metropolis, Bombay (now Mumbai), became a boom town where many Indians thought differences of caste and religion no longer counted: only ability did. The India of spinning wheels and hand looms was fading fast. With the government and many of the two-hundred-odd state enterprises near default, however, Prime Minister Narasimha Rao and Finance Minister Manmohan Singh redirected economic policy in 1991 toward privatization, greater freedom of enterprise from bureaucratic interference, and openness to foreign investment.

Segments of the population that might benefit hailed the change, but India's economic inequity and cultural complexity multiplied the grievances of those whose prospects were less sure. India's democratic institutions and the Congress party had been in decline since Indira Gandhi's abuse of them. Corruption remained a major issue, and commitment to the secularist synthesis that state and party represented was waning in an era of identity politics. In the 1990s, the government faced new challenges not only in outlying provinces or among minorities but also among the Hindu majority. In the northwest, separatist revolt continued among the Muslims of Kashmir. In the northeast, insurgency movements among the indigenous peoples of Assam targeted that state's often foreign-controlled tea plantations. All over India, migrants from backward zones crowded into places of greater opportunity, bringing people of different cultures and religions together in new ways. Muslims' migration to work in Middle Eastern oil-exporting states, and returning migrants' prosperity, sharpened jealousy of India's 120 million Muslims. Hindu backlash against changes that called attention to minorities was perhaps inevitable.

As India moved into the era of globalization and identity politics, several trends stood out. As in other postcolonial lands, old forms of unitary national mobilization, here the Congress party, declined. It made a comeback bid in the late 1990s with Rajiv Gandhi's Italian widow, Sonia, as party leader and candidate for prime minister. She rejuvenated the party by bringing in a younger generation of leaders at the state level, promoting people with expertise in economics and foreign policy, and requiring that 53 percent of party officials at all levels be women, Muslims, or low-caste people. Still, the party organization had decayed in many states. Her foreignness was an issue, even though she was a naturalized Indian citizen and heir to the Gandhi-Nehru legend. She had never held elective office. Her inexperience proved costly in April 1999 when she worked to topple the government headed by the rival Hindu nationalist party, boasting that she had the votes to form a Congress-led coalition but failing to do so. In the October 1999 election, the Congress party won barely a fifth of the seats in parliament, its worst defeat.

As the Congress party declined, up rose the Bharatiya Janata (Indian People's) party (BJP, founded 1982). This was only one of a network of Hindu identity movements, of which the oldest was the National Volunteer Corps (RSS in Hindi, founded 1925), out of which Mahatma Gandhi's assassins came. In contrast to the secularism enshrined in the Congress party and in India's constitution, arguably good for a multireligious, multiethnic country, the Hindu national-

ism of BJP supporters at first raised conflict levels alarmingly. Hindu militants' destruction of a sixteenth-century mosque at Ayodhya in 1992, built on a site many Hindus considered sacred, not only violated the constitution but touched off violence across India and left thousands dead. Still, after the 1998 and 1999 elections, BJP leader Atal Behari Vajpayee became prime minister not once but twice. He had proven more adroit than Sonia Gandhi in forming coalitions with small parties, promising in the process not to pursue policies offensive to secularists and Muslims. Vajpayee had also done things that appealed to a lot of Indians. Under him, India conducted its first nuclear tests in May 1998, prompting Pakistan to do likewise but also allaying Indian security worries about China. He engaged in a conflict with Pakistan over the contested border territory of Kashmir, but he also took steps to ease tensions, making an official visit to Pakistan. Both BJP and Congress were turning into large centrist parties, neither one able to rule by itself at the national level.

By the late 1990s, regional and caste-based parties dominated some states and held the balance of power nationally. The BJP government fell in spring 1999 when the state party from Tamil Nadu in the south, headed by former actress Jayalalitha Jayaram, withdrew. In the northern state of Uttar Pradesh, long a Congress bulwark, Mayawati, a dalit woman politician, mobilized low-caste voters behind her Majority Society party, while high-caste Hindus shifted to the BJP. Essential for such changes were laws reserving percentages of the seats on local councils (*panchayats*) for women, and part of those for women of low caste. Initiated in the more progressive states, this reform became national policy in 1993. Affirmative action policies providing for dalits to attend university or hold government jobs had made possible the rise of politicians like Mayawati. In the 1990s, India even acquired its first dalit president, K. R. Narayanan. Given that 3.5 percent of India's population belonged to the highest Brahmin

Indian women voting at Bahadurgarh, near New Delhi, February 1998. *Sherwin Crasto/©* *AP-Wide World Photos*

caste, while 16 percent were dalits, the implications of democratization in India were clear. The BJP's high-caste leaders might claim to represent all Hindus, but they would face challenges from dalits and low-caste Hindus as well as from Muslims or Sikhs.

The greatest challenge for all Indians was that human development lagged political democratization. More impressive in their achievements than ever, India's elites formed the second-largest English-speaking pool of technical expertise in the world, became leading entrepreneurs in Silicon Valley as well as in India, did much of the computer work and even ran telephone call-centers for U.S. business, reformed the country's economic policies, and reinvested billions in India. Yet many of India's 33 million widows, often still young and with no support but unwilling in-laws, depended on

charity to survive. Its high-tech success stories created fewer jobs for the less educated than the kind of industries, like textiles, that China favored. Female infanticide remained so prevalent that in some locales, the female-to-male ratio stood as low as 600 to 1,000; midwives earned more for killing a baby girl than for delivering a son. As the politics of caste, religion, gender, and ethnicity replaced common-front mobilization behind the Congress party, and as many Indians profited from the era of globalization, Indian inequalities survived, breached at points but still entrenched.

China Under the Communists

In number of people affected and depth of change, China has undergone the greatest revolution in history. It bears the mark of Mao Zedong (Mao Tse-tung, 1893–1976) to an exceptional degree, but his was never the only influence. In a sense, events since 1945 only continued the crisis touched off at the start of this century by the collapse of China's two-thousand-year-old synthesis of imperial state and Confucian culture. The crisis was not easy to end.

In the long run, Mao did better at revolution making than at state building. After the Communist triumph in the civil war of 1946–1949, the People's Republic of China (PRC) evolved through four phases: first, revolution under Communist rule (1949–1953); then the "socialist transformation" (1953–1961), which ran through the Great Leap Forward; next the "second revolution" (1962–1976), which climaxed in the Great Proletarian Cultural Revolution; and finally, the period of economic liberalization and "market socialism." Through these phases, the PRC went far toward creating a mass-mobilizing authoritarian state that was economically egalitarian and development oriented. The human costs were high, however; and the post-Mao "market socialism" eroded the old egalitariarism.

The First Phase of Communist Rule, 1949–1953

Outwardly, the second common front between Chiang Kai-shek's Guomindang (GMD) and the Chinese Communist party (CCP), formed in 1937, united China against Japanese invasion. Inwardly, competition between China's two nationalist movements persisted. At war's end, the United States, hoping to see China become a great power under the Nationalists, mediated an agreement between GMD and CCP. The agreement collapsed, and China lapsed into civil war in 1946. The GMD had many advantages, including larger forces (3 million fighters initially) and more foreign aid. But the Communists had a disciplined party, politically indoc- trinated military forces (1 million strong), command of guerrilla tactics, and commitment to mobilize the peasantry. Defeated on the mainland in 1949, Chiang and his supporters retired to Taiwan, which remained under GMD rule as the Republic of China. The CCP, with a 1947 membership of 2.7 million, had won control of a nation of almost 600 million people.

The period from the proclamation of the People's Republic in 1949 to 1953 formed a consolidation phase. Mao believed that China must have a "democratic revolution" before its socialist revolution. In this New Democracy phase, a common-front coalition including noncommunists would embody the "people's democratic dictatorship." While private property survived at first, the CCP was already restructuring Chinese life. It developed a triple organizational base of party, army, and government. The party controlled policy and had a hierarchical organization, from the Central Committee under Mao down to the village. To mobilize the populace, the regime created mass organizations, often with scores of millions of members, for such groups as youth, women, and peasant members of agricultural cooperatives.

Economically, the Communists had to cope with the damage done by years of war. The first task was to restore infrastructure and control inflation. To achieve land reform, cadres (party workers) then went into the villages, rousing villagers to stage public "trials" of landlords and redistribute their land. The Communists repeatedly used such methods to mobilize people for specific objectives. Tens of millions of families acquired land for the first time by becoming swept up in acts of collective violence that cost millions of lives. Their landownership did not last long. The organization of cooperatives soon began, with full collectivization to follow. Unlike Brazil or India, China restructured rural society as it modernized agriculture.

Social and cultural reform began with attacks on the family system idealized in Confucianism. The marriage law of 1950 equalized marriage and property rights for men and women. Though still emphasizing the family unit in many ways, the Communists encouraged children to denounce their parents as enemies of the revolution, rather than obey them blindly. Amid the patriotic fervor of the Korean War (1950–1953), denunciation of neighbors and relatives crescendoed into a reign of terror. The Communists insisted that literature and art serve political ends. They also widely employed thought-reform techniques—called "brainwashing" in Chinese slang—originally used to discipline the party. Individuals were drawn into a group, exposed to Mao's thought, and excited with a sense of belonging. Intense psychological pressure then created a fear of rejection and humiliation that led them to submit to indoctrination, repudiating old ideas and loyalties for Mao's new orthodoxy.

Industrialization was a major economic goal. China's foreign economic relations had previously focused on Japan, Europe, and the United States. After 1950, the Communists turned toward the USSR and tried to industrialize along Soviet lines, with Soviet technical assistance and loans, which they had to repay by exporting raw materials. The strategy worked poorly. China's economy was less developed in 1950 than the USSR's had been at the start of its first Five-Year Plan in 1928, and China's resources differed greatly.

The Socialist Transformation, 1953–1961

Like Stalin, Mao concluded that the resources for industrialization must come from agriculture and that collectivization was the way to extract them. The CCP ordered agricultural producers' cooperatives formed in 1953 and full collectives in 1955. Farm families lost their shares in the cooperatives and became wage laborers, though they retained small plots for their own use. By 1957, Chinese agriculture had been reorganized into about 800,000 collectives, averaging from 600 to 700 people each.

As collectivization progressed, the government began to nationalize business and industry. The first Five-Year Plan (1953–1957) projected heavy industrialization, with much slower growth in agriculture and consumer goods. Under the plan, China's industrial growth became the fastest in Asia.

By 1956, however, collectivization had run into trouble because of peasant reluctance, lack of qualified cadres, and disagreement in the Central Committee. Mao—ever enthusiastic for revolution—was unhappy at backtracking. Anxious to mobilize China's mostly Western-educated intellectuals and improve party discipline, he called for freer criticism of party and government under the classical phrase "Let a hundred flowers bloom."

At first intellectuals did not respond, but after repeated prompting, they loosed an unexpected torrent of criticism, which the government cut off in 1957 with an "anti-rightist" purge. Many intellectuals and cadres were subjected to "downward transfer" to the villages to end their "separation from the masses" and to boost agricultural output. The experience exposed important tensions among the leaders over the value of "mental" versus "manual" labor and of "expertise" as opposed to "redness" (ideological commitment).

Mao's solution to agricultural productivity problems expressed his revolutionary romanticism. China must mobilize the people's energies for a Great Leap Forward in industry and agriculture. Industrialization must be decentralized and combined with agriculture by merging the collectives into communes of twenty-thousand people or more. Private plots and most other personal possessions must go. Commune members would be organized into production brigades and teams that would work twenty-eight days a month. Children would be cared for in day nurseries, so that women could work full-time. Nothing better symbolized the Leap than the "battle for steel," the attempt to decentralize steel production in thousands of improvised furnaces scattered about the country.

Mao's approach to building communism proved too long on redness and too short on expertise. People could not stand the pace. For peasants used to performing all the tasks on small holdings, labor in production brigades performing a single task over a large, unfamiliar area proved very difficult. The decentralization of industry also backfired. Most products of the "battle for steel" were unusable. Many furnaces dissolved in the rain. In fact, the Leap plunged China into depression. The Leap's impact on agriculture caused an estimated 16 to 30 million additional deaths (2 to 4 percent of the population) between 1958 and 1960. Eventually, the 24,000 large communes were subdivided into 74,000 smaller ones.

China's leaders disagreed as never before about how to combine social and economic development. Senior functionaries more practical-minded than Mao—notably Liu Shaoqi (Liu Shao-ch'i), first vice chairman of the Central Committee and Mao's chosen successor, and

Deng Xiaoping (Teng Hsiao-p'ing), party general secretary—eased Mao out as chairman of the People's Republic, though he remained party chairman. Gradually, too, they shifted policy, restoring private peasant plots in 1962.

The Second Revolution, 1962–1976

Liu and Deng thought the time had come for organization and expertise, but Mao thought the party needed to change, either from within or by external force. He tried the first approach in 1962 with a Socialist Education Movement, under which many cadres and intellectuals were transferred downward to work among the peasants. Mao blamed the disappointing results on sabotage by people like Liu.

By 1965, Mao was ready to try changing the party from without. He launched the Great Proletarian Cultural Revolution to destroy the "four olds" (ideology, thought, customs, and habits) and complete the "transition from socialism to communism." Mao used the media to attack backers of Liu and Deng. He relied on the army, intensively indoctrinated under Marshal Lin Biao (Lin Piao), defense minister since 1959. Mao also mobilized youth, forming groups of teenagers into Red Guards—at least 13 million of them—by 1966. Mao charged them to "bomb the headquarters" of Liu and Deng. Armed with the little red books of quotations from Chairman Mao Zedong, the Red Guards bypassed the party and its Youth League to launch a reign of terror. Probably because of Mao's age and infirmity, his wife, Jiang Qing (Chiang Ch'ing), rose to a controlling position in the arts, media, and education. Attacked as "capitalist roaders" (advocates of moving China onto a capitalist road to development), Liu and Deng were toppled, and Lin Biao became first vice chairman of the Central Committee and Mao's heir-apparent.

The Cultural Revolution created for young Chinese some of the excitement that the Long March of 1935 had given their elders. The youth

of other countries also noticed: Chairman Mao's mobilization of young people to attack China's political and intellectual leaders helped inspire the global student activism of the late 1960s. In fact, the Red Guards included various interests: children of peasants, who felt they had been denied a fair chance for advancement; children of party functionaries, who sought to preserve their advantages; children of former landlords, who joined in attacking government offices in hopes of destroying records of their families' past. Soon, the Red Guards were fighting each other as much as the "four olds." By 1967, even Mao thought it was time to use the army to restrain the Guards. As millions of students followed party cadres in "downward transfer," the shock troops of the Cultural Revolution suffered the same fate as its enemies.

The Cultural Revolution lasted into Mao's last years, causing vast disruption despite some gains. Higher education was in disorder for a decade. Purging "proletarian culture" of foreign and traditional Chinese influences, Jiang Qing persecuted many artists and writers. On the other hand, Mao's zeal to close the urban-rural gap led to major advances in public health. China trained 1.6 million paramedics, or "barefoot doctors," and over 3 million health workers between 1966 and the late 1970s. Remarkably, economic growth continued despite the turmoil. GNP in 1970 was 40 percent higher than in 1965.

By 1969, efforts were underway to rebuild the party. Policy changes followed, such as normalization of relations with the United States in the 1970s. Deng Xiaoping re-emerged in 1973. But confusion lingered at the top. Mao tried to ease out Marshal Lin Biao, whose status as heir-apparent contradicted the rule of party control of the military. According to the official account, Lin then attempted a military coup in 1971 but failed and died while trying to escape to the Soviet Union. A new purge followed to discredit Lin. Jiang Qing and her associates—later derided as the Gang of Four—tried to continue the Cultural Revolution. She also aimed to become her husband's political heir.

Economic Liberalization

Mao died in 1976, shortly after Zhou Enlai (Chou En-lai, PRC premier since 1949). In the succession struggle, an opposing coalition first toppled the Gang of Four. Then a shakeout followed among coalition members. The Cultural Revolution officially ended in 1977. By 1980–1981, party vice chairman Deng Xiaoping (1904–1997) had become China's most important leader. Already old, he had survived the Long March, opposed the Great Leap, and endured disgrace under the Cultural Revolution and the Gang of Four.

With long memories of his hectic past, Deng faced the tasks of institutionalizing the Communist regime so as to end China's decades-long crisis of authority, charting a new course for economic development, and restoring the party unity shattered by the Cultural Revolution. Deng set about his tasks with the practical-mindedness that had made Mao distrust him. In many ways, Deng seemed successful, especially to foreigners. Then, in the spring of 1989, the bloody outcome of student demonstrations in Beijing exposed deep contradictions among his policies.

Signs of a new era had appeared by 1980–1981, in the last phase of the power struggle surrounding Deng's rise. The Mao personality cult gave way to criticism of Mao, and the Gang of Four was tried on charges stemming from the Cultural Revolution. Jiang Qing's claim that she acted only on Mao's orders turned her case into a virtual trial of her late husband. Yet the Deng regime could not repudiate Mao. He had been both China's Lenin and its Stalin: his "policy errors" of 1957–1976 might be repudiated, but an ideal image had to be saved to legitimate the regime. Henceforth, Deng and the party would interpret "Marxism–Leninism–Mao Zedong Thought" and restrain "leftist extremists."

Deng's key problem was the same one that faced reformers in other socialist countries in the 1980s. He masterminded economic reforms aimed at retaining the essential controls of a command economy while also allowing small private businesses to re-emerge and reopening China to foreign investment. To gain new technology, China expanded its foreign trade, especially with Japan. Dismantling the communes made the shift toward a market economy clearest in the countryside. To feed the people and raise capital for development, Deng offered peasants incentives, including the right to farm specific tracts of land under contract. Such stimuli, along with adoption of new technology, increased China's grain production by nearly half between 1976 and 1984. When most countries no longer could, the world's most populous nation still fed itself, increasing food supplies per person by one-third during the 1980s.

In China as in other socialist countries, however, economic liberalization raised hopes of political and cultural liberalization, which occurred only to a limited extent. For example, while dissidents still faced trouble, ordinary people could now busy themselves with non-political pursuits, as they could not under Mao. Deng rehabilitated mental labor, citing the need for scientists and technicians. The universities resumed operating, but China's secondary and university-level schools could still accommodate only a fourth of all applicants. Cultural life became freer. Even Confucianism, attacked under Mao, again enjoyed official interest.

Deng had seemed to favor democratization at times on his way to power, but anyone who thought he truly favored it was in for a shock. He might use market forces to boost production. As Marx wrote, society must pass through a capitalist stage before achieving socialism; China had skipped that stage and might need something of it. If Deng was a "capitalist roader" to that extent, however, his goals remained so-

Map 17.1 South and East Asia, 1990s

cialist. As he stated to party leaders in 1986: "Without leadership by the Communist Party and without socialism, there is no future for China. . . . Bourgeois liberalization means rejection of the Party's leadership; there would be nothing to unite our one billion people, and the Party itself would lose all power."[1]

During the 1980s, foreigners, and many Chinese, lost sight of this point. Economic and cultural change gave various groups a sense of empowerment—peasants, business people, students, intellectuals. Deng had not restructured politics to give them channels for real participation, but he also had not restored the party's authority as wielded before the Cultural Revolution. Deng's lack of interest in ideology demoralized party members, many of whom had no expertise aside from "redness." With Deng

距1997年7月1日

■■2天

■■■13557■秒

举办单位
新华社《中国名牌》杂志社   中国南方航空动力机械公司
中国革命博物馆   山东济宁菱花味精集团
一九九四年十二月十九日
                        诚信中央全息体(CCDI.)

Hong Kong reverts to Chinese sovereignty, July 1997. *Chinese soldiers
photograph each other in front of the countdown clock, Tienanmen
Square, Beijing. Greg Baker/© AP-Wide World Photos*

telling the public that "getting rich is glorious," officials and party functionaries began using their power to enrich themselves. Party and government sank into corruption and ineffectiveness. Startling results followed. Revenues fell as Chinese bent on getting rich ceased to pay taxes. A generational cleavage opened as the young lost interest in the party. The party became divided between "conservatives," authoritarians who opposed liberalization, and "liberals," some of whom preached a "new authoritarianism," arguing that China would develop faster with a strongly centralized government like Taiwan's or South Korea's.

With the gap between economic liberalization and political decay as backdrop, the seventieth anniversary of the May Fourth Movement (see Chapter 4) set the stage for confrontation in 1989. The 1919 movement had marked a milestone in the politicization of young Chinese and in the rise of nationalism. The regime planned a commemoration, omitting one of the original slogans: democracy. Students made their own plans, resulting in mass demonstrations in Beijing's Tienanmen Square and elsewhere, supported by many nonstudents. Faced with student hunger-strikers who said they would rather die than live without democracy, the government hesitated, then called troops into Beijing and declared martial law. "Conservative" premier Li Peng presided over what followed. The troops opened fire on June 4, massacring hundreds, perhaps thousands. Thousands were arrested; some were summarily executed.

Within another two years, Communist control collapsed almost everywhere else, but China still hewed to the path it had followed before Tienanmen. In 1993, Deng sought to ensure continuity by having his idea of the "socialist market economy" written into the constitution and giving top positions to several slightly younger men, chiefly Jiang Zemin, who became state president (he already controlled the party and the military).

As Chinese looked forward to regaining control of Hong Kong in 1997, China's economy was booming more than ever, with growth in GNP per person averaging 9.2 percent for 1990–1998. Foreign investment flooded into China, especially its port cities: $81.4 billion in 1994 alone. Foreign firms had liked China as a low-cost, high-quality production site in the 1980s. Rising incomes now made them value it as the world's largest consumer market, where five U.S.-based firms had sales exceeding $100 million each in 1994. China's exports, too, were growing, as evidenced by a trade surplus with the United States that grew from nothing in the mid-1980s to $57 billion a year by 1998.

Stated in terms of purchasing power (the purchasing power parity, or PPP, method of cal-culation) China's 1999 GNP of $4.1 trillion ranked second in the world. Stated without the adjustment for differences in purchasing power, Japan still had the second-largest GNP ($4.1 trillion in conventional dollars), and China came only seventh ($980 billion by this calculation). By either reckoning, when population was taken into account, Japan's GNP per person was very high, while China's was quite low. Most Chinese were far from rich; still, they had gained from the changes under Deng. In fact, if early 1990s growth rates continued, by 2010, China would regain the status it enjoyed for most of its history as the world's largest economy.

Deng's death in 1997, however, coincided with a slowdown that disclosed numerous uncertainties about China's economic prospects. By then, Uyghur Turks in China's Xinjiang Province were joking that the government, which used to say only socialism could save China, had started saying only China could save socialism. With time, the contradictions between China's economic and political paths indeed became more troublesome. By 2000, a deflationary economic crisis had set in. Consumer prices had been falling for two years; unemployment stood at 10 percent in urban areas and 30 percent in the hinterland. People hoarded what money they had, not only for fear of unemployment, but also because health care was no longer free. Praised ten years earlier for bringing longer, healthier lives to its people, China by 2000 had become one of the most unequal developing countries in access to health care (the United States was the most unequal of developed countries). Outside the southeastern coastal region, private enterprise remained limited, accounting for only a fifth of economic output and employment, with lack of capital a critical obstacle to company formation. Despite peasants' gains in independence, the state still owned the land, state firms bought the grain, landholdings were too small for efficient production, and the tax burden was higher than many farmers could support. Yet a rigid system of residence permits made it impossible to migrate freely inside China in search of opportunity and subjected those who went to the cities illegally to many disabilities, including unequal access to education for their children. All social problems, from female infanticide and child abandonment to an unacknowledged AIDS epidemic among people who sold blood to make money, were worse in the countryside, where some observers likened recent conditions to the inequalities of the 1930s, albeit at higher levels for all. It was no wonder that Chinese sought solace in movements like Falun Dafa. At the top, Li Peng, who had authorized the bloody repression of the Tienanmen demonstrators in 1989, a decade later still said there would be "zero tolerance" for opposition.

Contrasts between India and China have long fascinated observers of Asia. In the Mao era, China was not democratic politically but was more so than India in terms of social and economic change to improve ordinary people's lives. Yet despite India's stark inequalities, the fact that its governments were democratically elected meant that they could not become as unresponsive to distress as Mao did during the Great Leap Forward, or else they would lose the next election. Education offers another contrast: India did better in educating its elites; China did better in achieving mass literacy. India displayed regional variations so wide that some states, like Kerala in the south, achieved higher levels of social and economic development than China. In the 1980s, it seemed as if the bases laid down in the Mao period would enable Deng's "market socialism" to continue providing improvements for more of the people than in India. China's 1998 Human Development Index of 0.706, compared to India's 0.506, suggested that this was still the case, although the stresses that China displayed in development and democratization left open the question of whether the gap would widen or narrow.

If China's rapid growth raised questions about the mismatch between its politics and economics, so did the adequacy of China's resource base to sustain this growth. Home to 22 percent of world population, China had much smaller shares of vital resources such as cropland (7 percent of the world total), fresh water (7 percent), coal (11 percent), or oil (2 percent). Having long sustained its population through intensive agriculture, China put its self-sufficiency at risk by headlong economic transformation. Resource-poor Japan sustained its growth and prosperity by consuming vast amounts of resources from elsewhere in the world, as we shall see. Ultimately, as China looked toward becoming the world's largest national economy, ecological clouds overshadowed that prospect: Earth could not support 1.3 billion Chinese on the same scale as 127 million Japanese.

Japan: Re-emergence and Pre-eminence

When U.S. atomic bombs fell on Japan in 1945, its phenomenal rise seemed all undone. The war left 2 million Japanese dead, 40 percent of Japan's cities, its industry, and its agriculture in ruins. Yet Japan rose again to world power. The postwar U.S. occupation played a part in this revival, but the Japanese people's qualities were more important. Third in the world in GNP by 1970, Japan outstripped the Soviet Union by 1985 and became second in GNP only to the United States. Even if China would overtake Japan in time, for a country 10 percent smaller than California, with no significant natural resources, such an achievement excited global admiration. Increasingly since 1989, Japan has also faced difficulties. Both its difficulties and its successes reflect Japan's exceptional adaptation to tightening global interdepencence.

Reconstruction Under U.S. Occupation

Japan's reconstruction began under the nominally Allied, but actually U.S., occupation. Many changes made then produced lasting benefits, partly because they coincided with a new Japanese consensus for reconstruction, democratization, and demilitarization. Political reform began with prosecution of top war leaders. The emperor renounced the divine status that had been attributed to him, and a new constitution took effect in 1947. It transferred sovereignty from the emperor to the people, renounced war "forever," transformed the government into a British-style cabinet system, and guaranteed fundamental human rights. Further reforms mandated women's equality, extended the number of years of compulsory schooling, and tried to make higher education less elitist. The changes stopped far short, however, of the way Germany repudiated its wartime leaders and policies. As a result, Japan's Ministry of Education continued to teach that the war was not one of aggression and that Japan was never a colonial power. Japan's war record continued to create political and diplomatic problems decades later.

Like the U.S. New Deal, the occupation did give many Japanese a bigger stake in Japan's postwar order. One important reform was to break up the *zaibatsu* firms that dominated the prewar economy. Some old company names survived, but new organizational forms emerged. The occupation authorities brought labor legislation up to international standards and encouraged unionization, regarding it as part of democracy.

In the countryside, land reform virtually eliminated absentee landlords and reduced the proportion of tenant-operated farms below 10 percent. Average farm size was henceforth only 2.5 acres. The reform created a more egalitarian rural society, and technical improvements made the small farms very efficient. Together with land reform, tax reform gave Japan one of the world's most equitable income distributions. Equalizing the distribution not just of income but also of assets like land contributed vitally to Japan's later economic dynamism.

After the occupation ended in 1952, Japan continued to depend on the United States for aid and defense. A bilateral security pact provided for U.S. bases in Japan, and most Japanese remained opposed to large-scale rearmament. Low military spending became a factor in Japan's economic growth.

The Emergence of an Economic Superpower

In Japan's postoccupation era, economic growth became—even more clearly than in other countries—the driving force in its development. Prime Minister Shigeru Yoshida (1946–1947, 1948–1954) adopted policies designed to promote Japan's rebuilding. Known as the Yoshida Doctrine, these policies remained in place for the next forty years. Key points included limiting military spending, following the U.S. lead on issues of security and international relations, favoring producers rather than consumers, and promoting exports. With ambitious targets set under these policies, Japan's real economic growth, net of inflation, averaged nearly 10 percent a year until the 1970s. At the time, only Israel was growing faster, by a fraction of a point.

The global growth of the first postwar quarter-century probably benefited Japan more than any other country. Growth became a virtual religion. The Japanese took pride in international recognition of Japan's re-emergence, from the 1964 Tokyo Olympics to the Nobel prizes won by Japanese scientists. By 1970, Japan had begun to run trade surpluses, and its productive capacity had become almost as great as all the rest of Asia's.

Dependent on imports for most foodstuffs and for almost all energy and raw materials,

Japan suffered several shocks in the 1970s but responded well to them. Tensions had mounted in U.S.-Japanese relations since the late 1950s, as Japanese exports to the United States grew in volume, while U.S. exporters had trouble gaining access to Japan's markets. Facing serious balance-of-payments problems, partly because of the Vietnam War, the United States placed a 10 percent surcharge on imports in 1971 and suspended the convertibility of the dollar into gold. A U.S. embargo on soybean exports in 1973 further angered the Japanese, who depend on soybeans for protein. The United States also surprised the Japanese by announcing that President Nixon would visit the People's Republic of China. The Japanese had been led to expect consultation before such a reversal in China policy.

The oil shock that followed the 1973 Arab-Israeli war hit Japan especially hard. Dependent on imported petroleum for nearly three-fourths of its energy, Japan was more threatened than any other highly developed country by this crisis. Short-term effects of higher oil prices included negative trade balances and inflation. Average GNP growth fell to 5 percent per year for the 1970s.

The Japanese responded creatively to this new phase in their economic development. They searched for alternative energy sources. They moved away from heavy industries like steel and shipbuilding, which had eclipsed the light industries of the early postwar years, toward a new generation of "knowledge industries." These required less energy, less labor, and fewer raw materials and took advantage of Japan's high levels of skill and technology. Another reason for the change was that other East Asian economies, such as Taiwan and South Korea, were developing heavy industry and resented Japanese domination of their markets. The most important goal, however, was to move beyond importing and refining technologies developed elsewhere and to pioneer new technologies that Japan could export to earn

royalties. Quadrupling the funding of research and development, Japan became a technology exporter by 1980. In all, Japan probably adjusted more successfully than any other developed country to the new era of scarcity. Evidencing this successful adaptation, Japan's trade surplus mounted annually from $5 billion in 1981 to $86 billion in 1986, of which over $50 billion came from trade with the United States.

Under international pressure to redress such imbalances, Japan revalued the yen in 1985. Revaluation challenged Japan as had the shocks of the 1970s, but its responses opened a new growth period. The yen nearly tripled against the U.S. dollar, which bought 238 yen in 1985 but only 80 yen in 1995, a change that raised the price of Japanese exports but cheapened foreign goods for Japanese. The high yen thus made it easier for Japanese not only to import but also to invest abroad. They invested $21.7 billion in the United States in 1988 alone. For Japan's economic policy, revaluation implied a strategy aimed more at domestic rather than foreign markets. Austere living standards needed to rise. More foreign consumer goods needed to be allowed into the country, although the intricacy of Japan's market structures made that easier to say than do. The idea of creating a leisure economy in Japan prompted construction interests to invest heavily in theme parks and golf courses. With Japanese wages as high as U.S. or West German ones, revaluation required shifting some types of production to foreign labor markets. Now Japan began to undergo the "hollowing out" that U.S. or European industry had gone through with the shift from heavy industry to services. Japanese firms, however, cut costs so rigorously that Japan's exports began to rise in value again within a few years.

The late 1980s turned into a booming "bubble economy," which burst when the Tokyo stock market collapsed late in 1989, losing nearly $2 trillion (almost half of total market value) by 1993. Scandals linking major broker-age houses and the Finance Ministry to crime families (*yakuza*) further shook investor confi-dence. Land prices plunged, and the crisis spread to banking and manufacturing, causing layoffs and plant closings.

These events, about which more is said below, ended a boom; yet Japan's economy was still the world's second biggest. Japan's prob-lems were those of a mature, highly developed economy in an interdependent world. More than any other, Japan's had become a global economy, dependent worldwide for raw mater-ials and markets—a remarkable feat for a coun-try in ruins fifty years before.

Major Factors in Japan's Success

How had Japan done this? Many factors played a part. Land reform and income equalization during the occupation helped by stimulating agriculture and raising internal demand. So did limiting defense spending to 1 percent of GNP—a rate that still gave Japan the third-larg-est defense budget in the world. But some of the most important factors lie in the realm of busi-ness and government-business relations.

Commercial organization made a major dif-ference in Japan's growth. In place of the old *zaibatsu* firms, each a complex of interests dominating a single industry and controlled by a holding company, large-scale organizations known as *keiretsu,* or business groups, emerged by the 1960s. These grouped firms in different industries around a large bank or industrial firm. In the absence of anti-trust laws, the business groups could be very large. A key part of the group, the general trading company, conducted the group's foreign trade. Bigger than most U.S. export-import firms, the trading companies benefited from economies of scale and had large expert staffs. Because the business groups tended to raise capital internally instead of sell-ing shares, they were freer than U.S. firms to reinvest profits instead of paying dividends.

Having interests in several industries also made it easier for business groups to shift from fields where growth had slowed to others with better prospects.

Japanese labor relations, too, contributed to business success. Unions were typically com-pany unions, less militant than other industrial countries' industry-wide unions. Japanese cor-porations were less top-heavy than U.S. firms, less likely to segregate managers from workers, and keener on team spirit and corporate loyalty, qualities deep-rooted in Japanese society.

Though smaller than in other industrial countries, government also played a major role in Japan's economic development, In 1980, gov-ernment officials formed only 1.7 percent of Japan's working population, against 2.3 percent in the United States. Government revenues were also low; 22 percent of GNP in Japan in 1977; against 30 percent in the United States and 38 percent in West Germany. Partly because spending for defense and welfare was low, more of Japan's budget went for purposes that boosted the economy, like public works, on which so much was spent that Japan has been called a "construction state."

Fiscal conservatism enabled Japan to main-tain balanced budgets through 1966. After that, expanded welfare spending without offsetting tax increases produced an internal debt of $425 billion by 1983, roughly 60 percent as much debt per capita as in the United States at the time. One important consequence of histori-cally conservative government finance was Ja-pan's high savings rate: from 25 to 33 percent of GNP through the mid-1970s and still 19 percent in 1988 (in 1990, savings per household aver-aged $71,016 in Japan, compared to a U.S. rate of $28,125). Inducements to save included both low welfare spending and—until the 1988 tax reform—tax exemption for interest on postal savings accounts.

Special government agencies, particularly the Ministry of International Trade and Industry (MITI), played key roles in development. MITI led in targeting industries for development and phasing out others where Japan had lost its competitiveness. MITI worked with the large business groups, creating deliberative councils that brought officials and business leaders together to make policy, and preserving competition by bringing different firms together to work on any given project.

A distinctive approach to research and development underlay MITI-industry collaboration. Japan's funding for scientific research began to reach the level of other developed countries' only in the late 1960s. This was especially true of basic research, which tackles new problems for the advancement of science without immediate regard to practical applications. Basic research does more to advance science and industry in the long run, but applied research can yield huge profits. Having long stressed applied research more than basic, Japan reacted to criticism of its export surpluses and its history of exploiting others' discoveries by placing new emphasis on basic research. The founding of several cities for scientific research, starting with Tsukuba Science City, symbolized this thrust. Some key features of Japanese research did not change, however. Military priorities dominated U.S. research, but Japan's stayed consumer-oriented, and the private sector provided more of research funding—81 percent in 1985. MITI's capacity to lead declined by the late 1980s, once major firms had research budgets larger than its and the firms became less willing to share their findings. MITI responded by further emphasizing basic research.

Japan's industry-government collaboration would continue to face challenges, but the comparative significance of this collaboration was clear. Japan's pattern differed radically from communist economies, which eliminated competition for profits. It differed too from common Western ideas of the free market in that government helped chart the course of growth, rather than leaving the economy to itself or

intervening only to regulate it. The results spoke in Japan's favor.

Japanese Society and Economic Growth

Japan's postwar resurgence depended above all on its one abundant resource: its people. After the war, the Japanese faced daunting problems—food shortages, runaway inflation, unemployment, repatriation of 6 million Japanese from overseas, and a baby boom (1946–1948). But the same qualities that underlay Japan's earlier rise helped open an era of rapid growth.

With growth, certain social traits persisted. These included strong family ties and a sense of group solidarity recalling that of village life. Many Japanese assumed their commitment to their employers was for life, although in fact only a third of Japan's workers worked in large firms that guaranteed career-long employment. Tradition also affected the lives of Japanese women, despite legal equality. Until recently, most who worked when young withdrew into family life after marriage. An emphasis on education was another tradition that helped ensure Japan a highly qualified labor force. Examination pressures produced occasional student violence against teachers or even suicide; yet these remained less common than other types of youth-related problems familiar in the United States. Finally, while some other Asian societies were losing their traditional arts and crafts, the Japanese retained many of theirs—rich sources of distinctive design and workmanship.

In time, kimonos and scroll paintings became affordable luxuries for people among whom, by the 1960s, 80 to 90 percent saw themselves as middle class. Japanese men aspired to the image of the white-collar "salary man" employed by a large corporation. Population growth fell to about 1 percent per year by the 1970s, before declining to 0.2 percent in 1996. Low growth created a labor shortage. Despite ethnocentric reluctance to import workers, several hundred thousand foreign workers had reportedly entered Japan by the early 1990s. Rising wages and scarce workers provided reasons to emphasize the knowledge industries, automation, and robotics.

Meanwhile, urbanization progressed. The rural population fell to 8 percent of the total in 1989, down from 50 percent in the 1940s. Many rural Japanese combined work in town with agriculture. As the cities grew, the largest grew fastest. The population of greater Tokyo reached 8 million in the 1960s and 17 million by 1984, when it was the world's largest city.

The reduction in Japan's birth rate occurred voluntarily, reflecting the shift in attitudes that has accompanied urbanization and the rise of the middle class the world over. People came to prefer having few children so that family resources could be concentrated on their education and placement in society. With this shift in attitude, the proportion of students receiving higher education rose between 1965 and 1989 from 13 to 31 percent.

Rapid social change had its troublesome side effects. Severely crowded—half the population lived in 2 percent of the land area—Japanese remained poorly housed by European or U.S. standards. Yet housing costs were far higher in relation to income than in the United States or Europe. During the late 1980s, Japanese land prices rose to 75 times higher than U.S. prices. As in Third World supermetropolises, many workers spent as much as four hours a day commuting. Park lands and public facilities of all types were scarce, and industrial pollution was a familiar problem.

Urbanization and other factors took their toll on the extended family. By the 1980s, nuclear families (not including grandparents) accounted for 60 percent of Japan's 36 million households. But low public spending on welfare meant that the need for family support remained strong. Many workers had company health and retirement plans. National health insurance was instituted in 1961. The government expanded benefits by deficit financing, however. Demographic trends also threatened the stability of benefit programs because the percentage of the population aged sixty-five or over was growing faster than in the United States or many European countries.

Rapid change and the increasing isolation of the individual produced displays of alienation especially among the young. In 1960, leftist university students staged demonstrations—in which many other Japanese joined—against ratification of the new U.S.-Japanese security treaty. In 1968, student violence flared again, primarily directed against the poorly financed universities. A radical fringe group, the Japanese Red Army, remained active in international terrorism into the 1970s. In 1995, a doomsday cult, Aum Shinrikyu, shocked Japan by staging a nerve-gas attack in the Tokyo subway. By then, the collapse of the 1980s "bubble economy" had revealed socioeconomic strains that will require further comment below.

Political Consensus: Rise and Decline

For almost forty years, economic growth sustained an extraordinary political consensus. Postwar Japan produced many political movements, but by the mid-1950s these had sorted out into what has been called a one-and-a-half party system. From its coalescence in 1955 until the election of July 1993, the Liberal Democratic party (LDP), actually a conservative party, dominated every government. The next-largest party, the Japan Socialist party (JSP), polled fewer votes, and Japan had no leftist prime minister after 1948.

Japan is a constitutional monarchy with a government led by a prime minister. Within this system, distinctively Japanese realities prevail. We have already noted the policy framework known as the Yoshida Doctrine: an export-oriented industrial policy favorable to producers rather than consumers, and low military spending under the U.S. security umbrella. What really ruled Japan was a combination of interests known as the "iron triangle." At one corner stood big business, which supported the LDP by giving money and mobilizing employee votes. At the second corner stood the LDP, which influenced business by granting contracts or stalling legislation on topics businessmen disliked, like product liability. At the third corner stood the bureaucracy, which regulated business and was much more powerful than the politicians. Japan's bureaucracy was proportinately smaller than those of the United States or Germany, but its interference in the economy was very extensive, and vaguely worded laws enabled regulators to favor firms that backed the LDP. Carefully controlled markets also helped to limit foreign competition inside Japan and thus to support the widespread prosperity that gave most Japanese a stake in this system. Leadership came not so much from the government as from within the triangle, and prime ministers tended to produce less individual impact than in other countries.

In time the LDP yielded to the temptations of power and had to pay for its misdeeds. In April 1989, during the "bubble economy," a scandal over political contributions toppled Prime Minister Noboru Takeshita. In the July 1989 elections, the LDP met its first electoral defeat, as the JSP, then led by Takako Doi, the first woman to head a Japanese political party, won control of the upper house of parliament. Over the next two years, the JSP challenge faded, and the LDP remained in power. Yet scandals continued, climaxing in 1992–1993 with revelations that Shin Kanemaru, head of patronage for the biggest LDP faction, had taken money from a firm with mob ties and had over $50 million stashed in his home and office.

Ordinary Japanese were stunned to see corruption so extreme. The Kanemaru scandal raised an outcry, followed by splits in the LDP. In the 1993 election, the LDP retained more parliamentary seats than any other party but lost control of the government for the first time since 1955. The new government of Prime Minister Morihiro Hosokawa was an anti-LDP coalition of conservatives and socialists. Formation of this government looked like a turning point. A younger generation had come to power. Women assumed three cabinet posts, more than ever before, and Takako Doi became speaker of the lower house of parliament. Policy debate became more open; and members of the new cabinet talked of changing every aspect of the LDP system, the Yoshida Doctrine, and the "iron triangle." From one faction or another came proposals to apologize to other Asian countries for World War II, review constitutional limits on joining collective security arrangements, deregulate the economy, open Japan's rice market, and end corporate political donations.

As of 2000, the hopes for restructuring were still mostly hopes. The Hosokawa government fell after eight months, and the LDP soon regained power. Prime Minister Keizo Obuchi (1998–2000) shifted emphasis from long-term structural reform to a deficit-financed $400-billion plan to restart the economy and recapitalize the banks, policies continued by his successor after he died from a stroke. In the June 2000 elections, the LDP barely kept control of the lower house of parliament. Voters were losing faith in the party that since 1955 had governed Japan for all but eighteen months, but they did not yet trust any other party enough to give it more than a quarter of the seats in parliament. Nor had the younger generation inside the LDP yet managed to eclipse its old guard, which, to judge from its endless scandals or the decade-old economic crisis, had become part of Japan's problem.

The End of Hegemony

Japan's situation in the 1990s suggested not only that its postwar system had reached exhaustion but also that the era when one national economy could retain hegemonic status in the world had passed. The 1993 corruption scandal was far from the last. Revelations of police incompetence and corruption, including ignoring violence by the Aum Shinrikyu cult for years before its 1995 nerve-gas bombing in the Tokyo subway, eroded public trust. Health Ministry officials, perhaps in collusion with drug companies, ignored warnings that blood supplies were contaminated with the HIV virus, causing many Japanese hemophiliacs to die of AIDS. The 1995 Kobe earthquake, in a place experts had proclaimed safe from quakes, paralyzed the government and caused six thousand deaths, many of them avoidable. In 1999, a fuel-mixing accident at a nuclear power plant in Tokaimura produced radiation levels 10,000 to 20,000 times above normal and forced the evacuation of residents, most of whom did not know they lived next door to a nuclear facility. Japan's worst nuclear accident, this shook confidence in the nuclear power policy and mobilized unprecedented popular protest.

Japan had gotten out of past crises by expanding exports and spending on grandiose public works, and many of the key decisions—as in the case of the nuclear program—had been made out of public view. Vested interests had grown up around such policies. Japan's leadership in 2000 could still not stop reimplementing old formulas that had become counterproductive. As the birth rate fell, the population aged so much that the work force began to shrink in 1995 and some outlying localities became depopulated. Nevertheless, the government continued extending public works to remote locales. Although most bullet trains had lost money for years, in 2000 Japan launched a super-high-speed train, which went twice as fast (270 miles an hour) and required three times as much energy, even though residents of the locale the train served opposed it. The most important recent economic policies, the Obuchi stimulus package, greatly increased public debt. Soon, central government tax receipts could not cover debt service and pensions. Many local

governments were also bankrupt, efforts to bail out large banks cost over $200 billion, and the government had used the $3.8 trillion that thrifty Japanese had stashed in postal savings accounts for small business loans and works projects. Corporate bankruptcies, the virtual end of the system of lifetime employment, rising suicide rates, predictions that Japan would need 600,000 immigrants a year to maintain its work force, a surge of popular books about "individualism" and "personal responsibility," all signaled the need for a new start. Sociologists worried that the "third [postwar] generation" had never known hardship and were unwilling to work. Economists instead foresaw a "third revolution" (counting from the Meiji Revolution and post-1945 recovery), in which individual enterpreneurship, venture capital, and communications technologies, relying on handheld devices rather than personal computers, would launch a new growth wave.

It would take time to know which prediction was right. As they waited to see, world historians would also ask themselves whether the global pre-eminence that Britain exercised for over a century, that the United States enjoyed for a quarter-century after 1945, and that Japan enjoyed for a shorter time than that had vanished in a world of space-time compression.

The High-Performance Asian Economies

Several other Asian economies also achieved rapid growth, at least until financial crisis spread out of Thailand in 1997. The fastest growing were the four "little dragons": South Korea, Taiwan, Singapore, and Hong Kong, which reverted to Chinese sovereignty in 1997 but was supposed to remain economically distinct under a "one country-two systems" policy. The slower growing countries were Thailand, Malaysia, and Indonesia. Aside from the Euro-American democracies, these and Japan were the only economies in the world that had emerged from underdevelopment, if indeed all of these had. What explained their rise?

While they varied markedly in culture, these countries and Japan shared significant traits. After 1945, all of them had regimes that faced serious legitimacy problems, ranging from Japan's defeat in 1945 to imminent civil war among Malaysia's ethnic communities in 1969. And all these countries had to worry about repercussions of the Communist takeovers in China and North Korea. While the high-performance Asian economies were commonly authoritarian and repressive compared to the Euro-American democracies, their governments responded to their legitimacy problems with measures designed to spread the benefits of growth widely. These included not only measures that benefited the economic elites, such as the deliberation councils where government and business leaders joined in economic policy-making, but also others that gave common people a stake in the economy. Such mass-oriented policies included land reforms like those in Japan, Korea, and Taiwan; investment in rural infrastructure such as roads and bridges, which poor countries commonly neglect; educational policies that favored primary and secondary, as compared to higher, education much more than is common in developing countries; and income policies that produced some of the world's most egalitarian income distributions. Unlike the consumer subsidies that characterize the Third World version of the guarantor state, these policies amounted to transfers not of income or consumer goods but of assets that could further stimulate growth, either directly in the case of land reform and rural infrastructure, or indirectly in the case of policies that favored the rise of a healthy, skilled work force.

The egalitarian income distributions were especially important. If we compare the ratio between the shares of income going to the richest 20 percent and the poorest 20 percent of the population, these countries had ratios in the 1990s ranging from 3.4 for Japan and 5.2 for South Korea to 12 for Malaysia, compared to a 1996 ratio of 25.5 for Brazil. Globally and not just regionally significant, East Asia's record refutes the conventional economists' idea that high growth and income inequality must go together.

One critical feature of economic policy was that these countries early left behind the usual Third World development strategy of protectionist import substitution—if they ever subscribed to it. Japan targeted export-oriented growth from the 1940s on. South Korea abandoned import substitution for export-oriented industrialization in 1964, soon after the Park Chung Hee regime came to power. Corresponding policy shifts in Singapore and Indonesia occurred in 1963 and 1965. Most high-performance Asian economies had thus already accelerated their growth through export-led industrialization while other developing countries had still not yet seen the need for such a policy. This policy shift is vital, for productivity rises as production shifts from agriculture to manufacturing and from low-skill to high-skill manufacturing.

Governments' role in creating an environment that supports growth becomes clear in other respects, too. These regimes characteristically acted to secure property rights, even when their human rights records excited international criticism. They sought to assure a close fit between government and the economic elite through deliberation councils, like those in which the president of South Korea met with heads of the *chaebol*s (conglomerates) to set export targets. A particular priority was to establish an economic bureaucracy that would operate according to high professional standards, so creating a calculable operating environment for business and keeping inflation under better control than in most developing countries. Creating mechanisms through which government and business could collaborate to promote growth helped prevent one of the most common problems of underdevelopment, where businessmen seek to make money not by producing efficiently but by winning favors from the state ("rent-seeking," in economists' terms). Specific policies to promote small business were also adopted. In labor relations, the dominant note was to maintain government or company control over unions, neutralizing labor politically while meeting most of its demands. In Singapore, the National Wage Council, combining representatives of government, business, and labor, matched wage increases to productivity gains.

Financial crisis, beginning in Thailand in 1997, affected all these countries. Two years later, their stock markets were recovered somewhat, but underlying structural issues resembling Japan's—unsound banking practices and excessive corporate debt—remained unaddressed. Economic issues thus clouded future prospects for the Asian "tigers." Political issues, too, affected their future. Indonesia had experienced political as well as economic turmoil; Hong Kong had passed back under Chinese sovereignty; and the reunification of North and South Korea—which could have economic consequences more drastic than those of German reunification—began to seem more likely with South Korean president Kim Dae Jung's visit to the North in 2000. Still, for countries that had not developed comparably, the high-performance Asian economies provided some of the most important lessons that can be learned from recent world history.

Conclusion: The Fork in Asia's Developmental Road

After 1945, some Asian societies made the Third World's strongest bids for independence and reassertion. Their achievements depended on the same factors—with some further evolution—that governed the outcome of prewar independence struggles: adaptability to the tightening of global integration, maintenance of consensus about national identity and the organization of political life, governmental responsiveness to demands for mass participation in the benefits of change, and formulation of economic strategies to meet the people's needs and better the country's place in the world.

The post-1945 history of South and East Asia illustrates opposite extremes in responses to these factors. India and South Asia in general compose the region where both the status of women and overall human development—taking account of life expectancy, adult literacy, educational enrollment rates, and real incomes—are second lowest after Africa. India's free press and democratic government, characterized by high voter turnout and growing political influence for minorities, low-caste Hindus, and former Untouchables, creates bright spots in its record. Such, too, are the large technical elite, localized islands of high development, or the fact that a political system indifferent to mass distress in a way that would have shocked Mao yet has avoided the mass deaths from famine that his authoritarianism produced in China. The fact that India adhered to its protectionist import-substitution strategy until the early 1990s has further differentiated it from the high-performance Asian economies. Since then, however, economic restructuring and new political forces representing a wider range of social and regional interests have pointed toward a new era.

In terms of both women's status and overall human development, the performance of Southeast and East Asia is roughly midway between the performance of South Asia and of industrial countries elsewhere. Because it is still overall an underdeveloped country, in which market-oriented economic change began only after 1979, China presents a mixed profile. Mao's redistributive policies, by producing overall human development at a level nearly as high as that of rich industrial economies by some indicators, created essential bases for the post-Mao growth surge. By 2000, however, major questions confronting China focused on the character of the successor regime, how well it would conform to and support economic change, and how sustainable growth on such a scale would prove in a shrinking world.

Japan and the four "little dragons," did best in responding to globalization, in maintaining political consensus, partly by using economic policy as a means to that end, and in optimizing their economic and technological performance, domestically and in the world market. After 1989, Japan's lingering economic and political crisis indicated a need for significant structural reform and a new wave of Japanese-led technological innovation to restore high growth, although social changes associated with affluence and the aging of the population clouded this prospect. The "little tigers" also succumbed in 1997 to an economic crisis with traits resembling Japan's. Prior to the crisis, the high-growth Asian economies had convinced many analysts that what used to be called the Third World was no longer a single category because several Asian economies had risen out of underdevelopment. How well their performance sustains this assessment in the future, and how well Japan overcomes its crisis of the 1990s, will be very important for the world economy.

For the world historian, one key question about contemporary East Asia is easily overlooked in commenting on particular countries. As in the case of North America or Europe, if East Asia is to be a major center of productivity, how will it be configured? Considering that since 1975, U.S. trade across the Pacific has exceeded U.S. trade across the Atlantic in value, this question is especially important for the United States. While Japan has led the region in growth in recent decades, Japan's spectacular bid for hegemony flies in the face of thousands of years of Chinese pre-eminence in the region, suggesting, too, by its seeming exhaustion after 1989, that globalization may have ended the age

when one power can dominate the world system. Efforts at regional integration of the "Pacific rim" countries, along the lines of NAFTA or the European Union, have so far suffered from the tremendous diversity of this group of nations, especially when extended to include Australia or American nations bordering the Pacific, and from bad memories of Japanese aggression. Now that the "Pacific rim" has become as important in world affairs as the "Atlantic rim" was for the preceding five hundred years, East Asia will surely remain one of the world's centers of economic dynamism, perhaps even spreading its growth patterns by example to other developing countries. But East Asia will have problems of cohesion at least as great as those of North America or Europe.

Note

1. Quoted in the *Wall Street Journal,* June 16, 1989, p. A4.

Suggestions for Further Reading

India

Drèze, Jean, and Amartya Sen. *India: Economic Development and Social Opportunity* (1995).

Harriss-White, Barbara, and S. Subramanian, ed. *Illfare in India* (1999).

Lal, Deepak. *The Hindu Equilibrium.* Vol. 1, *Cultural Stability and Economic Stagnation: India, c. 1500 B.C.–A.D. 1980* (1988).

Rudolph, Lloyd I., and Suzanne H. Rudolph. *In Pursuit of Lakshmi: The Political Economy of the Indian State* (1987).

Wolpert, Stanley. *A New History of India.* 5th ed. (2000).

China

Davis, Deborah S., ed. *The Consumer Revolution in Urban China* (2000).

Far East Economic Review (Hong Kong).

Meisner, Maurice. *Mao's China and After: A History of the People's Republic* (1986).

Schram, Stuart. *The Thought of Mao Tse-tung* (1989).

Wang, James C. F. *Contemporary Chinese Politics*. 6th ed. (1999).

Japan

Hane, Mikiso. *Modern Japan: A Historical Survey*. 2d ed. (1992).

Ito, Takatoshi. *The Japanese Economy* (1992).

Iwao, Sumiko. *The Japanese Woman: Traditional Image and Changing Reality* (1993).

Kumagai, Fumie. *Unmasking Japan Today* (1996).

Look Japan (Tokyo).

McCormack, Gavan. *The Emptiness of Japanese Affluence* (1996).

Totman, Conrad. *A History of Japan* (2000).

High-Performance Asian Economies

Campos, Jose Edgardo, and Hilton L. Root. *The Key to the Asian Miracle: Making Shared Growth Credible* (1996).

Hofheinz, Roy, Jr., and Kent Calder. *The Eastasia Edge* (1982).

PART SIX

The World Today

CHAPTER 18

Toward the
Twenty-first Century

AS 1999 ENDED, THE WORLD AWAITED THE START OF A NEW CENTURY AND A NEW millennium. Would the hopes and fears that past prophets aroused about the idea of the millennium be fulfilled? Would the turnover on the calendar affect the world in more humdrum ways? Or might the calendar change make less difference than events before or after?

As the clock passed midnight on New Year's Eve in successive time zones, the worldwide electronic media broadcast the worldwide celebrations—the same fireworks bursting over changing scenes on the ground. Some broadcasters pointed out that technically, because of the way the Christian calendar count had started, the new millennium would not begin until 2001; but there seemed to be global consensus not to postpone the party. Less often did anyone note how extraordinary it was for what had begun as the religious calendar for one faith to have become a global standard. For Christians, 2000 might be the new "year of the Lord" (*anno domini,* A.D.), but it was also 2000 of what had become the world's "common era" (C.E.), part of the global apparatus of modernity, even for people like Jews and Muslims who had religious calendars in which a new millennium might not start for centuries. Was this a triumph for western civilization or just another part of a growing trend toward accepting globally agreed standards for doing things?

The start of preceding millennia, in both this and other calendars, had aroused widespread expectations about the end of the world. Such ideas were not absent this time, either. Yet now the most widespread worry was mundane: the "Y2K problem." If the "Y1K problem" had been the end of the world, the "Y2K problem" was its cybernetic equivalent, a data-processing apocalypse because software developers had not foreseen the need

Pope John Paul in Slovenia, 1999.   © *AFP/CORBIS*

to use more than two digits to record years. Globally, some $250 billion were spent to prevent computer-related disruptions in transportation, public utilities, financial transactions, defense, and so on. In any event, just as the real world did not end in 1000, the cyber world did not crash in 2000. Costly efforts kept that from happening and left lasting benefits in the form of computer systems that were better systematized and integrated.

Calendars and computers were not the only ways in which the global and the local intersected during the millennial year. Perhaps the institution most committed to observing the millennium was the Roman Catholic church. Pope John Paul II declared 2000 a Holy Year. A year-long series of events brought millions of pilgrims to Rome from all over the world and displayed the church's concern for many groups both within the fold—the young, the disabled, the poor—and without—Jews and others historically wronged in the name of religion. Embodying many keynotes of the late twentieth century—the growing visibility of the elderly, resurgent religious activism, anti-communism, public figures' vulnerability to terrorists' bullets—the Pope made a dramatic Holy Year pilgrimage to the Holy Land and also presided over a World Youth Day that drew two million young people to an open-air Mass in Rome. Papal calls for pardon included not only apologies to Jews but also calls on governments to reduce the poorest nations' debts, an idea shared by a global rainbow coalition of activists. Meanwhile, the Vatican demonstrated its market and media savvy by enlisting corporate sponsors for Holy Year events, organizing 70,000 volunteers to shepherd pilgrims, making marketing agreements for souvenirs from which the profits would subsidize poor pilgrims, authorizing a Los Angeles web-commerce firm to market reproductions from the Vatican Library, and publicizing Holy Year events over the Vatican website.

The millennial and global also threatened to come together less benignly. As 1999 ended, U.S. security forces monitored superpatriot and apocalyptic religious groups, making some arrests. Israeli security intercepted Christian millenarists coming to Jerusalem with apocalyptic expectations and plans. Alleged terrorist plots to disrupt crowded celebrations were discovered both in the United States and Jordan, with arrests in both countries. Those arrested had large amounts of bomb-making equipment, computer disks containing a ten-volume *Encyclopedia of Afghan Jihad,* intercontinental networks of connections, and plans directed at Christian pilgrims in Jordan and presumably also at New York City. Those arrested appear to have been followers of or inspired by Osama bin Laden, whom the United States blamed for the bombing of U.S. embassy buildings in Tanzania and Kenya in 1998 and for the bombing of a U.S. naval vessel in Aden harbor later in 2000.

To most historians, a new century had already begun with the collapse of communism (1989–1991). Some historians spoke of a "short twentieth century" that began in 1914. Others, taking crises like India's Great Mutiny (1857) or the U.S. Civil War (1861–1865) as reactions to a new stage in the tightening of global integration, spoke of a "long twentieth century" (1850–1991). For historians of either camp, the millenium celebrations may have been as much of a flash-in-the-pan as the fireworks that lit the sky. Yet they illustrated the complex interplay between the global and the local, the socioeconomic, the ecological, and the technological, that now forms the global context for the new era.

Globalization

Probably resulting more from space-time compression than from the Soviet collapse or the approach of 2000, signs of ending and beginning appeared all around. In the arts, for example, what had seemed "modern" in 1914 now seemed outdated. Although tall buildings continued to be built the world over, critics denounced the glass boxes and skyscrapers of modernism as dehumanizing, particularly when used to house the poor. Architecture was no longer about humankind overcoming nature; rather, in the information age, architecture needed to express the new struggle for human wisdom to triumph over mere knowledge, which humankind had once monopolized but now shared with computers and robots. In the visual arts, the abstraction that triumphed with Picasso and Matisse yielded ground partway to a new representationalism, but usually with ironic twists that challenged whether what seemed real was as it appeared. Andy Warhol's "pop" art reworkings of advertisements or movie stars' photos and Roy Lichtenstein's blowups of comic strip images helped start this trend in the 1960s and 1970s. A generation later, artists like Cindy Sherman and Barbara Kruger dissolved frontiers not only between art and popular culture, but also between media like painting and photography, and between "pure" art and feminist thought. Such art reflected an era when electronic images, video games, and theme parks offered a seductive "hyperreality," more real than everyday reality to many people.

If such changes had occurred only in the arts, they might have seemed less provocative; yet artistic changes corresponded to others in economics, politics, and society. The emerging sense of "globalization" was stimulated not only by global economic integration but also by the information technologies. The same technologies had changed politics, bringing live images

of bloodshed before people who once would not have seen the consequences of their or their leaders' decisions, and turning some politicians into would-be webmasters of virtual meetings where citizens could express their preferences, like consumers, without having to iron out their differences face-to-face in real meetings. Indeed, the changes in politics went beyond the electronic. Since the 1960s, many leftists had found the old Marxist politics of class repressive to women and minorities and had called instead for a "micropolitics" based on smaller groups and local interests. With superpatriot or neo-Nazi movements, the same kind of identity politics also rose on the far Right.

In the world of learning, too, a transdisciplinary movement of postmodern theory emerged, attacking as oppressive not only ideologies like Marxism but all "disciplines" and "grand narratives." A movement of postcolonial studies similarly extended its critique beyond the political, military, and cultural impact of imperialism, joining the postmodernists in attacking the very structures of knowledge—"disciplines" in more ways than one—that grew up in the era of imperialism and still structure universities the world over today. Both movements instead championed particular, local knowledge. Now that globalization has become an accomplished fact and not merely an idea, it is ironic that both movements reject the grand-scale theory or narrative required to explain a fact of global scale.

Just as some of the discoveries that did most to launch the "modern" in the early 1900s occurred in science and allied fields, the same was true in opening new vistas at century's end. Nowhere was this clearer than in psychology. However much Freud regarded himself as a scientist, later generations were not able to build cumulatively on his ideas in the way that is normal in science. Today, psychoanalysis and the case studies it produces seem closer to literature and literary interpretation than to em-

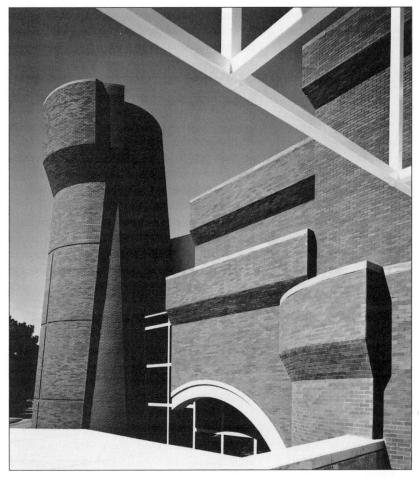

Post-modern architecture *both critiques modern conventions and reworks earlier styles. A sophisticated example, the Wexner Center for the Arts (1989) at Ohio State University was designed by Philip Eisenman and Richard Trott.*
Copyright ARTOG/D. G. Olsbarsky

pirical science; and psychoanalysts no longer have Freud's confidence that a patient's childhood explains his or her later development. The situation in the physical sciences differs in that recent developments have not so much questioned Einstein's breakthroughs as taken off in other fields, notably the information technologies and biotechnology. The two came together in 2000 when the announcement that the en-tire genome had been sequenced—perhaps that year's most "millennial" event—opened vast prospects for advances in medicine, hopes of a virtual Klondike for investors, and fears that genetic manipulation might produce destructive consequences.

In such respects, a new age seems to be opening. No one can entirely say what it will be like, but it is possible to discuss likely characteristics. Once again, the four themes of this book can guide us as we do.

From Global Interrelatedness to Globalization

The twentieth century will be remembered as a time when one centuries-old pattern of global integration collapsed and began to be replaced, after a transition, by a new and different pattern. What collapsed was the European-dominated pattern that reached its height in the nineteenth century and ended in the triple crisis of 1914–1945. The Cold War, the transitional period of superpower polarity that followed, was in many ways a prolongation of the 1914–1945 crisis. Between decolonization and the collapse of the Soviet Union, the world seemed to consist of three "worlds": first, the "free world" of the advanced, capitalist economies; second, the socialist countries; and finally, the "third world" of less-developed countries in Latin America, Africa, and Asia. However, this three-part pattern dissolved with the collapse of communism and divergences in the development of "Third World" countries.

The global pattern now forming differs from earlier patterns in several respects. Most obviously, geoeconomic competition has again eclipsed the geopolitical rivalry that seemed to become more important during the Cold War.

The number of power centers has also increased. Before 1914, the world had one major power center, Europe, although the European great powers competed with each other for hegemony within that center, and new, non-European powers—especially the United States—were vying for recognition. The world of 1945–1991 had two predominant power centers, the United States and Soviet Union, which rivaled each other for hegemony; with time, European integration and Japanese growth challenged the United States, and China challenged the Soviet Union.

Today, there are at least three regional power centers, located in Europe, North America, and East Asia. If the Soviet successor states can achieve enough stability, they may figure as a fourth power center. Whether any of these regional groupings can achieve hegemony within this new world of geoeconomic competition is an open question. The era of globalization may differ from the old European-dominated pattern in having multiple centers of power and productivity, no one of which will clearly dominate the rest. Whether globally or regionally, moreover, the ability of particular nations to exert dominance in the way that Britain did in the nineteenth century or the United States did for a quarter-century after 1945 seems questionable. Japan's ups and downs since the 1980s, and the prospect that China will again become Asia's largest economy, suggest that in a world of space-time compression and intensified economic competition, lasting dominance by any given power may give way to the ebb and flow that, in the 1990s, once again made the United States look more successful economically than Japan.

Globalization cannot be understood solely in terms of its concentrations of power and wealth, however. Both the political and economic significance of globalization, and the revolutionary character of the globalization process, require further consideration. The preceding review of changing patterns of global interrelatedness thus opens topics for further investigation.

Globalization and the Nation-State

As global integration tightened in the twentieth century, the nation-state officially remained the sovereign entity, answerable to no higher power. With the spread of nationalism in the colonial world, the number of nation-states roughly quintupled between 1914 and 1991,

Kosovo, 1999; Ethnic Hatred or Global Consumerism? *The old woman's dress speaks of villages left behind. The young refugees' dress speaks of desire for the common comforts of global modernity, far ahead. Dimitri Messinis/©AP-Wide World Photos*

until this particular political form covered the inhabited Earth. The endless reproduction of the nation-state model clearly suggested that it had been applied in settings where it did not fit well. As globalization intensified, several distinctive problems derived from this fact.

Of the 199 nations that competed in the 2000 Olympics, many were too small and too lacking in resources to flourish as nations—or even to make a good showing at the Olympics. Africa had become home to 55 nations, including several nearby island nations. While that was surely not the only factor, this number of nations, more than in any other region of compa-

rable size, perhaps explained some of Africa's decline since decolonization.

In Africa and the world over, the outward form of the nation-state usually masks a lack of the ethnic or cultural cohesion that the model assumes. In a few cases—notably the "neo-Europes" (see Chapter 1) like Canada, Australia, and the United States—the idea that the nation is mostly one of immigrants gives rise to pluralistic ideals of national identity that may abate, but not eliminate, some identity conflicts.

With exceptions like French Canada or, potentially, the heavily Hispanic regions of the U.S. Southwest, nations of immigrants are usually also insulated from regionally based separatist movements. In many other countries, growing interdependence and interaction have sharpened local ethnic or religious conflicts. Political disintegration has resulted in acute cases—notably the Soviet Union and Yugoslavia, two multinational states that authoritarian government and socialist-internationalist ideology had held together. In some cases, small ethnic groups like the Baltic nationalities clearly hoped to go it alone and later join regional blocs, like the European Union. As the Zapatista movement in Mexico's state of Chiapas shows, indigenous peoples have also become more assertive against the impact of both national and global pressures on their communities. Their access to the global electronic media also provides them a new shield against retaliation from national governments, which cannot afford to have brutal assaults on villagers broadcast all over the world.

Reproduced worldwide but internally fragile, nation-states have also proved unable to play the role once envisioned for them in organizing global interconnectedness. They were never the only actors in this process: business interests and religious movements, among many other examples, have always operated across borders. Yet great hopes were historically placed on maintaining international order through alliances among states, regional alliance systems like NATO, and—in the twentieth century— global organizations of states, first the League of Nations and then the United Nations. In the post–Cold War era, likewise, the feeling that no single state was large enough clearly contributed to the rush to join regional economic unions—not just the EU but also NAFTA and regional economic blocs formed in Latin America, Africa, and Asia. In the case of the United Nations, its many peacekeeping missions, and their failure to resolve conflicts like those of Bosnia and Kosovo, suggest that nation-states singly or collectively will not control the "world disorder" of the foreseeable future.

Yet nation-states will retain a salient role in the world disorder as units within which political and economic interests, social and cultural identities, are defined and expressed. No longer the building blocks of any monumental world order, they survive as fragments of the "modernity" of the preceding era, caught in a global web whose circuits we would have to be able to define in order to give a convincing definition of globalization. They are not the only such fragments.

Globalization and Economic Development

Already tightly interlinked by European imperialism, the world economy moved through several major twentieth-century cycles—the crisis period of 1914–1945, followed by the growth surge of 1945–1973, and the period of slowed growth and episodic recessions from 1973 to the present. Throughout, sharp classifications, with great economic significance, categorized the world's countries, ranging from the great powers and colonies of the pre-1945 period, to the "three worlds" of the Cold War years.

The idea that there could be three separate economic "worlds" was partly shaped by conditions of the 1929 Depression, when the collapse of international trade had made autarky—economic self-sufficiency—seem

more realistic as an economic policy than it could have seemed either earlier or later. For example, for Stalin, who launched his first Five-Year Plan in 1928, it seemed meaningful to create "socialism in one country" and then, after 1945, to create a self-contained socialist bloc. Likewise, in what later became the Third World, the 1930s trade-collapse set the stage, in already independent countries, for an economic policy based on import-substitution industrialization, high tariffs, centralized economic planning, and government initiative in founding enterprises. Pioneered in Turkey and Mexico in 1932–1933, such autarkist policy assumptions spread after decolonization, becoming a global hallmark of postcolonial nation building. Simultaneously, the efforts of the Soviet Union and the United States to surround themselves with other countries like themselves completed the picture of a world divided into three systems, two of them competing with each other in the Cold War, the third unorganized and unable to compete.

By the 1980s, if the capitalist economies were living through a period of difficulty, not only Soviet communism but also the Third World's "soft" developmental socialisms were failing. Except for the high-performing Asian economies, which mostly did so by the 1960s, Third World countries generally did not shift from protectionism to export-oriented industrialization until the 1980s. By the 1980s, too, the Soviets had opted for "restructuring" under Gorbachev, and Deng had decreed "market-socialism" for China.

By then, barriers that had separated the three economic "worlds" were falling like so many invisible Berlin walls. Backed by conservative economists, leaders like U.S. President Reagan or British Prime Minister Thatcher seemed convinced that not only socialism but also the economic wisdom of the 1930s, including the guarantor state and all forms of economic regulation, had failed, and that the economic wisdom of the 1830s, laissez-faire and the free market, had again proved right. Such was the advice given to countries like Russia or Poland as they abandoned the command economy, or to developing countries like India as it strove in the 1990s to abandon its "license raj," the regulatory "empire" (*raj*) created to hinder foreign interests in India.

If policymakers of the 1930s had reacted to a temporary shrinkage in world trade by misreading the long-term trend toward global integration, the policy shifts of the 1980s moved back forcefully into line with a globalizing trend that had grown much stronger by then, facilitating integration on all levels, from that of individual firms to the regional and global levels. International trade agreements, like two drafted in 1997 to end tariffs on information-technology products and telecommunications, further spurred growth. So did technological advances that launched new industries, as in communications or biotechnology, or the tripling of direct investment from rich countries in developing ones between 1990 and 1995. With such stimuli, the global opening and the tighter and denser economic linkages that developed with it seemed to create a changed economic world.

To some observers, indeed, it seemed as if the ups and downs over time that characterized economies historically had become less pronounced, if only temporarily, than spatial movements, where wealth flowed toward some points in the global economic network while draining away from others. Thus U.S. financial markets boomed in the 1990s, while Japan and Europe languished, and the former Soviet bloc collapsed. The fact that about 60 percent of international trade has flowed in recent decades among affluent nations, about 30 percent between them and poor countries, but only 10 percent among poor countries provides another way to map global economic inequality. The fact that poor countries' exports often take the form of agricultural or mineral raw materials has worsened this disparity. For many factors—from the way technological advance adds

value to manufactures, to substitution of synthetics for raw materials, and the impact of population growth on poor countries' ability to export—have caused a long-term decline in the fortunes of raw-materials exporters. Developing countries' manufactures have increased, but only from 10 percent of all manufactures traded in the world in 1950 to about 25 percent in the 1990s.

Critically important in the web of globalization, then, are the economic ties that these numbers express. As with nation-states, whose political importance has diminished but not ceased, the firms, markets, and international organizations that defined the economic world of the preceding era still play large roles; yet they, too, are now caught up in globalization processes that they cannot control. Some of the largest U.S., Japanese, and European firms have long had revenues exceeding the GNP of large nations. Among corporations, those that have internationalized most successfully have also seen their share prices soar. Yet these firms have also acquired new vulnerabilities. A U.S. fast-food company acquired restaurants in over a hundred countries before encountering challenges from the growing popularity of foods from other national cuisines. A U.S.-based soft drink company reached the point of generating 80 percent of its profits outside the United States, before seeing its market position sapped by challenges over quality control or ultracompetitive marketing practices. As such companies globalized, sending many of their "exports" to their own branches, "international trade" at times became hard to identify. Those who had cherished the old goals of import substitution and industrialization for developing nations found it impossible not to regard multinational firms as the new imperialist powers. Yet for others who did not understand why growing up in one country as opposed to another should deprive them of the everyday comforts of life, the desire to enjoy those firms' products and to participate in global patterns of mass consumption helped to define their desire for democratization and economic equality.

Economic globalization widened rather than narrowed inequalities in many ways, however. Worldwide, and even in the financial centers of the United States, competitive pressures, corporate crises, and "downsizing" deprived many people of their livelihoods, while a few grew rich. In an era that touted deregulation, business analysts awoke to the realization that banks in many countries were not well enough regulated by U.S. or European standards. Australia's relative immunity to the Asian economic crisis that radiated out of Thailand in 1997, for example, was attributed to its tighter safeguards on banking practice. A banking crisis somewhere, its effects spread worldwide by the electronic integration of financial markets, could trigger a global economic downturn. Meanwhile, the world's peoples grew ever more integrated into the world economy, not only as consumers but also as low-paid producers of products or the raw materials from which they were made. Even optimists who thought that the 1990s signalled the start of another long-term global growth spurt like that of 1945–1973 did not believe that the world economy had become immune to crisis. Nor, as the protesters who demonstrated at the 1999 World Trade Organization meetings in Seattle were saying, could optimistic assessments of economic globalization ignore the ecological and resource costs of economic growth—a point that will require further attention below.

Growth versus Human Development

For some analysts, these economic trends illustrated the difference between growth and development. During the Cold War, economists had long argued that widening economic inequality was the price of growth. The argument implied that the economic hardship endured by many in the 1980s and 1990s was a price worth paying. Other economists, citing not only cases like Brazil or India but also U.S. corporate heads who raised their own compensation astronomically while firing thousands of employees, saw growth without human development as destructive. To a degree, human development could occur with slow economic growth, as in Mao's China. The most successful combination, however, occurred when economic growth and human development reinforced each other. By the 1990s, the high-growth Asian economies (see Chapter 17), with their egalitarian income distributions, had unmistakably contradicted the old argument about inequality as the price of growth. There and elsewhere, government and nongovernmental organizations clearly had a role to play in seeing that basic health care, education, and other essential services were provided. The free market alone did not produce these goods. India's rural schools whose teachers never came, and its rural clinics that offered nothing but sterilizations, showed what could happen in the absence of public pressure for government to serve human needs.

Comparing the experience of different countries is a good way to appreciate the contrast between growth and development. In most affluent Euro-American economies, incomes per person were higher in the 1990s than ever before. In none of the former European socialist countries was this true. In the developing world, India and China both had higher incomes per person in the 1990s than ever before. Elsewhere in Asia, however, incomes were higher in twenty-one countries but lower in seven others. In other regions, the balance shifted in the negative direction. In the Arab world, per capita incomes were higher in the 1990s than before in two countries, lower in fourteen. In Latin America and the Caribbean, 1990s incomes were higher in twelve countries but lower in twenty-two. In sub-Saharan Africa, incomes were higher in eight countries, lower in thirty-five. In at least nineteen of the world's countries, eleven of them in Africa, incomes per person were lower in the 1990s than they had been in the 1960s, three decades earlier.[1]

Global economic inequality had widened not only across space but also over time. As of 1997, the ratio of western European incomes per person to those of the developing countries was 10 to 1. In 1950, the corresponding ratio would have been 5 to 1; in 1900, it would have been around 4 to 1.[2]

To assess development, and not merely growth, requires considering other indicators besides income. The income statistics need to be adjusted for differences in purchasing power. And quality of life needs to be measured in nonmonetary ways. One broad indicator of human development, used in earlier chapters, is the Human Development Index (HDI), which aggregates real GDP per person (in purchasing-power terms), life expectancy, and education, producing a statistic that varies from a high of 1 to a low of 0. Values from 0.8 to 1.0 signify high human development. Canada topped the 1998 list (0.935); Estonia just made it (0.801). Countries in between included the United States (0.929), Japan (0.924), Singapore (0.881), Hong Kong (since 1997 an autonomous region of China, 0.872), and Kuwait (0.836). Countries in the medium range, from 0.799 down to 0.500, included several that had ranked at the lower end of the high range a few years before: Malaysia (0.772), the Russian Federation (0.771), and Thailand (0.745). Others in the medium range included Cuba (0.783), Brazil and Saudi Arabia (both 0.747), Turkey (0.732), Iran (0.709), China (0.706), South Africa (0.697), Indonesia (0.670), Egypt (0.623), and India (0.563, having risen out of the low range in the last few years). Countries in the low range (below 0.500) in 1998 included Bangladesh (0.461), Haiti (0.440), and—last of 174 countries ranked—Sierra Leone (0.252). The global 1998 HDI stood at 0.712.

Grim measures of global inequality, these statistics proved that income per person only partly measures development. Here, Cuba out-ranked Russia; Saudi Arabia was even with Brazil; and China outranked India by nearly the same percentage that separated India and Haiti. These figures suggest as well that economic globalization, though a triumph for the free market in some sense, will have negative implications unless well studied and, indeed, regulated. Who will do this?

Globalization as Revolution

Globalization grew out of earlier forms of global interrelatedness but has become a structural transformation with revolutionary impacts and unanticipated features. Shaped by long-working processes of space-time compression, globalization encompasses new kinds of interrelatedness, including new realms of interaction over issues like human development, the environment and human rights, or a sense—heightened by population growth and ecological degradation—of global oneness and global citizenship.

Scholars so far have trouble explaining globalization. In part, it is a "global disorder," where it is difficult to identify all essential networks and where control points are sometimes nonexistent or hard to find. For example, global communications networks—fax machines, electronic mail, satellite broadcasts—have eroded the ability of governments to control the flow of information, creating mortal threats to regimes, like the Soviet Union, that depended on controlling what people think. In the case of the Internet, control seems almost a meaningless idea, except over the assigning of domain names.

The political and economic aspects of globalization, which we have emphasized so far, certainly show how it challenges conventional modes of explanation. For example, nothing better illustrates globalization than today's "virtual" economy, in which $1.5 trillion circulate electronically every twenty-four hours, eroding even the strongest nations' ability to control interest rates. With its instant communications,

"The world is becoming smaller" proclaims the sign on the pedestrian bridge over this crowded street scene in Dhaka, Bangladesh. The interaction of the global and the local, problems of population growth and technological diffusion—all the themes of the twentieth century blend in this view.
© *Mark Edwards/Still Pictures*

global credit flows, mobile markets, changeably transnational division of labor, and widened development gaps, the contemporary world economy combines global integration and spatial dispersal in ways that conventional maps or social-scientific theories are hard put to describe.

While thorough understanding of globalization may remain a task for the new century, clearly any analysis must take account of more than politics and economics. It must embrace both material and cultural aspects of globalization. In the interest of widening our understanding, we therefore continue our discussion by considering the themes of identity and difference, the mass society, and technology versus nature, which—as much as the theme of global interrelatedness—have guided this book.

Identity and Difference: Cultural Disequilibrium

In 1994, Nursultan Nazarbayev, an ex-Soviet functionary who had resurfaced as president of independent Kazakstan but who, as late as 1992, still opposed antagonizing the Russians, said:

"The world has changed. People are seeking their identities."[3]

The same statement could have come—sometimes less surprisingly—from thousands of leaders, in thousands of languages, around the world. For, as noted in Chapter 1, one consequence of global integration, already visible in the nineteenth century, was to work the production of cultural difference and resistance into the system in complex ways. Sometimes the result was crisis and rebellion, until resistance eventually culminated in decolonization. Sometimes the result was movements of self-strengthening through reform and adaptation, as in the Ottoman Empire or Japan. In the twentieth century, struggles of national liberation and the nonalignment movement continued to express such resistance. In the 1990s, even as global systems of new kinds—economic, technological, ideological—multiplied, a key challenge of understanding them was to assess the ways in which the politics of identity and difference worked its way into those systems.

For every person, what it means to live in the world has to be expressed in a local language, a local context. The local and the global grate together everywhere, endlessly and variably. As a revolutionary force, globalization has disrupted some communities—some nations have ceased to exist, countries and cultures have lost separateness—while reinforcing others or even making new kinds of communities possible.

Multiple Levels of Identity Politics

In particular, earlier chapters have noted the frequency with which reactions against globalization have taken shape as religious or nationalist movements. Religious revivalism has gained force all over the world in recent decades. Nationalism, often mixed with religion, has exerted powerful influence in places—like the former Soviet Union or Yugoslavia—where it had long been denied. Paradoxically, electronic communications have strengthened these movements that seem to resist globalization. Computers, for example, have globalized the reach of religious movements that might once have been local, while also facilitating the study—including study from a distance—of religious texts. Similarly, electronic communications have created new possibilities for nationalism. Palestinians migrating to Europe or North America in the computer age no longer virtually dropped out of their national struggle. Instead, in a newer sense of the word, they could remain virtual parts of it on a day-to-day basis. The age of jet planes, cellular phones, and fax modems had created a situation where human communities no longer had clear territorial boundaries: migrants in far parts of the world had the option to remain "plugged in," "on line." At the same time, globalization caused such people to acquire multiple identities: a permanent resident in the United States as well as a Palestinian activist, say, or a German-born leader in extremist political movements banned in Turkey.

Religion and nationalism, however, are not the only categories that serve to assert identity and difference in the midst of globalization. In many cases, the large communities that they define struggle to contain a micropolitics defined by bonds of race, ethnicity, class, and gender. As noted in Chapter 1 and since, one of the most persistent trends of the past century and more has been to critique contradictions in the way the grand slogans of classical liberal ideology about the "rights of man" were applied and to demand consistent application to all people. By the 1960s, the demand for equality was accompanied by demands for the acceptance of difference, and for accommodation of the rights and needs of groups defined by all types of special interests and needs, including sexual preference or physical disability.

As this occurred, larger communities that had once defined social and political consciousness often splintered or came under attack as oppressive. In the France of 1968, for example, worker solidarity came to be seen as oppressive to women. In some postcolonial nations—including India or much of Africa—nationalism came under challenge by groups who found themselves at a disadvantage in the postcolonial order. Connections between changes at the global level and these micropolitical realignments often appeared. To cite only a few, examples include the rise of environmentalism as a national and international political movement, as well as the way feminism gave women alternatives to ideologies unfriendly to gender issues and a new basis for international solidarity.

Revolutionary Implications of Identity Politics

Two facts seem particularly noteworthy about such situations. One is the far-reaching repercussions of some of these critiques. As an example like feminist critiques of the Marxist ideal of international worker solidarity reveals, what is at stake is not just the definition of communities or social bodies, but structures of power within those communities, and even the bodies of knowledge and theory used to explain and justify those realities. This is why the globalization revolution is as much cultural as material, and why its analysis requires new developments in social thought. This is why, to cite another example, postcolonial criticism attacks not just the power relations of the old European-dominated system, but also—following postmodernism in this—the very structures of cultural and social-scientific studies—the "disciplines"—that were developed in the universities and other institutions of that system. The same reasoning leads to attacks on all "grand theories" and "grand narratives," insisting, instead, on local and particular "knowledges" that are not reducible to local examples of something global.[4] Truly the maximum in asserting microlevel identity and difference, such attacks forbid the macrolevel

analysis required to understand globalization, even though the interactions between it and identity politics would seem to make each essential to the understanding of the other.

The other question that seems particularly salient for understanding reactions, on the level of identity politics, against globalization comes up especially in discussions of religious and nationalistic resurgences. This is the question—reinforced by the idea that modernity has reached a dead end—of whether such movements signify a re-emergence of something old, "traditional," even "primordial." Influential voices have been raised in support of the idea that such movements are throwbacks to things premodern, even ancient. Television commentators' habit of calling bitter conflicts "age-old" hatreds adds to such thinking the deceptive authority of electronic hyperreality.

But thoughtful analysis shows that however important the historical roots of today's resurgent ethnic and religious movements are, they are phenomena of their times, referring to the present as importantly as to the past. In the United States, for example, such themes of the Christian religious Right as abortion and school prayer could not have been big issues a few decades earlier, when abortion was uncommon, and when—precisely because sensitivity to issues of identity and difference had not been awakened—school students routinely recited some kind of prayer along with saluting the flag, the two together seen as one minor ritual for molding children of immigrants into God-fearing Americans. Ironically, by 2000, realization that Muslims outnumbered Episcopalians in the United States had awakened Christian rightists to the realization that school prayer was an issue that might not work reliably for them after all—one more sign of the movement's presentism.

Other religious revivalist movements show that their appeals to the traditional and the timeless are similarly subject to accommodation with changing circumstances. Before 1979, when Khomeini was in exile in France, his success in using tape-recorded cassettes to circulate his message inside Iran was widely noted—a perfect example of using modern tools of global communications to promote identity politics. Islamist intellectuals today, far from being "traditionalists," eagerly but selectively absorb postmodernist critiques of modernism to prove Islam's triumph over the secular modernism that used to threaten it. Of course, they do not absorb postmodernist critiques of "grand narratives" or of belief systems that attempt to explain everything.

It would not be hard to extend this survey around the world. India's resurgent Hindu nationalism selectively reworked themes out of a heterogeneous religious tradition to articulate grievances about contemporary conditions. The liberation theology that became popular in Latin America created enough of a contemporary challenge to the authority structure and teachings of Roman Catholicism that the conservative Polish pope, John Paul II, disciplined the movement forcefully.

What is true of religious resurgence is true, too, of resurgent nationalisms. In the Bosnian civil war, the supposed history of "age-old" conflict among Orthodox Christian Serbs, Catholic Croats, and largely Muslim Bosnians proved, when dispassionately studied, to be a narrative about the history not of anything ancient but of modern nationalism.[5] This narrative was constructed over the last two centuries by forcefully reworking a history of centuries of peaceful coexistence among people who shared the same ethnolinguistic identity but differed in religion. Nineteenth-century European models of nationalism emphasized ethnic and cultural homogeneity, a criterion that made the earlier coexistence of South Slavs of different faiths appear to some as a defect that needed to be "remedied." During the Bosnian civil war of the 1990s, this eventually happened through so-called ethnic cleansing—actually religious rather than ethnic, and more like geno-cide than cleansing. To South African President Nelson Mandela, a leader who used a radically different, conciliatory approach to end a conflict that could have turned out like Yugoslavia's, this is what happens when people "think through their blood and not through their brains."[6] The problem is a contemporary failure of vision, not an ancient history.

If one of the features of contemporary globalization, as argued in Chapter 1, is to create economic cores and peripheries on multiple levels, some nested inside others, much the same could be said of the politics of identity and difference. No longer just race, ethnicity, or religion, but now also class and gender, sexual preference, socioeconomic or physical disadvantage, and other traits have all interacted to define and subdivide the complex "hyphenated" identities that articulate our ties to other people and our points of contact with the various systems of globalization. Globalization is a revolution, then, in cultural as much as in material terms. Its local points of contact will all be subject to conflict and contestation, with implications that are also revolutionary. This will be the case not only because of the tightening of global integration and the new forms that it has taken on, but also because of the new meanings of the "mass society."

The Future of the Mass Society

One of the driving forces of globalization has been the explosive population growth that increased world population from 1.7 billion in 1900 to 6.1 billion in 2000, nearly 3.8 billion of them born since 1950. More than a matter of numbers, this demographic growth underlies the mass warfare, mass politics, mass communications, mass migration, and mass culture that characterize the world of globalization and identity politics.

A Third Demographic Transition?

Chapter 1 discussed population growth in terms of three demographic transitions, of which the first resulted from the prehistoric invention of agriculture. The European-centered second demographic transition interacted with the nineteenth-century dual revolution (political and industrial) to open the age of the mass society in major European and "neo-European" societies, including the United States, Canada, and Australia. Today, the question is whether the current, much larger population explosion, centered in the developing countries, constitutes a third demographic transition. The answer to this question will have important implications for all phases of human life, as well as for the balance between humankind and its natural habitat.

The idea that population growth could cause economic crisis is not new. In his *Essay on Population* (1798), Thomas Malthus argued that although humanity's means of subsistence could grow only by arithmetic increments, unchecked population growth would compound itself in a geometric progression. Strictly speaking, arithmetic progression means addition of a fixed factor ($2 + 2 = 4, 4 + 2 = 6, 6 + 2 = 8$). Geometric progression means multiplication by a fixed factor ($2 \times 2 = 4, 4 \times 2 = 8, 8 \times 2 = 16$), the result being a much faster increase.

Malthus's idea that unchecked population growth would outstrip increases in food supply has never been forgotten. Yet for a long time, exceptional increases in food supplies, resulting from the opening of new continents and improvements in agricultural yield, postponed the reckoning he predicted. Today, no more continents remain to open, world population is six times higher than in Malthus's day, and technological gains cannot necessarily produce new increments large enough to meet indefinitely expanding demand. After two centuries, Malthus's logic again haunts us.

The third demographic transition would reach completion only if birth and death rates eventually regained equilibrium at lower levels. In 2000, the best news on the global population front was that global population growth, after peaking near 2 percent in 1970 had fallen to 1.4 percent. Unlike the second demographic transition, in which nineteenth-century Europe's drop in birth rates coincided with the rising living standards made possible by industrialization, the recent decline in birth rates in poor countries occurred without improvements in living standards in many cases. The change probably resulted from advances in communications and education, especially female education, which correlates highly with reductions in fertility and infant mortality. Still, the annual addition to world population peaked at 87 million in 1989, with 90 percent of new births occurring in developing countries. In 1998, world population still grew by 78 million.

Population stabilization would require a much lower growth rate that hovered around zero (plus or minus 0.3 percent). By 1999, some thirty-two countries, home to 15 percent of humankind—essentially Japan, Russia, and most of Europe—had stable or falling populations. Elsewhere, the United States was growing at 0.6 percent in 2000, while China was growing at 0.9 percent. The aggregate rate for developing countries other than China was still 1.9 percent. The 2000 rate for sub-Saharan Africa was as high as 2.5 percent. All these rates had fallen in recent years. The extent to which economic development varied inversely with population growth rates could not escape notice.

The worst news about demographic change today, highlighted by these rate differentials, is probably the size that world population is predicted to assume before stabilizing. At the International Conference on Population and Development (Cairo, 1994), delegates from 179 nations studied high, medium, and low estimates, which predicted that world population would reach 11.9, 9.8, or 7.9 billion before stabilizing by 2050. Unwilling to accept the human and ecological costs of the high estimate, the delegates discussed ways of reaching stability between the medium and low estimates, focusing on human development issues, particularly universal primary education for girls, and family-planning services for the 120 million women who lacked them. Obstacles to stabilization at mid-to-low estimates included U.S. anti-abortion activists' opposition to family-planning aid, massive resentment of coercive family-planning programs in China and India, and the scale of Africa's needs.

Malthus believed that runaway population growth would inevitably end in "dismal peaks," when death rates would soar above birth rates because of war, famine, or disease. The world of the twenty-first century will face these risks and others, in a new configuration where questions of "security" cluster more around ecological issues than around the military issues that dominated Cold War thinking. Even short of the direst ecological scenarios, population growth will interact with other forces to produce some of the most distinctive features of the globalization revolution.

Masses in Motion

Global integration has been spurred by advances in transportation, like the advent of the automobile and aviation, and even more by recent improvements in communications. All have interacted to shrink time and distance and have combined with population growth to intensify human interactions in ways unimaginable a few decades before. The virtual obliteration of time and distance not only has stimulated the rise of identity politics, but also has created a world where it is as normal to migrate as to remain settled in one place. If some of this movement is voluntary, more of it is not, being driven instead by war, famine, or disease, or by the fantastic inequalities between

countries as close in distance—but far apart in quality of life—as Haiti and the United States.

Voluntary or involuntary, migration has become more common than ever before. The number of refugees, in the political sense of people fleeing persecution, increased from 2.5 million in the mid-1970s to 23 million in 1995. More than another 20 million people were internally displaced within their countries of origin for reasons such as famine or natural disaster. Examples included the 116,000 residents who fled the vicinity of Chernobyl (Ukraine) after the 1986 nuclear-plant disaster dispersed 180 tons of radioactive dust roundabout, or the many Bangladeshis fleeing the frequent floods and storms of their low-lying, densely populated homeland. Illegal immigrants were estimated globally at 10 million; most of these sought to cross economic gulfs like those that separated Mexico from California or Albania from Italy. Those migrating within their own countries in search of opportunity numbered 100 million in China alone, and several times that many worldwide.

One of the most common types of internal migration, often mentioned in earlier chapters, is rural to urban, usually prompted by overcrowding and declining opportunity in agricultural regions. Other migrants have been set in motion by authoritarian governments, as have the ethnic Chinese relocated to Tibet, Xinjiang Province, Inner Mongolia, and Manchuria in efforts to outnumber the indigenous Tibetans, Uygur Turks, Mongolians, and Manchurians, respectively. Some migrants have been evicted from their homelands, like the 1.5 million Kurds whom Saddam Husayn chased from Iraq into Turkey in 1991. Rising in frequency from an average of ten at any one time in the 1950s to 51 in 1992, then falling with the end of the Cold War to 25 in 1997, armed conflicts have provided the major negative factor behind migration.

What would do most to ease the pressures for migration would be greater global equality

Illegal Immigrants Enter Spain, August 2000. *Thirty-nine people had made the eight-mile crossing from Morocco in inflatable rafts. Ragel/EFE/© AP-Wide World Photos*

of opportunity and reductions in the human development gaps that yawn so wide among—and often within—societies today. With existing means for migration, however, the world will clearly remain a much more mobile place than in earlier periods.

The Mass Society and Democratization

As it struggles to complete its third demographic transition, then, the world of the twentieth-first century will also struggle with new meanings of the mass society. The twentieth century already knew many of these: huge demographic growth; proliferation of mass-oriented political systems, democratic or authoritarian; accelerated transport and communication; mass consumerism; the proliferation of new forms of popular culture; and wars

of all scales, including global ones. In the new millennium, the mix will become even more diverse, with more complex fusions of ethnicity and race, culture and cuisine, musical styles, business practice, and political ideas. Conflict and tension will persist in this mix, although some of their forms may change; and they will define agenda items for global politics. By 2000, some of the ways this would happen were already clear.

One of the most powerful themes running through recent global events has been a demand for democratization. This choice of words is deliberate: the *demand* for democratization has surely spread faster than realization of the demand. In the new century, such demands will continue to grow. Changes as far apart as the collapse of the Soviet Union and of apartheid in South Africa all point in this direction. According to one organization, Freedom House, which monitors the trend, the proportion of "democracies" has grown from 42 to 63 percent of the world's nations in a decade—although how democratic many of these are is surely questionable. China, the Arab world, and much of Africa lag the trend, but demand for democratization has grown everywhere.

If twentieth-century types of authoritarian mass politics seem to be in retreat, the democratizing trend will not be trouble-free and will not produce uniform results everywhere. Even in the historical Euro-American democracies, for example, the network of volunteer activities and associations that used to constitute the grassroots infrastructure of social and political life has weakened because of factors such as the growing prevalence of two-career families, the reliance on electronic rather than face-to-face communications, and the growth of lobbies and special-interest organizations.

Many other countries never had a well-developed "civil society," as scholars call the realm of autonomous, voluntary associations at mid-range between the individual and the government. In such countries, how to create "civil society" or how to nurture democratization in its absence will remain in question. Iran stands as a good example that a country with a constitution, a functioning parliament, contested elections, and strongly voiced demands for change and diversity may still not rank as democratic by criteria such as protection for civil rights or gender equality. In some countries, too, democratic processes may produce outcomes that endanger democracy. Many multiethnic nations, from the Soviet successor states to Africa, will face conflict between majority rule and minority rights. To cite a different problem, some experts fear—exaggeratedly, according to others—that Islamic activists' attitude toward democratic processes could be summed up as "one man, one vote, one time." In other words, the election that brought them to power would be the last one. Many countries, too, will have to fine-tune their electoral systems to try to keep

small parties from fragmenting politics to the point of obstructing governance. Still however rocky the democratizing trend may prove, the age of perennial dictators like Zaire's Mobutu, topped in 1997, or of rulers, like Iraq's Saddam Husayn, who close off their countries from the world, seems to be passing.

In the age of democratization, the world's societies will still differ in many ways. In foreign relations, for example, the old assumption that democratic nations have common interests, as they generally did during the Cold War, will become less sure, and conflicts among more or less democratic governments may increase.

The world's societies will also differ in the extent to which the masses are thought to be made up of individuals who have rights that must be protected. Attended by representatives of 160 countries and over two thousand nongovernmental organizations, the UN Conference on Human Rights (Vienna, 1993) illustrated this point. The Vienna conference touched off bitter controversy between "universalist" and "relativist" interpretations of rights issues. The "universalist" view is that human rights are the same everywhere: humanity must not be divided into blocs with unequal access to those rights. The "relativist" view is that individual rights depend on (are "relative" to) culture. For relativists, trying to set universal standards in human rights amounts to asserting moralistic domination of some cultures over others.

At Vienna, the universalist camp included the developed Euro-American countries, women's groups, and rights activists from around the world. The relativist bloc, led by China, Indonesia, Malaysia, Myanmar, Pakistan, Iraq, Iran, and Syria, insisted that rights depend on regional, cultural, and religious factors. Relativists argued, too, that a society has the right to defend the rights of the collectivity over those of the individual and that economic development takes primacy over human rights. Relativists further attacked the affluent countries' attempts to condition development aid on democratization and rights reforms: Was not development itself a human right?

UN High Commissioner for Human Rights Mary Robinson eloquently stated the opposing view. "Does universality negate cultural diversity? Are human rights at odds with religious beliefs? Are they a Western conception that is being imposed to advance global markets? Who can deny that all seek lives free from fear, discrimination, starvation, torture? When have we ever heard a free voice demand an end to freedom?" Ms. Robinson even reached an agreement with Chinese President Jiang Zemin in November 2000 for outside experts to advise China on changes needed for it to adhere to two treaties on human rights. As they shook hands, however, the air was thick with contradictory signals. China's top leadership, knowing that the world economy and the Internet were stronger forces for change than any treaties, was showing its readiness to get with the times. Yet during Ms. Robinson's visit, Jiang also showed his views on the universality of rights when he observed: "The Chinese government has always supported international exchange and cooperation in the area of human rights because each country has its own way."[7] The thousands of Falun Dafa believers recently sent without trial to Chinese labor camps knew what he meant, yet they might still have thanked Mary Robinson for engaging China in the global rights dialogue.

In the twenty-first century, then, promoting democratization and human rights is likely to prove as challenging as completing the third demographic transition or relieving the pressures that set migrants in motion. International movements supporting democratization and rights issues will persist as additional subsystems of the globalization process. Other, comparable movements and networks will concentrate around questions arising from the impact of the mass society on the natural environment.

Nature, Technology, and Globalization

Modern population growth and rapid technological change have posed for the future unprecedented questions about humankind's ability to assure its survival and well-being. With the advent of nuclear energy, some of the most threatening questions arose around the danger of nuclear war and mass destruction. But the needs of fast-growing populations turned humbler ecological and resource questions into security issues, as well. Whether by atomic weapons, or by the explosive population growth that an African commentator once called the "atomic bomb of the poor," humans acquired the ability to degrade or even destroy the natural world, before whose forces they had been helpless for most of their history. Advances in science and technology had done much to create this problem; they might help, too, to solve it. As ever, whether science and technology helped or hurt would depend on whether people used them wisely.

Food, Energy, and Climate: An Ecological Transition?

Since 1950, while world population has nearly tripled, the world economy has grown faster, from $4 trillion to $29 trillion. Were it not for vast inequalities in the distribution of this wealth and in human development, the fact that economic growth has outstripped population growth might seem like an unmixed blessing. Unfortunately, this growth pattern points to another problem even more basic than income inequity. For as long as the demographic transition in the developing countries remains uncompleted, does the whole world not also face the risk of an *ecological transition*, as growing populations consume natural resources faster than they can be replaced, until vital life-support systems collapse?[8]

This question literally becomes one of the Earth's *carrying capacity*. How many people can Earth support without losing the ability to sustain a desirable quality of life over the long term? Despite the difficulties of measuring carrying capacity, many signs today suggest that current world population already jeopardizes sustainability. A brief consideration of food, energy, and climate change will illustrate the seriousness of the problem.

Food Security Since 1950, while the world economy grew more than twice as fast as population, demand for grain, water, beef, and firewood roughly tripled, and consumption of seafood quadrupled. By 1989, all the oceans were being fished at or beyond capacity, and thirteen of fifteen major oceanic fisheries were declining. Grazing lands were not faring much better; they were declining in every country in Africa, for example.

By the 1990s, because fishers and ranchers could no longer increase production to meet demand, for the first time in history farmers faced that task alone. But their resource bases were also crossing thresholds beyond which use levels could not be sustained or expanded. Every major agricultural country was losing topsoil. Because of growing use for irrigation and citydwellers' needs, water tables were falling in major agricultural zones such as the U.S. Great Plains and Southwest, the Punjab (India), northern China, and southern Europe. Routinely, a number of important rivers no longer reached the sea because the water was all used for irrigation. The Colorado River was the best-known U.S. example. China's Yellow River dried up 600 kilometers from the sea in 1995. Three hundred Chinese cities had inadequate water supplies. The depletion of fossil aquifers—underground, water-bearing strata that are "fossils" in the sense of having been filled long ago and not being replenished from the surface, like the vast Ogallala aquifer under the U.S. Great Plains or those used for irrigation in Libya and Saudi Arabia—was perhaps more serious. Farmland was also being lost the world over to growing needs for housing and roads, as well as for shopping and recreation facilities.

These problems might seem less serious if farmers could increase the productivity of land and crops enough to feed each year's increment to world population. Between 1950 and 1990, they did this, thanks to improved crop varieties, increased fertilizer use, and irrigation. After 1978, however, limits on water supplies began to reduce irrigated area per person and force abandonment of marginal grainland. Geneticists' efforts to improve crops approached physiological limits on the efficiency of food production, although the bioengineering of the future might achieve gains in resistance to pests or diseases. Fertilizer use, after growing markedly for three decades, fell from 1989 on, largely because crops could not respond to more fertilizer than was already used on them. After decades of growth, grain exports from the world's leading exporters—Argentina, Australia, Canada, the European Union, and the United States—also began to level off in the 1990s.

One of the best ways to assess world food supplies is to consider *carryover grain stocks*, measured in the number of days of consumption that supplies on hand can support. Grains are a good indicator of food supplies in general. Directly consumed, grains provide half of world caloric intake; they also provide much of the rest indirectly, in the form of eggs, milk, and meat from grain-fed livestock. Maintaining minimal food security requires stocks sufficient for 70 days of world consumption. At less than 60 days, grain prices become unstable. After the bumper harvest of 1990, carryover stocks dropped, reaching a new low of 52 days of consumption in 1996. After declining from 1950 to 1993, real global prices for major grains consequently began to rise.

No doubt, researchers will continue to achieve breakthroughs, like a new rice variety under development in the mid-1990s, which

Drought in Ogaden Province, Ethiopia, April 2000. *Population growth, over-exploitation of fragile ecosystems, human-induced climate change, and bad government again take their toll.* Per-Anders Petterson/© Liaison/Newsmakers-Online USA

could raise production enough to cover world population growth for three years. Varieties genetically engineered for resistance to viruses and insects may provide similar gains. Each such gain provides, however, only an arithmetic increment to supply an exponentially growing demand. Questions of food scarcity and rising prices therefore will likely dominate coming decades and figure increasingly as major political issues. World population cannot stabilize fast enough to avert this scenario. Rising consumption levels in fast-growing Asian economies will also be a major factor, especially if China continues needing to import large amounts of grain, as it did in 1995 and is expected to do increasingly with time. Considering the huge grain deficits in prospect for most of the world, and taking food

issues together with those of energy and human-induced climate change, the economic stresses accompanying globalization may well dwarf those that followed on the OPEC oil price revolution of the 1970s.

Energy OPEC may have done the world a favor, for the price shocks of the 1970s drove home the point that the world has only a finite amount of oil. For the quarter-century preceding the 1973 embargo, the price of oil had been kept low, and world oil consumption had more than quintupled, to 20 billion barrels in 1973. Petroleum and related products had become the basis for much of the world's transportation, heating, and electric-power generation. Because they were produced in huge bulk, byproducts of the refining process had become the basic raw material for much of the chemical industry, even where other materials could have served as well. Plastics, synthetic fibers, even fertilizers were manufactured from petroleum derivatives. Between 1945 and 1973, then, the world consumed more and more oil and relied on it for more uses. Of course, there were gross regional disparities. The United States used disproportionately more petroleum than did most developing countries. The Soviet Union, an oil exporter and a command economy, used energy even more wastefully than the United States—and with less benefit to the average citizen.

The high consumption levels of the developed economies and the concentration of much of global oil reserves in a handful of culturally similar Middle Eastern states made OPEC possible. Conservation, development of non-OPEC petroleum sources such as Alaska's North Shore or Europe's North Sea, the shift to alternative forms of energy, and global recession then lowered world oil consumption from 1979 on. In 1980, oil prices also began to fall, dropping below $20 per barrel in 1986, the lowest price since 1975.

Oil prices and demand rose after 1986. By 2000, oil prices were again as high in nominal terms (half as high after adjustment for inflation) as in the 1970s: the oil crisis had not ended. Despite prodigious exploration between 1973 and 2000, about 80 percent of the oil produced still came from fields discovered before 1973, most of which were in decline, and total production had gone up less than 10 percent in twenty years. World production was expected to peak in 2010 and then drop rapidly for want of supply. Daily world consumption was about 70 million barrels a day as of 2000; but rapid economic growth, and the expansion of automobile production in a country like China, could increase demand markedly.

The OPEC shocks of the 1970s opened a time of searching for energy alternatives. At first,

it was common to point to coal and nuclear energy as alternatives. However, the role of coal burning in air pollution and acid rain was becoming a familiar issue. By the 1990s, China was almost unique in still relying—for want of choice—on coal to power its rapid growth.

Nuclear power's disadvantages were highlighted both by costs higher than those for other forms of electric power and by the nuclear plant disasters at Three Mile Island (Pennsylvania, 1979) and—vastly worse—Chernobyl (Soviet Ukraine, 1986). In the mid-1990s, East Asia was the only region where interest in increasing nuclear power generation persisted. As France had earlier, Japan tackled the challenge of building fast breeder reactors, which not only use plutonium as fuel but also produce more of this extremely radioactive substance than than they consume. By 2000, power plant accidents and realization that government had kept citizens in the dark about facilities located in residential areas had brought anti-nuclear activism even to Japan.

What would solve the world's energy problems would be not a quick technological fix but greater energy efficiency and development of nonpolluting, renewable energy sources. Efficiency gains realized since 1973 have already reduced the energy used to produce a dollar of GNP by over 50 percent for North America, Europe, and Japan. Further efficiency gains in heating, cooling, lighting, and transportation are possible, not only in developed countries but by the spread of efficient technologies, with modifications as needed, to eastern Europe and the developing world. Transportation, in particular, would ultimately have to become not only more efficient in energy use but less dependent on oil and the automobile. Signs of what might come appeared in the growing use of vehicles powered with natural gas or hydrogen, ongoing efforts to develop viable electric or solar-powered vehicles, improvements in rail transport, and efforts to equip cities—from Los Angeles to Cairo—with subways. In contrast,

China's efforts to develop a major auto industry raised new worries about petroleum usage, air pollution, and farmland to be turned into roads and parking lots.

Energy solutions for the twenty-first century will take the form of a solar-hydrogen economy based on conservation and a diversity of renewable, nonpolluting energy sources. As technical advances accumulated, the contours of such an economy began to take shape. In the 1990s, the energy sources with the highest annual global growth rates were wind power (22 percent a year) and solar photovoltaics (16 percent), compared to 2 percent each for oil and natural gas. Financially strapped farmers in North Dakota and comparable locales can now profit from a "second crop" by leasing rights to install wind turbines in their fields. Photovoltaics have long had applications in places where connection to a conventional grid was not practicable. The development of solar-cell roofing materials has now begun to offer more cost-effective possibilities for highly decentralized electricity generation off the roofs of buildings.

The nonpolluting substitute for fossil fuels will take the form of hydrogen, produced electrochemically by splitting water molecules into hydrogen and oxygen. Devices known as fuel cells can effectively produce electricity from hydrogen and are close enough to marketability that U.S. investor interest surged when oil prices rose in 2000. Poised to become the prime mover for the twenty-first century, much as the internal combustion engine was for the twentieth, fuel cells are suited for both stationary and mobile uses in a vast range of sizes, as well as for modular construction that enables them to undergo repair while continuing to function as uninterrupted power sources. Hydrogen fuel cells emit no byproduct but water.

In sum, the possibilities for meeting future energy needs appear more promising than those of limiting population or ensuring food security. Especially in the United States, however, business interests committed to fossil fuels will continue to delay using alternative technologies. Even with such conversion, climatic problems, mainly caused by past energy choices, will remain major threats to public health and sustainable development.

Human-induced Climate Change

In sharpening public awareness of atmospheric consequences of population growth, 1988 was the pivotal year when the "greenhouse effect" became front-page news. The term refers to what happens when the atmospheric concentration of certain gases, especially carbon dioxide, increases. The carbon dioxide absorbs infrared solar radiation, gradually warming the lower atmosphere. The 1980s became the warmest decade on record—until the 1990s became even warmer. In 1988, a year of severe heat and drought, the world also learned that the stratospheric ozone layer, which protects life on Earth from harmful ultraviolet radiation, was thinning not just in polar regions—a fact discovered several years earlier—but globally. In the early 1990s, the depletion rate was found to be twice as fast as previously thought. Climates are subject to wide natural variations, and the reasons for them are controversial. Even conservative climatologists now argue, however, for precautions against warming.

The greenhouse effect was indeed a global problem. Since 1970, less-developed countries, housing three-fourths of world population, have almost tripled their energy consumption, while industrial countries increased their energy usage by only a fifth (although starting at much higher levels). Tripling consumption meant much higher pollution levels, especially as numbers of automobiles—often lacking emissions controls—grew. As a result, some cities in developing countries had average concentrations of sulfur dioxide or suspended particulate matter—two major forms of atmospheric pollution—ten times as high as in the cities of affluent countries. A new ecological colonialism, found where multinational corporations relocated hazardous industries, such as asbestos or pesticides, to poor countries or where such countries keep environmental regulation lax to entice investors, worsened these problems. Accelerated by shortsighted development policy, deforestation also worsened air pollution. The cutting of the Amazon rain forest, for example, not only endangered unknown numbers of plant and animal species, many of which might produce substances of medicinal or other value, but also added to atmospheric carbon dioxide and disrupted the hydrologic cycle (the circulation of water between Earth and atmosphere through evaporation and rainfall).

Communist collapse revealed, however, that Eastern Europe had the worst pollution. Less efficient than the United States or Japan in energy usage, East European economies had produced some of the highest pollution levels ever recorded. In the Soviet Union, the health costs of pollution were estimated at $330 billion for 1987, or 11 percent of GDP. Not surprisingly, environmentalist "green" movements proliferated in Eastern Europe in the 1980s and became political parties upon the end of communism.

Among the greenhouse gases, the chief pollutant is carbon dioxide, produced mostly by burning fossil fuels, also by deforestation (decaying or burning plant matter releases carbon; live plants convert carbon dioxide into oxygen). Over the past century, atmospheric carbon dioxide has risen from 274 to 363 parts per million. Since 1989, carbon emissions have amounted annually to one ton a year for each human being on Earth; however, that figure masked emissions rates as far apart as 5.3 tons a year for every person in the United States and 0.3 tons a year for everyone in India or Indonesia. Other greenhouse gases included methane, from waste disposal and agriculture, and nitrous oxides, from fertilizers, industry, and motor ve-

hicles. Chlorofluorocarbons (CFCs) and halons posed a special challenge. Not long ago, CFCs were widely used in cleaning processes and cooling systems and as a blowing agent in aerosol cans and insulating foams. Halons are used in fire extinguishers. CFCs release chlorine, and halons release bromine; both chemicals rise into the stratosphere and react to break down ozone (oxygen's three-atom form).

The effects of these greenhouse gases make global warming a serious danger. Rapid warming would threaten biological diversity because many plants and animals would not be able to survive change in their habitats. Warming would also raise the danger of sea-level rise. Low-lying countries like Bangladesh, the Netherlands, and many island nations would be mortally threatened, as would the world's coastal cities.

Ozone depletion poses still other dangers. Ozone is harmful at ground level, where it forms the prime constituent of smog, hindering plant growth and lung functions. Stratospheric ozone, however, is vital: it is the only gas that prevents harmful ultraviolet radiation (especially UV-B wavelengths) from reaching Earth's surface. Ozone depletion makes exposure to the sun more dangerous. Increased exposure to ultraviolet radiation will raise the incidence of skin cancer and cataracts and may depress the human immune system, increasing the disease rates in general. UV-B exposure also lowers crop yields and kills marine organisms vital to the ocean food chain.

Experts now project that atmospheric concentrations of heat-trapping gases will double over the next fifty years, largely because of carbon emissions. At that rate, global temperatures will rise between 1.0 and 3.5 degrees Celsius over the next century, with far-reaching effects on sea levels, weather, and endangered species. The momentum of climate change is already too great to stop and cannot even be slowed without cutting use of fossil fuels and especially CFCs.

The issues of human-induced climate change, like those of food and energy, are global in impact, as well as national and local, and require action on many fronts. At the global level, environmental diplomacy and politics have become a major subsystem of globalization, almost as big a field of endeavor as superpower conflict was during the Cold War. While international environmental agreements go back a century, the pace has quickened, and 130 were concluded between the Stockholm Conference of 1972 and the year 2000. The Montreal Protocol on Substances That Deplete the Ozone Layer (1987) formed a successful case, where a favorable balance between costs and benefits facilitated agreement. Atmospheric concentrations of ozone-depleting substances consequently began to fall by the mid-1990s. The 1992 UN Conference on Environment and Development (the Rio de Janeiro "Earth Summit") and subsequent meetings sought to draft similar agreements to curb emissions of other greenhouse gases. To date, however, efforts to restrict other such gases, notably those resulting from combustion of fossil fuels, have proven less successful because the cost-benefit ratios are different for developed and developing countries, as well as for different groups among the latter. Some of the thirty-nine members of the Alliance of Small Island States would disappear, and Bangladesh would lose half its rice-growing region, if sea levels rose a meter or more, whereas China and India are more concerned about the bite that curbing carbon emissions would take out of their GDP growth.

In any event, political action about environmental issues is not only international, and governments are not the only actors. Since the 1960s, radical politics has in a sense turned from "red" to "green." Starting in Germany, Green political parties have emerged in some countries, and environmental issues have gained in interest everywhere. Often not overtly political, nongovernmental organizations committed to environmental issues have proliferated. Many such organizations operate across national boundaries, and some have participated in environmental diplomacy, as the World Meteorological Organization did in the negotiation of the Montreal Protocol of 1987. Global environmental activism has become interwoven with global electronic communications through the creation of websites that provide information on environmental issues. As with other facets of the global disorder, environmental action by both governmental and nongovernmental entities occurs on all levels, from the global to the national and the local. Some national governments play important roles in providing incentives for sound environmental practice and disincentives for unsound ones. For example, some European nations impose "carbon taxes" on the use of polluting fuels, while providing positive incentives in other ways. Similarly, a U.S. business magazine proposed a $.50-per-gallon rise in gasoline tax, to be offset by a 10 percent reduction in income tax. Some local governments, especially those of large cities with serious pollution problems, also contribute by promoting energy-efficient mass transportation as an alternative to the private automobile.

In 1992 the U.S. National Academy of Sciences and the Royal Society of London issued a report beginning: "If current predictions of population growth prove accurate and patterns of human activity on the planet remain unchanged, science and technology may not be able to prevent either irreversible degradation of the environment or continued poverty for much of the world." In 1998, leading scientists argued in the journal *Nature* that "global climate change could soon become the environmental equivalent of the Cold War" and that the shift to "carbon-free energy" could require an international effort comparable to the Apollo space program.[9] In the twenty-first century, security will depend as much on solving environmental and resource problems as it once depended on military strength.

Nuclear Arms and Weapons of Mass Destruction: 160 Million Chernobyls?

No scientific advance of the twentieth century roused greater fears and hopes than nuclear energy. Aside from important medical uses, however, most of the hopes ended in frustration. Advocates predicted nuclear power would provide much of the world's electricity, until problems with generating costs and safety clouded that vista. No exception to the rule that humankind always exploits technological advances for destructive purposes, nuclear weapons provided the fiery finale to World War II and then dominated both the superpower strategy of the Cold War and the arms control agendas that outlasted it. The unfinished task of controlling not just nuclear arms but all weapons of mass destruction will remain a top priority for the coming century and one of the stiffest tests of whether humans have the wisdom to achieve sustainable development.

A thorough discussion of nuclear weapons would cover many topics: characteristics and destructive impacts, modes of deployment, tactics and strategy, the difficulty of defense against nuclear attack, arms control, and proliferation (the spread of such weapons to powers that do not already have them). A comparable discussion of all means of mass destruction would consider not only nuclear arms but also chemical weapons, biological weapons, and ballistic missiles, which can be used to deliver warheads of any of the preceding types, as well as conventional explosives.

Because the U.S. and Soviet arsenals contained over 95 percent of the 55,000 nuclear warheads then in existence—enough to create a blast 160 million times as powerful as the 1986 Chernobyl disaster—discussions of weapons of mass destruction used to focus solely on the superpowers. This approach dangerously neglected proliferation and non-nuclear weapons, which poor countries can acquire far more

readily than they can obtain nuclear warheads. The end of the Cold War made it easier to redress this imbalance. We shall therefore focus on major issues for the new millennium: global militarization, the Cold War arms control record, and the newer global control agenda.

Global Militarization Today's world has undergone drastic militarization. Between 1945 and 1995, global military spending added up to $30–35 trillion. The U.S. nuclear weapons program alone absorbed $4 trillion.

Before World War II, military spending absorbed less than 1 percent of gross world product. In 1986, the figure stood around 6 percent. U.S. deficit debates drew attention to defense spending, which amounted to 6.5 percent of GDP in 1985. The weaker Soviet economy suffered from higher military spending—over 10 percent of GDP in the mid-1980s. The paradox of a USSR that was strong militarily but weak economically went far to explain Gorbachev's attempted restructuring (see Chapter 13).

U.S.-Soviet rivalry propelled increased military spending, but it was a global phenomenon with vast costs for developing countries. The United States and the Soviet Union stood first and third among the world's nations ranked by GNP. When poor countries devoted as large a part of GNP to military spending as did the United States or Soviet Union, the developmental impact was far worse. By 1997, U.S. military spending had dropped to 3.4 percent of GDP. However, countries whose military spending, reckoned as a percentage of their GDP, approached or exceeded the old U.S. rate of 6 percent included some of the world's most troubled economies: the Russian Federation (5.8 percent), North Korea (27.0), Afghanistan (12.5), Angola (8.8), Iraq (7.4), and Sierra Leone (6.9). In contrast, western European nations' military spending ranged between 1 and 3 percent. Japan's military spending remained at 1 percent of GDP, the historically low rate that had helped power Japan's phenomenal economic growth.

During the 1990s, global spending on armaments decreased, although it would take longer to determine whether this was a lasting benefit from the end of the Cold War or a consequence of economic stress in many countries. In either case, levels of military spending remained alarmingly high. Global totals of government expenditures on defense fell from $1,210 billion in 1985 to $804 billion in 1997, while global totals for the international arms trade fell from $89 billion in 1987 to a low of $34 billion in 1994, rising again to $46 billion in 1997. In some senses, the availability of arms for sale had increased. A major factor was the post-Soviet republics' economic hardships and their willingness to sell advanced weapons to earn hard currency. Sales by U.S. firms were far greater, however; and their British and French competitors together sold nearly as much. Israel was also a major contributor to global militarization in proportion to its size, averaging over $1 billion a year in arms sales in the 1990s.

Experts have long argued that military preparedness is the key to national security. During the Cold War, commentators on superpower military policy commonly maintained that nuclear preparedness was essential to deter nuclear attack, that "deterrence" was the best defense. However, the historical connection between arms buildups and eventual outbreak of war is very strong. Now that the Cold War has ended, what has been accomplished in arms control, and what needs to be done in response to global militarization?

Arms Control: The Cold War Record

The need to control the spread of nuclear weapons was realized very early. By the 1980s, numerous agreements had been negotiated. Multilateral agreements prohibited deploying nuclear weapons in the Antarctic, on the sea bed, in Latin America, in the South Pacific, and in outer space. The Nuclear Nonproliferation Treaty (NPT, 1968, renewed 1995) prohibited signatory states that did not have nuclear weapons from acquiring them. The Limited Test Ban Treaty (1963) prohibited nuclear testing in the atmosphere, in space, and under water; only underground testing remained possible. The 1996 Comprehensive Nuclear Test Ban Treaty (CTBT), if ratified, will finally prevent all tests.

The United States and the Soviet Union also reached important bilateral agreements. Notable among these were the SALT I and II (Strategic Arms Limitation Talks) agreements (1972, 1979), which limited missiles and certain weapons technologies. The United States did not ratify SALT II but observed its terms.

For several years after SALT II, the trend ran against arms control. In June 1982, the Soviet Union did state that it would not be the first to use nuclear weapons; the United States refused to do likewise, on grounds that NATO plans for defending Europe required the threat of first use of nuclear weapons. The idea of defense against missile attack also resurfaced in 1983 in the form of the U.S. Strategic Defense Initiative (SDI), popularly known as "Star Wars." SDI would rely on particle beams and lasers to destroy attacking missiles. In a time of mounting federal deficit, questions of cost and workability under combat conditions made SDI highly controversial.

Although such ideas still survive in U.S. defense policy, SDI was eclipsed by political change that opened new prospects for arms control. The first big breakthrough was the Intermediate Nuclear Forces Treaty (INF, 1988), which eliminated both intermediate-range (600–3,400 miles) and shorter-range (300–600 miles) land-based missiles. The treaty was highly significant for Europe, where such missiles were heavily deployed.

In perhaps the most radical arms cuts in European history, the Conventional Forces in Europe Treaty (CFE, 1990) went on to set equal limits on the military equipment of NATO and Warsaw Pact forces. With the breakup of the

Warsaw Pact (1991), the former member states distributed the cuts among themselves. Under another U.S.-Soviet agreement of 1990, the two states undertook to cease producing chemical weapons and to reduce their arsenals, with further reductions to follow when a global ban went into force.

The most important efforts to reduce superpower nuclear arsenals began just before the Soviet breakup. The first Strategic Arms Reduction Treaty (START I, July 1991) limited each superpower's numbers of delivery vehicles and warheads. Before START I could be ratified, the Soviet collapse left four successor states—Russia, Belarus, Ukraine, and Kazakstan—with nuclear weapons. Despite reluctance to become non-nuclear states bordering on nuclear-armed Russia, the other republics eventually agreed to ship their nuclear weapons to Russia for dismantling but asked international compensation for doing so. The United States committed billions of dollars to pay for weapons destruction or to buy the highly enriched uranium removed from dismantled warheads. The START II Treaty, signed by U.S. and Russian presidents Bush and Yeltsin in 1992 but still not ratified by Russia as of 1998, again lowered allowable numbers of warheads. In 1997, U.S. President Clinton proposed, depending on Russia's ratifying START II, negotiation of yet deeper cuts in a START III treaty. In fact, while internal politics delayed Russia's ratification of START II, economics kept it from maintaining the arms levels allowed under START I.

After 1985, then, arms control efforts accelerated in an unprecedented way. However, the Soviet breakup destroyed the framework in which the major agreements had been negotiated. Even the proposed START III ceilings would leave U.S. and Russian arms ceilings—2,000–2,500 strategic warheads apiece by 2007—menacingly high. It would take more START treaties and deeper cuts to bring other declared nuclear-weapons states—Britain, France, and China—into the arms control process. Beyond that, efforts at arms control would bring negotiators up against resentments provoked by the idea that some countries might possess nuclear weapons and others might not. Yet Soviet collapse and the progress made in limiting the two largest nuclear arsenals had shaped a new arms control agenda by making it easier to see the urgency of controlling weapons of mass destruction in general.

A Global Arms Control Agenda

The idea of "proliferation" derives from the historical spread of nuclear weapons from a U.S. monopoly to a possession of a handful of powers, among which the United States and the Soviet Union had the largest arsenals. Endorsing the idea of nuclear haves and have-nots, the proliferation concept will be questioned increasingly in future. Logically, the only solution is disarmament: the elimination by all countries of the weapons in question. However, the practical difficulties of achieving disarmament suggest that limiting the spread of dangerous weapons and the size of arsenals may be worthwhile steps toward that goal.

The end of the Cold War increased the danger that weapons of mass destruction would spread to nations that did not already have them, even to terrorists or other radical groups. In Russia, control over such weapons and military technologies has weakened, and high-placed Russians have been implicated in the procurement efforts of countries like Iran and Syria. Between 1991 and 1997, even highly enriched plutonium was exported from—or smuggled out of—Soviet successor states on at least four occasions. In Japan, the Aum Shinrikyu cult released the chemical agent sarin in the Tokyo subways in 1995 and was also experimenting with anthrax bacteria, a biological agent. Assessing proliferation thus requires considering not only nuclear arms but also chemical and biological weapons and ballistic missiles, which can be used to deliver nuclear, chemical, biological, or conventional payloads.

Even things as "low tech" as land mines count as weapons of mass destruction.

Countries known to possess nuclear weapons are the United States, Russia, Britain, France, China, India, and Pakistan. Israel is believed to possess nuclear weapons or to be able to assemble them quickly. Countries thought to be seeking nuclear weapons are Libya, Iran, Iraq, and North Korea. After Iraq's defeat in the Gulf War (1991), UN efforts to eliminate Iraq's weapons of mass destruction made Iraq the scene of an unprecedented experiment in arms control, which Iraq obstructed in every way possible. The Iraqi case proved that a country with a limited technological base can start a major nuclear-weapons program and largely hide it from international scrutiny. In the absence of sure ways to deal with this problem, future efforts to limit nuclear proliferation need to go beyond START I and II and make deep enough cuts to affect all nuclear powers.

While large-scale use of chemical weapons has not occurred since World War I, new concern about them emerged in the 1980s. Although only the Soviet Union, the United States, and France had possessed chemical weapons for many years, twenty countries—including Iraq, Iran, Libya, Egypt, Syria, Israel, Indonesia, Thailand, Vietnam, North Korea, and Taiwan— were suspected of having chemical weapons programs. Iraq used chemical weapons during the Iran-Iraq War; the use of chemical and biological weapons by Iraq was also a threat during the Gulf War. Compared to nuclear weapons, chemical weapons are easier and cheaper to produce, and their production and storage are harder to detect.

The list of diseases whose pathogens can be used for biological warfare is long; genetic engineering can make it longer. Biological agents can be highly effective in far smaller quantities than chemical agents and thus have greater potential as weapons of mass destruction. However, biological agents take longer to

work their course and may infect the users as well as the users' enemies. Partly for such reasons, historical evidence on use of biological weapons in warfare is sketchier than evidence on chemical weapons. However, ten nations are thought to have or be developing biological weapons, among them Iraq and North Korea. Iraqi officials have admitted stockpiling enough anthrax bacteria to kill the entire world population three times over; they ordered their original specimen from a U.S. mail-order firm. Following the Gulf War, illnesses among U.S. veterans, their families, and caregivers suggested that biological weapons had been detonated by U.S. attack on Iraqi storage facilities if not by Iraqi initiative. UN inspectors found, as well, that Iraq had missiles fitted with biological warheads. If population growth was the "nuclear bomb of the poor" in the twentieth century, a worst-case scenario for the twenty-first might picture biological weapons, which are easier and cheaper to produce than either nuclear or chemical weapons, as the "poor nations' nuclear weapons."

Ballistic missiles make a versatile delivery system for any of these weapons. For a long time there was no effective defense against missile attack, although one effective anti-missile defense system, the Patriot, was introduced in the Gulf War in January 1991. Because the technology required to develop ballistic missiles and satellite launch vehicles is the same, a government can easily hide a weapons-oriented missile program as a peaceful one. For all these reasons, the spread of ballistic missiles is a major facet of global militarization. Cruise missiles—essentially pilotless aircraft that can be used to deliver warheads—make proliferation even harder to control. Given the Global Positioning System (GPS), a system of satellites that emit signals for navigation, a cruise missile equipped with a low-cost GPS receiver can strike within feet of its target. When the GPS became fully operational in 1992, it ended what had been the technologically advanced countries' monopoly on accurate navigation. GPS technology has since become widely enough available to guide taxis as well as missiles.

Exporters of missile technology have included China, the Soviet Union (and now Russia), Israel, Brazil, India, North Korea, Sweden, and Argentina. Other countries that have at least deployed ballistic missiles include Algeria, Libya, South Africa, Iran, Iraq, Syria, Egypt, Saudi Arabia, Yemen, Pakistan, South Korea, and Taiwan. The fact that the list of exporters includes several countries that are not major industrial powers suggests that missile technologies will continue to spread. One of the lessons some nations drew from the 1991 Gulf War was that they should acquire the means to keep the United States from doing to them what it did to Iraq, whose Scud missiles had performed better than its tanks and artillery.

The extensive weapons programs that came to light in Iraq, and more recent reports that North Korea was close to developing nuclear weapons, prove the urgency of arms control for the coming century. Real safety from weapons of mass destruction requires not just preventing their spread but rather eliminating them completely or at least reducing them to the lowest achievable levels. Where does the world stand in that task?

The end of the Cold War helped global arms control in many ways. First, proliferation control, long eclipsed by superpower confrontation, came front and center among arms issues. Enough arms control treaties were concluded that the emphasis in arms control shifted both from negotiation to implementation, and from U.S.-Russian treaties to agreements among large numbers of countries. The reductions made in the START negotiations represented major steps toward reducing the immense gaps between nuclear haves and have-nots. The Nuclear Nonproliferation Treaty (NPT, renewed in 1995) and the Comprehensive Test Ban Treaty (CTBT,

1996) furthered nuclear weapons control globally. Controls on other weapons of mass destruction included the Chemical Weapons Convention (CWC, 1993) and the Biological Weapons Convention (BWC, formerly the Biological and Toxin Weapons Convention, 1972). Also important to mention are the Missile Technology Control Regime (MTCR, 1987, which is not a treaty but an agreement among developed nations to try to halt the spread of ballistic missile technologies), a convention prohibiting anti-personnel mines (1997), and the UN Weaponry Convention (amended 1998) to restrict highly injurious weapons such as plastic land mines. In 1998, agreement was also reached to launch negotiations of a Fissile Material Cut Off Treaty (FMCT) to ban production of highly enriched uranium and plutonium, needed for nuclear weapons.

Not all nations have signed any of these treaties and conventions. Yet by 1998, at least 185 nations had signed the NPT, 150 had signed the CTBT, 140 had signed the BWC, 114 were members of the CWC, and 129 had signed the 1997 convention against anti-personnel mines. These numbers are major gains, but more is needed to make the world safer. Desirable additional steps would include ratification of these agreements by the many signers that have not yet done so, additional regional treaties to create nuclear-free zones like those created for Africa and the South Pacific, replacing the MCTR with a binding treaty, and real elimination of anti-personnel mines, which maim civilians long years after war has ended.

Between signing a treaty and verifying compliance, a gulf looms. For a long time, experts warned that many forms of proliferation would be highly difficult to control. Limiting export of dual-use items, such as chemicals usable either for legitimate purposes or for making chemical weapons, or missile technologies usable either for launching satellites or for waging war, would be especially hard. Yet recent events have set precedents that show how much can be accomplished in arms control. To verify compliance, U.S.-Soviet agreements, starting with the INF Treaty, prescribed both satellite surveillance and on-site inspections. The terms imposed on Iraq after the Gulf War internationalized the system of intrusive inspection, making the United Nations the enforcer—a valuable precedent for an era when the main threats to global peace are likely to be regional conflicts. Experts also believe that verification of treaty compliance will be possible if arms control agreements include two requirements: on-site inspection and prior declaration by each state of its activities in the treaty-regulated field. The declarations provide a base line against which inspectors can verify compliance.

The framework of arms control agreements provides only the beginning of a web of restraints that raise the costs of noncompliance and may deter other states from violating the treaties. It remains unclear that the international community will always be willing to commit the resources to restraining violators that it committed in Iraq. Reducing global militarization will remain difficult, dangerous, and costly; eliminating weapons of mass destruction will be even harder. In a world that knows how to destroy itself but has trouble finding the resources to support sustainable development, the incentives to reduce spending on weapons of mass destruction are obvious. Will the wisdom to do so prevail?

Looking Ahead

Today, while thinkers focusing on identity and difference still reject global views, those struggling to theorize globalization see it as producing even these assertions of the local and particular. The global and the local interact in more and more ways, making up networks within the global web. In a world of space-time compression, globalization is a fact; we all have to try to understand the global disorder even while we wait for more refined theoretical explanations.

Clearly, globalization has both cultural and material dimensions. It includes both the messages transmitted over electronic networks and the software and hardware that transmit the messages. As a system that lacks any main center yet enables all users who observe common "protocols" or standards to communicate, the Internet offers, in fact, both a model for understanding globalization and one of its foremost subsystems. To think about the global and the local in the new century, let us therefore imagine a website with pages for each of the themes of this book and many links on each page to other sites containing text, images, and statistics.

With "globalization" written across the top of it in big letters, the Global Interrelatedness page is crowded with links. Some of these lead to the homepages of multinational corporations; interest groups that represent them; government agencies of economically powerful nations; or international organizations like the European Union, International Monetary Fund, or World Trade Organization. Pursuing those links yields the impression that globalization is a matter of global acceptance of "protocols" or standards that eliminate barriers to trade and investment and integrate the world's markets. Statistics on the growing rate and volume of global monetary flows may give us the impression that the world is getting richer, despite short-term crises here or there. Yet other links bring up the homepages of organizations like the UN Development Program, the Third World Network, and the Women's Environment and Development Organization. These remind us of the difference between growth and development, of the widening of income inequality within and among the world's societies, and of the remarkable extent to which the Left has turned "green."

Gender issues and worker rights raise our curiosity about the extent to which cultural, rather than material, issues define globalization. Exploring different links on the globalization page shows that it is in fact very much a cultural, and not only a material, process. Again in a way that recalls the structure of the Internet as a web with many nodal points but no center, many of the cultural linkages take the form of agreements to accept common standards, in matters ranging from religious belief to environmental issues or human rights. Others are new kinds of cultural "fusions," like the Afro-Celtic neo-folk or Tibetan-inspired "space music" that we might want to download to listen to while exploring our website.

Considering cultural issues quickly brings us to the Identity and Difference page, which abounds with signs of the adversarial tension between that theme and global interrelatedness. All together, these links show how identity issues, however individually disconnected from one another, form a global mosaic with an overall pattern. Some of these movements have always seen themselves as speaking to the entire world. The pope, who in the past spoke in Rome "to the city and to the world" (*urbi et orbi*), now can do so over the Vatican website when he is not actually traveling around the world. Other movements that are truly local can achieve global visibility through electronic communications, as, we have noted, do the Zapatistas of Chiapas in Mexico. Everywhere, the shift from the national to the regional or global as the most significant scale of spatial organization emboldens indigenous peoples, like Mexico's native Americans or Australia's aborigines, or stateless ethnic groups, like Scots, to greater assertiveness. Numerous links show, too, that some identity-based groups—U.S. super-patriots, German neo-Nazis—react against globalization by propagating messages of violence and hatred against those different from themselves. The most extreme cases, like the "Afghan" militants among Islamic activists, will avoid the publicity of websites but use other electronic means, such as cell phones, fax machines, or electronic funds transfers, not to mention electronic detonators, to carry out their far-flung missions.

The web pages for Mass Society and Technology—two themes that the twentieth century's explosive population growth inextricably intertwined—will also contain huge numbers of links. Some of these will lead to statistics that contrast the unfinished third demographic transition with the threat of an ecological transition—a massive loss of sustainability. Here, optimistic impressions of globalization as a matter of economic growth have to be weighed against costs of growth that conventional economic statistics do not measure. Demographic links lead to startling contrasts between the stable population sizes of many European societies and the continuing population growth elsewhere, to heart-wrenching scenes of the global AIDS epidemic, or to a rising tide of migration. Exploring the growing number of links on "democratization" provides evidence of its global spread, too, as well as of its incomplete realization in many lands.

One of the most important types of links pertains to the changing meanings of "security" now that Cold War thinking has yielded to concerns about food security, energy supplies, global warming, or the proliferation of weapons of mass destruction. Scenes of forests destroyed by reckless logging or acid rain, of rivers that run dry because of overuse for irrigation, of cities with skies darkened by smog or power outages illustrate the manifold linkages between the global and the local in environmental issues. Data on warheads being destroyed in Russia and the United States, on one hand, and of children maimed by land mines in poor countries, on the other, show that security still has military dimensions. Other links lead to pages showing how the work of governments and nongovernmental action groups to limit arms proliferation or control greenhouse gases have created additional global networks.

Coming back to our own homepage to consider the larger picture, we need time to reflect on the meaning of all we have seen. As we do, one of the oldest questions about history may come to us as the first to ask about the new millennium. What must humankind do to live together and provide equitably for their needs, without either making unsustainable demands on the environment or conflicting unmanageably with one another? This chapter has attempted to sum up some of the answers that emerge from the legacy of the twentieth century.

Notes

1. United Nations Development Program, *Human Development Report 1996* (New York: Oxford University Press, 1996), p. 3.

2. Patrick Karl O'Brien, "Intercontinental Trade and the Development of the Third World since the Industrial Revolution," *Journal of World History* 8:1 (1997), pp. 85–86.

3. Hugh Pope, "Back on the Silk Road," *Middle East International,* no. 487 (November 4, 1994), p. 13.

4. Gyan Prakash, "Introduction: After Colonialism," in Gyan Prakash, *After Colonialism: Imperial Histories and Postcolonial Displacements* (Princeton: Princeton University Press, 1995), p. 12.

5. Michael A. Sells, *The Bridge Betrayed: Religion and Genocide in Bosnia* (Berkeley: University of California Press, 1996).

6. Anthony Lewis, "Mandela the Pol," *New York Times Magazine,* March 23, 1997, p. 45.

7. United Nations Development Program, *Human Development Report 2000,* 113 (quotation from Mary Robinson); Erik Eckholm, "China's Rights Stand: Progress or an Irrelevance?" *New York Times,* November 27, 2000, page A8 (quotation from Jiang Zemin).

8. Lester R. Brown et al., *State of the World, 1987: A Worldwatch Institute Report on Progress Toward a Sustainable Society* (New York: Norton, 1987), pp. 26–27.

9. Lester R. Brown et al., *State of the World, 1993* (New York, Norton, 1993), p. 3; Brown et al., *State of the World, 1999* (New York, Norton, 1999), p. 35.

Suggestions for Further Reading

Appadurai, Arjun. *Modernity at Large: Cultural Dimensions of Globalization* (1996).

Bauer, Joanne R., and Daniel Bell, eds. *The East Asian Challenge for Human Rights* (1999).

Brown, Lester R., et al. *State of the World: A Worldwatch Institute Report on Progress Toward a Sustainable Society* (1984–2000, published annually).

Cohen, Joel. *How Many People Can the Earth Support* (1995).

Cole, Leonard A. *The Eleventh Plague: The Politics of Biological and Chemical Warfare* (1996).

Comaroff, John L. "Ethnicity, Nationalism, and the Politics of Difference in an Age of Revolution." In *Ethnicity, Identity, and Nationalism in South Africa: Past, Present, and Future,* edited by Edwin N. Wilmsen and P. A. McAllister (1996).

Danaher, Keven, and Roger Burbach, eds. *Globalize This! The Battle against the World Trade Organization and Corporate Rule* (2000).

Dryzek, John S., and David Schlosberg, eds. *Debating the Earth: The Environmental Politics Reader* (1998).

Gallagher, Nancy W. *Arms Control: New Approaches to Theory and Policy* (1998).

Geyer, Michael, and Charles Bright. "World History in a Global Age." *American Historical Review,* C, 4 (1995), 1034–1060.

Ghosh, Bimal, ed. *Managing Migration: Time for a New International Regime?* (2000).

Giddens, Anthony. *Runaway World: How Globalization is Reshaping our Lives* (2000).

Goldman, Ralph Morris. *Building Trust: An Introduction to Peacekeeping and Arms Control* (1997).

Hay, Colin, and David Marsh, eds. *Demystifying Globalization* (2000).

International Institute for Strategic Studies. *The Military Balance, 1998/1999* (1998, annual).

Kalb, Don, Marco van der Land, et al., eds. *The Ends of Globalization: Bringing Society Back In* (2000).

Kidron, Michael, and Ronald Segal. *The New State of the World Atlas.* 5th ed. (1995).

Maddison, Angus. *Monitoring the World Economy, 1820-1992* (1995).

O'Brien, Karl Patrick. "Intercontinental Trade and the Development of the Third World since the Industrial Revolution." *Journal of World History,* 8(1) (1997), 75-133.

Pierre, Andrew J., ed. *Cascade of Arms: Managing Conventional Weapons Proliferation* (1997).

Spencer, Jack. *The Ballistic Missile Threat Handbook* (2000).

United Nations Development Program. *Human Development Report* (1996-2000, published annually).

Went, Robert. *Globalization: Neoliberal Challenge, Radical Responses.* Translated by Peter Drucker (2000).

Wolfe, Patrick. "History and Imperialism: A Century of Theory, from Marx to Postcolonialism." *American Historical Review,* 102(2) (1997), 388-420.

World Bank. *World Development Reports* (1984-2000, published annually).

World Resources Institute. *World Resources* (1986-2000, annual).

Index

International Office of Public Health, 61

International organizations, 494; globalization and, 518. *See also* specific organizations

International relations: Cuba and, 382; from 1945 to 2000, 245–247

International zone, in Turkey, 200

Interracial relations. *See* Sex

Intervention: in Suez War (1956), 438; by U.S. in Latin America, 152; by U.S. in Mexico, 160

Intifada, 447–448, 451

Inventions: in Industrial Revolution, 9; in second Industrial Revolution, 30–31

Inventory system, just-in-time, 312

Investment: British, 110; foreign investments in U.S., 301; in Israel, 445; by Japan, 476; in Mexico, 93–94, 375; stock market crash and, 109

Iran, 431–436; European powers and, 199; government of, 432; Khomeini in, 433–436; oil embargo and, 263; overthrow of shah in, 263; politics in, 200; Qajar dynasty in, 194; revolution in, 83, 419; Safavids in, 193; shahs of, 200; Soviets and, 248; U.S. Embassy seizure in, 436. *See also* Persia

Iran hostage crisis, 263

Iranian Revolution (1979), 428; South Africa and, 406–407

Iran-Iraq War, 266, 435

Iraq: fascist movement in, 141; Iran-Iraq War and, 435; nuclear weapons in, 516; Persian Gulf War and, 266–268; PLO and, 448

Iron Curtain, 248–249

Iron Guard, in Romania, 139–140

Iron industry, 9

"Iron Lady." *See* Thatcher, Margaret

Iron triangle, in Japan, 480, 481

Irrigation, water resources and, 507

Islam, 423 (map); in Iran, 433; in Egypt, 50; in Middle East, 15–16, 419; Nigeria and, 177–178; revivalist movements in, 18; slave trade of, 8n, 174. *See also* Arab world; Middle East; Muslims; North Africa; Ottoman Empire; specific countries

Islamic empires, 15; Europe (1500) and, 6

Islamic Jihad, 176, 449. *See also* Holy War

Islamic militants, 441, 442. *See also* specific countries and issues

Islamic revolution, 419, 424–425

Isolation: China and, 205; end of U.S., 229–230; Japan and, 205

Israel, 200, 422–423, 442–451; Arab oil production and, 421; Arabs in, 444; Arab unity and, 424; Balfour Declaration and, 63; creation of, 202; Egypt and, 424, 438–439–440; Iran and, 432, 436; Lebanon invasion by, 446–447; Nasser and, 438–439; and neighboring countries, 443–444 (map); new settlements in, 448–449; OPEC oil embargo and, 263; "Oriental" Jews in, 446; Palestinians and, 447–451; Sadat in, 440; standard of living in, 450; Suez War (1956) and, 438. *See also* Arab-Israeli conflict; Arab world; Middle East; Palestine

Italy, 57, 129 (map); Allied invasion of, 233; fascism and, 122–123, 124, 125–128; imperialism by, 37–38; ouster from Ethiopia, 233; Somalia and, 396; in Triple Alliance, 60; unification of, 29; in World War I, 64. *See also* Ethiopia; Mussolini, Benito

Jabavu, John, 184

Jameson, Leander Starr, 182

Janata, Morarji Desai, 463

Japan, 192, 210–213, 216; alliance with Germany and Italy, 214–215; atomic bombing of, 235, 236; China and, 207, 209–210, 213, 226, 476; Christianity and, 8; code of, 227–229; commercial organization in, 477; computers in, 317; corruption scandal in, 480, 481; democratization and militarism in, 214–215; development of, 205; drive for empire, 220–221; economic changes in, 480–481; economic expansion of, 284; economic role of, 11; as economic superpower, 261, 475–477; European colonies in Asia, 456; Europe and, 205; expansionism in China, 207; foreign trade and, 10; globalization and, 484; GNP growth rate in, 333; government of, 210–211, 479–480; Great Depression and, 214; as Great Power, 9, 213–214; identity politics in, 459; imperialism in China, 35; industrial competition from, 295–296; industrial output of, 33; Meiji Restoration in, 212; military in, 211, 212, 213; in 1930s, 210 (map); nuclear accident in, 481; OPEC oil and, 421; Pacific region and, 251; Pearl Harbor and, 221, 226–229; population of, 457; productivity in, 312; racial equality and, 73; reasons for economic success, 477–478; reconstruction of, 475; Russian war with, 86; society of, 478–479; stock market collapse in, 476–477; Tokugawa shogunate in, 6, 193; treaties with, 206; turning point in World War II and, 230; United States and, 194, 206, 271–272, 376, 476; Vietnam and, 256; West and, 210–213; in World War I, 63; after World War II, 455, 474–481; World War II surrender of, 236. *See also* World War I; World War II

Japanese Americans, deportation of, 135

Japan Socialist party (JSP), 479, 480

Jaruzelski, Wojciech, 331–332, 343

Jayaram, Jayalalitha, 465

Jericho, 449

Jerusalem, 450; Israel and, 439; Palestinian-Israeli agreement and, 449; Sadat and, 440

Jewish State, The (Herzl), 201

Jews and Judaism: Holocaust and, 232–233; in Iran, 436; "Oriental" Jews in Israel, 446; Palestine homeland for, 63, 200; in Russia, 85. *See also* Arab world; Israel; Middle East; Zionism

Jiang Jieshi. *See* Chiang Kai-Shek

Jiang Qing, 469–470

Jiangxi soviet, 99–100

Jiang Zemin, 473, 506

Jihad. *See* Holy war; Islamic jihad

Jinnah, Muhammad Ali, 196, 197

Job Corps, 291

Jobs, 313; in Latin America, 355. *See also* Blue-collar workers; Employment; Unemployment; White-collar workers

John XXIII (Pope), Latin America and, 360

John Paul II (Pope): Holy Year (2000) and, 488–489; Latin America and, 360

Johnson, Lyndon B.: Great Society and, 291–292; Latin America and, 362; Vietnam War and, 258–259

Joint-stock corporations, 34

Joint ventures, in Hungary, 328

Jordan, 200, 201. *See also* West Bank of Jordan

Judaism, 15

Junk bonds, 301

Justicialist ideology, of Péron, 367

"Just in time" inventories, 312

Jutland, battle at, 63

Kádár, János, 328, 329

Kaiser (German emperor), 39–40, 43, 67

Kampuchea. *See* Cambodia

Kanemaru, Shin, 480

Kapp putsch, 130

Karpinsky, Len, 320–321

Kashmir, Muslims in, 464

Al-Kata'ib. *See* Phalange

Katanga Province, 388

Kazakstan, 498–499

Keiretsu (business groups), in Japan, 477

Kennedy, John E: Cuban missile crisis and, 244–245; Iran and, 432; Khrushchev, Berlin, and, 253; Latin America and, 361; televised debate by, 286; Vietnam and, 258

Kent State University, killings at, 289

Kenya, 167, 388–390; independence of, 390; women's groups in, 387

Kenyatta, Jomo, 390

Keynes, John Maynard, and Keynesian economics, 118, 119, 278, 298

Khamenei, Ali (Ayatollah), 435–436

Khatami, Muhammad, 436

Khedives, 46

Khomeini, Ruhollah (Ayatollah), 432, 433–436

Khrushchev, Nikita: change in Soviet Union and, 320–321; China and, 256; containment of, 251–254; Cuban missile crisis and, 244–245, 253–254; Gorbachev and, 323; ouster of, 326; reform and, 324–326; U.S. visit by (1959), 252

Kibbutz (Israel), 444

Kikuyu people, 388

Kimbangu, Simon, 176

Kim Dae Jung, 483

King, Martin Luther, Jr., 288–289; Gandhi, nonviolence, and, 199

Kinship: in Africa, 170, 171–173, 399, 400; in Egyptian society, 49–50

Kipling, Rudyard, 37

Kissinger, Henry, détente policy and, 260

Knowledge explosion, 284–285

Knowledge industries, in Japan, 476

Knowledge structures, globalization and, 490

Koestler, Arthur, 81–82

Kohl, Helmut, 310

Roosevelt, Franklin D.: Atlantic Charter and, 229; criticized as "socialistic," 105; embargo against Japan, 226; Mexico and, 162; New Deal and, 116-119; Poland and, 233-234; "Roosevelt Revolution" and, 117; on revolution, 119; at Yalta, 237, 238

Roosevelt, Theodore, survival of the fittest and, 30

Rough Riders, 30

Royal Air Force (Britain): Battle of Britain and, 224-225; raids on Germany by, 234-235

Royal Niger Company, 178

Rúa, Fernando de la, 369

Rubber, in Congo, 38

Ruhr region, French occupation of, 130

Rural areas: in Latin America, 148-149; migration from, 33-34, 278, 503

Rural society, in Russia, 321

Russell, Bertrand, 33

Russia: arms control and, 514-515; balance of power and, 28; Bloody Sunday in, 86; Bolshevik Revolution in, 11, 81-82; Bosnian crisis (1908-1909) and, 60; communism and, 103-104, 345-350; Crimean War and, 199; education in, 61; end of tsarism in, 83-86; industrialization of, 85-86; industrial output of, 32; invasion by western powers, 89; Iran and, 199; Japanese war with, 86; Lenin and, 86-90; mobilization of, 62; parliament in, 84; peasants in, 84; Persia and, 35; under Putin, 349-350; revolution of 1905 in, 89; revolutions of 1917 in, 56, 87-88, 89; society of, 85; in Triple Entente, 60; withdrawal from World War I, 66; World War I and, 63, 66, 80, 87; under Yeltsin, 346-348. See also Soviet Union

Russian Empire, 7

Russian front, in World War II, 225-226

Russian Mafia, 348

Russian Republic, Yeltsin and, 265, 339-340

Russo-Japanese War, 86, 213

Rwanda, Hutu refugees and, 392

Ryukyu Islands, 213

SA, 132; in Germany, 131

al-Sadat, Anwar, 424, 437, 439-440; assassination of, 440; Dinshawai incident and, 47

Safavid dynasty (Iran), 6, 193

Sahara desert, 169. See also Sub-Saharan Africa

Saigon, 259

St. Petersburg, as Petrograd, 87

Salazar, Oliveira, 122

Salgado, Plinio, 141

Salinas de Gortari, Carlos, 376, 377

SALT treaties: SALT I, 261, 514; SALT II, 262, 514

Samurai (Japan), 211

Sandinistas, in Nicaragua, 263

Sanitation, in Africa, 393

San Juan Hill, Roosevelt, Theodore, and, 31

Sankoh, Foday, 386

San people, 169

São Paulo, 157, 158, 352, 356

Sarajevo: Franz Ferdinand assassination in, 56, 57. See also Yugoslavia

Sarney, José, 372

Saro-Wiwa, Ken, 405

SASOL (South African Coal, Oil and Gas Corporation), 406-407

Satellite states, in Eastern Europe (1950s-1980s), 326-333

Sati (India), 195

Satyagraha, 96

Saudi Arabia, human development in, 420

SAVAK, 432

Savimbi, Jonas, 386

Savings: in Japan, 477; in United States, 301

Scandinavia: socialism in, 113. See also specific countries

Scapegoats, in United States, 309

Schlieffen, Alfred von, World War I and, 62

Schools: in Cuba, 382; in Japan, 213. See also Education

Sciences: Darwin and, 29; Einstein and, 30; Freud and, 30; in Germany, 45-46; globalization of, 490-491; in imperial Berlin, 43; in India, 462, 463; in Japan, 475; nature vs. technology and, 20-24; Pasteur and, 29. See also Technology

SDI. See Strategic Defense Initiative (SDI, Star Wars)

SDS. See Students for a Democratic Society (SDS)

Sea-level rises, 511

Seattle, WTO protests in, 273-274, 496

SEC. See Securities and Exchange Commission (SEC)

Second Industrial Revolution, 30

Second New Deal, 117

Second Republic, in Brazil, 370, 371

Second World War. See World War II

Secret police, in Soviet Union, 89, 324, 337

Secularism, Iran and, 435

Securities and Exchange Commission (SEC), 117

Security: of Israel, 442-451; of Japan, 475, 479; meaning of, 519; millennium celebrations and, 489

Security Council (UN), permanent members of, 242

Segregation: in United States, 288-289. See also Apartheid (South Africa)

Self-determination: Africa and, 174; Atlantic Charter and, 229; Latin America and, 152; after World War I, 77

Self-sufficiency, in African colonies, 175-176

Senegal, 176, 398

Senghor, Léopold, 398

Separatism, in India, 464

Serbia, World War I and, 56, 58

Serbs, 270

Serfdom, in Russia, 85

Service sector, 284; layoffs in, 304-305; in postindustrial society, 296

Settler colonies, 175; independence for, 177; South Africa as, 168

Sèvres, Treaty of, 74, 200

Sex: South African prohibition against interracial, 409. See also Gender

Sezer, Ahmet Necdet, 429, 431

Shaba Province. See Katanga Province

Shagari, Shehu, 405

Shah. See Iran; specific individuals

Shah-People Revolution (Iran), 432

Shaka (Zulu), in South Africa, 180-181

Shamir, Yitzhak, 447

Shandong Province, Falun Dafa and, 454-455

Shanghai, Japanese bombing of, 211

Shantytowns, 106, 356; in Brazil, 352

Sharia (Islamic religious law), 193

Sharon, Ariel, 446, 447, 451

Sharpeville massacre (South Africa), 410

Sheep, in Argentina, 153

Sherman, Cindy, 490

Shii Moslems, 433, 435

Ships and shipping: World War I and, 64; World War II and, 229, 230

Shogun (Japan), 211

Shona peoples, 390

Show trials, in Soviet Union, 324

Sicily, Allied invasion of, 233

Sierra Leone, 173, 177, 179, 386-387; independence of, 388

Sikhs, in India, 463

Silk route, interrelatedness and, 4

Silver, Chinese economy and, 6

Sinai, 438-439, 445, 446

Singapore: economic growth of, 481-483; in World War II, 227

Singh, Manmohan, 464

Single-party regime (Mexico), 374-375, 378

Sino-Japanese War, 207

Siqueiros, David Alfaro, 160

Sitdown strike, 116

Six-Day War (1967). See Arab-Israeli conflict

Sixties, The, 275-276

Slave labor, in Russia, 91-92

Slaves and slavery: African, 7, 8, 147, 173; African kinship and, 170; in Brazil, 148, 157; in Cuba, 378; debt peons and, 148-149; firearms and, 171

Slave trade: contact points in, 8; Islamic, 8n, 174

Slovakia, 342-343

Smuts, Jan, 183-184

Soccer, in Brazil, 158

Social action, collective, 296

Social classes. See Class

Social Darwinism, 30-31, 37-38; races among whites, 31

Social Democratic party: Bolshevik faction of, 87-88; Menshevik faction of, 87-88

Social equality, international comparison of, 313

Socialism, 494; in Africa, 398; in Arab world, 423, 438; Bolshevism and, 113; in Britain, 113-114; in Chile, 362; China transformed under, 468-469; communism compared with, 113; democratic, 105; in Egypt, 437-439; in France, 113; in German Reichstag, 45; in Great Depression, 113; in Hungary, 328-329; internationalist, 34; in Latin America, 362; of Mitterrand, 281-282, 297-298; in Nazi Germany, 132; Stalin and, 115; in Third World, 458; war socialism, 69; after World War II, 277; in Yugoslavia, 327-328. See also Marxism and Marxists

"Socialism in one country," 91–92, 322
"Socialism with a human face," in Czechoslovakia, 329
Socialist bloc, 11
Socialist party, in Germany, 113
Socialist transformation, in China, 466
Social revolutions, in Cuba, 380–382
Social roles, in Egyptian villages, 48
Social security, in Germany, 45
Social Security system, in United States, 277
Social stratification, on *Titanic*, 26–27
Social welfare, 10; French expenditures on, 297; in Germany, 45; government and, 68; in Japan, 479; in Scandinavia, 113. *See also* Welfare systems
Society: in Africa, 167–168, 171–173; in Asia, 194; in China, 468, 471–472, 474; corporatist, 127; critiques of, 500; in Cuba, 381; democratization and, 505–506; demographic transition in, 18–19; in Egyptian villages, 48–50; fascist, 123–125; in Germany, 131; in imperial Berlin, 40–46; in India, 193; in Japan, 478–479; in Latin America, 146–147, 354–356; mass, 18; in Nazi Germany, 132–135; in post-Soviet Russia, 346–350; in Russia, 85; technology and, 280–282; in Turkey, 202–204; after World War II, 221, 240–241, 276–277; World War I impact on, 68. *See also* Economy; Kinship; Mass society; Politics; Social stratification; Suburbs; Technology
Sokoto caliphate, 178, 179
Solar energy, 510
Soldiers: in revolutionary Mexico, 160; in World War I, 55–56, 64
Solidarity movement, 331; after Soviet Union, 343–344
Solomon Islands, 230
Solzhenitsyn, Alexandr, 326
Somalia, 390, 394–396; economy of, 394; Marxism in, 398; starvation in, 394
Somme River, battle at, 64
Somoza regime, in Nicaragua, 152
South Africa, 176, 186, 406–415; apartheid in, 408–410; De Beers conglomerate of, 385–386; diamonds in, 181–182; Dutch in, 180; Gandhi in, 96; gold in, 182; government of, 183–184; imperialism in, 180–185; majority rule in, 387, 397, 412–415; Namibia and, 174, 390; nonwhites in, 182, 184–185; politics and economy of, 182–184; post-apartheid provinces in, 414 (map); as settler colony, 168; Union of, 181; vote for black South Africans, 412–413; whites in, 180, 181, 186
South African National Congress (ANC). *See* African National Congress (ANC)
South African Native Convention, 184
South African party, 183
South Asia, 190, 191–192; culture in, 458–460; decolonization to reassertion in, 455–460; economies in, 458; in 1990s, 471 (map); post-1945 history of, 483–484
Southeast Anatolia Project (Turkey), 431
Southeast Asia, 191; domino theory and, 257; European expansion in, 194;

growth in, 11; Japan driven from, 236; population of, 457. *See also* Asia; Vietnam War; specific countries
Southern African Development Community (SADC), 397
Southern Rhodesia. *See* Zimbabwe
South Korea, 483; economic growth of, 481–483. *See also* Korea; Korean War
South Slavs: nationalism of, 57–58; Russia and, 60
South Vietnam, 258; United States and, 258; after Vietnam War, 259. *See also* Vietnam War
South-West Africa. *See* Namibia
Southwest Asia, 191; colonization of, 10; Israel and, 424; use of term, 191n. *See also* Middle East
Soviet bloc, 238, 250 (map)
Soviets (councils), in Russia, 87
Soviet Union, 11; Afghanistan invasion by, 262; Africa and, 399, 400–401; Arabs and, 437; Asia and, 208, 456; Battle of Stalingrad in, 230; Berlin and, 253; Carter and, 262; China and, 99, 247, 256, 467–468; collapse of, 11, 245, 247, 265, 320–321, 334–341, 341 (map); containment of, 251–254; Cuba and, 381, 382; Cuban missile crisis and, 245; Eastern Europe and, 262; Egypt and, 437, 438; Eighth Five-Year Plan in, 333; end of Soviet bloc in Eastern Europe, 340 (map); former, 345–350; GNP growth rate in, 333; government under Lenin, 89–90; Hitler's invasion of, 220, 221; industrialization of, 91; Iran and, 431; labor mobilization in, 231; Nazi invasion of, 225–226; Nazi-Soviet pact and, 138; Nixon and, 260–262; nonaligned nations and, 246–247; nuclear weapons of, 249, 513; openness in, 335, 336; pollution in, 511; secret police in, 89–90; Socialist bloc and, 11; at Tehran, 233; UN and, 242; western border changes (1914–1945), 239 (map); West Germany and, 261–262; in world economy, 261; after World War II, 242; Yalta and postwar world, 236–238. *See also* Russia; specific leaders
Soweto Civic Association, 411
Soyinka, Wole, 387
Spain: dictatorship in, 122; fascism in, 140; Latin America and, 147–150. *See also* Spanish Republic
Spanish America. *See* Latin America
Spanish-American War (1898), 149; Roosevelt, Theodore, and, 30
Spanish Civil War, 140
Spanish Empire, Spanish-American War and, 39–40
Spanish Republic, 122; Nationalist revolt against, 140. *See also* Spain
Spanish-speaking population, in United States, 356
Specialization, in cities, 15
Spending, during World War I, 69
Spengler, Oswald, on urban populations, 43
Spheres of influence, in China, 206
"Splendid isolation" policy, of Britain, 32

"Splendid little war," Spanish-American War as, 39
Squadristi (Italy), 125
Srebrenica, 270
Sri Lanka. *See* Ceylon
SS, in Nazi Germany, 232
Stagflation, 292, 294; Thatcher and, 298
Stalin, Joseph, 90, 248; dictatorship of, 321; European socialists and, 115; legacy of, 323–324; Lenin compared with, 92; Nazi-Soviet pact and, 138; Roosevelt, Franklin D., and, 233–234; Soviet Union under, 90–92; at Yalta, 237–238. *See also* Soviet Union
Stalingrad, Battle of, 230
Standard of living: in Africa, 391; in Argentina, 368; decline of, 295; economic slowdown and, 296; European Union and, 270; government guarantee of, 119; in Israel, 450; in Japan, 476; in South Africa, 407; in Soviet Union, 333; in Western Europe and Japan, 312
START treaties: START I, 515; START II, 515
Starvation. *See* Famine
Star Wars. *See* Strategic Defense Initiative (SDI, Star Wars)
Stateless societies, in Nigeria, 171
State-owned industries, privatization of, 279
States, in Africa, 171
Statute of Westminster (Britain), 183
Steam power, 9, 30; Germany and, 45
Steel industry, 9, 31; in Brazil, 159; in India, 111, 461; in United States, 272; worldwide, 111–112
Steinbeck, John, 102–103
Stock: joint-stock corporations and, 34. *See also* Great Depression (1930s); Wall Street crash
Stock market: collapse in Tokyo, 476–477; crash in Mexico, 376; crash of 1987 and, 300–301, 302; Great Depression and, 108–109; in Hungary, 342. *See also* New York Stock Exchange
Storm troopers, in Germany, 131
Strategic Air Command (U.S.), 249, 253
Strategic Arms Limitation Talks. *See* SALT treaties
Strategic Arms Reduction Treaty (START I, 1991), 515
Strategic Defense Initiative (SDI, Star Wars), 514
Stratification. *See* Castes; Class; Social stratification
Stress, in Russia, 347
Strikes: in France and Germany, 270; in 1912, 103–104; in Poland, 331; Reagan and, 302; sitdown, 116; Thatcher and, 298. *See also* Labor
Structural readjustment programs, of IMF, 357n
Student Nonviolent Coordinating Committee, 288–289
Students, in May Fourth Movement (China), 207–208
Students for a Democratic Society (SDS), 289
Submarines: *Kursk* sinking and, 350; in World War I, 63; in World War II, 229, 230

Sub-Saharan Africa, 385–387, 387–401; colonization of, 10; decolonization of, 388–391; Europe and, 165–167; France and, 400; independence in, 240; periods in, 387. See also Africa; specific countries

Subsistence agriculture, Great Depression and, 111

Suburbs: movement to, 285–286; voting population in, 304

Subversion, in Brazil, 371

Sudan, 176, 388

Sudeten Germans, in Czechoslovakia, 136–137

Sudetenland, German annexation of, 137–138

Suez Canal, 225; Britain and, 63; in World War II, 230

Suez War (1956), 438

Suffrage: universal manhood, 33. See also Voting and voting rights

Suffragettes, 33

Sugar, in Cuba, 378, 379, 380

Suicide, in India, 462

Süleyman Demirel, 427, 428–429

Sulfonamides, 241

Summit conferences: at Geneva, 251; Reagan-Gorbachev, 263–265

Summits, Franco-African, 397

Sunni Muslims, 433; in Turkey, 428

Sun Yat-sen, 84, 98–99, 207–208

Sun Yixuan. See Sun Yat-sen.

Superhighways, in Nazi Germany, 133

Superiority, of Europeans, 30

Superpowers: Africa and, 400–401; Japan as economic, 475–477; military vs. economic, 271–272; nuclear, 11; Soviet-U.S. conflict and, 245–246; after World War II, 221–222, 242

Suppression of Communism Act (1950, South Africa), 409

"Survival of the fittest," 29

Survival technologies, 21; in Africa, 388

SWAPO (Southwest African People's Organization), 390

Swaraj, 96

Swazi kingdom, 181

Swaziland, 181

Sweden, 113

Switzerland, woman's vote in, 33

Synthetics, in Nazi Germany, 133

Syphilis, cure for, 43

Syria: Arab-Israeli War (1973) and, 439; fascist movement in, 141; France and, 73; UAR and, 438

Taft-Hartley Law (United States, 1947), 283

Taiwan, 213, 456; economic growth of, 481–483; foreign aid to, 251

Takeshita, Noboru, 480

Tambo, Oliver, 410

Tamil Nadu, 464, 465

Tanganyika, independence of, 390

Tanks, in World War II, 222

Tanzania, 390

Taping Rebellion, 206

Tariffs: in Britain, 110; colonies and, 111; elimination of, 279–280; global integration and, 495; in Latin America, 150; in United States, 110

Taxation: approval of, 307; in British Nigeria, 165–166; corporate, 315; in France, 297; during Great Depression, 112–113; on inherited wealth (England), 35; national debt and, 303; of polluting fuels, 512; Reagan and, 299–300; reform in Japan, 475; Thatcher and, 299

Taylor, Charles, 386

Technical elites, in poor countries, 24

Technological innovation, 280

Technological unemployment, 109

Technology: airplane and, 64; computer revolution and, 284–285; economic change and, 284; in Egypt, 52–53; energy efficiency and, 509–510; in Germany, 45, 52–53; global integration and, 495; impact of, 280–282; in India, 463; Industrial Revolution and, 9; information, 20; in Japan, 476; in Latin America, 357; missile, 516–517; nature and, 4, 20–24; in "second Industrial Revolution," 30–32; Stalinist policies and, 322; weapons and, 30; World War II and postwar period, 241

Tehran conference, 233

Telegraph, 9

Television, 286–287

Temporary workers, 304, 313

Tension, globalization and, 12

Terrazas-Creel clan, 147

Terrorism, 489; by Arabs, 424; in Austro-Hungarian Empire, 58; in Israel, 446; Oklahoma City bombing and, 309; PLO and, 447–448

Tet offensive, 259

Thailand: economic growth of, 481; financial crisis in, 483

Thatcher, Margaret, 277, 294; conservative economics and, 298–299

Thermonuclear weapons, 249

Things Fall Apart (Achebe), 178

Third Reich, 132. See also Hitler, Adolf; Nazi Germany

Third Way, Clinton and, 315–318

Third World, 11, 19–20, 250 (map), 342; decolonization of, 455–460; emergence of, 221; Mexican Revolution and, 94–95; nationalism in, 252; nonaligned, 246; vs. superpowers, 456; urbanization in, 356. See also Developing world; Underdeveloped world; specific countries

Thoreau, Henry David, Gandhi and, 96

Thought control, in Soviet Union, 323–324

Three Mile Island, 509

Three People's Principles (Sun Yat-sen), 209

Tienanmen Square: Falun Dafa and, 454; massacres in (1989), 453, 473

Titanic (ship), 26–27

Tito, 326–328

Tobacco, in Cuba, 378

Togo, 174, 176

Togo, Heihachiro, 86

Tokugawa shogunate (Japan), 6, 193

Tokyo, 212; bombing of, 236

Tokyo Olympics, 475

Tolstoy, Leo, Gandhi and, 96

Tonkin Gulf Resolution, 258–259

Totalitarianism, in Nazi Germany, 133

Total war, in World War I, 68

Touré, Sékou, 388

Tourism, in Berlin, 43

Trade: Africa and, 167, 173; of Argentina, 365–366; of China, 473; with China, 205–206; of Cuba, 382; empires and, 6; global interrelatedness and, 5; globalization and, 495–496; Hungarian, 342; in India, 195; of Japan, 10, 475, 476; keiretsu and, 477; Latin American, 356–359; mercantilism and, 149; in Nigeria, 178–179, 401; Soviet, 335; after World War II, 278. See also North American Free Trade Agreement (NAFTA); Slave trade

Trade deficit: of Brazil, 370; of India, 462; of United States, 301, 312

Trade unions: in Germany, 45, 310; Solidarity as, 331; in World War I, 70

Trading networks, 5–6

Transportation, 9

Transvaal, 181; gold in, 182

Treaties: of Brest-Litovsk, 66, 67, 89; with China, 205–206; Comprehensive Nuclear Test Ban, 514, 517; Conventional Forces in Europe, 514; Egyptian-Israeli Peace Treaty (1979) and, 440; Intermediate Nuclear Forces, 264, 514; Israel-Egypt, 449; Israel-Palestinian, 449; with Japan, 206; Limited Test Ban, 514; Maastricht, 269, 270; Missile Material Cut Off, 517; Nuclear Nonproliferation, 514, 517; Ottoman-British free-trade treaty (1838), 199; of Paris (1856), 199; of Rome (1957), 255; of Sèvres, 74, 200; with Soviet constituent republics, 339; Strategic Arms Reduction, 515; of Versailles, 75, 76, 77–78; after World War I, 74–75, 76. See also SALT treaties

Trench warfare, in World War I, 64

Triple Alliance. See Central Powers

Triple Entente. See Entente Powers

Trotsky, Leon, 88, 89, 324

Truman, Harry, 248, 283, 361

Truman Doctrine, 248

Trusts, 34

Tsukuba Science City (Japan), 478

Tuberculosis, in Africa, 393

Tuchman, Barbara, 244

Tunisia, France and, 199

Turing, Alan, 284

Turkey, 199, 215–216, 421, 425–431; central planning in, 204–205; Cuban missile crisis and, 254; earthquake in, 417–419; heroes of independence in, 204; politics in, 202–205, 425–427; since 1990, 429–431; Treaty of Sèvres and, 200; in World War I, 63; after World War II, 248

Turkic languages, 14

Turkic people, 15

Turkic republics, 430

Tutsi people, 392

Tutu, Desmond, 387, 411, 413

Twentieth Century: assessment of, 315; beginning of, 28

Twentieth Soviet Party Congress (1956), 325

"Two Englands," 298–299